Encyclopedia of
COMMUNITY POLICING
and
PROBLEM SOLVING

Editorial Board

Encyclopedia of
COMMUNITY
POLICING
and
PROBLEM
SOLVING

Kenneth J. Peak | Editor

University of Nevada, Reno

Los Angeles | London | New Delhi
Singapore | Washington DC

Los Angeles | London | New Delhi
Singapore | Washington DC

FOR INFORMATION:

SAGE Publications, Inc.
2455 Teller Road
Thousand Oaks, California 91320
E-mail: order@sagepub.com

SAGE Publications Ltd.
1 Oliver's Yard
55 City Road
London, EC1Y 1SP
United Kingdom

SAGE Publications India Pvt. Ltd.
B 1/I 1 Mohan Cooperative Industrial Area
Mathura Road, New Delhi 110 044
India

SAGE Publications Asia-Pacific Pte. Ltd.
3 Church Street
#10-04 Samsung Hub
Singapore 049483

Publisher: Rolf A. Janke
Acquisitions Editor: Jim Brace-Thompson
Assistant to the Publisher: Michele Thompson
Developmental Editors: Carole Maurer
Reference Systems Manager: Leticia Gutierrez
Reference Systems Coordinators: Anna Villasenor,
    Laura Notton
Production Editor: David C. Felts
Copy Editor: Diane DiMura
Typesetter: Hurix Systems Pvt. Ltd.
Proofreader: Pam Suwinsky
Indexer: Karen Wiley
Cover Designer: Janet Kiesel
Marketing Manager: Carmel Schrire

Contents

List of Entries

Reader's Guide

The Reader's Guide is provided to assist readers in locating articles on related topics. It classifies articles into nine general topical categories: Changing Agency Culture; Crime Analysis: Technologies and Techniques; Evaluation and Assessment; Foundations: Evolution of Community Policing and Problem Solving; Future Considerations; Public Safety Issues; Supporting Legislation and National Organizations; Training and Curriculum; and "What Works"—Selected Strategies and Initiatives. Entries may be listed under more than one topic.

Changing Agency Culture

Agency Mission and Values, Changes in
Community Policing, Discretionary
    Authority Under
Community Policing: Resources, Time, and
    Finances in Support of
Customer-Based Policing
Decentralizing the Organization/
    Organizational Change
Implementation of Community Policing
Involving Local Businesses
Learning Organization
Measuring Officer Performance
Officers' Job Satisfaction
Publicity Campaigns
Recruiting for Quality and Diversity
Roles, Chief Executives'
Roles, First-Line Supervisors'
Roles, Middle Managers'
Roles, Officers'
Strategic Planning

Crime Analysis: Technologies and Techniques

CompStat
Computer-Aided Dispatch
Counterterrorism and Community Policing
Crime Analysis
Crime Analysts, Roles of
Crime Displacement
Crime Mapping
Global Positioning Systems/Geographic
    Information Systems
Hot Spots
Problem Analysis Triangle
Tipping Points of Neighborhoods
Website Uses by Local Agencies

Evaluation and Assessment

Citizen Surveys
Community Policing Self-Assessment Tool
    (CP-SAT)
Problem-Solving Initiatives, Assessment and
    Evaluation
Problem-Solving Initiatives, Examples of
    Assessment and Evaluation of

Foundations: Evolution of Community Policing and Problem Solving

Broken Windows Theory
Building Partnerships and Stakeholders
Citizen Patrols
Collaboration With Outside Agencies
Community, Definition of
Community Cohesion and Empowerment
Community Justice
Community Policing, Evolution of
Community Policing: What It Is Not
Community Policing and Problem Solving,
    Definition of
Community Prosecution
Crime Prevention Through Environmental
    Design
Directed Patrol, Studies of

Future Considerations

Public Safety Issues

Supporting Legislation and National Organizations

Training and Curriculum

"What Works"—Selected Strategies and Initiatives

About the Editor

Kenneth J. Peak, PhD, is a professor and former chairman of the criminal justice department at the University of Nevada, Reno (UNR). Beginning his career at Reno in 1983, he has been named "Teacher of the Year" by the UNR Honor Society and served as acting director of public safety. He has authored or coauthored 25 textbooks (several of which are now in their seventh editions) on community policing, justice administration, general policing, women in law enforcement, and police supervision and management; he has also published more than 60 journal articles and additional book chapters on a wide range of justice-related subjects. He has served as chairman of the Police Section, Academy of Criminal Justice Sciences, and is a past president of the Western and Pacific Association of Criminal Justice Educators. After beginning his criminal-justice career as a municipal police officer in Pittsburg, Kansas, he subsequently held positions as criminal justice planner for southeast Kansas; director of the Four-State Technical Assistance Institute, Law Enforcement Assistance Administration; director of university police, Pittsburg State University; and assistant professor at Wichita State University. He received two gubernatorial appointments to statewide criminal justice committees while in Kansas and holds a doctorate from the University of Kansas.

Contributors

James F. Albrecht
University of New Haven

Emmanuel P. Barthe
University of Nevada, Reno

Michael M. Berlin
Coppin State University

Theron L. Bowman
Arlington, Texas

Anthony A. Braga
*Rutgers University and
Harvard University*

Tom Cadwallader
*North Carolina Central
University*

David L. Carter
Michigan State University

Jeremy G. Carter
*Indiana University–Purdue
University Indianapolis*

Sharon Chamard
University of Alaska, Anchorage

Robert Chapman
U.S. Department of Justice

Gary W. Cordner
Kutztown University

Melchor C. de Guzman
*The College at Brockport, State
University of New York*

Rosemary DeMenno
*International Association of
Chiefs of Police*

Pamela M. Everett
Wayne State College

Joseph Ferrandino
Indiana University Northwest

Mora Fiedler
U.S. Department of Justice

D. Cody Gaines
Sam Houston State University

Larry K. Gaines
*California State University,
San Bernardino*

Daniel W. Gerard
*Cincinnati, Ohio, Police
Department*

Anne P. Glavin
*IACLEA and California State
University, Northridge*

Ronald W. Glensor
*Reno, Nevada, Police
Department (Retired)*

John R. Hamilton Jr.
Park University

Aaron A. Harnish
*Harrisburg Area Community
College*

Justin A. Heinonen
Michigan State University

Jerry Hoover
Feather River College

Brian Kauffman
Western Oregon University

Christopher S. Koper
George Mason University

Jonathan M. Kremser
*Kutztown University of
Pennsylvania*

Joseph B. Kuhns
*University of North Carolina,
Charlotte*

Jennifer L. Lanterman
University of Nevada, Reno

Susan A. Lentz
University of Nevada, Reno

Betsy Lindsay
*Housing Authority of the
County of Los Angeles*

Vivian Lord
*University of North Carolina,
Charlotte*

Cynthia Lum
George Mason University

Phillip M. Lyons Jr.
Sam Houston State University

Tamara D. Madensen
University of Nevada, Las Vegas

Jon Maskaly
University of South Florida

Robert Morin
Western Nevada College

Bernadette T. Muscat
California State University, Fresno

Richard W. Myers
*Colorado Springs, Colorado,
Police Department (Retired)*

Timothy N. Oettmeier
*Houston, Texas, Police
Department*

Willard M. Oliver
Sam Houston State University

Michael J. Palmiotto
Wichita State University

Cynthia E. Pappas
*Office of Community Oriented
    Policing Services*

Troy C. Payne
*University of Alaska,
    Anchorage*

Kenneth J. Peak
University of Nevada, Reno

Ken Pease
*Jill Dando Institute, University
    College London*

Elizabeth B. Perkins
Morehead State University

Jordan C. Pickering
University of Missouri, St. Louis

Steven Pitts
*Reno, Nevada, Police
    Department*

Rachel Boba Santos
Florida Atlantic University

Joseph A. Schafer
*Southern Illinois University,
    Carbondale*

Matthew C. Scheider
U.S. Department of Justice

Michael S. Scott
University of Wisconsin

Ellen Scrivner
Public Safety Innovations

Susan M. Shah
Vera Institute of Justice

Ronald C. Sloan
*Colorado Bureau of
    Investigation*

Deborah L. Spence
U.S. Department of Justice

B. Grant Stitt
University of Nevada, Reno

Cody W. Telep
George Mason University

Julie D. Wartell
The Analysis Group

Robert Wasserman
Strategic Policy Partnership

Sandra R. Webb
U.S. Department of Justice

Robert R. Weidner
University of Minnesota, Duluth

Deborah Lamm Weisel
*North Carolina Central
    University*

Robert L. Werling
*California State University,
    Stanislaus*

Robert V. Wolf
Center for Court Innovation

Jihong Zhao
Sam Houston State University

Chronology

1829: Robert Peel's Metropolitan Police Act of 1829 is enacted by UK Parliament; he becomes well known for his view that "the police are the public, and the public are the police."

1840s to 1930s: U.S. policing is in its political era.

1844: Full-time, preventive police force is initiated in the United States in New York City.

1905: August Vollmer is elected town marshal in Berkeley, California; as part of many "firsts," he soon began arguing that policing is multifaceted and should be viewed from multiple social science and medical perspectives.

1919: August Vollmer's article, "The Policeman as Social Worker" (*Proceedings, 26th Convention of the International Association of Chiefs of Police*, pp. 32–38), encourages police to develop programs to attack youth crime at its roots.

1930s to 1980s: U.S. policing is in its reform era.

1931: The Wickersham Commission issues 14 reports, including many recommendations that address police and politics, officers' standards and salaries, and use of women in policing.

1955: National Institute on Police and Community Relations (NIPCR) is founded at Michigan State University.

1965: St. Louis (Missouri) Police Department initiates the first computer-aided dispatch (CAD), which enhances its communications operation and improves patrol deployment.

1967: National Center on Police and Community Relations at Michigan State University begins to conduct national surveys on police-community relations.

1970s: San Diego (California) police, as part of several research projects in the department, conduct the first empirical study of community policing.

Early 1970s: Police patrol is redesigned based on motivators, leading to team policing, which was adopted by many agencies as a means of focusing on addressing community concerns and increasing police effectiveness by permanently assigning a group of police officers to a particular small geographic area or neighborhood; the team of officers was responsible for providing patrol and investigative services as well as developing appropriate police strategies and programs for that neighborhood.

1972: National Neighborhood Watch Program is founded within the National Sheriffs' Association.

1973: Oscar Newman coins the term *defensible space*.

1973: Team policing is examined in seven U.S. cities by Sherman, Milton, and Kelly in *Team policing: Seven case studies*.

1974: George Kelling and colleagues Pate, Dieckman, and Brown report their findings of the Kansas City preventive patrol experiment in *The Kansas City Preventive Patrol Experiment: A summary report*.

1975: RAND Corporation publishes *The criminal investigation process, Volume I: Summary and policy implications*, a report by Greenwood and Petersilia examining the role of detectives, concluding that the single most important factor in solving a case was contained in information supplied by the victim to the initial, responding patrol officer.

1977: Split-force patrol experiment is conducted in Wilmington, Delaware.

1977: C. Ray Jeffery refines and expands the crime prevention through environmental design (CPTED) theory.

1978: Police Foundation begins evaluating foot patrol in 28 New Jersey cities, with Newark as the primary evaluation site.

1979: Twelve police chiefs meet at a three-day seminar in Madison, Wisconsin, to explore the problem-oriented policing concept; emphasis is placed on examining policing's "means over ends" syndrome and to become more concerned with the "end product" of their efforts; the National Institute of Justice (NIJ) subsequently includes further development of the concept in its research program.

1979: Lawrence Cohen and Marcus Felson espouse their routine activities theory (which seeks to explain how physical and social environments create crime opportunities by the intersection of a "likely" offender, a "suitable" target, and the absence of a "capable guardian" against crime, such as a police officer or security guard) and the problem analysis triangle (which postulates that in order for a crime to occur, three elements, which form the crime triangle, are required: an offender, a victim/target, and a location).

1979: Herman Goldstein publishes "Improving Policing: A Problem-Oriented Approach" in *Crime & Delinquency*, advocating for problem-oriented policing: that police proactively identify and address root causes of problems.

1980s to present: Policing in the United States is in the community era.

1980: Situational crime prevention theory is espoused by Ronald V. Clarke in the *British Journal of Criminology* article, "Situational Crime Prevention: Theory and Practice."

1980s: Fear reduction studies in Houston, Texas; Newark, New Jersey; and elsewhere provide empirical data on the effectiveness of key community policing tactics.

1980: Response time analysis is conducted in the Kansas City (Missouri) Police Department.

1981: Analysis of Newark (New Jersey) Foot Patrol Experiment suggests several positive outcomes if police spend more time on foot in their neighborhoods.

1982: National Neighborhood Foot Patrol Center is established at Michigan State University.

1982: National Crime Prevention Council is founded.

1982: Research is conducted on experimental foot patrols in Flint, Michigan.

1982: Robert Trojanowicz conducts an evaluation of the Neighborhood Foot Patrol Program in Flint, Michigan, finding that it was a distinct success: crime and calls for service were down in the 14 experimental areas; with certain functions, foot patrol officers were more efficient than were motorized officers; and residents of the experimental foot patrol areas reported feeling safer in their neighborhoods.

1982: James Q. Wilson and George L. Kelling coauthor "Broken Windows: The Police and Neighborhood Safety" in the March issue of *Atlantic Monthly*.

1983: The first Executive Session on Policing is convened, cosponsored by the National Institute of Justice (NIJ) and Harvard's Kennedy School of Government, to consider policy recommendations for policing.

1983: The National Center for Community Policing is founded at Michigan State University.

1984: New York City Police Department launches its Community Patrol Officer Program (CPOP) to identify neighborhood problems and develop strategies.

1984: Evaluation of the Minneapolis Domestic Violence Experiment is conducted by Sherman and Berk in "The Specific Deterrent Effects of Arrest for Domestic Assault" in the *American Sociological Review;* they conclude that batterers who are arrested are less likely to re-batter than those batterers who are not arrested.

1987: Newport News (Virginia) study finds problem-oriented policing to be an effective approach to addressing many community problems; officers and researchers develop the SARA (scanning, analysis, response, assessment) problem-solving model.

1987: Evaluation commences of the Madison (Wisconsin) Police Department's new organizational design (both structural and managerial), intended to support community-oriented and problem-oriented policing in an Experimental Police District.

1988: George L. Kelling publishes "Police and Communities: The Quiet Revolution" in *Perspectives on Policing*, No. 1; he and Mark H. Moore also publish "The Evolving Strategy of Policing" in *Perspectives on Policing*, No. 4.

1988: Houston (Texas) Police Chief Lee P. Brown describes the development of Neighborhood Oriented Policing in the Houston Police Department; he later authors a "practical guide" for adopting community policing.

1989: Sherman, Buerger, and Gartin examine the Minneapolis' Repeat Call Address Policing (RECAP) program, indicating that police could identify the "hot spots" of repeat calls in a community and thereby devise strategies to reduce the number of calls for service.

1990s: Intelligence-led policing (ILP) is developed as a strategy in Great Britain, where crime levels had risen sharply.

1990: San Diego, California, is selected to host the first national conference on problem-oriented policing.

1990: Herman Goldstein's *Problem-Oriented Policing* is published by McGraw-Hill and Temple University Press.

1990: Robert Trojanowicz and Bonnie Bucqueroux's *Community Policing: A Contemporary Perspective* is published by Anderson Publishing Company.

1991: The U.S. Department of Justice launches Operation Weed and Seed, a key strategy of their antiviolence, antigang, and antidrug community revitalization programs with primary focus on high-crime neighborhoods; enforcement is used first to "weed" out crime, violence, and gangs and to stabilize the conditions in high-crime communities; then resources are identified and mobilized to "seed" the revitalization of the communities.

1993: Community Policing Consortium is founded, composed of the International Association of Chiefs of Police, the National Sheriffs' Association, the Police Executive Research Forum, and the Police Foundation.

1993: The Herman Goldstein Award is first offered, recognizing innovative and effective problem-solving efforts by police officers and agencies in the United States and abroad.

1993: Studies of repeat victimization and its implications for crime prevention are initiated in London (UK) by Graham Farrell and Ken Pease.

1993: "Tipping point" studies of neighborhood thresholds of crime (first noted in a paper by Thomas Shelling in 1971) begin to appear.

1994: The Violent Crime Control and Law Enforcement Act, authorizing $8.8 billion in expenditures over six years, is enacted.

1994: The federal Office of Community Oriented Policing Services (COPS) is created to distribute and monitor funds under the Violent Crime Control and Law Enforcement Act and provide numerous other functions related to and in support of community policing.

1994: Three-year Community Policing Demonstration Program is launched in 16 cities to design, demonstrate, and assess a comprehensive, departmentwide community policing prototype.

1994: CompStat *(comparative statistics* or *computer statistics),* a crime management process used in the problem-solving process, is introduced by the New York City Police Department.

1994: Bureau of Justice Assistance publishes *Understanding Community Policing: A Framework for Action.*

1995: Office of Community Oriented Policing Services funds 25,000 more officers; Lawrence Sherman authors "Hot Spots of Crime and Criminal Careers of Places" in *Crime Prevention Studies.*

1996: Office of Community Oriented Policing Services has funded more than 52,000 community policing officers and announces antigang, domestic violence, and problem-solving partnership initiatives.

1997: Office of Community Oriented Policing Services establishes a nationwide network of Regional Community Policing Institutes (RCPIs).

1997: National Institute of Justice establishes the Crime Mapping Research Center (CMRC).

1997: Systematic review of more than 500 crime prevention practices is prepared for Congress by Lawrence Sherman and colleagues, concerning which prevention programs work, do not work, are promising, and have not been tested adequately.

1998: Office of Community Oriented Policing Services announces that 75,000 new community policing officers had been funded nationwide; its monograph, *Problem Solving Tips: A Guide to Reducing Crime and Disorder Through Problem-Solving Partnerships,* is published.

1999: Office of Community Oriented Policing Services launches its *Problem-Oriented Guides* series, to summarize knowledge about how police can analyze and respond to specific crime and disorder problems.

1999: Office of Community Oriented Policing Services funds its 100,000th community policing officer.

1999: National evaluation of eight Operation Weed and Seed sites is performed, concerning their implementation and measurable outcomes related to crime and public safety. Although the results were not highly significant statistically, they were consistently favorable: seeding programs provided services that would not have been available without the program, additional structure and discipline were provided to young people in the area, six of the sites showed declines in Part I crimes (homicide, rape, robbery, aggravated assault, burglary, larceny, and auto theft).

2000: National evaluation of the problem-solving partnerships grant program is launched, wherein the federal COPS Office awarded grants to 468 police agencies to help solve crime and disorder problems, form community partnerships, and engage in problem-solving activities.

2000: Willard M. Oliver publishes his descriptions of three generations of community policing: (1) innovation (1979–1986); (2) diffusion (1987–1994); and (3) institutionalization, (1995 to the present).

2000: Office of Community Oriented Policing Services launches its Police as Problem-Solvers and Peacemakers program, awarding $1 million to five law enforcement agencies.

2001: Office of Community Oriented Policing Services launches two series of publications, *COPS Innovations* and *Problem-Oriented Policing Guides;* by 2011 more than 60 problem-solving guides had been published.

2001: The first *Problem-Oriented Guide,* authored by Michael S. Scott, was published, entitled *Assaults in and Around Bars*

2002: Center for Problem-Oriented Policing is created.

2002: The Crime Mapping Research Center evolves into the Mapping and Analysis for Public Safety (MAPS) program.

2003: The Department of Homeland Security (DHS) is formed, immediately hiring 80,000 new federal employees and committing $32 billion in 2003 toward safeguarding the nation.

2003: Office of Community Oriented Policing Services awards $23 million in grants to support the network of 31 RCPIs and the Community Policing Consortium (CPC); it also launches the Homeland Security Overtime Program (HSOP).

2006: An evaluation of gang hot spots policing in Chicago, Illinois, is funded by NIJ, to determine whether new policing strategies contributed to significant decreases in crime in the 2000s.

2007: Police use global positioning for monitoring police vehicle location across real time/space, for CompStat and other directed patrol strategies (e.g., hot spots policing).

2008: The second Executive Session is convened, cosponsored by NIJ and the Kennedy School of Government, on Policing and Public Safety.

2010: Predictive-policing conferences and articles emerge; predictive policing is a crime analysis tool using various analyses, technologies, and ILP for crime prevention strategies and tactics.

2012: In August, the Office of Community Oriented Policing Services announces that it will not continue funding the Center for Problem-Oriented Policing.

Introduction

Long before police agencies were organized and specialized for peacekeeping as we know them today, people expected designated village or community protectors to keep them safe from harm and to solve their problems. Beginning in the 9th century with Britain's citizen night watch, and continuing in about 1066 BCE with the function of the *shire reeve* (the forerunner of the modern-day sheriff), certain persons were assigned or volunteered to watch over their neighbors and to identify and address problems. Of course, policing has evolved tremendously since those early times, and today's community policing and problem-solving strategy—indeed, the contemporary community era of policing—represents the pinnacle of that evolution. At its root, however, community policing and problem solving remains a relatively simplistic endeavor: keeping the peace and maintaining order. As examples, and to begin to grasp the field, consider the following scenarios:

Scenario 1: During the late 1950s in a small midwestern town, the chief of police received several complaints concerning a growing nuisance: someone was allowing his chickens to run loose throughout the neighborhood. The chief summoned Officer John—an amicable, lank, grey-haired veteran lawman who probably could not remember when he had made his last arrest. The chief ordered the officer to deal with the problem and thus stem the neighbors' complaints. Upon Officer John's return to the station house a few hours later, the chief demanded to know whether he had resolved the situation once and for all; Officer John replied that he had. The chief demanded to know if John had arrested the owner of the vagrant fowl; Officer John replied that he had not. Pressing further, the chief demanded to know what Officer John had done to restore order to the neighborhood. "Well, chief," Officer John said, "I bought all the man's chickens,

and we loaded them all up and took them to my house and turned them loose in my yard."

Scenario 2: During the mid-1990s, a convenience store owner in a lower class area of a medium-size western city frequently called the police to complain about drug dealers conducting "business" at a pay telephone located at the store's front entrance; he was concerned about the drug dealers' presence, and that many children and other customers daily overheard the buying and selling transactions. Officer Ben went to the scene, assessed the problem, and then contacted the local telephone company to request that they reprogram the pay telephone so that it made only outgoing calls, thus removing the ability of the drug traffickers to receive incoming calls from customers. The traffickers were forced to leave the convenience store.

Viewed in the light of today's policing, the above scenarios might appear to be ludicrous (today's police officers can neither avoid making arrests nor use out-of-pocket resources to resolve neighborhood complaints) or incomplete (the drug dealers who vacated the convenience store may not have ceased their trafficking altogether, but merely took their business elsewhere). However, on closer examination the scenarios have one critical point in common: *Both officers solved the immediate problem using creative strategies that did not involve an arrest or other traditional, reactive, short-term measures.* Furthermore, these scenarios provide a glimpse into how policing was conducted during its infancy as it was developing and evolving in England, when the emphasis was on closeness to and working with the community to resolve neighborhood crime and disorder.

As will be seen below, the police have always known how to solve problems. The difference now, however, is that during policing's earlier eras, officers who confronted problems typically did not possess an in-depth understanding of the nature and underlying causes of those crime issues (becoming "street criminologists"), nor did they receive much guidance or support, or possess sophisticated methods (e.g., crime analysis, mapping tools, surveys) to support those efforts. The routine application of problem-solving techniques *is* new, however, and is grounded on two fundamental tenets: Problem-solving strategy can be applied by police officers (as well as non-sworn personnel) as part of their routine daily work to effectively reduce or eliminate neighborhood crime and disorder. It affords great challenges for today's patrol officers, making this a wonderful time in which to be engaged in the analytical and creative work of policing.

The Field

The seeds of community policing were sown in London in 1829, when Sir Robert Peel (the founder of London's police force) offered that "the police are the public and . . . the public are the police," and by establishing patrol beats, officers could get to know their citizens and thus have better opportunities to gather information concerning crime and disorder. In the United States, however, that close police-public association over time often led to powerful political influences and corruption (in terms of who was hired, promoted, and could bring in the most votes), which in turn led to the onset of the reform era in the 1930s (including the removal of the police from the community and political influence, the creation of civil service systems, and so forth); for the next half-century, police operated as though they alone could control crime and thus maintained a level of detachment from the public.

As a result, from the 1930s to the 1980s, the dominant police strategy under the reform era shifted to an emphasis on motorized patrol, rapid response time, numbers of arrests, and retrospective investigation of crimes; officer productivity was often measured quantitatively, including the number of miles driven during a duty shift, citations issued, arrests made, and so on. These strategies were not designed to address root community problems; rather, they were designed to detect crime and apprehend criminals—hence the image of the "crime fighter" cop.

Following the social unrest of the 1960s and 1970s, this schism between the police and the public became so wide—fomented by increasing crime rates, frequent race riots, and five national commissions calling for sweeping changes in policing—that police agencies were forced to open their doors to researchers and reveal their methods. Research findings indicated the reform-era police methods were ineffectual, so community policing began to gather momentum in the early 1980s and to develop partnerships between the police and those they served. In essence, the advent of community policing meant bringing back a modern version of Peel's "bobbie on the beat," with the police drawing on the public's fount of knowledge concerning where problems recur and which criminals repeatedly offend. Society came to understand that new police methods and measures of effectiveness were required. Current wisdom holds that the police cannot unilaterally attack the burgeoning crime, drug, and gang problems that beset our society, draining our federal, state, and local resources. Communities must police themselves.

Problem-oriented policing, which began to develop in the mid-1980s, was grounded in principles different from but complementary to community-oriented policing (thus, the term *community-oriented policing and problem solving* is widely used). Problem-oriented policing is a strategy that puts the community policing philosophy into practice. It advocates that police examine the underlying causes of recurring incidents of crime and disorder. The problem-solving process helps officers to identify problems, analyze them completely, develop response strategies, and assess the results. Police must be equipped to define more clearly and to understand more fully the problems they are expected to handle. They must recognize the relationships between and among incidents—for example, incidents involving the same behavior, the same address, or the same people. The police must therefore develop a commitment to analyzing problems—gather information from police files, from the minds of experienced officers, from other agencies of government, and from private sources as well. It can also require conducting house-to-house surveys and talking with victims, complainants, and offenders. It includes an uninhibited search for the most effective response to each problem, looking beyond just the criminal justice system to a wide range of alternatives; police must try to design a customized response that holds the greatest potential for dealing effectively with a specific problem in a specific place under specific conditions.

Thousands of police agencies both in the United States and abroad have now implemented new strategies and practices for addressing crime and disorder, focusing on training officers and agencies to conduct more in-depth analyses of recurring problems; obtaining problem-solving assistance from other government organizations, businesses, social service agencies, and the community at large; and evaluating the resulting efforts by going far beyond mere arrests or the issuance of citations or warnings.

These police agencies have broken away from their reactive, incident-driven methods that characterized the reform era. This change in philosophy and strategies goes far beyond merely creating a "crime prevention specialist" position, a "community relations unit," a foot or bicycle patrol, or a neighborhood mini-station. Today, community-oriented policing and problem solving involves radical changes in police organizational culture and structures, management styles, and external relationships. It requires a cultural transformation with the entire police agency, involving changes in recruiting, training, awards systems, evaluation, and promotions. Furthermore, new technologies have been designed to effect this change; and personnel training, evaluation, and reward systems have all been altered to accommodate this philosophy. At its core, this approach embraces a closer collaboration between the police, the public, and other governmental agencies, so as to develop more thoughtful crime control and prevention strategies. It is a long-term process that involves redefining the role throughout the ranks, from chief down to street officer.

To help to further discern community-oriented policing and problem solving as it compares with traditional policing, consider another scenario: In a relatively quiet neighborhood, police officers have recently responded to a series of disturbances. All of the disturbances—loud music, fighting, screeching tires, people displaying lewd behavior on and near the premises—appear to be related to a recently opened live-music dance club. In a month's time, police officers have been sent to the club to restore order on more than 50 occasions. As per traditional practice, swing- (evening) shift officers respond to the club and restore order for a short period of time;

later, graveyard- (night) shift officers often must return to the club after midnight to again restore calm. Usually when officers arrive, however, the offenders are already gone, so a report is taken and the officer returns to the patrol car and leaves.

Adopting the community policing and problem-solving approach, however, police would address this situation as follows, using the concept's SARA (scanning, analysis, response, assessment) problem-solving process:

While scanning the problem, the area patrol sergeant establishes that there have been large increases in the area's calls for service (CFS) on both shifts, that several realtors had contacted council members to complain about declining market interest in the area, and that a local newspaper was about to run a story on the increase in vehicle burglaries, noise complaints, fighting, and other criminal or inappropriate behaviors in and around the club's premises. Additional information is gathered from crime reports, the reporter who is writing the newspaper story, neighboring business owners, and the department's crime analysis unit. Information is also gathered concerning possible zoning and health department violations. Officers first arrange a meeting with the club manager-operator and representatives from the city's business licensing division, during which the consequences for continued problems are explained. This also results in the manager's removal of an unsavory employee and his "following" of drug users and other undesirable characters at the club. The hours of the club's live music are limited, and the manager and employees are trained in relevant sections of the municipal code covering disturbing the peace, minors in liquor establishments, trespassing laws, disorderly behaviors, and so on. The officers also arrange a meeting with the club's landlord, who agrees to install more lights in the parking lots and a "sound wall" around the business to buffer the area residents. A later assessment reveals that a reduction in CFS in the area was realized, and area residents, although not entirely happy with the continuing existence of the business, acknowledged satisfaction from their complaints; no further newspaper stories appeared regarding the noise and disorder in the neighborhood.

This scenario illustrates some of the differences between police responses to crime and disorder under the traditional reactive, incident-driven mode of policing and how a problem might be addressed under the community-oriented policing and problem-solving strategy.

Rationale for the Encyclopedia

It is apparent that the field of policing has witnessed tremendous change and growth during its span of nearly two centuries. With the ever-widening range of topics that now compose the field, there is no single extant reference source that captures the diverse and sophisticated nature of the discipline. In addition, with the increasing visibility of community-oriented policing and problem solving, and the fact that this strategy is both a science and a practice, there is a growing need for a single resource that explains the comprehensive nature of the field and is accessible to both experts and nonexperts. The *Encyclopedia of Community Policing and Problem Solving* was created to provide that service and to fill that void in the literature.

This encyclopedia is thus also intended to serve a diverse audience, providing a basic resource for high school and college/university undergraduate students, beginning graduate students of criminal justice and related social sciences, lay audiences seeking a nontechnical description of the field and its practices, practitioners wishing to keep abreast of the changes and updates in the field, and even the doctoral-level academic seeking a portal into the discipline.

Organization of the Entries

This encyclopedia has explicitly attempted to examine every substantive topic that pertains to community-oriented policing and problem solving. That is, of course, a lofty goal and one that, arguably, could not be achieved. Nonetheless, the editorial board and I have attempted to be as comprehensive as possible without being overly redundant. To accomplish this, the entries include several associated topics and cross-references.

To assist the reader in navigating the encyclopedia, a Reader's Guide is provided, which includes an alphabetical listing of the entries in nine broad categories or themes; then, within each theme the individual entries are also presented alphabetically. Finally, following each entry is a Further Readings section that can take the reader to the next level.

Note: It may be helpful for the reader to begin by reading entries in the "Foundations" section in order to better understand how community policing and problem solving evolved, several key definitions and practices, and a number of related concepts. Similarly, it may be good to defer reading entries in the "Future Considerations" section until last, after developing a contemporary understanding of the concept.

These nine thematic categories are arranged alphabetically, as follows: The first describes how the police agency's culture must be changed—in some cases, radically—to accommodate this strategy. The next category discusses crime analysis technologies and techniques that are needed and exist for performing the work of police problem solving, and the following section concerns methods for evaluating and assessing community-oriented policing initiatives.

Then an examination of the evolution and foundations of policing in general—and community policing in specific—are presented, to include its British origins and subsequent development in the United States (as it experienced movement through three distinct eras). The meaning and importance of community and partnerships is examined in this section as well as some of the early experiments and research studies of police functions. This category generally serves to explain how and why community-oriented policing and problem solving came into existence.

The next thematic category reviews the future of this concept; specifically discussed are the possible impact on community-oriented policing and problem solving that will be caused by future crime and demographics. Then several public safety issues are examined that lay at the root of the need for police problem solving; included are such crime problems as domestic violence, drug crimes, gangs, and youthful offenders.

The foci of the following category are the supporting legislation and organizations that helped to foment the development of, and funding, literature, training, and personnel for community-oriented policing and problem solving. Then, the requisite training and curriculum for sworn and non-sworn personnel are discussed.

Finally, a review is presented next of "what works"—selected examples of community-oriented policing and problem-solving strategies that are in use in a variety of settings, including colleges and universities, public housing, rural areas, and state patrol agencies. Furthermore, this section includes characteristics of community policing strategies for addressing the aforementioned public safety issues, including domestic violence, drug abuse, gangs, and other types of crimes.

To provide additional examples of and insight into the processes and practices of community policing and problem solving, selected case studies are shown describing actual problem-solving initiatives throughout the United States; most of the examples shown are winners or finalists for the highly reputed Herman Goldstein Award for Excellence in Problem-Oriented Policing, conferred annually by the Center for Problem-Oriented Policing. Each case study demonstrates the use of the SARA problem-solving model and includes the kinds of creative responses that police can develop to address crime and disorder.

Long entries, approximately 3,500 words in length, represent the most important and well-developed topics in the field, for which extensive and general research and theory exists. Medium-length entries, approximately 2,500 words in length, discuss subjects that have attained significance in the field as core topics. Short entries of 1,500 words for the most part describe topics that are relatively new to the field or that are less central to understanding community-oriented policing and problem solving.

It will be seen throughout that emphasis is placed on the practical or *applied* aspects of community-oriented policing and problem solving. Indeed, both esteemed practitioners as well as scholars have been selected to contribute the entries (and many of them possess both practitioner and academic experience). Responses to crime and neighborhood disorder must be realistically tied to available resources and police ingenuity. Furthermore, in these times of fiscal crisis and greater accountability, it is essential to know what works and will afford cost effectiveness. Policy decisions are also implicated, and the best way to make such decisions is through intelligent thinking, sound reasoning, and open discussions—thus being able to better effect long-term solutions to society's problems rather than short-term fixes.

Viewed in total, this encyclopedia provides a ready reference for comprehensively learning how, why, and what the police have done to effect a sea change toward bringing about a profoundly new and better approach to their mission of "serve and protect."

Acknowledgments

This project had its genesis with my being contacted by Jim Brace-Thompson, Senior Acquisition Editor with SAGE Publications. Jim, along with his staff, did the requisite marketing analyses to establish that such an encyclopedia was desirable and necessary; we remained in contact throughout the project duration, and Jim served as a valuable resource throughout. My primary point of contact as the project developed, however, was Carole Maurer, Senior Developmental Editor, whose steady hand at the keel (and exceptional editing skills) helped my editorial "apprenticeship" greatly and kept the project on course. SAGE Reference Tracking training and operation was provided by Laura Notton and Leticia Gutierrez. All of these SAGE professionals were exceedingly professional, patient, and efficient from beginning to end, and a huge debt of gratitude is owed to them.

I also appreciate the tremendous assistance of my editorial board, whose names and affiliations are listed in the front matter; I am obviously biased, but I have to believe that this group of experts is as stellar as any that could be convened for this purpose. They, too, realize that this project represents an exciting yet challenging opportunity to organize and convey the body of knowledge that comprises this discipline. I am very pleased and proud that they opted to join me in this effort. The board was most invaluable in reviewing the headword list that guided the essay contributions, and provided me with many names of possible contributors.

Certainly my editorial assistant—also one of my most capable and intelligent former students and now a successful academic in her own right—Pamela Everett, was key to this project as well. Pam concentrated on several key portions of each entry to ensure they met certain criteria and specifications. As has been the case during the nearly two decades I have observed Pam perform such tasks, her work was stellar.

Finally, this encyclopedia is most of all a testament to those contributing authors who devoted their time, effort, and expertise toward developing their entries and thus served to explicate community policing and problem solving. I wish each of them the very best in both their professional and personal endeavors.

Kenneth J. Peak

AGENCY MISSION AND VALUES, CHANGES IN

Values set forth the beliefs and expected norms that guide how an organization will fulfill its mission and act in a variety of complex situations. For the organization's members and the public, values provide agencies with a raison d'être, setting forth basic beliefs about how the organization's work will be carried out. In recent years, values have become a key means by which police agencies convey how they make choices in applying discretion and the standards the organization will live by to their members and the public. American policing has seen a marked evolution in values since the commencement of the 20th century, reflecting the change in policing strategy and orientation that has evolved during this time. This entry examines the evolution of those values, how such values have affected policing's mission, particularly the community policing mission, and how such values are articulated in police agencies.

The Evolution of Policing Toward a New Paradigm

Before the "professionalized" era of policing began, police values reflected political patronage and pre-bureaucratized municipal government. Starting at the turn of the 19th century, there was increasing clamor for reform of policing institutions, which were widely viewed as corrupt and ineffectual. The age of reform proceeded slowly, and did not gather

steam until the late 1940s and 1950s. Before that time—like most government institutions of the day—police mostly concerned themselves with serving the political powers to which they owed their livelihoods, including overlooking (or even assisting in) officeholders' crimes while punishing their opponents, even in the absence of wrongdoing. The values of fealty and malleability to political corruption defined the preprofessionalized policing era.

The values of policing began to change in the 1940s as cities instituted a number of reforms that began the move to more professionalized policing services. This included increased use of police vehicles, installation of radios for communication with headquarters, adoption of a military command structure, and an increasing recognition that the rule of law underlay effective policing. While corruption was still fairly widespread, it eventually became outside-the-norm as agencies shifted their mission to law enforcement. The new values for policing became adherence to the law, professional response to crime, and rapid response to citizen calls for service.

Subsequently, the President's Commission on Law Enforcement and Criminal Justice (1967), responding to the increasing crime rate in the late 1950s and early 1960s, set forth a strategy for dramatically increasing police professionalism and effectiveness. Improvements to police professionalism meant education, and through federal funding, millions of police officers studied for college degrees. The commission also urged equal treatment of all persons regardless of race or ethnicity, competency in solving crimes, and adherence to the rule of law.

Community relations became a priority, with police departments dedicating themselves to keeping their communities informed as to crime activities in their neighborhoods.

Amid the transformations of the professional era, police now comported themselves with higher professional standards, viewing themselves as representatives of the state whose primary function was law enforcement, and thus the only legitimate planners of crime-control policies and executors of anticrime actions (the professional era being characterized by reactive, incident-driven methods and emphases on quantitative results). Ordinary citizens were thus effectively shut out of dialogue on how to best police their own neighborhoods. This would change during the shift toward community-oriented policing in the late 1980s, when, despite half a century of its widespread adoption, the professionalized model was failing to control rising crime rates, and new sociological research challenged longstanding assumptions about policing best practices. Community policing would become the most significant reconceptualization of American policing since the early movement toward professionalization in the 1940s, and it required departments practicing it to commit to a new set of service-oriented values.

A paramount value of community-oriented versus crime-fighting policing is a change in the former's commitment to interacting with the community, mainly to communicate police concerns and press the community to report potential criminal activity through block watches and other local initiatives. Under community policing, no longer would police see themselves as the sole legitimate voice on what communities need to control crime; rather, police now saw themselves as partners in achieving safe neighborhoods. Police would seek to understand community disorder from residents' perspectives, aiming to improve daily life in those neighborhoods. Residents, in turn, would become more willing to share information that could improve policing services' efficacy.

Police would also be required to seriously consider recommendations resulting from this police-community dialogue to gain legitimacy, as residents would not trust police if it became apparent that police were unwilling or unable to uphold their end of the bargain. Giving "teeth" to community policing thus required decentralizing some policing services for neighborhood delivery, allowing community members and police to collaboratively determine how to solve local problems and allow police area supervisors to do so independent of broader shifts of departmental policy and resources. Acting on the results of police-community dialogue shows respect for the community. Respecting all who come in contact with police is another tenet of community policing. Police departments with a community policing orientation adopted a set of values that emphasized a sensitive, respectful demeanor in every police contact and a commitment to collaborate with people from all works of life on addressing neighborhood problems. This differed significantly from previous eras of policing, wherein citizens were treated with indifference unless they were victimized by criminals or they had committed a crime, in which case they were considered enemies of the law. Without demonstrating respect for all communities and their members, police departments would be unlikely to build the relationships of trust that are necessary to make the community-police partnership function.

A final distinguishing value of community policing is transparency. Community policing practitioners were to be transparent about their strategies, objectives, and tactics to demonstrate respect for the community's role in determining how their neighborhoods are policed. Critically too, police were to be transparent about their values, communicating their goal to be service oriented, respect democratic processes, accrue legitimacy, and work through collaboration and transparency.

Articulating a Police Agency's Values

O. W. Wilson, the reform superintendent of the Chicago Police Department, published a set of core values for that department in the early 1960s. In 1983, Lee P. Brown, while chief of police in Houston, Texas, also published a value statement for his department. Yet, most police agencies did little to explicitly define the core values that would guide their activities. In many agencies, police rules and regulations reflected values, but they were not stated as such—a firearms policy that dictates that fatal force could only be used to protect life, for example, reflected a desire to protect life above all else. Only in recent years has it become common for police organizations to more expressly list their values in writing.

Values can be explicitly articulated in departmental mottos—"to protect and to serve"—or policies and can encompass strategy, objectives, and intradepartmental norms (e.g., integrity). As in previous eras, they may also be implicit, inculcated through training or agency culture. Such implicit values are not always products of intentionally planned policy by command staff or political leadership; rather, values can also be generated by cohorts within police departments and society at large. Notably, values are often confused with assumptions about the nature of policing. For example, many assume that police agencies' primary function is arresting criminals, and many police officers see their responsibility as simply deterring lawlessness. In departments that practice community policing, this common misconception is remarkably false. Indeed, such assumptions about the nature of values in policing belie the development of distinct sets of values during the 20th century. As the history detailed above makes clear, each era of policing was defined most powerfully by a distinct shift in values.

In sum, the values of community policing are somewhat different from those of professionalized policing and far different from the values that existed in the political era of policing. While many tenets of professionalism remain important today, community policing directly seeks to solve problems identified by neighborhood residents and improve quality of life. This requires a commitment to a different set of values than the traditional, law enforcement-oriented policing, including transparency, respect, empathy, commitment to listening to and collaborating with ordinary citizens, problem solving, adherence to democratic principles, and service orientation. Community policing has been most significantly defined by this set of distinct values, regardless of how it has actually been carried out.

Robert Wasserman

See also Community Policing, Evolution of; Customer-Based Policing; Ethical Considerations; Immigrant Populations, Community Policing Strategies for; Police-Community Relations; Restorative Justice

Further Readings

Community Policing Consortium. (1994). *Understanding community policing: A framework for action*. NCJ 148457. Washington, DC: U.S. Department of Justice, Bureau of Justice Assistance.

Kelling, G. L., & Moore, M. H. (1988). The evolving strategy of policing. NCJ 114213. *Perspectives on Policing, 4*. Washington, DC: U.S. Department of Justice, National Institute of Justice.

Tyler, T. R. (2004). To better serve and protect: Improving police practices. In W. G. Skogan (Ed.), *Annals of the American Academy of Political and Social Science, 593*, 84–99.

Tyler, T. R. (2007). *Legitimacy and criminal justice: International perspectives*. New York, NY: Russell Sage Foundation.

Wasserman, R., & Moore, M. H. (1988). Values in policing. *Perspectives on Policing, 8*. Washington, DC: U.S. Department of Justice, National Institute of Justice. Retrieved from https://www.ncjrs.gov/pdffiles1/nij/114216.pdf

B

BRITISH ANTECEDENTS TO COMMUNITY POLICING

See Metropolitan Police Act of 1892

BROKEN WINDOWS THEORY

Broken windows is an influential criminological theory that posits that minor disorderly conditions left unchecked will result in neighborhood decline and increased serious criminal activity. James Q. Wilson and George Kelling originally presented it in the March 1982 issue of *Atlantic Monthly* magazine. Proponents of the theory credit the order-maintenance policing strategies derived from it with reducing crime in communities across the United States in recent decades. By contrast, critics of the theory submit that it is unproven and has been used to justify overly aggressive police tactics that infringe on individuals' rights and antagonize large segments of communities. This entry outlines the tenets of broken windows theory. It then presents a concise overview of the empirical research conducted to examine the validity of the theory. This entry concludes with a brief discussion of the criticisms leveled against policing practices based on the theory.

Tenets of Broken Windows Theory

Broken windows theory is based on two key notions. First, a primary source of fear in public spaces, along with fear of crime, is the fear of being bothered by disorderly people. This disorderly behavior—sometimes referred to as *social* disorder—need not be violent, or even criminal, to be fear inducing. Rather, unpredictable or unruly behavior by rowdy teenagers, addicts, drunks, and other loiterers can induce fear. Second, at the community level, disorder and crime are indirectly linked. A broken window is more than just an example, along with graffiti and litter-filled vacant lots, of *physical* disorder. Instead, that metaphorical broken window, left unrepaired, indicates that no one cares. Unchecked social and physical disorder manifests a breakdown of community controls, and thus become harbingers of more disorder and street crime, potentially including serious crime.

Because disorder can be as fear inducing as more serious crime, altering policing techniques can meaningfully address disorderly conditions, and thus make citizens feel safer. This premise is based in part on findings from an evaluation of a police foot patrol initiative in Newark, New Jersey. Whereas police departments with a crime-fighting focus will give low priority to enforcing laws against disorderly acts such as public drinking and drug use, this evaluation indicated that although the initiative did not result in less crime, citizens reported feeling safer as the result of officers who walked their beats (as opposed to patrolling from their squad cars) and proactively addressed disorderly behavior. According to Wilson and Kelling, the effective beat officer in Newark sometimes achieved results by enforcing the law, but just as often employed informal measures—including acts that likely would not survive legal challenge—to uphold neighborhood-specific standards of public order.

The idea that unchecked disorder and crime are causally linked is rooted in psychological research. In the late 1960s, the social psychologist Philip Zimbardo conducted research which showed that property which is demonstrably untended quickly becomes a target for vandalism and theft, even in "good" neighborhoods. From this research, Wilson and Kelling infer that "untended" behavior can result in a failure of community controls. Unaddressed instances of physical disorder and social disorder can beget further instances of disorder. As the frequency of such instances increases, law-abiding residents will alter their behavior to reduce their perceived risk of victimization. As their confidence in their ability to regulate public behavior diminishes, they may take steps from tending to stay inside their homes to moving to less disorderly neighborhoods. In sum, as social isolation waxes, informal social control wanes. In a community that experiences such a downward spiral, disorder intensifies and becomes more pervasive, and criminogenic conditions flourish.

According to Wilson and Kelling, it is crucial to address not only crimes committed against individuals, but also those that in the aggregate harm communities and neighborhoods. Through the lens of their theory, a single public drunk in a community is more than an individual engaging in behavior that is merely undesirable to others; instead, left unchecked, that drunk represents the first broken window. While the harm caused by that single individual is minimal, even inconsequential, this first broken window might lead to a thousand more, ultimately destroying the community. Thus, in their view, no disorderly act is "victimless." They lament the situation where laws designed to protect the rights of individual citizens restrict a police officer's ability to uphold the standards of his neighborhood beat.

Empirical Tests of Broken Windows

Research studies examining the explanatory validity of broken windows theory can be divided into two broad categories: those that examine hypotheses derived from the theory and those that evaluate the effects of broken windows-policing strategies.

Regarding the former, a handful of key studies have examined whether there is a relationship between disorder and serious crime; to the extent that there is, broken windows theory, and by extension order-maintenance policing strategies, would be supported. Wesley Skogan, in his 1990 study of 40 neighborhoods located in six cities, found a strong relationship between residents' perceptions of disorder in their neighborhoods and the likelihood that they had experienced robbery victimization. By contrast, Bernard Harcourt and Jens Ludwig (2006) conducted independent analyses of Skogan's data and found that the disorder-robbery relationship that Skogan identified disappeared upon excluding five neighborhoods from one of his six study sites (Newark, New Jersey). Harcourt and Ludwig also note that Skogan did not disclose that he found no relationships between disorder and the other four types of crime that he considered: burglary, physical assault, purse snatching, and rape. Also refuting broken windows are results of a study based on systematic social observation of Chicago neighborhoods by Robert Sampson and Stephen Raudenbush (1999). They found that disorder and three types of crime (burglary, robbery, and homicide) were related at the bivariate level. However, multivariate data analyses showed that, rather than being causally related, disorder and crime both originate from the same social and structural conditions. In light of this finding, they conclude that attempts by the police to stem crime by focusing on disorder, despite their political popularity, are ill advised. By comparison, Ralph Taylor (2001) found, based on his longitudinal study of Baltimore (Maryland) neighborhoods using multiple methodologies, that while disorder is a weak predictor of several types of violent crime, structural factors such as racial composition of a neighborhood are generally stronger predictors.

Despite the perception common among law enforcement policymakers that policing strategies focusing on minor offenses—alternatively referred to as "order-maintenance," "quality-of-life," "zero-tolerance," or simply "broken windows" policing—result in reductions in more serious crime, empirical evidence in support of this notion is mixed. Although arrest is just one of several tactics that police could employ to stem neighborhood disorder, including informal approaches, such as warning, counseling, and reminding, levels of misdemeanor arrests are often the sole measure employed in the study of broken windows-influenced policing tactics. Representative studies in this vein include George Kelling and William Sousa's (2001) examination of the relationship between misdemeanor arrests and several types of violent crime across New York City's 75 police precincts. Defining order-maintenance policing in this manner, they found that it made a significant contribution to the city's declining crime rates in the 1990s. Similarly, Hope Corman and Naci Mocan analyzed monthly crime data for New York City as a whole from 1970 to 2000. After statistically controlling for a number of potential rival causal factors, their results indicate a negative relationship between misdemeanor arrest rates and the rates for two types of crime: robbery and motor vehicle theft. Bernard Harcourt and Jens Ludwig (2006) take issue with the findings of each of these studies, impugning the methodologies on which they are based. They contend, for example, that in interpreting precincts' crime trends, Kelling and Sousa failed to account for a statistical phenomenon referred to as "mean reversion"—the idea that over time numbers (including crime rates) that increase the most will tend to be the ones that decrease the most.

Critiques of Broken Windows Policing

While the many advocates of broken windows-based policing strategies often credit them with dramatic reductions in crime, especially in the 1990s, many criminologists counter that factors such as the decline in the crack epidemic and demographic changes are more salient reasons for crime's decline. Moreover, critics say that some of the specific tactics commonly associated with broken windows policing, such as heavy use of stop-and-frisk and an emphasis on making arrests for petty and misdemeanor offenses, are not just ineffectual in fighting crime but are otherwise harmful. Such tactics are perceived by many as police harassment and have been identified as violating individuals' rights (e.g., when stop-and-frisks are carried out without probable cause). They also have been associated with cases of racial and ethnic bias (when members of minority groups are disproportionately targeted by police), thereby straining police-community relationships. It has also been pointed out that any

reductions in crime that result from the heavy use of stop-and-frisk and arrests for low-level offenses very well could be due *not* to the mechanisms described by broken windows theory, but instead to the enhanced surveillance that exemplifies these tactics.

Robert R. Weidner

See also CompStat; Fear of Crime; Foot Patrols; Hot Spots; Police-Community Relations; Policing, Three Eras of; Tipping Points of Neighborhoods

Further Readings

Harcourt, B. E., & Ludwig, J. (2006). Broken windows: New evidence from New York City and a five-city social experiment. *University of Chicago Law Review, 73,* 271–320.

Kelling, G. L., & Sousa, W. H. (2001). *Do police matter? An analysis of the impact of New York City's police reforms.* New York, NY: Center for Civic Innovation, Manhattan Institute.

Sampson, R. J., & Raudenbush, S. W. (1999). Systematic social observation of public spaces: A new look at disorder in urban neighborhoods. *American Journal of Sociology, 105*(3), 603–651.

Skogan, W. G. (1990). *Disorder and decline: Crime and the spiral of decay in American neighborhoods.* New York, NY: Free Press.

Taylor, R. B. (2001). *Breaking away from broken windows: Baltimore neighborhoods and the nationwide fight against crime, grime, fear, and decline.* Boulder, CO: Westview Press.

Wilson, J. Q., & Kelling, G. L. (1982, March). Broken windows: The police and neighborhood safety. *Atlantic Monthly, 249*(3), 29–38.

BUILDING PARTNERSHIPS AND STAKEHOLDERS

The earliest attempts to define and describe community policing emphasized partnerships and stakeholders. Although community policing pioneers did not have the luxury of 30 years of practical community policing experience, their vision of police and community as coproducers of safety was prophetic. Early iterations of community policing asked citizens to be the eyes and ears of the police. The police could then use citizen reports to "fight crime" and enhance community safety. Incredibly rapid societal, technological, and economic changes are forcing police to rethink their historically paternalistic and reactive roles. While in the earlier days of community policing, creating and maintaining partnerships were stated as desirable goals, building partnerships continues to be an objective of community policing, even in today's harsh economic climate. This entry describes this populist demand for more efficient and accountable police organizations, which can only be achieved by increased stakeholder identification, engagement, and collaborations.

Engaging Stakeholders

Police engage citizens through partnerships. Partnerships are developed by nurturing stakeholders. So the first rule of partnership building is to create an environment in which stakeholders are actively involved and valued. A conscious and meaningful effort must be made to provide opportunities for law enforcement and the public to build stronger relationships. Citizens need an avenue whereby they can express concerns to the police department, and the police need to be transparent and trustworthy to engage in dialogue with the public. Successful relationship building requires the police and public to recognize that each is a legitimate contributor to neighborhood safety and crime-reduction efforts. The cardinal rule in stakeholder and partnership-building endeavors is that the police must become the eyes and ears of the public as well as the public being eyes and ears for the police. The ultimate goal of framing the proper relationship with community stakeholders is to implement sustainable solutions that reverse neighborhood decay, thereby improving the quality of life for residents.

It is essential that the police, residents, businesses, and other government entities collaborate in addressing neighborhood crime and disorder. As an example, the Arlington (Texas) Police Department's (APD) community policing and problem-solving efforts entails partnerships and collaborative ventures with all such stakeholders. This collaboration allows the Arlington community to expeditiously identify emerging neighborhood challenges and logical and creative quality-of-life enhancing solutions. True collaboration requires open communication, collaboration across the entire domain of community concerns, an accountability system that places 24–7, geographic-based accountability in the hands of one person—not 10—and applying emerging technology as a force multiplier to benefit police and community collaborators. A community policing agency should have the organization structure and accountability systems that support partnership building. At the core of community, it was simply line-level officers having face-to-face contact with individuals, business owners, and other community organizations. It was important that the community had a direct line of communication with law enforcement that was open and candid.

Several key strategies rolled out during this new era of geographic accountability in Arlington included, but were not limited to, creating fixed beat areas with permanently assigned patrol officers, stressing problem-solving methods to prevent crime and disorder, and involving all rank structures in the 24-hour beat accountability model. Geographic policing provides an interconnected relationship between the line-level officers, residents, and business tenants that encompass the officer's geographic area of responsibility. Patrol officers are taught from the initial academy training days and through extensive postacademy training to be proactive and develop problem-solving tactics. This process starts with developing relationships with area residents, businesses, and faith-based organizations to name just a few. Officers partner with area apartment community and business owners, helping relationships thrive and develop a cooperation that takes hold within the community. Self-sustaining accountability systems result from these police-initiated stakeholder alliances. Business council meetings can be facilitated by the Chamber of Commerce. The Chamber uses peer pressure to ensure retailers are responsible and commercial corridors are maintained in pristine condition. They also recruit investors for problem or neglected properties creating financial incentives for those owners to sell.

The nexus to economic development becomes very clear when police partnerships result in building physical structures and securing environments where economic transactions occur. Partnering with the development community and nonprofit community development corporations is an emerging police best practice that serves as a catalyst for "building communities out of crime." Generally, such practices will result in reductions in crime, increased quality of life for residents, enhanced departmental communication across all layers of the organization, and higher officer job satisfaction. The geographical accountability structure has greatly strengthened stakeholder engagement through relationship building.

A Variety of Programs and Activities

Engaging other governmental partners is essential for building collaborative partnerships with the community. The power of forging ongoing intergovernmental collaborations is evident in Arlington's National Night Out activities. There is no other single event where all stakeholders within the community can come together, including district attorneys, city employees, elected officials, religious leaders or faith-based organization representatives, judges, prosecutors, corrections administrators, public and private school leaders, business leaders, and other community leaders, activists, and residents, are prominently visible and demonstrating their commitment to community. By having such diverse participants, initial relationships are formed, existing relationships are strengthened, and networking increases.

Time and resources must be invested into police partner–initiated efforts. The department should ensure attendance from all levels of the organization at weekly, monthly, and quarterly meetings held by community organizations and citizens. Trust building is facilitated when stakeholders can place a face with a name. Barriers are brought down, destroying the perception of law enforcement as a secret, rigid governmental operation. Information that can be shared with businesses and citizens should be routinely disseminated through newsletters, e-mail systems, social media, and face-to-face contacts with beat officers. Providing such information furthers the idea that relationships with citizens are needed and everyone is part of the team effort.

Keeping the public informed about police activities is also about reaching audiences that might not normally consider partnering with the department. By using a vast array of social media tools—Facebook, Twitter, and YouTube—police can interact with their existing partners and open the door for new ones to join their efforts. Agencies can also engage in such activities as hosting a virtual ride-along on Twitter (some of which have been named "Tweet-Alongs"). While riding with an officer, a citizen might sit in the patrol car passenger seat and send Twitter-message calls for service and traffic stops. Doing so shows the sort of work that officers do on a daily basis that gets little attention or recognition. Simply put, police are telling their story directly to their customers and supplementing the filtered version provided by traditional news outlets.

The traditional community-oriented policing and problem-solving approach encourages citizens to take pride and ownership in the community, for example, by engaging in preventive patrols of the neighborhood. The agency's Crime Prevention Unit can facilitate such patrol programs by training citizens, teaching them about patrol, reporting procedures, and identifying suspicious activity. By inviting program participants to patrol briefings and providing sanitized versions of crime intelligence reports to enhance their patrols, the agency can ensure that program participants feel part of the team. Another new development for engaging stakeholders is a citizens-on-patrol mobile program, wherein the police agency provides city-issued, marked vehicles to civilian program members. The members are then assigned to "hot spot" areas to patrol, similar to how patrol officers are assigned.

Municipal police and sheriff's agencies can also develop various community watch organizations throughout the city or county. Those groups can serve to foster collaboration and familiarity between agency officials and citizens. Through these organizations, citizens learn to anticipate, recognize, and appraise the crime risks in their neighborhoods, and how to take action that can reduce opportunities for them to be victimized. The police cannot be everywhere all the time, so this partnership between citizens and the police is important to reduce neighborhood crime. Promoting positive interactions within a neighborhood may displace negative activities, and the community may be able to take back their neighborhoods, increasing optimism and tranquility. The faith-based community is also an abundant resource for partnerships. An example is Arlington's Clergy and Police Partnership (ACAPP), a coalition of clergy from every faith and denomination that partners with the department and is available to respond to crisis situations in the community. There is a formalized training program where clergy are taught basic police principles and periodically ride along with officers. Upon graduation, clergy are entrusted with providing calm in crisis situations, assisting in certain crime issues when ministers are requested, and offering a variety of support, from serving youths to crime victims of all ages.

Conclusions

There are many ways in which an organization can engage with the community to increase public safety and reduce crime and disorder. To police effectively, partnerships between law enforcement and the citizenry, the business community, other city departments, law enforcement agencies, social service organizations, and so on, are required.

Theron L. Bowman

See also Citizen Patrols; Citizen Police Academies; Citizen Surveys; Collaboration With Outside Agencies; Community, Definition of; Community Cohesion and Empowerment; Community Justice; Restorative Justice; Social Capital; Volunteers, Police Use of

Further Readings

Correia, M. E. (2000). Social capital and sense of community building: Building social cohesion. In R. W. Glensor, M. E. Correia, & K. J. Peak (Eds.), *Policing communities: Understanding crime and solving problems* (pp. 75–82). Los Angeles, CA: Roxbury.

Couper, D., & Lobitz, S. (1991). *Quality policing: The Madison experience.* Washington, DC: Police Executive Research Forum.

Gardner, J. (1994, September). There is more than a ray of hope for America's future: Rebuilding America's sense of community. *Journal for Quality and Participation, 17*(5). Retrieved from http://www.worldtrans.org/qual/Americancommunity.html

Gurwitt, R. (1993, August). Communitarianism: You can try it at home. *Governing, 6,* 33–39.

Osborne, D., & Gaebler, T. (1992). *Reinventing government: How the entrepreneurial spirit is transforming the public sector.* Reading, MA: Addison-Wesley.

Wilson, L. J. (1995, April). Placing community-oriented policing in the broader realms of community cooperation. *The Police Chief, 62*(4), 127.

CENTER FOR PROBLEM-ORIENTED POLICING

The Center for Problem-Oriented Policing serves as a source of information for police practitioners and academics both in the United States and abroad. The center's publications, training modules, case studies, awards program, and annual conference can serve as an initial point of inquiry when police attempt to address crime and disorder through the use of problem-oriented policing. The sole mission of the center is to advance the concept and practice of problem-oriented policing in order to assist the police in more effectively addressing neighborhood problems of crime and disorder. This entry discusses the means by which the center attempts to accomplish this mission.

Purpose and Mission

The Center for Problem-Oriented Policing is a non-profit research organization, established in 2002 to advance the development and practice of problem-oriented policing. Essentially, this is a strategy involving the clear definition and analysis of a crime problem, and then developing and implementing the most effective way of dealing with it. The center includes a content-rich website that features the following informational products:

- Problem-Oriented Guides for Police series
- Manuals on various topics related to problem-oriented policing and situational crime

prevention (i.e., strategies that involve environmental changes for reducing the opportunities for crime and increase its risk, such as the installation of surveillance equipment in a parking lot experiencing vandalism)
- Basic instructional information about the history and elements of problem-oriented policing and situational crime prevention
- A model academic curriculum in problem-oriented policing and situational crime prevention
- Hundreds of interactive instructional modules that train and challenge officers' problem-solving skills
- A virtual library of readings on problem-oriented policing and situational crime prevention
- Online collections of reports, case studies, and conference presentations of problem-oriented policing and situational crime prevention in practice
- A collection of problem-oriented policing and situational crime prevention publications that have been translated from the original English to other languages

In addition, the Center for Problem-Oriented Policing sponsors an annual conference and awards program that further help to disseminate knowledge about problem-oriented policing and situational crime prevention.

The Center for Problem-Oriented Policing represents a framework for advancing several long-standing goals for improving policing, namely to improve the collaborative efforts of police practitioners and scholars through the development and dissemination of a professional body of policing knowledge.

The Center for Problem-Oriented Policing and its Problem-Oriented Guides for Police series seek to serve much the same purpose for the police profession that other organizations and publications have served for other professions: a centralized, comprehensive compendium of professional knowledge to inform and improve—and sometimes to standardize—its practitioners' substantive work.

History

The idea for the Center for Problem-Oriented Policing grew out of Herman Goldstein's conceptual work on problem-oriented policing and subsequent efforts to experiment with and evaluate the concept. More particularly, it resulted from two initiatives funded by the U.S. Department of Justice's Office of Community Oriented Policing Services (COPS Office).

The first initiative was a visiting fellowship awarded to Michael S. Scott (the author of this encyclopedia entry) for 1998 to 1999. Scott is a former student of and research assistant to Goldstein, and former police administrator with extensive experience introducing problem-oriented policing principles and methods to police agencies. Scott spent a year assessing the progress made over the course of the prior 20 years across the policing profession in adopting a problem-oriented approach to police work. He reviewed the research literature; interviewed experts; visited police agencies in the United States, the United Kingdom, and Canada that had adopted problem-oriented policing approaches; analyzed problem-oriented policing project reports; and drew upon his own knowledge of problem-oriented policing's principles to inform a set of recommendations to the COPS Office that both reflected on progress made to date and recommended future directions. Among those recommendations was the creation of an accessible body of knowledge about how police could most effectively address the wide range of public-safety problems that comprised the essence of their work.

The second federally funded initiative that led to the creation of the Center for Problem-Oriented Policing was an open solicitation by the COPS Office to develop problem-solving tools for police practitioners. A group of scholars interested in problem-oriented policing, comprising Michael Scott, Herman Goldstein, Ronald Clarke, John Eck, Rana Sampson, and Deborah Lamm Weisel, submitted a proposal to the COPS Office to design and develop prototypes of guidebooks for police practitioners on best practices for addressing selected public-safety problems. Between 1999 and 2001, this group, in consultation with several U.S. police agencies and the COPS Office, designed the Problem-Oriented Guides for Police series and produced 20 guidebooks on selected problems. Through a subsequent award of funding, the guidebooks were field-tested in four U.S. police agencies (Newark, New Jersey; Savannah, Georgia; Chula Vista, California; and Raleigh, North Carolina).

Two members of the original group, Michael Scott and Ronald Clarke, decided to pursue additional funding from the COPS Office to continue work on the guides and to create a website to disseminate the guides more widely. They recruited Graeme Newman, a criminologist with substantial expertise in publishing and website development. Scott, Clarke, and Newman then established the center and incorporated it as a nonprofit organization, with Scott as the director, and Clarke and Newman as associate directors, a structure that continues as of this writing.

Structure

By design, the Center for Problem-Oriented Policing is not a brick-and-mortar organization with central offices and permanent staff. Rather, it operates as a collaboration of a wide array of individuals and organizations. It is run out of the office of its director, originally in Savannah, Georgia, and now in Madison, Wisconsin, where Scott is also a clinical professor at the University of Wisconsin Law School. Its associate directors, Clarke and Newman, are on the faculty at Rutgers University and the University at Albany, respectively. Library research for the problem-oriented guides is conducted principally at the Rutgers University Library, drawing from its extensive criminal justice collection and the special expertise of its criminal justice librarian, Phyllis Schultze. Website development and maintenance is performed at the Professional Development Program at the University at Albany. Conference planning, award-program administration, writing and editing guidebooks, and other administrative support functions are performed by scholars and professionals, working as paid consultants, and operating from their offices across the United States and abroad (including in the United Kingdom, Australia, Norway, Italy, and Estonia).

A Problem Classification Scheme

Soon after launching the Problem-Oriented Guides for Police project, the project team, led by Clarke and Eck, began mapping the universe of public-safety problems that police are commonly called upon to address. This work took two different approaches. The first approach was to start with a theoretical construct about how policing problems might be categorized. Using routine activity theory (which seeks to explain how physical and social environments create crime opportunities by the intersection of a "likely" offender, a "suitable" target, and the absence of a "capable guardian" against crime, such as a police officer or security guard) as its basis, Clarke and Eck developed a scheme that organized policing problems according to two dimensions: the nature of the problematic behavior and the nature of the setting in

which the behavior occurs (see Table 1). This scheme could be made even more refined if additional dimensions of problems were to be factored in, such as the times when problems occur, the types of people involved in problems, the scope of the problem, or the degree to which a problem was concentrated in terms of time, place, or persons involved.

The second approach to mapping the universe of policing problems was atheoretical: It was a running catalogue of known, common policing problems, broken down to whatever level of specificity seemed reasonable given what is presently known about the problem. Under this scheme, "theft" would be too broad to be useful as a category because while police can prevent and address certain kinds of theft in similar ways, other types of theft require distinct approaches (for instance, police have different strategies for auto theft than they do for bicycle theft). It is to this latter catalogue that the Center for Problem-Oriented Policing has referred when selecting the topics for the Problem-Oriented Guides for Police series. To date, the center has produced guides on 72 of these specific problems, or roughly 30% of the catalogued policing problems.

Table 1   The Beginnings of a Problem Classification Scheme

	Behaviors						
Environments	Predatory	Consensual	Interpersonal Conflict	Incivilities	Endangerment	Protest and Political Action	Misuse of Police
Residential							
Recreational							
Offices							
Retail							
Industrial							
Agricultural							
Educational							
Human service							
Public ways							
Transport							
Open/							
Transitional							

Source: Author.

As the Center for Problem-Oriented Policing has published more guides, it has become useful to develop another method of categorizing topics. A scheme of overlapping categories has been developed to allow readers to see guide topics similar in a significant respect clustered together. At present, the guides have been listed and cross-listed in the following categories of problem types: alcohol and drug; burglary and theft; business related; disorder and nuisance; frauds; gang related; misuse of police resources; robbery; school and college related; sex related; traffic; vehicle related; violence; and youth and juvenile related.

The Problem-Oriented Guides for Police Series

Within the Problem-Oriented Guides for Police series are three distinct guide series: *Problem-Specific Guides, Response Guides,* and *Problem-Solving Tools.*

The *Problem-Specific Guides* cover the specific behavioral problems that police are commonly called upon to address. Each of these guides follows a standard structure: describing the nature and scope of the problem, the harms caused by it, and the known factors that contribute to it; suggested research questions to develop a thorough understanding of the problem at the local level and measures for determining what impact police are having on the problem; and responses to the problem that are believed—on the basis of research and reliable police practice—to be either effective or of limited effectiveness in addressing the problem.

Response Guides take the reverse approach of the *Problem-Specific Guides*: They cover common police responses to crime and disorder, explaining what is known—again, from research and reliable police practice—about how those responses are intended to achieve policing objectives, what types of problems they are likely to be effective in addressing, and considerations for how police can make the response most effective and fair. Among the topics of *Response Guides* are enforcement crackdowns, street lighting, asset forfeiture, and crime prevention publicity campaigns.

The *Problem-Solving Tools* series covers research and analysis methods that police will likely find helpful in analyzing and assessing problems. Among the topics in print are assessing responses to problems,

analyzing repeat victimization, and measuring displacement and diffusion (i.e., the phenomenon whereby a specified crime problem is relocated to other times and places and therefore the root causes of the problem are not addressed) of benefits.

The web-based versions of the Problem-Oriented Guides for Police series are enhanced with links to references, glossary terms, and related problem-oriented policing projects, and additional photographs. Conversion of the guides to formats suitable for electronic reader devices is under way.

To supplement the Problem-Oriented Guides for Police series, the Center for Problem-Oriented Policing also has produced several special publications. The topics of those currently available are crime analysis for problem solving, the local police response to terrorism, and the political executive's role in problem-oriented policing. A manual on implementing problem-oriented policing in a police agency and a manual on intelligence analysis and problem solving are also in production.

International Problem-Oriented Policing Conference

The Center for Problem-Oriented Policing also sponsors the annual International Problem-Oriented Policing Conference, originally launched and sponsored by the Police Executive Research Forum from 1990 to 2003. The conference attracts police practitioners, analysts, and scholars to discuss a variety of topics pertinent to the practice of problem-oriented policing and situational crime prevention. Sessions are of several types: those on how certain communities addressed specific problems; those that provide instruction on problem-solving skills and methods; and those that share experiences with the administration of problem-oriented policing. The conference is hosted by police agencies committed to adopting a problem-oriented approach to policing and is held in a different city in the United States each year.

The Herman Goldstein Award for Excellence in Problem-Oriented Policing

As part of the annual conference, the Center for Problem-Oriented Policing sponsors the Herman Goldstein Award for Excellence in Problem-Oriented Policing, also having assumed sponsorship of this program from the Police Executive Research Forum. Since the program's inception in

1993, approximately 1,000 problem-oriented policing projects have been submitted for consideration. Each year, on the basis of a standardized judging process by expert judges, the projects that best exemplify the principles and methods of problem-oriented policing are recognized with awards. The police officers, analysts, and community members who were closely involved with the problem-solving effort then present their work to the attendees of the annual conference. In recent years, attendees have also participated in the judging process. In addition to recognizing exemplary work, the presentation of the work and subsequent posting of the project reports on the Center for Problem-Oriented Policing website help disseminate good problem-oriented policing practice across the whole police profession.

The Center for Problem-Oriented Policing has also collected and made accessible on its website the problem-oriented policing project reports submitted to a similar awards program in the United Kingdom, the Tilley Awards. This award program, open only to British police agencies, is sponsored by the U.K. Home Office (which works to support visible, responsive, and accountable policing and problem solving) and named in honor of Professor Nick Tilley, a leading scholar on problem-oriented policing who is affiliated with Nottingham University and the Jill Dando Institute of Crime Science at University College London.

Virtual Library

To further supplement the Problem-Oriented Guides for Police series and the Goldstein and Tilley award reports, the Center for Problem-Oriented Policing website also has built up an extensive virtual library of publications and reports pertinent to both problem-oriented policing and situational crime prevention. It includes many publications and reports referenced in the Problem-Oriented Guides for Police series (where permission has been granted by the copyright holder); background readings on problem-oriented policing, situational crime prevention, and problem research and analysis; other especially relevant guides and manuals published by other publishers; unpublished problem-oriented policing documents (so-called gray literature); a glossary of terms particular to problem-oriented policing, situational crime prevention, and crime analysis; and links to other relevant organizations' websites.

Learning Center

The Center for Problem-Oriented Policing website also contains several instructional modules to help users learn about problem-oriented policing's principles and methods. These include an interactive learning exercise in which the user adopts the role of a police consultant, hired to help a community improve its response to a serious street prostitution problem. The module allows the user to learn about both the problem of street prostitution and the problem analysis process, and to receive feedback on the basis of the user's work. There is also a Problem Analysis Module (PAM) that guides users through real-world problem solving, allowing them to respond to questions about their problem with real information and data. The module is designed to guide users toward effective responses to their problem and away from responses less likely to be effective. There is also a video-based instructional module on the problem of speeding in residential areas; basic information about the elements and principles of problem-oriented policing and situational crime prevention; a video of police scholar Samuel Walker interviewing Goldstein, the original proponent of problem-oriented policing; a model academic curriculum (designed for a 14-week undergraduate course, but adaptable to other levels and lengths); and a summary and examples of the 25 techniques of situational crime prevention.

Translated Works

The Center for Problem-Oriented Policing has had many of its publications translated into other languages and made these versions available on its website. The most-often translated publication is *Crime Analysis for Problem Solvers,* either the American or the British version. As of 2012, this publication has been translated into Chinese, Czech, Dutch, Estonian, Farsi, German, Italian, Japanese, Korean, Latvian, Portuguese, Slovenian, Spanish, Swedish, and Turkish. Several other publications of the Center for Problem-Oriented Policing have also been translated into Spanish, Portuguese, Turkish, Slovenian, and Hebrew.

The Center's Future

In August 2012, the Office of Community Oriented Policing Services announced that it would not continue funding the Center for Problem-Oriented Policing. This marked the first time since the center began its work in 1999 that it would not receive this allocation. Because of the timing of the decision, the center was left with little time to seek alternative funding arrangements. Therefore, many if not all of the programs and activities described in this entry may be discontinued, unless new funding is secured. A high priority for the center is to preserve its website so that the vast amount of information contained therein will continue to be available to and accessible by the public. —Ed. Note

Michael S. Scott

See also Community Oriented Policing Services, Office of; Community Policing: Resources, Time, and Finances in Support of; Community Policing and Problem Solving, Definition of; Problem-Oriented Policing: Elements, Processes, Implications; Problem-Oriented Policing, Goldstein's Development of

Further Readings

Eck, J. E., & Clarke, R. V. (2003). Classifying common police problems: A routine activity approach. In M. J. Smith & D. B. Cornish, *Theory for practice in situational crime prevention: Crime prevention studies, Volume 16*. New York, NY: Criminal Justice Press. Retrieved from http://www.popcenter.org/library/crimeprevention/volume_16/TitlePages.pdf

Goldstein, H. (1990). *Problem-oriented policing.* New York, NY: McGraw-Hill.

Scott, M. S. (2000). *Problem-oriented policing: Reflections on the first 20 years.* Washington, DC: U.S. Department of Justice, Office of Community Oriented Policing Services. Retrieved from http://www.cops.usdoj.gov/Publications/e03011022.txt

Website

Center for Problem-Oriented Policing; http:// www.popcenter.org

CITIZEN PATROLS

Citizen patrols are organized groups of volunteers who actively engage in activities aimed at deterring and reducing crime in their communities. These patrol groups can be found throughout the world, are diverse in their member demographics and organizational structures, and often work directly with specific police agencies. As with other forms of positive citizen engagement with the police, citizen patrols can complement community policing and problem solving by providing a coordinated approach to crime fighting and enhancing police efforts. This entry describes various types of citizen patrols found within the United States, the purpose and general functions of these groups, research findings concerning their impact on crime levels, and the major controversies surrounding citizen patrol organizations.

Types of Patrols

Citizen patrols are an integral part of U.S. history. From vigilante groups who sought justice for victims in the Wild West, to volunteer watchmen who guarded towns at night while sheriffs slept, to formal neighborhood watch organizations created in the last century, people other than police have always played a role in addressing community crime. Efforts to organize citizens interested in patrolling neighborhoods to prevent crime became common in the 1970s, and the prevalence and popularity of these groups grew tremendously in the 1980s. Citizen patrols, an extension of the aforementioned crime prevention efforts, are called various names, such as "policing volunteers," "volunteers on patrol," "citizen observer patrols," "community action patrols," and "police partners."

Citizen patrols can be divided into two general categories: sanctioned (or police-sanctioned) and unsanctioned. In 2012, the Citizens on Patrol National Organization recognized more than 80 police-sanctioned citizen patrols in 19 different states. While no official list of unsanctioned citizen patrols exists, two of the most widely recognized organizations are the Guardian Angels and the Minutemen. There are several noteworthy similarities and differences between sanctioned and unsanctioned citizen patrols.

Similarities

Almost all citizen patrols groups are staffed by non-sworn neighborhood residents, although many jurisdictions do not prevent off-duty officers from participating in these groups. Most groups, therefore, consist of unpaid volunteers who join based on a desire to take an active role in reducing crime or to assist others who live in their community. Those who participate in the patrols often wear identifiable uniforms and drive in marked vehicles (i.e., have magnetic signs on the exterior of their personal vehicles) to increase their visibility and clarify the purpose of their activities.

Differences

Sanctioned citizen patrols groups tend to work directly with a specific police agency. These groups may be started, organized, and funded by police, who may also provide sanctioned groups with equipment such as radios, binoculars, cell phones, uniforms, or vehicles. These citizen patrols usually report directly to their sponsoring police agency, and a specific officer or department staff member may be assigned to help coordinate the patrols and respond to community issues or events reported by the group.

Alternatively, unsanctioned groups operate independently from police agencies; they are usually initiated, organized, and financed through private funding sources or by patrol members who support their own efforts through volunteer time, donations, and fund-raising. This independence allows for other organizational differences. For example, while members of sanctioned citizen patrols must usually undergo a criminal background check and meet specific background criteria, the criteria for membership may be different and based on the personal preferences of the groups' leadership (e.g., political biases, lifestyle, or personality characteristics). Also, while many police agencies have developed formal written rules or guidelines to manage patrol volunteer behaviors and activities, unsanctioned groups may operate using less formal strategies and procedures.

Purpose and Functions

Although citizen patrol groups vary in their ties to police agencies and organizational structures, the general and primary objective of most patrols is to prevent crime. They differ, however, from other community-based crime prevention efforts, including neighborhood watch organizations. Neighborhood watch groups are formed to increase residents' vigilance over unregulated public spaces (e.g., parks) and encourage the reporting of suspicious activities observed on or near their neighbors' properties. This increased vigilance occurs in the course of residents'

everyday regular activities and, typically, neighborhood watch members monitor neighborhood activities from their own properties. Citizen patrols offer more than increased vigilance, however, and involve routine and formal observations of community properties, streets, and other public places. Like neighborhood watch, patrol groups monitor and report suspicious activities to police, but they actively search for criminal activities in their communities during regularly scheduled patrols, either in vehicles or on foot. Therefore, citizen patrols are typically considered more proactive than neighborhood watch organizations in their efforts to detect and prevent crime.

Citizen patrols attempt to create a visible presence within neighborhoods to reduce residents' fear of crime and deter potential criminals. In addition to visible patrolling and reporting activities, citizen patrols may also provide various community services. These services include traffic control, vacation checks, routine welfare checks on senior or disabled persons, checks of businesses during and after business hours as well as providing aid to stranded motorists, staffing safety fairs to collect fingerprints from children and teens, and providing extra patrol in high crime locations. Some groups also monitor Internet chat rooms to identify and report piracy, fraud, and pedophiles who solicit children. These services help to reduce police resource burdens and increase the effectiveness or distribution of available police services.

Members of sanctioned citizen patrols typically engage in much more passive behaviors. These patrol members simply act as additional "eyes and ears" and report suspicious activities to police. Patrol group members are not authorized to take enforcement action, are rarely permitted to carry weapons, and are instructed to avoid questioning or engaging in physical contact with potential suspects. Police officers or department personnel typically provide training, although the duration and quality of training can vary significantly depending on police policies and protocols and the types of activities patrol members are expected to perform.

For example, some citizen patrols participate in radar programs, in which volunteers use a police-issued radar unit to monitor vehicle speeds in neighborhoods and school zones. Offenders' license plates and vehicle descriptions are documented and submitted to the police agency, which then sends letters to the registered owners informing them of the observed violations. To become part of the program, members must first successfully pass a background check, attend a basic radar training class, and practice using the radar units in the field under police supervision.

Members of some unsanctioned organizations engage in more active intervention efforts. Individuals on patrol take direct action to disrupt crimes in progress if they happen to observe an incident. They also attempt to apprehend offenders and make citizen arrests. Basic training is provided to help members prepare to handle the situations they will likely encounter and ensure that they understand specific legal issues associated with attempts to take action against offenders.

As an example, the Guardian Angels are an unsanctioned citizen patrol group that began patrolling New York City subways in 1979. Their operations have since extended to cities throughout the world. Members are unarmed, but attempt to deter criminals through their presence and willingness to intervene if a crime is observed. Their signature red berets and t-shirts with insignia make them recognizable to the public. Members of the Guardian Angels receive training that includes CPR instruction and information concerning how and when a legal citizen's arrest can be made.

Effectiveness

Very few research studies have been conducted on citizen patrols. Some studies have tried to determine the characteristics of residents who are most likely to join these organizations. These studies have produced disparate findings. The type of person most likely to join citizen patrols appears to be at least partially dependent on contextual variables, including characteristics of the patrol organization and the targeted community. Research also shows that patrol effectiveness can be negatively impacted by a variety of factors, including waning volunteer interest, the monotony of surveillance activities, absence of strong leadership, and other organizational problems.

Research on the effectiveness of citizen patrols in reducing crime is virtually nonexistent. The limited research available includes little more than descriptive case studies that cannot adequately assess the impact of citizen patrols on crime. One of the most

rigorous studies of a citizen patrol used a quasi-experimental design to examine the impact of the Guardian Angels on New York subways. The study found that the group did not significantly change overall or long-term perceptions of passenger safety. Additionally, decreases in crime were not observed in areas patrolled by the group in vehicles. The research noted that such insufficient crime data made it difficult to detect meaningful changes in crime levels. A two-year study sponsored by the U.S. Department of Justice in the 1980s reached a similar conclusion. This study could not find conclusive evidence concerning the effectiveness of Guardian Angel patrols due to difficulties in measuring deterrence effects. Despite these inconclusive findings, at least one survey found evidence to suggest that people in middle-class communities believe citizen patrols have the potential to increase neighborhood safety.

Controversies

Members of sanctioned citizen volunteer groups have been the focus of sensational national headlines for overstepping their legal bounds. One example was the February 2012 shooting in Sanford, Florida, of an unarmed 17-year-old boy, Trayvon Martin. George Zimmerman, a local crime watch volunteer in a gated community, admitted shooting Martin and was charged with second-degree murder. Zimmerman claimed he acted in self-defense after Martin attacked him. This incident led to widespread outcries that such patrols at times overstep their legal bounds (e.g., in this case, violating a primary rule among neighborhood watch volunteers that they not carry a concealed weapon). Another controversial aspect of the case was Florida's "stand your ground" law, which gives citizens broad latitude to use deadly force against an attacker if they believe their life is at risk. Likewise, other sanctioned volunteer groups, including citizen patrols, have been accused of engaging in vigilante activities since patrol members are not always able to distinguish neighborhood residents from outsiders. However, most of the controversies surrounding citizen patrols involve unsanctioned patrol groups.

Police, media, citizens, and other critics have accused unsanctioned citizen patrol groups of taking the law into their own hands and of becoming socially destructive forces in communities.

For example, while the Guardian Angels have enjoyed tremendous popularity, with many people hailing their efforts to prevent crime as heroic, the group has also generated a significant amount of negative publicity. Many Guardian Angel members directly contributed to crime and disorder. The New York police arrested or issued summons for hundreds of Guardian Angel members who committed offenses, including failing to pay subway fares. Also, several members were killed after instigating altercations while on patrol. Tension between the Guardian Angels and the police was common in the 1980s, with both groups issuing accusatory public statements—the Guardian Angels accused police of being lazy and ineffective, while the police accused the citizen patrol group of being nothing more than criminals and publicity hounds. Furthermore, in 1992, the group's founder and CEO, Curtis Sliwa, admitted to fabricating stories of several crime incidents, including his own kidnapping and accusations of police abuse, in order to bolster the image of his organization.

Another unsanctioned citizen patrol group, the Minutemen, has generated similar controversy. Formed in 2007 with more than 1,000 volunteer members, the Minutemen started conducting armed patrols along the Arizona-Mexico border. Members referred to themselves as "undocumented border patrol agents." Then both U.S. President George W. Bush and Mexican President Vicente Fox publicly referred to the Minutemen as a vigilante group. Police have expressed concern over the potential violence that could result when armed Minutemen members confront smugglers or inadvertently engage border patrol authorities. The group adamantly insists that volunteers with racist tendencies are turned away, but members of the organization have been repeatedly accused of racism, xenophobia, and white supremacist beliefs. A similar citizen patrol group with reported member ties to the Minutemen, called the American Border Patrol, was listed as an anti-immigrant group on the Southern Poverty Law Center's website.

Despite these controversies, citizen patrol groups and other citizen-based crime prevention efforts will likely remain a part of U.S. culture. Police resource limitations and public fear of crime continues to generate interest in these alternative crime reduction initiatives. However, new research is needed to better understand the current prevalence, functions, and effectiveness of citizen patrol groups.

Tamara D. Madensen

See also Citizen Police Academies; Neighborhood Associations; Non-sworn Personnel and Volunteers, Use and Training of

Further Readings

Gauna, K. (2011, April 4). Citizen group uses controversial methods to patrol the U.S.-Mexico border. *Cronkite News*. Retrieved from http://cronkitenewsonline.com/2011/04/citizen-group-uses-controversial-methods-to-patrol-the-u-s-mexico-border/

Kenney, D. J. (1986). Crime on the subways: Measuring the effectiveness of the Guardian Angels. *Justice Quarterly*, 3(4), 481–496.

Levitz, J. (2009, September 8). Volunteer 5–0: Civilian patrols grow as recession puts citizens on guard. *Wall Street Journal*. Retrieved from http://online.wsj.com/article/SB125235840966590631.html

Robertson, C., & Schwartz, J. (2012, March 22). Shooting focuses attention on a program that seeks to avoid guns. *New York Times*. Retrieved from http://www.nytimes.com/2012/03/23/us/trayvon-martin-death-spotlights-neighborhood-watch-groups.html?_r=2pagewanted=all&

Website

National Association of Citizens on Patrol; http://www.nacop.org/index.htm

CITIZEN POLICE ACADEMIES

Many local law enforcement agencies operate citizen police academies for the public to learn about police procedures; such academies have become a popular approach to developing police-community relationships. Citizen police academies are condensed versions of regular law enforcement academies and exemplify the philosophy of community policing. Community policing is premised upon two related theories. The first theory is problem-oriented policing, which maintains that police should address the root causes of problems and spend time solving the problems. The second theory is community-oriented policing. This theory provides that police cannot be successful without the cooperation of their citizens and that the police should form partnerships with citizens in order to address crime and community problems. Citizen police academies are intended to build partnerships between the police and the communities. Citizen police academies can foster cooperation, facilitate communication, provide education to the public about the police, and improve police-community relations. This entry describes the origins, curriculum, and operation of citizen police academies as well as various modifications to this model.

Origins

The citizen police academy traces its origins to England. In 1977, the Devon and Cornwall Constabulary in Middlemoor, Exeter, established a Police Night School. The purpose of the school was to teach people about police organizational structure, operations, and practices. The school met one night each week for 10 weeks. Class sessions were taught by police personnel who volunteered their time to teach the citizens. The Constabulary's program was popular, and police instructors learned that citizens knew little about police organization, practices, and operations. They also learned that citizens were genuinely interested in learning about police organization and police work. The success of this police night school resulted in other constabularies in England organizing and operating police night schools for citizens.

The Orlando (Florida) Police Department organized and implemented the first citizen police academy in the United States in 1985. The Orlando Citizen Police academy was modeled after the constabulary's police night school program in England. The Orlando Citizen Police Academy consisted of a 10-week program with citizens meeting once each week. The Orlando program consisted of a broad-based curriculum that provided citizens with knowledge of police organization, operations, and procedures in a classroom setting. Citizen students were also provided with opportunities for first-hand experience with police work. Citizen students were able to participate in ride-alongs with police officers. The Orlando Citizen Police Academy was highly successful and other law enforcement agencies throughout the United States quickly followed with the development and implementation of citizen

police academies. There is no single, generic citizen police academy model. Although most citizen police academies have followed the Orlando Citizen Police Academy model in developing citizen police academies, each law enforcement agency that operates such an academy organizes its program and constructs its own curriculum based on the characteristics of its jurisdiction. In a little over a 25-year period, citizen police academies are being operated by many small, medium, and large law enforcement agencies all across the United States. Citizen police academies have become popular in improving police-community relations and in implementing the philosophy of community policing.

Curriculum

The curriculum of citizen police academies is based on classroom lecture, demonstrations, and participatory activities. Citizen police academies generally run between 10 and 13 weeks, with the class meeting once a week. The curriculum of citizen police academies includes topics such as an overview of departmental organization, officer selection, officer training, ethics, and internal affairs. Operations topics include patrol procedures, accident investigations, communications, traffic enforcement, K-9 operations, police officer safety, and use of force. Investigations topics include general criminal investigations, narcotics, child abuse, family violence, property crimes, and violent crimes. Legal-issue topics include arrest, search, seizure, evidence, constitutional law, and juvenile law. Crime prevention topics include drug awareness, gang awareness, auto theft prevention, neighborhood crime watch, statistics, and planning. Criminal justice system topics include the federal criminal justice system, state criminal justice system, judges, attorneys, probation officers, parole officers, and social workers. Citizen police academies also include components that are hands on and participatory. Participatory activities include firearms safety, firearms training, fingerprinting procedures, mock vehicle stops, defensive tactics, baton training, domestic violence role-playing scenarios, and ride-alongs. Participatory activities may also include tours of firearms ranges, dispatch centers, and jails.

Each law enforcement agency formulates its own curriculum for the citizen police academy. Staffing of the academies is an important element in ensuring they serve the purpose of building police-community relations. Successful citizen police academies require support from the department's administrators and line police officers. Departments assign an officer to serve as the program coordinator. Coordinators develop the curriculum, schedule activities, recruit instructors, and serve to foster the building of citizen-police relationships. Law enforcement agencies recruit instructors for citizen police academies from personnel within their department. Agencies also use criminal justice professionals from law enforcement, the courts, and corrections.

Operation

Citizen police academy classes generally have between 25 and 35 students. Agencies will advertise and recruit citizens to enroll in citizen police academies. The goal is to have a citizen class that represents a cross section of the community. Citizens who are interested in participating in the citizen police academy must complete an application form containing basic information. Agencies perform criminal history checks on the applicants to determine whether they have a criminal record. Some agencies will automatically reject a citizen applicant who possesses a prior criminal history, while other agencies will weigh whether to accept such an application on a case-by-case basis (such as the nature and extent of one's criminal record). Agencies generally establish a minimum age requirement of 18 years and prefer that the applicant live or work within the jurisdiction.

Citizen police academies represent a small expense relative to an agency's overall budget. Agencies will experience minimal expenditures for materials such as handouts, binders, shirts or some other related identifying apparel, and advertising. The most significant expenditure is for labor costs for the police personnel teaching the citizen police academy class sessions (however, many people instruct for free, such as prosecutors, experts on such subjects as financial crimes and social services, etc.). Some law enforcement agencies charge participants an application fee and tuition. Citizen police academies may be operated by one law enforcement agency or a partnership consisting of two or more agencies. A partnership-based citizen police academy allows for smaller agencies to combine personnel expertise and financing, whereas each

agency may find it infeasible to operate a citizen police academy on their own. The last session of a citizen police academy is the graduation ceremony where the citizens who have successfully completed the academy are honored and receive a graduation certificate.

Variations

Some law enforcement agencies have modified the traditional, general citizen police academy model in order to tailor the academy to certain groups of citizens. Some agencies have developed and implemented a teen academy. This form of citizen police academy is open only to teenagers who were residents of the jurisdiction. The focus of the teen academy is more hands-on activities than lecture in a classroom. Young people's interest in citizen police academies has prompted the development of teen (also termed *youth*) police academies, which teach young people about policing but also provide the opportunity for the police to solicit their ideas and feedback. Another modification of the citizen police academy concept is the cultural academy. The cultural academy tailors the citizen police academy model to address community policing and different ethnic cultures in the jurisdiction. Cultural academies address many of the same topics addressed in the citizens police academy, however, special attention is dedicated to the specific issues of interest to the specific group. Finally, some agencies have adapted the citizen police academy concept to focus on the business community. The purpose of this program is building relationships between law enforcement and the business community in an effort to reduce crimes against businesses. The curriculum of the business police academy provides a general overview of law enforcement organization and operations, with specific emphasis placed on topics and crimes specific to businesses.

Citizen police academies have succeeded in two main respects. First, they provide a cross-section of citizens with an understanding of the organization, operation, issues, and complexities of law enforcement. Second, citizen police academies have fostered communication and the building of partnerships between law enforcement and citizens in accordance with the philosophy of community policing.

Robert Morin

See also Building Partnerships and Stakeholders; Citizen Patrols; Community, Definition of; Community Cohesion and Empowerment; Customer-Based Policing; Police-Community Relations; Publicity Campaigns; Volunteers, Police Use of

Further Readings

Aryani, G. A., Alsabrook, C. L., & Garrett, T. D. (2003, January). The business police academy: Commercial loss prevention through education. *FBI Law Enforcement Bulletin,* 72(1), 10–14.

Aryani, G. A., Garrett, T. D., & Alsabrook, C. L. (2000, May). The citizen police academy: Success through community partnerships. *FBI Law Enforcement Bulletin,* 69(5), 16–21.

Barlow, S., Branch, J., & Close, G. (2009, March). Citizen police academies: A model for small agencies. *The Police Chief,* 77(3).

Bonello, E. M., & Schafer, J. A. (2002, November). Citizen police academies: Do they just entertain? *FBI Law Enforcement Bulletin,* 71(11), 19–23.

Cohn, E. G. (1996). The citizen police academy: A recipe for improving police-community relations. *Journal of Criminal Justice, 24*(3), 265–271. doi:10.1016/0047-2352(96)00011-6

Palmiotto, M. J., & Unninthan, N. P. (2002, March-April). The impact of citizen police academies on participants: An exploratory study. *Journal of Criminal Justice, 30*(2), 101–106.

Raffel, W. E. (2005). Citizen police academies: The importance of communication. *Policing: An International Journal of Police Strategies & Management, 28*(1), 84–97. doi: 10.1108/13639510510580995

Schafer, J. A., & Bonello, E. M. (2001). The citizen police academy: Measuring outcomes. *Police Quarterly, 4*(4), 434–448.

Volunteers in Police Service Program. (2008). *Citizen police academies: Introducing law enforcement to the community.* Retrieved from http://www.pdfio.com/k-2267486.html

Citizen Surveys

An integral part of modern policing is getting feedback from the community being served. Traditionally, police obtained citizen feedback by holding community meetings in venues such as local churches, community centers, or schools. With the advent of computers and the increased ability to analyze data, many police departments have borrowed the concept of marketing surveys from the private sector to evaluate community demands and how they respond to community needs.

Citizen surveys provide multiple advantages to police agencies. The first lies in the relatively low cost associated with the administration of the surveys and tabulation of the results. A well-designed survey can be printed numerous times and used over multiple years. The second benefit lies in the ability to study results over time. Of course, comparisons are more easily made if the survey instrument remains the same from year to year. A third benefit is that the analysis of the survey data can be carried out relatively quickly, allowing the police agency to engage the community about the results. Finally, citizen surveys help in making the community feel that their police department is interested in their concerns. Citizen surveys not only inform the police about problems in the community, but they also serve to reinforce the relationship between the public and law enforcement agencies. This entry begins by presenting the reasons for citizen surveys. Next, it describes the survey instrument in general. Finally, this entry discusses the focus and scope of citizen surveys.

Reasons for Citizen Surveys

Many law enforcement agencies are constantly juggling the demands of the public and uncertain budgetary constraints. This has forced many police officials to reconsider how police services can be rendered in the most efficient, yet economical way. Citizen surveys can be instrumental in helping shape policies aimed at improving police services and the broader police-community relationship. However, the use of citizen surveys has been resisted by some police agencies and officers because these data collection efforts are perceived as a tool to malign their agencies.

Because of this perception, it is important that any jurisdiction that considers implementing police citizen surveys have absolute buy-in from the police community. Acceptance of citizen surveys is gained by demonstrating that the questions and results will be used to inform the police agency about the community's needs, problems, and concerns. It is also important to remind police officials that citizen surveys are a good tool to capture and measure citizen attitudes concerning their performance. There are very few instances when the police are able to gather such feedback from the community, and the implementation of citizen surveys could prove invaluable in terms of showing how a department is doing a good job in the community.

Finally, citizen surveys can play an important role in program evaluation or to gauge public attitude concerning a change in police activities. For example, if a police department has recently implemented a specific antispeeding program, citizen surveys may provide valuable data concerning this particular program that may not be captured with other data collection techniques. With the feedback from the community, the police department can then judge whether or not the program is having the desired impact in the community.

The Survey Instrument

Survey Frequency

For citizen surveys to reach their optimal efficacy, they should be carried out on a regular basis. Law enforcement agencies that survey their citizens only once, without any further attempts at data collection, will obtain only a snapshot of the community's concerns. Ideally, law enforcement agencies should survey citizens once a year, creating a database of information that can be compared from year to year. Furthermore, yearly citizen surveys provide the police leadership with the ability to look at trends and variations across time and geographic settings. Finally, carrying out citizen surveys on a yearly basis demonstrates a law enforcement agency's continued interest in community problems.

Survey Construction

As with any data collection endeavor, law enforcement agencies need to ensure that the instrument used to survey citizens is valid and reliable. Lists of questions should be grouped by theme or category. For instance, one section may address crime problems in the neighborhood, another may be directed at attitudes or feelings toward the police, while yet another may seek information on how to resolve particular community concerns.

Once the categories have been established, the specific questions designed to collect information on these categories need to be developed. Relying on previous and tested surveys is one approach, because it allows law enforcement agencies to avoid "reinventing the wheel." However, some jurisdictions may have specific problems that have not been addressed by previous instruments. Multiple-choice style surveys are recommended to limit the number of possible answers received and ensure the usability of the survey information.

A crucial element of survey construction involves the origin of the questions. Law enforcement agencies must refrain from being the sole agents in the construction of the survey. Agency-created surveys may lead to a one-sided view of problems, and the community may criticize the entire effort. A more balanced approach is to invite different community stakeholders—business owners, social services personnel, community group leaders, and other organizational leaders—to be part of the survey construction. The stakeholders can raise certain points that police officials may not have thought of as being important. Furthermore, involving community stakeholders ensures that all parts of the community have a say in this crucial information-gathering process. The inclusion of community leaders needs to occur at all steps of the survey creation process, not just at the beginning stages. This helps to ensure that the community considers the instrument to be valid, reliable, and a true reflection of their concerns.

Survey Administration

Once police officials are satisfied with the integrity of their survey instrument, an appropriate sample size for their jurisdiction needs to be determined and a proper survey administration method decided on. An important element in the sample selection is that the citizens surveyed be representative of the broader community. This means that whatever sampling method is used, every single person in the community has a chance of being selected for the survey. Any indication that those surveyed are not a representative sample of the community may yield doubts about the process and resentment about the results.

Law enforcement agencies have the option of doing mail surveys, e-mail surveys, web-based surveys, or phone surveys. Each method offers advantages and disadvantages, which vary from jurisdiction to jurisdiction. Traditional mail surveys run the risk of the citizens not returning the survey instrument, leading to a low response rate. E-mail surveys require that the agency have a master list of citizen e-mails, something that is not always feasible. Web-based surveys require that the citizens go to a website where the survey is hosted, and this may lead to an unrepresentative sample of the population, as not everyone will go to the website or will have the technical capacity to do so. Finally, phone surveys allow the agency to target certain neighborhoods by using programs that are able to generate lists of phone numbers for residents living in a certain area. While popular, phone surveys have run into a problem with the advent of cell phones, as many citizens no longer have traditional telephone land lines, and it has become more problematic to use phone numbers as indicators of geographic residence.

Collecting and Coding Data

Once the method of survey administration has been selected, the next step involves collecting the data in a systematic fashion for future analysis. The data collected from the surveys should be entered into a spreadsheet program. To facilitate analysis, it is helpful to designate specific coding schemes for each question so that the data are entered in a numeric format as opposed to a string or character format. For example, if a particular question asks if the citizen is a renter or a home owner, a coding scheme could be renter = 1, owner = 2, and not applicable = 3.

Depending on the number of surveys collected, some jurisdictions may opt to have the data coded by external entities such as the local university, private companies, or volunteers. For example, local colleges or universities may be glad to help in such a research endeavor as it offers their students real-life examples of survey implementation. In return, the law enforcement agency does not have to undertake the sometimes tedious coding aspect of the citizen surveys.

Analysis

Once the data have been entered into a spreadsheet and all of the survey information has been compiled, the important task of analyzing and giving meaning to the information begins. This responsibility usually falls to a data analyst who will interpret the raw numbers and contextualize their meanings. Some law enforcement agencies have an in-house crime or data analyst who can do this work, but in case an agency does not have such personnel,

reliance on local research entities (once again, a university or local college) is a viable option.

The analysis can be very descriptive, providing the percentage breakdown for responses to each question, and sometimes can include the use of inferential statistics to predict future trends based on the community input.

Geographic information systems, or mapping programs, will also allow the analyst to show the results based on different geographic regions in the concerned jurisdiction. For example, the citizen survey results can be broken down by neighborhood, census tract, block group, or even street level.

Survey Results

Having analyzed the data, the law enforcement agency should engage in an internal department-wide discussion concerning its survey results. Do these results make sense? What explanations could there be for the information provided by the citizen survey? What steps can the agency take to address some of the community concerns?

When these basic questions have been addressed, it is crucial for police officials to create a summary report, addressing the major findings of the citizen survey and detailing how the police agency is going to address what the community has brought to its attention. This summary report needs to be shared with the community, preferably using multiple media outlets—newspaper, television, radio, and even the department's website and social media—so the citizens can see the outcome of the survey. Providing the citizens with feedback may also increase future participation in the data-gathering efforts as the citizens may feel included in the problem-solving process.

Other Considerations

When creating questions for the survey instrument, it is important to refrain from questions that the agency has little interest in or plans doing little about. For example, if a police agency has no plans to address a crime problem differently, it makes little sense to ask the community if they would like this problem solved differently. In essence, the citizen survey should be a serious and concerted effort to collect information that will help the police agency guide and mold its future operational agenda.

Another consideration concerning citizen surveys is asking questions that may yield negative comments. Law enforcement agencies should not be afraid to hear criticism from the community they serve. In that vein, citizen surveys should devote a set of questions on public satisfaction with the rendering of police services. These can include questions concerning the public's satisfaction with various police actions, such as traffic stops, police demeanor, public interactions, and the approach to various disorder problems such as drinking in public. Negative responses concerning the public's view of the police may be based on genuine public safety problems or on mere misunderstandings between the public and the police. Regardless of the basis, the police-community relationship can be strengthened by identifying and addressing the concerns reflected by these responses.

Citizen surveys are a good tool to identify where such misunderstandings can occur in the police-community relationship, and the police agency can then address these misunderstandings with public education, police training, or a combination of the two. A good example of such an effort would be a citizen academy whereby citizens spend a few hours or a few days learning about how police officers approach their jobs and the different situations they are asked to face on a daily basis.

Focus and Scope

Focus

A recurring question when it comes to police surveying citizens involves who should be the focus of such an inquiry. There are some arguments that the respondent should only include people who have had police contact in a given period of time. The reasoning is that citizens who have had no police contact at all are ill equipped to judge and evaluate police performance. Similarly, those who have never been victimized may have a biased view of their neighborhood's safety level. On the other hand, some would argue that citizens can still have a valid opinion of the police without having had direct contact with them.

Many citizen surveys address this problem by having a bifurcated survey instrument whereby the first part comprises general questions that all citizens can answer, and the second is reserved for those citizens who have had prior contact with the police and wish to comment on their experience with that interaction.

Scope

Citizen surveys can be used in a variety of ways. The most direct and simple is to ask citizens what they consider to be the biggest crime problem in their neighborhood. However, citizen surveys need not be seen in such a limited light. Law enforcement agencies can use citizen surveys to learn about other elements of their communities and how these are related to the complexities of crime problems.

Citizen surveys could be used to gather data on neighborhood characteristics, for example, the number of bars on each street, the number of parks available to the children in a certain neighborhood, the number of grocery outlets, or the number of liquor stores. Citizen surveys could also inform police officials that citizens find current bus schedules inadequate or that street lighting is in dire need of repair. While these are not directly related to crime, it is imperative to know about the characteristics of one's jurisdictions to be able to fully understand the crime picture. Citizen surveys can often be a valuable tool to supplement knowledge of one's community.

Emmanuel P. Barthe

See also Crime Analysis; Customer-Based Policing; Police-Community Relations; Publicity Campaigns

Further Readings

Alpert, G. P., Flynn, D., & Piquero, A. (2001). Effective community policing performance measures. *Justice Research and Policy, 3*(2), 79–94.

Alpert, G. P., & Moore, M. H. (1993). Measuring police performance in the new paradigm of community policing. In G. P. Alpert & A. R. Piquero (Eds.), *Community policing: Contemporary readings* (pp. 215–232). Prospect Heights, IL: Waveland Press.

Langworthy, R. H. (1999). *Measuring what matters: Proceedings from the Policing Research Institute meetings.* Washington, DC: U.S. Department of Justice, National Institute of Justice.

Poyner, B. (1993) What works in crime prevention: An overview of evaluations. In R. V. Clarke (Ed.), *Crime prevention studies* (Vol. 1). Monsey, NY: Criminal Justice Press.

Rosenbaum, D. P. (2007, March). Police innovation post 1980: Assessing effectiveness and equity concerns in the information technology era. *Institute for the Prevention of Crime Review, 1,* 11–44. Retrieved from http://www.sciencessociales.uottawa.ca/ipc/pdf/kr1-rosenbaum.pdf

Rosenbaum, D. P., Graziano, L. M., Stephens, C. D., & Schuck, A. M. (2011). Understanding community policing and legitimacy-seeking behavior in virtual reality: A national study of municipal police websites. *Police Quarterly, 14*(1), 25–47.

Scheider, M. C., Rowell, T., & Bezdikian, V. (2003). The impact of citizen perceptions of community policing on fear of crime: Findings from twelve cities. *Police Quarterly, 6*(4), 363–386.

COLLABORATION WITH OUTSIDE AGENCIES

Community partnership is the touchstone of community policing and problem solving. Indeed, to address crime and disorder, a basic premise is that the police must cooperate with the community and encourage the public to come forward with information. In so doing, the police engage in such activities as meeting with neighborhood groups, participating in business and civic events, working with social agencies, and taking part in youth programs. This entry examines how, under community policing and problem solving, the police and community together define priorities and even determine the allocation of limited resources.

Fundamentals of Collaboration

Collaboration can take the form of activities such as patrol officers talking to local business owners to help identify their problems and concerns; visiting residents' homes to offer advice on security and crime prevention; developing, disseminating, and tabulating questionnaires with residents and business owners as respondents; and helping to organize and support neighborhood watch groups and regular community meetings. The department might also consult with community members about gang and drug suppression tactics, disorderly youth activities, and so on.

Every level of the department must actively engage in external relations and solicit the concerns and suggestions of community groups, residents, leaders, and local government officials. Such collaborative efforts constitute multilateral problem solving. Indeed, problem solving is based on the assumption that crime and disorder can be reduced in small geographic areas by carefully studying the characteristics of problems in the area and then applying the appropriate resources. Such collaboration also reinforces trust, facilitates the exchange of information, and leads to the identification of other areas that could benefit from the mutual attention of the police and the community. Police and external groups will not always agree on which specific problems deserve attention first or which specific responses will work best; nonetheless, officers must serve as catalysts for joint police and community problem-solving endeavors.

Many problems of crime and disorder can be successfully addressed *only* if there is such collaboration between the police and community. For example, proper lighting affords crime prevention benefits by providing surveillance, deterrence, detection, and liability and fear reduction. Assume that a determination is made that more and better lighting is needed to decrease crime incidents at a local park. The police do not possess such expertise, so they seek the services of a specially trained lighting expert from the local utility company to determine the proper number, locations, and types of lighting that can reduce public risk of crime victimization—while also maintaining the attractiveness of the particular area. Other examples include those community problems requiring the assistance of the prosecutor's office to draft new ordinances (such as curfews) and the health department to condemn an abandoned home that is frequented by drug users.

Collaborating With Nongovernment Agencies

Nongovernment agencies and institutions constitute an important community asset. Every member of the police organization can contribute to the development of a comprehensive list of available government and private resources, to include names, addresses, phone numbers, and a description of services. This information should be easily accessible to allow patrol officers, supervisors, and dispatchers to provide references to community members. The chief or sheriff should enlist the support of these private agencies in their community policing efforts.

Representatives from such organizations can be invited to participate in training sessions on community policing and problem solving. Depending on the nature and scope of the problem addressed, the composition of problem-solving teams might include representatives from the community, government agencies, and social agencies. The department must develop close cooperative links with all community policing partners who contribute to the problem-solving process, and explicit procedures must be established that facilitate the appropriate use of resources.

As indicated above with the lighting example, some types of problems require collaboration with specialized organizations or agencies. To reduce domestic violence, for instance, police might work with women's groups or agencies that maintain safe houses for abused women and their children. Furthermore, because there is a correlation between spousal assaults and excessive drinking by the perpetrators, especially at illegal after-hours clubs, the police and community may find themselves exploring ways to close down certain clubs with the help of local zoning and city planning boards.

Collaborating With Other Governmental Agencies

Collaboration with other government agencies may also be advisable and even necessary for the police. Offenders with alcohol problems might be required to attend rehabilitation programs run by a city or county agency. Police may find themselves working with the local health or fire departments to raze an abandoned building that has not only become a fire trap and an eyesore, but also a known crack house. Prosecutors' offices may be contacted about creating a new graffiti law or to establish a curfew in an area, developing an ordinance barring prostitutes and their clients from frequenting certain problem areas, or revoking a trouble spot's liquor license. Code and zoning laws may need to be used for dealing with people who engage in land-use violations such as harboring inoperative vehicles; allowing their yards to contain junk, trash, and debris; or maintaining a home business and thus causing a neighborhood disturbance.

City and county offices have considerable powers for maintaining neighborhood safety and appearance, up to and including the ability to demolish homes or businesses that constitute public nuisances. Police have also called on nearby military bases for a variety of purposes, including firefighting and maintaining general order in the aftermath of natural disasters.

Possibilities for collaboration with federal, state, and local agencies are thus nearly without limit because the problem-solving process itself relies on the expertise and assistance of a wide array of social and government agencies and community resources; furthermore, problem solving involves addressing crime by confronting problems at the grassroots level.

Elected and appointed administrators must also understand the law enforcement agency's community policing and problem solving strategy and participate in its development. Mayors, city managers, legislative representatives, and other government executives must be active partners in the collaborative process, and work to ensure the movement toward "community-oriented government" at the local level. Political leaders and service providers need to find ways to direct available resources at the jurisdiction's critical social problems, such as alcohol and drug abuse, domestic violence. They must realize that police agencies alone do not possess the resources for addressing problems. Regular communication with the heads of these other government agencies will go a long way toward securing their assistance and allowing them to prepare their personnel for the day when their services will be required.

Collaboration in Action: A Case Study

This case study, taken from a western state, shows how police sought out assistance from outside agencies in their problem-solving effort. The effort involved the use of the SARA (scanning, analysis, response, assessment) problem-solving model.

Scanning revealed that there were about 10,000 annual calls for service (CFS) to the police from a lower-income area in which there were five housing complexes in close proximity; most CFS involved domestic disturbances, noise complaints, violent crimes, and gang-related activities. Citizens who were interviewed by officers expressed considerable fear and tension, wrought by the gangs and graffiti, assaults, fights, and shots fired. Analysis confirmed several hot spots existed in the area when compared with the city at large. A survey instrument—developed by the officers with assistance from the local university—was administered to business owners, residents, and apartment managers and uncovered many problems not revealed by the crime analysis. First, the primary fear of residents concerned gangs and graffiti, and they welcomed neighborhood watch and business watch programs. Apartment managers neither knew their rights nor communicated with each other; as a result, evicted renters often moved from one housing unit to another nearby unit.

An environmental survey was accomplished by a police officer having expertise in crime prevention as it relates to environmental design, such as means of ingress and egress by criminals; street intersections were photographed for the city streets department; and abandoned homes were videotaped for the health, zoning, and fire departments. Speed surveys were performed by citizen volunteers, a lighting survey was done by the local utility company, and landscaping that mainly consisted of rocks was noted (which were used by many youths to destroy apartment windows). The officers, armed with this information and data, called for a collaborative city-wide approach. To begin implementing responses, a graffiti ordinance was drafted by the city attorney. A gang enforcement team was created and sent to perform field interrogations of people in the area, identify gang members, and generally establish a presence. A curfew was placed on use of the public park, and known gang members were contacted and informed of the curfew and the project crackdown in general. Bike and foot patrols complemented vehicle patrols, and immediate results were realized in catching juvenile gang members in the act of burglarizing automobiles. A resident council consisting of people from the five apartment complexes was established as were neighborhood and business watch programs and target hardening (i.e., strengthening building security) efforts. Apartment managers were trained in screening and evicting tenants and in recognizing different types of gang graffiti. A latchkey program was initiated for children whose parents worked and were not home when children got out of school. The local power company provided free consulting services concerning area lighting. Junk "yard cars" were removed after checking to see if stolen. A neighborhood cleanup campaign was launched and dilapidated houses were demolished. The city and residents jointly cleaned, painted, and repaired the park. Pyracantha, a thorny evergreen shrub, was planted around fences to serve as a crime barrier. A follow-up survey found less crime, less fear of crime

by area residents, an improved environment, and ongoing self-help efforts by residents in the area.

Kenneth J. Peak

See also Building Partnerships and Stakeholders; Community, Definition of; Community Cohesion and Empowerment; Customer-Based Policing; Neighborhood Associations; Publicity Campaigns; Social Capital; Volunteers, Police Use of; Website Uses by Local Agencies

Further Readings

Correia, M. E. (2000). Social capital and sense of community building: Building social cohesion. In R. W. Glensor, M. E. Correia, & K. J. Peak (Eds.), *Policing communities: Understanding crime and solving problems* (pp. 75–82). Los Angeles, CA: Roxbury.

Goldstein, H. (1987). Toward community-oriented policing: Potential, basic requirements, and threshold questions. *Crime and Delinquency, 33*(1), 6–30. doi: 10.1177/0011128787033001002

Osborne, D., & Gaebler, T. (1992). *Reinventing government: How the entrepreneurial spirit is transforming the public sector.* Reading, MA: Addison-Wesley.

Wilson, L. J. (April, 1995). Placing community-oriented policing in the broader realms of community cooperation. *The Police Chief, 62*(4), 127–128.

COLLEGES AND UNIVERSITIES, COMMUNITY POLICING STRATEGIES FOR

Community policing is well suited to colleges and universities, which are designed to promote a culture of academic inquiry, engagement, outreach, and openness among students, faculty, staff, and administrators. Community-oriented policing and problem-solving strategies are in keeping with this philosophy.

The U.S. Department of Justice's Office of Community Oriented Policing Services (COPS Office), defines community policing as "a philosophy that promotes organizational strategies, which support the systematic use of partnerships and problem-solving techniques, to proactively address the immediate conditions that give rise to public safety issues such as crime, social disorder, and fear of crime."

A 2008 report by the Department of Justice's Bureau of Justice Statistics (BJS), based on a survey of campus law enforcement agencies, indicated community policing is widely used by campus public safety agencies in the United States. The report found more than two-thirds (69%) of campus law enforcement agencies incorporated community policing into their security policies.

Community policing activities on college campuses include assigning patrol officers to specific geographic areas, collaborating with citizen groups, and meeting regularly with faculty, staff, and citizen groups. Other manifestations of community policing cited in the BJS report included designating a staff member to address specific crime-related issues, such as self-defense programs (69%) and drug and alcohol prevention programs (73% and 67%, respectively). In addition, the BJS report found that nearly all four-year colleges and universities with 2,500 or more students provided crime prevention programs, including general crime prevention and sexual assault prevention programs.

It is widely believed by police, academics, and college and university administrators that a properly administered community policing program can build an environment of trust, partnerships, prevention, and problem solving on college and university campuses. After briefly describing the history of community policing on college and university campuses, this entry discusses the implementation and practices of community policing on campuses as well as the structure of community policing and attributes of community policing officers.

History

According to Bonnie S. Fisher and John J. Sloan III (2007), modern community policing programs on college campuses have their roots in the 1980s, when several campus crime victims and their families brought lawsuits alleging that inadequate campus security contributed to the death or injury of students. Public policy makers at the federal and state levels began focusing their attention on campus security, one result of which was enactment of the Crime Awareness and Campus Security Act of 1990, as amended (known as the "Clery Act" and named for Jeanne Clery, a Lehigh

University student who was murdered in 1986). The act requires all colleges and universities to maintain, report, and make available to the public detailed campus crime statistics on an annual basis.

A key characteristic of community policing, according to Fisher and Sloan, is a closer degree of cooperation between police and community members in finding ways to mutually deal with crime. This is evidenced by the assignment of patrol officers to specific locations for sustained periods of time to work with community members. Similarly, according to Gary J. Margolis and Noel C. March (2008), policing a college or university campus requires a level of sensitivity and professionalism that will resonate within the postsecondary educational environment—and only through a combination of enforcement and education can the campus police attempt to achieve a crime-free campus. Campus police, like their state and local counterparts, must adhere to the tenets of preventive, relationship-oriented, community-focused policing if they are to achieve their mission.

Implementation and Practices on U.S. Campuses

The development of a community policing program begins with the agency's mission statement, which includes clearly stated values, beliefs, and goals of the campus police organization. Elements of a community policing program include

- Strong leadership of the agency to develop and implement the concept
- Development of sworn officer and non-sworn staff training in community relations and problem solving
- Development and maintenance of formal outreach programs to student, faculty, and other organizations on the campus
- Provision of specialized training for some staff members, such as crime prevention, drug and alcohol recognition and prevention, and sexual assault prevention
- Development and provision of general crime prevention programs and education to the campus community
- Regular engagement with key stakeholder groups on the campus

Campus public safety organizations that make a commitment to the community policing philosophy are likely to have some or all of the following types of programs in place: geographic patrol areas, ride-along programs, safe ride or walk programs, crime prevention, campus safety information at first-year student orientations, sexual assault and drug and alcohol prevention programs, and property identification programs.

One example of a school with an array of crime prevention programs is California State University, Northridge, where a crime prevention unit provides safety workshops on general safety as well as on specific safety issues such as residential security, identity theft prevention, and pepper spray defense. Three of the nationally recognized Rape Aggression Defense (RAD) System's self-defense courses are offered twice per year, including semester-length classes for men and women (through a partnership with the university's department of kinesiology). The crime prevention unit conducts more than 160 programs per year and regularly conducts campus events throughout the semester that highlight topics such as bicycle security and laptop theft prevention.

Surveys by the U.S. Department of Justice indicate that most large colleges and universities in the country offer crime prevention programs, including preventing sexual assaults, through an array of services to students, as well as classes, orientation sessions, brochures, and videos. For example, the Department of Education's Office for Safe and Drug-Free Schools in a white paper advocated the use of the SARA (scanning, analysis, response, assessment) problem-solving process for designing, developing, and evaluating substance abuse prevention programs on college campuses. Campuses first perform surveys or obtain data concerning actual levels of substance abuse; then, if a problem is discerned, authorities work to develop appropriate responses. Getting campus involvement from a number of constituencies is critical to the success of such substance abuse prevention programs. These groups include students, student activity directors, residential life, faculty, marketing and communications specialists, and senior administrators. Enforcement and access control are sound prevention techniques, but strategies may also include elements of community policing: meetings, outreach, and education.

Community Policing Structure

Michigan State University (MSU) was among the first universities to develop a community policing philosophy and structure, transitioning to this mission and strategy in late 1986. Bruce Benson, the then–chief of police, invited all department members to give input into the development of a new mission statement, which emphasized not only a safe but also an "ethical, people-oriented" environment. Operationally, the adoption of a community policing philosophy was carried out by assigning dedicated community policing officers to specific areas of the campus. Eventually, the campus was divided into six community policing areas, each with its own assigned officer, a local office, and phone. In 2012, the MSU campus was divided into four areas, with a team assigned to each area. Each team had a supervisor, two team leaders, five officers, one detective, and a representative of both the parking and safety services divisions.

Attributes of Community Policing Officers

The University of South Florida (USF) was also an early adoptee of the community policing philosophy, initiating its efforts in 1992. Robert Johnson (1995), former chief of the USF police department, in a monograph published by the International Association of Campus Law Enforcement Administrators, outlined the following desired characteristics of a campus community policing officer:

- An officer who is interested in the problems of crime and disorder; this officer recognizes the broader role of the police in maintaining public order and in providing a wide range of services
- An officer who derives job satisfaction from seeing the benefits of his or her labor and receives positive feedback from the job
- An officer who can adapt to a community/ neighborhood perspective of law enforcement, and is willing to make contacts in the community and work with people in the area served
- An officer who is self-confident and challenges conventional wisdom, while exploring a wide range of alternatives for handling community problems
- An officer who is innovative and willing to explore new ways of solving problems and looks for the source of problems rather than a quick fix

- A officer who is creative and resourceful in the job, is well organized and able to think both conceptually and in the abstract
- An officer who is objective in making decisions and makes those decisions based on collected data—not jumping to conclusions when making a decision but basing decisions on available information
- An officer who has a broad perspective based on prior work experience, education, and an understanding of diverse cultures (pp. 37–49)

The 2008 BJS survey on campus law enforcement found that campus police were more likely than local police agencies to assess recruits' community relations skills prior to hiring them. Among the skills more likely to be assessed by campus police were analytical problem-solving skills, understanding of cultural diversity, and assessment of skills related to mediation and conflict management.

Conclusion

Community policing has major benefits in a college or university setting. Colleges foster a tradition of openness, inquiry, and discourse. Community policing emphasizes the systematic use of partnerships, problem solving, and the development of an atmosphere of trust and customer service. It is no surprise that community policing is the dominant philosophy in the nation's larger institutions of higher education. Indeed, in an environment that stresses a strong service-oriented style of policing, the community policing and problem-solving approach is tailor-made for working with challenges involving faculty, staff, and students.

Anne P. Glavin

See also Community Policing and Problem Solving, Definition of; Place-Based Policing; Youthful Offenders, Community Policing Strategies for

Further Readings

Bureau of Justice Assistance. (1994). *Understanding community policing: A framework for action.* NCJ 148457. Washington, DC: U.S. Department of Justice. Retrieved from https://www.ncjrs.gov/pdffiles/commp.pdf

Fisher, B. S., & Sloan, J. J., III. (2007). *Campus crime: Legal, social, and policy perspectives* (2nd ed.). Springfield, IL: Charles C Thomas.

Johnson, R. P. (1995). *Community policing on campus.* Hartford, CT: International Association of Campus Law Enforcement Administrators.

Margolis, G. J., & March, N. C. (2008, May-June). Campus community policing: It all started with us. . . . *Campus Law Enforcement Journal, 38*(3), 22–23.

United Negro College Fund. (2009, June). *Campus community policing at historically Black colleges and universities: Final evaluation report.* Fairfax, VA: Author. Retrieved from http://www.cops.usdoj.gov/Publications/e071026295-HBCU-Final-Report.pdf

Woolfenden, S., & Stevenson, B. (2011). *Establishing appropriate staffing levels for campus public safety departments.* West Hartford, CT: International Association of Campus Law Enforcement Administrators. Retrieved from http://cops.usdoj.gov/files/RIC/Publications/e061122378_Est-Approp-Stfg-Levels_FIN.pdf

Website

U.S. Department of Justice, Community-Oriented Policing Services; http://www.cops.usdoj.gov

COMMUNITY, DEFINITION OF

Traditional definitions of *community* emphasize commonality and similarity, but do not address the diversity and complexity that exist in many communities. Traditionally, the police viewed the community through a single lens, but community policing embraces a multifaceted view. Each interpretation impacts the roles and relationship between the police and the community. This entry discusses how the definitions of community have changed and affected the roles and relationship between community and police over time.

Changing Roles

The common police motto "to protect and serve" assumes the role of police to be caretakers of the community. It also suggests that the role of the community in addressing crime is passive. That may be an effective role if a community is small, demographically similar, and experiences low levels of crime. But in the burgeoning, disparate, and crime-impacted communities of urban and suburban areas, the caretaker role is only one of many responsibilities police must assume to impact the challenges of crime.

In the 1970s, crime prevention initiatives were introduced throughout the United States to bring police and communities closer together. Police departments were awarded grants to address various crime problems by involving the community, with a secondary goal of improving community relations. Crime prevention programs focused on the reduction of a crime problem identified through extensive crime analysis. The goal of these programs was to educate residents about what they could do to reduce their chances of becoming victims. One traditional strategy employed by many police departments was organizing block watches and training residents in target hardening (i.e., strengthening the security of their residences and businesses). The new skill set for the area patrol or crime prevention officer included basic crime analysis, public speaking, and community organizing. Overall, these programs achieved their goal of reducing crime, but the success was often short lived because the police, not the community, were viewed as the entity responsible for crime reduction.

In the late 1970s and early 1980s, community policing was introduced as a new philosophy that looked at changing and more clearly defining the roles of not only the police, but the community as well. It is a proactive approach that relies on partnerships and problem solving to address crime and quality-of-life issues. It provides a process for engaging the community and building a long-term collaboration including, but not limited to, police, residents, businesses, faith communities, schools, government agencies, and nonprofit service organizations. Police and community are problem-solving partners actively engaged in all aspects of the police problem-solving process—SARA, for scanning, analysis, response and assessment. They share responsibility for problem solving.

Through scanning and analysis, the police no longer prioritize the crime problem based solely on reported crime. Police listen to the community's priorities that often include unreported crime, nuisance crimes, and broader issues such as lack of quality education or employment opportunities, and limited government and social services. By enlisting the community's experience and resources throughout the problem-solving process, effective and targeted responses are planned, implemented, and assessed.

In addition to the aforementioned crime prevention skills, police have acquired skills in surveying their communities, complex crime and community analysis, communication technology, and conflict resolution. They also seek information and an understanding about community risk and protective factors. Crime is viewed as symptomatic of larger issues that negatively impact community safety and well-being. Examples of risk factors include poverty, unemployment, low literacy, poor health, and family issues. Protective factors include stable housing, employment, successful schools, and community involvement opportunities.

Key to successful implementation of community policing is an understanding of the targeted community from many perspectives. The community analysis may include, but not be limited to, population size, age, race or ethnicity, income, education levels, language, culture, and religion. Housing developments, business sectors, formal and informal community leaders, interest groups and other stakeholders need to be identified. The police also need to know the history of the community. Without a thorough and ongoing analysis, the community policing process may not be inclusive and the response to community problems and long-term effectiveness of community policing may not be realized.

Future Roles, Directions, and Challenges

A new philosophy and direction in community policing is community governance. It involves partnerships not only within communities but also across all sectors of local government within a jurisdiction. The overall goal of this approach, broadly stated, is to improve and maintain quality of life through collaboration and shared decision making. Local government leaders, including police chiefs, look beyond the institutions they lead to an inclusive process of genuinely engaging and working with the community and agency counterparts. Because the community's problems are complex, the solutions require a multifaceted, multiagency approach.

The new roles for police and other government employees therefore include facilitator, consensus builder, collaborator, and community builder. It moves from a single agency being responsible for problem solving to a shared responsibility that fully engages the community. Drew Diamond and Deirdre Mead Weiss (2004) discuss that at the heart of community governance is organizational transformation that requires a change in organizational culture, increased accountability, information sharing, resource sharing, changes in recruitment, training of upper and middle management and line staff, agency cross-training, and evaluation of service-oriented police officers and government employees.

Once the community is trained and engaged in community governance, then problems can be solved and trusting relationships built among police, other government agencies, and community residents. A skilled and capable group of committed community stakeholders can be leaders in addressing various problems and reducing the burden on government agencies, especially during a time of diminished resources. More informed citizens make better decisions and can provide support to various government agencies.

Community crime prevention, community policing, and community governance all share the same challenge: maintaining and sustaining the partnership with the community. In the field of crime prevention, the average life expectancy of the block watch is short. Concerned residents come together to address a crisis, but when the crisis is over, they are less involved. When police begin to see targeted crime increase, they need to provide ongoing support to maintain the block watches and to connect residents with resources to solve other problems they identify. When this strategy is employed, crime can be reduced and long-term impact sustained.

The challenges to community policing and community governance often stem from a history of poor relations between the police and the community, a lack of trust, and unsuccessful attempts to work together. In high-crime communities, residents may fear retaliation if they work too closely with the police and other government agencies. There may also be a general lack of interest within the community and agencies to work together in partnership. In diverse communities, there may be isolation among groups and lack of understanding of different cultures. Within government agencies there are employees who resist change and choose to maintain the status quo and undermine efforts to implement community governance. The solution to these challenges is a commitment from leadership and dedicated staff who are responsible for facilitating and sustaining

the partnership between the community, police, and other government agencies.

Betsy Lindsay

See also Broken Windows Theory; Collaboration With Outside Agencies; Community Cohesion and Empowerment; Immigrant Populations, Community Policing Strategies for; Neighborhood Associations; Operation Weed and Seed; Police-Community Relations; Policing, Three Eras of; Problem-Solving Process (SARA); Social Capital

Further Readings

Cohen, D. (2001). *Problem-solving partnerships: Including the community for a change.* Washington, DC: U.S. Department of Justice, National Criminal Justice Reference Service.

Diamond, D., & Weiss, D. M. (2004). *Advancing community policing through community governance: A framework document.* Washington, DC: U.S. Department of Justice, Office of Community Oriented Policing Services.

Flynn, D. W. (1998, July). *Defining the "community" in community policing.* Washington, DC: Police Executive Research Forum.

Francisco, V. T., Fawcett, S. B., Schultz, J. A., Berkowitz, B., Wolff, T. J., & Nagy, G. (2001, April). Using Internet-based resources to build community capacity: The community tool box. *American Journal of Community Psychology, 29*(2), 293–301.

Hillery, G. A., Jr. (1955, June). Definitions of community: Areas of agreement. *Rural Sociology, 20*(4), 111–124.

Manning, P. K. (1997). *Police work: The social organization of policing.* Prospect Heights, IL: Waveland Press.

Niven, R. (2011, December 8). The role of social media in community building and development. *The Guardian.* Retrieved from http://www.guardian.co.uk/voluntary-sector-network/community-action-blog/2011/dec/08/facebook-social-media-community-development

Scott, M. S., & Goldstein, H. (2005). *Shifting and sharing responsibility for public safety problems.* Washington, DC: U.S. Department of Justice, Community Oriented Policing Services.

Stevens, D. J. (2002). *Policing and community partnerships.* Upper Saddle River, NJ: Prentice Hall.

Trojanowicz, R. C., & Moore, M. H. (1988). *The meaning of community in community policing.* East Lansing: Michigan State University, The National Center for Community Policing. Retrieved from http://www.cj.msu.edu/~people/cp/themea.html

COMMUNITY COHESION AND EMPOWERMENT

While there is no agreed-upon definition of *community cohesion,* there is general consensus that it includes the following elements: (1) people in the community share common values, respect each other, and have a common identity; and (2) people in the community share goals and responsibilities and are willing to work with others. Empowerment is the result of community cohesion; it refers to the ability of neighborhood residents to work together to decide what is best for the community and to transform these decisions into action and desired outcomes. Community cohesion and empowerment are processes rather than outcomes; that is, they entail an ongoing effort by people in the community to work together to achieve shared goals. Fostering a strong sense of community is one of the principles of community policing, and it follows that key roles for the police include identifying and addressing issues of neighborhood crime and disorder in order to prevent victimization and fear of crime. This entry discusses how the police and other governmental leaders can empower citizens so that they may have a stake in and provide formal assistance with crime and disorder reduction.

Theoretical Background

The concept of community cohesion (also known as *social cohesion*) was a big focus of the work of the early University of Chicago (Illinois) urban sociologists who developed social disorganization theory. In particular, Clifford Shaw and Henry McKay discovered that the residences of juvenile delinquents were concentrated in certain parts of Chicago; these geographic patterns were essentially the same from one decade to the next, regardless of which ethnic group was living in these delinquent-clustered neighborhoods. These "zones in transition" were home to a variety of other social problems, including high rates of poverty and unemployment, ethnic and racial heterogeneity, residential instability, and female-headed households. These areas that fostered juvenile delinquency were disorganized because of the social and ecological conditions of the neighborhoods. One such condition was ethnic and cultural diversity, which can result in social instability, as it can lead to communication problems and a lack of shared experiences and cultural values, which then promotes fear and lack of trust of one's neighbors. Because there are few shared values concerning appropriate behavior, disorganized neighborhoods also have problems with regulation of undesirable public activity, particularly on the part of youth. In other words, there is a deficit of *informal social control*—the mechanism through which conformity to norms and laws is brought about by institutions such as families, churches, and community groups, and the influence of peers and neighbors, rather than the police, courts, or corrections, or other government agencies. Informal social control occurs when people take action toward the betterment of the community.

More than 60 years after the development of social disorganization theory, the idea of crime being largely due to low informal social control resulting from neighborhood-level factors continues to be an important area of criminological research. In an influential study of 343 Chicago neighborhoods by Robert Sampson and his colleagues (2007), social cohesion and trust was measured by surveying residents about how strongly they agreed with five statements, among them "this is a close-knit neighborhood," "people around here are willing to help their neighbors," and "people in this neighborhood can be trusted." Informal social control was similarly measured with five questions asking residents how likely their neighbors could be counted on to intervene in various situations, including "children were spray-painting graffiti on a local building," "a fight broke out in front of their house," and "the fire station closest to their home was threatened with budget cuts." Sampson and colleagues' work shows that *collective efficacy,* a concept encompassing both social cohesion and informal social control, was the best explanation for levels of violent crime in neighborhoods, even taking into account prior homicide rate, concentrated disadvantage (which includes poverty, receipt of public assistance, female-headed households, density of children, and percentage of black residents), immigrant concentration, density of friendship ties, and residential stability.

World Bank Model of Community Empowerment

Recently, the World Bank has been promoting community empowerment as a means to combat poverty. Its model, which includes four elements, is also suitable for understanding the role of community empowerment in decreasing crime and increasing quality of life. The first element of the model has two aspects: (1) inclusion and participation, which entail bringing decision making to the lowest possible level; and (2) community groups having authority and control over resources. Pushing decision making down to the lowest levels possible is presumed to expand citizen involvement and thus increase a feeling of democracy. The membership of such groups often excludes the young, the poor, minorities, renters, recent immigrants, and so on. Increasing the participation of underrepresented groups can be very difficult, but it is important to do so because these groups typically make up a large percentage of the population in neighborhoods most in need of empowerment. Special efforts must be made to involve as many different types of people as possible, as methods of outreach that work reasonably well with middle-class, middle-aged, white homeowners may not be effective with poor, young, minority residents.

The second element of the World Bank model is access to information. This goes beyond just being aware of what government is doing, and implies a two-way flow between government and residents. Indeed, a two-way communication between citizens and government is essential. It is important for empowerment that residents are able to learn about and take advantage of opportunities and are kept informed of pending projects and developments in their area. For example, if there are plans to locate a police substation, halfway house, or prison in the neighborhood, public hearings should be held in advance to obtain residents' input and feedback. Similarly, if there is the potential for something desirable to come into the neighborhood, learning about it early through public hearings can give the community some leverage to ensure that it benefits.

Accountability is the third element of the empowerment model. This refers to the ability of citizens to call public officials to account for their use of resources, policies, and actions. As with the access-to-information element, accountability is a two-way exchange: The community brings its concerns to the attention of public officials without haranguing them, and public officials respond to the community's concerns by taking appropriate action to address those concerns. However, the environment in the broader community can influence the government's

responsiveness. For example, if the general consensus in the community is that it is not appropriate for residents to be involved in government decision making, then government officials may be less likely to be responsive to community concerns. Another important factor with regard to responsiveness is the size of the community group. The concerns of a small group can be easily but perhaps erroneously dismissed as not representing the "face" of the neighborhood.

The final element of empowerment, and the most essential, is local organizational capacity: the ability to work together, organize, and mobilize resources to solve problems of common interest.

How to Achieve Community Cohesion and Empowerment

Bringing about social or community cohesion and empowerment in neighborhoods that are the most disadvantaged—those with the most poverty, despair, and crime—is one of the most vexing issues for community organizers. A typical first step is to organize neighborhood gatherings, such as block parties, to bring neighbors together in the hopes that social connections among people will be developed and strengthened. While this is perhaps a desirable goal, it is now fairly clear from research on community that it is not enough that people like and trust each other to achieve empowerment. Indeed, dense personal ties and social networks among neighborhood residents can sometimes reduce the empowerment of a community. This seems like a paradox, but what can happen in densely connected communities is that residents and those with whom they have close ties become insular. That is, they focus almost exclusively on their own interests, and are reluctant to look beyond these boundaries for help addressing their problems.

Community cohesion, while alone not enough for empowerment, is a necessary component. Despite the potential for insularity discussed above, bringing neighbors together to meet each other, ideally to work on a small project like a neighborhood cleanup, is essential. Neighbors do not need to become friends, but they do need to identify shared concerns, and eventually, strategies to address these concerns. Much has been written about how to motivate group action. There must be clear incentives and immediate rewards if people are to work collectively. Strong leadership, good communication, and recognition of volunteers' efforts are also important to ensure continued involvement.

Communities with many different organizations and voluntary associations have higher levels of collective efficacy. In what has been termed the "power of weak ties," a group can be more effective when it has multiple connections with other groups external to itself rather than strong connections among individuals within the group. When neighborhood groups work with other organizations, such as businesses, nonprofit organizations, churches, schools, libraries, and other governmental agencies (such as the police), the capacity of the community to effect positive change is further enhanced. This is demonstrative of "bridging" social capital, which in this context concerns social networks and relationships, bonding people, establishing bridges between them, and stressing the importance of community groups working together. The successful use of bridging social capital is associated with community empowerment. As a caveat, it cannot be assumed that just because groups agree on what the problems are they will work well together. Some groups may not have experience collaborating or are suspicious of other groups that may be seen as competitors for resources.

Community Empowerment and Community Policing

If citizens are to engage in collective action that involves collaboration with police, they must trust the police and believe in their legitimacy. Yet the traditional policing strategies and suppressive tactics used in high-crime neighborhoods, such as aggressive stop-and-frisk and crackdowns, can have the effect of eroding trust and perceived legitimacy. Further, communities that feel alienated from the police may lose the ability to exert informal social control. In these circumstances, an effective partnership between police and the community may not be possible until the damaged relationship is rebuilt.

An example of how to do this comes from Boston, where the Ten Point Coalition, a group of activist black clergy who were initially hostile to the police gradually changed their views after they formed relationships with officers who were working to combat youth violence. The ministers had legitimacy in their communities and were able

to shield the police from criticism when they did things the ministers thought were good for the community. The coalition held the police accountable, publicly calling them to task when necessary but also praising them when appropriate. As the police worked with the coalition, they came to see the community as not just providers of information about crime (to which the police, as "experts," would make decisions about how to respond and implement the response), but as coproducers of public safety. Making the police more accountable actually worked to the benefit of the police, for when Operation Ceasefire, a program to reduce youth gang-related violence and homicides, began years later, there was already a solid network of relationships among practitioners and community members. The Ten Point Coalition was included as a way to provide transparency and accountability to minority communities. The coalition served as an intermediary between the police and the community in high-crime, predominantly black and Hispanic neighborhoods, and helped craft legitimacy that affected police operations in those neighborhoods. The police agreed to refrain from tactics perceived as racist and abusive, and in exchange, the leaders were able to convince neighborhood youth to stop gang-related violence. If violence continued, other organizations, such as law enforcement, probation and parole, and social workers stepped in to engage in a process known as "pulling levers."

Another example is the Chicago Alternative Policing Strategy, which was developed in the early 1990s in response to a failure of the traditional methods of preventive patrol and rapid response to calls for service to adequately control crime. This was not a problem unique to Chicago; there was a growing realization across the country of the necessity to change what police do and how they do it. Community advocates and city leaders in Chicago saw that reforms done in other cities did not usually involve citizens and recognized the value of including citizens, for they had local knowledge, different capacities and resources than police, and the ability to monitor police and hold them accountable for their actions. Soon, police officers were assigned to beat teams and expected to become familiar with those small areas. Monthly community beat meetings were held, where police meet regularly with residents. The mayor's office and the Chicago Police Department trained the police and citizens in successful problem solving to reach out and encourage residents to get involved. The beat meetings were not just one-way flows of information, but entailed police and citizens working together to identify problems and come up with solutions that involved the police and the community. They were also a forum to assess the effectiveness of the solutions and consider alternative responses.

Beat meetings contributed greatly to the development of community empowerment. Their regularity and format provided an opportunity for citizens to participate continuously and directly in local-level decision making. There were also deliberative decision procedures—residents and police would create a list of crime and safety problems, prioritize the list, and pool their information to analyze the problems. They decided what to do and who would do it, and then assessed the effectiveness of their responses. If they were successful, they would move on to other problems; if not, they would develop different approaches to deal with the problems. Finally, citizens came to understand that their involvement in the beat-meeting process could directly influence what the police did and whether it worked.

Sharon Chamard

See also Involving Local Businesses; Neighborhood Associations; Police-Community Relations; Social Capital; Tipping Points of Neighborhoods

Further Readings

Braga, A. A., & Winship, C. (2006). Partnership, accountability, and innovation: Clarifying Boston's experience with pulling levers. In D. L. Weisburd & A. A. Braga (Eds.), *Police innovation: Contrasting approaches and perspectives* (pp. 171–187). New York, NY: Cambridge University Press.

Fung, A. (2001) Accountable autonomy: Toward empowered deliberation in Chicago schools and policing. *Politics & Society, 29*(1), 73–103.

Ipsos-MORI. (2007). *"What Works" in community cohesion*. London, England: Department for Communities and Local Government.

Ohmer, M., & Beck, E. (2006) Citizen participation in neighborhood organizations in poor communities and its relationship to neighborhood and organizational collective efficacy. *Journal of Sociology and Social Welfare, 33*(1), 179–202.

Sampson, R. J. (2004). Neighborhood and community: Collective efficacy and community safety. *New Economy, 11*, 106–113.

Sampson, R. J., Raudenbush, S. W., & Earls, F. (2007). Neighborhoods and violent crime: A multilevel study of collective efficacy. *Science, 277*, 918–924. doi:10.1126/science.277.5328.918

Shaw, C. R., & McKay, H. D. (1942). *Juvenile delinquency in urban areas*. Chicago, IL: University of Chicago Press.

COMMUNITY JUSTICE

Community justice is a concept that addresses how criminal justice operations should be carried out in areas where public safety is a major problem. A definition of community justice, provided by David Karp and Todd Clear (2000) is that it encompasses all crime prevention and justice activities that include the community in their processes and have as their primary goal the enhancement of community quality of life. Such initiatives include crime prevention, community policing, community defense and prosecution, community courts, and restorative justice.

There are two assumptions that are inherent within the idea of community justice. The first assumption is that within established jurisdictions, such as states or large cities, there are important differences from one community to another, so criminal justice strategies need to be customized to each community. Criminal law applies equally to everyone, but criminal justice strategies, if they are to be successful, will need to take different forms in different locations. The second assumption is that formal systems of social control, such as the criminal justice system, are not the main means of providing public safety. Rather, informal social controls—such as families, neighbors, social organizations, and friendship relations—form the most important foundation for public safety. Community justice builds on the differing strategies of formal social control (e.g., the criminal justice system), depending on the specific problems facing the local area, and aims to strengthen the capacity of informal social control (e.g., families, schools) within that location.

The bridge between community justice and community policing lies in the fact that, whereas community policing focuses on the police role being broadened to include community collaboration to produce public safety, the focus of community justice lies in the fact that public safety involves broad collaboration between the formal criminal justice system and the community. This entry discusses community justice concepts applicable to all elements of the criminal justice system (law enforcement, courts, and corrections), how each element of the criminal justice system is affected by community justice, and concludes with models for operation.

Important Concepts in Community Justice

An important concept inherent in community justice is that of *informal social control*. Informal social control mechanisms include schools, churches, families, friends, clubs, social groups, and nonprofit agencies. *Formal social controls* include elements of the criminal justice system: law enforcement, courts, and corrections. The reason for the emphasis on strengthening informal social controls is that research has demonstrated that these controls have a stronger and longer-lasting effect on reducing crime.

In general, those who offend are aware that if they are apprehended by the police, tried in court and found guilty, they will be sent to prison. Such awareness, though, does not seem to prevent these people from offending. On the contrary, studies around the world have long shown that informal control mechanisms (family, neighbors, neighborhood, and peers) are more likely to prevent crime than formal control mechanisms (courts, police, and correctional facilities).

Another concept that is discussed with regard to community justice is that of *place*. The place where a person lives can determine the schools that person's children attend, leisure-time activities, the places at which the person eats, and so on. Infrastructure is also important: Transportation, public works, adequate education opportunities, and proper housing all play a role in how place affects those who live there. The focus of police on people committing crimes has increasingly given way to a focus on places: the particular physical locations in which offenders act, because crimes do not occur randomly in space; instead, they are highly clustered in small geographic areas, and this concentration tends to remain stable over time.

The term *community* can be defined many ways, but when discussing community justice, it refers to neighborhoods, which are smaller geographic areas within a larger geographical entity. *Neighborhoods* and *community* are often be used interchangeably in discussing community justice.

How Neighborhoods Affect Community Life

Community justice argues that neighborhoods differ greatly in the degree to which they experience criminal activity and criminal justice. To determine where criminal activity is occurring, information about specific neighborhoods can be examined through the use of crime mapping to determine hot spots, the places where crime appears to be most concentrated. Crime mapping can also be used to examine noncriminal data in order to develop a more accurate picture of needs of a particular community.

Community Policing and Community Justice

Community justice is often seen as being the same as community policing, but there is a difference. Community policing is both a comprehensive strategy of policing and a philosophy of law enforcement, whereas community justice is a strategy and philosophy of criminal justice as a whole, including policing, the courts, and corrections.

Basic community policing tenets certainly inform a part of the strategy for community justice. Because the police adopted the philosophy of community policing in the 1980s, they have been seen as the first element of the criminal justice system to engage the community in public safety. Over the past 30 years, the police have worked to refine the concept of community policing and incorporate it as a standard operating procedure in providing public safety to the community. This section discusses the important concepts of community policing that apply to community justice.

The two aims of community-oriented policing are to improve community relations and to prevent crime. Academic studies showed that rethinking and retooling the philosophy of policing was necessary to put community policing and problem solving into practice. As a result of these studies, the concept of community policing was based on community-building strategies and problem-oriented strategies. Strategies developed from the broken windows theory—which holds that crime results from public disorder and therefore the solution to crime is to use police to create order—have also recently been incorporated into the community policing concept. Because community policing emphasizes creating better communities by expanding the responsibilities of police beyond arresting offenders and investigating crimes, it fits well into the community justice framework.

The concept of problem-oriented policing also fits well into the community justice framework because it emphasizes looking for root causes of problems and long-term solutions to the problems that are identified. As the practice of problem-oriented policing has expanded and grown philosophically, a number of resources have been developed that the police can utilize in partnering with communities to address problems.

According to Karp and Clear, community justice has a broad focus and contains five core elements: (1) neighborhoods, (2) problem solving, (3) decentralization of authority and accountability, (4) community quality of life, and (5) citizen participation. Next we briefly discuss each of these core elements.

1. Community justice operates at the neighborhood level. Karp and Clear believe that, although criminal law jurisdictions involve political boundaries (i.e., states, municipalities, and governments), from the standpoint of community life, these legal parameters mean very little. Communities implement their state's criminal laws, but community life in those jurisdictions is quite different in terms of their crime and its control. Under the community justice ideal, criminal justice activities are adapted to the unique circumstances of crime and community life within each community.

2. Community justice is problem solving. Although traditional criminal law is often an adversarial contest between the accused and the state, Karp and Clear argue that, under community justice, crime is a series of public safety problems to be solved in order to improve community life. Problem-solving approaches involve information, deliberation, and mutual interest for a resolution. The underlying philosophy is that citizens share a set of values and concerns and, with proper information, can find solutions to problems. High-crime areas receive greater attention and investment of resources, as residents inform criminal-justice workers about quality of life problems.

3. Community justice decentralizes authority and accountability. Rather than being hierarchical or paramilitary in nature, Karp and Clear assert that community justice approaches utilize nontraditional alignments, with staff reporting to citizen groups, managers in one organization (e.g., policing) networking with managers of another organization (e.g., probation or prosecution) in order to improve coordination and to generate ideas and action. Like the community policing and problem-solving officer who organizes community anticrime campaigns, mediates neighborhood disputes, and coordinates responses to problems by involving professionals from other agencies, under community justice a social worker might place an at-risk youth in a drug treatment program, or a transportation planner might alter traffic flow through a highly visible drug market. Solutions to public safety problems will nearly always require organizational integration.

4. Community justice gives priority to a community's quality of life. While traditional criminal justice concerns itself with persons who commit and are arrested for crimes, community justice strives to improve the quality of community life. Because an offender has been convicted and punished does not mean that justice has prevailed in its broadest meaning. Under community justice, the aim is to also strengthen the capacity of communities for self-regulation and realization of the collective aims of welfare. In this view, justice is not exclusively the purview of individuals involved with the justice system, but also a collective experience in everyday life.

5. Community justice involves citizens in the justice process. In community justice initiatives, every role involves the capacity of the citizen to influence the local practice of justice. Even the least involved citizens may influence justice system practices by attending and participating in meetings in which crime and disorder are discussed. Citizens volunteer their time to work on particular projects, provide support to victims, assist offenders in their reintegration back into the community, and carry out community crime prevention activities. Others assume more formal roles as members of advisory boards, to provide structured input into community justice practices.

The community policing approach also requires changes in the way police officers are trained. Rather than an emphasis on command-and-control techniques, officers are trained in mediation and conflict resolution so that they can prevent problems and improve relationships with citizens. In academy and

in-service training sessions, officers are also introduced to the concept of problem solving and how to
address the problems they encounter.

The Courts and Community Justice

Of the three elements in the criminal justice system—
law enforcement, the courts, and corrections—
the courts appear to be the least community oriented. One reason is that courts work with cases
and do not concern themselves about the places
where the offenses occurred. They also have a formal process where specific steps are followed in
a prescribed order. Courts are usually detached
from communities because, being bound by law
and precedent, they do not require input from outside sources on how they should operate their system. Many court reformers have worked to retool
court processes, procedures, and jurisdictions so
that community-oriented philosophies are incorporated within the broader context of individual
protections.

The courts have two functions: adjudicat-
ing complaints and sanctioning wrongdoers.
Community justice advocates do not see the adjudication function as a contest in which one side
wins and the other side loses. It is argued that the
court process should be less formal in its approach
and should strive for outcomes that are just to all
those who are affected. Community justice challenges the sanctioning function of the courts in two
ways. First, those who advocate for community-
oriented penalties (such as house arrest) tend to
desire broader choices of case outcomes than are
now available to judges. Second, a high priority is
given to what is thought of as *voice:* The victim,
the offender, and the community should have an
opportunity to explore and explain to the court
what is desired as the best outcome of the sanction
once it is selected.

Under community justice, punishment takes a
backseat to the needs of the victim and community to restore some of the losses suffered because
of the crime. Restorative justice—an approach to
dealing with offenders whereby they are urged to
accept responsibility for their offenses by meeting
with and making reparations to victims as well as
to the community—is seen as a viable and positive
way to determine a meaningful sanction that takes
into account the needs of the victim, the offender,
and the community.

Corrections and Community Justice

Compared to law enforcement and the courts, the
correctional function has come late to the concept
of community justice. Correctional operations are
usually organized into two types: institutional corrections and field service or community corrections.
Institutional corrections include physical facilities such as jails and prisons, whereas field services
or community corrections include probation and
parole activities. In the United States, most forms of
corrections occur in the community.

In corrections, the most significant change from
traditional practices is that community justice
seeks to align itself with and increase the capacity
of informal social controls at the community level.
The focus in community justice is on neighborhoods
and local communities for both types of correctional
operations to ensure appropriate services are delivered, embracing directly the interests of victims and
communities, problem solving to find long-term
solutions to entrenched difficulties, and restoration
to repair the losses suffered by victims of crime and
the social damage caused by the crime.

Integrating Traditional Correctional Thought Into
the Community Justice Framework

The traditional concerns of corrections do not
disappear under community justice; rather, they are
incorporated into community justice priorities. The
most important of these is the neighborhood and
community focus of community justice, and most of
the traditional correctional agenda is shaped by this
orientation. Offender management becomes community focused, with correctional workers becoming
involved with key members of the offender's interpersonal network to support the offender, to strengthen
network ties, and to establish new ties. Correctional
workers must understand the risk the offender represents to the people in that network and to others
in the community, but balance that valid concern for
risk with the need to establish supports.

Two very significant ways that community justice workers ensure an offender progresses toward
reintegration into society is through the combined
strategies of treatment programs and problem-
solving efforts. Treatment programs control and
reduce risks, while problem-solving strategies identify ways those risks may be overcome through new
offender and community approaches.

Finally, punishment, surveillance, and control are aspects of community justice, but they are used as tools to help the offender reintegrate into society rather than just ends in themselves. Thus, under a community justice orientation, traditional themes of corrections remain but are subordinate to the considerations of community justice.

How Community Justice Changes the Traditional Correctional Functions

Probation, as well as parole, involves community supervision, which means that its operations occur in the community and its clients live in the community. Often, traditional probation services will locate offices downtown, near courthouses, or far away from the clients they serve. In a community justice framework, these offices are moved into the communities, closer to the clients, where correctional officers can be more in touch with the neighborhood. This allows the correctional officers to assist clients in establishing supports and following through with a court's restitution order. By locating in the neighborhood, community justice probation tailors its efforts to the particular neighborhood.

Most jails are community based because they operate within the boundaries of a particular community such as a county. Because jail stays are of limited duration, there is a need to have the offenders emotionally prepared for reentry into the community. Three principles appear to be important in the application of community justice principles to the jail: informal social controls, transition planning, and restoration or restitution. Informal social controls create supports in the community to assist an offender in the return to the community, transition planning helps prepare an offender for the return to the community, and restitution or restoration provides the means to help an offender perform restorative services in the community.

Of all the correctional functions, prison appears to be the most removed from a community justice orientation. Typically, offenders are away from the community for several years. Offenders must make many adjustments when they are released from prison and return to the community. Prisons are positioned to make that process of adjustment easier. While in prison, offenders can be readied for release through education, job skills training, impulse control treatment, drug rehabilitation, and establishment of community supports.

Community justice in reentry can function similarly to community justice in probation: through a neighborhood center that provides an array of services to newly released offenders, their families, and other residents. The main additional function of a neighborhood-based reentry center is participation in the transition process that begins with the last stages of incarceration. The role of key people in the offender's reentry is developed and mutually understood by the local residents and the offender alike. Through community guardianship, civic leadership, workforce development, and supportive health care and housing, offenders can find the necessary supports to provide a successful reentry into the community.

Future Issues in Community Justice

The idea of community justice is fairly new, having been introduced around the turn of the 21st century. However, it can be argued that many of the concepts and activities cited under the community justice framework have been included in the criminal justice system for quite some time.

There are several issues that may affect implementation of community justice tenets. One issue is the need for evidence showing that community justice is effective. A second issue is that of politics: If it is recognized by policymakers that this is a valuable method of providing public safety, then support and funding will follow.

John R. Hamilton Jr.

See also Broken Windows Theory; Center for Problem-Oriented Policing; Community Cohesion and Empowerment; Community Prosecution; National Center for Community Policing; Problem-Solving Courts; Restorative Justice; Social Capital

Further Readings

Clear, T. R. (2007). *Imprisoning communities: How mass incarceration makes disadvantaged neighborhoods worse.* Oxford, England: Oxford University Press.

Clear, T. R., Hamilton, J. R., & Cadora, E. (2011). *Community justice* (2nd ed.). London, England: Routledge.

Goldstein, H. (1991). *Problem-oriented policing.* New York, NY: McGraw-Hill.

Karp, D. R., & Clear, T. R. (2000). Community justice: A conceptual framework. In *Criminal Justice 2000.*

Washington, DC: National Criminal Justice Reference Service.

Sampson, R. J., Raudenbush, S. W., & Earls, F. (1997). Neighborhoods and violent crime: A multilevel study of collective efficacy. *Science, 277,* 918–924. doi:10.1126/science.277.5328.918

Shaw, C. R., & McKay, H. D. (1942). *Juvenile delinquency in urban areas.* Chicago, IL: University of Chicago Press.

Tonry, M. (1996). *Sentencing matters.* New York, NY: Oxford University Press.

Trojanowicz, R. C., & Bucqueroux, B. (1990). *Community policing: A contemporary perspective.* Cincinnati, OH: Anderson.

Wilson, J. Q., & Kelling, G. L. (1982, March). Broken windows: The police and neighborhood safety. *Atlantic Monthly, 249*(3), 29–38.

Zehr, H. (2002). *The little book of restorative justice.* Intercourse, PA: Good Books.

COMMUNITY ORIENTED POLICING SERVICES, OFFICE OF

The Office of Community Oriented Policing Services (COPS Office) is a grant-making component of the U.S. Department of Justice that is responsible for advancing public safety through the promotion of the community policing philosophy. To achieve its mission, the office has developed a variety of grant programs for local law enforcement agencies that provide funding to hire community policing officers, procure law enforcement technology, hire civilians, support innovative responses to specific public safety problems, and provide research, training, and technical assistance resources. This entry describes the origins and history of the office, summarizes its most significant programs and activities, and describes the most comprehensive efforts to evaluate its effectiveness.

History

Origins and Legislation

During the 1992 presidential election, crime was at historically high levels in the United States, and there was little public confidence in the ability of the government to develop effective responses to it. In addition, police practitioners and researchers were growing increasingly skeptical of the ability of traditional law enforcement models characterized by routine patrol, rapid response, follow-up investigations, and arrests to alone be sufficient to reduce crime.

At the same time, notions of community policing that emphasized the public and police working together as partners to develop longer-term solutions to crime problems and having the police take on proactive roles in crime reduction were increasingly seen as viable approaches to guide public safety efforts. These notions coalesced around the campaign pledge from then-presidential candidate Bill Clinton to put 100,000 new community policing officers on the streets of the nation. The notion of community-oriented policing appealed to both advocates of get-tough crime control approaches, who focused on the policing aspect, and to adherents of prevention and community enhancement, who focused on the community aspect. After his election, President Clinton worked with Congress to craft a comprehensive bill that addressed crime and public safety and included funding for police.

With bipartisan support, on September 13, 1994, the Violent Crime Control and Law Enforcement Act (the Crime Act) was signed into law. The Crime Act allocated $8.8 billion dollars over six years for Title I, the Public Safety Partnership and Community Policing Act of 1994. This represented an unprecedented investment in local law enforcement; prior to the Crime Act the total federal investment in the entire criminal justice system had never significantly exceeded $1 billion. One of the most controversial aspects of the legislation was the concern that the investment amounted to "federalizing" what had traditionally been state and local functions. As a result of this concern, attention was given to designing a program that did not preempt local autonomy and control, yet achieved specific program goals that the federal government had determined.

To administer these funds, on October 9, 1994, then-Attorney General Janet Reno created the Office of Community Oriented Policing Services, a separate office within the Department of Justice that would report directly to the Associate Attorney General.

Title I outlined four specific goals:

1. Increase the number of law enforcement officers interacting directly with members of the community.

2. Provide training to law enforcement officers to enhance their problem-solving, service, and other skills needed in interacting with members of the community.

3. Encourage the development and implementation of innovative programs to permit members of the community to assist state, Indian tribal government, and local law enforcement agencies in the prevention of crime.

4. Encourage the development of new technologies to assist state, Indian tribal government, and local law enforcement agencies in reorienting the emphasis of their activities from reacting to crime to preventing crime.

To achieve these goals, the COPS Office developed various grant programs and training and technical assistance initiatives, the primary of which are described below.

Programs and Funding

One unique aspect of COPS grant program funding is that it provides funding directly to units of state, local, and tribal government as opposed to block grant programs that provide funding to states to then administer to local jurisdictions. This has enabled the office to have direct contact with thousands of law enforcement agencies across the nation.

Initially, the office emphasized simplicity of the application process in order to reduce administrative burdens on grantees and to ensure that funds quickly reached recipients, with the office touting its "one page application." In addition, the office allowed significant flexibility on the part of agencies to interpret and implement community policing as they saw fit to their local circumstances.

As the office grew and as notions of community policing became increasingly clarified, the application process also evolved. Although still simplified relative to many other federal programs, the office has required agencies to meet a greater number of programmatic and administrative requirements. The office has also provided increased guidance to agencies in terms of the community policing activities that are desired under these grants while still allowing for great latitude in local autonomy and control.

Starting in 2010, the office underwent a significant overhaul of the community policing aspects of the hiring grant program application process. In addition to having all applications submitted online, agencies are now asked to select specific public safety problems that are most relevant to their jurisdiction and to present a comprehensive community policing and problem-solving plan to address them. In addition to other factors such as crime and fiscal need (which first became a part of the application process in 2009), agencies are now evaluated based on the comprehensiveness of their plans relative to others. Applications also ask agencies if they are willing to commit to undertake specific self-selected organizational changes as a condition of their grant. Finally, the office now requires that agencies complete a community policing self-assessment tool at the beginning and end of their grant.

Although COPS Office grants have placed an emphasis on community policing from the outset, diminishing funding resources have introduced greater selectivity in award processes and additional programmatic requirements that are designed to increase the leverage grant dollars have to advance the philosophy of community policing. To date, it remains to be seen if this new strategy has resulted in grant programs that produce greater adoption of community policing or public safety outcomes than previous hiring programs.

As can be seen in Figure 1, the percentage of COPS Office funding that is discretionary as opposed to earmarked by Congress has fluctuated over the years. Beginning in 1998 and reaching its peak in 2006, a progressively increasing percentage of the COPS Office budget included funds earmarked by Congress for specific jurisdictions. These earmarked funds were primarily in the areas of police technology and methamphetamine reduction initiatives. In 2007, Congress placed a one-year moratorium on the earmarking of grant programs. Over the years, COPS discretionary funding has focused primarily on officer hiring and technology, but has also been used to support a variety of other grant programs and initiatives.

Hiring and MORE Technology Grants

Less than a month after signing the Crime Act, the COPS Office awarded nearly $200 million in hiring grants to hire 2,700 community policing officers; and on May 12, 1999, the office announced that it had achieved the goal of providing funding for 100,000 officers (although it would take additional time for them to be fully deployed). By 2012, the COPS Office awarded more than $14 billion in grant funding to more than 13,000 law enforcement agencies (of the approximately 18,000 law

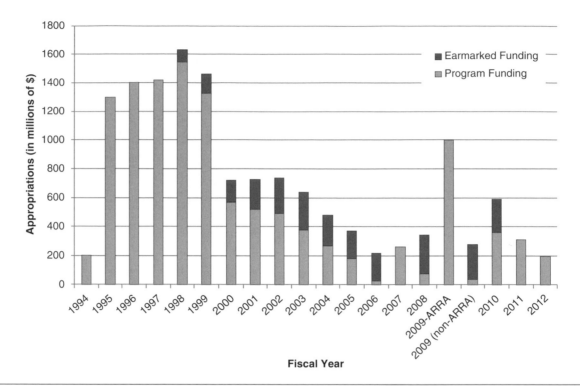

Figure 1   COPS Office Funding, FY1994–FY2012

Source: U.S. Department of Justice, COPS Office.

enforcement agencies in the United States) to hire 123,000 additional officers.

Initially hiring grants were limited to 75% of an entry level officer's salary and fringe benefits up to a three-year cap of $75,000. Agencies were required to provide a 25% local match and to retain the officers for a minimum of 12 months after grant expiration. In addition, the Crime Act requires that half of COPS funding be provided to cities with populations above 150,000 and half to cities with populations below 150,000 and (the "population split" requirement) that one-half of 1% of total funding available be provided to every state and territory (the "state minimum" requirement).

Both the population split and state minimum requirements were the subject of much debate during the initial negotiations regarding the legislation. There were those within the Department of Justice, the administration, and a number of influential outside experts who argued for a program that focused greater resources on high-crime cities in order to have the greatest impact on crime. However, in the end, it was determined that the majority of the funding going to significantly smaller number of high-crime cities was not a politically viable approach, and that the primary goal of the program was to advance the

state of policing in law enforcement agencies of all sizes, and thus these requirements were maintained.

In 2009, the COPS Office received $1 billion through the American Recovery and Reinvestment Act to invest in officer hiring. For this year, the 25% local match and cap requirements were waived and the federal investment increased to 100%, still with a one-year retention requirement for agencies. This waiver of the local match continued into the 2010 and 2011 hiring programs, although these programs were much smaller in scope. In 2012, legislation reinstituted the 25% local match, but raised the three-year cap for an entry level officer's salary and benefits to $125,000.

From 1995 to 2001, the COPS Office also provided funding to law enforcement agencies through its second largest grant program, the Making Officer Redeployment Effective program (MORE program). The MORE program provided funding to hire civilians and procure technology (e.g., mobile computers, records management systems, booking and arraignment technology, in-car computers) that result in time savings and in the redeployment of officers to street. In the most straightforward of cases, civilian staff directly replaced desk-duty officers, who then could be deployed to the street. In other cases, agencies were asked to measure and count the time savings resulting from the technology and report these totals back to the COPS Office. This program struck the balance between the law enforcement community's desire for funding for technology and civilians with the administration's desire to achieve its stated goal of putting 100,000 officers on the street. The accuracy of this reporting system was the subject of much debate. As can be seen in Figure 2, counting this redeployment is important, because nearly 42,000 of the initial officers that were counted toward the 100,000 officer goal were "redeployed" officers as a result of this investment.

One of the earliest challenges and criticisms of the office was the concern that federal dollars would merely supplant rather than supplement local funds. COPS grant conditions specify that funds must be used to supplement and not supplant local funds and the office monitors for these issues. Although individual instances of supplanting have been identified and the actual extent of any potential supplanting will never be able to be fully determined, all of the major studies regarding the grant program have examined this question and have concluded that supplanting is not a significant issue and that COPS-funded officers did result

in significant increases in sworn force strength above that which would have occurred without it.

Innovative Grant Programs

In its earliest years, the COPS Office also provided funding for a variety of smaller grant programs that focused on encouraging innovation around specific types of public safety problems and issues. Through the COPS in Schools program, the office provided funding to hire approximately 6,800 school resource officers that would work in and around primary and secondary schools. In 1995 and 1998, the office funded the creation of domestic violence partnerships through the Community Policing to Combat Domestic Violence Program and promoted researcher and law enforcement partnerships through the Problem Solving Partnerships program. In 1996, the office funded an antigang initiative that provided funding for agencies to develop community policing strategies around grant issues. Most notably perhaps, the office also developed and continues to operate a large Tribal Resources Grant Program that provides officers, equipment, and training to federally recognized tribal law enforcement agencies.

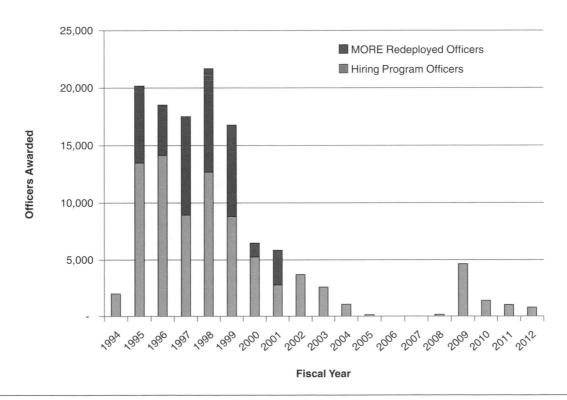

Figure 2   COPS Office Redeployed and Hiring Program Officers
Source: U.S. Department of Justice, COPS Office.

Training, Publications, and Policing Research

The office also invests significantly in policing research, training and technical assistance initiatives, and the creation of a variety of publications and deliverables. From 1994 to 2001, the COPS Office worked with the National Institute of Justice to make the largest-ever documented single investment in policing research of over $46,000,000 to explore practices to improve the quality of police services. The portfolio of studies included examinations of police patrol, firearms violence, and many local research projects that communities used to better understand their own public safety problems.

The COPS Office is also responsible for the largest investment in law enforcement training in the last century through the Community Policing Consortium and the national Regional Community Policing Institutes. Although with diminishing funding, the training capacity of the office has been considerably reduced; to date, the office claims to have trained over 700,000 community members, law enforcement and government officials in various aspects of community policing and public safety topics primarily through its 28 (at its peak) regional institutes.

The office has also developed hundreds of publications and products on a variety of public safety topics, including police and private security partnerships, early intervention systems, racial profiling, homeland security, fear of crime, police citizen interactions, officer recruitment and hiring, ethics and integrity, and police leadership. The office has distributed over 4 million of these products to police practitioners. The office also provided funding for the creation of the Center for Problem-Oriented Policing (the POP Center). The POP Center is an attempt to consolidate all of the research and academic knowledge regarding specific public safety problems and distill it into a format that law enforcement agencies can use to inform their own problem-solving activities. As of 2012, the POP Center has produced more than 80 publications and a variety of other resources around specific public safety topics, and they account for nearly one half of all COPS Office publication distributions.

Evaluations of Effectiveness

By its sheer scale, COPS Office funding has provided an unprecedented opportunity for researchers to examine the ability of federal funding to influence officer hiring, crime rates, and the promotion of an organizational philosophy (community policing) and to examine the ability of police officers to impact crime. Numerous government officials, criminologists and economists have attempted to address these questions through the use of multiple methods examining COPS funding over time. Three of the largest and most comprehensive studies are described in this section.

The National Evaluation of the COPS Program

The earliest comprehensive attempt to evaluate the effectiveness of the office was completed in August 2000 by the Urban Institute. The Urban Institute was provided funding from the National Institute of Justice to conduct an independent evaluation of all aspects of the first four years of COPS Office operations and funding. A team of researchers used a variety of methods to reach their conclusions, including examining internal COPS Office records, conducting telephone surveys, and using case studies and site visits of COPS grantees.

The study found that the COPS program was effectively administered in that COPS Office funding was efficiently distributed directly to and used by local communities. In addition, researchers found little evidence of supplanting but rather determined that the federal investment did in fact add additional officers to the streets and agencies were likely to retain a high percentage of COPS-funded officers. At the time of this evaluation, many of the MORE technology grants were still not fully operational, but researchers did find that officers were being redeployed as a result of these grant funds.

They also found that COPS Office funding did advance the adoption of community policing in local jurisdictions, but researchers also pointed out that COPS funding likely provided fuel to movements toward community policing that were already accelerating. Questions regarding the impact of COPS funding on crime or other public safety outcomes were outside of the scope of this initial evaluation; in later years, however, others attempted to address these issues.

Government Accountability Office

After the national evaluation was released, multiple researchers (including those funded by the COPS Office) attempted to estimate the effect that

Community Oriented Policing Services, Office of

COPS Office grants had on crime rates using various statistical models and at times reached contradictory findings. As a result of these studies, in 2004 the Government Accountability Office (GAO) was asked by Congress to conduct its own evaluation of the effectiveness of COPS Office grants. Similar to the previous studies, the GAO examined a comprehensive database including observations of 4,247 COPS-funded agencies, on crime, officer hiring, COPS funding, other federal investments in local communities, surveys of police practices, and other factors contributing to crime from 1990 to 2001.

The study found that COPS grants significantly increased sworn officer levels above the levels that would have been expected without these funds and that COPS grants produced significant negative impacts on violent and property crime rates. For the years 1994 to 2001, the GAO found that crime rates reduced due to the COPS Office grant expenditures amounted to about 8% of the total decline in index crimes and 13% of the total decline in violent crimes from 1993 levels. Overall, they found that a 1% increase in the size of the police force decreased property crime by .25% and violent crime by 1%. They also found that agencies that received COPS grants had larger increases in the average levels of reported use of problem solving, place-oriented policing, and community collaboration practices than agencies that did not receive COPS grants.

Flypaper COPS

In 2007, two economists at the University of Maryland sought to address the question of the effectiveness of COPS Office grants on crime rates and of the long-term impact that hiring officers had on law enforcement staffing levels. They examined annual data from 2,074 cities and found that for each COPS-funded officer, agencies had a longer term expansion of their force by .70 officers. They stated that COPS grants were like flypaper that "stuck where they hit." In addition they found that COPS-funded officers and technology produced significant reductions in four of seven index crimes in the years following their hire and procurement.

Conclusion

The Crime Act and the subsequent creation of the COPS Office is the single-largest-ever federal investment in law enforcement. The office has been responsible for the hiring of more than 100,000 community policing officers and has developed a variety of programs and initiatives designed to advance the community policing philosophy in U.S. law enforcement. Since inception, funding for the office has diminished considerably from its initial highs, but it is still working to provide resources to the law enforcement field.

Matthew C. Scheider

See also Center for Problem-Oriented Policing; Community Policing, Evolution of; Community Policing: Resources, Time, and Finances in Support of; Community Policing Consortium; Community Policing Self-Assessment Tool (CP-SAT); Police Training Officer (PTO) Program; Regional Community Policing Institutes; Violent Crime Control and Law Enforcement Act of 1994

Further Readings

Evans, W. N., & Owens, E. (2007). COPS and crime. *Journal of Public Economics, 91*(1–2), 181–201. doi: 10.1016/j.jpubeco.2006.05.014

Heaton, P. (2010). *Hidden in plain sight: What cost of crime research can tell us about investing in police.* Santa Monica, CA: RAND.

Johnson, C. C., & Roth, J. A. (2003). *The COPS program and the spread of community policing practices, 1995–2000.* Washington, DC: The Urban Institute.

Koper, C. S., Moore, G., & Roth, J. A. (2002). *Putting 100,000 officers on the street: A survey-based assessment of the federal COPS program.* Washington, DC: The Urban Institute. Retrieved from http://www.sas.upenn.edu/jerrylee/research/cops_levels.pdf

Muhlhausen, D. B. (2001). *Do community oriented policing services grants affect violent crime rates?* (Report no. CDA01–05). Washington, DC: Heritage Foundation, Center for Data Analysis.

Roth, J. A., Ryan, J. A., & Koper, C. S. (2000, August). *National evaluation of the COPS program—Title 1 of the 1994 Crime Act.* NCJ 183643. Washington, DC: The Urban Institute. Retrieved from https://www.ncjrs.gov/pdffiles1/nij/183643.pdf

U.S. Government Accountability Office. (2005, October). *COPS grants were a modest contributor to declines in crime in the 1990s.* GAO-06-104. Washington, DC: Author. Retrieved from http://www.gao.gov/products/GAO-06-104

Zhao, J., Scheider, M. C., & Thurman, Q. C. (2002). Funding community policing to reduce crime: Have

COPS grants made a difference? *Criminology and Public Policy, 2*(1), 7–32. doi: 10.1111/j.1745-9133.2002.tb00104

COMMUNITY POLICING, DISCRETIONARY AUTHORITY UNDER

Underlying any discussion of community policing and discretion is a curious dichotomy. If the public were polled about ideal policing, many would respond favorably to the idea that police should be firm, fair, and impartial—a common image of a state or metropolitan police officer. But others would respond that more individualized policing, such as that in small towns where the officer knows everybody and everybody knows the officer, is the ideal. Yes, the small-town officer treats different people differently, but it is because she or he knows them personally, knows their history, knows what to expect from them, and knows what will work to set them straight. Basically, the public wants equal and consistent enforcement of the law, but they also want the police to use discretion when dealing with individuals.

Studies of policing over the last 50 years, in big cities and small towns, have demonstrated that police officers have broad discretion. Today, an open and important question is whether community policing has changed that discretion. A common argument is that police officers who work closely with the community need even more flexibility and authority in order to adapt their activities to neighborhood needs and to implement creative problem-solving responses that satisfy multiple constituencies. If, however, at the same time the community is given a stronger voice in determining how it is policed, it might be just as likely that police discretion is reduced as community discretion is enhanced.

Police Discretion

The exercise of discretion is nearly inevitable in policing. When performing their traditional core functions, police officers make many choices from a range of possible actions or inactions available to them—choices that are not specifically prescribed by law, policy, procedure, or rule. Some laws are outdated, while others are unpopular with the public (e.g., marijuana laws, motorcycle helmet laws). Still others are vague, unconstitutional, or lack enforceable sanctions. Legislatures pass laws and fail to abolish others, for a variety of purposes, only one of which is to establish clear expectations and guidelines for enforcement through police action. In contrast to most laws, some police organizational policies specifically aim to guide officers in their use of discretion, but the infinite number of hypothetical scenarios that police might encounter makes it nearly impossible to anticipate everything, resulting in guidelines that depend heavily on officers using their judgment.

Another complication is that the multiple purposes that laws and policies seek to achieve sometimes conflict with one another. In such instances, police must decide which objectives take precedence over others. For example, during a public demonstration held in the streets, police may find that the objective of keeping traffic avenues clear conflicts with the objective of safeguarding citizens' rights to peaceful protest. Similarly, one police policy might emphasize that officers should be sympathetic and responsive toward crime victims' needs and wishes, while another policy requires mandatory arrest in misdemeanor domestic violence situations, even if the victim specifically asks that the offender not be arrested.

In addition, police and other criminal justice resources are simply too limited to allow police to enforce all laws exhaustively. Most communities would not tolerate full enforcement of the law, even if resources would allow it, preferring a degree of police tolerance, especially for minor legal transgressions. The very capacity of the criminal justice system to continue functioning in many communities depends to a great extent on the police not fully enforcing the law. Sudden or prolonged increases in police arrest activity can seriously challenge the capacity of any criminal justice system.

Perhaps the most profound types of discretionary decisions made in policing are the decisions to use force and to enforce the law through arrest or citation. In regard to the use of force, sociologist Egon Bittner famously described the core of the police role as "the distribution of nonnegotiably coercive force employed in accordance with the dictates of an intuitive grasp of situational exigencies." What Bittner meant is that the police are regularly called to the scenes of trouble, and often find it through their own initiative. These situations are frequently confusing, if not chaotic. In these situations, police officers are authorized to use reasonable force, if necessary, in order to quell the trouble. Their decisions about whether the use of force is necessary, and if so, how much force to use, are largely discretionary, within the relatively broad constraints imposed by the law. Decisions are made by the officer or officers on the scene, based on their "intuitive grasp" of the circumstances (the "situational exigencies") as they unfold.

Police decisions about whether to arrest are discretionary too. Generally, police are authorized to arrest (1) with a warrant issued by a court, (2) whenever a person commits any crime in their presence, and (3) whenever they have probable cause to believe that a felony (serious) crime has been committed and that a particular person has committed it, even if the probable cause is based on second-hand or third-hand information. In regard to warrantless arrests, which are the most common, law and official policy rarely say that the police *must* arrest. Most often the laws and policies say, or are interpreted as meaning, that the police *may* arrest, leaving discretion in the hands of ordinary police officers.

The most ubiquitous discretionary situations encountered by police are the decisions whether to stop drivers who violate traffic laws and, once traffic stops are made, whether to cite the drivers and, further, whether to search the vehicle for evidence or contraband. Many observed traffic violations are minor in nature (such as driving five miles over the speed limit or failing to signal a lane change) and therefore frequently ignored by police, or at most, addressed with a warning. By the same token, poor driving causes many deaths and injuries every year and a huge amount of property loss, so traffic policing and its associated discretionary decision making should not be dismissed as a trivial matter. As well, when officers decide to issue citations to drivers, fines are routinely in the hundreds of dollars today and can result in the loss of driving privileges, which in turn can have serious consequences for employment and income. Moreover, police commonly engage in traffic enforcement as a method of controlling more serious crime in an effort to locate illegal guns and drugs, to locate persons with outstanding arrest warrants, to disrupt illegal drug and prostitution markets, to deter burglars and thieves from prowling neighborhoods, and so forth.

Studies have shown that about half of traffic stops result in a citation. Similarly, although it is harder to measure, it is estimated that when police have probable cause to make an arrest, they do so only about half the time. Across all incidents that they handle, police use force no more than 5% of the time, and even in full-custody arrests, only about 20% entail a degree of force beyond mere handcuffing. In other words, police use of their authority is significantly mediated by discretion.

As these figures demonstrate, the most obvious consequence of discretion is that police often choose *not* to enforce the law, thus softening the impact of the criminal law on people's lives. With discretion, officers get to choose how to handle various situations, and at least half the time when an arrest could be made or a citation issued, they choose underenforcement or some other version of leniency. Because of discretion, officers' actions can be affected by sympathy and empathy, and officers have the opportunity to practice "justice tempered with mercy"—to choose what they consider to be the most fair or just resolution of the situation, even if that entails not enforcing the law.

One potential problem with discretion and underenforcement arises if the police are more lenient toward members of majority groups and higher-status individuals than they are with others. Analyses often indicate that members of minority groups are disproportionately arrested for minor offenses and disproportionately subject to searches following traffic stops. In other words, the overall picture is one of underenforcement, but often the enforcement that *is* undertaken is differentially applied to racial and ethnic minority groups. This pattern of police discretionary decision making—often called racial profiling but perhaps more accurately called racially biased policing—might be accounted for by legitimate situational factors, but it might also be a reflection of conscious or unconscious bias.

An inherent byproduct of discretion, and thus perhaps the most fundamental challenge associated with it, is inconsistency. Discretion gives police officers leeway in deciding how to handle encounters and confrontations based on an "intuitive grasp" of each situation. Ultimately, some people caught with a marijuana cigarette get arrested and some do not, some drivers who fail to signal their turns get citations and some do not. This brings into focus two competing conceptions of justice and fairness—one perspective says that fairness is treating every rule-breaker the same, while the other perspective says that fairness is treating each person *as a person*, according to his or her unique circumstances.

Discretion and Community Policing

The question here is whether community policing affects these longstanding realities of police discretion, and if so, in what ways. One straightforward possibility is that community policing puts officers into closer relationships with neighborhood residents, increasing the chances of favoritism in enforcement and other actions. That is, a permanently assigned beat officer considering whether to arrest an individual for drinking in public, whether to cite a driver for failing to stop at a stop sign, or whether to require a husband to leave home in response to a domestic dispute, might be influenced by familiarity with the person, and in particular, might be more likely to choose leniency. This could become problematic if the seriousness of the person's behavior merited a stricter response, and it could lead to inconsistency if the officer did not make the same choices when dealing with neighborhood nonresidents.

Increasing police officers' familiarity with neighborhoods and their residents is an overt objective of community policing. Advocates of community policing argue that police officers have broad discretion anyway and they can use it more effectively when they know who's who—that it is better for police to make decisions based on intimate knowledge about the people involved rather than deciding in a vacuum, uninfluenced by individuals' particular circumstances or community concerns. However, as noted above, a competing conception of fairness is that police decisions should be made without regard to the specific people involved, but rather in a way that is even and consistent. A clear resolution of this centuries-old debate is not possible, because most people are willing to support both perspectives, depending on the situation.

Another common characteristic of community policing is the tailoring of enforcement and other police activity to the needs and priorities of different neighborhoods. One neighborhood might be very concerned about residential speeding while another might not. Similarly, residents of one neighborhood might be offended by drinking in public, while the same behavior might be widespread and tolerated in another neighborhood. If meeting community needs and providing policing *for* the community and not *to* the community are taken seriously, then community policing is likely to result in differential enforcement across neighborhoods.

Differential policing across neighborhoods might be produced by the discretionary decision making of individual beat officers, or it might result from higher-level decisions that are also discretionary. If the former, it could be argued that community policing expands the discretion of patrol officers, as it officially licenses them to make judgments about what is and is not tolerable in different neighborhoods and then to act accordingly. In the latter case, though, if it is a beat team sergeant or area commander (typically a lieutenant or captain) who decides what types of behavior will or will not be tolerated in different neighborhoods, then discretion still abounds, but it is mostly in the hands of police managers, not street-level officers.

Police discretion exercised at the neighborhood or community level is not limited to whether officers respond to law infractions by arrest, but extends to strategic alternatives to enforcement. In a community in which police have helped to establish a youth peer court—an alternative to formal processing in the juvenile system—police officers might routinely refer local youth who commit infractions to the peer court rather than to the juvenile justice system. In a neighborhood beset by drug crimes, police might opt to emphasize civil law enforcement against residential and commercial properties that are facilitating the drug crimes while deemphasizing intensive criminal drug enforcement. This could result in a wholesale reduction in criminal law enforcement across the neighborhood.

To some degree, police officers have always had and exercised the kinds of discretion described above. Quite possibly, community policing has not expanded police discretion at all, but has merely recast it in several ways. It has brought discretion more out into the open, while raising the question of who should exercise that discretion: street officers or managers (or the community). Also, it has increased the likelihood of familiarity in everyday police decisions, which does not necessarily expand discretion but does introduce complications that have the potential to lead to favoritism and ethical dilemmas.

Bringing police discretion more out into the open has long been advocated by reformers. Police officers have historically exercised "low-visibility" discretion and police agencies have traditionally pretended that officers simply enforce the law. This has been a convenient and comfortable pretense, allowing police executives to avoid public acknowledgment of discretion and avoid having to explain why their officers engage in differential application of the law. While greater transparency about discretion is bound to be painful and challenging for police leaders, it should ultimately result in more honest public discussion and greater public understanding of the complex police mission.

Bringing police managers more into the decision-making arena also has the potential to add greater consistency and accountability to police use of discretion. Managers usually have more experience, they should have a clearer sense of the big picture and think strategically, and they are in better positions to coordinate actions and decisions across the police organization. Also, since there are fewer managers than street-level officers, it is easier to place accountability on them. From a cautionary perspective, though, managers are one or two levels away from the immediate action, plus they may sometimes pass the buck and avoid both decision making and accountability. Overall, shifting discretion more toward police managers has potential for improving decisions and enhancing consistency, but it is not a panacea and it calls for striking the right balance between street-level and management perspectives.

The increase in familiarity that comes along with community policing has already been discussed. As noted, it should be a plus but it does add complications. Agencies implementing community policing might need to develop policies designed to guide officers in decision-making situations when the officers are familiar with the people involved, and closer supervision might be needed to ensure that improper favoritism does not arise. When community policing is implemented, training and leadership in professional ethics probably becomes even more important than usual for police in order to help officers properly navigate through tricky and morally ambiguous situations.

Perhaps the greatest impact of community policing on police discretion would occur if the community was truly empowered to set priorities and make more decisions on its own behalf. If neighborhood residents decided that public drinking was acceptable, or at least a low priority for them, and this actually drove police enforcement, then it would seem that police discretion would be reduced, not expanded. Similarly, if a community decided that it wanted youthful offenders handled informally rather than arrested, and officers followed suit, police discretion would be effectively reduced.

What these two scenarios describe, of course, is community-driven community policing rather than police-driven community policing. This model has been tried in some jurisdictions, but the general consensus is that police-driven community policing is much more common. Cynics would argue that police have been unwilling to really share power with the community. But it is also important to realize that the police have a sworn responsibility to uphold the law and abide by the Constitution—neighborhood residents do not. Moreover, neighborhood residents are not always (or usually) in complete agreement about priorities and tolerable behavior—in the absence of consensus, the police still get called to emergencies and disputes and they still have to make decisions. At best, then, some form of power sharing between the police and local communities may be seen. But it would be irresponsible of the police to abdicate their authority and responsibilities, including the discretion that inevitably characterizes their work.

Discretion and Problem Solving

To this point, this entry has mainly focused on police discretion in regard to enforcement and other traditional activities, and how that might be affected by community policing. One aspect of community policing that has not been directly addressed is problem solving, or problem-oriented policing. If police take a problem-oriented rather than incident-oriented approach to policing, how is discretion affected? For the most part, the answer parallels the preceding discussion. When police work closely with neighborhood residents in identifying and responding to problems, the issue of familiarity comes in, with its associated pluses and minuses. Also, police who focus their attention on problems are likely to end up addressing different problems in different neighborhoods, leading to inconsistency across the jurisdiction. And if police give neighborhood residents significant say in identifying and prioritizing their own problems, they have to watch out for the tyranny of the majority and make sure that problem solving does not boil down to tasking the police with keeping such persons as the homeless or mentally unstable people in line and keeping outsiders out.

While most discretion issues associated with problem-oriented policing are not new or unique, there are two that deserve some further mention. One is that the problem-solving process (e.g., the SARA model) provides some structure to decision making. The expectation that problems will be carefully identified and thoroughly analyzed increases the likelihood that they will be well understood before any police action is taken. Then, it is expected that a range of responses will be given consideration before choosing those responses that have the best fit with the specific problem being addressed, including the best evidence that they will work in the type of situation being faced. This systematic approach stands in contrast to most traditional police work, in which officers make quick discretionary decisions based on their "intuitive grasp" of the circumstances. To be sure, problem-oriented policing does not eliminate the occurrence of emergencies and other crises in which quick decision making is required, but it expands the sphere of police work within which more thorough analysis and calmer thinking can precede police action.

Finally, police problem solving often leads to "third-party policing," in which the police work with code enforcement, private security, neighborhood watch groups, landlords, and others who have different forms of authority, influence, and leverage over potential offenders or particular locations. Third-party policing has sometimes been criticized as an unobtrusive means of expanding surveillance and as a sneaky way for the publicly accountable police to get others to do some of their "dirty work." Not often mentioned is that it probably does reduce police discretion, inasmuch as it represents a delegation of police responsibilities to other formal and informal institutions. Both the police and the third parties to whom responsibility is delegated must be accountable for how that authority is ultimately exercised.

Gary W. Cordner and Michael S. Scott

See also Ethical Considerations; Problem-Oriented Policing: Elements, Processes, Implications; Problem-Solving Process (SARA); Traffic Problems, Community Policing Strategies for

Further Readings

Bittner, E. (1970). *The functions of the police in modern society*. Washington, DC: Government Printing Office.

Brown, L. P. (1985). Police-community power sharing. In W. A. Geller (Ed.), *Police leadership in America: Crisis and opportunity* (pp. 70–83). New York, NY: Praeger.

Eith, C., & Durose, M. R. (2011). *Contacts between police and the public, 2008*. NCJ 234599. Washington, DC: U.S. Department of Justice, Bureau of Justice Statistics. Retrieved from http://www.bjs.gov/content/pub/pdf/cpp08.pdf

Gaines, L. K., & Swanson, C. R. (1999). Empowering police officers: A tarnished silver bullet? In L. K. Gaines & G. W. Cordner (Eds.), *Policing perspectives: An anthology* (pp. 363–371). Los Angeles, CA: Roxbury.

Goldstein, H. (1963, September). Police discretion: The ideal versus the real. *Public Administration Review, 23*(3), 140–148.

Goldstein, J. (1960). Police discretion not to invoke the criminal process: Low-visibility decisions in the administration of justice. *Yale Law Journal, 69,* 543–589.

Greene, J. R. (2000). Community policing in America: Changing the nature, structure, and function of the police. In J. Horney, R. Peterson, D. L. MacKenzie, J. Martin, & D. P. Rosenbaum (Eds.), *Policies, processes, and decisions of the criminal justice system* (Vol. 3) (pp. 299–370). NCJ 182410. Washington, DC: U.S. Department of Justice, National Institute of Justice.

Mastrofski, S. D., Worden, R. E., & Snipes, J. B. (1995). Law enforcement in a time of community policing. *Criminology, 33*(4), 539–563.

Peak, K. J., Stitt, B. G., & Glensor, R. W. (1998). Ethical considerations in community policing and problem solving. *Police Quarterly, 1*(3), 19–34.

Weisheit, R. A. (2005). Rural police. In L. Sullivan & M. Simonetti Rosen (Eds.), *Encyclopedia of law enforcement* (Vol. 1; pp. 411–412). Thousand Oaks, CA: Sage.

COMMUNITY POLICING, EVOLUTION OF

One of the best ways to fully grasp the concept of community policing, including key aspects and critical elements of community policing, is through an understanding of the historical evolution of community policing. This entry explores the historical context of community policing, commonly recognized eras of policing, portents of community policing, antecedents of community policing, reasons for implementation of community policing, approaches to community policing, the development of community policing over the past three decades, and future prospects for community policing.

Historical Context

To understand community policing, it is important to look at the historical context in which community policing developed. In their early work on community policing, George Kelling and Mark Moore (1988) distinguish between and summarize salient features of three *eras* of policing: the political era, the reform era, and the community policing/problem solving era.

The political era dates from the introduction of municipal police forces in the 1840s and continued until the early 1900s. Prior to this, many colonial cities had a night watch system, an outgrowth of the English pledge system. The political era was characterized by close ties between police and politics. Local police commanders had frequent contact and communication with political leaders and ward bosses. Police priorities were set in conjunction with these political figures. While it has been argued that the close relationship between police and local politicians increased police legitimacy and responsiveness to the community, it has also been argued that local politicians and ward bosses often acted in their own interest rather than the public interest and that this era of policing was characterized by corruption and discrimination against minorities.

The reform era took hold in the 1930s, reached its peak in the 1950s and 1960s, and began its decline in the 1970s. August Vollmer, a former police chief and first professor of police administration, was one of the first advocates of the reform era in the early 1900s. The reform era was characterized by a professional crime fighting approach, reliance upon routine patrol, quick response to calls for service, and criminal investigations. The reform era is said to be both a reaction to the corruption of the political era and in keeping with the growing trend toward scientific management. Policing is generally viewed as having become far more professional and police organizations far more sophisticated during this era.

The community policing/problem-solving era, which began in the late 1970s, developed over the past three decades and continues into the 21st century, albeit in a very different form from its origins. The community policing era is characterized by close working relationships between the police and the community, attention to quality of life and problem solving. Policing is generally viewed to have become far more attentive to community concerns during this period and police organizations became more decentralized.

Each era of policing is characterized by differences in public perception of the primary sources of police legitimacy and authority, view of the police function, organizational design, external relationships between the police and the community, demand management (how police are summoned and the police resources allocated), principal programs and technologies, and measures of success.

Portents

The reform era of policing was marked by relatively calm and quiet police-public relationships between 1920 and 1960. For the most part, police and public order did not engender highly visible or significant public policy issues. Professionalism grew, though many police departments adopted a highly discretionary watchman style of policing characterized by incident-driven methods and emphases on quantitative outcomes, emphasizing order-maintenance over enforcement, particularly with regard to less serious offenses. This changed dramatically with the civil unrest and riots of the 1960s. Police thinking, tactics, and resources changed significantly during this period, and the changes centered primarily on police relations with communities, particularly minority communities. The *Report of the National Advisory Commission on Civil Disorders* issued in 1968 and popularly known as the Kerner Commission Report, cited hostility between ghetto residents and police as a primary cause of the racial disruptions. Aggressive preventive patrol and roving task forces were singled out for negative comment by the report. Lack of redress for complaints against police conduct and lack of minority representation on police forces were also cited.

Antecedents

Early evidence of concepts associated with community policing can be traced to the latter part of the political era and beginning of the reform era. In

New York City, junior police leagues were initiated and the police made school visits to inform children that police work involved making the neighborhood a better, safer place to live. Emphases were on service, improved relationships with the community, and quality of life.

More recently, police-community relations units were instituted in response to the civil disorder and social tensions of the 1960s. These programs have often been criticized as generally existing to make the agency look good, limited to segregated units of police departments, and largely cosmetic in nature. While these programs may have failed to accomplish their intended goals, viewed from an evolutionary perspective, their recognition of the importance of citizen cooperation with the police and the importance of responding to diverse community needs may have laid the groundwork for community policing. While community policing and community relations are clearly different, the former probably could not have developed without the groundwork of the later.

Many team policing projects were instituted in the 1970s in response to the 1967 President's Commission on Law Enforcement and the Administration of Justice recommendation of more frequent, informal contact between police and the public. The overarching goal of the commission was to study crime, those who commit it, those who are its victims, and what could be done to reduce it. The Commission issued more than 200 recommendations in those areas, including how the police could be brought closer to their communities, which it termed the "community-service function of the police." Team policing has often been described as a step toward the development of community policing. The theory behind team policing was to improve police services to neighborhoods, have officers work in close contact with communities to prevent crime and maintain order, and improve officer morale. Team policing was never fully implemented in most of the cities studied, and the results of team policing experiments were generally not impressive.

Research in the 1970s also contributed to the development of community policing. Foremost among this research was the Kansas City preventive patrol experiment, which investigated two unproven, though widely accepted assumptions underlying the primary method of traditional policing, automotive preventive police patrol. Many academics and practitioners assumed that visible police presence deterred potential offenders and diminished the public's fear of crime. Analysis of the data from the Kansas City experiment revealed no significant differences between different levels of patrol coverage and reported instances of crime, nor any significant differences in citizens' attitudes toward police services, citizens' perceptions of fear, police response time, and citizen satisfaction with response time. The Kansas City study demonstrated that routine preventive patrol did not deter crime or contribute to the public sense of security. Traditional methods of policing were not reducing crime nor reassuring the public.

Reasons for Implementing Community Policing

Community policing was implemented to prevent and reduce crime and improve relationships between police and citizens. Crime rose steadily from the early 1960s through the early 1980s. The mid-1980s brought further increases in crime, particularly violent crime, often linked to drug-related criminal activity. Inner-city violence, particularly homicides involving young African American men, captured headlines across the urban United States. Quality of life in communities deteriorated as a result of rising crime, violence, and poverty. The early community policing literature argued that community policing had the potential to prevent and reduce crime and disorder, curb growing violence, and alleviate fear of crime and disorder.

In addition to rising crime, the growing isolation of the police from the community and complaints of police brutality and indifference, especially in minority communities, substantially contributed to the development of community policing. Among the primary reasons for the growing isolation of the police from the public were the emphasis on police as crime control professionals and the reliance on routine automotive patrol. As a result of the growing focus on enforcement and reliance upon automotive patrol, informal contacts between police and citizens were reduced and the bond between police and citizens weakened. At the same time, aggressive patrol tactics adopted in response to rising crime and civil disobedience increased the likelihood of hostile confrontations between police and citizens and contributed to increasing complaints against the police. The community policing literature strongly suggests that community policing could improve communication and trust between police and citizens, reverse the growing distance and isolation of the police from the public, and reduce citizen complaints of brutality and indifference.

Community Policing Approaches

Although aspects of community policing appear to have been widely implemented in U.S. police departments since the late 1970s, the concept of community policing is subject to widely varying approaches. Some label any program to improve police and community relationships as community policing. As community policing became more established and began to spread across the United States, approaches evolved along with the practice of community policing, albeit somewhat unevenly. Jerome Skolnick and David Bayley argue that at its core, community policing requires increased public participation in enhancing public safety and the maintenance of public order.

The numerous approaches to community policing have both advantages and disadvantages for diffusion and development of the practice. On the one hand, the varying approaches can serve as a barrier to its spread and makes evaluation difficult. On the other, they may actually facilitate implementation. Community policing means different things to different people; it is an intangible construct appealing to different audiences for different reasons. One of the reasons for the varying approaches is that aspects of community policing are shaped, at least in part, by forces within specific police agencies and local jurisdictions related to local history, concerns, politics and real or perceived problems. This makes establishment of a strict historical timeline chronicling the development of community policing difficult. Nevertheless, it is possible to make certain generalizations.

Development of Community Policing

The era of community policing began in the late 1970s, following the civil unrest of the 1960s and the Kansas City preventive patrol experiment and team policing projects of the 1970s. Willard Oliver categorizes the era of community policing as falling within three generations: innovation, 1979–1986; diffusion, 1987–1994; and institutionalization, 1995–present.

Innovation

The innovation generation began during the late 1970s after certain long-held beliefs in the law enforcement community, such as the effectiveness of routine preventive patrol, were placed in doubt,

sparking a search for what would work. This first stage included early work on problem-oriented policing and broken windows theory, which focused on dealing with neighborhood disorder, public drunkenness, panhandling, prostitution, and other urban quality-of-life offenses as a means of reducing crime and citizen fear. Community policing experiments, test sites, and demonstration projects implemented during this phase focused on major urban areas, were generally funded by grants, and typically involved a single intervention. Widely publicized early efforts include the Newark, New Jersey, and Flint, Michigan, foot patrol experiments; the Houston, Texas, Neighborhood Oriented Policing Project; and the Newport News, Virginia, Problem-Oriented Policing effort.

Early community policing efforts and experiments involved strong emphasis on foot patrol. Two well-known experiments occurred in Newark, New Jersey, and Flint, Michigan. In both of these cities, the terms *foot patrol* and *community policing* were used interchangeably. The Newark experiment hypothesized that increased foot patrol would lead to reduced fear of crime, the actual incidence of crime, reduced victimization, a larger percentage of arrest rates in the foot patrol areas, increased police officer job satisfaction, and improved citizen relations in foot patrol areas. The Newark experiment found that "residents were aware of the different patrol levels in their neighborhoods" and that police patrols were "overwhelmingly popular." The hypotheses that foot patrol would lead to a reduction in crime and victimization were not supported by the findings of the Newark experiment. However, the experiment did produce findings of decreased citizen fear and increased officer job satisfaction.

The Flint foot patrol program is said to have demonstrated both the efficiency and effectiveness of foot patrol officers who were judged to be able to carry out a wide range of activities as community organizers, dispute mediators, and service brokers. There were indications that mutual respect between police officers and the community was growing. It appears that these results were achieved as a combination of the nature of foot patrol, which encouraged far more officer-initiated activities, such as home and business visits and instruction with regard to community organizing, leadership, and problem solving. Officers were given broad flexibility to carry out their tasks, encouraged to be creative, and take ownership of their patrol beats.

Houston, Texas, experimented with Directed Area Response Teams (DART), to increase positive interaction between police and communities during this early phase of community policing. It also implemented Project Oasis, which involved strategies aimed at reducing fear and encouraging community revitalization before eventually selecting Neighborhood Oriented Policing (NOP) as its new policing style. NOP facilitated interaction between officers and citizens for the purpose of identifying crime and noncrime problems. It incorporated both a managerial philosophy and operational approach. Officers were relieved of traditional random, vehicular patrol responsibilities and assigned to work with citizens, community associations, and businesses in designated neighborhoods. However, NOP was so poorly received by patrol officers that the acronym was dropped, although the elements of the program continued for a time.

Newport News, Virginia, implemented problem-oriented policing during this period. Problem-oriented policing is sometimes considered a precursor to or a subset of community policing. Police identify, analyze, and respond to the underlying circumstances that create incidents. Problem-oriented policing involves scanning, analysis, response, and assessment (SARA). The Newport News, Virginia, community policing experiment demonstrated that police officers could learn and apply problem-oriented policing techniques to their daily routines and through them enhance cooperation among them, the public, and other agencies.

Diffusion

The next generation of community policing, the diffusion generation, began in the mid- to late 1980s and continued through the early to mid-1990s. It was marked by the diffusion of community policing to medium and large metropolitan law enforcement agencies throughout the United States. Community policing efforts during this period were generally, although not always grant funded, and involved multiple components, such as specialized units, foot patrol, partnership efforts, and problem solving. New York City's Community Patrol Officer Program (CPOP), Baltimore County, Maryland's Community Oriented Police Enforcement (COPE) program and Hartford, Connecticut's Cartographic Oriented Management Program for Abatement of Street Sales (COMPASS) are some of the better-known examples of community policing programs that were implemented during this stage.

In Baltimore County, COPE teams worked with local patrol officers to identify conditions that did not respond to conventional patrol methods, but might instead use other resources of government agencies. COPE teams had extensive contact with residents and were well aware of the importance of fear reduction. COPE was generally viewed as a success and led to the development of Community Foot Patrol Officers (CFPOs). In 2010, with a $10 million federal grant awarded to the city, 25 newly hired officers were assigned to foot patrol.

New York City's Community Police Officer Program (CPOP, which was instituted in 1984 and ended in the early 1990s) included elements similar to the Baltimore County COPE program. CPOP officers were permanently assigned to beats covering approximately 18 city blocks. They were responsible for getting to know the community, uncovering problems, facilitating solutions, and increasing the reciprocal flow of information between the police and the public. The CPOP program was subsequently expanded on a citywide basis.

Institutionalization

The present generation of community policing began in the mid-1990s and is characterized by the institutionalization of community policing and its spread to small-town and rural police agencies. Community policing efforts during this generation were widespread, tended to involve multiple strategies such as improved police-citizen communication and community partnerships, increased attention to quality-of-life offenses, and targeted enforcement of violent drug offenders. The Violent Crime Control and Law Enforcement Act of 1994 and extensive federal spending facilitated the institutionalization of community policing on a large scale. However, despite clear evidence of extensive implementation of community policing, the true nature and extent of implementation, depth of institutionalization, and level of institutional commitment remain unclear. Barriers to implementation of community policing have been well documented and include rank-and-file resistance to community policing; leadership, management, and organizational issues; and uncertainty concerning the ability of community policing to achieve its stated goals, particularly crime prevention and reduction. Just as community policing was reaching its zenith in the mid-1990s after 15 years of gradual expansion, a new movement, CompStat, which focused on crime reduction, was rapidly developing and expanding.

CompStat

CompStat, which refers to comparative statistics or computer statistics, carries a general agreement, at least in theory, that community policing represented a fundamentally new approach to policing, a paradigm shift in the relationship between police and citizens that offered hope in reducing crime and improved police-citizen relationships. However, there is wide disagreement whether CompStat is a paradigm shift representing a new era of policing or whether it is an administrative tool or innovation. Each side of the debate has numerous supporters and makes compelling arguments. Of greater significance in this discussion is the extent to which community policing and CompStat are compatible.

The questions are both theoretical and practical. Many proponents of CompStat argue that community policing and CompStat are not mutually exclusive and can be implemented simultaneously. There is evidence to suggest coimplementation, that both strategies have been implemented independent of each other and operate on parallel tracks within the same jurisdiction. Recommendations to integrate the strategies include incorporating policing values, goals and practices in CompStat, and using it to focus on crime analysis, problem-solving approaches, and building partnerships.

Increased homeland security and antiterrorism-related responsibilities assumed by local police, especially after 9/11, suggest a potentially workable approach toward integrating community policing and CompStat. Law enforcement and homeland security officials agree that intelligence is the key to preventing and disrupting terrorist activities. There is also growing attention to intelligence-led policing, which employs a problem-solving approach to identify and target threats. By targeting enforcement toward individuals engaged in serious criminal activity based on specific information and intelligence, it should be possible to avoid broad use of aggressive patrol tactics that were a contributing factor to the racial tensions of the 1960s, and, more recently,

resurfaced in the form of complaints against aggressive quality-of-life enforcement associated with CompStat.

In theory, community policing and CompStat can work together to reduce crime and improve community relationships, particularly in the context of an intelligence-led policing approach. To a certain extent, police leaders have had to balance conflicting priorities: enforcement, service, and order-maintenance. In practice, the issues are quite complex. Is it possible for police leadership to have two equally important priorities: crime reduction and improved police-citizen relationships? Do community policing and CompStat require different leadership styles or are the styles compatible? Can the police enforce the law, reduce crime, and enjoy good police-community relationships? These are all issues that require further research and will help to determine the future direction of community policing.

Michael M. Berlin

See also Broken Windows Theory; Community Policing and Problem Solving, Definition of; CompStat; Counterterrorism and Community Policing; Intelligence-Led Policing; Kansas City Preventive Patrol Experiment; Police-Community Relations; Policing, Three Eras of; Team Policing; Terrorism, Future Impact of Community Policing on

Further Readings

Berlin, M. M. (2012). The evolution, decline and nascent transformation of community policing in the United States: 1980–2010. In D. Palmer, M. M. Berlin, & D. K. Das (Eds.), *The global environment of policing* (pp. 27–48). Boca Raton, FL: CRC Press.

Commission on Civil Disorders. (1968). *Report of the national advisory commission on civil disorders.* New York, NY: Bantam Books.

Kelling, G. L., & Moore, M. H. (1988). The evolving strategy of policing. NCJ 114213. *Perspectives on Policing, 4.* Washington, DC: U.S. Department of Justice, National Institute of Justice.

Peterson, M. (2005). *Intelligence-led policing: The new intelligence architecture.* NCJ 210681. Washington, DC: U.S. Department of Justice, Bureau of Justice Assistance. Retrieved from https://www.ncjrs.gov/pdffiles1/bja/210681.pdf

Skolnick, J. H., & Bayley, D. H. (1988). *Community policing: Issues and practices around the world.*

Washington, DC: U.S. Department of Justice, National Institute of Justice.

Willis, J., Mastrofski, S., & Kochel, T. (2010). *Maximizing the benefits of reform: Integrating CompStat and community policing in America.* Washington, DC: U.S. Department of Justice, Office of Community Oriented Policing Services.

Wilson, J. Q., & Kelling, G. L. (1982, March). Broken windows: The police and neighborhood safety. *Atlantic Monthly, 249*(3), 29–38.

COMMUNITY POLICING: RESOURCES, TIME, AND FINANCES IN SUPPORT OF

Police leaders, employees, and community stakeholders are sometimes unaware of the resources, time, and finances needed to support a community policing program. The extremely challenging economic conditions of the early 21st century have resulted in severe resource constraints for police agencies of all sizes across the United States. It is apparent that short-term, if not long-term, macroeconomic conditions have restricted police departments' access to new budget resources. In many cases, police departments have had to lay off employees and curtail their budget expenditures.

More than thirty years into the community era of policing, and specifically, community policing problem-solving strategies, now allow police agencies to discern both external and internal resource needs and opportunities for further advancing community policing. This entry examines those needs and opportunities.

A New Norm

The current economic cycle with its resource constraints is forcing police agencies into a "new norm." While access to new tangible resources is part of the new norm, there is no indication that the public will relax its expectations that police continue to lead local efforts to reduce crime and enhance community safety. Thus, police departments are facing a dilemma that challenges them to not only be accountable stewards of community safety and security but also to participate in resource-reducing budget-balancing initiatives. Some agencies have sacrificed community policing efforts to maximize their capacity for call response. Police agencies that have deployed special community policing units have the discretion to eliminate those units. However, for departments that have deployed or desire to deploy community policing and problem solving, the creation and continuity of community policing operations, even in tough economic times, requires both external and internal efforts.

Political Leaders and Other Stakeholders

Commitment to community policing begins with the political leadership and police leadership. Typically comprised of the mayor and city or town council, the political leadership of a city must be willing to support, embrace, and facilitate communitywide acceptance of community policing efforts. These leaders are in a position where they can promote the philosophy and ascertain community needs, such as in community meetings, informal and written communications with constituents, and public forums. City management executives can likewise embrace and support this effort.

Leadership of a community policing effort requires a police chief with omnidirectional influence and leadership capabilities. He or she must be adept at managing internal change processes while eliciting external community support. This leader must be visionary and influential and possess the commitment to creating and improving communitywide policing efforts. The leader must understand the value of education and the capacity of internal systems to enhance police legitimacy. Such a leader must also have the administrative virtuoso to assess and address internal work environment needs while concurrently stepping outside of the agency to gauge citizen interest, expectations, and accessibility for implementing and continuing a community-centric policing strategy. The leader should be willing to look at other police organizations, preferably of similar size and organizational structure that have successfully implemented a community policing philosophy to identify compatible programs and see how and where resources were deployed. The community policing leader must understand and expect internal philosophical challenges but be sufficiently committed to avoid derailment from the mission. Once an agency has accumulated sufficient information to develop a community policing implementation strategy, the implementation stage can begin.

Police organizations interested in embracing a community policing philosophy must also understand the resource needs and requirements in order to implement and sustain community policing in their communities. Internal police and external community resources are required. The political leadership, government executives, police leaders, and employees must work together with the community to create and maintain a viable community policing effort. In the following sections, external resource needs are addressed first, followed by internal requirements and opportunities.

External Resources

An active and engaged citizenry is a cornerstone of any successful community policing philosophy and its corresponding programs. Engaging more citizen volunteers to co-police communities seems to at least partially address the human resource constraints of the current economy. Many citizens may want to be active and engaged in their communities and be available and responsive to police personnel with whom they can readily interact and communicate. Others may want transparent and direct access to information, data, and alerts—a level of access that allows them to communicate directly with neighborhood cohorts without having to go through a police representative. To create and sustain this level of citizen accessibility to information and data, police departments may consider adding tools such as social media, read-only web-based data access, and any one of many emerging subscription services that proactively "push" important information out to citizens instead of waiting for them to initiate access. Access to information can motivate citizens to become more active in other efforts, such as citizen patrols, community watch, and neighborhood associations. Research has shown that high-crime neighborhoods where citizens formed community watch and citizen-on-patrol groups in their neighborhoods experience 80% to 90% reductions in crime within the first year. By the police deploying relatively small numbers of officers to serve information upon which community groups act, crime and workload can be reduced, allowing redeployment or repurposing of "reactive" police resources.

External resources in business, nonprofit, and faith-based communities can also be engaged. On one hand, the business community represents sources of crime and police workload; but on the other, it represents economic stability and development, jobs, and even philanthropic resources. Safe and secure environments around business locations can deter crime, but they can also facilitate business development and economic prosperity. Thus, police and the business community are not only crime reduction partners but also economic development partners. Business prosperity creates local government revenue, which can be reinvested in police operations.

Police agencies can extend their outreach efforts to school districts; nonprofit organizations, particularly those in the social service arena; other city or county operations; as well as other local, state, and federal government entities. Local police can partner with other local agencies to combat conditions that tend to be corollaries of crime. For example, a partnership with the library system may allow police to influence literacy and education, inverse correlates of criminality. Partnering with parks and recreation departments can be just as impactful. Parks and recreation departments often provide facilities and structured programs for youth. Such structured programs help youths to redirect their time and energy from crime and mischief to productive behavior within a supervised environment. These kinds of local partnerships largely use existing external resources that can enhance police partnerships, reduce police workload, and improve both the short- and long-term outcomes with regard to reducing community crime and increasing safety.

Internal Efforts

There are two basic models for delivery of community policing services: specialist and generalist. Which model to use is a decision made internally by the organization.

The specialist model typically designates a person, people, or special unit to deliver community policing services to the community. The special unit provides proactive police services while patrol officers remain dedicated to emergency call response. This special community policing unit consists of community policing officers with responsibility for delivery of proactive community policing services in designated areas across the jurisdiction. A community policing officer (CPO) or neighborhood police officer (NPO) is assigned to each neighborhood policing district (NPD). The CPO or NPO bears the primary responsibility for identifying and serving the quality-of-life needs of citizens, groups, and stakeholders within the community.

The generalist approach to police service delivery allocates to every employee, both sworn and non-sworn members, responsibility for effecting the community policing philosophy. Under the generalist approach, every employee in every segment of the organization should understand and be capable of articulating the individual role and responsibility in delivering community policing services. Because every employee within a police organization interacts with the public on some level, each interaction can become a community policing effort. For example, records clerks regularly provide copies of police incident and accident reports to citizens. To them, every citizen contact is an opportunity to talk about citizen engagement. Thus, when citizens pick up reports, records clerks can ask them about their engagement in volunteer opportunities, community watch groups, and citizen patrol efforts. Records clerks can also assess citizens' willingness to lead or assemble a neighborhood effort to create and operate a new volunteer initiative. Telephone report operators have similar opportunities. When taking citizen crime reports by telephone, report operators can converse with a motivated crime victim, who may be ready to engage in citizen volunteer activities. Report operators can ask citizens about their involvement in volunteer efforts or suggest volunteer opportunities sponsored by the police department or another agency. Volunteerism—whether it is with a citizen-on-patrol group, the elementary school Parent-Teacher Association, or with a nonprofit social service organization—is a key factor for a safe and orderly community.

Most interactions between citizens and police occur during police patrol. Therefore, the organizational structure of the patrol function should support the efficient delivery of accountable community policing services. Geography-based police patrol deployment and accountability systems can provide such support. The Arlington (Texas) Police Department's Geographic Community Policing model is one example. Arlington has approximately 380,000 residents. Under this model, the city is divided into four primary policing divisions, each serving a population of approximately 95,000 residents, and balanced proportionately based on average workload. Each of the four districts is commanded by a police deputy chief, who is subordinate to an assistant police chief and the chief of police. Each deputy chief serves as the "chief of police" in that district. Reducing the city into smaller but structurally similar divisions allows each patrol district to have operational autonomy to serve the district's citizens in accordance with their unique characteristics yet remain accountable within a larger structure to the department's mission and vision. Each police patrol district is then subdivided into three smaller *sectors*, with each serving a population of approximately 32,000 people and commanded by a police lieutenant with 24/7 accountability for service delivery. The size of each sector is primarily determined by workload. Each sector is further subdivided into three *beats*, each of which is supervised by a police sergeant with 24/7 accountability. One sergeant per sector and one lieutenant are assigned to each of the three patrol shifts. Sergeants in each sector work as a team, as do lieutenants, across sectors to ensure adequate coverage and accountability. Officers on each shift, as well as investigators are assigned to beats.

Such geographic-based accountability systems have additional benefits. Investigator workload may be reduced, freeing investigators up for more proactive work or acute investigative focus. As a result, their mind-set changes from clearing cases to preventing crime. Citizens hail this type of geography-based service delivery system because it places accountability for service delivery into the hands of one person, making it easier and less time-consuming to have service delivery issues addressed.

Investments

No discussion of tools and resources needed for community policing can be complete without addressing the need for additional people, equipment, and tools to facilitate and operate a community policing program. While additional people and equipment resources may be needed, one of the greatest agency resource is the internalized commitment to creating and maintaining communities that can be safe everywhere, for everyone, all the time. Intangible assets such as corporate commitment, drive, and vision may reduce the size of investments needed for tangible resources like more people and equipment. To the extent a generalist service delivery approach is adopted across an entire organization where commitment to enhancing legitimacy, community service, and partnering with citizen, business, faith-based, nonprofit, and other governmental entities occurs, the need to deploy additional specialized resources lessens. Conversely, to the extent agencies view community policing as an artificial overlay onto core police services may result in a perception that additional costly resources are needed to supplement current operations.

Thus, police departments that are committed to community policing will implement and sustain training programs and selection systems that result in hiring personnel with the characteristics that allow them to thrive in a community policing environment. One example of an innovative, post-recruit academy training strategy is the PTO program that was created and perfected by the Reno (Nevada) Police Department. The police chief and leaders bilaterally communicate with personnel—sworn and non-sworn—across all job categories using communiqués from newsletters to e-mails, in-person meetings, briefings, and informal hallway and parking lot conversations.

As a result of budget constraints brought on by challenging economic conditions, it seems that for the foreseeable future, new personnel and equipment resources will not be available to police departments. Police leaders and managers must find a way to continue to secure communities without the large investments in personnel and equipment that were formerly available. One might logically conclude that police must now look to others for assistance in facilitating the security and orderliness of community, such as the citizens of the community. Enhancing citizen's willingness to obey the law and creating opportunities for citizens to more easily and readily engage in volunteer activities can help citizens become coproducers of community safety with the police.

Earlier iterations of community policing sought to get citizens to serve as the "eyes and ears" of the police. However, police can also become the public's eyes and ears—or effective purveyors of information—by expanding their data and information systems and mass communications capabilities. By providing access to meaningful microlevel information, the police facilitate community engagement and enhances neighborhood safety. Engaging citizens and all police employees provide, access to underutilized available resources, requires little additional investment, frees up police officer time for redeployment or repurposing, and helps to ensure a continuity of service levels, even during fiscally austere times.

Theron L. Bowman

See also Agency Mission and Values, Changes in; Building Partnerships and Stakeholders; CompStat; Police Training Officer (PTO) Program; Roles, Chief Executives'; Strategic Planning

Further Readings

Brown, L. P. (1992, March). *Community policing: Bring the community into the battle against crime.* Speech at the 19th Annual Lehman Lecture Series, Long Island University, Brookville, NY.

Eck, J. E., & Spelman, W. (1989). A problem-oriented approach to police service delivery. In D. J. Kenney (Ed.), *Police and policing: Contemporary issues* (pp. 95–111). New York, NY: Praeger.

Kelling, G. L., & Bratton, W. J. (1993). Implementing community policing: The administrative problem. NCJ 141236. *Perspectives on Policing, 17,* 1–11. Washington, DC: U.S. Department of Justice, National Institute of Justice.

U.S. Department of Justice. (2003). *Call management and community policing: A guidebook for law enforcement.* Washington, DC: U.S. Department of Justice, Office of Community Oriented Policing Services.

COMMUNITY POLICING: WHAT IT IS NOT

To inform the continued discussion and debate about what community policing *is*, one should begin by deducing what community policing is *not*. This is not an easy task, as most articles, books, and monograms discuss community policing in the context of other concepts, tools, approaches, and perspectives, which can prove to be confusing rather than provide clarity. To better define the parameters of community policing, the following discussion analyzes from a variety of perspectives what community policing is not: It is not problem-oriented policing; it is not a monolithic program; it is not line-officer-based management of the department; it is not about the number of partnerships a department has; it is not a softer version of policing; it is not public control over the department; it is not police-community relations; it is not the end of police service delivery evolution; and it is not a silver bullet for all that ails departments and communities.

Not Problem-Oriented Policing

Community policing is not problem-oriented policing. These two concepts are discussed in tandem, and most literature cites problem solving as an essential element of community policing, but there are some major differences that can be delineated between the two.

The first is that problem-oriented policing can be done internally without broader police-community interactions and feedback. Through internal data analysis of crime reports and calls for service, arrests, and other available police data, community problems can be identified within the policing organization. Then, these problems can be analyzed, responses formulated, and the outcomes of action assessed without input from the community stakeholders, which is a prerequisite foundation for community policing. Second, problem-oriented policing is a tool used by police to enhance their law enforcement and order maintenance capabilities and capacities. Thus, it is not a broader organizational management philosophy as community policing is. The two can work in tandem, but they can also be utilized mutually exclusive of one another: They are complementary but not interchangeable. A department can employ a problem-solving approach without committing to community policing, but in order to community police, some level of problem-oriented policing is required.

Not a Cookie-Cutter Strategy or Program

Community policing is not a monolithic program that can be easily transferred from one department directly to another. Many researchers have viewed community policing programmatically and many departments have implemented the concept from this orientation. However, community policing is not a program, which suggests rigidity in structure, similarity in process, and uniformity in outcome expectancy, even though there are some basic foundational precepts which constitute community policing in practice (such as the attainment of

partnership and the focus on solving problems in conjunction with community stakeholders). In contrast to a programmatic orientation, community policing is intended to be an innovative approach to police management that can be implemented through the use of specific tools tailored to the environment in which it is utilized.

Examples of this are the quality policing approach of the Madison, Wisconsin, Police Department and the Chicago Alternative Police Strategy (CAPS). Since departments differ greatly in size and environment within the constraints of shifting goals, problems, and populations, a programmatic approach that can be applied within any agency is often not practical throughout the organizational field. Although many departments still view community-oriented policing (COP) officers as a separate structure within the police department, a more holistic view of community policing is emerging in which all police officers within the department are COP officers and the department employs tools rather than programs. From this perspective, community-oriented policing is more flexible, innovative, variant, and suited to particular needs rather than the programmatic approach, which limits all of these features and their potential applications within different departments. While community policing can include programs within its application, it is not a program in itself.

Line officers are expected to be proactive and "own" the problems in their assigned patrol area, using their discretion to deal with these problems directly. The reality is that many patrol officers are still not assigned to specific beats in many agencies, their discretion is more limited than this portrayal, the policing organization is still quite hierarchal and top-down, and most patrol officers still spend their time responding to calls for service or being reactive in contrast to the proactivity desired in community policing.

Taken together, these realities suggest that this conceptual notion of community policing has not been attained in most policing organizations and that the management and decision making in these organizations is still done by upper management and line supervision, not by the line officer. A more holistic view of community policing encompasses each level and actor within the organization playing a role, and the bottom-up approach, while important in executing this version of policing, has not been fully implemented in many agencies.

Community policing is not about obtaining a certain number of partnerships within the community, but rather the results that derive from the partnerships. The consensus in the literature over a long time period is that partnerships are a central tenet of community policing. A partnership implies a bond with a certain level of responsibility from each partner. In the community policing era, partnerships are a means to an end (i.e., greater community interaction with the police process, more inclusiveness on the part of police and enhanced communication between the police and the public) rather than being an end in themselves. Thus, while partnerships are a central and important component of community policing, it is not the existence of partnerships that matters but what results from the utilization of partnerships for both the police and the community. From this perspective, partnerships are more important in terms of process and outcomes (how they are used and what they produce) than structure (how many partnerships are present and to what degree).

Not a Softer Version of Policing

Community policing is not a softer version of policing. The focus on law enforcement and order maintenance as detailed by James Q. Wilson is still prevalent in the community policing era, as is Egon Bittner's notion that police hold a monopoly on the legal, public use of force within our society. These tenets have not changed with the advent of community policing: Police still enforce laws, maintain order, make arrests, serve warrants, run surveillance, and use lethal and nonlethal force. Community policing does not mean police are softer on the criminal elements within any given jurisdiction. Rather, it simply means they use standard policing tools and processes on criminals while focusing on being more inclusive of the law-abiding citizens and institutions within the community. The "us versus them" mentality of the past traditional policing model did not make this differentiation of two publics, but community policing does.

Thus, the police do not change their approach in dealing with citizens that break the law, but instead change their approach to citizens that are impacted by crime (e.g., residents and business owners) to gain their assistance and approval in dealing with

criminal behavior. In this light, community policing is not a softer version of policing relative to those who break the law, but it is softer in engaging and enabling the law-abiding community elements to better perform their well-established functions and fulfill their newly established role.

Not Public Domination of the Police

Community policing is not public control over the police department. The concept of partnerships is central to community policing, but literal partnerships involve equal investment, equal benefit, equal liability, and equal loss. Rather, police in the contemporary community era of policing often involve the community participants in more of a network format, with police still principally responsible for the outcomes that result.

These network structures take different forms, including, but not limited to, community meetings in which citizens can express concerns and identify problems to police actors as well as receive information from the department; citizen review boards that involve citizen oversight of police officer behaviors to enhance accountability, though these differ in strength and scope; community policing offices or storefronts staffed by local residents volunteering their time; neighborhood watch areas conducted by citizens in contact with local policing departments; and other various network arrangements that include the public in the process of policing to varying degrees.

However, none of these arrangements denote public control over the police department. While public inclusion is a lynchpin in the community era because it was often lacked in the previous eras, this involvement is not control. Rather, interaction and cooperation of the police and the community becomes more important than who is "in control" of the organization and its actions.

Not Mere "Community Relations"

Community policing is not the same as police-community relations. Police organizations can employ a wide variety of tools to improve or enhance community relations without making changes to organizational structures or processes that community policing requires. Police can deploy public information officers; enhance their public information available through department websites; hire outside consultants or firms to enhance their image; hold community meetings without a broader connection to actions taken; increase officer training in areas of ethics, diversity, and communication; and countless other forms of action meant to enhance police-community relations. This is not the same as community policing for several reasons.

First, community policing requires enhanced relations with certain segments of the public but this is to achieve greater ends, while police-community relations is a means to more limited ends than those of community policing. Second, community policing is a broader organizational concept of which one component is police-community relations, which is more limited in nature. Third, police-community relations is measured by mood of the citizenry (i.e., whether the citizens are satisfied, angry, confident, or some other feeling toward the police), whereas community policing is measured by outcomes such as citizen participation, less crime, fewer citizen complaints, increased contact with police and residents, and a variety of other outcomes. There is a connection and a synergy between community policing and police-community relations, but the two are not the same.

Community policing is not the end of police service delivery evolution. Policing, as an important social institution, has come a long way since its inception in the United States. From the political era, to the professional era, and now the community era, police services have evolved greatly along with the society the police represent. Community policing, when viewed from this perspective, is not the end of police evolution but an important era in the process of policing a rights-based democracy. A wide spectrum of community policing exists within U.S. policing because policing organizations are evolving at different paces in different political, traditional, and social environments. The wide range of policing organization forms in the United States—local, county, state, specialty, and federal for example—also influence the promulgation of different types of community policing, depending on the agency. Thus, community policing is not the end of police service evolution in the United States but rather one more important step toward reconciling the public with the police contracted to secure the citizenry, a relationship that had frayed in previous eras. This ties together the need for innovation and explains why a programmatic approach does not define community policing: It is a means to an end and not an end in

itself. As policing agencies learn from community policing, the concept will evolve as the political and professional eras did prior.

Not a Panacea for Problems

Community policing is not a silver bullet for all that is wrong in policing or the communities they serve. The implementation of community policing is difficult, as is getting buy-in from the internal members of the organization and for external stakeholders. It is difficult to enact changes to such traditional institutions as policing organizations, and community policing requires a commitment to change structures and processes while redefining the range of measureable outcomes, which is far easier said than done.

A department that truly and fully enacts and implements community policing will often experience many difficulties in doing so, meaning it is not a panacea for all the problems inherent in the profession of policing. It will not eliminate corruption, inefficiency, misuse of power, authority, or discretion, and the other problems that are characteristics of policing organizations, regardless of era. In this sense, there are as many issues that arise from community policing as the change is intended to alleviate. One of these issues is the relationship with the public. Simply claiming to be practicing community policing does not mean the department will involve community stakeholders to the level required, nor does it mean the community will respond to their responsibilities in assisting police and policing their own neighborhoods. Thus, community policing is but one aspect of community development and in itself will not solve the problems a community faces, but it is intended to be one leg of the stool in accomplishing that goal.

Joseph Ferrandino

See also Community Policing, Evolution of; Community Policing and Problem Solving, Definition of; Generations (Three) of Community Policing; Policing, Three Eras of; Problem-Oriented Policing: Elements, Processes, Implications

Further Readings

Bureau of Justice Assistance. (1994). *Understanding community policing: A framework for action.* NCJ 148457. Washington, DC: U.S. Department of Justice. Retrieved from https://www.ncjrs.gov/pdffiles/commp.pdf

Cordner, G. W. (1999). Elements of community policing. In L. K. Gaines & G. W. Cordner (Eds.), *Policing perspectives: An anthology.* Los Angeles, CA: Roxbury.

Gianakis, G. A., & Davis, G. J., III. (1998). Re-inventing or re-packaging police services? The case of community-oriented policing. *Public Administration Review, 58*(6), 485–498.

Lurigio, A. J., & Skogan, W. G. (1994). Winning the hearts and minds of police officers: An assessment of staff perceptions of community policing in Chicago. *Crime & Delinquency, 40*(3), 315–330.

Nicholl, C. G. (2000). *Community policing, community justice, and restorative justice: Exploring the links for the delivery of a balanced approach to public safety.* Washington, DC: U.S. Department of Justice, Office of Community Oriented Policing Services.

Rosenbaum, D. P., & Lurigio, A. J. (1994). An inside look at community policing reform: Definitions, organizational changes and evaluation findings. *Crime & Delinquency, 40*(3), 299–314.

Skolnick, J. H., & Bayley, D. H. (1988). Theme and variation in community policing. *Crime and Justice, 10,* 1–37.

Sparrow, M. K. (1988). *Implementing community policing.* NCJ 114217. U.S. Department of Justice, National Institute of Justice. Retrieved from https://www.ncjrs.gov/pdffiles1/nij/114217.pdf

COMMUNITY POLICING AND PROBLEM SOLVING, DEFINITION OF

Community policing and problem solving are two relatively new and distinct yet complementary concepts for addressing neighborhood crime and disorder. As a single philosophy, community policing and problem solving involves the systematic use of police-public partnerships and problem-solving techniques to proactively address the conditions that give rise to public safety issues, including crime, social disorder, and fear of crime. Because this approach was created in response to and is in stark contrast to the previous reform (or professional) era of policing that lasted for nearly a half century, it is important to understand the underlying precepts of that era; therefore, this entry begins by examining its basic tenets. Then the definition and purposes of community policing are discussed, followed by an examination of the transition to and basic elements of problem-oriented policing. To further explain and demonstrate the

primary differences between the two philosophies, included in this discussion are examples of both traditional policing methods as well as problem-solving approaches to crime and disorder.

Traditional Policing Methods Under the Reform Era

From about 1930 to 1980, police reformers sought to remove the police from under the powerful political influences over police that existed from about 1840 to 1930 (known as the political era of policing) and to enhance the professional nature of their work. Therefore, police work was defined almost exclusively in terms of efficiency, and administrators sought to strengthen their control over rank-and-file officers. This new professional model—with police as "crime fighters"—demanded an impartial law enforcer who related to citizens in neutral and distant terms. The emphasis on professionalization also shaped the role of citizens in crime control. Similar to physicians who cared for health problems and teachers for educational problems, the police would be responsible for crime problems. Citizens thus became passive in crime control, their role becoming limited to calling police and serving as witnesses when asked to do so. The advent of the patrol car further removed the police from their neighborhoods, and foot patrol, which was common during the political era, was viewed as an unnecessary frill.

For all its shortcomings, under the previous political era, the police link to neighborhoods and politicians had been close. During the reform era, however, citizens were no longer encouraged to go to "their" police officers or districts; officers were expected to drive marked cars randomly through the streets, reactively respond to calls for service (CFS), and be typically evaluated by such measures as the numbers of arrests made, calls handled, and even the number of miles driven during a shift.

During the late 1960s, however, problems began to arise under the reform model, including the following:

- *Crimes began to increase and research suggested that conventional police methods were not effective.* The 1960s witnessed riots in several major cities; protests against the Vietnam War; assassinations of President John F. Kennedy, Robert F. Kennedy, and civil rights leader

Rev. Martin Luther King Jr.; and the riot at the 1968 Democratic National Convention in Chicago. During this period, many people and institutions questioned the police and their function and role.

- *Fear of crime rose.* As a result, citizens abandoned parks, public transportation, neighborhood shopping centers, churches, and entire neighborhoods.
- *Many minority citizens did not perceive their treatment as equitable or adequate.* They protested not only police mistreatment, but lack of police services.
- *The antiwar and civil rights movements challenged the legitimacy of police.* Students resisted police, minorities rioted against them, and the public began to question police tactics.
- *Some of the concepts on which the reform era was founded were found to be without basis.* Studies showed, for example, that emphases on random patrol and rapid response times did not equate to increased arrests and fewer crimes committed.

As Mark Moore and George Kelling observed in 1983,

In professionalizing crime fighting, the "volunteers," citizens on whom so much used to depend (were) removed from the fight. If anything has been learned from the history of American policing, it is that, whatever the benefits of professionalization (e.g., reduced corruption, due process, serious police training), the reforms . . . ignored, even attacked, some features that once made the police powerful institutions in maintaining a sense of community security. (p. 58)

There developed among the public and the police a growing awareness that the community can and *must* play a vital role in problem solving and crime fighting. Thus, came into being the community era of policing.

Community Policing

In the early 1980s, the notion of community policing emerged as the dominant school of thought concerning policing in order to reunite the police with the community. From the beginning, it was touted as an overarching philosophy, not a specific tactic;

it was, furthermore, advanced as a proactive, decentralized approach (pushing more decision-making ability down to the patrol officer level) that was designed to reduce crime, disorder, and fear of crime by assigning the same officer in the same neighborhood on a long-term basis. Community institutions such as families, school, and neighborhood and merchants associations are seen as key partners with the police in creating safer, more secure communities. The community's views have greater status under community policing.

Community policing is a long-term process that involves fundamental institutional change and a cultural transformation within the organization. It is not merely an adjunct to or a division within a police agency, nor is it simply implementing foot and bicycle patrols or neighborhood stations. It redefines the role of the officer on the street, from crime fighter to problem solver, and includes a decentralized organizational structure and changes in personnel recruitment, training, awards and evaluation systems, and promotions. It therefore begins with related instruction in the recruit academy, emphasizing that today's police officers are to seek proactive and creative resolution to crime and disorder.

Lee P. Brown, former police chief in New York City; Atlanta, Georgia; and Houston, Texas, wrote,

In essence, we are bringing back a modern version of the "cop on the beat." We need to *solve* community problems rather than just *react* to them. It is time to adopt new strategies to address the dramatic increases in crime and the fear of crime. I view community policing as a better, smarter and more cost-effective way of using police resources.

Community policing has been applied in various forms by police agencies in the United States and abroad and differs according to the community needs, politics, and resources available. A few examples are the Neighborhood Oriented Policing and the Directed Area Responsibility Team programs (Houston, Texas); Community Patrol Officer Program (Brooklyn, New York); Citizen-Oriented Police Enforcement (Baltimore County, Maryland); and the Community Mobilization Project, the Basic Car Plan and the Senior Lead-Officer Programs (Los Angeles, California).

Once the police organization and the community are entrenched in addressing problems of crime and disorder, it then becomes necessary to further formalize the police-community approach to solving those problems. Next the complementary concept of problem solving is discussed.

Problem Solving

Origin and Rationale

Problem-solving efforts in policing are nothing new; police officers have always tried to solve problems. The difference is that in the past, prior to the community era of policing, officers received little guidance, support, or technology from police administrators for dealing with problems. Therefore, the routine application of problem-solving techniques *is* new, and is premised on two truths: Problem solving can be applied by officers throughout the agency as part of their daily work, and routine problem-solving efforts can be effective in reducing or resolving problems.

Problem-oriented policing was grounded on different principles than community policing; however, as noted above, they are complementary, hand in glove. Problem-oriented policing is a strategy that puts the community policing philosophy into practice. It advocates that police examine the underlying causes of recurring incidents of crime and disorder.

Herman Goldstein is considered by many to be the principal architect of problem-oriented policing. His 1977 seminal book *Policing a Free Society* is among the most frequently cited works in police literature. A 1990 work, *Problem-Oriented Policing,* provided a rich and complete exploration into problem-oriented policing. Goldstein was frustrated with the traditional method of policing and its emphases on response times, arrests, and so on. As a result, Goldstein argued for a radical change in the direction of efforts to improve policing to a much more direct, thoughtful concern with substantive problems. He argued that the police must define more clearly and understand more fully the problems they are expected to handle; develop a commitment to analyzing problems; and be encouraged to conduct an uninhibited search for the most effective response to each problem, looking beyond just the criminal justice system to a wide range of alternatives.

The first step in problem-oriented policing, therefore, is to recognize that incidents are often merely overt symptoms of problems, with officers acquainting themselves with some of the conditions and factors that cause them. Furthermore, everyone in the police agency contributes to this mission, not just a few innovative officers or a special unit or function.

Chris Braiden, former Superintendent of Police in Edmonton, Alberta, Canada, described problem-oriented policing using an analogy from the medical community:

> The doctor (police officer) talks to the patient (community) to identify a problem. Sometimes the solution lies solely with the patient (community); for example, a change of diet (the owner agrees to remove an eyesore or an abandoned automobile). Sometimes it calls for the doctor (police officer) and patient (community) to work together, i.e., a change of diet plus medicine (organizing the neighborhood to help shut down a "blight" establishment). Sometimes only the doctor (police) alone can solve the problem, i.e., surgery (heavy law enforcement). Sometimes we have to accept the fact that the problem simply cannot be solved, e.g., terminal illness (poverty).

The Role of the Street Officer

A major area where problem-oriented policing departs from the traditional policing style lies with the view of the line officer, who is given more discretion and decision-making ability and is trusted with a broader array of responsibilities. Problem-oriented policing values officers who are creative thinkers, urging them to take the initiative in trying to deal more effectively with problems in the areas they serve. Officers are therefore challenged and have opportunities to follow through on individual cases and analyze and solve problems. Problem-solving officers do more than handle calls for service; they use the information gathered in their responses to incidents, together with information obtained from other sources, to get a clearer picture of the problem. They then address the underlying conditions.

SARA Problem-Solving Process

The SARA problem-solving process (for scanning, analysis, response, assessment) guides officers by providing the tools necessary to accomplish problem solving. The four steps and their core components are discussed in the following subsections.

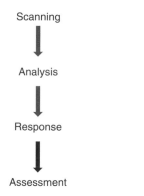

Scanning

Analysis

Response

Assessment

Figure 1   A Problem-Solving Process

Source: Eck, J. E., & Spelman, W. (1987). *Problem-Solving: Problem-Oriented Policing in Newport News* (p. 43). Washington, DC: U.S. Department of Justice, National Institute of Justice.

Scanning

Scanning initiates the problem-solving process. Officers first look for a pattern or persistent, repeat incidents, and whether or not a problem exists. A problem is simply a group of two or more incidents that are similar in one or more respects, causing harm to the public. The primary purpose of scanning is to conduct a preliminary inquiry to determine if a problem really exists and whether further analysis is needed. During this stage, priorities are established if multiple problems exist and a specific officer or team of officers assigned to handle the problem.

Analysis

This is the heart of the problem-solving process; it is critical to the success of a problem-solving effort. The purpose of analysis is to learn as much as possible about problems in order to identify their causes. Officers gather information from sources inside and outside their agency about the scope, nature, and causes of problems. Tools such as the problem analysis triangle can be employed; examining the *offender*, the *victim*, and the *location* helps officers to visualize the problem and understand the relationship between the three elements.

Response

After a problem has been clearly defined and analyzed, officers confront the ultimate challenge in problem-oriented policing: the search for the most effective way of dealing with the problem. To develop tailored responses, problem solvers review their findings about the three sides of the problem analysis triangle and develop creative solutions that will address at least two sides of the triangle. Depending on the problem, responses may be wide ranging and involve private and other government organizations (e.g., prosecutor's office for new ordinances, health department to condemn an abandoned home being frequented by drug abusers).

Assessment

In this step, officers evaluate the effectiveness of their responses. Criteria might include numbers of arrests, levels of reported crime, response times, clearance rates, citizen complaints, and various workload indicators, such as calls for service and the number of field interviews conducted. Assessment determines whether the responses implemented were effective; if not, the information gathered during analysis is then reviewed and new solutions developed and implemented.

Michael J. Palmiotto and Kenneth J. Peak

See also Center for Problem-Oriented Policing; Community, Definition of; Community Oriented Policing Services, Office of; Community Policing, Evolution of; Community Policing: What It Is Not; Problem-Solving Initiatives, Assessment and Evaluation; Problem-Solving Process (SARA)

Further Readings

Braiden, C. (1992, November). Community policing: Nothing new under the sun. In *Community oriented policing and problem solving* (p. 21). Sacramento: California Department of Justice.

Brown, L. P. (1991, September). Community policing: Its time has come. *The Police Chief, 62*, 10.

Eck, J. E., & Spelman, W. (1989). A problem-oriented approach to police service delivery. In D. J. Kenney (Ed.), *Police and policing: Contemporary issues* (pp. 95–111). New York, NY: Praeger.

Goldstein, H. (1977). *Policing a free society*. Cambridge, MA: Ballinger.

Goldstein, H. (1990). *Problem-oriented policing*. New York, NY: McGraw-Hill.

Moore, M. H., & Kelling, G. L. (1983, Winter). "To serve and protect": Learning from police history. *The Public Interest, 70*, 49–65.

Peak, K. J., & Glensor, R. W. (2011). *Community policing and problem solving: Strategies and practices* (6th ed.). Columbus, OH: Pearson.

Trojanowicz, R. C., & Bucqueroux, B. (1990). *Community policing: A contemporary perspective.* Cincinnati, OH: Anderson.

Moore, M. H., & Trojanowicz, R. C. (1988). *Corporate strategies for policing.* Washington, DC: U.S. Department of Justice, National Institute of Justice. Retrieved from https://www.ncjrs.gov/pdffiles1/nij/114215.pdf

COMMUNITY POLICING CONSORTIUM

The Community Policing Consortium (CPC) was developed in 1992 as part of an effort by the U.S. Department of Justice (DOJ) to ensure local law enforcement agencies had the training and technical assistance they needed to carry out community policing initiatives. The Office of Community Oriented Policing Services (COPS Office), created in 1994, along with the Regional Community Policing Institutes (RCPIs), created in 1997—both within the DOJ—created an infrastructure of knowledge and innovative training to support CPC's hiring and technology programs. The rotating of responsibility for the management of the CPC among each of its members for each funding cycle brought a systematic accountability and buy-in for five law enforcement stakeholder groups—the International Association of Chiefs of Police (IACP), the National Sheriffs' Association (NSA), the National Organization of Black Law Enforcement Executives (NOBLE), the Police Executive Research Forum (PERF), and the Police Foundation—whose support of community policing was seen as critical to its ultimate acceptance by law enforcement agencies and the communities they served. After briefly describing the origins of the CPC, this entry discusses the CPC's training material content, its outreach and publications, and several of its major initiatives.

Origins

The CPC was created to promote community policing and transform the relationship of law enforcement agencies with their communities. It was a partnership of the five leading law enforcement organizations named above.

The mission statement of the CPC was to advance community policing strategies that allow individual citizens and community organizations to work as full and equal partners with law enforcement agencies and other public and private organizations in the effort to enhance quality of life. The CPC provided services to the field to implement community policing, and information to assist practitioners and scholars who were interested in the philosophy of community policing.

The Bureau of Justice Assistance within the DOJ provided initial funding to the five partners for a project in which they provided community policing consultantships to five demonstration sites and produced a foundational document on community policing entitled *Understanding Community Policing: A Framework for Action.* In 1994, funding and oversight for the consortium was transferred to the Office of Community Oriented Policing Services, after its creation under the Violent Crime Control and Law Enforcement Act of 1994.

The COPS Office, under its mission, offered grants for programs that hired officers to engage in community policing, so the consortium targeted its services to these grantees. The COPS Hiring Program grantees were required to participate in training and the consortium services were designed to fill that need. In later years, until its closure in June 2006, the consortium engaged in a number of special projects that helped agencies deal with emerging public safety issues.

Content

Over the life of the consortium, the partners were asked to leverage their organizational expertise in specialized subject areas. While the training materials emphasized community policing from a local perspective—community partnerships, problem solving, strategic planning and assessment, and cultural diversity—each organization had its own core area under which it offered training and technical assistance.

The IACP focused on operational topics such as the technology management, personnel needs and strategies, performance evaluations and organizational transformation. The NSA had similar core topics, but its courses were developed and conducted with the understanding that sheriff's offices are county-level elected offices with different community relationships than police departments.

NOBLE developed much of the community-based content with courses on topics such as cultural diversity, community partnerships, and strategies for cross-cultural communication and partnerships. PERF developed a series of courses based on problem solving. The Police Foundation's core courses were on strategic planning and police ethics.

The consortium delivered its training in a variety of ways because the COPS grantees were spread throughout the United States, and each had a requirement of completing two courses on community policing during the life of their award. The most-used mechanisms were two-day regional training sessions focusing on a particular topic. These sessions were designed to be interactive, enabling agencies to network and collaborate around central themes in community policing. Almost 90% of the COPS grantees completed their training requirements in this manner. The CPC also used mentor sites, where an agency with experience in community policing would host peer exchanges with another agency's supervisors and executives for informal learning. Train-the-trainer instruction was designed to teach CPC core subjects to local trainers, who could then integrate the content into academy and in-service programs.

Outreach and Publications

Along with the training and technical assistance, the consortium partners developed an information dissemination program to provide up-to-date information on trends in implementing community policing and promising practices at the local level. Several monographs were published in addition to the first *Framework* guide, including *Staircase to Strategic Planning, National Business Leadership Strategies: A Guide to Engaging the Private Sector in Community Policing Initiatives,* and *Creating and Maintaining Partnerships.*

The NSA published the three newsletters of the consortium: *Community Links,* which told stories about community successes; *Community Policing Exchange,* the primary newsletter for law enforcement; and *Sheriff Times,* a county-level publication to support training for sheriffs.

Major Initiatives

As the core training was taking hold through the 1990s, it became apparent through focus groups, surveys, and CEO symposia, that there was a need for additional services that addressed more sophisticated coordination and integration of community policing strategies if organizational transformation was to be achieved. The COPS Office and the consortium partners developed several major initiatives that addressed these special needs. The results showed how community policing tools could be used to address a multitude of emerging public safety issues.

Community Engagement Program

The Community Engagement Program became a signature service for the consortium. Developed as a joint project by all five member organizations, the Community Engagement Program was a one-and-a-half-day event facilitated by a consortium team but featured a group of about 30 local participants, with a ratio of four citizens to every law enforcement officer in the room. The purpose was to use community policing as a foundation to build relationships between the police and often frustrated community members who felt they were not being included in identifying and solving public safety problems in their neighborhoods. From the beginning, it was clear that the engagement event itself was only part of the community engagement process. CPC staff prepared a toolkit that taught the participating law enforcement agency how to recruit and select participants, choose the site, and follow through on action steps that result from the event.

Reduction in Gun Violence

In partnership with U.S. attorney's offices, the consortium facilitated regional partnership symposia to implement Project Safe Neighborhoods, a DOJ initiative to reduce gun violence. The symposia featured local law enforcement and local prosecutors addressing policy and implementation challenges and issues specific to their jurisdictions, identifying needed community resources, and planning strategically for partnerships with their communities. The expected outcome was to set the stage to bring the CPC's signature product, a community engagement event, to their jurisdiction.

Hiring in the Spirit of Service

This initiative was designed to counteract a widely held view that the best police officers are those who have tactical skills and like the adventure of responding to serious criminal activity. The initiative explored the concept of changing the way officers are recruited, trained, and retained to attract candidates who are service minded, have strong communication skills, and enjoy interacting with citizens. A guide was published based on recommendations from a focus group of police psychologists.

Blueprint Series

The Executive Blueprint Series was designed to engage senior law enforcement managers in planning for community policing innovations. Each event was a two-day forum in which decision makers analyzed common factors impacting agency operations as they created steps to align all functions with their community policing mission. The topics were Organization and Management (NSA), Patrol and Investigations (IACP), Internal Inspections and Investigations (Police Foundation), Personnel Administration and Training (PERF), and Partnerships and Community Outreach (NOBLE). These sessions were offered in 2001 through 2002.

Sandra R. Webb

See also Community Oriented Policing Services, Office of; Regional Community Policing Institutes; Violent Crime Control and Law Enforcement Act of 1994

Further Readings

Buerger, M. E. (1998). Police training as a Pentecost: Using tools singularly ill-suited to the purpose of reform. *Police Quarterly, 1,* 32.

Community Policing Consortium. (1998). *Understanding community policing: A framework for action.* NCJ 148457. Washington, DC: U.S. Department of Justice, Bureau of Justice Assistance.

Sprafka, H., & Kranda, A. H. (2008, January). Institutionalizing mentoring in police departments. *The Police Chief, 75*(1), 46–49. Retrieved from http://www.policechiefmagazine.org/magazine/index.cfm?fuseaction=display_arch&article_id=1375&issue_id=12008

COMMUNITY POLICING SELF-ASSESSMENT TOOL (CP-SAT)

Many police leaders espouse combining community partnerships and problem-solving activities with more traditional methods of law enforcement to form what is now considered the prevailing policing paradigm of community policing. Nevertheless, in spite of a shared understanding about its conceptual composition and the significant investments in and efforts to implement community policing, it has remained operationally ill defined. Consequently, law enforcement agencies have implemented the philosophy through widely varying sets of practical strategies and tactics, with differing levels of breadth and intensity.

To help address this perceived weakness and facilitate the alignment of community policing philosophy and practice, the U.S. Department of Justice, Office of Community Oriented Policing Services (the COPS Office) sponsored the development of the Community Policing Self-Assessment Tool (CP-SAT). This entry explains what the CP-SAT was designed to measure and how it is implemented.

Design

The CP-SAT, developed in 2010, was designed to establish a common and shared understanding of the definitional elements of community policing and ensure those concepts are carried out across ranks and functions within an agency. Also, it was meant to create an organizational assessment process and tailored survey questions that would assist individual agencies with measuring their implementation of community policing.

The resulting CP-SAT, developed in partnership with consulting firm ICF International, Inc., and the Police Executive Research Forum (PERF), comprises a series of audience-specific questions based on the definitions of the elements of community policing: community partnerships, problem solving, and organizational change. Data is collected by surveying community partners and sworn and civilian staff. Sworn and civilian staff is surveyed about the community policing practices that they employ, and community partners are queried about their perceptions and to provide feedback. From this data, a law enforcement agency can objectively assess its level of community policing and identify areas that need improvement. Although this tool effectively helps agencies understand to what extent they have implemented community policing practices, it really is about measuring and informing their journey, as opposed to focusing on the destination.

The Value of a Comprehensive Self-Assessment

Policing is extremely complex and dynamic work. Agencies rarely have a comprehensive and representative picture of how their line-level and other employees are implementing the overarching philosophy in their day-to-day duties. Compounding the difficulties inherent to understanding where an agency stands in terms of its desired community policing implementation is that law enforcement agencies are largely hierarchical, their work is distributed by time and place, and few systems or processes are in place to capture the work outputs of community policing. These fundamental constraints drove the development of an organizational self-assessment tool that would assist agencies in understanding their implementation status as they move toward community policing, and their own implementation goals.

In other words, the CP-SAT helps to identify what individual officers do in order to translate the community policing philosophy into practice. For example, when responding to a call for service, are officers perceptive to repeat problems? Do they take steps to further understand the problem by examining the nature and circumstances of the affected victims, the environmental conditions, and those perpetrating the crimes? Do the agency and its employees engage different segments of the community in meaningful collaboration around crime and disorder problems, establishing priorities for collective efforts and in shifting and sharing responsibilities for addressing problems? While the answers to these questions are rarely simple, to date there have been limited ways for agencies to even begin to collect information about what is happening at the line-level related to community policing practice. Organizational assessments are widely used in both the private and public sectors across many disciplines, yet they are not a systematic part of the policing craft. The CP-SAT brings the strengths of organizational self-assessment and combines a specific, detailed focus on the community policing

components that reflect the vision for police work in the 21st century.

The CP-SAT Process, Content, and Report

The CP-SAT was originally established as a process for assessing organizationwide implementation of community policing through a set of pen-and-paper surveys. A crucial objective that was identified as essential to the successful development of the CP-SAT was to create a tool and process that balanced the need for appropriate scientific standards of rigor, while minimizing burden to respondents and agencies. Depending on the size of the agency, it is intended to be administered to most or all agency personnel. There is also inherent benefit to personnel who, through seeing practical (or operationalized) examples of how different community policing concepts are implemented through day-to-day police work, can come away with new ideas for their own work. However, larger agencies may choose to capture a representative picture of their community policing by drawing a sample that reflects the geographic and temporal distribution of officers, or their differing assignments and functions.

Through field testing, it was determined that the biggest time investments involved the respondents' time to complete the survey, and the administrative aspects of distributing the survey forms, collecting the completed forms, and entering the survey responses into a database. To mitigate these shortcomings, the number of CP-SAT survey questions was decreased and the assessment was moved to a web-based survey software platform. These changes served to reduce the average time required to complete the survey to less than 15 minutes, while also allowing for increased automation and administrative efficiency of the assessment process, which eliminated the need for hard-copy survey distribution, collection, and data entry.

The CP-SAT currently includes 108 questions that are specific to different respondent types: line officers, supervisors, command staff, civilian staff, and community partners. Screening questions and automated skip patterns ensure that questions that are irrelevant to the existing duties or activities of a respondent are not posed. Some questions are phrased in a way that is relevant for all respondent types, while others are specific to the span of control (i.e., the optimal numbers of employees that one person can supervise) or relevant to the responsibilities of a specific respondent type. The survey logic reflects these distinctions. For example, "to what extent do you make contact with a wide range of community members to assess community priorities" is an activity that can be relevant to a range of respondent types, and thus it is posed to everyone. However, "to what extent are community partners represented in planning and policy activities (e.g., budgeting, citizen advisory panels)" is most relevant to those who are in a position to establish and implement policy, and this is an example of a question received by only those at the commander or equivalent rank. Community partners' roles are especially unique, and therefore questions such as "to what extent does the law enforcement agency involve community members in solutions to community problems" are posed solely to those partners.

The CP-SAT survey questions are designed to assess the three central areas of community policing: *community partnerships, problem solving,* and *organizational transformation.* The survey sections are organized by these three areas.

Community Partnerships

This module of the CP-SAT collects information on and measures four broad concepts: engagement with a wide range of partners, partnerships with government partners, partnerships with community organizations and local businesses, and community engagement more generally.

Engagement With a Wide Range of Partners

These questions examine the extent to which there is active participation of numerous types of potential community partners with the agency. These potential partners include other law enforcement agencies, other components of the criminal justice system, other government agencies, nonprofits that serve the community, the local media, and individuals in the community.

Government Partnerships

These questions examine the range of partnerships with non-law-enforcement government agencies in the community, to include parks, public works, traffic engineering, code enforcement, or the school system, as well as the depth of the engagement with these partners.

Community Organization and Local Business Partnerships

These questions examine the range of nongovernment partnerships, which include block watch groups, faith-based organizations, neighborhood associations, nonprofit service providers, media, local businesses, and youth clubs. The depth of engagement with these community organizations and local business partnerships is assessed.

General Engagement With the Community

These questions examine the extent to which the agency reaches out to the local community to involve it in the community policing process.

Problem Solving

Problem solving is defined as the process of engaging in the proactive and systematic examination of identified problems to develop effective responses. This module of the CP-SAT captures a snapshot of the department's problem-solving approaches and activities.

The problem solving module measures five concepts, four of which specifically relate to the SARA (scanning, analysis, response, assessment) problem-solving model, and one that identifies overall problem-solving practices.

Organizational Transformation

Organizational transformation, also commonly referred to as *organizational change,* refers to the alignment of policies and practices to support community partnerships and proactive problem solving. The results presented here represent a snapshot of the department's principles of organizational transformation.

The organizational transformation module measures four concepts: agency management, personnel management, leadership, and transparency.

Agency Management

Under community policing, changes to agency management are imperative to infuse modern management practices with community policing principles. These changes can influence climate and culture, leadership practices, formal policies and procedures, and labor relations. These CP-SAT questions specifically examine agency management as reflected through resources and finances; planning and policies; and organizational evaluations.

Personnel Management

Personnel systems and processes have a profound impact on everything from the type of employees who are attracted to a particular agency, to the expectations against which they are evaluated, to training and development that support their growth and performance. These CP-SAT questions specifically examine recruitment, selection, and hiring; personnel evaluations and supervision; training; and geographic assignment of officers.

Leadership

Leaders not only must model the behavior they expect to see throughout the organization, but they also set the tone for their agency's direction and style of policing through decision making, policies, and other means of exerting formal and informal influence. These CP-SAT questions examine the work, actions, and behaviors of leadership, such as the chief or sheriff and top command staff, when it comes to supporting community policing.

Transparency

By emphasizing partnerships, agencies inherently commit to becoming more transparent. The community in general, and more specifically formal partners engaged in meaningful collaboration, must receive relevant information on crime and disorder and matters of police business that impact them. These CP-SAT questions examine the extent to which the agency is open and forthcoming with the community about crime and disorder and police operations.

CP-SAT Summary Report

At the conclusion of the assessment process, the agency executive receives a report that summarizes their data in a user-friendly format, incorporating charts, graphs, and tables. The information within the report is provided in a way that clearly highlights the results so that executives and others can quickly identify areas of relative strength and weakness. This information is important in that it can assist the agency and its leaders in identifying training needs, as well as to inform strategic planning efforts and the creation of benchmarks and goals. Beyond planning, the results can also help them gain a better

understanding of community perceptions about the agency and their engagement work. It can also help establish a dialogue within the agency about the level and style of its particular approach to community policing. Finally, while it may not be central to the purpose of the assessment process, having objective data can help the agency promote its professionalism, and community policing advances and successes, which can all positively influence its standing with the community, appointed and elected officials, and other stakeholders.

There are several cautions to how the data will be construed or used. First, although the process is designed to protect the confidentiality of individual responses, officers may be skeptical about the extent to which this is taken seriously. For that reason, part of the communication strategy for embarking on the CP-SAT process entails assuring officers that at no time will the agency have access to any individual survey data. Also, the results are not to be used to "grade" an agency, but rather the CP-SAT is designed in the spirit that in order to make improvements an agency must be aware its existing levels of practice. Related, it is not intended to be punitive, nor would it be fair for an agency undertaking the process to be criticized for its CP-SAT results, which is likely to be the first objective picture of its community policing implementation. However, some, including elected or appointed officials, the media, community members, or even agency employees, may use the results to malign an agency's leaders. The COPS Office carefully weighed each of these risks against what are believed to be the benefits of the CP-SAT and decided that the value of the tool far exceeds any misinterpretation of the tool or results.

The Imperative for Assessing Community Policing

Every day, officers and other employees use a variety of strategies and tactics, many of which fall under the rubric of the philosophy of community policing, yet there are no universal approaches or even sufficient direction for how the various elements are systematically applied through specific police practices. The CP-SAT is intended to bring consistency to the implementation of the community policing philosophy.

Community policing is commonly accepted by many police practitioners for its effectiveness in addressing crime and disorder and in improving citizen satisfaction with police services. The malleability of the philosophy has resulted in community policing taking on a form that often looks very different across practicing agencies, into what is essentially a buffet of potential activities—legitimately and appropriately influenced by local policing traditions, organizational cultures, management prerogatives, community makeup, and agency resources—from which an agency can choose to implement. However the lack of consistency around the practice of community policing has compounded the difficulty of determining what impact that community policing has on public safety outcomes such as crime reduction, fear of crime reduction, and increased citizen satisfaction. The CP-SAT is intended to bring greater definitional and operational integrity and precision to the philosophy, which over time may assist in establishing norms of practice around community policing.

Robert Chapman and Mora Fiedler

See also Building Partnerships and Stakeholders; Community Oriented Policing Services, Office of; Community Policing and Problem Solving, Definition of; Implementation of Community Policing; Problem-Solving Process (SARA); Roles, Chief Executives'; Roles, First-Line Supervisors'; Roles, Middle Managers'; Roles, Officers'; Strategic Planning

Further Readings

Michigan Regional Community Policing Institute. (1999). Transformational leadership and community policing: A road map for change. *Police Chief, 67*(12), 14–22. Retrieved from http://www.cj.msu.edu/~people/cp/roadmaparticle.html

Taylor, B., Heinen, B., Mulvaney, R., Weiss, D., Chapman, R., Scheider, M., Diamond, D., Cronin, C., & Conlon, A. (in press). *Community policing self-assessment tool: Documenting today and planning for tomorrow.* Washington, DC: U.S. Department of Justice, Office of Community Oriented Policing Services.

Wilson, J. M. (2004, Fall). A measurement model approach to estimating community policing implementation. *Justice Research and Policy, 6*(2), 24.

COMMUNITY PROSECUTION

Inspired by the popularity and success of community policing strategies, prosecutors in the early 1990s began experimenting with an approach to addressing crime that came to be known as *community prosecution*. Because community prosecution was inspired by and built upon community policing, the approaches share characteristics—most significantly, perhaps, an emphasis on making centralized, anonymous agencies more neighborhood specific and personal. This entry describes community prosecution's components, history, and impact on community policing as well as presenting Denver's (Colorado) community prosecution initiative as an example.

Components

The definition of community prosecution continues to evolve. In some respects its definition changes with every office that practices it. Still, researchers and practitioners have identified components that distinguish it from traditional prosecution: community engagement, partnership, and problem solving.

Community Engagement

Community prosecution seeks to engage communities in various ways. The purpose of community engagement is to build bridges between prosecutors' offices and their constituents in pursuit of safer communities and improved public confidence in justice. Through community engagement, prosecutors tap public knowledge and resources, try to identify the most pressing crime and safety problems, and enlist local resources in fashioning effective responses. Tools of community engagement include conducting surveys, hosting and attending public meetings, creating community advisory boards, and establishing storefront offices that encourage community members to walk in off the streets with complaints, concerns, and questions.

Partnership

Community prosecution emphasizes going beyond the prosecutor's office in search of information, know-how, and resources to address office priorities. Through partnerships with other government agencies, community-based organizations and individuals, community prosecutors seek to build better cases and solve community problems. A number of community prosecution programs are characterized by closer working relationships with police departments. In Indianapolis, Indiana, for example, community prosecutors were assigned offices in stationhouses to answer officers' questions, help officers build better cases, and develop collaborative crime-control and prevention strategies.

Problem Solving

Community prosecution uses varied and innovative approaches to address crime and public safety issues. The idea is not just to prosecute cases but to use data and local knowledge to craft new crime prevention strategies and to address problems that are not overtly crime related—for example, a community's lack of constructive after-school activities.

History

Two of the earliest advocates of community prosecution were Multnomah County (Oregon) District Attorney Michael Schrunk and Kings County (New York) District Attorney Charles J. Hynes. They were inspired, in part, by frustration with rising caseloads. Despite putting more and more people behind bars, especially at the peak of the crack epidemic during the mid-1980s, many prosecutors felt they were having little impact on crime. The overwhelming amount of work, and the fact that many offenders were returning to criminal activity as soon as they were released, fostered a desire for new responses, and many, like Schrunk and Hynes, turned to community policing as a model.

Schrunk launched his Neighborhood D.A. Program in 1990 by assigning a single prosecutor to a commercial district in Portland, Oregon, where low-level offending was felt to be harming economic revitalization efforts. The prosecutor's first focus was illegal camping, which local businesses considered a public nuisance, an impediment to neighborhood development, and a source of petty criminal activity. Since arresting transients hadn't solved the problem, the community prosecutor addressed the issue by engaging multiple city agencies in cleanup efforts, forming a volunteer citizen patrol to alert authorities to the presence of illegal campers, and supporting initiatives to link transients to housing and other services.

The effort contained many of the elements common to community prosecution programs: a geographic focus, an interest in low-level offending, and an attempt to harness a wide range of local resources to not only mitigate a current problem but to prevent future offending.

In 1991, Hynes similarly adopted a geographic approach, organizing many of the more than 400 prosecutors in his office into five zones. He also adopted a "vertical" prosecution strategy—that is, he required prosecutors to follow felony cases from grand jury presentation through sentencing rather than handing cases off to colleagues at every stage of the court process.

Hynes has supported numerous initiatives with a neighborhood problem-solving focus. For example, in 2000 he helped establish the Red Hook Community Justice Center to improve public safety in a crime-ridden neighborhood in southwest Brooklyn, New York. Hynes has also developed programs that offer alternatives to incarceration and treatment-based diversion, which have been cited as examples of community prosecution.

Part of the interest in community prosecution can be traced to the support of the U.S. Department of Justice, which, beginning under Attorney General Janet Reno in the 1990s and continuing through successive administrations, invested millions of grant dollars in community prosecution programming across the country. By 2004, an American Prosecutors Research Institute survey found that 37.8% of offices self-reported practicing community prosecution. In recent years, national community prosecution conferences have drawn participants from virtually every corner of the United States, from offices large and small, urban and rural.

A number of elected district attorneys in high-profile jurisdictions, such as Cook County (Chicago), Illinois; Philadelphia, Pennsylvania; and New York, New York, have successfully run for office promising to implement (or restore) community prosecution approaches.

The nature of community prosecution has evolved over the years. In its early stages, community prosecution was frequently promoted as a tool to address low-level offending. In recent years, however, advocates of community prosecution have emphasized the strategy's capacity to tackle more serious crime—such as gang violence, large-scale drug dealing, and armed robbery.

Impacts

Despite the growing use of the term *community prosecution,* most of the evidence of its success is anecdotal and formal research measuring program impacts is limited. Two studies—one of the Multnomah County Prosecutor's Office published in 2007 and another of the U.S. Attorney's Office in Washington, D.C., published in 2001—claim reductions in crime associated with community prosecution initiatives. Both studies found that crime reductions were greater in the neighborhoods studied than in comparison neighborhoods, although they acknowledge that other factors, such as economic development, may have also played a role.

An Example: Denver's Initiatives

Denver's district attorney's office—through the use of community justice councils, accountability boards (using community volunteers to determine restorative sanctions for offenders), and a community court—has encouraged the community to take an active leadership role in helping to identify crime and quality-of-life problems and to develop strategies for addressing them. One tool is a "connect the dots" exercise, where community prosecution staff meet with neighborhood residents and ask them to discuss local concerns. Using large posters listing all the issues raised, citizens place green dots next to any issues they feel are neighborhood problems and place red dots next to the issues they deem the most important. This affords the group a concrete measure of which issues are of greatest collective concern.

Denver prosecutors also worked to create a community court that hears youth offenses in a high-crime neighborhood, holding offenders accountable for their behavior while also providing services to them to lessen the likelihood of their reoffending. Many such courts utilize the "youth jury model," where the offender admits having committed the offense, the police officer involved in the youth's detention indicates that such a disposition is appropriate, and the offender and parent or guardian give consent to such a disposition; the members of the panel then question the offender, deliberate, and assign appropriate consequences, which always include some form of community service.

Community prosecutors also survey residents to decide where to focus their efforts; one such survey resulted in addressing problems of family violence, drug sales, and alcohol-related crimes.

Robert V. Wolf

See also Broken Windows Theory; Building Partnerships and Stakeholders; Citizen Surveys; Community, Definition of; Crime Prevention Through Environmental Design; Hot Spots; Involving Local Businesses; Problem-Solving Courts; Problem-Solving Process (SARA)

Further Readings

Boland, B. (2007). *The response of Multnomah County to neighborhood crime: 1990–2005*. Alexandria, VA: National District Attorneys Association. Retrieved from http://www.ndaa.org/pdf/pub_multnomah_county_07.pdf

National Association of Youth Courts. (n.d.). *Facts and Stats*. Retrieved from http://www.youthcourt.net/?page_id=24

National District Attorneys Association. (2009). *Key principles of community prosecution*. Alexandria, VA: Author. Retrieved from http://www.ndaa.org/pdf/final_key_principles_updated_jan_2009.pdf

Nugent, M. E., Fanflik, P., & Bromirski, D. (2004). *The changing nature of prosecution: Community prosecution vs. traditional prosecution approaches*. Alexandria, VA: American Prosecutors Research Institute. Retrieved from http://www.ndaa.org/pdf/changing_nature_of_prosecution.pdf

Porter, R. (2011). *Choosing performance indicators for your community prosecution initiative*. Washington, DC: Association of Prosecuting Attorneys. Retrieved from http://www.ndaa.org/pdf/final_key_principles_updated_jan_2009.pdf

Thompson, A. C., & Wolf, R. V. (2004). *The prosecutor as problem-solver: An overview of community prosecution*. New York, NY: Center for Court Innovation. Retrieved from http://www.courtinnovation.org/sites/default/files/prosecutor_as_ps.pdf

Weinstein, S. P. (2011). *Community prosecution: A decade into the 21st century*. Retrieved from http://www.apainc.org/files/DDF/CP%20%20Decade%20into%2021st%20Century%20FINAL.pdf

Wolf, R. V. (2010). *Community prosecution and serious crime*. Alexandria, VA: National District Attorneys Association. Retrieved from http://www.courtinnovation.org/sites/default/files/documents/CP_SC.pdf

Wolf, R. V., & Campbell, N. (2004). *Beyond big cities: The problem-solving innovations of community prosecutors in smaller jurisdictions*. NCJ 213474. New York, NY: Center for Court Innovation. Retrieved from http://www.courtinnovation.org/sites/default/files/beyond_big_cities.pdf

Wolf, R. V., & Worrall, J. L. (2004). *Lessons from the field: Ten community prosecution leadership profiles*.

Alexandria, VA: American Prosecutors Research Institute. Retrieved from http://www.courtinnovation .org/sites/default/files/cp_lessons_from_the_field.pdf

COMPSTAT

CompStat is a term that refers to comparative statistics or computer statistics. It is the systematic collection, analysis, and mapping of crime data and police performance measures toward addressing crime, while also holding police managers accountable for their own and their officers' performance as measured by these data.

CompStat originated in 1994 at the New York City Police Department (NYPD) as a multilayered approach to reducing crime, improving quality of life, and establishing better accountability for personnel and resource management. A principal aim of CompStat was to engage NYPD's precinct captains in employing problem-solving strategies and tactics to address neighborhood problems in their areas of command. As such, it represents a departure from conventional policing, which is characterized by organizational inflexibility, central authority, and limited discretion. Based on key features of community policing, problem solving, and broken windows theory, CompStat places the accountability for managing crime problems directly on the shoulders of a police organization's mid-level managers (generally captains or commanders, depending on the agency's size).

While critics argue the NYPD approach may not suit all agencies, CompStat-like programs were quickly adopted by agencies nationwide and abroad as a result of the NYPD's highly publicized successes. This entry discusses the origins, expansion, premises and purposes, evaluation, current status, and future of this major tool for use in community policing and problem solving.

Origins

In 1994, William Bratton was appointed as the police commissioner for the NYPD and with the assistance of Deputy Chief Commissioner Jack Maple implemented CompStat. Four NYPD detectives are credited with creating the term as they were entering data onto a 5.25-inch floppy disk using a small business software package named SmartWare. The outdated computer operating system (known as DOS, for disk operating system) they were using restricted the officers to eight characters to name the file. One officer yelled out "CompStat," and that in essence was the term's humble beginnings. The implementation of CompStat as an organizational management tool and accountability system is credited to Jack Maple. He was a lieutenant in the New York transit authority police department when Bratton appointed him to deputy commissioner in 1994. Maple is credited by many as the architect of the department's CompStat program, which placed accountability on precinct commanders to use crime statistics to examine problems at rigorous weekly meetings with the department's top officials.

Bratton's policing approach differed in many ways from other police leaders who under community policing models were decentralizing decision-making authority to patrol officers. Bratton identified precinct commanders as being better suited for the task of decision making because young officers were inexperienced at addressing many of the serious issues facing New York City. Prior to his appointment as head of the NYPD, Bratton was head of the city's subway system, which under his leadership showed significant reductions in crime. That success led to his appointment as head of the NYPD by then-Mayor Rudolph Giuliani, who wanted the same reduction in crime throughout the city.

Overcoming Conventional Crime Fighting Methods

Prior to CompStat, NYPD generally had a three- to six-month delay in reporting crime statistics, which made it nearly impossible to provide officers with meaningful or timely analysis. NYPD's precincts had the ability to perform crime analysis but did not do so systematically. Precinct captains simply did not consider the analysis of crime data or crime reduction as their principal responsibility. This was traditionally common among police departments across the nation, where reactive, incident-driven patrol was seen as more important and detective and patrol bureaus rarely communicated or collaborated.

CompStat was developed as a means of restructuring departments to overcome these issues by ensuring that all precincts generated weekly crime activity reports so that precinct captains could be held accountable for meeting performance objectives. Over time, crime data were computerized and compiled into a CompStat book, offering timely information that was then compared and evaluated at city, precinct, and patrol levels. Commanders quickly realized that their role had significantly changed and they could no longer simply respond to crime. They were now required to find innovative ways to think about suppression, intervention, and prevention. To ensure that this message was heard by commanders, the NYPD began holding regularly scheduled meetings in which the precinct captains and their staff would meet with the department's executive staff to discuss crime trends and issues.

These meetings created an intimidating environment for commanders, who had to stand before their peers and executive staff and discuss their approaches to crime problems. During the meetings, three large screens flashed maps that used geographic information systems to show the number of crime incidences in the commanders' areas of responsibility. As the presentation progressed, commanders were asked questions to identify their crime problems, to discuss the tactics and strategies they were using to address the problems, and to describe what, if any, collaborative partnerships were formed to solve them. Participants then brainstormed about how to respond to the crime problems, and suggested strategies to assist commanders in their approaches. Commanders were required to report progress at subsequent meetings to ensure accountability.

The use of various data sources has expanded considerably as CompStat evolved. Other data used in the analysis process include census demographics, arrests, citations, response times, calls for service incidents from dispatched calls, officers' use of vacation and sick time, use of force reports, and citizens' complaints of officer misconduct. Academics and practitioners alike have maintained that CompStat has played an indispensable role in significantly reducing crime in New York City. Furthermore, its impact on increasing police accountability practices is significant and cannot be ignored. Reports by officers of increased job satisfaction as a result of being empowered by the problem-solving process to address crime more successfully is an added benefit of the CompStat process.

Objectives

Since being implemented by the NYPD, CompStat has been adopted by agencies across the United States and abroad. A national survey by the Police Foundation of U.S. agencies found that 58% of large agencies (100 or more sworn officers) had either adopted or were planning to implement a CompStat-like program. CompStat's weekly or monthly crime reports from readily available crime data provide officers citywide timely information to address problems in their assigned areas.

CompStat teaches police commanders how to think about crime in terms of suppression, intervention, and prevention. When explaining their crime problems to the department's executive staff and peers they not only identify a problem, but also explain what tactics they have employed to address crime patterns, resources they have and need, and with whom they have collaborated. Follow-up by top brass further ensures accountability.

CompStat begins with the identification of specific operational objectives. This is a principal responsibility of an agency's leadership and management. In the case of CompStat, the objectives relate to crime and quality-of-life uses. Four key features of CompStat are as follows:

- *Accurate and timely intelligence:* Effective responses to crime and criminal events require that officers have accurate knowledge of crime types, when they are occurring, and who the criminals are. The accuracy of criminal intelligence increases the likelihood of effective responses.
- *Effective tactics:* Effective response tactics require careful analysis of timely intelligence information.
- *Rapid deployment of personnel and resources:* An array of personnel and resources from patrol and various other areas of the agency may be required to address a problem. The collaboration of expertise in different areas of the agency is critical to successful response strategies.
- *Relentless follow-up and assessment:* Problem-solving efforts require rigorous follow-up and assessment. It serves to identify successes as well as needed changes in analysis and response strategies. It also serves to identify effective responses that may be applied to future similar problems.

Presentation of CompStat Data

Provided in this section are some fundamentals about how to present, compare, and map data. Although some of this information may be complex, the three steps of the process are presented here as an overview of what is available with CompStat analyses. The three steps are as follows:

1. This step involves presenting data in a way that everyone in the department—from the chief executives to patrol officers—can understand the information and utilize it to address crime problems. There are many different ways to present data, including showing simple increases and decreases, percentages (including over time or between specific time frames); ratios; ratio by population, mean, median and mode; pie charts, bar charts, line graphs, histograms, and so on.

2. The next set in a data presentation involves identifying the relationship between two or more crimes. The statistics used to accomplish this are called *measures of association*. They provide the crime analyst with information that determines the strength of a relationship between crimes and assists with making predictions. For example, a crime analyst may be interested in determining if a relationship between use of closed-circuit television (CCTV) cameras at convenience stores and the incidence of robberies exists. The analyst can gather the data and calculate any association using the statistical measure Pearson's *r* to determine the strength of any relationship and its direction. If a strong relationship is found between the two variables (CCTV and robbery), it may be presumed with some reliability that the two are closely related. Simply, convenience stores with CCTV have a lower incidence of robbery than establishments without this prevention technology. It is important, however, that the analyst is cautious in making predictions because a strong positive relationship does not necessarily prove that a connection exists; it may only serve as a clue to causation. These methods of analyses allow for analysts and commanders to adjust personnel and resources to shifts where problems are occurring. The data may also be displayed by different areas of town, shifts, or smaller geographic beats. Changes in crime patterns by these spatial (location) and temporal (time) means help commanders see the big picture.

3. Crime mapping is the final step in the process. Crime mapping provides analysts an opportunity to display complicated data and analysis into a simple illustration (map). Mapping software also allows analysts to overlay various datasets over one map.

For instance, an area map may be generated to depict areas where recently paroled burglars live and the incidence of car and home burglaries. Criminology theories explain that burglars typically commit their crimes within a circle of where they live, work, and play. If police are seeing a rash of burglaries and three parolee residences are in the middle of that map hot spot, police may want to further investigate the possibility that one or more of the parolees are responsible.

Organizational Structure for CompStat

Weekly Crime Reports

Weekly crime reports are a concise summary report of crimes and arrests that occurred during the week. The identification of crime patterns and a discussion of response strategies are included in these reports. The NYPD required that each of its 76 precincts, 9 police service areas, and 12 transit districts develop weekly crime reports, which were collated and entered into a citywide database by the department's CompStat Unit, allowing for the analysis of crime data and patterns in a number of ways, including by day, hour, week, month, year, and geographic area. Weekly crime report data can provide precinct commanders and top management important information about current and emerging crime trends, and top management can also use the data to evaluate and compare performance metrics between precincts and commands.

Crime Control Strategy Meetings

The underpinning of CompStat is accountability at the precinct captain (commander) level. Crime control strategy meetings, also referred to as CompStat meetings, are held twice weekly and attended by commanders and agency executives. CompStat meetings are viewed as an opportunity to motivate commanders to improve operational performance. They also provide an opportunity for commanders to impress peers and executives. Each commander is responsible for presenting his crime data and responses to the group. Discussions revolve around the presentation of statistical crime data and illustrations using crime mapping. The focus of the meetings is to provide an opportunity for dialogue among commanders and agency executives about strategies to reduce crime at the precinct level. As a performance measure, the meetings provide the department's leadership an opportunity to evaluate the knowledge, skills, abilities, and effectiveness of commanders to deal with crime as well as manage resources.

Commander Profile Reports

Commander profile reports are an important measurement tool generated from CompStat data. These reports include information about each commander's date and years of rank, education, training, and performance evaluations. Data to evaluate a commander's management skills and abilities include overtime used by personnel assigned to the command, sick time usage, on-the-job injuries, citizen complaints, and vehicle accidents. The NYPD viewed this profile as an important tool for executives to evaluate a commander's ability to manage personnel and resources.

Replication and Small Agency Use

A study conducted by the Police Foundation revealed significant variation in CompStat programs implemented by law enforcement agencies across the country. It also found that larger agencies were more likely to implement CompStat-like programs. This, according to the study, may be related to larger agencies' interest in CompStat's ability to increase middle management accountability and controls, which have been a major area of concern for policing.

Vincent E. Henry in his 2002 book *The CompStat Paradigm* argues that the future of CompStat is the ability of agencies of any size to tailor it to their own particular needs. Jon Shane, retired Newark, New Jersey, police captain, Police Foundation fellow and faculty member at New York's John Jay College, identifies CompStat as the wave of the future. It has been used in agencies of various sizes, from NYPD's 34,500 officers to departments with 12 or fewer officers. While CompStat operations may vary, patrol strategies based on broken windows theory and problem-oriented policing, with their emphasis on crime data collection and analysis and tactical responses, are common among agencies of varied sizes. Below are some examples of smaller agencies that have implemented CompStat-like programs:

Police in Tuscaloosa County, Florida, used crime data from the department's records management system to illustrate problem areas using crime

mapping software and used that information to develop responses.

Paradise Valley, Arizona, is a resort community adjacent to Phoenix and is especially plagued with burglary problems. The chief, command staff, and six sergeants in the 36-officer police agency meet monthly to discuss problems. The agency's computer-aided dispatch system (CAD) provides data for analysis of crime problems. Volunteers are utilized for neighborhood patrols.

Washington State Police instituted an accountability driven leadership model based on the principles of CompStat. This model expands the concept of CompStat to other areas of public safety and management to include budgetary practices, forensic laboratory services, and identifying children and seniors who are at risk of becoming crime victims.

Fulton County, Georgia, adapted the CompStat process into its jail operation in an effort to comply with a consent decree with the federal government concerning jail living conditions. The sheriff conducts "audit meetings" where commanders are required to present strategies to the group for resolving jail-related problems. Significant improvements were reported during the first nine months of the CompStat "audit" process.

The experiences of smaller agencies show that the CompStat process may be implemented with success using limited computer analysis capabilities. Still, most agencies today have some computerized capabilities to capture incident and crime data, whether they use CAD, records management system (RMS), or a stand-alone system using spreadsheet databases such as Microsoft Excel. The key is to organize and present the data so that executive staff and commanders can understand and use it for analysis and formulation of responses.

CompStat Plus

Bratton was appointed as the chief of the Los Angeles Police Department (LAPD) in 2002 with a commitment to improve what he viewed as the agency's lagging ability to address crime problems. During the course of inspecting various commands, Bratton discovered that unlike the NYPD, police managers in Los Angeles did not respond well to threats of disciplinary action for nonperformance.

He also felt that it was necessary that every police station (precinct) in the LAPD perform at its maximum capacity. CompStat Plus was implemented as an enhanced application of Bratton's efforts at the NYPD. The plus adds the use of more in-depth auditing methods, mentorship, and close collaboration to that of CompStat's foundational principles of management and accountability.

The Newton area of Los Angeles was the testing ground in 2004 for CompStat Plus. This densely populated, economically depressed section of the city was rife with serious crime problems, including the presence of 52 street gangs. Three clear strategies were implemented: (1) an analysis of underperformance by police in Newton and a focus on solutions to complex problems, (2) dialogue between stakeholders to identify problems, and (3) a collaborative partnership between stakeholders to address the problems. The promise of CompStat Plus for the LAPD is evidenced by an 11% drop in violent crimes in the Newton area only four weeks after its implementation.

Concerns

The potential for manipulating data to satisfy bosses is a major criticism and concern about CompStat. A survey by the *New York Daily News* of 1,200 retired NYPD officers who worked during the CompStat era revealed concerns during 2008, which was the time period covered in the survey. Respondents included 100 captains and other supervisors. Issues related to changed or distorted crime reports were identified by 168 respondents. Complaints about supervisory pressure to decrease the eight Part I or index crimes (murder, forcible rape, robbery, aggravated assault, burglary, theft [except auto], auto theft, and arson) also raised data integrity concerns However, the questionnaires did not attempt to measure the frequency of any manipulation, none of the respondents were asked to identify specific acts of misconduct, none admitted to having done it themselves, and a police spokesman stated that a large number of respondents could have been recalling the same incident. Still, the survey clearly elicited disturbing answers; of the 160 retired officers who indicated they were aware of changes in crime reports, more than three-quarters said the changes were unethical.

Evaluations of Effectiveness

Many questions about the effectiveness of CompStat remain unanswered. Critics argue the NYPD may not be representative of most other departments and that a significant drop in crime nationally during the initial year of CompStat may account for much of what is cited as CompStat-related successes. An evaluation of CompStat in Fort Worth, Texas, by Hyunseok Jang and colleagues, found significant increases in nuisance arrests and property crimes. While there was no significant impact on violent crime, there was a significant reduction on total number of the eight aforementioned Part I index offenses. The evaluations of CompStat in New York and Fort Worth (Texas) indicate that it has promise, but it is clear that, concurrently, a rigorous auditing system should be instituted to maintain the integrity of the crime reporting operation.

Future of CompStat

The future of CompStat does not lie in its survival as a tool of upper management but as a tool of the street officer. All of the principal reform movements in policing have relied on line-level officers and investigators having current, ongoing knowledge of the criminal activity in their beat. Agencies have been improving their internal information management and communications infrastructure for this purpose, making it possible for any member of any police agency to create CompStat-like analyses at their discretion. CompStat has evolved from a simple file name to a technique and a belief system. It must therefore be understood by management and then pushed down to both supervisors and rank-and-file police officers.

CompStat is now used to address crime and quality-of-life issues in police agencies around the United States and in other parts of the world. The strength of CompStat lies in its management and accountability factors. As such, it has been referred to as a new police paradigm that has revolutionized law enforcement management and practices.

Ronald W. Glensor

See also Broken Windows Theory; Crime Analysis; Crime Mapping; Crime Prevention Through Environmental Design; Global Positioning Systems/ Geographic Information Systems; Predictive Policing

Further Readings

Buerger, M. E. (2005, January-February). COMPSTAT: A strategic vision. *The Associate*, 18–23.

DeLorenzi, D., Shane, J. M., & Amendola, K. L. (2006) The CompStat process: Managing performance on the pathway to leadership. *The Police Chief, 73*(9).

Eterno, J., & Silverman, E. (2010, February 15). The trouble with CompStat: Pressure on MYPD commanders endangered the integrity of crime stats. *New York Daily News*. Retrieved from http://articles. nydailynews.com/2010-02-15/news/27056291_1_compstat-crime-reports-commanders

Grant, H. J., & Terry, K. J. (2005). *Law enforcement in the 21st century*. Boston, MA: Allyn & Bacon.

Henry, V. E. (2002). *The CompStat paradigm: Management accountability in policing, business and the public sector.* Flushing, NY: Looseleaf Law.

Jang, H., Hoover, L. T., & Joo, H-J. (2010). An evaluation of CompStat's effect on crime: The Fort Worth experience. *Police Quarterly, 13*(4), 387–412. doi: 10.1177/1098611110384085

Shane, J. M. (2004, May). CompStat design. *FBI Law Enforcement Bulletin, 73*(5), 12-19.

Varga, A. (2011). CompStat: Too big for small department? *Law and Order, 3,* 34–37.

Weisburd, D. L., Mastrofski, S., McNally, A. M., Greenspan, R., & Willis, J. (2003). Reforming to preserve: CompStat and strategic problem solving in American policing. *Criminology and Public Policy, 2*(3), 421–456. doi: 10.1111/j.1745-9133.2003.tb00006

COMPUTER-AIDED DISPATCH

A computer-aided dispatch (CAD) system is a highly specialized computer system that uses telecommunications and geographic display to support police and other first responders, such as fire and ambulance services. Specific to police, CAD is used to dispatch officers to incident locations about which citizens have called for police services, to record officers' self-generated activity, to facilitate communication between police officers and dispatchers who support officers in the field, as well as to keep track of calls for service, officers' locations, and their activities. Because a CAD system tracks the activities of officers on all service calls, it is an important source of data for community policing. This entry details the two key types of data that CAD systems produce—unit history data and calls for service data—and discusses the uses of the latter in community policing.

Unit History Data

CAD systems produce data from each communication that has been entered into the system by the officers and the dispatchers about officers' activity while in the field (i.e., unit history data). In unit history data, each record denotes a specific communication between an officer and a dispatcher. For example, an officer who pulls over a vehicle may look up the license plate of the vehicle to determine whether it is stolen or may ask the dispatcher to run a person's driver license for warrants. Detectives conducting investigations also communicate with dispatchers about interviews they are conducting and their other activities. Each record in the data contains a date and time and description of the activity. Depending on the CAD system, the format and content of unit history data can vary.

Unit history data is primarily used for examining resource allocation and determining staffing levels for an agency, since it provides the most detailed information about officer activities. For example, the data contain the number of officers dispatched to each call and the amount of time each officer spends on a call. Thus, unit history data can be aggregated and examined to determine whether current staffing levels are appropriate (i.e., are the correct number of officers assigned to a particular shift), as well as to anticipate whether additional officers will be required over time. These data are also used to determine police geographic boundaries within the jurisdiction (i.e., redistricting), which supports the community policing practice of assigning officers to a particular geographic area.

Calls for Service Data

CAD systems also produce data about incidents that officers are dispatched to or incidents they have discovered themselves. In calls for service data, each record represents one call for service. These data are different from unit history data where each record represents a correspondence between the dispatch and the officer over the computer system, in that calls for service data reflect a snapshot of the entire call after it is over. For example, where unit history data show the time spent on the call by each officer who was dispatched to the call, calls for service data show the total time of the call from when the first officer arrived on the scene to when the last officer cleared the call.

Although there may be some differences from one CAD system to another, in general the following are the key characteristics that are collected for each call for service: the unique incident or record number; the location of the call, which often includes the location name, address, and beat or other police geographic area; the dates and times when the call was received, when the call was dispatched to an officer, when the first officer arrived at the scene, and when the call was cleared; the officer who was assigned the call; the type of call; the priority of the call; the disposition or final outcome of the call; and a short narrative describing the circumstances of the call.

There are two categories of calls for service. The first category is *citizen-generated* calls for service. These calls are the most common, as they are the calls for service that are initiated by a citizen or another source external to the police department. In other words, they reflect the community's demand for police service. Because the role of police in society is to assist with all problematic activity and the police respond 24 hours a day, 7 days a week, they receive many more than just calls for service about crime. In fact, a conservative estimate is that under 25% of citizen-generated calls for service result in a crime report, making most of the citizen-generated calls for service about something other than crime. Calls for service in most communities include, but are not limited to, the following:

- Criminal calls, such as robbery, burglary, theft, homicide, rape, shoplifting, fight, assault, trespassing
- Traffic-related calls, such as accidents, assist motorist, traffic signal down, speeding
- Disorder calls, such as disturbances, neighbor disputes, juvenile trouble, narcotics activity, loud party, suspicious vehicle or person, trespassing
- General calls, such as 911 hang-up, burglar alarms, welfare checks, loud noise, missing person

Calls for service types do not often represent the exact nature of the activity about which the citizen is calling, but the classifications are used by dispatchers to classify the activity to guide officers in their initial response. For example, domestic violence calls for service typically require two officers to respond.

The second category of calls for service is called *officer-generated* calls for service. These are calls in which officers proactively identify problematic activity in the field and inform the dispatcher about the time, location, and the nature of activity. Officer-generated calls typically contain similar information as citizen-generated calls, but in most CAD systems are distinguished as being generated by an officer. These types of calls most often involve officers stopping vehicles for traffic violations, stopping individuals for suspicious behavior, and conducting directed patrol or stopping at individual locations. The number of officer-generated calls for service is highly influenced by the volume of citizen-generated calls for service, because the number of citizen-generated calls influences the amount of time officers have to generate calls themselves. That is, for police departments, answering citizen-generated calls for service is the highest priority, thus when there are more citizen-generated calls for service to answer, officers have less time to generate calls themselves, and vice versa.

Uses of Calls for Service Data for Community Policing

Where citizen-generated calls for service are used to determine the needs of the community, officer-generated calls are used to determine the workload and focus of officers during their uncommitted time. For example, multiple citizen-generated loud party calls for service at an apartment complex indicate residents are not happy with the loud party activity, whereas the number of DUIs in an area does not indicate how many DUIs actually occurred but how many were identified by officers, since typically citizens do not report DUIs. Consequently, citizen-generated calls for service are more often used for community policing efforts, specifically informing the community of issues and identifying problems.

An important tenet of community policing is sharing information with the community so that the police and the community can work together to identify and resolve problems. Citizen-generated calls for service data are often shared with community members to inform them of activity in their own neighborhoods, to provide them with information on areas of the community where they might want to live, send their children to school, or locate a business, and to encourage citizens to assist police by letting them know of additional issues. The dissemination of calls for service information is typically done through neighborhood association meetings, block and crime watch meetings, and the Internet.

Another important tenet of community policing is identifying and addressing crime and disorder problems. Because many of the problems that society and police face are not crime related, citizen-generated calls for service data are an important tool in the problem-solving process. Both small problems, such as repeat calls from one location and large problems, such as false burglar alarm calls throughout a city, are identified using calls for service data. Calls for service data of either category are also used to better understand the nature of noncriminal problems, for example, speeding in residential areas, false burglar alarms, disorderly youth in public places, loud car stereos, and misuse and abuse of 911.

Lastly, calls for service data are less precise for examining crime incidents than crime data from crime reports written by officers. Even though crimes that are reported to or discovered by the police start as a call for service, the calls for service data about these criminal incidents do not accurately represent them. For example, the dates and times in calls for service data reflect when each call was received and dispatched to the officer, when the officer arrived, and when the call was cleared, but not the date and time when the crime actually occurred. That is, a victim can call on Monday morning about her car being stolen on Saturday night. Also, the location listed in call for service data is the location where the call originated, which may not be the location where the crime occurred. Given these limitations, calls for service data are used in analyses of noncriminal problems identified by citizens and officers rather than in crime incident analyses.

Rachel Boba Santos

See also Community Policing and Problem Solving, Definition of; Crime Analysis; Crime Mapping; Measuring Officer Performance; Problem-Solving Process (SARA)

Further Readings

Alleman, T. (1996). *Introduction to computing in criminal justice*. Upper Saddle River, NJ: Prentice Hall.

McEwen, T., Ahn, J., Pendleton, S., Webster, B., & Williams, G. (2002). *Computer aided dispatch in support of community policing, final report*. NCJ 204025. Alexandria, VA: Institute for Law and Justice. Retrieved from https://www.ncjrs.gov/pdffiles1/nij/grants/204025.pdf

Pattavina, A. (Ed.). (2005). *Information technology and the criminal justice system*. Thousand Oaks, CA: Sage.

Santos, R. B. (2012). *Crime analysis with crime mapping* (3rd ed.). Thousand Oaks, CA: Sage.

COUNTERTERRORISM AND COMMUNITY POLICING

Terrorism as a form of conflict and war has existed for centuries. However, it began to receive special consideration in the United States after the attacks of September 11, 2001, in which hijackers crashed two planes into the World Trade Center in New York City, one plane into the Pentagon in northern Virginia, and an additional plane into a field in Pennsylvania. These attacks were perpetrated by the terrorist group al Qaeda. The attacks resulted in nearly 3,000 deaths and billions of dollars in damage to the U.S. economy. Although there had been other terrorist attacks on the United States, the 9/11 attacks were a defining moment. After the attacks, the Department of Homeland Security was created and police departments across the country began to include counterterrorism and homeland security in their departmental missions.

Terrorism and counterterrorism became an important part of policing, and community policing can play an important role in a police agency's counterterrorism efforts. Positive community relationships and partnerships, a component of community policing, is an effective strategy for police to obtain information, including terrorist intelligence. This entry defines terrorism and counterterrorism and discusses community policing's role in counterterrorism.

Terrorism

Terrorism is a socially constructed term that is fraught with ideology; one man's terrorist may be another man's freedom fighter. Definitions often depend on perspective. Most of the definitions have two primary components: political motivation and massive destruction often aimed at civilian populations. In terms of political motivation, terrorist groups attempt to change the political or social structure in their own country or other countries. Islamists terrorists perpetrate terrorism to spread the Muslim religion or some form of Islamic law. Other terrorists, left-wing and right-wing, attempt to change or support a government ideology. In terms of destruction, terrorists see massive destruction to infrastructure and casualties as a way of demonstrating their powerfulness. These acts instill fear and cause overreaction on the part of their enemies and generate support from others who see their targets as enemies. One way of examining terrorism is to consider terrorist acts as crimes.

There are different kinds of terrorism, including state-sponsored terrorism, dissent terrorism, religious terrorism, and criminal terrorism. State-sponsored terrorism consists of terrorists acts perpetrated against another country or against groups or populations within the country who are opposed to the state. The U.S. Department of State has identified Cuba, Iran, Sudan, and Syria as state sponsors of terrorism. Dissent terrorism refers to groups within a country that use terrorism as a way of overthrowing their government. They attempt to institute a government that is consistent with their ideas. Religious terrorism is most associated with groups in the Middle East and Asia. These groups are attempting to instill their religious beliefs on other people and countries.

The primary concern regarding terrorism has been attacks from groups outside the United States, especially those conducted by Islamists. However, there are groups within our borders who are willing to perpetrate terrorism on U.S. citizens. Today, terrorists on U.S. soil for the most part can be categorized as eco- and animal-rights terrorists, right-wing terrorists, and Islamic terrorists. Eco- and animal-rights terrorists have conducted a number of attacks on businesses and universities. The eco-terrorists' attacks have been sporadic, focusing on businesses such as automobile dealerships and timber companies that they believe are harming the environment. Animal-rights terrorists have bombed university and corporate laboratories that used animals in their research. These two groups have not caused many deaths or injuries, but they have caused considerable property damage.

Although there have been several left-wing groups in the United States—anti-government "patriot" groups, right-to-life extremists, eco-terrorists, and animal-rights extremists, all who are or were attempting to achieve their political aims and committing crimes and acts of terrorism—their numbers and activities have subsided over the years. Today, there are numerous right-wing groups and militias in the United States that periodically conduct terrorist attacks and activities. They include the Ku Klux Klan, neo-Nazis, patriot groups, and skinhead groups. The most significant of these attacks was the 1995 bombing of the Alfred P. Murrah Federal Building in Oklahoma City, Oklahoma, which resulted in 168 deaths. The main perpetrator, Timothy McVeigh, did not see himself as a terrorist, but believed he was fighting government oppression. This is a theme used by a number of groups that have planned terrorist acts. Others are racially motivated against minorities.

Since the 9/11 attacks, there have been instances of homegrown Muslim terrorists. Some of these terrorists have attempted to commit terrorist acts in the United States, and others have traveled to Afghanistan and other Muslim countries to become terrorists. In 2010, Faisal Shahzad, a Pakistani American, parked an SUV loaded with explosives in Times Square in New York City. Although the bomb did not detonate, he was arrested and charged with attempting to use a weapon of mass destruction. Shahzad pled guilty and was sentenced to life in prison without parole. Anwar al-Awlaki, an American citizen born in New Mexico, was a radical Muslim imam located in Yemen. He advocated the destruction of the United States and exhorted American Muslims to attack the United States. He was a part of al Qaeda in Yemen and recruited new jihadists for the organization. He was associated with over a dozen conspiracies to commit attacks on U.S. soil. He was killed in Yemen by a U.S. drone attack in 2011. Since the 9/11 attacks, several cases of attempted terrorism have been bungled or thwarted by authorities. Such plots, because they always occur in a local community, affect local law enforcement.

Counterterrorism

Counterterrorism is the combined efforts of federal, state, and local law enforcement as well as homeland security agencies to uncover terrorists and their plots and to prevent attacks on U.S. soil and U.S. interests. Since the 9/11 attacks, there has been substantial government reorganization to facilitate counterterrorism. A number of agencies within the U.S. Department of Homeland Security as well as the Federal Bureau of Investigation (FBI) play an active role at the federal level. Local and state police agencies are also active in counterterrorism.

Joint Terrorism Task Forces

The Joint Terrorism Task Forces (JTTF) under the FBI counterterrorism division have primary responsibility for coordinating counterterrorism. The task forces consist of 18 federal agencies as well as state and local police representation. They operate in 100 U.S. cities and are based out of the FBI field offices. Personnel assigned to these offices include investigators, analysts, linguists, and SWAT experts.

The 9/11 Commission, which in 2004 released a report on the events leading up to the 9/11 terrorist attacks, was critical of U.S. intelligence operations for a lack of sharing information and coordinating activities. The JTTFs assist in reducing this problem. All the agencies assigned to the task forces bring their intelligence information to the table where it can be collated and compared to information from other member agencies. This allows for a more comprehensive view of activities and problems. Also, once information about a plot or activity is discovered, the information can flow horizontally and downward to agencies in the potentially affected areas. This top-down process helps to ensure that local authorities have information about potential terrorists and their plots.

Fusion Centers

Whereas the Joint Terrorism Task Forces operate at the national level, fusion centers are owned by state and local entities with funding support from the federal government and located in states and major urban areas throughout the country, for the receipt, analysis, gathering, and sharing of threat-related information between all levels of government. Primarily staffed by personnel with expertise in law enforcement, criminal intelligence, counter terrorism, military operations, counter-narcotics and international affairs, there are often representatives from a number of other areas such as emergency services, energy, hospitality and lodging,

telecommunications, private security, public works, real estate, transportation, and social services. All of these agencies can provide intelligence about attacks. Public health officials monitor trends in diseases and can recognize a biological attack should there be a sudden and substantial increase in a communicable disease. Private security officials can report suspicious activities around critical infrastructure that are potential terrorist targets. Real estate transfers can be monitored for suspicious purchases of homes and businesses. Businesses that sell precursor chemicals that can be used to make explosives can be monitored. Essentially, the fusion center allows for the surveillance and monitoring of a wide range of activities that potentially could be involved in terrorist plots.

Community Policing and Counterterrorism

The 9/11 attacks caused the police and the public to view with suspicion Arabs and Muslims in their communities. It was feared that there were numerous terrorist cells located in cities and towns across the United States. There was some discussion that the police should abandon community policing and move to an oppressive-tactics model so that the police could use intense investigations, traffic stops, field interrogations, and high-visibility law enforcement to ferret out terrorists. Some advocated that this style of law enforcement would be more effective in identifying terrorists.

However, this operational approach has been shown to be ineffective, especially when seeking from citizens information about crime and criminals. When citizens are exposed to oppressive police operations, they often develop negative attitudes toward the police and consequently are less likely to cooperate with them. Such tactics can curtail information flowing to the police.

To gain information from the public, police officers must have positive working relationships with the citizenry, an objective of community policing. Such relationships may result in citizens reporting suspicious persons and activities. For example, in 2008, the FBI arrested six radical Islamist men who were plotting an attack on soldiers at Fort Dix in New Jersey. The plot was uncovered when one of the men took a video of them practicing shooting their automatic weapons to a store to have the video converted to a DVD. The store clerk, upon watching the video, called the police, who later called in the FBI. The plot was uncovered as a result of a citizen providing key information to the police. The key to this public reporting is good relations between the police and public.

A number of departments have taken this a step further by appointing police liaisons who work with Arab and Muslim communities to establish better relations and possibly recruit Arab and Muslim citizens for the police force. As an example, the New York City Police Department started a cricket league. Cricket is a popular sport in many countries with large Muslim populations, including India and Pakistan. The cricket league was designed to improve relations with the Muslim community. Many people in Arab and Muslim communities immigrated to the United States from countries that had oppressive police forces, so they tend to be distrustful of the police. This means that departments must take extraordinary measures to develop more trust among these populations.

Public Education Programming

Police departments historically have used public education programs to inform the public about problems. There have been programs focusing on drugs, crimes, fraudulent activities aimed at the elderly, seatbelts, and driving under the influence, to name a few. Police departments can also initiate public education programs to encourage citizens to assist the police with identifying possible terrorists and suspicious activities. For example, because hotels have been the targets of terrorists, the "if you see something, say something" program has been implemented in a number of hotel chains. This program encourages staff to be more observant and report suspicious people and activities in hotels to police.

The police can also conduct such public education programs for the general public. The public can be educated on how to observe and survey their surroundings. They can be educated about which activities should be considered suspicious, especially with regard to possible terrorist activities. An education program can focus on the cues that terrorists might exhibit. Because citizens must know how to report a suspicious person or activity that they observe, reporting procedures are often part of public education programs. Such programs can result in the police receiving valuable counterterrorism information.

Community Partnerships

Another community policing strategy in counterterrorism is community partnerships. The first type is partnerships with citizens and businesses. In the past, most of these partnerships concentrated on addressing crime, including neighborhood watches and neighborhood police-citizen councils. Information on how to detect and report suspicious activity can be disseminated at these forums. Because terrorists typically will attempt to procure firearms or weapons of mass destruction, businesses that sell firearms or materials that can be used for weapons of mass destruction can become a focus. Such partnerships can substantially expand a police department's intelligence gathering.

The police can also focus on local industries that are possible terrorist targets, such as factories and public utilities. Industries often are considered dead zones in terms of police coverage and concerns because the police do not patrol these areas unless called. Such industries are largely self-sufficient, and their properties have private security apparatuses that include guards, access control, and cameras, all designed to keep people out. At the same time, though, these apparatuses can be used to observe people and activities in and around the area's perimeter. Security personnel who observe suspicious persons or activities are encouraged to report them to the police. This process can be facilitated by developing periodic meetings between police and security personnel. These meetings can serve to discuss suspicious persons and activities as well as operational tactics so that improvements can be passed to other security personnel. Police departments in Dallas, Texas, and Las Vegas, Nevada, currently have these types of partnerships.

Community Policing and Counterterrorism Intelligence

The joint terrorism task forces and fusion centers provide a structure for collating, analyzing, and disseminating terrorism intelligence information. As departments collect information, it is fed into the fusion centers and ultimately the joint terrorism task forces. However, community policing is an important tool at ground zero for collecting this information. Community policing is in a position to develop intelligence information because officers have substantially more contact with citizens and activities in their communities. If police have proper working relationships with citizens, citizens will provide them with needed information. This information is then forwarded to the department's crime analysis unit for analysis.

Crime analysis units collect information about people, activities, and events. These units maintain files on people and suspicious activities. As officers provide information, it is entered into these files. At some point, the sum of the information in the files begins to provide a better understanding of the what, when, where, and how crime. Once this occurs, the department can begin to focus on people and activities either to prevent a terrorist event or to collect more information. Community policing officers, as a result of their relations with the community, are in the best position to collect additional information. Thus, community policing plays an important role in developing leads about possible terrorist attacks.

Larry K. Gaines

See also Crime Analysis; Intelligence-Led Policing; Police-Community Relations; Terrorism, Future Impact of Community Policing on

Further Readings

Gaines, L. K., & Kappeler, V. E. (2012). *Homeland security.* Upper Saddle River, NJ: Prentice Hall.

Jenkins, B. M. (2010). *Would-be warriors: Incidents of jihadist terrorist radicalization in the United States since September 11, 2001.* Santa Monica, CA: RAND.

LaFree, G., & Dugan, L. (2009). Research on terrorism and countering terrorism. In M. Tonry (Ed.), *Crime and justice: A review of research* (Vol. 38; pp. 413–477). Chicago, IL: University of Chicago Press.

CP-SAT

See Community Policing Self-Assessment Tool

CRIME ANALYSIS

Crime analysis, the second stage of the SARA (scanning, analysis, response, assessment) problem-solving process, represents the heart of the process.

Comprehensively analyzing a problem is critical to the success of a problem-solving effort. Effective tailor-made responses cannot be developed unless people know what is causing the problem. Thus, the purpose of analysis is to learn as much as possible about problems in order to identify their causes; officers must gather information from sources inside and outside their agency about the scope, nature, and causes of problems.

Some people describe crime analysis as an art, others as a science, and still others as a discipline. Crime analysis can be any or all of these. Crime analysis is the study of crime trends and patterns, the art of turning data into information, and the practice of statistical, investigative, and problem-solving support.

The focus of crime analysis varies from one agency or jurisdiction to another, and from one crime analyst to another. This entry describes the evolution of crime analysis and then goes into more detail on the types of crime analysis, the many applications, and related technologies. This entry concludes with a discussion of the future of crime analysis. While crime analysis in general is discussed, the primary focus is specifically on crime analysis for community policing and problem solving.

One might be tempted to circumvent or give only passing attention to the analysis phase of the problem-solving process, believing that the nature of the problem is obvious, succumbing to pressure to quickly solve the problem, or feeling that the pressure of calls for service (CFS) precludes having time for detailed inquiries into the nature of the problem. However, as will be seen, problem solvers must resist these temptations or they risk addressing a problem that does not exist or implementing solutions that are ineffective in the long run.

Evolution

Crime analysis was first recognized as a discipline in England in the early 19th century with the advent of the first modern police force. The detectives were tasked with collecting, collating, and analyzing police information to help solve crimes. Early crime analysis, including pin mapping, began in the United States about a century later. The first major incentive driving crime analysis in U.S. police agencies came in the 1970s with funding provided by the Law Enforcement

Assistance Administration (LEAA). Federal grants allowed police departments to set up crime analysis units (often referred to as *Integrated Criminal Apprehension Program* units because of the LEAA program focus) as well as receive training and establish evaluation programs. A 2010 survey by the U.S. Department of Justice Bureau of Justice Statistics found that this is a growing field: While only 38% of all municipal police and county sheriff's agencies used crime analysis, 96% of all such agencies serving jurisdictions of more than 100,000 population did so; moreover, while only 27% of all such agencies employed crime mapping capabilities, 94% of these agencies serving jurisdictions of more than 100,000 population did so. Many police departments, primarily in rural areas or very small agencies, have not had the resources for crime analysis or exposure to the value of crime analysis.

Crime analysts may be situated in a variety of divisions within the department, including administration, investigations, technology, records, crime prevention, community or neighborhood policing, or as a stand-alone position. However, in many police departments, the majority of the officers, and many in the command staff, are not aware of where crime analysis fits in their agency. As a result of this confusion, crime analysts are often asked to wear a variety of hats. Crime analysts' responsibilities range from preparing administrative statistics to tactical bulletins, from creating crime prevention materials to maintaining an investigative database. Education and training backgrounds also vary greatly in the crime analysis field. Early analysts started as records clerks, dispatchers, or in other administrative positions, had no related higher education, and were promoted with on-the-job training. While a handful of analysts have doctoral degrees, the majority have a college education and an increasing number have master's degrees. However, as training and certification programs and college degrees focused on crime analysis have begun to develop, the field has begun to be populated with individuals who have more specialized knowledge of crime analysis, crime prevention, and the linked field of environmental criminology (the study of crime and victimization as they relate to particular places and how people conduct their activities and are influenced by place-based or spatial factors).

Classifications

Crime analysis generally includes four types of analysis—administrative, tactical, strategic, and operations. Problem analysis, a primary form for community policing and problem solving, is often categorized as a part of strategic analysis but has distinct differences applicable to community policing and problem solving. These are explained in the following subsections.

Administrative

Administrative analysis refers to the analysis of statistics used for weekly, monthly, quarterly, or annual reports. While administrative analysis is often done using crime or other police data, the products are not generally used for crime investigation, reduction, or prevention purposes. A common example of administrative analysis is the Uniform Crime Reports (UCR) that the Federal Bureau of Investigation (FBI) collects from law enforcement agencies annually. A similar report created by the FBI is the National Incident-Based Reporting System (NIBRS). The goal of NIBRS is to collect more detailed, incident-based data about each crime, rather than just overall counts. Most law enforcement agencies report UCR statistics, but many states and jurisdictions have chosen not to report to NIBRS until they have sufficient resources and abilities. In some police agencies, UCR reporting is administered through the crime analysis unit, while in others, the records unit is responsible.

Besides UCR/NIBRS reporting, there are a multitude of other types of administrative crime analyses. These might include examining the potential effect of a new shopping mall in the city or estimates on changes in crimes and calls for service for the city to annex an area. There may be a need for analysis for a demographic study, a grant application, or decisions on whether to issue alcohol licenses. Police agencies may also produce statistics, charts, and maps to distribute to the news media or to present to elected officials and community groups.

Tactical

In tactical analysis, analysts are looking to identify the offender, solve a series of crimes, or predict where the next crime may happen. It is the examination of who, what, when, where and how a crime or crimes have occurred. In smaller agencies, tactical analysis may include reading crime reports on a daily basis and entering information for certain crimes into a database. Jurisdictions with a great deal of daily crime have to rely more on technology and may only review reports that either come to the attention of an analyst or are a part of a series or pattern. Depending on the agency's records management system, some data may not be entered or there may not be the ability to extract all data needed for analysis. Key data for tactical analysis include crime type, date, time, location, victim and suspect information, and method of operation. Depending on the crimes that are tracked, or for a particular series or trend, other analysis data might be weapon, point of entry, drug type, security, surrounding area type, and vehicle descriptors.

Tactical analysis is important support for both patrol and investigations. Examples of tactical analysis products may be a map of a spike in vehicle burglaries on the graveyard shift, a bulletin about a recent spate of vandalism where there is suspect information, or a map and temporal chart depicting the most likely locations and times for the next fast-food restaurant robbery. Tactical analysis is focused on real-time, short-term crime problems, and having a variety of data sources readily available is important. While the focus is on solving the crime(s), data such as offender information (arrests, parolees/probationers, registrants, field interviews), vehicles (registration and photos), property information (type of property, ownership), and other relevant data are often included in the analysis products.

Operations

The study of police policies and practices is a type of analysis that is sometimes performed by crime analysis or another administrative support unit within the department. This may include resource allocation (e.g., patrol deployment, investigative assignments, and other staffing), response time studies, or redistricting (e.g., shifting the boundaries of the beats). The internal data to be analyzed may come from the records management system (RMS), computer-aided dispatch (CAD) system, or other files such as patrol logs, investigator case-tracking systems, or databases developed for specific purposes, such as an officer-involved shooting database.

Depending on the need, external data may also be integrated. For instance, for patrol deployment, census and land use data would be incorporated. Some operations analyses may be conducted annually and some projects may arise on an as-needed basis.

Strategic/Problem Solving

Strategic/problem-solving analysis relates to longer-term crime and disorder issues. The study of these broader issues is often based on criminological theory with a focus on environmental criminology. These environmental criminology theories—rational choice, routine activity, crime pattern, repeat victimization, and situational crime prevention—have a huge influence on how data are analyzed, how crime problems are assessed and responded to, and how crime reduction and prevention efforts are undertaken. Problem analysis requires knowledge of not only crime trends in the jurisdiction but also knowledge of what works in policing, research and evaluation skills, and the ability to communicate with diverse audiences. Problem analysis is the one type of crime analysis that requires the analyst to get out from behind the computer in order to be effective.

Crime analysts have conducted analysis for problem solving since Herman Goldstein wrote the seminal book *Problem-Oriented Policing* in 1990. But, the subdiscipline of problem analysis was really defined with the publishing of Ronald Clarke and John Eck's *Crime Analysis for Problem Solvers in 60 Small Steps* in 2005. A definition of *problem analysis* is as follows: process conducted within a police agency in which formal criminal justice theories, research methods, and comprehensive data collection and analysis procedures are used in a systematic way to conduct in-depth examination of, develop informed responses to, and evaluate crime and disorder problems. This definition greatly expands the role of the crime analyst.

Strategic/problem-solving analysis uses crime and other policing data, but in different ways than tactical, operations, and administrative analysis. One major difference is the need for long-term (e.g., at least one year but preferably more) data to determine if the problem is a persistent one. Instead of querying a database for individual people or crimes, incidents (e.g., crimes, calls for service, or complaints) are analyzed for trends over time. For instance, through administrative analysis, one might see that violent crimes are higher for the current year than the previous year. Problem analysis starts by drilling down with the goal of identifying the underlying causes—first looking at just the robberies, then commercial versus residential versus street, then within each of these subcategories. In this regard, one might detect that within commercial robberies, convenience store robberies are causing this upward trend. Once the specific crime problem has been identified, further analysis will begin to reveal why certain convenience stores are getting robbed at a higher rate than others.

Analysis of a convenience store robbery problem goes beyond looking at the total statistics and making a map of the incident locations. Problem analysis relies on theories and evidence about what is known regarding this crime problem. One needs to look not just at aspects of the criminal incidents, such as suspect and victim characteristics, but at factors surrounding the crime. For a thorough analysis of a problem, primary data collection is a necessity. One might examine land use, lighting, street access, and convenience stores that have not been robbed. Problem analysis also includes analyzing all sides of the "crime triangle": What is known about offenders, victims, and locations for this problem? What other questions can be answered? One aspect of the analysis is to examine repeat victims and places to determine how closely the problem fits the 80–20 rule (where 20% of criminals account for 80% of crime). In the convenience store example, it is likely that a small percentage of stores or locations account for the majority of the robberies. Further analysis needs to be done on the top locations versus the locations with no or low numbers of robberies to determine why these places are higher risk.

A common means of primary data collection are surveys and interviews. If the problem is place based, environmental surveys can be conducted to collect data on possible contributing factors. Interviews or surveys can also be done of stakeholders, victims, and offenders. Once all of the data are collected regarding offenders, victims, and locations, the data can then be analyzed. Problem analysis is not a simple, quick, or easy process. Thorough problem analysis requires multiple people, data, and discussions in order to identify the underlying causes of the problem as well as the most effective responses and how best to assess the overall effort at reducing or eliminating the problem. Aspects of problem analysis are often applied within an overall policing strategy.

Applications

Crime analysis has been used in many different policing philosophies and strategies. From its initial application to investigations and solving crimes and reporting statistics, crime analysis is now well integrated into many of the strategies being practiced by police departments in the 21st century. Some of the more common ones include CompStat, predictive policing, intelligence-led policing, community policing, and problem-oriented policing. All have different foci but share the "data-driven" feature. How crime analysis is applied for each varies widely across departments. At the minimum, crime analysts are collating data and producing maps and reports. The other end of the spectrum has crime analysts as leading members of problem-solving teams.

For community policing and problem solving, crime analysis techniques and processes can be integrated at many levels. Crime analysis can identify problems and assist with collecting data, analyzing the data, helping inform the team on the best responses, and assessing the results of problem-solving efforts. Crime analysis is important in producing and sharing information with stakeholders, both internal and external to the department. Crime analysis may play a role in creating new databases, developing surveys, and partnering with outside evaluators.

While crime analysis has generally been associated with local policing agencies, an increasing number of other criminal justice agencies as well as other governmental agencies are applying aspects of crime analysis. One can now find crime analysts in prosecutors' offices, state correctional departments, and community supervision agencies. There are aspects of crime analysis being performed in nonprofit agencies as well as major commercial organizations. City and state governments have adopted versions of CompStat and community policing. Looking at crime and disorder trends with stakeholders throughout the jurisdiction is an effective way of reducing and preventing crime.

Data and Technologies

Crime analysis could not occur without data, and technology has enhanced crime analysis efficiency and effectiveness immensely. There are a wide variety of databases and information technology for crime analysis as well as tools that can be used to conduct analysis.

Data and Information Technology

Almost all police agencies have the aforementioned computer-aided dispatch (CAD) and records management system (RMS). This is often the basis for the data that is analyzed—calls for service and crime incidents and arrests. Additionally, there may be a number of other local and state crime-related databases that can be accessed for analysis. At the state level, this includes databases for traffic crash data, parolees, sex offenders, and other registrants. Locally, probation and prosecution agencies have their own databases, and a growing number of jurisdictions have automated vehicle locator (AVL) databases, global positioning system (GPS) offender tracking, license plate readers, and closed-circuit television video (CCTV).

In addition to the typical crime-related databases, a wealth of other data are available to help in crime analysis. Many of these come from noncriminal justice government agencies. These include, but are not limited to, fire or emergency medical service, tax assessor, land use, census, department of motor vehicles, street lights, parks, schools, and health and human services (e.g., clinics, shelters, halfway houses). Relevant data also exist in a wide variety of nongovernmental venues, such as business associations (e.g., retail, motel, pharmacy, and restaurant), community organizations, and neighborhood groups.

As police departments implement these new technologies, crime analysis can go beyond using the information solely for investigations and take advantage of the wealth of data that are collected to map and analyze contributing factors. A vital aspect of crime analysis for community policing and problem solving is having the right data to better understand the underlying causes of the specific crime or disorder problem.

Crime Analysis Tools

Crime analysis tools include investigative tools, geographic information systems (GIS), spreadsheets, and link analysis (i.e., analysis using sophisticated software that examines large amounts of seemingly independent and unrelated data into a more connected, cogent product and is particularly helpful with crimes involving counterterrorism, organized crime, and drugs). Most crime analysis functions can be accomplished with the most basic spreadsheet, database, and GIS tools. Some agencies also utilize graphical user interfaces (GUI) or custom applications to assist with repetitive tasks and products. These tools may be free of cost to a police agency because they were either developed with government funding or offered at no cost by the developer, or they can cost hundreds of thousands of dollars. With the growth of Internet technology, new tools have arisen to collect data from the public, such as crime reports or complaints of abandoned vehicles and graffiti and to make and share crime maps. Crime analysis tools can help make a crime analyst's job easier, but the most important thing is to truly understand the data and the outputs from the tools that are being provided to officers and the public.

Future of Crime Analysis

Crime analysis is still an evolving field. The type and amount of resources available for crime analysts has grown exponentially. From the 2,100-member International Association of Crime Analysts, which offers training, certification, website resources, and an active listserv to the Center for Problem-Oriented Policing, which provides a wealth of guidebooks and tools to aid problem analysis, crime analysts are supported extensively in their endeavors. As the policing field increasingly moves toward being data driven and problem oriented, the reliance on crime analysis will likely be expanded and accepted.

Julie D. Wartell

See also CompStat; Crime Analysts, Roles of; Crime Displacement; Crime Mapping; Global Positioning Systems/Geographic Information Systems; Hot Spots; Predictive Policing; Problem Analysis Triangle; Problem-Solving Process (SARA)

Further Readings

Boba, R. (2003). *Problem analysis in policing.* Washington, DC: Police Foundation.

Clarke, R. V., & Eck, J. E. (2005). *Crime analysis for problem solvers in 60 small steps.* Washington, DC: U.S. Department of Justice, Office of Community Oriented Policing Services.

Goldstein, H. (1990). *Problem-oriented policing*. New York, NY: McGraw-Hill.

Gwinn, S., Bruce, C., Cooper, J., & Hick, S. (Eds.). (2011). *Exploring crime analysis: Readings on essential skills* (2nd ed.). Overland Park, KS: International Association of Crime Analysts.

Jones, G., & Molina, M. (2011). *Crime analysis case studies*. Washington, DC: U.S. Department of Justice, Office of Community Oriented Policing Services.

Ratcliffe, J. H. (2008). *Intelligence-led policing*. Cullompton, England: Willan.

Reaves, B. A. (2010, December). *Local police departments, 2007*. NCJ 231174. Washington, DC: U.S. Department of Justice, Bureau of Justice Statistics. Retrieved from http://bjs.ojp.usdoj.gov/content/pub/pdf/lpd07.pdf

Santos, R. B. (2012) *Crime analysis with crime mapping* (3rd ed.). Thousand Oaks, CA: Sage.

Schmerler, K., & Velasco, M. (2002). Primary data collection: A problem solving necessity. *Crime Mapping News, 4*(2), 4–8.

White, M. (2008). *Enhancing the problem-solving capacity in crime analysis units*. Washington, DC: U.S. Department of Justice, Office of Community Oriented Policing Services. Retrieved from http://www.cops.usdoj.gov/Publications/e020827126.txt

CRIME ANALYSTS, ROLES OF

Crime analysts have served many roles in a policing agency. Crime analysts may do statistical reporting, tactical and strategic analysis, investigative support, crime scene diagramming and link analysis charts, crime research, and everything in between. Crime analysts also play an integral role in community policing and problem solving through their roles as data managers and analysts, as researchers, and as members on the problem-solving team. This entry introduces the various roles of crime analysts and then goes into more detail on the roles of analysts for community policing and problem-solving agencies. The entry concludes with a discussion of the future roles of crime analysts in policing.

Traditional Roles

The three types of crime analysis that predominate in policing are administrative, tactical, and strategic. Within these categories, crime analysts perform many varied roles. An analyst in a smaller agency often has to fill all of these roles, perhaps even within the same day at the office. While most analysts are cross-trained to perform all of these roles, in large departments they may specialize and spend most of their time on only one of them. This may be determined by where they are located within the agency's organizational structure (e.g., chief's office versus patrol or investigative division), the most frequent consumers of crime analysis products in their agency (i.e., management, community policing officers, or detectives), their skills, or any combination of the above.

When crime analysts are in the role of *administrative analyst*, they are generally conducting tallies of crime and arrest reports, calls for service, workload analysis, or other administrative statistics. Because every law enforcement agency is obligated to provide Uniform Crime Reports data to the FBI, oftentimes this responsibility falls on the crime analyst who is most familiar with the data and may be already doing similar monthly or quarterly reports for the police chief or sheriff.

The role of *tactical analyst* has become common in the past two decades, as analysts play a larger role in identifying crime patterns, trends, and series to support both patrol officers as well as investigators. The role of the crime analyst in the performance of *strategic analysis* varies widely. This may include working on long-term problems, assisting with research projects, technology acquisition, or organizational change issues. Strategic analyst is the role that is most closely related to the role of analyst as a problem solver.

Another role that may arise for crime analysts is that of *intelligence analyst*. Intelligence analysts were predominantly in federal and state agencies and task forces until September 11, 2001. With the substantial increase in funding and focus on homeland security, many local police agencies created and hired "intel" analysts to work at fusion centers (entities located in states and major urban areas throughout the country, and deal with the receipt, analysis, gathering, and sharing of threat-related information across all levels of government) as well as within city and county agencies. Crime analysts may serve an intelligence-gathering role in some agencies, focusing on organized crime, terrorism, or homeland security; however, to date they have not been involved with community policing and problem solving.

Analysts as Problem Solvers

In 2005, the U.S. Department of Justice's Office of Community Oriented Policing and the Center for

Problem-Oriented Policing published Clarke and Eck's *Crime Analysis for Problem Solvers in 60 Small Steps*. This seminal book defined, expanded, and enhanced the role of the crime analyst—namely as someone who is integral to community policing and problem solving. The very first step in the manual is "Rethink your job." While crime analysts are often serving in whatever role their immediate supervisor, manager, or chief thinks they should be doing, the idea of rethinking the role is important not just for the analyst, but for the entire agency. As the authors noted, this role includes the following:

- Becoming a crime expert
- Knowing what works in policing
- Promoting problem solving
- Taking your place on the project team
- Learning about environmental criminology (the study of crime as it relates to opportunity and place)
- Honing your research skills
- Communicating effectively
- Enhancing your profession

Analysts may do some of these for their roles in administrative, tactical, and strategic analysis, but one needs to be able to do all of these to be a successful problem-solving analyst. Much like investigators specialize in a type of crime, analysts should gather expertise on the long-term, persistent crime problems on which they are working. For instance, if a jurisdiction is experiencing a problem with vehicle thefts, the role of the crime analyst is to know not only who, what, where and when, but also why (specifically for that jurisdiction's problem), what works to reduce vehicle theft, and who has done similar work. This also relates to knowing the theories and application of environmental criminology and related research. Understanding situational crime prevention approaches (i.e., strategies to increase the perceived risk or decrease the perceived benefit) is greatly beneficial for creating effective responses to the problem.

Policing agencies that are using the SARA model (scanning, analysis, response, assessment) for problem solving can benefit greatly from their crime analysts' efforts. While many agencies and analysts see their role in problem solving as the SARA *analysis* phase, analysts can also play a role in *scanning* (helping to identify underlying problems), *response*

(knowing what works and which are the most effective strategies), and *assessment* (measuring if what the problem-solving effort set out to accomplish was indeed accomplished). This expanded role of the crime analyst requires leaving the computer and collecting primary data, interacting with stakeholders, and being an active part of the problem-solving team. These "new" activities may be a challenge for some analysts; in addition, sworn personnel may not be as comfortable with crime analysts in this role. Crime analyst problem solvers may have to take the initiative in integrating their role into the larger process, including proactively participating in meetings, offering expertise beyond just making a map or charts, and getting out in the field with the officers to better understand the problem.

In the problem-solver role, analysts should be comfortable speaking to a room full of police officers, police managers, or community members about what they have learned about the problem from the analysis and suggested responses. Analysts should also be able to present the information to a room full of analysts or researchers with more technical results or questions for discussion. While crime analysts are playing a supporting role in problem solving throughout the country, most "successes" that are publicized still relate to apprehending offenders, not long-term problem-solving efforts. As the crime analysis profession continues to mature, the enhanced role of the crime analyst should also be reflected in future presentations, publications, and policing practice.

The Analyst of the Future

The role of the crime analyst—from analyzer of statistics to creator of link analysis charts to conductor of surveys—has evolved immensely since the position initially began to appear in law enforcement agencies in the late 1970s. The field has evolved from police personnel affixing pins in maps to show locations of crimes, to highly complex spatial analysis; from reporting on how many incidents happened last month to predicting when and where a crime is likely to show up next; and from producing charts for officers to leading problem-solving efforts. Although technology can greatly enhance the many roles of the crime analyst, the analyst's critical thinking, research and communication skills, and effective use of the technology are vital to problem solving and effective crime prevention and reduction. The crime analyst of the future will need to be astute to the research on what works and doesn't work in policing, intelligent about when and how to implement the most effective technologies, and able to work as part of a problem-solving team.

Julie D. Wartell

See also CompStat; Crime Analysis; Crime Displacement; Crime Mapping; Global Positioning Systems/ Geographic Information Systems; Hot Spots; Non-sworn Personnel and Volunteers, Use and Training of; Predictive Policing; Problem Analysis Triangle; Problem-Solving Process (SARA); Situational Crime Prevention

Further Readings

Clarke, R. V., & Eck, J. E. (2009). *Crime analysis for problem solvers in 60 small steps.* Washington, DC: U.S. Department of Justice, Office of Community Oriented Policing Services.

Gwinn, S., Bruce, C., Cooper, J., & Hick, S. (Eds.). (2011). *Exploring crime analysis: Readings on essential skills* (2nd ed.). Overland Park, KS: International Association of Crime Analysts.

White, M. B. (2008). *Enhancing the problem-solving capacity of crime analysis units.* Washington, DC: U.S. Department of Justice, Office of Community Oriented Policing Services. Retrieved from http://www.cops.usdoj .gov/Publications/e020827126.txt

CRIME DISPLACEMENT

One of the hallmarks of community policing efforts has been the focus of police resources on those locations most in need of policing services. The hope is that focusing on those locations most in need of police services will lead to a reduction in crime. Research has consistently shown that there are a small number of locations, often called *hot spots*, where crime occurs and that consume the vast majority of police services. Once these hot spots are identified, place-based interventions are used to combat the crime problem at these locations. Researchers have determined that these place-based interventions can often successfully reduce crime in these hot spots, although there is concern that crime may simply be displaced to other locations. In other words, the place-based intervention produces a false positive benefit, but the crime problem has not been resolved. This entry discusses the related concepts of displacement and diffusion of benefits associated with place-based interventions and examines the prevalence of each of these effects. The entry then concludes with the newest methods for examining potential crime displacement effects.

Types of Displacement

Crime displacement represents an offender's natural adaptation to place-based policing interventions to avoid detection. There are six recognized types of displacement that can occur:

1. *Temporal*—Offenders choose to commit crimes at a different time, such as avoiding police presence that is limited to a particular time of day.

2. *Tactical*—Offenders switch tactics to avoid detection, such as switching from selling drugs in open-air markets to selling inside of a dwelling.

3. *Target*—Offenders switch targets to avoid detection, such as switching from burglarizing single-family homes to apartments.

4. *Types of crime*—Offenders choose to commit a new type of crime, such as switching from burglarizing residences to businesses.

5. *Perpetrator*—Offenders that are arrested are replaced by new offenders, such as arrested drug dealers from a gang being replaced by other members of the gang.

6. *Spatial*—Offenders choose to offend in locations outside of the police intervention, such as prostitutes moving to different street corners not being watched by the police.

The most frequent concern of place-based policing interventions has been spatial displacement, and as such has been the most frequently researched type of displacement.

From a criminological perspective, displacement should be a concern of researchers and practitioners who are examining place-based policing interventions. Deterministic theories of crime causation, those that state crime is the product of some characteristic of the offender (e.g., subcultural values, lack of self-control, strain), suggest that displacement is an inevitable consequence of place-based policing initiatives. According to these theories of crime, removing the opportunity to commit crime does not resolve the underlying characteristic of the offender. As such, the offender will either commit crime regardless of the police presence and be detected or continue to look for an opportunity to commit crime that will be less likely to result in detection. When crime is examined from the rational choice perspective, displacement becomes a concern because offenders will make rationally bound decisions about offending based on perceptions of risk and reward. Both of these explanations suggest the crucial nature of examining potential displacement effects associated with place-based policing interventions.

Since the development of the concept of crime displacement in the late 1970s, a number of research studies have looked for the existence and extent of crime displacement associated with place-based policing initiatives. The earliest research studies confirmed the existence of crime displacement, although the results were highly questionable due to the difficulty in measuring the problem. Reviews of the displacement literature have routinely suggested that displacement should indeed be a concern for criminological researchers, although the effects may have been exaggerated. Two independent reviews of displacement literature conducted in the early 1990s suggested that in the vast majority of research studies there was little to no evidence of displacement. In the remainder of studies, there was some evidence of displacement, although there were few studies that showed substantial amounts of crime displacement. All the studies reviewed showed no examples of complete displacement, where all of the crime is displaced in one of the six forms mentioned above.

A more recent review of the displacement literature suggests that the results of place-based and hot spot initiatives may be even more promising than originally anticipated. This analysis focused on studies that had been recently conducted using improved technology and more standardized operational measures of displacement. The results again suggest that displacement was observed in about one in every four studies. Importantly, the results suggested that when displacement did occur, the amount of crime displaced was less than the amount of crime reduced in the target area. These results suggest that the early critics of place-based policing interventions may have been overly pessimistic.

The displacement of crime need not be viewed exclusively as a negative consequence of place-based interventions. Crime displacement can be either benign or malign. *Benign displacement* refers to examples where crime has indeed been displaced with one of the six methods specified above; however, the effects of this displaced crime are less harmful to the community than the original type of crime. For example, interventions can spatially or temporally displace prostitutes to work in locations or at times of day that are less harmful to the community. Additionally, benign displacement could force armed robbers to begin committing burglaries instead. Although burglary is harmful to the community, armed robbery is more harmful because it is more likely to involve violence. In both scenarios, the crime problem has been displaced, although the displaced crime is not as bad as the original crime.

The second type of displacement, *malign displacement*, suggests that crime displacement has an adverse effect greater than the original crime targeted. This would be the case if, for example, open air drug markets are displaced from a downtown street corner to an area that is proximate to schools. The spatial displacement of the drug market from the street corner to the school is seen as an adverse consequence associated with the place-based intervention. Both benign and malign displacement are undesirable; however, malign displacement is of greater concern to researchers and law enforcement officials alike.

Diffusion of Benefits

Early on in the research into place-based policing initiatives, researchers realized that there could be types of displacement that were not considered adverse to place-based interventions. Early researchers were referring to a type of positive displacement in which the crime control benefits of the place-based intervention extended beyond the target area. A number of early researchers noted the potential phenomenon and termed it the *free rider effect*, the *bonus effect*, and the *halo effect*. The idea behind all of these terms suggests the positive nature of the intervention permeating into areas not specifically targeted, a process that has formally become known as the *diffusion of benefits*.

There are two types of diffusion of benefits processes that can be observed: deterrent and discouragement. Deterrent diffusion of benefits processes works by increasing the perception of risk for offenders in a given situation. In essence, offenders are deterred from committing crime because of fears of detection and apprehension by police in the area. The second type of diffusion of benefits process, discouragement, relies upon alteration of the perceived effort necessary or rewards to be collected. In other words, discouragement works by making offenders think that more effort will need to be expended or less reward will be obtained in the commission of the crime. Although there is a fundamental difference between the diffusion of benefits processes, both seem to work equally well at preventing crime.

Research investigating the diffusion of benefits of place-based crime control initiatives suggests the process behaves similarly to traditional crime displacement processes. Specifically, recent research finds that in approximately one in four studies there is evidence of diffusion of benefits processes. In essence, one in every four place-based initiatives will significantly decrease crime in areas that are not targeted with the intervention. Researchers have long been calling for more research on the diffusion of benefits processes; compared to crime displacement very little is known about the phenomenon. Currently, researchers are not certain whether diffusion of benefits processes are the result of a specific part of a place-based initiative or something unrelated to the intervention. Some have suggested that in order to maximize the potential diffusion of benefits effects associated with a place-based intervention, researchers should randomly vary the level of enforcement. The thought is that if the levels of enforcement are randomly varied, offenders will consistently overestimate the risk of detection at any given moment. However, this notion remains unsubstantiated.

The Future of Crime Displacement Research

Despite the evidence that suggests fears of crime displacement may have been exaggerated in the past, the concept of displacement and diffusion of benefits have become staples of place-based policing strategies. Furthermore, place-based policing strategies have become a staple of community policing programs and now represent an effective tool to combat crime. Therefore, crime displacement is a concept that will remain important in the research and practitioner literature. As such, new tools and approaches need to be designed to effectively measure and detect crime displacement when it occurs.

One of the common critiques of early displacement literature was the notoriously difficult nature of accurately measuring displacement. Although all types of crime displacement are difficult to measure, the difficulties in measurement of spatial displacement have been repeatedly highlighted. The focus on spatial displacement stems from the concerns that it is the most problematic type of displacement. In fact, the majority of studies examining crime displacement have focused on spatial displacement, and many of the early studies relied upon a variety of different measures for detecting spatial displacement. Early on in displacement research, the most rigorous studies relied on comparing control areas to areas where interventions were introduced. Although this method is superior to the methods previously introduced, it still suffers from a number of problems that pose serious threats to the validity of the study being conducted. Chief among these problems are identifying a priori where crime will be displaced.

In the early 2000s, researchers from the United Kingdom addressed the issues associated with measuring spatial displacement through the creation of the *weighted displacement quotient*. Unlike previous measures, the weighted displacement quotient was designed to estimate the amount of displacement or diffusion of benefits from a place-based intervention using three concentric zones that were defined by researchers. In the center zone, Zone A, researchers could measure the amount of crime in a specific geographical area before and after an intervention. The next zone out, Zone B, completely surrounds Zone A and is the place where crime is most likely to be spatially displaced by an intervention. The third and final zone, Zone C, represents a control area that completely surrounds Zone B. The thought is that Zone C crime levels should remain unchanged by an intervention due to its distal location to Zone A; however, Zone C was a good control area because it allowed for a control area that was spatially proximal to Zone A and thus would have similar crime rates to Zone A. The size of each zone can be varied according to the needs of the researcher, but typically the distances are based on what is termed the *distance-decay function*, which refers to the belief that a relationship exists between the distance from an offender's home to a potential target location—specifically, that most crimes are committed nearer rather than farther from the criminals' own homes because the costs to the criminal in terms of time, energy, and money increases with distance. The size of Zone B, the buffer zone, should be selected based on the likely travel patterns of the offender.

The specific math used in calculating the weighted displacement quotient is outside the scope of this entry; however, it is noteworthy to mention the ease with which the value is interpreted. The weighted displacement quotient will always yield a value between −1 and +1. The closer the value is to −1 suggests that the displacement effects exceeded the crime reduction benefits of the intervention. The closer the value is to +1 suggests the diffusion of benefits effects were greater than the direct effect of the intervention. In essence, the buffer zone saw greater decreases in crime than did the target area. A value close to 0 suggests that there was no displacement or diffusion of benefits effects noted in the research. It is important to note that the weighted displacement quotient only examines the displacement effects of the intervention, not whether crime was reduced in the target area.

The weighted displacement quotient has become the gold standard for measuring spatial displacement. The strength of the measure over previous methods, in addition to relative ease of calculation and interpretation, have aided in the success of the measure. Additionally, results from those studies that have used the weighted displacement quotient have yielded results that are substantively similar to previous studies. Essentially, spatial crime displacement occurs with regularity; however, the effects of the displacement are rarely substantial in magnitude. Furthermore, diffusion of benefits also occurs with regularity; however, the crime reductions in other areas are rarely as large as the reductions in the target area.

Jon Maskaly

See also Crime Analysis; Crime Mapping; Hot Spots, Place-Based Policing; Predictive Policing

Further Readings

Barnes, G. (1995). Defining and optimizing displacement. In J. E. Eck & D. L. Weisburd (Eds.), *Crime and place.* Crime Prevention Studies (Vol. 4). Monsey, NY: Criminal Justice Press.

Bowers, K. J., & Johnson, S. D. (2003). Measuring the geographical displacement and diffusion of benefit effects of crime prevention activity. *Journal of Quantitative Criminology, 19*(3), 275–301.

Bowers, K. J., Johnson, S. D., Guerette, R. T., Summers, L., & Poynton, S. (2011). Spatial displacement and diffusion of benefits among geographically focused policing initiatives. *Journal of Experimental Criminology, 7*(4), 347–374. doi: 10.4073/csr.2011.3

Braga, A. A., Weisburd, D. L., Waring, E. J., Green, L., Spelman, W., & Gajewski, F. (1999). Problem-oriented policing in violent crime places: A randomized controlled experiment. *Criminology, 37*, 541–580. doi: 10.1111/j.1745-9125.1999.tb00496

Clarke, R. V. (2000). Situational crime prevention: Successful studies. In R. W. Glensor, M. E. Correia, & K. J. Peak (Eds.), *Policing communities: Understanding crime and solving problems: An anthology* (pp. 182–225). Los Angeles, CA: Roxbury.

Clarke, R. V., & Weisburd, D. L. (1994). Diffusion of crime control benefits: Observations on the reverse of displacement. In R. V. Clarke (Ed.), *Crime Prevention Studies* (Vol. 3; pp. 165–183). Monsey, NY: Criminal Justice Press.

Eck, J. E. (1993, Summer). The threat of crime displacement. *Problem Solving Quarterly, 6*(3), 1–2.

Hesseling, R. B. P. (1995). Displacement: A review of the empirical literature. In R. V. Clarke (Ed.), *Crime Prevention Studies* (Vol. 3; pp.197–230). New York, NY: Criminal Justice Press.

Repetto, T. A. (1974). *Residential crime.* Cambridge, MA: Ballinger.

Weisburd, D. L., & Green, L. (1995). Measuring immediate spatial displacement: Methodological issues and problems. In J. E. Eck & D. L. Weisburd (Eds.), *Crime and place.* Crime Prevention Studies (Vol. 4; pp. 349–361). Monsey, NY: Criminal Justice Press.

CRIME MAPPING

Crime mapping is the process of taking events and displaying them spatially across a certain geographic space. It allows the user a different perspective on crime and disorder problems as events can be seen in the context of social spaces, geographic clusters, and temporal variations. Crime mapping has evolved from simply plotting criminal incidents on a paper map with pins to complex analysis techniques that allow the prediction of future crime locations. Researchers and police officials have also seen the benefit of mapping not only crime, but other geographical elements which help paint a fuller picture of the underlying criminal phenomenon. Mapping is an important adjunct to community policing and problem because it allows analysts to map, visualize, and examine patterns of crime. This entry discusses the development, mechanics, and many applications of crime mapping as it serves to inform crime analysis.

Advent of Crime Mapping

The use of crime mapping or looking at incidents in a geographic space has been a popular tool in the social sciences. In the 1920s and 1930s, sociologists in Chicago examined the impact of social disorganization on crime rates and used geographic analysis to show how different sections of the city experienced differing crime rates based on their poverty levels. It became clear that looking at social problems and their eventual solutions from a spatial perspective was an additional tool that researchers, city planners, and law enforcement agencies could adopt. In policing circles, before the advent of computers, police officials would use color-coded pins to identify crime locations on a paper city map.

Over time, police officials could discern whether there were patterns in certain neighborhoods, whether crime migrated from one area to the next, or whether a police response had the desired effect of reducing crime in a particular neighborhood. During the early 1990s, the paper map and color-coded pins in the chief's office were replaced by computer screens, keyboards, and databases. The advent of computerization and technology would allow crime mapping to enter its next phase and become the scientific, accurate, and predictive tool it is today. Technological innovations in policing include mobile data terminals (MDTs), computer mainframes, easily accessible desktop software, client/server technology, for example. The MDTs installed in patrol cars allow for the sharing of information among dispatchers, officers on patrol, and citizens requesting police assistance. All of this information is stored on departmental computer mainframes and is now easily accessible using desktop software.

Crime Mapping Mechanics

Computerized crime mapping relies on geographic information systems (GIS) software. There are several out-of-the-box packages available to the public, and there are more elaborate mainframe systems for large agencies to consider. Most police departments can use desktop GIS programs that are connected to the various databases created by the police department. Spatial analysis programs operate by allowing the user to overlay different layers of data or information on a virtual or computerized map. The map usually represents the jurisdiction, with a street network and other geographic attributes such as parks, water features, and major roads and highways. The user can rely on numerous different types of maps, ranging from the city level, the county level, the state level, the national level, all the way up to the international level. Most police agencies, however, will rely on the city level or the county level to plot and analyze their data.

The geographic map is the initial layer that is represented when using a GIS program. It is also known as the *base map*. Base maps can be obtained from other municipal agencies such as the planning bureau or the engineering department, or they can be purchased from private companies that specialize in creating these geographic layers. Modern advances in computerized cartography now allow police agencies to purchase city maps based on satellite photos that depict, with photo quality, all the different geographic aspects of their jurisdictions.

Geocoding

Once the base map is displayed on the computer screen, the user imports different data sets (e.g., calls for service or incident reports) and overlays each type of data onto the geographic base map. The merging of the two layers (the event layer and the geographic layer) is achieved through a process called *geocoding*, whereby each event's location is matched to the location on the base map. Geocoding is a crucial step in crime mapping because an event that does not have a designated location or address field cannot be plotted onto the base map, resulting in missing data.

Crime mapping relies on accurate data collection, proper report writing, and constant vigilance by law enforcement officers. As a rule, most crime mapping efforts will report the geocoding rate of a map representing crime events to indicate the level of missing data (e.g., a geocoding rate of 80% tells the map reader that 20% of the incidents in the original database were not able to be plotted on the map and interpretations of the displayed data need to take that into account).

Modern crime mapping programs are able to display numerous data layers simultaneously, allowing the user an unlimited arena when it comes to analyzing crime trends and patterns. Perhaps the most operationally useful tool in most crime mapping programs is the ability to query the spatially plotted events. For instance, after having plotted a year's worth of robberies on a map, a crime analyst or police officer can query this map by creating a new layer showing only the robberies occurring on Saturdays between 1 a.m. and 3 a.m. and involving the use of a weapon. With this ability to refine data, analysts and crime mappers are able to examine the spatial distribution of very specific crime types.

Other Considerations

Crime mapping's visual representation can sometimes be misleading or factually inaccurate. It is up to the map creator to divulge all of the relevant methodological constraints and decisions encountered while creating the map. For example, the scale or size of the icons selected to represent criminal incidents can be misleading to the uninitiated eyes. Oversized red dots can lead the map reader to conclude that there is a severe crime problem, whereas a smaller icon size might lead them to a different conclusion.

Another consideration is to make sure that the right type of symbology is applied to crime maps. If a map creator wants to show the concentration of crime in an area, a simple dot map will not suffice because incidents occurring in the same location will only be displayed as a single dot when they are overlaid on top of each other. In this case, a map with graduated symbols, or even a density map may be more appropriate.

Types of Police Data Commonly Mapped

Calls for Service

Generally, police agencies produce three main types of data. The first is calls for service, which are usually requests from local residents for police assistance. An officer may also generate a call for service by letting the dispatcher know that officer encountered a situation which requires assistance. The majority of calls for service are resolved informally or found to be without cause; hence, most calls to

the police do not produce a formal incident report. Mapping calls for service remains a good way to measure police activity and the type of demands the local population expects from their law enforcement agency. By mapping calls, law enforcement officials can allocate resources differentially based on need, and police resources can be targeted to certain neighborhoods that produce a disproportionate number of calls for service.

Incident Data

The second type of police data is known as incident data, which represent events deemed serious enough by the police to be documented in a formal incident report. For example, if a victim claims to have been robbed and the police determine that a robbery did in fact occur, then an incident report is filed. If there is insufficient evidence of a claim, then no report is filed. Mapping incidents is a good way to represent the true crime picture of an area or jurisdiction. Law enforcement officials can get a visual snapshot of where crime occurs in a given timeframe. As discussed below, crime mapping allows map creators to plot incidents based on different characteristics and police agencies can choose to focus on victims, offenders, or problem locations.

Arrest Data

The third type of police data is known as arrest data and represents the information gathered when an individual is taken into police custody. Arrest data usually includes information about the crime type, demographics about the offender and the victim, the location of the crime, and other contextual data such as time of day, weather conditions, or whether the victim and offender knew each other. Mapping arrest data allows police officials to determine many aspects of offender behaviors. Mapping the location of an offender's home versus the arrest location can provide the police valuable information concerning the offender's journey to crime. Officials can also examine repeat arrestees to see whether they are rearrested for similar offenses, whether they are arrested in similar areas, or to measure the length of time between each arrest.

Approaches to Crime Mapping

Law enforcement agencies have a variety of options when it comes to crime mapping. At the most basic level, locations of known criminal incidents are mapped. More advanced techniques may include an analysis of crime displacement after a police intervention or an examination of a neighborhood's crime history over time. Some examples of the different approaches to crime mapping are discussed in the following subsections.

Crime Triangle

Situational crime prevention theory and routine activities theory postulate that in order for a crime to occur, three elements, which form the crime triangle, are required: an offender, a victim or target, and a location. Given this premise, crime mapping can present a complete representation of the criminal phenomenon by plotting each element of the crime simultaneously. Another approach using the crime triangle is to look at where most offenders are arrested, or where most victims report being victimized. By plotting incidents over time, police officials are also able to see the bigger picture when it comes to each element of the crime triangle. Once the offenders, victims, and places are plotted spatially, crime mapping can be used to see if there are any relationships or patterns that would explain the criminal events on the map. For example, the police may be able to determine that offenders are victimizing stores that are near freeway exits as these provide an easy escape route. Similarly, the police may be able to ascertain that all robbery victims in the last month were between the ages of 19 and 22 years, and all reported having small electronic devices taken from them. Knowing this, police officials may start a crime prevention campaign targeted to this specified group in order to reduce future robberies.

Repeat Incidents

Crime mapping can also be useful in terms of identifying criminogenic locations, or hot spots. Criminal justice research has shown that crime is not truly random, and that there are some social and spatial characteristics that facilitate criminal activity. For example, stores located in proximity to schools are more likely to experience property crimes such as burglary, vandalism, or petty theft. Similarly, crime hot spots have been found to occur around liquor stores, nightclubs, and other settings where criminal activity is less easily detected and people have more anonymity.

By focusing on areas where there are multiple incidents occurring within a short time frame, police officials are able to identify criminal hot spots. Once these hot spots are identified, a targeted response can be tailored to "cool" the problem area. For example, a problematic park with high rates of vandalism may be closed by the city at night to reduce future problems. Other tactics may include not allowing people to loiter, increasing lighting, and installing cameras in the park. By using crime mapping to identify criminal hot spots, police agencies are able to be more proactive in their crime reduction efforts because they are aware of the problem locations and structural characteristics that enable crime to occur at these places.

Displacement

Crime mapping can also be used for more advanced analysis of crime problems. For instance, law enforcement agencies can use crime mapping to see how criminal incidents change given a police intervention. Using crime mapping to measure the displacement of crime, or the movement of crime, is an example of how crime mapping can be used throughout the entire crime reduction effort. While the first effort lies in identifying where the problems occur, the second effort helps police officials gauge the efficiency of their response.

Getting the Most From Crime Mapping

In many law enforcement agencies, crime mapping occurs in the crime analysis unit. These specialized units are charged with collecting different sources of data, analyzing these data, and providing police officials with summary reports. These reports are usually comprised of charts, tables, and other visual and spatial representations of the crime problem in their jurisdiction. Given the specialized nature of crime mapping and crime analysis, law enforcement agencies may have a dedicated crime analyst on staff to carry out or supervise these functions, as the involved computer programs require a certain degree of knowledge, skill, and sophistication to produce the appropriate reports.

Remaining up to date in terms of the software and other technological developments in the field is also important. In this fast-evolving field, and as with global positioning systems (GPS) in automobiles, computer programs are routinely updated, offering new techniques, options, or settings. It is crucial for crime analysts to have the latest hardware and software tools at their disposal. Another consideration may be how to best disseminate the information produced by the crime analysis unit to the patrol officers on the street: online, by e-mail, through a local network, or by printing paper maps.

Finally, to get the most out of crime mapping, law enforcement agencies can integrate crime mapping into their organizational and operational plans. In the past, crime mapping was seen as just an additional tool to illustrate where crime was occurring. Today, with its advanced capacities, crime mapping is able to link together many sources of data to present a comprehensive picture of crime, disorder, and other community issues. By integrating information from local businesses, census data, citizen surveys, and officer activity reports, police officials can monitor in real-time the successes and pitfalls of their policing strategies. Numerous police agencies have incorporated CompStat (comparative statistics, or computer statistics) into their organizational frameworks, and up-to-date information and spatial analysis through crime mapping have been crucial in helping these agencies address crime and disorder problems in a more efficient manner.

Emmanuel P. Barthe

See also Hot Spots; Problem-Oriented Policing: Elements, Processes, Implications; Situational Crime Prevention

Further Readings

Boba, R. (2001). *Introductory guide to crime analysis and mapping*. Washington, DC: U.S. Department of Justice, Office of Community Oriented Policing Services.

Clarke, R. V., & Eck, J. E. (2003). *Become a problem-solving crime analyst: In 55 small steps*. London, England: Jill Dando Institute of Crime Science.

Eck, J. E., & Weisburd, D. L. (1995). *Crime and place*. Monsey, NY: Willow Tree Press.

Harries, K. (1999). *Mapping crime: Principles and practices*. Washington, DC: National Institute of Justice.

Rich, T. (1995). *The use of computerized mapping in crime control and prevention programs*. (Research in Action series). NCJ 155182. Washington, DC: U.S. Department of Justice, National Institute of Justice.

Weisburd, D. L., & McEwen, T. (1997). *Crime mapping & crime prevention*. Crime Prevention Studies (Vol. 8). Monsey, NY: Criminal Justice Press.

CRIME PREVENTION THROUGH ENVIRONMENTAL DESIGN

Crime prevention through environmental design (CPTED) is a method of preventing or minimizing crime in an area by methodically and purposefully designing the space. CPTED is a valuable adjunct to the SARA (scanning, analysis, response, assessment) problem-solving process for addressing persistent crime problems. It poses four questions: What is the problem (*scanning*)? Why here (*analysis*)? What can be done to solve the problem (*response*)? How well did our responses work (*assessment*)? CPTED has been one of many crime prevention strategies to show a great deal of success in reducing crime in an area. Many cities and counties now require that plans for new buildings be certified by the National Institute of Crime Prevention or some similar professional body for CPTED qualities. CPTED emphasizes five primary design approaches to reduce crime: natural access control, natural surveillance, territorial reinforcement, activity generation, and place maintenance. This entry briefly reviews the origins of CPTED, follows with a discussion of these five design approaches, the five types of information needed for effective CPTED planning, and concludes with a brief overview of the directions in which CPTED research and applications are heading in the future.

Development

CPTED was developed by C. Ray Jeffery in the early 1970s. In his original writing, Jeffery expressed a generally pessimistic attitude about the current state of criminological theories to find solutions to the crime problem. Jeffery stated that criminologists needed to pay greater attention to how environmental conditions could be related to crime prevention, and involve changes to the physical environment as well as increased citizen involvement and proactive policing. Jeffery further stated that it is necessary to determine the source of crime, wherever the source may be. In essence, Jeffery was trying to settle a long-standing debate within criminology about whether the causes of crime were within the offender (intrinsic) or represented contextual elements that influenced the offender's behavior. Jeffery ultimately concluded that the causes of crime identified by previous researchers were in fact overstated simplifications that failed to take into account both individual differences and environmental contexts. Jeffery argued that to reduce crime it is necessary to address the ecological considerations that serve to evoke criminal behavior.

When discussing CPTED, many textbooks will also include the concept of defensible space as described by Oscar Newman at about the same time Jeffery was writing about CPTED. Although the two concepts are similar, they are based on fundamentally different theoretical models of human behavior. CPTED seeks to design any space in such a manner that it is difficult for would-be offenders to gain access to a target without being detected; whereas the concept of defensible space seeks to design spaces in such a manner that would-be offenders know the space is exclusively for legitimate users with a legitimate purpose. The difference between the two is nuanced, but an easy way to understand the difference is to consider defensible space a *physical determinist* argument, although Newman vehemently opposed it being labeled as such. It might be said that, while the two had similar ideas about environmental influences on behavior, Newman believed in a more of a cause-and-effect relationship, whereas Jeffery allowed for other influences on behavior. In fact, public housing projects were built based on Newman's ideas, including the need to increase the potential for residents to see and report likely offenders, and thereby allow residents to control the physical environments in which they reside. Many environmental criminologists feel that Newman's concept was developed without considering human behavior. The CPTED is based on models of human behavior, whereas defensible space theory argues that specific design features will work to prevent crime.

When CPTED was first published as a theoretical model of criminal behavior, it was not hailed as a revolutionary way of examining and subsequently preventing crime in society. Rather, many criminologists reacted to the publication of the book with general apathy or outright hostility toward the biological implications of CPTED. Additionally, many criminologists saw a number of potential problems with the use of CPTED. The chief problem was believed to be displacement of crime, whereby crime that was prevented at one location that had been well designed would simply be displaced to another area without the improved design. Furthermore, there was a lack of specific strategies for reducing the opportunities for crime in the environment. As a result of the apathetic response to it, CPTED became an underused tool for researching and preventing criminal behavior.

Interest in CPTED was largely reinvigorated by Tim Crowe in the early 1990s when he developed a comprehensive list of guidelines to reduce opportunities for crime. Crowe provided a list of guidelines that could be empirically examined by researchers while also serving as guidelines for police, policymakers, and those responsible for designing space. Also during this time, researchers began to develop methodological tools that could estimate the displacement effects of CPTED strategies. The results from these early studies examining displacement found that there was often no displacement of crime and when there was evidence of displacement, it was far from the total displacement of the crime problem hypothesized by criminologists. In other words, although some crime appeared to be displaced to a new location, there was still a decrease in crime associated with the use of the CPTED strategies.

CPTED gained even more popularity as successful policy intervention with the spread of community policing throughout the United States and the world. Law enforcement agencies that were transitioning to the community policing model were fond of prevention strategies like CPTED, because both focused on using innovative methods to solve the underlying problem responsible for crime in an area.

Design Approaches

The entirety of CPTED as a crime-prevention approach, as noted earlier, comes down to five principles: natural access control, natural surveillance, territorial reinforcement, activity generation, and place maintenance. While each of these principles is presented separately, CPTED solutions tend to represent multiple principles in one implemented design feature. All of the CPTED strategies revolve around one common theme: the rational offender. Each strategy is designed to change the offender's rationale by increasing the risk of detection or increasing the amount of effort necessary to commit a crime. The more the risk can be increased or the more effort the offender has to expend, the less likely that person will choose to commit crime in a location.

Natural Access Control

Natural access control strategies refer to those strategies used to force would-be offenders to enter and exit a place through one designated spot. Access control can include the implementation of physical barriers such as fences, gates, and doors. Access control devices are used to prevent offenders from easily accessing a location where they can then commit crime. Even in locations with high volumes of customers coming and going, access control is still an effective method of prevention. In these situations, the access control point does not serve to make accessing the target more difficult; rather, it increases the perception that an offender's presence will be detected by someone within.

Natural access principles expand beyond place-specific solutions and have been used with a great deal of success at more macro levels. Research suggests that crime in neighborhoods can be reduced by making entry into the neighborhood more difficult for would-be offenders. Making entry more difficult can be done by altering traffic patterns and adding traffic control devices. For instance, adding a series of one-way streets that force traffic to follow a set pattern within neighborhoods increases the risk of detection for offenders who must follow a specific path and increase offenders' expended effort by forcing offenders to learn the traffic pattern while locating potential targets. Similar results can be obtained by creating a number of cul-de-sacs in the neighborhood to force all traffic to use specific streets to traverse a neighborhood.

Natural Surveillance

Natural surveillance refers to the proper placement and use of windows, lighting, and landscaping to increase the ability of those passing by a location to observe the activities that are occurring within and take appropriate action. Appropriate action could be summoning the police or property owner to the area to assist someone else who is being victimized.

Additionally, natural surveillance can allow potential victims to observe and potentially avoid an area where would-be offenders are waiting to victimize them. By increasing the natural surveillance in an area, the hiding places available to would-be offenders who are hoping to capitalize on surprising their victims are removed.

Increasing natural surveillance tends to be accomplished fairly easily. This can be done by increasing the output wattage of light bulbs or the height of lighting structures, but additional light is not always necessary to maximize visibility. Oftentimes increases in natural surveillance can be accomplished by trimming back trees and shrubs or removing objects from windows that block the view from outside. When designing structures, it is important to minimize the number of blind corners where people must walk.

Territorial Reinforcement

Territorial reinforcements serve to delineate ownership of space. Using territorial reinforcement is a method of communicating to would-be offenders that this space belongs to someone else and they are not welcome to use it. Territorial reinforcement can be accomplished simply by using sidewalks, planter beds, and certain types of fences. These devices can serve to communicate that offenders are clearly in another person's space and should not be there.

Additionally, the use of territorial reinforcement help increase natural surveillance by allowing outside observers to determine if someone is in a space where that person does not belong. In other words, if territorial reinforcement is in use, then neighbors should be able to determine whether a person belongs in a certain area and summon for help if not. There is a good deal of overlap between territorial reinforcement and access control measures, although there are clear differences between the two. Access control devices are designed specifically to keep a person out of an area or force them to pass through an area at a certain point; territorial reinforcement prevents a person from entering into an area undetected. Metaphorically speaking, access control refers to a barrier or guardrail on the freeway whereas territorial reinforcement is the painted lane lines. The paint does not prevent a driver from coming into someone else's travel lane; it just serves to alert both drivers.

Activity Generation

The concept of activity generation revolves around attracting legitimate users to a space to dissuade potential offenders from occupying the same space. Activity generation involves bringing in legitimate users to a space that was previously seen as unpalatable due to crime or environmental conditions that were perceived to be adverse. Legitimate users of space are those people who wish to use the space for its intended, noncriminal purpose. Activity generation can involve bringing in needed services or businesses to an area that serve to attract legitimate users of a space. This can include holding special events in the area (e.g., street vendors or craft shows) or implementing recreational facilities (e.g., public parks or athletic fields). The thought is that the legitimate users of the space will dissuade potential offenders or illegitimate users of spaces. As a result of the increased number of legitimate users in a space, potential offenders choose to stop offending or are displaced to another space to offend.

Some argue that activity generation is a potentially counterproductive component of CPTED because it simply brings in additional targets to a location. However, this argument rests on the assumption that there have been no other changes made to a space. Research suggests that bringing in legitimate activity to an area that has been otherwise improved can bring increased natural surveillance and bolster territorial reinforcement measures. By reinforcing environmental changes that have already been made in an area, activity generation leads offenders to decide to stop offending or move to a different space to continue offending. Activity generation is unlikely to work as a solution in isolation but will serve to reinforce other strategies that have been implemented.

Place Maintenance

Place maintenance refers to a strategy whereby the physical environment is maintained, making the space desirable for legitimate users and undesirable for illegitimate users. The concept is closely related to the ideas presented in broken windows theory and utilized by law enforcement agencies in order maintenance policing strategies. These theories and strategies rely on the idea that disorderly conditions, in the form of unkempt areas, suggest a breakdown in both formal and informal social control and

invite crime into an area. The concept of place maintenance proposes that keeping up the appearance of space serves to portray high levels of social control and ownership in an area, suggesting that a potential offender's conduct is likely to be challenged or reported by legitimate users of the space.

Place maintenance not only involves the suggestion of elevated levels of social control and ownership, but also ensuring other crime prevention strategies are still functioning. Research suggests that in many spaces, offenders will remove, intentionally tamper with, or otherwise defeat crime prevention features that have been implemented. However, through the process of place maintenance the presence and effectiveness of these destructive efforts can be overcome before illegitimate users and crime return to a space.

Effective CPTED Planning

The evidence suggests CPTED is an effective strategy for modifying a space or designing a new space to minimize the potential crime problems associated with this new area. To effectively implement any of the five CPTED principles listed above, it is necessary to collect certain information that will allow law enforcement agencies and legitimate users of the space to implement CPTED successfully. If this information is not collected, the effectiveness of CPTED could be severely limited. This information can be seen as akin to the information that is collected during the scanning phase of the SARA (scanning, analysis, response, assessment) model in problem-oriented policing.

The first type of information that needs to be collected is crime analysis information, which will allow problems (in existing spaces) or potential problems (in planned spaces) to be identified. Logically, it is difficult to prevent crime without knowing what types of crimes are likely to be prevalent in an area. Additionally, it is necessary to collect land use information and detailed observations of the space. This information will help identify the potential problems that need to be addressed with the CPTED strategies. Furthermore, it is helpful to collect information (e.g., demographic and perceptual) regarding the legitimate uses of the space under consideration. This information can assist in identifying appropriate and effective solutions that are responsive to the needs and concerns of legitimate users. Although collecting this information may be seen as cumbersome, the effectiveness of CPTED depends on it. The more complete the information, the better the understanding of extant and potential problems, thereby increasing the effectiveness and support of CPTED solutions.

The Future of CPTED

Despite the fact that CPTED has been shown to be an effective strategy for addressing crime problems, recent research has focused on methods of improving and extending its effectiveness. This work extending CPTED has been termed *2nd Generation CPTED* (CPTED2) and was helped in large measure by a 1997 article by Greg Saville and Gerry Cleveland that encouraged CPTED practitioners to also consider the social and psychological issues beyond the built environment. The work of CPTED2 seeks to expand CPTED beyond focusing on the environmental factors that contribute to criminal behavior to addressing the causes of criminal behavior in the environment. In other words, CPTED2 seeks to treat the underlying causes of crime, thought to be weak social ties among neighborhood residents, rather than simply focusing on and treating the symptoms as the original CPTED has done. The work of CPTED2 does not seek to replace the original CPTED, but rather seeks to expand upon this work by incorporating additional principles that will assist in designing crime out of spaces (particularly neighborhoods). Although CPTED2 is still in its infancy, researchers generally agree upon the addition of five additional crime prevention principles that revolve around creating strong neighborhoods where crime prevention activities will likely be successful: neighborhood identity, community development, sustainable neighborhoods, healthy neighborhoods, and community empowerment. As with the original principles of CPTED, there is a great deal of overlap between these principles. Proponents of CPTED2 argue that incorporating these new principles will strengthen the ability to use principles from CPTED to solve crime problems in these neighborhoods.

Neighborhood Identity

The principle of neighborhood identity speaks to the necessity of a community to have an identity. This allows those who reside within the neighborhood to identify with the area and other people living within the neighborhood, as well as the perceptions people have of the neighborhood. If people can relate to a place it makes relating to their neighbors that much easier and the relationships more meaningful. Neighborhoods without this sense of identity have a difficult time implementing crime prevention strategies that rely on the principles of natural surveillance, territorial reinforcement, and activity generation.

Community Development

The principle of community development speaks to the necessity of communities to bring neighbors together to meet and interact. This can be accomplished through local events (e.g., block parties or community centers) or through locations where large numbers of residents congregate on a regular basis (e.g., churches or schools). The key to building strong communities is getting neighborhood residents to interact, which is facilitated by these events and locations. Interaction among residents builds a sense of community, which can allow crime prevention efforts to be implemented more effectively.

Sustainable Neighborhoods

The principle of sustainable neighborhoods speaks to the idea that neighborhoods should be designed around the concept of self-sufficiency. In other words, neighborhoods should be able to provide all of the services needed by residents, such as a post office and grocery stores. Although it may be unrealistic for a single neighborhood to provide all such services for residents, the more services than can be found within the neighborhood, the better. The less community members must travel outside of the neighborhood, the more contact neighbors will have and the stronger the community will be. This again reinforces the concept of community and increases the likelihood that crime prevention strategies will be successful.

Healthy Neighborhoods

The principle of healthy neighborhoods speaks to the necessity for communities to engage in those behaviors that are productive for the development of the community. Communication is key to the concept of healthy communities. Creating strong social ties within the neighborhood rests on the ability of residents to be able to communicate their wants and needs to others in the community. This not only draws community members closer together but also allows for community members to solve problems more effectively. Again, the more residents communicate with one another, the stronger the community is and the more likely that crime prevention strategies will be successful.

Community Empowerment

The principle of community empowerment speaks to the ability of the community to recognize and communicate its wants and needs with those outside of the community. It is unrealistic to assume that any community will ever be fully self-sufficient, and as such it is necessary for community members to be able to effectively communicate with those outside of the community. This communication can come in the form of requests for services from city governments or requests for information from nearby communities. Due to the arbitrary boundaries between communities, multiple communities can be afflicted by the same problems. Community empowerment allows communities to reach across these boundaries to learn from and problem-solve with other communities in the area. The more empowered that communities are, the more likely they will be able to create effective crime prevention strategies.

Jon Maskaly

See also Broken Windows Theory; Crime Analysis; Crime Displacement; Crime Mapping; Hot Spots; Place-Based Policing; Problem Analysis Triangle; Problem-Solving Process (SARA); Situational Crime Prevention

Further Readings

Atlas, R. I. (2008). *21st century security and CPTED: Designing for critical infrastructure protection and crime prevention.* Boca Raton, FL: Auerbach.

Cisneros, H. G. (1995). *Defensible space: Deterring crime and building communities.* Washington, DC: U.S. Department of Housing and Urban Development.

Clarke, R. V. (1997). *Situational crime prevention: Successful case studies* (2nd ed.). Albany, NY: Harrow & Heston.

Crowe, T. D. (1991). *Crime prevention through environmental design: Applications of architectural design and space management concepts.* (National Crime Prevention Institute). Boston, MA: Butterworth-Heinemann.

Dickout, D. (2006). A community based approach for creating safer night-life spaces: 2nd Generation CPTED in action. *CPTED Journal, 2,* 25–32.

Felson, M., & Boba, R. (2010). *Crime and everyday life* (4th Ed.). Thousand Oaks, CA: Sage.

Jeffery, C. R. (1977). *Crime prevention through environmental design* (2nd ed.). Beverly Hills, CA: Sage.

Newman, O. (1972). *Defensible space: Crime prevention through urban design.* New York, NY: MacMillan.

Newman, O. (1996). *Creating defensible space.* Washington, DC: U.S. Department of Housing and Urban Development.

Sarkissian, W. (2003). Stories in a park. Second-generation CPTED in practice: Reducing crime and stigma through community storytelling. *CPTED Journal, 2,* 34–45.

Zahm, D. (2005). Learning, translating, and implementing CPTED. *Journal of Architectural and Planning Research, 22*(4), 284–293.

Zahm, D. (2007). *Using crime prevention through environmental design in problem solving.* (Problem-Oriented Guides for Police, Problem-Solving Tools Series, No. 8). Retrieved from http://www.popcenter.org/tools/cpted

CUSTOMER-BASED POLICING

The traditional police view that the priorities of police and the focus of their work is the sole domain of the police has been part of the organizational transformation required to implement the philosophy of community policing. As community policing evolves, the needs and desires of the consumers of police services (police customers) takes on a greater importance. Community policing, as a philosophy, challenges the traditional police thinking that "we're the experts; we'll tell *you* what you need."

Customer-based policing is but one element of the philosophy of community policing. It focuses on the consumers of police services and develops and tailors services for the needs and priorities of the customers. Just as intelligence-led policing relies on data to solve problems and guide police activity, customer-based policing relies on the consumers to identify problems and participate in the solutions. In customer-based policing, consumer input is valued and is used to guide organizational decisions. This entry discusses the key elements, characteristics, and challenges associated with customer-based policing.

Key Elements and Characteristics

The adoption of customer-based policing includes all three of the key elements of community policing as defined by the Community Oriented Policing Services (COPS) Office: community partnerships, organizational transformation, and focus on problem solving. In transforming the organization, police leadership is challenged to overcome the resistance to yield more influence to the consumers of police services. In customer-based policing, consumers play a role in organizational processes such as selection of officers and supervisors and evaluation of organizational effectiveness.

The characteristic most identified with customer-based policing is that of building community partnerships. As police shift from working only with traditional partners (governmental social service agencies, hospital emergency rooms, etc.) to connecting with nontraditional partners (Boys & Girls Clubs, neighborhood-based, nongovernmental social service agencies, etc.), a focus on customers requires the use of new methods. Input from community members guides the prioritization and delivery of services.

Empowered line-level police officers serve more as a direct link to the customers in a community policing agency. As the officers take increasing ownership of their geographically defined area, they are better able to glean subtle information from residents that sharpens their ability to identify and analyze problems. This accompanies a shift of the planning and establishment of the street officer's priorities from internal sources to be more inclusive of external customer input.

Police agencies that have adopted customer-based policing share several characteristics. First, they employ multiple means of collecting feedback and input on services, such as customer satisfaction. Multiple methods are necessary to get the broadest perspective. For example, if an agency handed out satisfaction response cards only to everyone who received a speeding ticket, the confrontational nature of enforcement tasks would likely bias the response information. Examples of feedback methods used would include the following:

- *Callbacks of crime victims.* Agencies use volunteers and employees to telephone persons listed on crime incident reports to both inquire about any additional information that could be helpful to the case and receive feedback on the quality and nature of the service received.
- *Website-based response and feedback methods.* Consumers of police services can go to the agency's website and leave direct feedback.
- *Community surveys.* This can be a police stand-alone survey or part of a larger survey on all city services or community quality-of-life indicator surveys. After developing a representative sample, a survey is mailed out requesting that respondents provide input on services and list their priorities.
- *Feedback response cards.* Officers may distribute such cards every time they have contact with a customer, or the cards may be clearly identified in a display placed at the front desk of police stations or at other public locations.
- *Social media.* Agencies are increasingly using social media as a means to connect with community members. Comments left on social media sites provide insight into what some members of the community think about police services.

Customer-based police agencies may conduct periodic meetings, geographically disbursed across the community, to reassess priorities with direct input from customers who drive the discussion. Representatives of a customer-focused police agency might be regular guests on radio or television talk shows, not only to educate the audience, but to solicit customer input and ideas. Employees throughout an agency that embraces customer-based policing demonstrate that they are accessible and eager to hear from the consumers of their service.

Police departments that practice customer-based policing are likely to expand how customers can access their services. Other computer-based services such as social media can both push and collect valuable consumer information. Along with the decentralization of the delivery of services, customer-based policing may provide distributed access points throughout the community, such as interactive kiosks and customer-focused storefront stations.

Challenges

The strength of the relationships can be tested in a customer-based police environment. Historic roles for the police in determining the deployment of assets, training and equipment needs, and establishing performance expectations can be heavily influenced by a strong dose of customer demands. Tensions may arise when the analysis of the police yields one set of priorities but the community backs other priorities. A strong customer-driven agency will recognize the need to step back, engage consumers in meaningful dialogue about the community's condition and problems, and jointly develop collaborative priorities. The more the line-level beat officer is involved, the more likely that the police representatives in this partnership show insight for the problems expressed by the consumers.

Enforcing laws may be another source of tension in a customer-based agency. Most consumers do not wish to become "customers" as the receiving end of a traffic citation. While residents generally are concerned about the impact that speeding and loud cars have on the quality of life in their neighborhood, they do not want to be the target of traffic enforcement themselves. This is an example of the peripheral benefits of a customer-based police agency. If residents have a healthy working relationship with "their" beat officer, they are likely to engage the officer in a less tense conversation about things that bother them, like the speeding ticket they received the day before. In return, beat officers well trained in the ways of customer-based policing will be skilled at listening and showing empathy for one of "their" customers, while still reinforcing the importance of voluntary compliance with traffic laws and the necessity of conducting enforcement measures.

It is the strength and quality of the relationships developed between the police and consumers in a customer-based agency that will overcome many of the traditional tensions inherent in policing. If residents in a neighborhood hold a high level of trust for the officers they know, they are more likely to tolerate a secretive operation resulting in a high profile deployment by special police units, even if they weren't previously made aware of the circumstances requiring it. Customers who are well connected with officers may be less likely to assume the worst when the media reports on a controversial action by a member of the department. And the media may be more likely to report on positive interactions between police and consumers when the department is centered on customer service.

As the fiscal crisis spread with the recession of 2007 to 2009, police departments faced at least frozen budgets and for many, severe budget reductions. The trend for the use of volunteers to augment police employees increased with the growth of the fiscal crisis. Recruiting volunteers will more likely get results within a customer-based police agency. Beat officers with relationships with residents are ideal recruiters for volunteers, and citizen participation in program like citizens' academies is likely due to the satisfaction consumers have for the customer-focused services they receive.

The discussion on customer-based policing cannot overlook the reality that citizens represent external customers, but there are many internal customers for police agencies as well. Patrol officers are consumers of the work by records, investigations, and crime labs; the reverse is also true. Other municipal governmental agencies may represent internal customers, and outside policing agencies such as county sheriff offices, state police agencies, and federal or tribal police departments can be both consumers and providers of services. This highlights an important need for the customer-based agency to develop an organizational culture that fosters a strong customer service orientation throughout every level of the department. A police leader might recognize when such a culture has evolved in the department when the leader hears a police officer refer to an arrestee as a customer absent sarcasm that may have previously accompanied such a remark.

Richard W. Myers

See also Building Partnerships and Stakeholders; Citizen Surveys; Decentralizing the Organization/ Organizational Change; Intelligence-Led Policing; Involving Local Businesses; Non-sworn Personnel and Volunteers, Use and Training of

Further Readings

Garner, G. W. (2003, June). Exceptional customer service. *Law and Order*, 103–106.

Gurwitt, R. (1993). Communitarianism: You can try it at home. *Governing, 6,* 33–39.

University of New Hampshire Cooperative Extension. (n.d.). *Community building: Strengthening sense of community*. Retrieved from http://extension.unh.edu/resources/representation/Resource000625_Rep647.pdf

Wilson, L. J. (1995, April). Placing community-oriented policing in the broader realms of community cooperation. *The Police Chief, 62*(4), 127–128.

CYBERCRIME AND COMMUNITY POLICING

Cybercrime encompasses a broad range of criminal activity involving electronic devices. Due to the progressive nature of technology in recent years, it is difficult to establish a specific, yet comprehensive, definition for *cybercrime*. Generally, an accepted definition includes the electronic manipulation of data through addition or deletion of files or a theft of information. Specific offenses include, but are not limited to, identity theft, cyberstalking via social network sites or e-mail, child pornography, cyberbullying, embezzlement, theft, and various forms of fraud.

Cybercrime is complex and difficult for police to address through either traditional forms of policing or community policing. Often the victim and offender do not know each other because the crime is perpetrated solely through the anonymity of electronic means. Those who do become aware they have been victimized may be unsure that the police can help. This entry further details cybercrime and the community policing response to such crimes and offenders.

Cybercrime

The U.S. Department of Justice describes broad categories of cybercrime rather than detailing specific criminal offenses. While specific offenses do exist, cybercrime is most easily understood in broad categories.

First, the computer itself can be targeted for unlawful reasons like theft of personal information or release of viruses. Cybercriminals can commit identity theft by retrieving personal information from the user or owner of a computer without the victim's knowledge. That information can be sold or manipulated for use in further criminal activity. Computer viruses can be created and installed to inhibit the proper operations of computer hardware and software. Oftentimes the viruses' stealth of operation leaves the user unaware that the computer is infected.

Second, the computer can be used as the mechanism for criminal activity. Examples include fraud, harassment, child pornography, and illegal sales. Using a computer as an instrument of a crime allows an offender to commit an offense without being physically present at a crime scene. The fact that cybercrime is perpetrated over the Internet makes identification of the offender more difficult.

Third, the final category includes the computer being used as a secondary means for committing a crime; for example, housing databases that support illegal activity. Traditionally these items existed in physical form, but now they can be stored electronically, making the evidence easier to conceal and destroy. Examples of this category include possession of child pornography and electronic bookkeeping that details illegal business operations and profits.

Cybercrime is relatively easy to commit yet very difficult to detect. It is common for victims not to realize that they have been the victim of a cybercrime. Many times the programs and technologies used to facilitate cybercrime can infiltrate a computer without the victim's knowledge. Nefarious programs can transmit personal data for months or even years before the owner of the computer realizes what has been taking place. Offenders often target businesses due to large monetary assets, but individuals can also be targeted. The popularity of mobile devices has led to increased insecurity and vulnerability of users' private information. The Internet allows for worldwide connectivity and the remote transfer of data. Computers and mobile computer devices have become common throughout the world. Mobile devices often do not have the security software and layers of safety present in personal computers.

Some police officers, however, do not have the requisite training to understand the complexity of computer systems and corresponding crimes. When investigations do occur, the physical evidence that is seized is fragile and requires significant forensic analysis for the data to be compiled and organized in preparation for prosecution. For these reasons, police departments may submit the evidence to a centralized forensics laboratory for investigation, but some departments have created their own forensics unit with specially trained officers.

Relative to traditional criminal offenses, cybercrime is young and evolving quickly as new technology emerges. Challenges exist in that oftentimes suspects are individuals who are technologically savvy or have more computer-based expertise than the average person. Offenders who possess superior knowledge often understand the functionality and safeguards of computer systems more than the owner of the device. Offenders engage in cybercrime for a variety of reasons, including personal gain, maliciousness, and revenge.

The effect of cybercrime is widespread and has the potential to devastate a diverse population of individuals and businesses. The offenses can involve complex solutions or remedies. This does not mean that solutions are impossible. Efforts can be made to identify specific problems in local jurisdictions and educate the public in cybercrime prevention strategies.

Cybercrime and Community Policing

Police implementation of community policing to address cybercrime differs from that to address other types of crime because the problem often exists in both electronic and physical communities. The Internet joins people together based on common interests, activities, and beliefs, together creating risks comparable to what often exist in physical communities. The SARA (scanning, analysis, response, assessment) model of problem solving that is used in community policing is still applicable with regard to cybercrime.

Police must shift from a reactive position toward a more proactive position in order for community policing to adequately address cybercrime. Specifically, the challenge is to examine the overall problem of cybercrime within a community rather than focusing on specific incidents and viewing them as being self-contained and unrelated. Traditional responses generally view incidents in isolation, rather than as part of a larger problem. By utilizing the SARA model of problem solving, police deal with the origins of the problem. In addition, police recognize the connectedness of incidents, as well as factors and circumstances that cause the overall problem.

During the problem-solving process, it is crucial to involve citizens in decision making. In the community policing model, citizens are viewed as recipients of police service much like customers of a business. As a result, problem solving involves a high level of interaction between police and citizens. Information flows continuously from citizens to police and back as the SARA process evolves. Citizens' accessibility to police is essential for program success.

Police often request assistance from community agencies to help them address the problem of cybercrime. For instance, police may contact local banks to determine if banks are informing their customers of the risks related to online banking. Police may also contact computer repair stores and encourage stores to offer a customer vulnerability assessment to determine if an individual's computer is infected or at risk. Businesses' involvement benefits the problem-solving process in that they bring a host of resources that are unavailable to police and private citizens.

Police integrate the SARA model to cybercrime in the following manner. Police scan and determine the localized problems as the first step in the SARA model. To address cybercrime, police utilize crime report data, citizen interviews, and personal observations in an effort to answer questions about the scope of the problem. For example, what specific types of cybercrime are taking place within the jurisdiction? How significant of a problem is cybercrime? Are citizens reporting cybercrime victimization or does it generally go unreported? By not addressing the problem, does it make the problem worse?

Next, police expand on the problems identified during the scanning step by conducting analysis. For example, what are the causes of cybercrime? What other crimes, if any, have derived from cybercrime victimization? What are the most basic forms of victimization? What resources are available to abate cybercrime?

Police then develop a variety of responses, the third step, by considering the following questions: What have other communities done to remedy the cybercrime problem? What are possible interventions that might work? Who is needed to implement each possible response plan? What are the sources of data that will be gathered?

The final step is assessment, which involves the police examining the outcome. Was the intervention plan implemented correctly? Were the listed goals obtained? Have new challenges arisen and, if so, how can they be addressed? During the assessment stage, it is important to distinguish between process evaluation and impact evaluation. Process evaluation considers whether the plan was implemented correctly, while impact evaluation examines whether the identified problems increased or declined as a result of the intervention plan.

One successful goal of community policing is a reduction in the overall incidents of repeat victimization. While a complete elimination of cybercrime is both unattainable and unrealistic, citizens should not fear being victimized repeatedly. The police work to obtain prevention and reduction where it is possible while still recognizing the total elimination of cybercrime is unlikely. The strength of community policing lies in empowering citizens to help improve their own communities. It is essential that a community-based crime prevention model is specific to the variety of cybercrime that is taking place within a particular community.

Aaron A. Harnish

See also Community Policing and Problem Solving, Definition of; Problem-Solving Process (SARA)

Further Readings

National Institute of Justice. (2004). *Forensic examination of digital evidence: A guide for law enforcement.* Washington, DC: U.S. Department of Justice. Retrieved from http://www.ojp.usdoj.gov/nij/pubs-sum/199408.htm

National Institute of Justice. (2007). *Investigations involving the Internet and computer networks.* Washington, DC: U.S. Department of Justice. Retrieved from https://www.ncjrs.gov/pdffiles1/nij/210798.pdf

National Institute of Justice. (2008). *Electronic crime scene investigation: A guide for first responders.* Washington, DC: U.S. Department of Justice. Retrieved from http://www.ojp.usdoj.gov/nij/pubs-sum/187736.htm

Office of Justice Programs. (2007). *Digital evidence in the courtroom: A guide for law enforcement and prosecutors.* Washington, DC: U.S. Department of Justice. Retrieved from http://www.ojp.usdoj.gov/nij/pubs-sum/211314.htm

DECENTRALIZING THE ORGANIZATION/ ORGANIZATIONAL CHANGE

Of the three key characteristics of community-oriented policing—community partnerships, problem solving, and organizational transformation—the most challenging is often the transformation of the organization. While each police agency is unique and the difficulties to implement community policing will vary, an almost universal characteristic of police agencies is resistance to change. Decentralizing is one of many significant organizational changes that facilitate the delivery of police services with a community policing philosophy. This entry explores why police resist change, the various steps and recommendations for organizational transformation, and how a decentralized department or agency operates in the modern policing arena.

Barriers to Transformation

Before exploring the nature of organizational transformation necessary to support community policing, it may be useful to consider why police resist change.

- Police officers work in one of the most dynamic environments of any profession: the streets. More specifically, police are not confined to controlled environments such as an office, or within clearly defined boundaries of most outdoor work environments. Unlike other service jobs, police enter areas forbidden to others and also have to enter dangerous environments as a routine course of their jobs.

- Every day is different for police officers. While officers in some assignments, such as traffic-enforcement officers, may focus on the same tasks each day, many factors can contribute to making each shift worked as different and unique for specialized officers as for generalized patrol officers.

- Vigilance is required for the ever-present but unknown threats during each work shift. While some police officers develop hypervigilance that results in unhealthy lifestyles, most officers are able to find a balance that allows them to decompress during their off-duty time and, while working, between calls for service.

- Balancing vigilance requires safety, security, and comfort; the police organization itself provides the police the safety of "home base" where they are surrounded by others who understand their stress and the risks faced daily. In a world of constant and dynamic change, the department is a source of security and normality. In a career with long, irregular shifts and required work during off-duty hours, such as training, court appearances, and extra assignments, some police see their colleagues more than their own families.

- Organizational transformation is a direct threat to the steadiness and security sought by the police within their "home away from home." Police are well trained and instinctive about reacting to threats, and the force with which they can resist change should not be underestimated.

Organizational Transformation

Despite the predictable and sometimes vehement resistance to changing the organization, transformation is possible, and it is necessary for community policing to be implemented. Development of community partnerships and problem solving, the other two key characteristics of community policing, requires a retooling of traditional police structure and function.

In traditional police organizations, there is a strong hierarchical command structure that requires line-level officers to seek approval for any deviation from a tightly scripted set of duties and methods. A simple example: An officer in a traditional department would need to seek approval to leave his assigned beat to drive home an elderly woman whose car was just totaled in a crash. In the context of the community policing philosophy, an empowered officer would keep his supervisor and dispatch aware that he would be outside his area for a few minutes as he drove the woman home; the officer might further take steps to contact a relative of the woman to follow up on the woman's well-being later in the day.

Some agencies have tried to provide guidance on the management of officer discretion in an empowered department. One way agencies have done this is by issuing decision-making guides, often printed on small cards easily carried in a pocket. These typically pose several questions to guide an officer's decision making:

- Is it legal?
- Is it ethical?
- Is it consistent with the values of the police department?
- Is it the right thing to do?
- Is it within the rules and regulations of the police department?
- Are you willing to justify it if called upon?
- If the answer to all of these questions is *yes*, don't ask, just do it!

Empowering employees is merely one aspect of the organizational transformation. Some police leaders have learned that simply handing out cards without many of the other transformative elements in place results in confusion in the workforce, supervisors who suddenly question their role, and an unanticipated reaction by officers who also are threatened by an expanded role in decision making and respond with "just tell me what you want me to do."

While there is no prescribed sequence of the organizational changes that accompany implementing the philosophy of community policing, it is illustrative to consider transformation as a foundation upon which to build the delivery of community policing. The building blocks for this foundation include organizational structure, policy, leadership and decision making, geographic ownership, personnel management, and the tools of the trade.

Hiring/Promotion

Because most police agencies were not constructed with the community policing philosophy, employees' tenure is spread out along a continuum of many years. As the transformation begins, the department should have a vision of what the "new" organization will be, and recruit and hire employees who will contribute to that new vision. This requires retooling the selection processes as well as other personnel management aspects such as promotional tests. Leaders must consider the long-term implications of the choices they make on who to hire and who to promote. Training and evaluation systems also should reflect the vision of community policing. Leaders, especially first-line supervisors, must lead in a manner that empowers and mentors employees with the support they need to increase their decision-making capacity.

It is easier to implement changes in hiring and promoting than it is for well-established leaders to alter their course. New employees who are brought in within the context of transformation don't have to unlearn the old ways and learn new ones. For senior leaders, however, even if they are championing the change, their years of training and experience in more traditional methods can be challenging to overcome. Police departments are not unlike most organizations as employees at all levels take their cues from the behaviors of the leaders. As difficult as it may be, senior leaders overseeing a transformation must learn and practice the new methods and adopt the new philosophy in highly visible ways.

Structural Changes

Many agencies implementing the community policing philosophy have created visible structural changes, which often can be leading indicators that change is afoot. The traditional hierarchical pyramid may be flattened, lessening the number of ranks in the structure, and accompanying the change to push more and more decision making to the lowest possible level. Changes in policies to provide more guidance for employees to make decisions at their level, together with organizational values, may influence employee behaviors more than rules. The old mantra "employees will do that which is counted or measured" requires changing evaluation systems to put a priority on developing community relationships and collaboratively focusing on solving problems.

Traditional policing typically means revealing only that which is necessary for the good of the mission. In community policing, securing the trust of the community is fundamental, and the transparency shown by the agency directly reflects the level of trust that follows. Again, this characteristic must emanate from the top leaders. Effective leadership includes transparency with the employees throughout the agency as well. Employees who feel a mutual level of trust with their leaders are far more likely to embrace a new level of empowerment.

Strategic Planning

While strategic planning is well established in policing, under the community policing philosophy it requires evolution to support the new methods and structure. Community input is of increased importance in a community policing environment, and there must be ways for citizens to provide input during all phases of the planning.

Within the big picture view of transforming an organization, the single largest hurdle to overcome is the organizational culture. While the definition of *organizational culture* may be grossly simplified as "it's how we do things around here," the nuances and subtle uniqueness can be easily overlooked when planning change. The deepest roots of resistance to change lie in the culture. Here also are the unwritten practices and expectations that don't automatically change with newly promulgated policies and procedures. Leaders must patiently and steadily reinforce the healthiest aspects of the culture while leading employees away from unhealthy or deficient practices. While policies and plans can be changed with the stroke of a pen, culture change can take years because it requires overcoming the inherent resistance and protective behaviors of long-term employees.

Culture change and all the other cumulative organizational changes that accompany a shift to community policing will occur under some process, whether planned or unplanned. It is more likely to occur sooner rather than later if a strategic plan for change is developed and widely known and used. Strategic plans for change often include several key ingredients:

- Leadership conducts a thorough assessment of the organization's current state, as well as defines a future vision of where the organization is headed. A planning process that outlines the path from the current to the future evolves along with the organization.
- At some point in the planning process, employees from throughout the organization are engaged in the process. Under the theory that employees must be able to see the "what's in it for me?" in order to fully embrace the changes, involving representatives of all employee levels helps spread the vision for the future change. Also, representation from consumers of the police services might benefit the process.
- For those employees who are not part of the formal planning process, strong and effective communication methods seek to inform and educate about the purpose behind the changes and how the process is progressing. The more extreme the nature of the changes, the more communication is needed.
- As the planning begins to provide specific change ideas, employees and perhaps the community at large will need education and training on the benefits of the changes and how the changes will affect them.
- As an organization's evolution into community policing continues, the process should continue to monitor progress and measure the effectiveness of the changes. This keeps the process timely and relevant and strengthens the organization's resolve to sustain the philosophy of community policing.

Modifying Technologies

The process above is useful to illustrate another change in the transformation that often makes an early appearance: the need to modify technologies. This can vary from the technologies needed to gather and analyze information for the planning and implementation, to evaluative technologies to help measure effectiveness and outcomes, to technologies needed to facilitate the partnership with the community. Shifting the use of technology from solely gathering basic crime data to creating highly interactive communication and education streams represents a significant investment and change within police organizations.

Decentralization

Another organizational change that is prominent under a community policing philosophy also leads into the second theme for this entry: decentralization. Police departments' structure usually is a reflection of their operating philosophy. When the organizational chart physically looks like a pyramid, there is probably a strong top-down chain-of-command style. As the pyramid flattens, reducing the number of ranks and pushing decision making to lower levels, it embodies more of the philosophical elements of community policing.

A strong indicator of decentralization is structuring the delivery of police services geographically rather than temporally. Traditional agencies are structured by the various work shifts, defined by the time of day. Decentralized community policing puts officers in charge of well-defined geographic areas often referred to as *beats, sectors, zones, neighborhoods,* or other descriptive terms. While officers are still likely to be assigned to specific shifts and often work the same hours, they are recognized more for their specific assigned beat. Along with this definition comes a heightened sense of ownership. In its simplest terms, the officer "owns" the beat, and the beat "owns" the officer. The officer is expected to become well acquainted with the residents, businesses, and other occupants of that beat. The community is expected to collaborate with the beat officer in identifying neighborhood problems and developing sustainable solutions.

Agencies that embrace the vision of the community policing philosophy as being everyone's responsibility tend to avoid creating specialized units defined as "community policing" teams. Rather, most department functions are structured around the framework of the geographic beats, facilitating both internal and external collaboration. For example, an agency may organize around several beats and within the grouping, assign detectives, traffic officers, and other support services like K-9 and evidence technicians.

These supporting specialists would approach their work as supporting the needs of the basic beat officer, participating in the community problem identification and solutions efforts. From a customer-service perspective, decentralization might include introducing decentralized locations for citizens to acquire services, such as precinct or district stations. Traditional agencies that have multiple precincts or districts operate with the beat officers under the control and direction of empowered area commanders. In contrast, in the community policing atmosphere, the beat cops are empowered to provide the services needed and desired by their community members, with the area commander providing logistical and leadership support centered on the individual beats.

Under a decentralized community policing model, beat officers are expected to know and collaborate with all relevant and available services, both governmental and nongovernmental. While support services, such as precinct investigators and evidence technicians, may be available to them, they may also call on neighborhood-based resources outside the role of their employing agency. Some agencies structured around the decentralized model have developed neighborhood-level advisory committees to provide direct input and feedback from community members. In many decentralized agencies, success is not defined by measuring individual outputs by an officer, but instead by measuring outcomes within an area of responsibility. A beat officer who takes ownership of the crime patterns and quality of life in the assigned beat is more likely to secure the steady support and participation by community members within that beat.

As the recession of 2007 to 2009 deeply affected police agencies across the United States, some agencies responded by retreating on the decentralization of police services. Decentralized structures are sometimes perceived to be more costly than centralized, due to the need for site-specific leadership, police stations, and the latest technologies. It is not uncommon to hear police leaders who are facing massive budget reductions propose closing or consolidating some of their precincts or districts. A compromise may be to keep the most visible, direct-service delivery elements, such as patrol officers and precinct houses, decentralized while consolidating or centralizing the "back room" support services that are not evident to consumers, such as communications, evidence and property handling, major crimes investigations, and records management. This balance may provide for the highly desired element of ownership for the fundamental core service (patrol) while using cost-effective centralized support services where ownership of a piece of the community is not crucial or relevant to their mission.

Richard W. Myers

See also Agency Mission and Values, Changes in; Building Partnerships and Stakeholders; Collaboration With Outside Agencies; Customer-Based Policing; Implementation of Community Policing; Involving Local Businesses; Measuring Officer Performance

Further Readings

Eck, J. E. (2004). Why don't problems get solved? In W. G. Skogan (Ed.), *Community policing: Can it work?* (pp. 185–206). Belmont, CA: Wadsworth.

Gilmartin, K. M. (2002). *Emotional survival for law enforcement: A guide for officers and their families.* Tucson, AZ: E-S Press.

Jenson, C. J., III, & Levin, B. H. (2005, January). *Neighborhood-driven policing: A series of working papers from the futures working group.* Proceedings of the Futures Working Group (Vol. I). Washington, DC: Federal Bureau of Investigation. Retrieved from http://www2.fbi.gov/hq/td/fwg/neighborhood/neighborhood-driven-policing.pdf

DEMOGRAPHICS, FUTURE IMPACT ON COMMUNITY POLICING

When community demographics change—for example, when communities becomes more diverse—how police agencies carry out community policing also changes because of alterations in the makeup of the agencies and in the focus of their service. Relationship building within the community is affected, as is the nature of problems that the police will seek to solve through community collaboration. By studying future demographic trends, police leaders can lead agencies into new relationships with growing populations and identify possible problems. Changes are likely in many aspects of policing, such as the diversity of the composition of police agencies, police and social services provided, crime patterns and problem solving, the importance of effective communication skills, and the kinds of technology needed. This entry outlines how demographic changes impact the practice of community policing.

Effects of Demographic Change

Changes in demographics are a function of two drivers for population: birth and death rates, and migration. In developed countries, birth rates are steady or declining, and throughout the world people are living longer. There are numerous reasons for migration, and migration is not limited to a certain demographic group such as young people. Aging and migration pose significant impacts on the future of community policing. As once-homogenous populations change to include multiple faiths, languages, and races, policing is destined to change. Over time, the net effect of all these changes can be challenging to forecast; some of the individual factors are presented here to illustrate potential impacts.

Aging populations are a logical outcome as health care evolves and becomes more accessible globally. Average life expectancy is longer than at any time in history, and it could continue to increase with medical advancements such as stem-cell therapy and complex artificial body parts. The growth of medical treatments and devices poses new crime opportunities, ranging from an expanding number of addictive drugs to theft of medical devices and vital organs.

As populations age, the nature of crime may change. Historically, violent crime offenders came from a youthful cohort. As people age and personal wealth grows, they become a fruitful target for financial crimes. Some police agencies with a strong community policing philosophy have provided specialized training for officers related to senior citizen problems, such as frauds, scams, extortion, and senior abuse. Crimes within senior housing and by caregivers, including family members, are increasing as the population ages. Community policing officers require a keen understanding of the range of social and fiscal services available to all crime victims, as well as subtle signs of elder abuse.

Senior citizens are using computers and the Internet at a growing rate, making it more likely they will be victimized by the plethora of scams and schemes to separate people from their money. Internet-based crime, whether the victim is aged or not, continues to pose technical and jurisdictional challenges for the police. Local police agencies may be overwhelmed by the sheer volume of fraud cases, both traditional and online. As many online scams are generated from continents away, confusing jurisdiction parameters limit the ability of community policing officers to assist victims.

The median age of police officers is likely to rise as people live longer. Since the recession of 2007 to 2009 in the United States, there has been growing criticism of police pension plans and postemployment medical insurance benefits. As medical-cost growth outpaces inflation, the prospect of more out-of-pocket expenses with a fixed income has resulted in police officers serving longer. This trend may be offset locally as some police officers rush to retire before threatened reductions in pension programs are implemented. While these seemingly contradicting trends may serve to cancel each other out, police departments may welcome the chance to retain older officers, due to the decline of the traditional police candidate's cohort. The falling birth rate in the United States may signal an ever-declining pool of police applicants in the traditional age group of 21 to 35 years old.

Demographic changes will impact police recruiting beyond the shrinking cohort of young applicants. Increases in the immigrant population result in the need for more multilingual officers. Diversifying the workforce helps police departments better relate to their unique community makeup. Many cultural nuances are brought along with immigrant populations. Police officers who understand the rituals and practices of the people who live in their communities are more likely to secure cooperation and partnerships in their problem-solving efforts. Minority recruitment can be paradoxical; the greater the gap between a police department and segments of its service area, the less likely that the minority group will yield applicants. As people flee countries characterized by oppressive military and law enforcement, their fear and mistrust of police in their country may immigrate with them to their new country.

Community policing agencies may offer periodic nonnative language versions of their citizens' police academy. In the United States, the most common of these would be Spanish-language versions because of the large population of immigrants from Latin America. Agencies also are customizing their programs for localized populations such as Hmong and Somali. Translating department brochures and official reporting documents is commonly done in diverse communities. As the police rely more on web-based services and social networking, the need to translate may expand into online services as well.

Training needs for the police grow as their service population diversifies. Policing is largely a person-to-person, transactional business. Difficulties in communicating between the police and the people they serve diminish many of the strengths of community policing, such as community partnerships and solving problems. While automatic translation technology may eventually mitigate communication challenges, police officers will still require training in cultural nuances. For example, a police officer might pat or rub the head of a child in an endearing manner with no negative consequences in a typical American household. In certain Asian cultures, however, this may result in the parents being highly offended and far less likely to be cooperative with the officer. Immigrants who have recently arrived from countries where the police are feared and survival frequently relies on one's ability to flee may run from the police, so officers must be trained that such behavior may not always be a sign of guilt. Police officers with little knowledge of Islam may enter a mosque without removing their shoes, creating a high level of tension and perceived disrespect for the very people they are there to assist.

Police departments successful at recruiting officers from minority cultures and religions may face unexpected needs to accommodate their new employees in ways that other employees may view as unnecessary or unfair. Some police departments in the United States and Canada have allowed police officers who are Sikh to wear turbans with their uniforms. Other agencies have accommodated facial hair for religious or medical purposes. Even a native, majority population can present challenges for the police environment; as the Millennial Generation has begun to populate police jobs, the growth and popularity of tattoos among this generation has caused some departments to consider revising their appearance standards.

Differences in workgroup members' value systems can result in tensions. In the United States, baby boomer leaders and supervisors who oversee the work of younger generations grapple with conflicting priorities and perceived differences in work ethic. Communication styles and technology preferences are also among the intergenerational issues. Tension and conflict over differences among demographic groups can be a police concern. For example, a minority group that has long been fighting for recognition and equality in a community may see its influence diminished by another minority group that is younger or rapidly growing. The police must show equal interest for both groups to avoid perceptions of disparate services. With diversity comes a higher expectation of tailoring police services to meet the specialized needs of diverse communities.

Impact on Community Policing

Police department policies are likely to evolve as a community changes. At the urging of transgendered people, police departments are developing specific policies that provide their officers direction on conducting searches on people who self-identify with a gender other than the one of their birth. The deaf and hard-of-hearing community encourages police agencies to grow their capacity to communicate with sign language and assistive technologies for phones and computers. Growing complexity in demographics will require a commensurate development of policies and procedures.

Demographic and population forecasts are derived from several sources, such as trend analysis of census data, immigration rates, and global birth rates. Depending on the sources, many such forecasts suggest that the United States is changing from a country where Whites make up the majority to a majority-minority country, or one where minorities collectively make up the greatest share of the population. While the range of dates when this will likely happen is broad, many are forecasting this outcome by the year 2050. Traditional strategic planning in policing may encompass a future time frame of two to seven years, but few police planners or leaders are pondering the demographic forecasts for 2050. The Society of Police Futurists International (PFI) was formed in 1991 to encourage the use of forecasting and futures research in policing. Many of the potential impacts of the forecasted demographics shifts have been explored by PFI members as well as in the publications of the Futures Working Group (FWG), a collaboration between PFI and the Federal Bureau of Investigation. Membership and active participation in these futures-oriented organizations is representative of a fraction of police agencies, both within the United States and internationally.

Community-oriented, problem-solving police agencies have likely made significant changes in organizational structure, mission, and methodologies. Adopting a futures research component is helpful in preparing the organization to become more adaptable and innovative in its community-relationship building and problem solving.

Changing a community policing organization to adapt to demographic shifts is similar to making any kind of significant organizational change. Police departments generally have a bias for the status quo, with employees eschewing sweeping changes while defending "how things are done around here." Police leadership during demographic shifts should support and promote developing organizational capacity to change, apply futures research and forecasts, and expedite meaningful changes to better serve all demographic groups.

Community-oriented, problem-solving policing is centered on the people of a community and the problems they face. The philosophy of such agencies is more proactive than the reactive methods used under traditional policing. As communities become more diverse, the police may take more of a leadership role through policy development, training for both the community and its police officers, recruiting for diversity in the ranks, and even facilitating dialogue and growth for other community institutions. The stronger the partnerships among the police and the people served by the police, the higher the likelihood of success in identifying and solving community problems and preventing crime and disorder.

Richard W. Myers

See also Building Partnerships and Stakeholders; Community, Definition of; Community Cohesion and Empowerment; Elderly Victimization, Characteristics of; Elderly Victimization, Community Policing Strategies for; Immigration: Issues, Law and Police Training; Recruiting for Quality and Diversity

Further Readings

Cetron, M. J., & Davies, O. (2008). *55 trends now shaping the future of policing.* Charleston, SC: CreateSpace.

Schafer, J. A. (Ed.). (2007). *Policing 2020: Exploring the future of crime, communities, and policing. Proceedings of the Futures Working Group,* Washington, DC: U.S. Department of Justice, Federal Bureau of Investigation.

Retrieved from http://www.policefuturists.org/pdf/Policing2020.pdf

Schafer, J. A., Buerger, M. E., Myers, R. W., Jensen, C. J., III, & Levin, B. H. (2012). *The future of policing: A practical guide for police managers and leaders.* Boca Raton, FL: CRC Press.

Websites

The Futures Working Group; http://futuresworkinggroup .cos.ucf.edu/index.php

Police Futurists International; http://www.policefuturists.org

DIRECTED PATROL, STUDIES OF

Directed patrol is a strategy that uses problem-solving techniques to improve the efficiency of police-patrol activities. Directed patrol tends to focus the activity of officers in areas where there is high crime or other problems. Historically, police asserted that random police patrol deterred crime. Research debunked this belief and led police agencies to consider ways to better utilize their officers. Using a problem-solving paradigm, various police activities, including police patrol, were assessed. Directed patrol, with its reliance on problem solving, one of the pillars of community policing, plays an important role in making community policing successful.

Early Patrol Strategy

When Sir Robert Peel established the London Metropolitan Police Department in 1829, he determined that the purpose of uniformed agents of social control was to reduce crime and fear of crime in the communities they served. It was believed that a uniformed police presence would deter criminal activity. The logical thing for officers to do was stroll through neighborhoods as a sort of advertisement that the community was safe and protected. This activity was believed to deter criminals from committing crimes and, at the same time, to provide a sense of security to the law-abiding citizens. This policing "myth" endured until the 1970s.

Kansas City Preventive Patrol Experiment

Although not specifically a study of directed patrol, the Kansas City preventive patrol experiment convinced police administrators that there were more efficient and effective ways of deploying their officers than random patrol. Beginning in October 1972 and continuing through 1973, the Kansas City Police Department permitted researchers to examine the effectiveness of random patrol. Patrol was eliminated in some districts so that officers only responded to calls for assistance and then returned to other patrol districts. Patrol was enhanced in some districts, with patrol units doubled and sometimes tripled, while it remained the same as before in districts used as control groups for research purposes.

At the conclusion of the research, change in crime rate was used as one measure of patrol effectiveness. It was assumed that crime would go up in districts where patrol was eliminated, remain unchanged in districts where the number of patrol units remained the same, and go down in districts where patrol was enhanced. Instead, the research found no change in the crime rate in the combined districts. In effect, random patrol had no measurable influence on crime.

One significant finding was that approximately 60% of an officer's time was uncommitted. This meant that officers were waiting on calls for service. Police managers began to consider that this time could be better spent in a directed form of police patrol.

Directed Patrol: A Change of Paradigm

Capitalizing on the Kansas City preventive patrol experiment, police managers began to alter the use of patrol. They told their officers to focus their efforts in high-crime areas—which in effect meant that for officers on the street, they could be anywhere in their beats. But without specific direction on where to go and what to do, officers simply continued to patrol in the same manner in which they had been done for decades.

In the 1980s, a paradigm shift began to occur in policing. The ineffectiveness of "professional era" police tactics—that is, reactive, incident-driven methods and emphases on quantitative outcomes such as number of calls for service, arrests, and so forth—was becoming apparent. Television images of water hoses and police dogs being used on peaceful demonstrators and police use of nightsticks to beat protestors led the public to question police tactics. This, in turn, led to authors suggesting that police-patrol strategies may alleviate the social pressure that was building in the United States.

With researchers questioning long-held beliefs about patrol, a new management strategy emerged. Community policing, as it became known, released officers from being tied to a radio waiting for calls. One of the elements of community policing is decentralization of decision making. Community policing is based on an officer communicating and forming partnerships with citizens to determine how best to resolve the problems that the community views as important. Community policing also allows officers to implement strategies that will deal with the problems. These community partnerships and problem solving strategies led to the concept of directed patrol.

Focus of Directed Patrol

There are two types of directed patrol. One type is a short-term patrol strategy that is crime specific. When crime analysis determines a "hot spot" (a location where certain crimes cluster), directed enforcement can be used to reduce or eliminate the problem. Driving-under-the-influence (DUI) checkpoints, gun buy-back programs, and stings to inhibit prostitution, drug sales, or robberies will usually involve a short-term change of patrol activity. The patrol strategy is based on the response deemed appropriate by the officer(s) involved in the problem solving. Although not crime related, crowd control at a major event or an anticipated problem location (e.g., dignitary visit, major sporting event) also involve short-term changes in patrol activity.

The second type of directed patrol involves a longer-term change of patrol activity. To determine if one-man patrol units are as effective as two-man patrol units, it is necessary to change current tactics to test one strategy against another. The same is true for foot patrol versus motor patrol, horse patrol versus foot/motor patrol, bike patrol versus other forms of patrol, and so on. If a new patrol strategy is going to be used, it is necessary to give the new strategy appropriate time to be evaluated.

Research on Directed Patrol

Considering the long history of policing, directed patrol is a recent management strategy. However, there is a significant body of research that is being developed to study the effectiveness of this new strategy.

Research on directed patrol has usually been done to determine the effectiveness of a change in patrol strategy. If the research is conducted by the agency conducting the program or engaging in a change of strategy, the research is usually evaluative in nature. The purpose is often to justify a short-term change of resource allocation. The results of this research usually involve descriptive statistics (e.g., numbers of warrants served, street value of drugs seized, numbers of DUI arrests made).

If the studies are conducted by academic researchers, the results are usually analytical and based on longer-range results of a change in patrol strategies. Often the research will use inferential statistics and can be found in legislative reports and scholarly journals.

Evaluative Research

When an agency conducts a short-term, directed patrol strategy, it usually employs an evaluative research design that describes the need for the action and the results. This type of research is very pragmatic. After agencies set up driver's license checkpoints, gun buy-back programs, or DUI checkpoints, they will often release to news agencies the number of citations issued, guns removed from the street, and arrests made. These indicators of police activity reflect positive police efforts to keep the community safe.

Rarely do departments release data that cast a negative light on the department. However, both positive and negative evaluations are used to make internal changes in police strategy and also to evaluate teams, internal departments, or individual officers. As indicated above, the effectiveness of the program is based solely on data that indicate the positive effect of the program and is rarely used in comparative evaluations with other programs unless the comparison is a positive reflection of the most recent program.

Analytical Research

Scholars use analytical designs to conduct their research. Analytical research tends to be more neutral. Such researchers are rarely interested in short-term outcomes; their focus is usually on long-term effectiveness of police strategies. They may focus such results as social or psychological effects of changes in strategy. Studies that examine the use of foot patrol on reduction of community fear of crime or the relationship of an officer's job satisfaction and approval of community policing would be examples of this type of research.

Analytical research often uses statistical analysis to evaluate findings. Unlike evaluative research, analytical research is more likely to use higher levels of data. The purpose of the research is not to find approval or disapproval of a program or strategy. The purpose of analytical research is to analyze several variables and determine if a difference occurs or if a correlation exists. The researchers will then propose reasons for the change and comment on whether the change is positive or negative.

Directed patrol is an important evolution in policing. Thus, research that will help police agencies to determine if directed patrol is working and what type of directed patrol works best for a specific department is important to criminal justice.

Robert L. Werling

See also Building Partnerships and Stakeholders; Crime Analysis; Hot Spots; Learning Organization; Place-Based Policing; Problem-Solving Initiatives, Assessment and Evaluation

Further Readings

McGarrell, E. F., Chermak, S., & Weiss, A. (2002, November). *Reducing gun violence: Evaluation of the Indianapolis Police Department's directed patrol project.* NCJ 188740. Retrieved from https://www.ncjrs.gov/pdffiles1/nij/188740.pdf

Peak, K. J., & Glensor, R. W. (2011). *Community policing and problem solving: Strategies and practices* (6th ed.). Upper Saddle River, NJ: Prentice Hall

Sherman, L. W., & Weisburd, D. L. (1995). General deterrent effects of police patrol in crime "hot spots": A randomized, controlled trial. *Justice Quarterly, 12*(4), 625–648.

DOMESTIC VIOLENCE, CHARACTERISTICS OF

Domestic violence is generally not a crime; rather, the term is descriptive of the serious social problem of violence located largely within the family structure. In general, domestic violence is also often considered a pattern of behavior which may escalate. Within the legal system, the term *domestic violence* is used to encompass a variety of crimes, ranging from battery and assault to false imprisonment, kidnapping, stalking, rape or sexual assault, and homicide. Such crimes, when identified as domestic violence, have raised issues of enforcement, prosecution, and sentencing. Crimes associated with domestic violence may involve mandatory arrest policies or laws, a suspect being held in jail for a specified number of hours before conditional release is permitted, and unique criminal sentences such as batterer counseling.

Although early scrutiny of domestic violence focused on wife abuse, the legal system and state legislatures now acknowledge gender neutrality; that is, the perpetrator or victim of domestic violence may be any person regardless of gender or sexual orientation. In addition, state and local laws vary widely in defining domestic violence: it may include crimes perpetrated by spouses or intimate partners, or persons who have been in such a relationship. Victims or perpetrators may be children, siblings, or the elderly such as parents or grandparents. Most recently, states have begun to include violence in dating relationships within their definitions of domestic violence.

In the U.S. criminal justice system, domestic violence crimes are those most often termed crimes against persons. They generally involve physical violence or threats of violence. Physical violence includes not only beating but also kicking, pulling hair, burning, shoving, and choking. Recently, states have begun to enact strangulation laws specifically aimed at domestic violence. Threats of violence or of harming the victim or loved ones, intimidation, and coercion are criminal acts often associated with domestic violence. In many cases, domestic violence crimes are charged as misdemeanors unless there is substantial bodily harm. Finally, crimes against property that are commonly associated with domestic violence include destruction of property and vandalism, theft, and trespass.

Understanding the general characteristics of domestic violence and its evolution as a crime provides the setting for the role of modern community policing in combating such violence. After a brief historical perspective of domestic violence, this entry provides an overview of contemporary victims and offenders, the risk factors for violence, and the characteristics and responses of victims and perpetrators as they relate to law enforcement's response to domestic violence.

Historical Perspective

Before the 19th century, wives were considered the property of their husbands and had no legal identity. The head of the family was not only legally responsible for his wife's actions but also had a duty to maintain order in the family—including the correction of his wife. A man's authority also extended over his children and all members of his household. Given this history, it is not surprising or unexpected that wives were often blamed for their own physical or emotional abuse. In colonial America, the local vicar or parish minister might well counsel her to be a better wife, although the spouse might also be advised to be a more patient husband.

As wives gained independent legal status during the second half of the 19th century, the husband's duty and authority became more uncertain. Early feminists identified financial stress and alcohol consumption as triggers for domestic violence, but saw the root of wife abuse in the rule of men. Then, during the same period and well into the 20th century, the issue of family privacy further obscured the issue of domestic violence, particularly in the middle and upper classes. As a matter of private shame, domestic violence could be a family secret. When it was made public, legal authorities were frequently reluctant to intervene directly, except when required in cases of extreme violence.

In the modern era, establishing services and shelters for battered women in the early 1970s was quickly followed by the recognition of civil protection or restraining orders. In the 1980s, the role of the criminal justice system in combating domestic violence centered on police response and the law. Today, in addition to such social and legal responses, preventive measures include increased public awareness and education.

Victims and Offenders

As noted above, domestic violence offenders and their victims are largely defined by their relationship. It can be argued that throughout much of history a husband's legal authority over his household led to the toleration of a degree of violence in the family. Indeed, a wife's "provocation" was at times even a defense for physical violence. There were also other ways for a man to control his household. A husband could, for example, deny his wife physical luxuries, even necessities, or deprive her of contact with family and friends, thus isolating her. Or, he could even have her committed to a mental institution. Today, it is still recognized that domestic violence is often about power and control.

In the 1980s, the Domestic Abuse Intervention Project of Duluth, Minnesota, first publicized the Power and Control Wheel based on the experiences of domestic violence victims: It identifies how men use intimidation, emotional abuse, male privilege, economic abuse, isolation, blaming, and children within a physically, and often sexually, violent intimate relationship (see Figure 1). Contrasted with the Power and Control Wheel is the Equality Wheel, also developed by the Domestic Abuse Intervention Project, defining relationships based on shared responsibility, respect, economic partnership, and trust (see Figure 2).

While research indicates that men are generally more aggressive than women, male violence is most likely to involve other males. Violence associated with women is more likely intimate violence. Although it is commonly believed that the vast majority of victims of domestic violence continue to be women, studies and surveys stress that men may also be victims, and domestic violence occurs in same-sex relationships. The degree to which women are abusers in intimate relationships continues to be much debated: When a woman has committed an act of domestic violence, is she the primary abuser in the relationship, or is mutual battery involved, or did she act in self-defense, as is commonly argued? In this analysis, understanding the dynamics of domestic violence becomes crucial: Women in abusive relationships may initiate a violent act, believing that such action will prevent further violence or limit its severity.

In addition, it is widely recognized that domestic violence crosses class, race, and ethnicity. It occurs in rural as well as urban communities. Perpetrators and victims include professionals with college educations and workers who have not completed high school. Domestic violence also crosses cultures. Research suggests that culture impacts attitudes, beliefs, and norms regarding the toleration, or acceptance, of domestic violence, and reporting it. This may be particularly evident in immigrant communities, where language can be an obstacle to communication with service providers or the

Figure 1   Power and Control Wheel

Source: Domestic Abuse Intervention Project, Duluth, Minnesota.

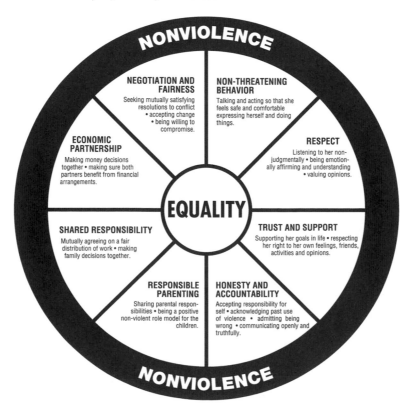

Figure 2   Equality Wheel

Source: Domestic Abuse Intervention Project, Duluth, Minnesota.

police. Underreporting remains a particular concern for minority communities as well. Fear and shame can equally deter victims from revealing their abuse. A reluctance or aversion to dealing with the police also remains common. For the victim who is an immigrant living illegally in the United States, reporting abuse may simply not be seen as an option—even though under the federal Violence Against Women Act, if certain conditions are met, removal, or deportation, proceedings will not be initiated against battered noncitizens.

Given the diverse demographics of domestic violence, it is not surprising that one size does not fit all in regard to the characteristics of such violence. Researchers will use different labels in regard to their findings, and the legal system, police, and service providers will also often use different terms in describing the characteristics, motivations, and risk factors of victims or abusers. Thus, domestic violence may, for example, be termed *marital violence*, *intimate partner violence* or even *terrorism*, *dating violence*, *mutual battering* or *couples violence*, and *lesbian* or *gay violence*. In these categories, differences in the levels or character of the violence may be apparent.

In regard to abusive men, research indicates that some may be physically aggressive and violent only in the home, whereas others may be generally aggressive and violent. Individuals in the latter group are more likely to come from a violent family and have been a victim themselves of child abuse. Intimate partner violence is often characterized by the issues of power and control referenced above. Abusive men are likely to be extremely possessive and jealous. In addition, they may have negative attitudes toward women. Violent women are also likely to have histories of child abuse (i.e., being abused as a child). In contrast, there are intimate relationships where mutual violence exists. Research suggests that male physical violence is more likely to cause injury, primarily because men are physically stronger and larger. In such mutually violent relationships, alcohol consumption by both parties is common.

It is widely recognized that alcohol impacts reasoning and cognitive abilities and may lower or remove inhibitions. In addition, intimate partner violence and mutual violence may be motivated by a desire to have control, to be more powerful. As noted above, jealousy is common. Research also suggests that stress generally may be a risk factor or trigger for violence. Economic stress, in particular, is often a precursor to violence if there are family financial problems or unemployment. While risk factors may predict domestic violence, often service providers and the criminal justice system are not able to intervene to address the problem of violence until the domestic violence is reported by the victim, a family member, neighbor, or other third party.

Responses to Domestic Violence

Responding to domestic violence in the modern era primarily centers on the criminal justice response to such violence from the initial call and arrest to prosecution and sentencing. Victims and offenders, however, also react and respond to the violence in their lives.

Victims and Offenders

For victims, certain responses to a beating or other acts of domestic violence may, in fact, contribute to what is often termed a *cycle of violence*. In an ongoing abusive relationship, the victim may change his or her behavior in response to a beating, possibly being very vigilant regarding the offender's verbal and physical cues and in complying with his or her demands. Victims may stay in a relationship involving domestic violence for many reasons, from love and hope to financial dependence and low self-esteem. This does not mean that the victims necessarily become helpless, as many victims have a variety of coping strategies such as problem solving, emotional withdrawal, or even fighting back. When domestic violence has escalated to extreme threats or acts of harming pets and child abuse, or the direct threat, "I will kill you," leaving may be the only option, but research suggests that doing so is also the most dangerous option.

The actions of the offender are central to the cycle of violence. Often the offender is a skilled manipulator, and after an acute violent episode, there is likely to be a honeymoon phase: The offender expresses remorse, promises that the violence will not happen again, and may even buys flowers or other gifts. The victim then may begin to hope. But, eventually the tension builds again; verbal abuse escalates and the cues appear until an episode or outburst of physical violence occurs, and the cycle resumes. These cycles in intimate partner violence often escalate in frequency and severity. Many states have implemented domestic violence fatality review teams. These panels examine the chronology and circumstances surrounding homicides, or suicides, in domestic violence cases, and attempt to identify possible interventions that can prevent other instances of domestic violence and deaths.

Criminal Justice Response

Today police agencies are most often the first responders to domestic violence incidents and thus are an essential part of a wider response to domestic violence, offering shelter and services to victims. Victims who escape violent relationships often need medical care, economic assistance, housing, employment, and basic skills training. Victims may also need to relocate or even change their identities. Hospitals commonly have protocols addressing domestic violence, and a majority of states have laws addressing domestic violence in the workplace aimed at protecting and assisting victims. Today there is a National Domestic Violence Hotline as well as statewide hotlines and networks that offer assistance.

The criminal justice response to domestic violence is multilayered. It will likely begin with a domestic violence call. Here, police officers are critical actors. Throughout much of the 20th century, police officers generally responded to domestic violence calls by either sending the batterer away, calming the situation, or mediating between the parties, or in cases of extreme violence, arresting the offender. Officers were often reluctant to intervene in what were then viewed as a family matter and generally disliked domestic violence calls. Such attitudes were influenced by perceptions of their danger, that they resulted in little reward, and that they were not "real police work." Following the grassroots movement to address domestic violence in the 1970s, police agencies and legislatures began to address the role of arrest. Proponents of proarrest policies have long argued that arrest sends the message that beating your spouse or partner is a crime, and it may also give the victim an opportunity to escape the relationship. The message in public service announcements became: No one deserves to be beaten.

In response to this debate, police agencies began to impose proarrest or mandatory arrest policies and many states also enacted mandatory arrest laws limiting police officer discretion. These laws basically require a police officer to arrest a suspected offender where there is probable cause to believe that person has committed a criminal act involving domestic violence. Significantly, the officers need not witness the incident (historically, to make misdemeanor arrests without warrants, officers would have to witness the offense). All states today authorize warrantless arrests for misdemeanor domestic violence cases where probable cause exists. Exceptions to the mandatory arrest requirement may exist, for example, if the suspect is no longer present at the scene. In such cases, though, an officer may seek an arrest warrant for the suspected offender.

In some jurisdictions, mandatory arrest laws led to high rates of mutual arrest (i.e., both parties being arrested). In response to this issue, a number of states enacted "primary aggressor" laws requiring that police officers attempt to determine whether there is a primary aggressor and who it is. Officers will then generally arrest and book only the primary aggressor. Although policies and statutes vary widely, today it is also common to have detention holds placed on domestic violence arrestees—the primary aggressor must be held in jail a certain number of hours before conditional release—which may give the victim the opportunity to leave the abuser and service providers and domestic violence advocates the extra time needed to assist the victim.

Prosecutor's offices also have their own policies regarding domestic violence cases, and may even have designated domestic violence teams or personnel. An important issue here is the burden of proof. How will the prosecutor prove beyond a reasonable doubt (the legal requirement for criminal conviction) that a crime has been committed? This is particularly problematic when victims change their minds regarding the charge or refuse to testify. Victims may be reluctant to testify because of fear, because they are financially dependent on the offender, or because they may not want their abuser jailed.

In the 1990s, some prosecutor's offices developed "no drop" policies, that is, proceeding to trial without the victim's cooperation if there is sufficient evidence such as photographs of the scene and victim as well as police officer testimony. Nevertheless, in cases where victims refuse to testify despite a subpoena to do so, prosecutors and judges face difficult decisions: Should a victim who does not cooperate be jailed for contempt of court, particularly if the victim's testimony is considered vital for a conviction, or should the charges be dropped or dismissed? As early as the 1980s, some prosecutor's offices began to hire victim advocates to contact victims and assist them through the legal and court process, in an effort to familiarize them with the justice process and ensure there were no surprises for victims at trial. Today, victim advocates also work within police agencies.

Although the effectiveness of proarrest policies and laws continues to be debated, arrest is generally the first step to prosecution, conviction, and sentencing. In domestic violence cases today, sentencing is likely to include mandatory counseling for offenders as well as jail time. Counseling often focuses on the offenders' mental health status, including personality disorders, and emphasizes behavioral changes. Evaluation of the short- and long-term impacts of counseling programs on deterrence and stopping the violence is ongoing.

Beyond state and local criminal justice responses to domestic violence, the federal government has also been active in addressing domestic violence in recent decades. For example, perpetrators of domestic abuse who use firearms in the commission of domestic violence–related crimes face possible federal prosecution. Also, federal law requires that civil protection orders for victims be recognized and enforced across state borders in all jurisdictions. The federal Violence Against Women Act of 1994, and its amendments, have also been of particular importance in funding domestic violence training, services, and research.

Today, it is reported that fewer people are experiencing domestic violence. While strides have been made in public awareness and education and in criminal justice policies and responses, domestic violence remains a serious social problem. Debate continues to drive new awareness, research, and policies.

Susan A. Lentz

See also Domestic Violence, Community Policing Strategies for; Violent Crime Control and Law Enforcement Act of 1994

Further Readings

Buzawa, E. S., & Buzawa, C. G. (2002). *Domestic violence: The criminal justice response* (3rd ed.). Thousand Oaks, CA: Sage.

Eigenberg, H. M. (Ed.). (2001). *Women battering in the United States: Till death do us part.* Prospect Heights, IL: Waveland Press.

Feder, L. (Ed.). (1999). *Women and domestic violence: An interdisciplinary approach.* New York, NY: Haworth Press.

Frieze, I. H. (2005). *Hurting the one you love: Violence in relationships.* Belmont, CA: Wadsworth.

Gosselin, D. K. (2009). *Heavy hands: An introduction to the crimes of domestic violence* (4th ed.). Upper Saddle River, NJ: Prentice Hall.

Matthews, D. (Ed.). (2004). *Domestic violence sourcebook.* Detroit, MI: Omnigraphics.

McCue, M. L. (2008). *Domestic violence: A reference handbook.* Santa Barbara, CA: ABC-CLIO.

National Institute of Justice. (n.d.). Retrieved from http://www.nij.gov/topics/crime

DOMESTIC VIOLENCE, COMMUNITY POLICING STRATEGIES FOR

Domestic violence, also known as *intimate partner violence*, is dangerous not only for the victim but also for the law enforcement officers who respond to these service calls. Efforts to intervene and prevent intimate partner violence are important not only for the primary victim but also for any secondary victims such as children who are growing up in an environment filled with violence and abuse. In recent years, greater emphasis has focused on the long-term detrimental consequences of simply witnessing abuse. Given the cyclical nature, intensity, and potential lethality of this crime, greater efforts are being made within law enforcement, the criminal justice system, and the community to address intimate partner violence. This entry examines strategies for applying community policing to this critical issue.

Community Policing to Address Intimate Partner Violence

In 1996, the Community Policing to Combat Domestic Violence Initiative was created within the U.S. Department of Justice's Community Oriented Policing Services Office to encourage local law enforcement to create innovative ways to address intimate partner violence. Given the complexity of intimate partner violence and the varied needs of those trying to escape and survive this crime, it became necessary to not focus on a single agency for support, but rather to create a collaborative effort to provide wrap-around support to those victimized. In recognition of the need to provide multiple, layered supports, federal grant monies enabled local law enforcement agencies to hire police officers, purchase technology, and expand services for housing, health and mental health, and victim services. At the community level, law enforcement and service providers were encouraged to work together through an equal partnership to determine ways to intervene and prevent intimate partner violence.

In the initial year of funding, the program awarded nearly $47 million to more than 300 agencies that used the monies to focus on training, problem solving, and implementing organizational change to streamline and provide more effective services. In subsequent years, monies were targeted toward creating investigative units, expanding services in rural and tribal communities, assisting underserved populations, and addressing stalking. The latter is common in domestic abuse situations, particularly during times of estrangement or after a relationship has ended.

These federal monies provided for intervention at different points along the abuse continuum—before violence begins, during an incident to stop the immediate abuse, and after victimization to address recidivism. Improved responses focused on all potential victims, as well as all potential offenders with the recognition that children who grew up exposed to domestic violence could repeat the pattern later in their own teen and adult relationships. Given the longitudinal nature of the cycle of violence, intervening early and often can help to break this violent and abusive pattern.

Early education-awareness programs can discuss violence within relationships, types of abusive behaviors, the impact of abuse, and healthy partnerships. Other aspects of these programs can include the importance of reporting, what to do if abuse is suspected, and school and community resources—all of which work to address and alleviate violence in teen and young adult dating relationships. More research is needed to evaluate these types of programs because studies based on the limited data collected have produced mixed results regarding the programs' effectiveness. Evaluations show increased knowledge of the types of abuse and available resources, but not necessarily reductions in victimization.

Some jurisdictions used monies to create a tiered approach to deter offenders from abusing partners. The varied response recognizes that some offenders respond well and are deterred from future acts of violence simply through police intervention. Other offenders are more resistant and added layers of intervention are needed, such as arrest, restraining orders, or offender-intervention programs. Likewise, there are gradations in the services that victims need. As such, a one-size-fits-all approach to addressing intimate partner violence is not appropriate and, in fact, could be quite dangerous.

Of equal importance is to focus intervention efforts on both the victim and the offender. The combined intervention strategy allows for the provision of services to better address the needs of both partners in the violent relationship. Some crime prevention strategies have included increased police surveillance and patrol; electronic ankle bracelet monitoring for high-risk offenders; pendant alarms and preprogrammed cell phones for victims; alarm-activated recording devices with two-way communication, allowing victims and law enforcement officers to speak directly; and video camera surveillance for high-risk victims. Subsequent evaluations of tiered approaches found a reduction in the number of intimate partner violence calls, as well as longer intervals between violence.

Other communities focused on developing an assessment instrument to help law enforcement identify those cases that were most likely to escalate in an attempt to predict and prevent potential lethality. Although some instruments exist, they do not effectively predict lethality in intimate partner violence cases. Regardless of the lack of an accurate assessment tool, some factors that put law enforcement on heightened alert for escalation include threats of violence, harassment, violations of protective orders, prior use of a gun, and engaging in other types of crimes, such as stalking, trespassing, and vandalism.

Monies were available to collect aggregate data on intimate partner violence, which provides valuable insight into the extent of the problem within the community. These data are critical to understand the context and history of assaults, to determine the potential for escalation and lethality, and to find out whether there are other types of abuse or neglect occurring within the domicile. Funding also provided for research to evaluate the efforts under way. This is essential, as measurement helps organizations and collaborative partnerships to identify critical gaps in strategies or resources; areas for targeted improvement; redundancies in service delivery; as well as efficient and effective practices. Research also allows for promising practices to be replicated in other communities.

Specialized Courts

There are several hundred courts throughout the United States that focus specifically on intimate partner violence cases. The inception of these courts is part of a larger movement to have specialized courts to deal with difficult and complex problems and populations including drugs, mental health, and drunk driving. Those who work in these courts see the importance of having all court personnel trained to deal with the specific case at hand. Domestic violence courts personnel are trained to understand the dynamics of an abusive relationship, the inherent power imbalance, and the various tactics used to control, threaten, coerce, and manipulate the victim. In addition, these courts deal with only these types of cases, making all personnel equally familiar with the history and dynamics of the victim and offender as they go through the court process. Those working within this court do not have to get up to speed each time with new clients. Given the repeated and cyclical nature of intimate partner violence, greater familiarity is gained through a court that only addresses these types of cases. Furthermore, domestic violence can contribute to more timely responses, fewer delays, more appropriate referrals for assistance, and greater accountability when conditions of the court are not met or followed. Ultimately, cases can be handled effectively in a specialized domestic violence court.

In this setting, one judge or a handful of judges, depending on the size of the community and the extent of the problem of intimate partner violence, will work with a team of law enforcement and service providers to develop a case plan for the offender. Treatment programs (such as substance abuse and mental health counseling) and even criminal sanctions may result if the offender fails to comply with the case plan. Domestic violence courts also aggressively pursue prosecution of severe cases, even if a victim recants or no longer wants to participate. Victimless prosecution relies heavily on the testimony provided by law enforcement and witnesses, photographs, medical reports, 911 calls of assaults in progress to build a case of violence, abuse, and aggression against the victim. Law enforcement plays a critical role in helping prosecutors identify the most severe and chronic cases from the multitude of arrests made each day. This partnership helps prosecutors to focus efforts on increasing safety, while also helping those victims who are in the greatest need of assistance from the courts.

Publicized convictions can serve to maximize the general deterrent effect. The lack of victim participation may reduce the offender's urge to retaliate given that the victim has not played a role in the outcome. An unintended consequence of victimless prosecution is to further reduce victim discretion and control. While evaluations indicate victim satisfaction with the court process, the impact of these courts on recidivism requires further research.

Family Justice Centers

The beginning of the 21st century saw the dawn of a new one-stop program to house intimate partner violence intervention services in a single facility. The Family Justice Center model seeks to increase victim survival and independence, address immediate and long-term needs, and promote recovery. Before the one-stop approach emerged, victim services were dispersed across the community, an approach that still exists in some places. This makes it cumbersome for individuals, who can have trouble going from one location to another, especially when they are dependent on public transportation or when timing is critical because of work, school, or familial responsibilities. In addition, dispersed services can force victims to repeat their needs, retell their story, and become exhausted from having to go from one organization to another, and back to a previous one for more assistance. Fragmented service provision can breed frustration, discontent, and feelings that it is easier just to go back to the abuser.

The San Diego Family Justice Center (http://www.familyjusticecenter.org) was the first of its kind to provide victims with advocacy, safety planning, law enforcement assistance, documentation of injuries for investigation and prosecution, legal assistance and court accompaniment, assistance for people with disabilities, medical and mental health care, housing options, transportation, child care, faith-based services, and a host of other essential interventions all in the same location. The San Diego Family Justice Center became a model program that has since been replicated.

In October 2003, President George W. Bush announced the creation of the President's Family Justice Center Initiative. With the infusion of federal monies, multidisciplinary one-stop service centers to address intimate partner violence, sexual assault, and elder abuse cropped up in urban, suburban, and rural communities throughout the United States. The importance of Family Justice Centers as an effective tool in addressing family violence has been recognized by continued funding through the Violence Against Women Act (VAWA).

The Family Justice Center model is identified as a best practice in the intervention and prevention of intimate partner violence with documented outcomes of reduced homicide, increased safety, and increased victim independence and empowerment. In addition, evaluations of this model showed reduced victim fear and anxiety, greater willingness to participate in the criminal justice system, greater prosecution of offenders, and increased community support for victim services. Research based on evaluations, focus groups, and client feedback surveys has also shown that an effective Family Justice Center must have ten key components: (1) colocated multidisciplinary services to increase safety and support; (2) proarrest policies to increase offender accountability; (3) policies incidental to arrest and enforcement to reduce revictimization; (4) victim safety and advocacy as the highest priority; (5) victim confidentiality as a priority; (6) prohibition against offenders seeking services from the Family Justice Center; (7) community history of collaborative efforts to address family violence; (8) strong support from local elected officials and policymakers; (9) strategic planning; and (10) strong and diverse community support.

Community Interventions Beyond the Criminal Justice System

There are a number of community-based interventions under way to address intimate partner violence outside of the scope of the criminal justice system, but these efforts are helpful for law enforcement with reporting, investigating, and reducing intimate partner violence. The medical community, law schools, and hairdressers all have been key players in these efforts.

The American Medical Association (AMA), the American Academy of Pediatrics, and the American College of Obstetricians and Gynecologists in 1999 recommended guidelines for screening and referrals for suspected victims of intimate partner violence. The AMA recognized that medical personnel may be the only individuals to see the repercussions of abuse. When injuries are viewed, it is important to follow a screening protocol to determine the nature of the injuries and to document the abuse. Likewise, medical professionals should discuss intimate partner violence with patients whom they suspect may be abused or those who are statistically at a higher risk of violence, such as those who are pregnant. Documentation about specific incidents can play a vital role in an investigation and subsequent prosecution. Some jurisdictions have created partnerships between medical practitioners and law enforcement in an attempt to ascertain the victim's abuse history. A study of these efforts indicated that victims were more willing to talk to someone from the medical community than to a law enforcement officer about their injuries and the abuse. Despite the promises that this continued partnership may hold for greater insight into abuse and injury, medical personnel are at times reluctant to provide routine screening for intimate partner violence due to a lack of training regarding appropriate responses, referrals, and follow-up.

Many law schools around the United States offer student advocacy services for victims, especially those who experience intimate partner violence. Some student legal clinics assist with the legal paperwork associated with restraining orders, as well as divorce and custody matters. Others provide court accompaniments to help victims navigate legal proceedings in a courtroom setting. These programs provide important low-cost or even free legal assistance for the victims, as well as invaluable experience for future legal practitioners.

While not an intuitive partner in the efforts to alleviate intimate partner violence, cosmetology programs are beginning to train hairdressers to identify and respond to domestic abuse. This new partner is important because a salon may be one of the few places a victim can go without an abuser in tow. Likewise, the victim may have a long-standing relationship with her hairdresser and may confide details of the abuse. Similarly, hairdressers may be able to see bruising at the scalp or bald patches that have occurred during violent incidents. Given the ability to talk in private, hairdressers can provide an ear to listen, resources for assistance, and some degree of follow-up at subsequent visits. These efforts have proven to be helpful in rural locales where victims may face added stigma in seeking services or where resources are not readily available. While hairdressers should not replace professional counseling or therapy, they can be a first line of identification, disclosure, discussion, and referral.

Important factors associated with designing effective community responses to intimate partner violence include the following: (1) Community partners are essential to increase awareness and build skills; (2) increasing awareness and skills related to cultural competence are essential to reach out to underserved victim populations; (3) law enforcement, victim services, and allied professionals must work together on mutual and shared goals; and (4) the entire community plays a role in increasing resources, identifying victims, and reporting victimization, all of which contribute to greater intervention and ultimately prevention of intimate partner violence and abuse.

Bernadette T. Muscat

See also Domestic Violence, Characteristics of

Further Readings

Catalano, S., Smith, E., Snyder, H., & Rand, M. (2009). *Female victims of violence.* NCJ 228356. Washington, DC: U.S. Department of Justice, Bureau of Justice Statistics. Retrieved from http://bjs.ojp.usdoj.gov/content/pub/pdf/fvv.pdf

Reuland, M., Morabito, M. S., Preston, C., & Cheney, J. (2006). *Police-community partnerships to address domestic violence.* Washington, DC: U.S. Department of Justice, Office of Community Oriented Policing Services. Retrieved from http://cops.usdoj.gov/files/RIC/Publications/domestic_violence_web3.pdf

Sadusky, J. (2004). *Bridging domestic violence intervention and community policing: Partnership and problem-solving tools.* Washington, DC: U.S. Department of Justice, Office of Justice Programs, Office on Violence Against Women. Retrieved from http://www.vaw.umn.edu/documents/bridgingdv/bridgingdv.pdf

Sampson, R. (2007). *Problem-oriented guides for police, problem-specific guides series, No. 45.* U.S. Department of Justice, Office of Community Oriented Policing Services. Retrieved from http://www.cops.usdoj.gov

Sherman, L. W., & Berk, R. A. (1984, April). The specific deterrent effects of arrest for domestic assault. *American Sociological Review, 49*(2), 261–272.

Smith, E. L., & Farole, D. J. (2009). *Profile of intimate partner violence cases in large urban counties.* NCJ 228193. Washington, DC: U.S. Department of Justice, Bureau of Justice Statistics. Retrieved from http://bjs.ojp.usdoj.gov/content/pub/pdf/pipvcluc.pdf

U.S. Department of Justice. (2001). *Toolkit to end violence against women.* Washington, DC: U.S. Department of Justice, Office on Violence Against Women. Retrieved from https://www.ncjrs.gov/pdffiles1/206041.pdf

DRUG CRIMES, CHARACTERISTICS OF

The use and abuse of illegal drugs is connected to a significant amount of crime around the world. Drug crime is not just a problem of violations of drug control laws and regulations, but is also a significant contributing factor to a large amount of violent and property crime as well as social disorder. While drug laws have been continually evolving, the correlation of drugs and crime is not recent, and attempts to address drug crime have long been a focus of local, state, and federal law enforcement agencies. What has become clear to many who work to enforce drug laws is that drug crime is not something we can expect to eliminate through arrest and regulation alone.

The extent of drug use while people commit crimes is also quite high, and seems to be related to where the offender lives: for example, one survey found that 49% of persons arrested tested positive for at least one illicit drug in Washington, D.C., while 87% of arrestees in Chicago, Illinois, tested positive for an illicit drug. Additionally, many arrestees tested positive for more than one illegal drug at the time of arrest—from 15% in Atlanta, Georgia, to 40% in Chicago. The most common substances present at time of arrest, in descending order, are marijuana, cocaine, opiates, and methamphetamine.

Finally, the annual financial cost of combating drug abuse is significant as well. For fiscal year 2013, the federal Office of National Drug Control Policy was appropriated more than $13 billion to reduce drug use and availability through (1) substance abuse prevention, (2) substance abuse treatment, (3) domestic law enforcement, and (4) interdiction and international counterdrug support.

A common perception of a drug crime consists of an open-air drug deal where a street dealer and a drug user exchange a small amount of an illegal drug for cash. While this type of crime is common, there is a wide range of crimes associated with and caused by drug use and abuse. This entry briefly describes the characteristics of drug crimes by grouping them into three broad categories: drug-defined, drug-influenced, and drug-involved.

Drug-Defined Crimes

Drug-defined crimes are crimes where the primary offense is a violation of a criminal statute that prohibits or regulates the possession, manufacture, or distribution of drugs that have the potential for abuse. This is a substantial category of drug crime, as according to the Federal Bureau of Investigation, more than 1.6 million arrests are made each year for drug-abuse violations. The common perception example described above would fall into this category, with state-to-state variations in the severity of the crime depending on the type and amount of the drug in the offender's possession, whether there is also evidence of intent to sell or distribute, and the offender's prior criminal record. Federal law may also come into play depending on the volume and trafficking patterns involved in distribution.

Another type of drug-defined crime would be the cultivation or manufacture of illegal substances, such as in marijuana grow houses or methamphetamine labs. Many people think of drugs being cultivated or manufactured in other countries and smuggled into this country, and this is largely true for drugs such as cocaine, MDMA (ecstasy), heroin, and marijuana. It also appears to be true for two of the newest drug threats: synthetic cannabis and bath salts, a set of designer drugs that often contain substituted cathinones. However a wide variety of organic and synthetic drugs are grown or manufactured within the United States as well, including marijuana, methamphetamine, PCP, and LSD. The size of the operations to cultivate and manufacture these drugs can vary dramatically, from large marijuana grows in rural areas to "shake-and-bake" method methamphetamine labs no larger than a plastic drink bottle. The latter means of manufacturing methamphetamine is simple and requires little technical knowledge: all that is required is a two-liter soda bottle, a few cold pills, and a few household chemicals. The mix of chemicals in the soda bottle can explode—if there is only a little oxygen inside the bottle, or it is shaken or opened in an incorrect manner—and become a giant fireball. The result can be devastating, and a number of severe burns and fatalities have resulted. Police officers across the nation are being trained in how to handle these new mobile labs.

This category of drug-defined crime also includes the diversion of legal but regulated drugs from their legitimate purpose to an illicit one. For example, the redistribution of prescription drugs—such as hydrocodone (found in Vicodin), oxycodone (known as OxyContin), ketamine (an anesthetic most often used in veterinary practice), and benzodiazepine (common in anti-anxiety medications like Valium or Xanax)—for nonmedical use. This has become a growing concern for policymakers in recent years as many users of these drugs do not see them as being in the same dangerous category as illegal drugs. There is a perception among many youth today that because these drugs are prescription drugs they are safer to use, but no narcotic is safe once it has been diverted from its intended purpose.

Diversion of legal narcotics can take place in different ways, including raiding family medicine cabinets, using altered or fraudulent prescriptions, doctor-shopping (going to a series of physicians to collect multiple legitimate scripts), and theft from hospitals and pharmacies. Diversion can also be the act of one person for a small amount of a drug, or part of a more sophisticated enterprise involving multiple people in the systematic diversion of drugs. The Internet has become one of the primary tools used to systematically divert prescription drugs, and for the schemes to work it requires multiple people to be complicit in the crime, from the website staff to unscrupulous doctors.

Drug-Influenced Crimes

The second broad category of drug crimes is drug-influenced crimes, where the primary criminal act is not the possession of an illegal substance but where drugs were a significant factor in the commission of the crime. Work by the Arrestee Drug Abuse Monitoring Program suggests that about half of the people who are arrested—regardless of the offense—test positive for an illicit substance at the time of their arrest. The most obvious example of a drug-influenced crime is when a drug user commits a crime in order to obtain the money needed to buy illegal drugs. Thefts of cash, but also of items that can be easily sold for cash, are common. In addition to stealing in order to buy drugs, others may simply steal the drugs themselves. In recent years with the increase in the abuse of prescription drugs, pharmacies across the country have seen a growing risk of robbery of their stock.

Prostitution is also frequently a drug-influenced crime, and crime statistics regularly bear out a strong link between street prostitution and street drug markets. The prostitute may be the drug user looking for a fast way to get money for drugs, but it is not uncommon to find prostitutes who are the girlfriends of men with serious drug addictions who engage in prostitution to support their partners' drug habit. Pimps also regularly exploit the substance abuse problems of prostitutes they are trafficking to better control them. This exploitation is frequently compounded by subjecting the prostitutes to a wide range of psychological abuse and physical violence. Fear of their pimp, combined with the psychological and physical effects of substance abuse, can easily trap individuals in the sex trade for prolonged amounts of time.

Another example of drug-influenced crimes is when an offender commits a crime while under the influence of drugs, such that the pharmacological effects of the drug are a contributing factor to their behavior. The influence of the drugs does not excuse their behavior, but it is a factor for understanding motivations and actions. For example, the chronic use of stimulants (including cocaine, PCP, and methamphetamine) is frequently associated with hostility and aggression, and homicidal tendencies and paranoia can also occur in users. It is not hard to see how a disagreement in which one or more individuals are high on stimulants could quickly escalate into violence. Other drugs, like MDMA for example, can have a significant impact on the ability of the body to feel pain in addition to causing changes in perception and judgment. Drug users under the influence of these and other stimulants can be volatile and unpredictable, especially in pursuit of the money or drugs needed for their next high, posing a danger to law enforcement officers responding to crimes they commit. In other cases, the influence of the drug may endanger the family and friends of the user, placing them at increased risk of being a victim of violence simply by proximity to the user. There is also a growing body of research on the impact that witnessing violence has on children, providing evidence that even when children are not the direct victim of violence it still places them at greater risk for behavioral problems and victimization in the future.

A final type of drug-influenced crime is when participants in the drug trade commit crimes in order to maintain their business. These are primarily crimes relating to distribution rather than use, and many offenders do not actually use drugs themselves. Drug-influenced crimes of this type can range from simple assaults to homicide, money laundering, bribery and corruption of public officials, and human trafficking. Crimes may occur between rival dealers or gangs fighting over turf and clients in a neighborhood up to large cartels involved in trafficking product and profits across international borders. Estimates of the extent of the international drug trade are hard to establish since it is not a legitimate business paying taxes or issuing profit and loss reports, but there is widespread agreement that drugs make up a significant percentage of transnational organized crime, worth billions of dollars annually to the cartels and organizations controlling the different drug markets around the world.

Drug-Involved Crimes

The third category of drug crimes is drug-involved crimes, where the connection between the drug use and the crime may be less overt than in the previous two categories. Potentially harder to identify, these are nonetheless crimes that may have the greatest impact on a community at large. The drug-using lifestyle ultimately puts those near the user—both in terms of social networks and geographic proximity—at a greater risk of criminal victimization.

For example, simple street market dealers operating in open-air drug markets bring with them a variety of additional criminal activities to the neighborhoods where they operate beyond the exchange of illicit substances, including violence, property crime, and prostitution. The residents of the immediate neighborhood may not actually be involved in the drug market at all, and frequently the majority are not, but their risk of victimization is significantly increased because of their proximity to the drug-defined and drug-influenced crime of the market. Communities along international borders and major national trafficking routes are similarly at risk due to rival distributor and transporter disputes as well as from the connections between drug trafficking and the trafficking of weapons and people. Given the potential for violence and lack of judgment caused by substance abuse, it can be difficult for a community to put an end to the drug trade in their neighborhood, even when the majority of the people who live there do not support or condone the activity.

A second example of a drug-involved crime is child abuse and neglect. Based on work by the Substance Abuse and Mental Health Services Administration (SAMHSA) and the National Center on Addiction and Substance Abuse, there are potentially upward of 9 million children living in homes where an adult uses illicit drugs. These children are commonly referred to as *drug-endangered children*. Because of what we know about the impact that drug use can have on behavior and judgment, these children are at an increased risk of suffering emotional or physical abuse or neglect as a result of living in a home with a drug user. Research has also consistently shown that children who suffer abuse and neglect, as well as children of substance abusers generally, are more likely to become substance abusers themselves. Such drug-involved crime has the potential to lead to all types of drug-related crime in the future if efforts are not made to systematically intercede on behalf of these children and get them access to the treatment, counseling, and other support services they need to break the cycle of substance abuse.

The use of drugs by pregnant women also presents both short- and long-term risks to their future children, and the risks to infants with prenatal exposure to drugs are also frequently included in the discussion of drug-endangered children. Where every state has a variety of statutes concerning child abuse and neglect, drug-involved or otherwise, some states have also begun to criminalize prenatal drug abuse, with sanctions ranging from involuntary commitments to treatment to fines and jail or prison sentences. A key factor in the ability of a state to interfere criminally or civilly on behalf of an unborn child in instances of prenatal substance abuse is whether the state defines a fetus as a person.

A third type of drug-involved crime relates to drug manufacturing and environmental law. The manufacture of synthetic drugs such as methamphetamine, PCP, and GHB produces a significant amount of hazardous waste, but the clandestine-lab "cooks" producing these drugs are not concerned with waste disposal regulations. While research is still ongoing on the long-term environmental hazards associated with clandestine labs, it is possible that residual contamination may affect the ground, buildings, and even the water supply for many years after a clandestine lab has moved or been shut down, unbeknownst to subsequent owners or tenants. Although synthetic drug manufacturers are not the primary target, a number of federal and state environmental laws apply to damage created by the clandestine labs.

It is difficult for communities to combat and prevent the drug-related crimes of possession, diversion, manufacture, and distribution. The crime directly influenced by drug use and abuse adds a significant additional burden to ensuring the health and safety of communities. Once this final group of drug-involved crimes is added into the discussion, the full, substantial extent of drug crime becomes clear. Drug crime is a problem that cuts across crime types and international borders, and affects a wide range of victims, making it a significant challenge for communities, researchers, policymakers, and law enforcement.

Deborah L. Spence

See also Drug Crimes, Community Policing Responses for; Gangs and Their Crimes, Characteristics of; Gang Crimes, Community Policing Strategies for

Further Readings

Center for Behavioral Health Statistics and Quality. (2011). *Results from the 2010 national survey on drug use and health: Summary of national findings*. Rockville, MD: U.S. Department of Health and Human Services, Substance Abuse and Mental Health Services Administration.

Drug Enforcement Administration. (2011). *Drugs of abuse: A DEA resource guide*. Washington, DC: Author.

National Alliance for Drug Endangered Children. (2011). *Drug endangered children: A resource CD for professionals*. Washington, DC: U.S. Department of Justice, Office of Community Oriented Policing Services.

National Drug Intelligence Center. (2011). *National drug threat assessment*. Washington, DC: U.S. Department of Justice, National Drug Intelligence Center.

National Institute on Drug Abuse. (2010). *Drugs, brains, and behavior: The science of addiction*. NIH Pub Number: 10–5605. Bethesda, MD: Author.

National Institute on Drug Abuse. (2011). *Prescription drugs: Abuse and addiction*. NIH Pub Number: 11–4881. Bethesda, MD: Author.

Office of National Drug Control Policy. (2011). *Epidemic: Responding to America's prescription drug abuse crisis*. Washington, DC: Author.

United Nations Office on Drugs and Crime. (2011). *World drug report 2011*. New York, NY: United Nations.

DRUG CRIMES, COMMUNITY POLICING STRATEGIES FOR

While law enforcement plays an important and leading role in any community's attempt to control drug crime, addressing the causes and conditions that lead to drug crime requires a multifaceted approach that works to interrupt supply as well as demand. The community policing principles of problem solving and multidisciplinary collaboration are well suited to addressing both. This entry discusses why community policing is an effective philosophy to employ to address drug crime and provides some examples of specific strategies for different types of drug crime that are built on the community policing philosophy.

Weaknesses of a Traditional Approach

A comprehensive approach to reducing drug crime requires thinking about drugs as a product in a marketplace. The marketplace may be illicit, but it functions with many of the same principles as legitimately traded goods. There are people who want a product and are willing to pay for it, and there are manufacturers, growers, and distributors who are interested in making money through meeting customer needs. Traditional law enforcement techniques largely focus on interrupting the supply side of this market. Those in possession of drugs are sought out and arrested and the product is confiscated. Law enforcement around the world is capable of seizing millions of kilograms of illegal drugs year after year. But there are a number of weaknesses to this approach's ability to eliminate drug crime.

First, simple market principles tell us that when supply is reduced, the cost of the product increases because demand remains. Arresting dealers and traffickers may significantly increase the cost drug users have to pay to get their product of choice, but given what we know about the nature of addiction and the impact that drugs can have on the ability to act rationally, increases in costs are unlikely to deter serious users from seeking their high. If anything, employing this market disruption approach on its own comes with the risk of increasing drug-involved crime, as users resort to more dramatic efforts to obtain their drug of choice and dealers work to protect their supply lines and profit margins.

Second, this traditional approach fails to account for the sheer volume of the market for illegal drugs and its international nature. Despite thousands of local, state, and federal law enforcement officers exclusively focused on counternarcotics enforcement working to seize illegal drugs and interrupt supply, drugs still make it to the streets at prices users can afford. In 2010, the Drug Enforcement Administration alone made more than 30,000 arrests and confiscated more than three-quarters of a million kilograms of cocaine, heroin, methamphetamine, and marijuana.

The third thing the traditional supply-side approaches do not fully account for is the varying characteristics of the drugs, their users, and the neighborhoods in which they are found. All of these factors will contribute to different crime problems in different areas, and one approach will not work equally well in all situations. For example, arresting a street dealer in an open-air market may help law enforcement officers seize a small amount of product and take a dealer temporarily off the street, but it may not help identify the higher-level suppliers or do anything about the various violent and property crimes being committed by that dealer's users. Similarly, large-scale operations may have the ability to bring down a particular regional network or even a cartel that deals in a particular drug that is traditionally trafficked, like marijuana or cocaine, but such operations may not work against drugs that can be manufactured at the user level, like methamphetamine, or the supply chains that were actually legitimate prior to their diversion to illicit use, as in the case of prescription drugs.

Finally, the traditional approach does not adequately address the demand side of the drug market. Some users are arrested, but simple possession generally carries relatively short sentences. At the end of their sentences, arrestees most often return to their communities still being drug users. Furthermore, law enforcement cannot realistically arrest everyone who is a user of illicit drugs. According to the National Survey on Drug Use and Health, an annual survey conducted by the Substance Abuse and Mental Health Services Administration found that more than 8% of the U.S. population ages 12 years and older used an illicit drug in the prior month, with a recent usage rate of more than 20% for individuals between the ages of 18 and 25 years. Yet the percentage of the population under the supervision of adult correctional authorities (both state and federal) is only about 3% of the adult population, and the majority of those are not serving time for drug offenses. Efforts to arrest even more users would likely overwhelm an already heavily burdened correctional system.

To truly address demand, we must look to prevention and treatment, programs that are not part of the traditional enforcement milieu. Prevention programs attempt to keep as many people as possible from becoming addicted to drugs in the first place, and treatment programs help those who do start to stop. Attacking the supply side alone may not be enough of an incentive to get drug cultivators and manufacturers out of the business, but addressing the demand side can further reduce the profitability of being in the business. Logically, if the market is not there, the drug crime associated with the market should decline as well.

Benefits of a Community Policing Approach

A community policing approach can help address these weaknesses. This is because community policing brings to the drug problem an emphasis on problem solving and collaboration with other stakeholders. The use of problem-solving techniques and multidisciplinary collaboration is not only critical to addressing the demand for drugs, but also can greatly enhance the ability to attack the supply.

The first step in any problem-solving process is to clearly define and understand the problem to be addressed. Taking the time to carefully study the problem before responding allows a law enforcement agency to design responses that are more likely to work in a specific environment. Drug-related crime covers a wide range of criminal behaviors, but not all will be present in every local market. A community must start by identifying the types of drug crime that it experiences. This might also include identifying the most commonly used drugs and separating the drug crime by drug type and then developing separate responses to address each distinct drug problem. Effectively addressing crime problems related to small volume of clandestine

methamphetamine or PCP labs requires a different approach than what would be best employed against problems related to the smuggling of cocaine or marijuana by international cartels or to the diversion of prescription drugs.

Once the specific drug and crime problem is clearly defined, then decisions can be made about what responses a community wishes to deploy. If the community keeps in mind the two-pronged approach of addressing both supply and demand, it will quickly realize that there is no one agency that can fully address the problem. Effectively addressing a drug crime problem requires work by a combination of law enforcement agencies, the courts, corrections agencies, treatment providers, other social service providers, prevention experts, educators, medical practitioners, pharmacists, retailers, and even neighborhood groups of private citizens.

Once the specific drug problem is defined and those responsible for addressing it are identified, then strategies that will address both supply and demand can be developed and deployed. In developing strategies, it can be helpful to picture the drug problem as three-legged stool: One leg represents prevention, one leg interdiction, and the third treatment. Strategies that are successful in knocking down one leg will help control and reduce crime, but strategies that address more than one leg have a better chance of bringing long-term change with improved public health and safety for the community.

Examples of Community Policing Strategies

Community policing is an inherently locally driven approach; therefore the following examples are not meant as model strategies or endorsements of particular approaches. They are instead presented as examples of the application of community policing approaches to a variety of drug crime problems including open-air drug markets, dealing in private properties, methamphetamine manufacturing, substance-abusing repeat offenders, and the diversion of prescription drugs.

One approach for addressing overt, open-air drug markets pairs traditional undercover law enforcement work to build prosecutable cases against the street dealers with efforts by community groups and social service providers to directly engage the dealers and their families with the aim of giving the dealers permanent alternatives to dealing drugs. Close partnership with the prosecutor's office means that dealers can be confronted with the serious threat of conviction and incarceration, but if they choose to get out of the drug business, a wide array of city and community services are put at their disposal to help them build a life away from crime. In some of the neighborhoods where this strategy has been employed, the results were immediate and dramatic, with documented declines in drug crimes and violence as well as improved relations between the residents and law enforcement.

Following are some additional strategies the police have employed to address open-air drug dealing:

- *Policing the area in a highly visible fashion.* Visible policing (including foot patrol) may disrupt the drug market and make it inconvenient for sellers and buyers to engage in drug transactions.
- *Enforcing the law intensively.* The effect of such a crackdown is dependent on the drug market that is targeted and the amount of resources available. Methods include street surveillance and intelligence gathering, hotline for area residents, and increases in drug treatment services.
- *Using intelligence-led investigative work.* Information from drug hotlines and local residents can help to identify and analyze a problem. In addition, an arrest may produce information if officers debrief the offender, and drug buyers may lead undercover officers to drug locations.
- *Arresting drug buyers in "reverse stings."* This response serves to impact the demand side of the market and is most successful against new or occasional drug users. Police in Miami, Florida, found that the process of being arrested, charged, and forced to appear in court and having a vehicle impounded acted as a deterrent.

In another attempt to determine what is most effective in street-level drug enforcement interventions, a federally funded research project reviewed a number of rigorous academic studies evaluating a wide range of street-level drug law enforcement interventions. Their findings were instructive in terms of determining what is effective.

First, regarding the use of police crackdowns—where police engage in stepped-up escalations in law enforcement activities—for drug dealing and use, researchers discovered the following:

- Crackdowns are largely ineffective in disrupting drug problems, such as use, dealing, and drug offenses.
- Crackdowns appear to have more success addressing associated crime problems, such as property crime and violent crime. However, a common problem was the displacement of drug and crime problems to other areas and times of day.
- Crackdowns tend to have minimal, short-term effects on drug, crime, and disorder problems.

Next, the researchers also looked at *community-wide approaches*, which include police interventions that typically are unfocused and involve partnerships with individuals and entities such as local councils, community groups, regulators, inspectors, business groups, and other crime-control agencies. Such programs revealed small and generally insignificant decreases in crime, drug calls, and drug consumption, along with greater citizen satisfaction with the police. Foot and bike patrols showed small reductions in drug-related arrests. Shop fronts (also known as "cop shops") revealed improvements in quality of life, reductions in fear of crime, and increased police satisfaction in the community.

Finally, the researchers examined initiatives that centered on problem-oriented policing—with extremely positive results—more than 70% (24 out of 34) of the problem-oriented policing evaluations reported positive effects on drug outcomes. Almost 80% (19 out of 24) of the problem-oriented policing evaluations reported positive effects on nondrug outcomes, such as property crimes, violent crimes, and disorder offenses.

The major policy implication that emerged from this body of research was that the police will be most effective at reducing street-level drug problems when they work with community partners, whether the partnerships operate within a problem-oriented policing context or not. To reduce street-level drug problems, police need to improve police-citizen relations, forge partnerships with nonpolice agencies, utilize a range of civil remedies, and leverage additional resources to deal with a community's drug problems.

Some communities will define their problem as one of drug markets in leased residential properties as opposed to on the street. An example of a community policing response to this challenge pairs traditional law enforcement practices like knock-and-talks (knocking and asking to talk with a resident without a warrant), buy-busts (an undercover buy), and probation and parole searches with civil actions and prevention-based environmental design strategies. This set of tactics requires building collaborative partnerships with probation officers, city code-enforcement officers, and the landlords themselves. Once law enforcement officers identify problem properties, then depending on the locality, a variety of civil actions can be employed to motivate the landlord to make changes to the property with the goal of deterring future drug problems. These might range from fines to even the loss of the property through civil suits. In communities that have made use of this approach, the landlords who worked with the police to evict problem tenants and improve their properties saw the best successes at preventing future problems with their rental units and therefore helped eliminate a long-standing drug crime problem.

Faced with challenges of small methamphetamine labs, communities across the country have worked in concert with state legislatures and retailers to control access to the precursor chemicals needed to manufacture the drug, including pseudoephedrine (found in many allergy and cold medications) and anhydrous ammonia (found in fertilizer). The Combat Methamphetamine Epidemic Act of 2005 brought minimum national standards to precursor controls, but it built on some of the successful strategies that had already been implemented at the state and local levels to restrict the amount of precursors that can be legitimately purchased at any one time and improved the regulations over storage and transit of the chemicals. In addition, successful approaches to addressing clandestine labs often include prevention and awareness campaigns, where law enforcement partners with the community to engage everyone in understanding how to recognize the signs of a clandestine lab. Individuals like landlords and utility workers routinely enter private properties, but if they do not know what they are looking at, they may not realize they are looking at a crime scene.

Communities that have been the most successful at eliminating their clandestine lab problems are those that mix a number of activities that cross a range of professional disciplines.

Many users who are arrested for possession are not violent felons, but their addiction puts them at high risk for repeat offending, costing the criminal justice system a lot of time and money as they cycle through the process multiple times. Without access to treatment, these offenders represent a law enforcement problem that can never be solved. Treatment courts, which are grounded on the same principles of problem solving and partnerships that define community policing, have proven to be effective at breaking this cycle of crime and addiction. Some treatment courts follow a preadjudication model (conviction and sentencing is deferred pending program completion), others a postplea model (the offender pleads guilty but the sentence is vacated pending program completion). In both models, the court partners with treatment and social service providers to assist offenders with whatever they need to get and stay clean, and if they successfully complete the program their charges (or convictions) are set aside. Some treatment courts also bring police into the project partnership, recognizing that they can play an important role in helping addicts get access to the treatment they need and are more likely to do so if they are presented with opportunities to see that treatment can work.

Finally, many communities looking to address a problem of prescription drug diversion have begun to make use of community policing approaches. Partnerships between law enforcement officers, regulators, and pharmacists are crucial to helping combat problems of diversion at the distributor level, but what many communities experience is a problem of diversion from private households. Youths may raid their homes' medicine cabinets and bring whatever they can find to school or to parties to share with their peers. Not only is this illegal, it is also highly dangerous as they may unwittingly ingest dangerous combinations of drugs, resulting in emergency room visits, long-term health side effects, or even death. Unless the school catches the drugs or the party causes a nuisance problem resulting in a 911 call, law enforcement officials are unlikely to even know that these diversion problems are occurring. Developing partnerships with schools, parents, and pharmacists is crucial to being able to prevent the crime before it occurs. Helping schools develop effective drug-control strategies for students with legitimate prescriptions, educating parents on carefully storing and monitoring their own prescriptions, educating youth on the dangers of taking nonprescribed narcotics, and working with pharmacists to develop disposal programs that allow people to easily empty their medicine cabinets of unused medications in an environmentally responsible way can successfully ameliorate the diversion problem. Waiting until after a crime takes place to respond traditionally puts community health and safety at risk.

There are many illegal drugs and many types of drug crime. If law enforcement agencies work in concert with other stakeholders to carefully define their community's specific problems and develop responses to address both supply and demand, they will have the best chance at not just controlling drug crime but reducing it, and improving the overall health and safety of the community for the long term.

Deborah L. Spence

See also Building Partnerships and Stakeholders; Collaboration With Outside Agencies; Community Policing and Problem Solving, Definition of; Drug Crimes, Characteristics of; Problem-Solving Courts; Problem-Solving Process (SARA)

Further Readings

Davis, R. C., & Lurigio, A. J. (1996). *Fighting back: Neighborhood antidrug strategies.* Thousand Oaks, CA: Sage.

Harocopos, A., & Hough, M. (2005). *Drug dealing in open-air markets.* Washington, DC: U.S. Department of Justice, Office of Community Oriented Policing Services.

Huddleston, W., & Marlowe, D. (2011). *Painting the current picture: A national report on drug courts and other problem solving court programs in the United States.* Washington, DC: U.S. Department of Justice, Bureau of Justice Assistance.

Kennedy, D. M. (2009). *Deterrence and crime prevention: Reconsidering the prospect of sanction.* New York, NY: Routledge.

Mazerolle, L., Soole, D. W., & Rombouts, S. (2007). *Crime prevention research reviews No. 1: Disrupting street-level drug markets.* Washington, DC: U.S. Department of Justice, Office of Community Oriented Policing Services. Retrieved from http://cops.usdoj.gov/files/RIC/Publications/e04072678.pdf

National Alliance for Model State Drug Laws. (2011). *Controlling methamphetamine precursors ephedrine and pseudoephedrine: A brief history of controls and current initiatives.* Santa Fe, NM: Author.

Office of National Drug Control Policy. (2012). *National drug control strategy.* Washington, DC: Author.

Reuter, P. (Ed.), & National Research Council. (2010). *Understanding the demand for illegal drugs.* Washington, DC: The National Academies Press.

Saleem, O. (1996). Killing the proverbial two birds with one stone: Using environmental statutes and nuisance to combat the crime of illegal drug trafficking. *Dickinson Law Review, 100*(4), 685–732.

Scott, M. S., & Dedel, K. (2006). *Clandestine methamphetamine labs* (2nd ed.). Washington, DC: U.S. Department of Justice, Office of Community Oriented Policing Services.

ELDERLY VICTIMIZATION, CHARACTERISTICS OF

As the number of older adults increases, so too does the victimization and abuse of these individuals. *Elder abuse* is any knowing, intentional, or negligent act by another person that causes injury, harm, or even death to an elderly person. The abuse can be a one-time act or ongoing, and the perpetrator can be a stranger, although typically it will be a relative, friend, acquaintance, or a caregiver. The perpetrator knowingly causes distress to the older adult through a variety of different actions. As people age, they may become more physically fragile: weaker bones, thinner skin, with medical conditions that diminish mobility and independence. Some individuals may become dependent on family and caretakers or become isolated, with limited access to communication and decreased visits from friends and relatives. These factors contribute to the severity of consequences for older victims of various forms of victimization and abuse. This entry outlines the types and consequences of elder victimization and abuse and the systems in place for investigating and reporting such cases.

Types of Abuse and Victimization

Physical Abuse

When considering victimization and abuse, most people think of physical violence against another person that causes injury. While all abuse is a crime, there are milder forms of physical abuse, such as a push, shove, or grab. Threats of greater physical violence also fall within the spectrum of abuse, as does an actual act of a slap, punch, or kick. Escalated forms of physical abuse include burns and branding, strangulation, sexual assault, and murder. A variety of weapons can be used in the commission of violent acts: for example, belts, sticks, baseball bats, knives, guns, and lighters, stoves, and other sources of fire. Liquids can also be used as weapons, including accelerants and extremely hot liquids to scald or burn the older adult. In some cases, a caregiver has drawn a scalding hot bath or turned on a shower to the highest temperature, placed the older adult in the water and left. Such an act of physical abuse can cause severe scalding burns on the victim. Other types of weapons include ropes, scarves, ligatures, plastic bags, or any object that can be used to asphyxiate a person. While the commission of an act falls within the spectrum of abuse, so too does the omission of an act such as depriving an older adult of sustenance needed for basic survival, medications, or hygiene—all of which can contribute to serious medical problems or death.

Another form of physical abuse that is experienced by older adults is sexual abuse, which includes any nonconsensual sexual act, such as forcing an older adult to have sexual intercourse, oral sex, or anal sex. Digital penetration or the forced penetration of foreign objects and weapons also falls within the definition of sexual assault. Forcing another person to watch or engage in a sexual act with a third party also constitutes sexual abuse. Sometimes an older adult may be sexually victimized in the process of changing, cleaning, or bathing.

Neglect

While most people think of *physical* forms of abuse, the statistical reality is that someone is more likely to be victimized by acts of neglect. There are three types of neglect: active, passive, and self-neglect. *Active neglect* refers to acts in which someone knowingly fails to provide food for nutrition, liquids for hydration, hygiene, clothing, and shelter, including appropriate temperature control based on the season. A common form of active neglect occurs when a caregiver intentionally fails to move someone who is confined to a bed or chair, contributing to bed sores. Another form occurs when an older adult is left unattended by family, friends, or caretakers for short or extended periods of time. Similarly, restraining an older adult, locking the person in a room, or moving a needed wheelchair or walker out of reach, resulting in extended periods of confinement, are also forms of active neglect. Furthermore, active neglect may include removing telephones, eyeglasses, or hearing aids. All of these intentional and knowing acts are forms of active neglect that may be used to control, decrease independence, and isolate the other adult.

Passive neglect occurs when someone unknowingly fails to provide adequate nutrition, hygiene, or medications. While this is not intentional, serious health problems or death can still occur. Finally, *self-neglect* occurs when an older adult is unwilling or unable to request help in obtaining nutrition, hygiene, shelter, or medications. The older adult may refuse assistance due to a diminished mental or physical ability, depression, social isolation, substance abuse, fear of losing independence, or not wanting to be a burden on another person. Some older adults do not want a home health care provider for fear that they will be sent to an institutional setting. As a result, the older adult may not seek needed assistance. Signs of self-neglect include the following: hoarding, failure to take medications or medical treatment, poor personal hygiene, inappropriate clothing, poor housekeeping, bewilderment and confusion, and failure to take routine safety precautions. While there may be a family member or caretaker who is willing and able to provide assistance, the older adult may refuse, thereby contributing to her or his diminished well-being.

Emotional Maltreatment

Another form of abuse is *psychological* or *emotional* maltreatment. These words are often used interchangeably and refer to any verbal or non-verbal action that seeks to cause harm or distress to another person. This type of harm can include threats of physical injury, calling someone demeaning names, or belittling the person. In the case of older adults, this can also include telling them that they are progressing toward senility, dementia, or Alzheimer's, or making them feel they are crazy or "losing it."

Financial Victimization

There are several forms of financial exploitation and abuse of older adults. This can include stealing money, assets, jewelry, collectibles, electronics, or other personal items. Changes in an adult's financial situation due to the unexplained disappearance of money, funds, or transfers of money out of accounts and investments are possible signs of financial abuse. Excessive ATM withdrawals, online transactions, or credit card purchases should also be suspect, especially if the older adult is bedridden, lacks a computer, or is not technologically savvy enough for online banking and investing. Some family members or caretakers may coerce an older adult into making changes to his or her will, power of attorney, estates, trust, titles, policies, or signature cards with financial institutions to gain greater control of and access to finances.

Marketing fraud is another type of financial abuse whereby strangers prey upon and target older adults through various programs, gimmicks, and seminars. For example, free lunch programs offer a complimentary meal and an opportunity to invest in a bogus program. Older adults are quite often the victim of personal information scams whereby they will be contacted by an alleged representative of a legitimate company to update computer records or files. The scam artists may convince the victim to divulge personal financial information, which is then used to perpetrate fraud, financial abuse, or identity theft. Marketing fraud can also occur through e-mail, cold calls, text messages, direct mail, online, or television. These tactics include phishing, advance loans or credit, real estate scams, or fraudulent notification of lottery winnings, prizes, or sweepstakes. The goal of each of these efforts is to find an older adult, befriend the person, and ultimately swindle money by encouraging the person to purchase an item or make an investment.

Other Victimizations

Older adults may also be victims of property crimes including breaking and entering, home invasions, vandalism, and mugging. While these crimes mostly account for financial losses to the older adult, the victim may be physically harmed in the process. Likewise, after the home is invaded by a predator, an older person may be afraid to stay in the home. This type of crime can shatter one's independence and can be all the more devastating when the person has lived many years in the home, married, and raised children there, but now is too afraid to stay due to fear for personal safety.

Identification and Reporting

As outlined in the previous section, there is a wide array of abuse that can occur. Further, there are three types of abusers: known persons in the home, employees in an institutional setting, and strangers. Generally, abuse occurs within the home and the abuser is a family member, a spouse, caretaker, friend, or acquaintance. Across the life span, an individual is most likely to be abused by someone who is known, rather than a stranger. The second major category of abuser is someone who works within in an institutional setting such as a hospital, nursing home, assisted living, or transitional-living environment. However, there is crossover between the two environments. For example, a nurse may visit an older adult in a home setting and abuse the person there. Likewise, an older adult may be abused by a spouse, family member, of friend while living in an institutional setting. The third type of abuser is a stranger who may randomly enter a person's home, mug the person on the street, or may be a telemarketer or other type of solicitor. The stranger engages in random crimes and is the least prevalent type of abuser of the elderly.

There are several indicators of abuse or maltreatment, and their presence should be reported to the appropriate authorities such as law enforcement agencies and adult protective services (APS) for further evaluation and investigation. Warning signs indicative of abuse or maltreatment include bruises, particularly those that are on the fleshy parts of one's body such as the buttocks, inner arms, or thighs. Such bruises are questionable given the location of the mark, because fleshy body parts do not readily bruise. However, a bruise in and of itself on an older person may not be indicative of abuse, as older adults often bruise easily, which can be exacerbated by certain medications. Likewise, bruises or scratches on the bony parts of one's body such as the hands, knees, elbows, nose, chin, and forehead may be indicative of a fall, but not necessarily abuse. Thus, it is important to look at the totality of the person's condition, including other bruising, pressure marks, abrasions, burns, untreated injuries of various stages of healing, or ligature marks on the wrists or ankles indicative of restraint. Also, any changes in a person's behavior should raise a red flag. Possible changes include alterations in one's routine or daily activities, or a sudden shift toward states of hypersensitivity, anxiety, or depression. Changes in diet, appetite, and thirst can also indicate problems, as can corresponding weight loss or gain. The onset of substance abuse and the overuse or underuse of medications are problems that should be explored further. Any regressive behaviors such as sucking one's thumb, rocking, biting, or bedwetting should also raise concerns. Other red flags are older adults with bed sores, unattended medical needs, poor hygiene, soiled clothes, or bed sheets that have not been changed. Possible indicators of sexual abuse include bruising or bleeding around the breasts, genitals, or anus, as well as the presence of sexually transmitted diseases (STDs).

It is the responsibility of anyone who suspects abuse to report maltreatment to the appropriate authorities. Most states have mandatory reporting laws for elder abuse, but laws vary widely as to who is a mandated reporter and what should be reported. Mandated reporting laws for elder abuse are not nearly as comprehensive or standardized as child abuse reporting laws. This is compounded by the potential for isolation and limited social networks of older adults, which can contribute to long-term abuse before it is ever identified. As such, it is imperative that everyone look out for an older adult and reports suspicious actions or behaviors. It is equally important for family members and friends to conduct regular unannounced home visits, make frequent phone calls, and invite the older adult to outside activities and excursions. Each of these contacts provides the observer with a better sense of changes in behavior and cognition, and also builds a relationship in which a disclosure of abuse can be made.

Once a case of suspected abuse or victimization is reported, the case is typically referred to APS. A county-based program that provides assistance to older adults over the age of 65 years or dependent adults with a disability between the ages of 18 and 64 years, APS is responsible for investigating reports of abuse for those who live in any setting—a private residence, group home, or an institution. If the investigation confirms abuse or victimization, APS staff will arrange for advocacy services, out-of-home placements, or even conservatorship, if merited. APS also provides referrals, conducts outreach, and engages in awareness campaigns to increase the community's knowledge of a variety of topics relevant for their target population, including elder abuse and victimization.

Bernadette T. Muscat

See also Domestic Violence, Characteristics of; Domestic Violence, Community Policing Strategies for; Elderly Victimization, Community Policing Strategies for

Further Readings

Litwin, H., & Zoabi, S. (2004). A multivariate examination of explanations for the occurrence of elder abuse. *Social Work Research, 28*(3), 133–142.

Nerenberg, L. (2007). *Elder abuse prevention: Emerging trends and promising strategies.* New York, NY: Springer-Verlag.

U.S. Government Accountability Office. (2011, March). *Elder justice: Stronger federal leadership could enhance national response to elder abuse.* GAO-11–208. Washington, DC: Author. Retrieved from http://aging .senate.gov/events/hr230kb2.pdf

Websites

Clearinghouse on Abuse and Neglect of the Elderly; http://www.cane.udel.edu

International Network for the Prevention of Elder Abuse; http://www.inpea.net

National Adult Protective Services Association; http://www .apsnetwork.org

National Center on Elder Abuse c/o Center for Community Research and Services; http://www.ncea.aoa.gov

National Committee for the Prevention of Elder Abuse; http://www.preventelderabuse.org

ELDERLY VICTIMIZATION, COMMUNITY POLICING STRATEGIES FOR

As individuals age, their fear of crime and of becoming a victim increases. While older adults can be the target of specific types of financial crimes and identity theft, the statistical reality is that as people age, they are less likely to be victimized. Still, as the number of older adults increases, the need to protect this population also increases. Greater efforts are being made within communities across the United States to address fear of crime, decrease potential vulnerabilities, raise awareness of possible sources of victimization, and provide referrals for intervention, counseling, and other pertinent services. Law enforcement officials are playing a significant role in these community-based initiatives. This entry discusses several such efforts and initiatives.

Triads

Three national organizations—American Association of Retired Persons (AARP), the International Association of Chiefs of Police (IACP), and the National Sheriffs' Association (NSA)—agreed in 1988 to work in collaboration to address crime prevention for older adults within communities. These organizations recognized the vulnerabilities of older adults, as well as the short- and long-term impact of victimization, including health consequences, emotional stress, financial burdens, possible loss of independence, and even death. Older adults also may be isolated and lack resources, compounding the trauma of victimization. These factors were at the forefront of early deliberations and the recognition that more must be done to assist older adults. The organizations created the Triad model to reduce victimization, improve quality of life, educate and seek community input to identify and implement solutions, and improve relationships between law enforcement and older adults. Triads, found in communities nationwide, are comprised of volunteers who are older adults, law enforcement, and community organizations working with the target population. After their inception, Triads expanded their outreach to people with physical, developmental, and cognitive disabilities.

A Triad develops and implements crime prevention and intervention programs that are applicable to the community within which it is located. Prevention is addressed through community education and awareness, while intervention includes helping older adults after victimization. The level and type of services that may be needed varies upon the victim and the type of crime. Triads work to streamline and explain the criminal justice process, provide referrals, decrease trauma, and serve as a resource for older adults who have been victimized. Triads work to reduce the fear of crime by dispelling stereotypes about crime, while simultaneously identifying ways to reduce vulnerabilities. Of equal importance is providing older adults with crime statistics by geographic area, including what, when, and where crimes are taking place. It is critical to provide information about creating safe living spaces, locks and alarms, and to highlight the tactics criminals use to gain entry to one's residence (such as misrepresenting themselves as service technicians or salespersons). Triads work with law enforcement agencies to provide a free cell phone that is programmed to call 911 for emergencies. Each of these efforts contributes to an older adult's sense of safety and well-being. Informational meetings can also serve as a good opportunity for older adults to network and socialize, and for organizations to recruit volunteers. These goals are achieved through ongoing dialogue and information exchange, as well as training between Triad partners and the community they serve.

Triads use multiple avenues in an attempt to reach as many older adults as possible. Some effective communication tools include print media, community bulletin boards, websites, billboards, newsletters, community calendars, and neighborhood and housing groups, associations, and authorities. Targeted publications for retirees or veterans can assist with outreach, as can faith-based organizations. Public service announcements (PSAs) and broadcasts on public access channels are important avenues. Some locations provide senior centers and Meals-on-Wheels programs with placemats carrying information on the signs of abuse and neglect, as

well as the corresponding physical, behavioral, and psychological indicators of trauma. The placemats also provide recipients with information on how to receive help through a hotline number, which can be answered by a Triad volunteer. Speakers bureaus are another avenue to reach older adults by having different individuals speak to community groups for older adults. Senior centers that provide meals can be good venues for a luncheon speaker.

Some Triads have a buddy system whereby a volunteer is assigned to an older adult. The volunteer can conduct welfare checks for his or her assigned buddy through phone calls and home visits. Home visits allow the volunteer to identify potential vulnerabilities and signs of abuse or neglect, so he or she can contact law enforcement officials or give referrals. Volunteers also can observe changes in seniors' behavior, health, diet, hygiene, and emotional well-being, all of which may be associated with abuse, maltreatment, or neglect. The buddy system also helps to identify, develop, and bolster support networks that seniors need to share information and maintain independence. Some Triads have a Telephone Reassurance program where a volunteer will call an older adult on a daily basis to check in, determine needs, and provide a resource. Some Triads also provide extensions of the buddy program, including Safe Walks, Adopt-a-Senior programs, and escort partnerships. Each program pairs a younger person with an older adult to provide accompaniment for exercise, medical visits, grocery shopping, religious services, and community events. These efforts reduce the older adult's vulnerability while walking, traveling, and engaging in daily activities.

Neighborhood watch programs offer older adults the opportunity to observe and report suspicious activities. Some Triads take this a step further by recruiting law enforcement officers to do more concentrated patrols, or even to reside, in senior housing or other parts of the community that are densely populated by older adults. The added police presence can serve as a deterrent and contribute to residents' perceptions of safety and security.

Some Triads work with older adults for disaster preparedness or in the aftermath of a natural or human-made disaster. Triads can assist with the creation of emergency kits, as well evacuation planning, particularly for individuals with special needs. Triads work with emergency management organizations for emergency planning; to conduct door-to-door outreach and distribute needed resources to older adults after a disaster; and to locate, map, and provide referrals during critical times. A Triad volunteer can also work with emergency management organizations to identify potential in-home dangers.

Triads also serve an important role in policing because many law enforcement agencies lack the budget to staff programs that address older people's needs. Triad volunteers can assess the community and work with law enforcement personnel to address the needs the volunteers identify. Triads evolve and adjust based on identified concerns, which further helps law enforcement agencies work toward results-driven activities. Triads can help crime victims navigate the criminal justice system and identify resources. Some Triads even have a dedicated senior phone line within the law enforcement department that is staffed by volunteers who encourage callers to report suspicious activities or crimes. These volunteers can also alleviate some of the workload for law enforcement agencies by addressing chronic callers or taking calls that are outside the scope of policing.

State-level Triads are responsible for training and providing technical assistance, as well as pertinent legislative updates. State Triads can also share information about starting a Triad, promising practices, and program evaluation efforts.

Seniors and Law Enforcement Together (SALT) Council

One of the steps in Triad formation is to create a Seniors and Law Enforcement Together (SALT) Council, which meets monthly and is typically comprised of a high-level law enforcement administrator such as the sheriff or police chief, as well as key community leaders. The council is meant to serve in an advisory capacity for the local Triad. For example, the Triad will identify crime-related concerns or fears, often through a community survey. Once the data are collected and analyzed, the Triad presents the findings to the SALT, which will help the Triad to identify needed resources, determine capabilities, and prioritize needs. The council reviews identified needs and provide recommendations as to how to address these concerns. SALT meetings are an opportunity to have an open and frank discussion about ideas and potential resolutions. Effective SALT Councils work to implement and stabilize one program at a

time from the list of identified priorities. Once progress is made and the issue is addressed, then other priorities can be adopted. The council is not meant to be a review board or policymaking body. All daily operations and personnel decisions are managed at the local Triad level, not with the SALT Council.

Safety Training and Resources (STAR) Initiative

The Safety Training and Resources (STAR) Initiative was created through the collaborative efforts of the Community Safety Institute (CSI), the National Sheriffs' Association (NSA), and the U.S. Department of Justice's (DOJ) Office of Community Oriented Policing Services (COPS). The STAR Initiative is a community-based, citizen-driven program that provides law enforcement agencies and emergency responders with training and a database of resource information for disaster preparedness for critical incidents such as large-scale human or natural disasters and terrorist attacks. Training and dissemination of information is provided through a joint effort of law enforcement personnel and Triad volunteers.

There are numerous benefits associated with the STAR Initiative for Triads, law enforcement agencies, first responders, and the larger community. First, community involvement is crucial in planning to know what to do and where to go when a crisis occurs. Next, when a network is in place, law enforcement officers and first responders can focus on triage and helping those in the greatest need. This helps to minimize duplicated efforts and redundancies in services. Finally, vulnerable populations such as older adults benefit through the coordinated efforts of trained partners, as well as a database where resources can be accessed quickly. The STAR Initiative can help to save lives and minimize property losses.

Fatality Review Teams

Elder Abuse Fatality Review Teams (EA-FRTs) exist to identify the types of deaths that occur due to abuse, such as intimate partner violence or neglect in a care facility. Despite research that indicates that elder abuse hastens death, teams to review the correlation between abuse and death for older adults lack sophistication. In 2001, the U.S. Department of Justice's Office for Victims of Crime (OVC) developed technical assistance to create Elder Abuse Fatality Review Teams to examine how adult protective services, law enforcement, prosecutors, victim service providers, and home care professionals were responding to the increasing prevalence of elder abuse.

One of the advantages of EA-FRTs is to raise awareness about the potential lethality of elder abuse. The team approach encourages those who work directly with older adults, members of the criminal justice system, home care professionals, as well as those in political power, to question whether an older person's death is the result of natural causes or due to abuse or neglect. The review teams also work together to decide how to protect older adults from abuse, improve police and agency protocol to address elder abuse, and increase resources for older adult victims. If an older adult dies, it is the responsibility of the review team to determine if the cause of death was due to abuse or if the death occurred under suspicious circumstances. If the team determines that the death was due to abuse or neglect, then it is also the team's responsibility to determine how to prevent similar deaths from occurring in the future.

Another advantage rests in the knowledge and expertise about elder abuse that team members bring to the table. Together, they can network and educate one another about the signs and symptoms of abuse, as well as various ways to address intervention and prevention. Team members work together to educate the public about the potential contributing factors to elder abuse, and the patterns of behavior that can lead to lethal elder abuse. The team can also identify offender behavior and a victim's situation, which may accurately predict lethality. Working together, professionals gain a sense of gaps in service delivery, advocate for increased funding and changes in local and state legislation to better address elder abuse, and streamline agency protocol to better serve victims. Finally, team members can help each other with vicarious trauma through open discussion and shared grief when dealing with the death of a victim of elder abuse. When this occurs, team members forge stronger bonds to work more cooperatively, and in turn, reduce the potential for burnout.

Fatality Review Teams function when all team members have access to information about the case at hand, even the information that would otherwise be deemed confidential. Team members must keep all information confidential, which can be solidified through policies or a signed memorandum of understanding (MOU) against involuntary disclosure of deliberations, medical and mental health records, legal proceedings, discovery, criminal history, and in-home supportive services involved in the case that is examined. Information is a key component in creating a full and clear picture of the circumstances surrounding the death under review, as well as analyzing if there was a systematic response to the case. The end result of the review is to develop a comprehensive set of appropriate recommendations for all team members to take back to their respective organizations for self-evaluation and improved policies to address elder abuse. Review teams are able to examine both open and closed cases, as well as deaths that occurred in institutional and residential settings.

Multiple systems are involved in addressing and responding to elder abuse prior to a victim's death. As a result, a full system analysis is essential to determine the ways in which the systems worked effectively or where there were gaps in service delivery. While sharing information is of vital importance, it is equally important to provide safeguards for protecting information as it is transferred through electronic, and often unsecured, networks.

A key step in a case review is to develop a chronology of the events surrounding the abuse and untimely death, identifying interventions or lack thereof, and recommendations for system change.

Bernadette T. Muscat

See also Domestic Violence, Characteristics of; Domestic Violence, Community Policing Strategies For; Elderly Victimization, Characteristics of

Further Readings

National Association of Triads. (n.d.). *About NATI: Who we are, what we stand for, and the services we provide your community.* Alexandria, VA: Author. Retrieved from http://www.nationaltriad.org/About_NATI.htm

National Association of Triads. (2007). *STAR: Safety Training and Resources: Law Enforcement Officer Training Instructor Handbook.* Alexandria, VA.: Author. Retrieved from http://www.nationaltriad.org/STAR_Program/STAR%20LE%20Instructor%20Handbook_1.pdf

Orange County Triad. (n.d.). *Safety for seniors.* Orange, VA: Author. Retrieved from http://search.yahoo.com/search;_ylt=A00G7hqXXtNQsWUAAlFXNyoA?p=Tria

ds+aarp&ei=UTF-8&fr=yfp-t-701&xargs=0&pstart=1
&b=11&xa=6BPHIyt0fEFs9v_19Q0
CKA—,1356115991

Otto, J. M., & Quinn, K. M. (2007). *Summary report adult protective services programs state administrative structures.* Springfield, IL: National Adult Protective Services Association. Retrieved from http://www .apsnetwork.org/Resources/docs/Administrative%20 Structure%20Report.pdf

Stiegel, L. A., American Bar Association, Commission on Law and Aging, & Office of Office for Victims of Crime. (2005). *Elder abuse fatality review teams: A replication manual.* Washington, DC: American Bar Association & U.S. Department of Justice, Office for Victims of Crime.

Websites

American Association of Retired Persons (AARP); http:// www.aarp.org

Administration on Aging, U.S. Department of Health & Human Services; http://www.aoa.gov

American Bar Association Commission on Law and Aging; http://www.abanet.org/aging

Clearinghouse on Abuse and Neglect of the Elderly, University of Delaware, Department of Consumer Studies; http://db.rdms.udel.edu:8080/CANE

The Community Policing Consortium; http://www .communitypolicing.org

COPS, U.S. Department of Justice; http://www.cops.usdoj.gov

National Adult Protective Services Association; http://www .apsnetwork.org/About/policy.htm

National Center on Elder Abuse; http://www .elderabusecenter.org

National Clearinghouse on Abuse in Later Life, Wisconsin Coalition Against Domestic Violence; http://www.ncall.us

National Committee for the Prevention of Elder Abuse; http://www.preventelderabuse.org

ETHICAL CONSIDERATIONS

With community policing's emphasis on problem solving and the creation of active police and community relationships, coupled with increased independence and latitude given to officers, community policing naturally generates increased concerns in the area of ethics. It has long been acknowledged that increased officer discretion is an area rife with ethical considerations. The decentralization of police departments and increased interaction with the public in attempting to implement solutions to crime and disorder problems further heighten concerns about police ethics.

Given the responsibility of law enforcement in U.S. society to "serve and protect," it is not surprising that proper ethical conduct is a paramount concern in policing. As American society has become increasingly diverse in terms of race, ethnicity, culture, socioeconomics, and philosophies, the task of enforcing the law ethically, fairly, and uniformly has become increasingly more difficult. This entry examines the role of ethics in policing in general and community policing in particular. It also discusses the moral dilemmas police officers may face and ethics training for officers.

Ethics and Policing

Ethics is generally concerned with the study and analysis of what constitutes good or bad, right or wrong behavior. For present purposes, *ethics* shall be defined as the study of the general nature of morals and the specific moral choices an individual makes in relating to others; in this case, as they apply to police conduct. *Morality* shall be defined as principles or standards with respect to right or wrong conduct. These principles of behavior as right or wrong relate to one's interactions with others. In this sense, a moral being is one who takes the welfare of others into account. Here, the most basic of all moral ideas comes to mind: the Golden Rule. Simply stated, the Golden Rule is to do unto others as you would have them do unto you (Matthew 7:12, *Bible*).

The present analysis involves moral ideas and standards as they apply to the police profession, which can be subsumed under the general rubric *professional ethics.* From this conceptualization it can be deduced that ethical police behavior is quite simply, moral behavior in a professional (police) setting.

A logical question that might be asked is, "How are police ethics different from any other ethics?" The difference lies with the distinctive demands placed on police in the roles they play and situations they encounter. For example, police officers can, under their position of authority, take away someone's freedom by arrest or by use deadly force, if necessary, in the performance of their duties. From a social scientific perspective, this attribution of rightness or wrongness in terms of morality is somewhat problematic because a goal of science is value-free objectivity, and labeling someone as moral or immoral is somewhat of a contradiction. Nonetheless, this analysis will proceed by borrowing assumptions and ideas from social control theory. Here, it is assumed that individuals are born amoral, that is, with no concept of morality. Starting with no conception of morality, a person generally goes through the process of socialization where one becomes a more or less moral person. It is the idea of "more or less" that is important because this moral status of the individual members of society is assumed to vary along a dimension from amoral to highly moral. For the sake of anchoring this continuum, we might think of the almost totally amoral psychopath on one end of the continuum. Such individuals are totally self-interested and not concerned about others. They only concern themselves with the effect their behavior has on others to the extent that it might benefit or harm their own interests. At the other end of the continuum is the Mother Teresa-type individual, who is virtually selfless and gives continually and freely to others. This cognitive dimension, therefore, represents the individual's intentions or motivations for behavior relative to others. Clearly there is more to being a moral person than whether one has good intentions or motivations relative to others. This is where the behavioral dimension fits in.

The behavioral dimension of morality is exactly that—namely, the behavioral outcome of one's behavior vis-à-vis other individuals. Here one's behavior can vary from immoral (very harmful behavior) to highly moral (giving, kind, loving, etc.) behavior. Common sense would dictate that there must be a relationship between these two dimensions. To more clearly conceptualize this relationship, see Figure 1.

If a person is on the amoral end of the cognitive dimension, there is no reason for that person to choose to do moral actions, except for reasons of self-interest. Such an amoral person may behave in moral ways but is doing the right thing for the wrong reason. The same is true, to a lesser extent, of those who are deterred from committing socially unacceptable acts due only to the fear of punishment. They are not refraining from doing the wrong things because they are wrong, but rather out of the fear of negative consequences. However, amoral persons will easily choose the nonmoral or harmful behaviors which might benefit them because they do not possess the internal control which makes them take others into account. Conversely, the individual who has evolved toward the moral end of the cognitive dimension chooses moral actions more often than not, and for the right reasons. For example, in a Good Samaritan situation the individual offers assistance, not for what it will benefit him, or because he is afraid of being punished by violating a Good Samaritan statute, but rather because it is the kind, considerate thing to do. This type of individual would want the other person to help him or her if their positions were reversed. It should be noted that human nature being what it is, we all, even if we are more or less moral beings in a cognitive sense, will from time to time choose immoral behaviors, perhaps out of selfishness, greed, lust, or other imperfections.

Ethical Dilemmas and Moral Ambiguity

Admittedly, the explanation above represents a very simplistic conceptualization of what is moral and, therefore, ethical conduct. However, given this approach there would be very few situations that might seem morally ambiguous. In fact, the only morally ambiguous situation that should exist for

Figure 1 Dimensions of Morality
Source: Author.

a moral police officer is one that truly represents an ethical dilemma. Ethical dilemmas are those situations that are no-win in nature. Such situations are best examined in terms of means and ends. A genuine moral dilemma exists when the achievement of a good or moral end can only be accomplished through the use of morally tainted means. Often police officers find themselves in role conflicts, which can quickly lead to such dilemmas. An example would be the officer who is put into the position of giving a friend or a relative a traffic citation. The conflict is between the role as an impartial public servant, who is sworn to serve and protect all citizens, and the role as a friend or relative.

Other kinds of situations in the policing context which may appear to be dilemmas are those where all choices are wrong. However, upon close examination such situations may not really be dilemmas after all. For example, the illegal wiretapping of an organized-crime figure's home or false testimony given to ensure that a public menace is put in prison might sometimes, though wrong, be justified in the minds of some people as necessary for the public good. The question here is, If the action can be justified *morally*, is it in fact *wrong*; or put another way, "Does the end justify the means?" If man-made rules such as the exclusionary rule (the Supreme Court's determination that evidence obtained illegally is inadmissible at trial), legal requirements for arrest, or laws on search and seizure interfere with justice or what is right, then in those situations are those rules wrong? The hitch is that the police, above all, are not to break the law, nor are they arbiters who can decide the validity of the law.

The problem here is that if an officer uses a morally questionable means to achieve what is personally believed to be a morally acceptable end and continues to engage in these practices, the morally questionable means can become habitual. If the officer defines arrest and incarceration as morally good ends, then the officer may feel justified in using a morally questionable means, such as violating an individual's Fourth Amendment rights, to achieve that good end. Further, if the officer makes a habit of violating people's rights, that habit may become generalized as a way to deal with all people.

Ethical Awareness

From the above discussion, it can be inferred that ethics and morality are learned. They are taught and learned through the process of socialization. This is, indeed, an instance of life-long learning; however, the most important lessons are those that are learned during the early years of one's life. It is unlikely that an inherently amoral police recruit can be transformed into a moral one. Given the process whereby one's moral makeup is shaped, it is simply not possible, through an educational curriculum, to transform a person into a moral being; it is too late for such a change to occur. The desire to do the right thing for the right reason is ultimately up to the individual. To perceive that a moral dilemma or problem exists, the individual has to be a moral being in the first place. Put another way, only one who cares about being a good person and doing what is right can appreciate ethical and moral questions. The person to whom there is no concern about doing the right thing in the right way for the right reasons does not have the prerequisites to become sensitized to moral issues. For this reason, police agencies wishing to have the highest possible moral standards must recruit those who already possess a moral disposition.

Given that a police department does the best within its ability to recruit those with a moral disposition, of what good then are training sessions in ethics? First of all, the intent of ethics training sessions is not to teach ethics, but rather to heighten ethical awareness. Heightening ethical awareness should cause officers to be increasingly aware of the ethical dimensions of their everyday conduct. Individuals with a moral disposition do not necessarily consistently examine their own behavior with sufficient prudence to discover every ethical shortcoming. For example, a male officer may think nothing of telling what he considers slightly off-color jokes to coworkers without realizing that the jokes may offend female officers. Similarly, an officer may use slang expressions to refer to members of a minority group without considering that those terms can be offensive.

Training designed to heighten ethical awareness can sensitize individuals as to how their conduct is perceived and interpreted through the eyes of others. If officers truly are disposed to be moral, this sensitization should reinforce the ethical and moral content of their behavior. This, in turn, should enhance their integrity, allowing them to confront their jobs from a perspective that permits them to deal fairly and consistently with others. Such ethical and moral sensitivity should preclude them from ignoring incompetence, brutality or corruption, or characteristics of organizations that social scientists call "structural immorality." They should also be less tolerant of institutionalized racism and other discriminatory practices.

Ethical Concerns Unique to Community Policing

Policing is clearly a unique profession where questions of the ethical correctness of behaviors are confronted daily. The next issue to be addressed is what specific factors cause community policing to face even more unique and ever-present ethical concerns.

First of all, the success of community policing, more so than any other facet of policing, is based on the image that the police force portrays to the community. Since the problem-solving component of community policing requires officers to team up with citizens in a joint attempt to handle neighborhood problems, it is vital that police are perceived as fair, equitable, and trustworthy. In our increasingly heterogeneous society, cultural, language, and lifestyle differences can impede communications between divergent individuals and groups. Further, some neighborhoods may be composed of individuals and groups of divergent origins, and police officers may be put in the difficult position of having to facilitate teamwork among people who do not get along. As if their increased responsibilities were not enough, officers are still in the position of having to intervene in citizens' lives to enforce the law. This includes making arrests, writing citations, breaking up late-night parties and rowdy social gatherings where citizens may resent police interference into their affairs. Thus, officers are forced to be both bad guys and good guys. As they attempt to accomplish this they must do everything possible not to play favorites and be fair and treat all citizens equally.

Two other closely linked factors associated with community policing that can play a significant role in generating ethics problems are increased discretion and decentralization of decision making. In its attempt to address situations that give rise to crime-related issues, community policing requires officers to actively engage community players, including individual citizens, various citizen organizations, service providers, other government agencies, the media, and private businesses, in joint problem-solving strategies. Individual officers have the freedom or discretion to be creative and develop appropriate response strategies

to perceived problems. Clearly these partnerships require that police have the trust and respect of these potential partners. Additionally, for this approach to work, officers must be intimately involved in the community and have increased discretion to implement new and creative efforts determined by the immediate problems they face. This is where the decentralization of decision making is necessary.

In this new role, officers must walk the tightrope between being friends and perhaps losing objectivity, and being partners responsible to the entire community and not certain interests. A potential problem that can arise in this situation is the issue of gratuities and the "free cup of coffee." Whatever the motive of the giver, the "norm of reciprocity" puts the receiver in a position of owing the giver something. Even if the cup of coffee is given by the proprietor of a restaurant as a kindness and out of general appreciation for the police officer's service to the community, the officer who receives it likely will feel that he or she owes the giver, and the reciprocity might take many forms as the future unfolds. Some reciprocal actions may seem harmless in a moral sense, such as checking the business after hours, but checking one person's business should not be done at the expense of not checking others, or in any way taking away from other citizens' equal access to the officer's time and presence.

At the same time, it should be noted that if the officer refuses the free cup of coffee, he or she might offend or hurt the feelings of a giver who has no ulterior motives. In these instances, officers can explain that they do not accept free gifts from anyone and that they would be violating departmental policy were they to do so.

Another area of concern brought about due to the implementation of community policing is the dynamics of the supervisor-street officer relationship. Given the increased independence and autonomy of the community policing officer, the supervisor is removed from the immediate actions the officer is performing. The supervisor becomes less of a watchdog and more of a resource to be utilized as the officer sees fit. Supervisors then serve as the source of ethical and practical guidance and direction, not the authoritarian figure the officer strives to please by making arrests and citations and avoiding citizen complaints. In their new role, supervisors must not only be examples of what moral, ethical police should be, but they must continue to sensitize officers to ethical problems as they surface and offer guidance as necessary. As is the case in all law enforcement organizations, the practice of ethical and moral behavior must be advocated and exemplified from the top down; that is, ethical and moral behavior must be practiced and preached from the chief down through all ranks.

Because the success of community policing is dependent on the need to be perceived as fair, unbiased, and truly concerned with "justice for all," ethical concerns in community policing center on the more frequent and intense interactions officers have with all facets of the community. As mentioned earlier, this includes individual citizens, various citizen organizations, service providers, other government agencies, the media, and private businesses. In their capacity as problem solvers working with these various constituencies, community policing officers may confront conflicting demands to satisfy different parties; for example, rival gangs, a gang versus a citizen group, rival political groups, and any other combination of competing interests. In such situations, treating the different parties with respect and negotiating fairly and openly with the different parties is essential for community policing to work. At the same time, officers are bound by oath to enforce the law and protect individual and community interests. Here the exercise of discretion must be done fairly and equitably.

In the final analysis, ethical problems confronting community police officers may not be that much different from those faced in traditional policing. The concern under community policing is that ethical behavior takes on an even more important role. Working closely and effectively with individuals outside the police force demands a high level of respect and trust from those individuals. Thus, recruiting ethical and moral persons into the police ranks is now even more important. Then, training to sensitize these new officers to the ethical considerations that abound in their new role must occur. Last, but certainly not least, senior officers on up through the chief must be ethical and moral role models who will always support their personnel as they take on the challenge of being partners with the community in dealing with crime.

B. Grant Stitt

See also Mentoring; Police Mission; Recruit Academy Training

Further Readings

Cohen, H. S., & Feldberg, M. (1991). *Power and restraint: The moral dimension of police work.* New York, NY: Praeger.

Delattre, E. J. (1994). *Character & cops: Ethics in policing.* Washington, DC: AEI Press.

Kleinig, J. (1996). *The ethics of policing.* New York, NY: Cambridge University Press.

Peak, K. J., Stitt, B. G., & Glensor, R. W. (1998). Ethical considerations in community policing and problem solving. *Police Quarterly, 1*(3), 19–34.

Pollock-Byrne, J. M. (1989). *Ethics in crime and justice.* Pacific Grove, CA: Brooks/Cole.

EVIDENCE-BASED POLICING

In a 1998 lecture for the Police Foundation, Lawrence Sherman stated that police should base their strategies and tactics on what has been shown, through systematic and scientific study, to be effective. Although this was by no means a new idea (e.g., many people had called for research into police practices during the upheaval of the 1960s and 1970s), this idea gained traction and began to develop into what is now a widely recognized perspective of both scholars and decision makers known as *evidence-based policing*. Evidence-based policing posits that high-quality knowledge from research, analysis, and evaluation should be included in tactical, strategic, managerial, and community-oriented conversations about law enforcement. An example of evidence-based policing would be a police commander avoiding heavy reliance on reactive responses and random patrol and focusing more on proactive and directed patrol deployment, given that the latter approaches have been shown in numerous research studies to be more effective in reducing and preventing crime. This entry discusses elements of the evidence-based policing approach, aspects of the approach in practice, and evidence-based policing's connection with problem-oriented and community-oriented policing.

The Evidence-Based Policing Approach

Aside from being grounded in the idea of incorporating high-quality research into decision making, evidence-based policing does not specify the aspects of police practices to which research might be applied, the sources from which research is obtained, or even the method by which the research is generated. Although evidence-based policing has been criticized as only centering on a "what works" framework (i.e., focusing on outcome evaluation about what works to prevent crime), a wide range of police issues beyond crime prevention and control strategies, including internal efficiency, managerial concerns, or community relations, can be informed by research. Others have criticized evidence-based policing for being an overly academic venture, focusing on university-generated research. However, evidence-based policing is about incorporating research into the conversations of the police, no matter the source of that knowledge. Although a large portion of research knowledge has been generated by researchers, information may also arise from an agency's research and planning units, crime analysts, commanders, or other personnel.

Further, while the crux of evidence-based policing is its focus on the use and generation of knowledge from high-quality research and analysis, "high quality" does not mean that decisions must be made based only on experimental research, which is generally considered the gold standard of evaluation research. Critics of evidence-based policing have equated the idea of evaluation research with randomized controlled experimentation. Police practices can be informed by other forms of data analyses. Thus, while quality is an important factor when considering which research evidence to employ in making decisions, quality research can take a number of forms, including experiments and quasi-experiments, statistical modeling and analysis, crime analysis, systematic social observations, rigorous ethnographic and qualitative approaches, or surveys. Indeed, in Cynthia Lum, Christopher Koper, and Cody Telep's *Evidence-Based Policing Matrix,* multiple types of experimental and quasi-experimental evaluations are included in this evidence-to-practice tool. The goal of evidence-based policing is to use the best available research for decision making.

Evidence-based policing, and evidence-based crime policy more generally, reflect contemporary values associated with both accountable democratic governance as well as medical practice. With regard to accountable governance, evidence-based policing reflects a value in modern liberal democracies that there must be evaluable and objective accountability for government spending and actions. An evidence-based approach is one way to ensure that the large amount of public funds allocated to law enforcement are being spent on activities that actually do what they are intended to do, whether those intentions are to improve community safety, police legitimacy and fairness with the public, or internal efficiency. Additionally, general accountability to the public regarding the police mandate—to prevent, reduce, and detect crime, and to deliver services in a fair, constitutional, and legitimate manner—are things difficult to assess in unbiased ways, without systematic analysis and research.

From a medical perspective, findings from high-quality evaluations of medicinal treatments and doctors' techniques are believed to be useful in healing patients and also minimizing their harm from malpractice. In this approach, nonevidence-based approaches and informal sources of information may be archaic and dangerous and should be minimized. Evidence-based policing draws from these ideas, emphasizing that when police make decisions on how to reduce crime, improve internal efficiency, or interact with the public, these practices should not be based on hunches, anecdotes, feelings, best guesses, or even "best practices" based on group consensus, all which could lead to biased or ineffective policing and management. Rather, decisions should at least include and acknowledge high-quality information, analysis, research, and transparent knowledge so that the most informed decisions can be made and that harm can be avoided. Both the medical and criminal justice fields have had disturbing examples of practitioners using interventions despite knowledge from evaluations that show they either do not work or that they cause harm. A common example in the medical field is prescribing antibiotics for the common cold. In criminal justice, such examples include Drug Abuse Resistance Education (DARE), boot camps for juvenile offenders, and random reactive patrol.

Using research evidence to guide police practices has been seen as an important step forward in the professionalization of American law enforcement agencies. Scholars of evidence-based policing have pointed out numerous benefits from police departments adopting an evidence-based perspective that includes research as part of their tactical, strategic, and managerial conversations. These benefits can include reducing crime and fear, improving community satisfaction with the police, and reducing internal problems with personnel. Evidence-based approaches can assist with identifying interventions that backfire or harm people, and also provide systematic approaches to saving agencies time and money. The approach uses more objective methods of decision making, and can improve police legitimacy, transparency, and accountability by providing objective justifications for police actions. Because assessment and evaluation are important aspects of an evidence-based policing approach, evidence-based policing has the potential of alerting agencies to problems within their information management systems, and may indirectly improve data collection and crime analysis, as well as information sharing. Other police strategies, such as problem solving and community policing, require collecting information as well as evaluating interventions, which are implicated in an evidence-based policing approach.

Evidence-Based Policing in Practice

Despite the logic and benefits of evidence-based policing, its objectives have not been fully realized in policing, nor is it without its critics, as already discussed. Numerous scholars writing for the 2008 *Ideas in American Policing* lectures for the Police Foundation, including David Bayley, Stephen Mastrofski, Lawrence Sherman, David Weisburd, Cynthia Lum, Geoff Alpert, and James Willis, have pointed out a gap between what has been discovered in policing research and current police practices. As Weisburd asserted in his lecture, the best example of the disconnect between the evidence in policing and its use in practice is the failure of agencies to regularly adopt place-based or "hot spot" approaches that target specific problems at specific geographic locales. This is despite strong evidence that crime concentrates at small geographic places, that targeting police efforts on community problems at specific places is a highly effective way of reducing crime, and that crime is not displaced to other locations as much as commonly believed. Police in most places continue to practice random, undirected patrol with officers working in traditional police beat areas, including locations that do not have crime problems.

Police continue to employ reactive, case-by-case procedural approaches to crime, rather than proactive, holistic, multiagency, and problem-solving strategies. When they do use the latter strategies, they often do not have the resources or the motivation to sustain them. Instead of becoming mainstays in patrol or investigations, they become ad-hoc efforts or efforts linked to special programs, units, or research projects. In this way, evidence-based policing is very similar to problem-oriented policing (POP) and community-oriented policing (COP), suffering from similar problems such as sustainability and institutionalization into law enforcement culture and mentality.

There are many reasons for the gap between police research evidence and its use in practice. Some scholars focus on the supply of research in order to meet requirements for academic publication and tenure, while showing less interest in the demand for research by police agencies. Hence, such researchers may gravitate toward topics of less practical interest to police. Further, they may have little incentive to publish practitioner-friendly versions of their work in practitioner-oriented publications. Even if researchers are motivated to consider the practical demands for knowledge, translating research concepts into tangible practices may prove challenging, given the many complexities of police organizations, practice, and amenability to change (it may be easy, for example, to recommend that police do hot spots policing or problem-oriented policing, but operationalizing these recommendations may be more difficult).

In turn, very little demand for research has arisen from police agencies traditionally. Law enforcement continues to be heavily reliant on a procedures-based approach, which is markedly different from an evidence-based approach. Even with the advent of numerous alternative models for police deployment (such as problem- and community-oriented policing, team policing, and intelligence-led policing), the reactive, procedures-based approach continues to dominate. Although procedures can certainly reflect research evidence, most police procedures are reactive, and based on standard responses to crime events and resolving issues from a legal perspective. When approached with research, police chiefs may cite lack of resources and the analytic or operational capacity to carry out research projects, officer resistance, or possible political backlash as reasons for not emphasizing evaluation or pursuing changes to deeply ingrained police procedures and practices. There may also be resistance to academics and researchers based on the belief that they know little about the realities of policing or the belief that experience is a more valid decision-making base than systematically collected knowledge.

Despite these concerns, debates, and arguments, research evidence is becoming more accepted among police leaders. This has been facilitated in part by federal agencies such as the Office of Community Oriented Policing Services, the National Institute of Justice, and the Bureau of Justice Assistance, which fund police agencies and their crime prevention projects. These agencies now regularly incorporate principles of evidence-based policing into their law enforcement grant solicitations. For example, solicitations encourage applicants to show they will use the most rigorous methods to evaluate policing interventions. Or, funding may be conditioned on the requirements that grantees use evidence-based interventions and programs. Although squabbles about "which evidence" or "what type of evidence" continue, there has been considerable change in the acceptance of the need for a more evidence-based approach, at least at the level of funding and research leadership.

Connection With Problem-Oriented and Community-Oriented Policing

An important topic to probe is the relationship between evidence-based policing and problem-oriented policing (POP) and community-oriented policing (COP). Evidence-based policing is highly compatible with, and in some cases required by, problem-oriented and community-oriented policing approaches. Not only can POP and COP strategies and tactics be examined using systematic and scientific processes, but the problem-solving process itself implies a scientific approach.

Problem-oriented approaches, as envisioned by Herman Goldstein, put forth a systematic and scientific approach to understanding and addressing crime problems rather than individual incidents. Consider the problem-solving SARA model (scanning, analysis, response, assessment) coined by John Eck and William Spelman (1987). In its entirety, this approach reflects the scientific method of observation and hypothesis testing. The response called for by the SARA model is not just any response, but one that is based on the nature of the problem as well as existing knowledge from research and evaluation on tailoring solutions to those problems. The assessment in the SARA model clearly requires evaluation, the results of which are used to determine if the response was appropriate.

Further, believability of those evaluations is central to making the decision as to whether or not the response was appropriate, also implicating values of an evidence-based approach. Finally, problem-oriented policing as a general strategy has itself been evaluated and shown to have positive effects. An evidence-based policing approach therefore would encourage the use of problem-oriented strategies.

Community-oriented policing approaches, including those components that are separate from problem-oriented policing, can also benefit from evidence-based policing. Although the effects of specific community policing practices on crime vary, evidence-based policing is more broadly concerned about the impact of research on all types of issues police confront—not just crime. Community policing approaches may thus be informed by research on a variety of issues including crime, citizen satisfaction, traffic safety, police legitimacy, or fear of crime. Similar to crime and evaluation data, information on knowledge, attitudes, and priorities from the community as well as results of tests of community-oriented policing strategies can be collected systematically and scientifically. An evidence-based approach to policing, for example, might result in a decision not to use DARE as a way to reduce juvenile delinquency and drug use, if research has shown it does not reduce either delinquency or drug use and also does not improve police relations with high-risk juveniles.

A great deal of research evidence has been generated about problem-oriented and community-oriented policing approaches that could be used to guide police decisions about these practices. Numerous positive evaluations and reviews of problem-solving policing approaches have been conducted, many of which are found in the *Evidence-Based Policing Matrix*. Five systematic reviews, including David Weisburd, Cody Telep, Joshua Hinkle, and John Eck's review of problem-oriented policing; Anthony Braga's review of hot spots policing (which has overlaps with problem solving); Christopher Koper and Evan Mayo-Wilson's review on crackdowns on gun carrying in hot spots; Lorraine Mazerolle, David Soole, and Sasha Rombouts's review of law enforcement in drug hot spots; and Braga and Weisburd's review on pulling levers approaches, all show positive effects of proactive problem-solving approaches by police agencies.

With regard to community policing more generally, there are also high-quality research studies that can serve as sources of information for police decision making. This includes research on police legitimacy and also some evaluations of different types of community policing interventions, such as neighborhood watch, community meetings, door-to-door visitations by the police, and foot patrol. The evidence with regard to the effect of community policing on crime reduction remains weak, although some efforts such as multiagency problem solving with strong and tailored community components are promising. A review by Trevor Bennett and his colleagues (2008) of neighborhood watch programs was generally positive about this program's ability to reduce burglary, although others have reviews that the crime-control benefits of community policing have been less optimistic. On the other hand, Pate and colleagues' 1986 report of the Police Foundation's landmark studies of community policing in Newark and Houston suggest that community policing strategies reduce citizens' fear and improve their satisfaction with police. There is also research conducted by Tom Tyler, Stephen Mastrofski, and Raymond Paternoster and colleagues which suggests that the way police treat victims, suspects, and witnesses can affect citizen perceptions of police legitimacy, and that fairer treatment by police may have long-term benefits in terms of increased compliance with the law.

Final Thoughts

Evidence-based policing should be considered a decision-making perspective for the police, not a panacea. It is grounded in the idea that policies and practices should be supported by evidence and analytics, not blindly determined by them, and that research is not ignored. The challenge for police will be how to partner with researchers and analysts to convert research into tangible forms so that it can become part of the conversation about how to reduce crime, increase legitimacy, or address internal problems.

Cynthia Lum and Christopher S. Koper

See also Community Policing (All); Crime Mapping; Directed Patrol, Studies of; Hot Spots; Learning Organization; Place-Based Policing; Problem-Oriented Policing (All); Problem-Solving Initiatives, Assessment and Evaluation; Problem-Solving Initiatives, Examples of Assessment and Evaluation of; Problem-Solving Process (SARA)

Further Readings

Bennett, T., Farrington, D., & Holloway, K. (2008). *Does neighborhood watch reduce crime?* (Crime Prevention Research Review No. 3). Washington, DC: U.S. Department of Justice, Office of Community Oriented Policing Services. Retrieved from http://cops.usdoj.gov/files/RIC/Publications/e040825133-res-review3.pdf

Braga, A. A. (2001). The effects of hot spots policing on crime. *Annals of the American Academy of Political and Social Science, 578*(1), 104–125. doi: 10.1177/0002716201578001007

Eck, J. E., & Spelman, W. (1989). A problem-oriented approach to police service delivery. In D. J. Kenney (Ed.), *Police and policing: Contemporary issues* (pp. 95–111). New York, NY: Praeger.

Goldstein, H. (1979). Improving policing: A problem-oriented approach. *Crime & Delinquency, 25*(2), 236–258. doi: 10.1177/001112877902500207

Koper, C. S., & Mayo-Wilson, E. (2006). Police crackdowns on illegal gun carrying: A systematic review of their impacts on gun crime. *Journal of Experimental Criminology, 2*(2), 227–261.

Lum, C. (2009, August). Translating police research into practice. *Ideas in American Policing, 11*, 1–16. Washington, DC: Police Foundation. Retrieved from http://www.policefoundation.org/content/translating-police-research-practice

Lum, C., & Koper, C. (2013). Evidence-based policing. In G. Bruinsma & D. L. Weisburd (Eds.), *The Encyclopedia of Criminology and Criminal Justice*. Springer-Verlag.

Lum, C., Koper, C., & Telep, C. W. (2011). The evidence-based policing matrix. *Journal of Experimental Criminology, 7*, 3–26.

Lum, C., Telep, C., Koper, C., & Grieco, J. (2012). Receptivity to research in policing. *Justice Research and Policy, 14*(1), 61–96. doi: 10.3818/JRP.14.1.2012.61

Mastrofski, S. D., Snipes, J. B., & Supina, A. E. (1996). Compliance on demand: The public's response to specific police requests. *Journal of Research in Crime and Delinquency, 33*(3), 269–305.

Mazerolle, L., Soole, D. W., & Rombouts, S. (2007). *Crime prevention research reviews No. 1: Disrupting street-level drug markets.* Washington, DC: U.S. Department of Justice, Office of Community Oriented Policing Services. Retrieved from http://cops.usdoj.gov/files/RIC/Publications/e04072678.pdf

Pate, A. M, Wycoff, M. A., Skogan, W. G., & Sherman, L. W. (1986). *Reducing fear of crime in Houston and Newark: A summary report.* Washington, DC: Police Foundation. Retrieved from http://www.policefoundation.co/sites/pftest1.drupalgardens.com/

files/Pate%20et%20al.%20%281986%29%20-%20
Reducing%20Fear%200f%20Crime%20in%20
Houston%20and%20Newark%20%28Summary%20
Report%29%20.pdf

Sherman, L. W. (1998). *Evidence-based policing.*
Washington, DC: Police Foundation.

Sherman, L. W., Farrington, D. P., Welsh, B. C., &
MacKenzie, D. L. (Eds.). (2002). *Evidence-based crime
prevention.* New York, NY: Routledge.

Tyler, T. R. (2006). *Why people obey the law.* Princeton,
NJ: Princeton University Press.

Weisburd, D. L. (2008, January). Place-based policing.
Ideas in Policing No. 9. Washington, DC: Police
Foundation. Retrieved from http://www
.policefoundation.org/pdf/placebasedpolicing.pdf

Weisburd, D. L., Telep, C. W., Hinkle, J. C., & Eck, J. E.
(2010). Is problem-oriented policing effective in
reducing crime and disorder? Findings from a Campbell
systematic review. *Criminology & Public Policy, 9*(1),
139–172. doi: 10.1111/j.1745–9133.2010.00617

Website

Evidence-based Policing Matrix; http://gemini.gmu.edu/
cebcp/Matrix.html

EXECUTIVE SESSIONS ON POLICING

In the early 1980s, Harvard University's John F. Kennedy School of Government and the Program in Criminal Justice Policy and Management developed a series of Executive Sessions with the purpose of allowing practitioners and academics to meet, confer, and search for effective means of addressing important public problems. More specifically, these Executive Sessions were created to generate a "sustained conversation" among a "core group of members selected for their ability to provide leadership to a practice field," and to produce "learning and transformation in a practice field through continuing dialogue, digestible publications, and education."

The basic model of an Executive Session is a series of five or six three-day meetings, usually held over a period of three years, in which 25 to 30 high-level practitioners and academics engage in a creative dialogue with a view to redefining and proposing solutions for substantive policy issues.

This entry discusses the two Executive Sessions on policing that have thus far been coordinated by Harvard University to address significant concerns faced by police over the last three decades, and to discuss, analyze, and recommend policy revisions to improve police and criminal justice effectiveness for the future.

Criminal Justice Research

Following the recommendations of the President's Commission on Law Enforcement and Administration of Justice in 1967, the policing and justice professions were tasked with engaging in research-supported strategy development to enhance the performance of the criminal justice sectors. As a result, Congress passed the Omnibus Crime Control and Safe Streets Act of 1968, which led to the creation of the National Institute of Law Enforcement and Criminal Justice (NILECJ), the predecessor of the National Institute of Justice (NIJ), the research and evaluation component of the U.S. Department of Justice.

Notable research projects were conducted through the 1970s and 1980s (e.g., the Kansas City preventive patrol experiment in 1974 and the RAND Study on criminal investigation in 1976), resulting in considerable recommendations to improve police organizational performance. However, even when related policy and procedural revisions were implemented, there was little impact on the rising violent and serious crime rates and the expanding illicit drug trade. Government leaders, police agency administrators, and the public noted the need for further change.

First Executive Session on Policing, 1983–1991

The first Executive Session was convened in 1983 and was jointly coordinated by the National Institute of Justice and the Harvard University Kennedy School of Government. This session's members included the U.S. Attorney General, mayors from large U.S. cities, police chiefs, and criminal justice academics noted for significant police-related research. The predominant goal of these sessions was to develop recommendations to enhance police policy and deployment effectiveness through the start of the new millennium. The critical strategy and policy recommendations that resulted after the first Executive Session was community policing, an initiative designed to incorporate community cooperation and partnership into a prioritized problem-solving approach to reduce crime and improve community confidence in the police.

Furthermore, a number of significant papers were published during and following this first session. These papers—which laid the foundation of community policing and are available from the Kennedy School of Government (see "Further Readings" below) and were viewed as the basis for the revolutionary strategic changes that dramatically affected police deployment practices in the 1980s and 1990s—were compiled into a series called *Perspectives on Policing.*

Second Executive Session on Policing, 2008–2014

Of course, since these significant publications were issued, several factors, including the attacks of September 11, 2001, have led to tremendous changes in U.S. policing and society. So the second Executive Session on Policing and Public Safety was initiated in 2008 and faces new challenges. It consists of two phases. The first phase of the second session took place at the Harvard University Kennedy School of Government from 2008 through 2011. This session was again staffed by noteworthy professionals and criminal justice academics, but took the additional step of including union officials, psychiatrists, prosecutors, attorneys, and civil liberty advocates.

In addition to the events of 9/11, other major developments have been of extreme relevance since the conclusion of the first Executive Session. A national trend arose and has continued that has witnessed the drastic reduction of violence and serious crime rates across the United States. Some of this can be attributed to advanced technology that has permitted comprehensive crime analysis and improved forensic investigation. Of equal importance has been the need to implement effective counterterrorism protocols following the 2001 terrorist attacks. This has expanded the responsibilities of law enforcement to include understanding transnational and global perspectives on crime and terrorism. And finally, the economic downturn of 2008 to 2012 has overwhelmingly impacted government spending on policing and justice administration, thereby creating challenges for police executives in maintaining agency efficacy, equity, and efficiency.

In response to the above events, the participants of the second Executive Session have already published a number of papers that have evaluated the critical contemporary issues facing police administrators. These works, called the *New Perspectives in Policing,* are also available from the Kennedy School of Government.

Another phase of the second Executive Session will meet at Harvard University through 2014 to address the current concerns of government leaders and criminal justice administrators. It is anticipated that the resulting publications will have an equally significant effect on policing and justice administration endeavors.

James F. Albrecht

See also Community Policing, Evolution of; Crime Analysis; Crime Mapping; Foot Patrols; Hot Spots; Kansas City Preventive Patrol Experiment; Place-Based Policing; Police-Community Relations; Strategic Planning

Further Readings

Albrecht, J. F. (2011). Analyzing the implementation and evolution of community policing in the United States and Scandinavia. In M. de Guzman, A. M. Das, & D. K. Das (Eds.), *Strategic responses to crime: Thinking globally, acting locally* (pp. 3–26). Boca Raton, FL: CRC Press.

Harvard University, John F. Kennedy School of Government, Program in Criminal Justice Policy and Management. (n.d.). *Executive Sessions.* Retrieved from http://www.hks.harvard.edu/programs/criminaljustice/research-publications/executive-sessions

Harvard University, John F. Kennedy School of Government, Program in Criminal Justice Policy and Management. (2012). *Research & Publications.* Retrieved from http://www.hks.harvard.edu/programs/criminaljustice/research-publications

Moore, M. H., & Hartmann, F. X. (1999). *On the theory and practice of "executive sessions."* Retrieved from http://www.hks.harvard.edu/var/ezp_site/storage/fckeditor/file/pdfs/centers-programs/programs/criminal-justice/exec_sessions_theory.pdf

Office of Justice Programs, National Institute of Justice. (2009). *What is an executive session?* Retrieved from http://www.nij.gov/topics/law-enforcement/administration/executive-sessions/what-is.htm

President's Commission on Law Enforcement and Administration of Justice. (1967). *The challenge of crime in a free society.* Washington, DC: Government Printing Office.

Fear of Crime

When fear of crime became a significant political issue in the United States in the 1970s and 1980s, reducing fear soon became a police objective. This situation helped spur the development of community policing in the 1980s and 1990s. However, the importance of fear of crime within the explicit missions of most police departments has waxed and waned over the past 20 to 30 years. Many police departments give lip service to reducing fear, but relatively few can actually point to activities specifically targeted at fear reduction, and fewer still measure fear of crime in a thorough and systematic manner.

One of the reasons that fear of crime is important is that it affects communities negatively. If parents prohibit their children from playing in a park because of their fear that something bad will happen to the children, then the park goes unused and becomes more susceptible to crime and disorder. If neighborhood residents stay in at night because they are afraid of being mugged, then the neighborhood's streets and sidewalks become even more dangerous. If people cease shopping in a certain part of town because they do not feel safe there, the businesses eventually close. People whose fear of crime in their own neighborhoods is high move to other neighborhoods or other jurisdictions if they can afford to do so. In other words, fear of crime affects individual behavior and also the health of communities. This entry explains what causes people to become fearful of crime, how fear of crime can be measured, and how police can use a problem-oriented approach to respond to residents' fear of crime.

Understanding Fear of Crime

Fear of crime is a very popular topic among criminologists and other social scientists, not to mention journalists, politicians, and the general public. However, the term *fear of crime* is used rather loosely and inconsistently in research and public discussions. It is best understood as an emotion or feeling. People who fear crime experience anxiety, concern, alarm, or dread caused by a belief that crime will happen to them or to others close to them. Fear is not the same as a perception of a dangerous environment or a belief in the likelihood of becoming a crime victim—rather, these are possible *causes* of fear, not indications of fear *per se*. Similarly, it is not the same as believing that crime is increasing—having such a belief might cause one's fear to increase, but not necessarily, especially if one expects that the victims of increasing crime will be "others," such as people who live elsewhere or who engage in risky behaviors.

Unlike reported crime and even personal crime victimization, fear of crime is not measured nationally on an annual and official basis. Consequently, it is not possible to determine, with confidence, during what period fear of crime has been the highest or the lowest, or where in the nation it is increasing or decreasing. Most of the many studies of fear of crime have been small-scale studies in single sites. National polling organizations such as Gallup occasionally measure the level of fear of crime, but not every year, and not in such a way that one could compare, say, New York to Los Angeles.

With those caveats in mind, what do we know about fear of crime? Here are a few conclusions drawn from the work of leading scholars:

1. Common cues to crime danger include darkness, unfamiliar environments, lack of companions, suspicious bystanders, and signs of incivility or disorder.

2. The most common behavioral reaction to fear of crime is to avoid unsafe areas at night.

3. Older people often report high levels of generalized fear of crime, but when asked about specific sources of fear or behavioral reactions (e.g., afraid to go out at night), their responses are typically similar to those of middle-aged people.

4. School-age youths and young adults usually report the highest levels of fear of crime, but are least likely to adopt constraining or precautionary behaviors.

5. Women usually report higher levels of fear of crime than men. This seems to be driven by fear of sexual assault, which influences fear of burglary, mugging, strangers, dark streets, and other conditions.

6. Women and older people are most likely to take precautionary measures in response to their fear of crime.

7. Fear of crime tends to be higher among minority residents and urban dwellers.

8. Perceived risk of victimization has one of the strongest effects on fear of crime.

9. Fear of property crimes is often higher than fear of personal crimes, reflecting a rational understanding that property crimes occur much more frequently than violent crimes.

10. Many people get most of their crime information from the mass media. Where people get their information affects their fear of crime, with TV news and tabloid newspapers having the most impact. Interestingly, though, people often can distinguish local news stories from those that are more distant and less likely to be relevant to their lifestyle and surroundings.

Beyond these generalizations, it is apparent that fear of crime, causes of fear, and the consequences of fear vary—they fluctuate over time, they vary between different jurisdictions, and they vary among groups of people. This is not particularly surprising, but it means that, logically, the priority that police and others should give to reducing fear of crime should shift over time and should vary among different jurisdictions and different subsets of the population. It would clearly be a mistake to merely assume that fear of crime in a specific city, town, or county fits the national profile, without looking into it more closely. To avoid making this assumption, it is necessary to measure fear of crime systematically and repeatedly.

Community Policing and Fear of Crime

For many years, police assumed that the logical approach to reducing fear of crime was to reduce crime itself. The fallacy of this assumption eventually became evident. While fear of crime *is* related to actual crime, the connection is far from linear or straightforward. The most fearful individuals are not necessarily those who have suffered the most crime or who are most at risk of victimization. The most fearful communities are not necessarily the ones with the most crime. Over time, fear of crime does not necessarily go up or down in correlation with the amount of actual crime, as demonstrated over the last two decades, during which crime has decreased substantially but fear of crime does not seem to have followed suit.

In the early 1980s, two studies of foot patrol had a major impact on police thinking in relation to fear of crime. In Newark, New Jersey, an experiment was conducted that involved adding foot patrols in some neighborhoods and eliminating it in others. Just as in the famous Kansas City (Missouri) preventive patrol experiment, in which the impact of different levels of motorized patrol was tested, there was no impact on crime due to foot patrol in Newark. Unlike Kansas City, though, neighborhood residents in Newark noticed the fluctuations in levels of foot patrol, and when they had foot patrol, they felt safer. A study in Flint, Michigan, had similar results. The clear-cut positive effect of foot patrol on fear of crime grabbed the attention of police strategists, in part because earlier studies of professional era motorized patrol and rapid response had such discouraging results.

In the space of a few years, renewed interest in foot patrol expanded into the widespread adoption of community policing. Many police agencies saw that foot patrol would be of limited utility for them (because of low population density, for example) but sought other ways of capturing some of the value of foot patrol, including fear reduction—this led to bicycle patrol, police storefronts and ministations, beat teams, specialized community policing officers, and a host of other alternatives to routine motorized patrol, along with increased police-citizen contact, more personalized policing, more opportunities for community input, more information sharing between police and the public, police-community partnerships, and systematic multiagency collaboration in support of community safety.

The available evidence generally supports the view that community policing (not just foot patrol) makes people feel safer. Increased police-public contact, whether through foot patrol, police visits to homes and stores, or more formal meetings and other organizing efforts, seems to reduce fear of crime directly, or else indirectly through the mechanism of enhancing public confidence in the police. Studies have also shown, however, that when community policing efforts become too diffuse and unfocused, their effects on fear of crime and other outcomes tend to diminish.

Broken Windows and Fear of Crime

A very important catalyst for the conceptual leap from foot patrol to community policing was the broken windows theory articulated in 1982 by James Q. Wilson and George Kelling. The question they addressed was how foot patrol made people feel safer when the actual amount of crime seemed unaffected. Their conclusion was that it was more than just increased police visibility, "felt presence," and a recognizable beat officer. In addition to those benefits, they observed that foot patrol officers were more likely to address minor crimes, disorder, incivilities, and signs of crime than were officers patrolling in cars. Why is that important? Because citizens often identify those very same types of low-level incidents and conditions, such as graffiti and disorderly youth, as "signs of crime," that is, evidence that their neighborhoods are not safe. When people see the police doing something about these signs of crime, they are reassured.

The broken windows theory goes on to postulate a domino effect—that if minor crime and disorder are tolerated, then more serious crime creeps in,

residents who can afford to do so will move out, property owners will fail to maintain their homes and businesses as well as they should, and a downward spiral grips the neighborhood. This extended theory, tying together passive policing, disorder, and serious crime in a pattern of urban decay, has not been successfully verified through in-depth empirical studies. The front end of the theory, though, is well supported—when disorder and minor crime are left unchecked, neighborhood residents feel unsafe, but when police address these types of low-level conditions, residents feel safer.

Problem-Oriented Policing and Fear of Crime

A problem-oriented approach to fear reduction has even greater potential than broad-based community policing or broken windows for the simple reason that it is, by definition, more targeted. Community policing tends to be expansive and diffuse rather than focused, and it is aimed principally, although not exclusively, at enhancing police-community relations and the public's trust and confidence in the police. Strategies based on the broken windows theory are explicitly directed toward minor crime, disorder, incivilities, and similar kinds of incidents and conditions—these have been shown to be associated with fear of crime in many neighborhoods, but certainly are not the sole or universal causes of fear of crime. It is quite a testament to both of these approaches that they have been relatively successful at reducing fear of crime, inasmuch as neither is specifically or primarily targeted at fear reduction.

The problem-oriented approach begins with a simple premise—fear of crime is a problem worth addressing. Then, in line with the well-known SARA process (scanning, analysis, response, assessment), a problem-oriented approach has several basic features:

Scanning to determine if fear of crime is a problem, whether it is increasing or decreasing, where it is most acute, and which groups or types of people suffer the most from it

Analysis to determine more specifically the causes of identified fear of crime problems within the jurisdiction, recognizing that these causes might differ between neighborhoods, change over time, and vary among categories of residents

Responses that are tailored and targeted to the jurisdiction's specific fear of crime problems and their causes

Assessment of responses once they are implemented, to determine if they are working to reduce fear of crime, and if not, why not

Addressing fear of crime in this way is not a theoretical proposition. When the Baltimore County, Maryland, police department took a problem-oriented approach to fear reduction in the 1980s with its Citizen Oriented Police Enforcement (COPE) program (discussed below), it was measurably more successful than previous efforts using saturation patrol and traditional crime prevention techniques. A problem-oriented approach to school crime and disorder in Charlotte, North Carolina, led to decreased fear of crime among students and teachers. The national evaluation of Reassurance Policing in the United Kingdom, focusing on the particular problem of juvenile nuisances for comparison purposes between sample agencies, concluded that those sites that implemented problem solving most successfully had the best results in public reassurance. Several systematic evaluations of problem-oriented policing targeted at street-level drug markets have documented reductions in fear of crime.

An important factor that inhibits more of this kind of problem-oriented policing is that targeting fear of crime has lagged behind targeting crime itself. Over the past 30 years, police agencies have dramatically enhanced their capacity to target crime through crime analysis, crime mapping, and repeat complaint analysis. Today, these kinds of analyses support directed patrol, targeted patrol, hot spots policing, and intelligence-led policing. Instead of spreading officers and other resources uniformly or randomly across the entire jurisdiction, police agencies now target their resources in a more strategic way to deal with crime and disorder. The evidence is strong that this targeted approach is more effective at reducing crime and disorder than traditional practices. Unfortunately, police agencies have not developed the same kind of targeted approach to fear reduction.

Even if they wanted to do so, most police agencies could not immediately implement a targeted approach to fear reduction because they nearly all lack data on fear of crime. This is a big challenge. Police agencies more or less automatically produce data on crime and calls for service as part of their normal operations. These data are then analyzed to help target crime and disorder. But police agencies do not normally or routinely produce data on fear of crime—it requires extra effort. Most agencies have never realized how much value such data would have, or they have decided that it would be too difficult to obtain.

Measuring Fear of Crime

When the Baltimore County Police Department began its COPE strategy in the early 1980s, its initial challenge was to identify neighborhoods in which to implement fear reduction efforts. At first, officers relied heavily on crime statistics, news items, suggestions from political leaders, and their own personal experiences and observations. What they discovered was that these information sources could be useful for scanning to identify neighborhoods where fear of crime *might* be high, but further investigation was required. For example, the rate of burglaries in a neighborhood might be higher than normal, but it had not caused an increase in fear of crime. Or a referral from an elected county official might actually represent the concerns of just one vocal neighborhood resident, not a widespread concern.

The police department eventually settled on a strategy that involved both interviews and community surveys. The first step was to verify that there really was a fear of crime problem in a neighborhood. This typically involved speaking to at least a handful of neighborhood leaders and residents. If the preliminary evidence seemed to indicate that there was a problem worth tackling, then a more systematic door-to-door canvass was undertaken. During this canvass, residents were asked to complete a short questionnaire, and then they were interviewed about problems in the neighborhood that concerned them.

The purpose of the interviews was to diagnose the problem(s) in the neighborhood. Officers had a few standardized questions to use to begin the interviews, but were encouraged to follow up on items mentioned by residents and probe for underlying issues and specific information. Most interviews lasted only a few minutes, but some took longer. Officers had the opportunity to introduce themselves, explain what they were doing in the neighborhood, and secure commitments for ongoing assistance.

The purpose of the short questionnaire was to measure the fear of crime problem. These questionnaires were not employed in every neighborhood in which the COPE officers worked, but they were used quite often. Generally, the questionnaires were administered when the officers first did their neighborhood canvass, and then again a few months later. This before-and-after measurement made it possible to determine whether the level of fear had gone up or down, or stayed the same, once the COPE officers had implemented their fear reduction measures in the neighborhood. The cumulative results of these surveys administered in multiple neighborhoods were instrumental in showing that the police department's fear reduction efforts were making an impact.

This kind of interviewing and surveying in targeted neighborhoods is within the reach of agencies that are committed to community policing and that want to reduce fear of crime. Other approaches can also be used to collect data, including communitywide surveys, community meetings, key person interviews, and environmental audits. Today, social media provide another source of information about the public's fears and concerns. The main objective, of course, is to correctly identify real fear of crime problems as opposed to illusory concerns, and then to analyze those problems in order to figure out what is causing them. At that point, responses that specifically address the problems and their causes can be formulated and implemented.

Responses to Fear of Crime

Community policing and broken windows incorporate some responses that are associated with fear reduction, such as personalized policing, community engagement, collaboration with other agencies, and attention to minor crime and disorder. Another tried and true response is crime prevention through environmental design (CPTED). However, it is crucial to keep in mind that the causes of fear in any situation can be very specific and idiosyncratic, so one-size-fits-all responses should be avoided. Moreover, once a fear of crime problem is carefully identified and analyzed, it often becomes obvious what the response should be.

In one Baltimore County case, for example, COPE officers became aware that the residents of a senior citizen high rise had largely stopped shopping in a nearby commercial strip, instead taking buses to shop at a more distant mall. The officers' first assumption was that the cause was a group of "paint huffers" who had taken to using an adjacent park to abuse inhalants, mainly spray paint in aerosol cans. The officers were already familiar with this developing problem and had begun targeting it in various ways.

When officers surveyed and interviewed the elderly residents of the high rise, however, it turned out that they were largely unaware of the paint-huffing problem in the park. Their real concerns were mainly twofold: (1) They feared crossing the busy street to get to the close-by shopping area; and (2) they feared the aggressive panhandlers who had become common on the sidewalks in the shopping area (some, but not most, of whom were also paint huffers).

Officers were able to address these two problems once they had been identified. They worked with traffic engineers to lengthen the time provided by walk lights and improve the visibility of crosswalks. To address the panhandling problem, they took several steps, including getting a more workable county ordinance passed so that aggressive panhandlers could be arrested, implementing a publicity campaign aimed at discouraging shoppers from giving money to the panhandlers, and convincing local merchants not to sell alcoholic beverages (or spray paint) to anyone already intoxicated. These measures were largely successful at reducing the causes of fear in the shopping area, and many of the senior high rise residents resumed shopping there.

The key features of a problem-oriented approach to the problem of fear of crime are careful identification, thorough analysis, and then the application of responses that are tailored to the specific nature and causes of the fear problem being addressed. Fear of crime is not identical to other crime and disorder problems that police tackle, but the problem-solving principles that should be used are the same.

Gary W. Cordner

See also Broken Windows Theory; Citizen Surveys; Crime Mapping; Neighborhood Associations

Further Readings

Cordner, G. (2010). *Reducing fear of crime: Strategies for police.* Washington, DC: U.S. Department of Justice, Office of Community Oriented Policing Services.

Ferraro, K. F. (1995). *Fear of crime: Interpreting victimization risk.* Albany: State University of New York Press.

Kenney, D., & Watson, S. (1998). *Crime in schools: Reducing fear and disorder with student problem solving.* Washington, DC: Police Executive Research Forum.

Pate, A., Wycoff, M. A., Skogan, W. G., & Sherman, L. W. (1986). *Reducing fear of crime in Houston and Newark: A summary report.* Washington, DC: Police Foundation. Retrieved from http://www.policefoundation.co/sites/pftest1.drupalgardens.com/files/Pate%20et%20al.%20%281986%29%20-%20Reducing%20Fear%20of%20Crime%20in%20Houston%20and%20Newark%20%28Summary%20Report%29%20.pdf

Simon, J. (2007). *Governing through crime: How the war on crime transformed American democracy and created a culture of fear.* New York, NY: Oxford University Press.

Skogan, W. G. (2006). *Police and community in Chicago: A tale of three cities.* New York, NY: Oxford University Press.

Taft, P. (1986). *Fighting fear: The Baltimore County COPE project.* NCJ 103756. Washington, DC: Police Executive Research Forum.

Tuffin, R., Morris, J., & Poole, A. (2006). *An evaluation of the impact of the National Reassurance Policing Programme.* London, England: Home Office.

Weisburd, D. L., & Eck, J. E. (2004). What can police do to reduce crime, disorder, and fear? *The Annals of the American Academy of Political and Social Science, 593,* 42–65. doi: 10.1177/0002716203262548

Wilson, J. Q., & Kelling, G. L. (1982, March). Broken windows: The police and neighborhood safety. *Atlantic Monthly, 249*(3), 29–38.

FLINT, MICHIGAN, EXPERIMENT

The Flint, Michigan, foot patrol experiment is one of the first evaluation studies of a community policing program and also one of the first policing studies to include measures of citizen fear of crime. The three-year evaluation study assessed how foot patrol affected citizen perceptions, officer attitudes, and crime and disorder. Overall, the intervention had a beneficial impact on a number of indicators, suggesting that foot patrol could be an effective program for both community outreach and crime reduction. Foot patrol is frequently a component of community policing programs. Foot patrol officers are typically expected to do more than just use surveillance and presence to deter crime. Foot patrol inherently involves more direct police-citizen interaction than officers spending their shift responding to 911 calls in automobiles or driving randomly through their beat in a patrol car. Officers can use this increase in citizen contact to help promote joint police-citizen efforts to address and prevent crime. This was the goal of efforts in Flint. In this entry, the context in Flint leading up to the experiment is explained in more detail. The goals and design of the intervention are then described before turning to the results of the program.

Background

The Flint Neighborhood Foot Patrol Program began in January 1979, with $2.6 million in funding provided by the Charles Stewart Mott Foundation for the intervention and for an evaluation by a research team at Michigan State University led by Robert Trojanowicz. The grant helped establish the National Neighborhood Foot Patrol Center in the School of Criminal Justice at Michigan State. As the project began, both the City of Flint and the Flint Police Department were undergoing difficult times. Flint, located about 66 miles northwest of Detroit, is the birthplace of General Motors and many Flint residents were employed by the automaker. Downsizing by the company led to high unemployment rates in the late 1970s, and many residents left the city to seek opportunities elsewhere. The unstable economy and departure of many residents contributed to increased crime in the city as well. At the time of the experiment, Flint had the sixth highest homicide rate in the country.

The Flint Police Department was not only dealing with increased rates of violent crime but also a series of internal problems that helped exacerbate racial tension in a city with a history of racial strife. In one notable incident, an African American female officer and a white male officer got into a fight at police headquarters about who would drive their patrol car. The fight eventually led to other officers becoming involved and at some point, shots were fired and the female officer was wounded. Police also shot and killed a 15-year-old boy who was trying to escape the police by climbing over a fence, leading to anger among many residents. A Michigan state trooper was accidentally shot and killed by a Flint police officer in an undercover operation with the Flint Police Department. The instability in both the city and the department led to a great deal of animosity between residents and police and a general feeling that police could not effectively work with the community or address crime in the city.

The Flint Neighborhood Foot Patrol Program was seen as a way to get citizens more involved in crime prevention efforts and to encourage both the development of neighborhood organizations and increases in positive communication between the police department and Flint residents. While the study officially began in January 1979, the planning process had begun in November 1977. The goal was to develop a program using input from police, citizens, and policymakers to ensure that the final product was a program that was appropriately designed for the local context of Flint. Police and the research team also believed that citizens would be more supportive of the program if they were given the opportunity to give extensive input during the design phase.

Design

The Mott Foundation created 10 goals for the Flint program. The Michigan State Research team evaluated whether or not these goals were met and also provided technical assistance to the Flint Police Department throughout the project. These goals included reducing actual and perceived crime; increasing citizen perceptions of safety; and increasing protection for women, children, and the elderly. The project was also intended to increase community awareness of crime problems and to encourage citizens to both report crime and assist in police efforts to address crime. The evaluation was also designed to examine the activities of foot patrol officers, how foot patrol fit in with other units in the department, and whether training affected foot patrol officer performance.

The foot patrol treatment was a major change from standard, random preventive patrol in automobiles that had been the norm in Flint (and almost all other agencies). Officers were not expected to only focus on deterring crime through their presence. Instead, officers were encouraged to help coordinate and build block watch groups or other organizations to make citizens active partners with the police in crime prevention efforts. Foot patrol officers also were instructed to use referrals to social service and other government agencies as a means of addressing problem situations. Law enforcement and arrest were not assumed to be the only or best response to many of the problems officers faced, and the intimate knowledge of the community that comes with foot patrol was expected to make

officers better able to judge what actions would be appropriate. Unlike the inherently reactive nature of motorized responses to calls for service, foot patrol was expected to be more proactive as officers would help address minor problems before they escalated into serious situations. Additionally, officers were expected to encourage community members to take preventive efforts that could contribute to crime reduction.

The program focused on 14 neighborhoods that contained about 20% of the city's population. These neighborhoods were not just in the central business district but covered a range of areas, both in terms of geography and socioeconomic status. Twenty-two officers were assigned to foot patrol in these neighborhoods. The experiment operated between January 1979 and January 1982. One methodological challenge for the study was maintaining control groups for the 14 treatment neighborhoods. As the intervention became more popular over the course of the three-year evaluation period, some of the original control areas also received foot patrol. Thus, while the study is commonly referred to as the Flint foot patrol experiment, it is not truly a randomized controlled experiment, because control areas were not maintained for the entire study. The analysis of crime data discussed below uses a less rigorous before and after research design.

The project team used four main sources of information to evaluate the project. First, a number of interviews were conducted. All of the foot patrol officers were interviewed each year of the project, as well as a sample of motor patrol officers to serve as a comparison group. The study team also interviewed clergy, business owners, and community group leaders who were assumed to be particularly well informed about police activity in the experimental neighborhoods. To assess the views of the general public, a sample of experimental area residents was interviewed each year to examine change over time, and a second random sample of interviews were conducted with residents in the second and third year of the project.

Crime incident data and calls for service for the 14 experimental areas were examined, comparing data from 1978 (the year before the program began) to data from 1979, 1980, and 1981, when the program was in operation. As noted above, comparison data were available for 14 similar neighborhoods that did not initially receive foot patrol, although some of these neighborhoods began receiving treatment in 1981. Researchers also monitored foot patrol activity logs to assess what officers were spending their time on. Media coverage of the intervention was also closely examined and coded.

Results

The Flint study showed overall positive results in a number of areas. In terms of citizen views, general levels of satisfaction with the police increased over time, as did feelings of safety. By 1981, 64% of citizens were satisfied with the program and 68% felt safer in their neighborhoods. About 90% of surveyed citizens knew about the program and 72% had either seen or had a personal interaction with a foot patrol officer. Over 60% responded that foot patrol officers had encouraged reporting crimes and becoming more involved in crime prevention efforts. About half of citizens had suggestions for improving the program, and most of these concerned expanding the program. Citizens wanted more night foot patrols, smaller foot patrol areas to increase the visibility of officers, and more total officers in the program.

The Flint Neighborhood Foot Patrol Program also had impacts on reported crime and calls for service. This was a contrast from the Newark, New Jersey, foot patrol experiment conducted in the mid-1970s by the Police Foundation, a policy and research organization in Washington, D.C. From that study, the general consensus about foot patrol was that it could have a beneficial impact on citizen attitudes toward the police, but not necessarily an effect on actual crime. The number of incidents in the 14 treatment areas in Flint declined from 4,085 in 1978 to 3,371 in 1981. Only robbery and burglary did not show declines, and this could be attributed to the fact that these offenses typically took place at night and foot patrol officers worked during the day. Additionally, these crime declines were more dramatic in the first two years of the program, which makes sense because the treatment area was expanded greatly in year three and so treatment was less intensive. Calls for service also showed a substantial decline, dropping from 678 in 1978 to 384 in 1981. Researcher observations suggested that less serious nuisance incidents were being handled by the foot patrol officers instead of being reported by phone. Although these results suggest fairly substantial drops in calls for service and a smaller drop

in overall crime, the findings should be interpreted with some caution because of concerns about the methodological rigor of the research design used. Any study that relies on before-and-after comparisons of crime data is subject to potential threats to internal validity or the believability of the results because there could be factors other than the intervention that explain the changes in crime.

Citizens were also asked about whether foot or motor patrol officers performed better on a number of tasks. In preventing crime, encouraging citizen self-protection, working with juveniles, and following up on complaints, foot patrol officers received substantially higher ratings. Motor patrol officers were rated more highly on responding to complaints, in part because of their greater ability to respond quickly to emergency calls. Generally, however, survey respondents felt foot patrol officers did a much better job of connecting with residents in crime prevention efforts.

From the perspective of foot and motor patrol officers, foot patrol officers were more likely to believe that building relationships with residents and teaching them about crime prevention were important goals for the police. In terms of job satisfaction, foot patrol officers tended to express more enthusiasm for their work and were less likely than motor patrol officer to express dissatisfaction with their job. Foot patrol officers also overall felt safer when working than motor patrol officers, in part because they felt more connected with the communities they were patrolling. Because of a better understanding of these communities, foot patrol officers felt that resorting to the use of force would be less necessary, and these officers also believed, to a greater extent than motor patrol officers, that citizens would come to their aid if needed.

The overall positive results from the study led Flint residents to approve a special tax increase to hire 76 additional foot patrol officers in 1982 to expand the program citywide to 64 total foot patrol areas. Unfortunately, subsequent budget cuts forced cutbacks in motor patrol and led to some tension between foot and motor patrol officers. Nonetheless, residents were satisfied and reassured enough by the initial three year-program to accept an additional tax in an economically difficult time in Flint in order to expand foot patrols.

As with most policing studies, there were some implementation issues that arose during the intervention. One problem was motor patrol officers not viewing foot patrol officers as doing real police work. Over the course of the experiment, adjustments were made to ensure that foot patrol officers were responding to all types of calls (when possible) and not leaving motor patrol officers to deal with the most serious calls. As noted above, an additional issue was the expansion of the program to other neighborhoods in the third year without additional resources (i.e., more foot patrol officers). This led to a dilution of treatment across the experimental sites. Finally, there was variation across the foot patrol officers in terms of performance. While officers were encouraged to work closely with juveniles and make referrals to social service agencies when possible, the training in this area was weak, and some officers infrequently made use of referrals. Additionally, getting officers to interact closely with citizens was sometimes challenging. Officers frequently interacted with business owners, but engaging with citizens, particularly in efforts to create citizen organizations, took some extra effort.

Despite the need for caution about the crime findings from Flint, the study overall suggests that foot patrol can be an effective way to enhance citizen engagement with the police and reduce overall fear of crime. The Flint study demonstrated that foot patrol can be an important component of community policing programs attempting to build bridges between the police and community members. Foot patrol in Flint helped build positive relationships between citizens and the police and enhanced the ability of both police and residents to prevent crime.

Cody W. Telep

See also Citizen Surveys; Fear of Crime; Foot Patrols; Measuring Officer Performance; Officers' Job Satisfaction; National Center for Community Policing; Problem-Solving Initiatives, Assessment and Evaluation

Further Readings

Police Foundation. (1981). *The Newark foot patrol experiment*. Washington, DC: Police Foundation.

Trojanowicz, R. C. (1982). *An evaluation of the neighborhood foot patrol program in Flint, Michigan*. East Lansing: Michigan State University, The National Neighborhood Foot Patrol Center. Retrieved from http://www.cj.msu.edu/~people/cp/evaluate.html

Trojanowicz, R. C. (1983). An evaluation of a neighborhood foot patrol. *Journal of Police Science and Administration, 11*(4), 410–419.

Trojanowicz, R. C. (1986). Evaluating a neighborhood foot patrol program. The Flint, Michigan project. In D. Rosenbaum (Ed.), *Community crime prevention: Does it work?* (pp. 157–178). Beverly Hills, CA: Sage.

Trojanowicz, R. C., & Banas, D. W. (1985). *Job satisfaction: A comparison of foot patrol versus motor patrol officers*. East Lansing: National Neighborhood Foot Patrol Center, Michigan State University.

Trojanowicz, R. C., Kappeler, V. E., Gaines, L. K., & Bucqueroux, B. (1998). *Community policing: A contemporary perspective* (2nd ed.). Cincinnati, OH: Anderson.

Trojanowicz, R. C., & Smyth, P. R. (1984). *Manual for the establishment and operation of a foot patrol program*. East Lansing: National Neighborhood Foot Patrol Center, Michigan State University. Retrieved from http://www.cj.msu.edu/~people/cp/fpmanual.html

FOOT PATROLS

One of the hallmarks of community policing has been reintegrating the police with the communities they serve. Although this reintegration was done using a number of methods, one of the most popular methods involved reinstituting neighborhood foot patrols. Foot patrols remove officers from patrol cars and deploy them to patrol a smaller area on foot. The goal of foot patrol is twofold: to break down social distance between the police and citizens in the neighborhoods they serve, and to prevent crime by increasing the likelihood of an officer being close enough to deter would-be criminals. The implementation of foot patrols is not a novel concept associated with community policing; rather, it has seen support ebb and flow over time. This entry discusses the use of foot patrols through the eras of policing, focusing especially on the community policing era. The entry concludes by reviewing recent research questioning the common misconceptions about whether foot patrols are an effective crime prevention strategy.

Historical Overview

Foot patrols were originally the primary method used for police on patrol prior to the advent of the automobile in the first half of the 20th century (some agencies, but not all, also used horses and bicycles for patrol). With reforms associated with transitioning toward a more efficient and effective police department, many officers were eventually removed from their traditional foot patrols and placed in motor vehicles. This shift in police deployment practices fundamentally changed the relationship of the police with the communities they served. No longer were police officers available to easily develop relationships with the communities they served; rather, they were responding to calls for service. Instead of routinely seeing a police officer walking through a neighborhood, now residents would only see police officers in the neighborhood if a call for police service brought them there. Some scholars claim that this was partially responsible for the increased crime rates in communities in the 1970s and 1980s.

With the transition toward community policing commencing in the 1970s, police agencies were looking for methods of reconnecting officers with the communities they served. However, research suggests that foot patrols were, initially, one of the most least effective programs associated with community policing in the United States, owing to the lack of rapid police response to crimes as well as preventive patrols for crime reduction.

Despite these concerns, foot patrols were frequently implemented as crime reduction strategies due to their intangible benefits. These benefits included reductions in fear of crime and improved informal social control mechanisms among neighborhood residents. Subsequent research conducted on the efficacy of foot patrols found that although they were not effective in reducing crime, they significantly decreased perceptions of fear of crime; in other words, residents felt safer upon seeing foot patrols. This decreased fear of crime was found in a number of cities around the United States, thus bolstering police confidence in the use of foot patrols. In sum, foot patrols were then seen as an ineffective method of actually reducing crime that had, at best, a moderate likelihood of reducing the levels of fear of crime in neighborhoods.

Recent Research on Foot Patrols

Police administrators in a number of cities around the United States, including Newark, New Jersey, and Philadelphia, Pennsylvania, have remained optimistic about the potential crime reduction benefits of foot patrols. These police administrators, with the help of criminological researchers, have started examining the effectiveness of foot patrols, taking into account relevant theoretical considerations. The researchers are implementing findings from the hot spot and deterrence literature to assist in designing effective foot patrol campaigns. The results from Philadelphia and Newark are discussed independently and then compared.

Philadelphia

In an effort to examine the effectiveness of foot patrols as a targeted intervention strategy, researchers, in conjunction with the Philadelphia Police Department, randomly selected 120 hot spots of violent crime located throughout the city. Fifty of these hot spots were randomly selected to receive targeted foot patrols to address the levels of violent crime in the areas. The police department specifically assigned personnel responsible for patrolling these geographically defined areas by foot; officers were in these areas 16 hours per day, five days per week, for three months. Unlike previous randomized experiments with foot patrol initiatives, researchers ensured that the officers were provided with clear instructions and remained in the target area during the intervention.

The results from the study suggest that foot patrols were associated with a reduction in the number of incidents of violent crime compared to similarly situated control areas. The researchers in Philadelphia note that there was some evidence that the implementation of foot patrols was associated with crime being displaced to other areas, but that the displacement was less than the crime reduction in the targeted areas. After accounting for the displaced crime, the foot patrols reduced violent crime by 23% compared to the control areas in the same period of time. In addition, after the foot patrol officers were reassigned to regular beats around the city, a number of residents called the police department inquiring about the whereabouts of the foot patrol officers. This suggests that, like earlier studies, this study increased perceptions of safety among neighborhood residents and achieved crime reduction benefits. Interestingly, the residents who called inquiring about the whereabouts of the officers lived in neighborhoods typically characterized by tense police-community relationships.

Newark

A similar experiment was conducted in Newark, although it consisted of only one treatment area that was selected because it was one of the areas in the city with the highest levels of violent crime. In this study, a team of 15 police officers patrolled a complex of apartments on a nightly basis. The complex was designed in such a manner that the officers on foot patrol were able to access places in the complex that were impossible to reach with, and could not be seen from, an automobile. The results from the study suggest that over the course of one year officers made high numbers of positive contacts with citizens in the target area and were able to decrease violent crime in the neighborhood. When the results are disaggregated by crime type the results differ for some crimes, like robbery. The research suggests that although there was an initial reduction in the amount of robbery, there also was evidence of temporal and spatial displacement. In other words, the targeted foot patrols served to deter robbery in the location at the times they were present; however, the offenders moved to other locations or chose to offend at times when officers were not on duty.

Implications for Foot Patrol

The results from these two studies suggest that foot patrol might indeed be a plausible crime reduction strategy for law enforcement agencies under certain circumstances. Unlike previous studies investigating the effectiveness of foot patrol, both of the studies discussed above were targeted interventions that were specifically deployed due to abnormally high levels of violent crime in the area. In previous studies, the effects of foot patrols were assessed based on random selection by the researchers and police administrators. Additionally, both of these studies were conducted in relatively small areas that police officers could randomly be expected to cover on foot. It is interesting to note that both studies found evidence of crime displacement associated with the interventions. While the displacement effects were greater in magnitude in certain cities for certain crimes, the evidence suggests that future research and implementations of foot patrols should consider the displacement effects associated with the interventions. Despite the presence of displacement in both studies, neither study found evidence of complete displacement. In other words, the foot patrols worked to reduce crime in the area and the crime that was displaced was lesser than the original magnitude of crime. These results suggest that in the right situation and with some strategic planning by administrators, foot patrols remain a viable crime control strategy.

Jon Maskaly

See also Broken Windows Theory; Crime Displacement; Fear of Crime; Flint, Michigan, Experiment; Hot Spots; Place-Based Policing; Situational Crime Prevention

Further Readings

Cordner, G. W. (1986). Fear of crime and the police: An evaluation of a fear reduction strategy. *Journal of Police Science and Administration, 14,* 223–233.

Kelling, G., & Coles, C. (1996). *Fixing broken windows: Restoring order and reducing crime in our communities.* New York, NY: Touchstone.

National Research Council, Skogan, W. G., & Frydl, K. (Eds.). (2004). *Fairness and effectiveness in policing: The evidence.* Washington, DC: National Academies Press.

Piza, E. L., & O'Hara, B. A. (2012). Saturation foot-patrol in a high-violence area: A quasi-experimental evaluation. *Justice Quarterly, 29,* 1–26. doi: 10.1080/07418825.2012.668923

Ratcliffe, J. H., Taniguchi, T., Groff, E. R., & Wood, J. D. (2011). The Philadelphia foot patrol experiment: A randomized controlled trial of police patrol effectiveness in violent crime hotspots. *Criminology, 49*(3), 795–831. doi: 10.1111/j.1745–9125.2011.00240

Rosenbaum, D. P., & Lurigio, A. J. (1994). An inside look at community policing reform: Definitions, organizational changes, and evaluation findings. *Crime & Delinquency, 40*(3), 299–314.

GANG CRIMES, COMMUNITY POLICING STRATEGIES FOR

Because of their geographic and demographic expansion, involvement in crime (e.g., firearm transactions, gun violence, drug sales and use, burglaries, car thefts, and murder), as well as the psychological and social damage they can cause, gangs can have a significant impact on a community's quality of life. Traditional police attempts at gang reduction and elimination (e.g., suppression tactics such as arrests) alone have not resolved the gang dilemma. Under the community policing model, the police and the community collaborate to adopt strategies and develop tailored responses to the gang problem. Forging such police-community partnerships can be difficult, but they are integral to the community policing approach of understanding the gang problem.

This entry discusses the coordinated, multifaceted community policing approach that has demonstrated successes with gangs. In addition, community policing and problem-solving strategies—foremost among them being the SARA (scanning, analysis, response, assessment) problem-solving process—that have been employed are discussed.

Defining Gangs and Gang Members

The first step in developing a strategy for addressing gang problems is for a jurisdiction to develop a statutorily determined definition of a gang and a gang member. In order to confirm that there are gang problems in a particular jurisdiction, developing a common understanding of the term *gang* is necessary. Furthermore, simply because another jurisdiction believes it is suffering a "gang problem" does not mean that is the case or that such a problem exists in other nearby jurisdictions. Therefore, enforcement, suppression, prevention, and intervention—as well as multiagency collaboration—will be better served if everyone is working with a common definition.

Although no model gang definition appears to be in use among various agencies across the nation (such as with penal and traffic codes), one approach is for local police agencies to adopt the definition of a criminal street gang set forth in U.S. Code, Title 18, Section 521: "ongoing groups, clubs, organizations, or associations of five or more individuals that have as one of their primary purposes the commission of one or more criminal offenses." A federal survey of police gang units found that only 60% of gang units used a statutorily determined definition of gang, while 21% of the units employed their own definition and 20% used no definition. Similarly, about half used a statutory definition to classify a "gang member," while 36% of the units followed their own definition and 14% had no definition.

A Comprehensive Approach

There is now a sizeable body of literature describing police and community responses to gang problems. Most of these responses employ a three-pronged approach—prevention, intervention, and suppression (discussed below)—which, when used within the overarching SARA problem-solving process, has been shown as affording the best chance of achieving and sustaining success.

A central premise of community policing and problem solving is that gang problems—like any other crime problems—are local. Therefore, their solutions must be based on careful analysis in order to completely and accurately understand the local problem.

One of the most effective tools for a law enforcement analysis of local problems is the SARA problem-solving process, which consists of four sequential steps: scanning, analysis, response, and assessment. This section discusses the kinds of activities that occur within each step when using SARA to address gang problems.

Scanning

Scanning means problem identification, so as a first step, officers should identify problems on their beats and then look for a pattern or persistent repeat incidents. At this juncture, the question that might well be asked is, "Do we have a 'problem'?" A problem consists of two or more incidents that are similar in nature and scope, causing harm, and therefore are of concern to the police and the public.

Gang members' crimes such as violence and drug dealing may be identified as the problem, but the consequences may be wider reaching and include such things as vandalism, disrupted traffic, neighborhood disorder, aggravated assaults, or increased public fear of crime. Once the problems and their consequences have been fully identified, it is necessary to determine if the problems are indeed gang related.

To properly scan, the agency and community must ask the following kinds of questions:

- How does our community define a gang and gang member?
- How are our gang crimes tracked? Do the police identify, isolate, and tabulate those crimes committed by gang members?
- What appear to be the predominant crimes gang members commit?
- What information sources are available concerning gangs—schools, social service groups, the juvenile court, hospitals?
- How many gangs appear to be operating in our jurisdiction and for how long? What are the demographics of their memberships?

- How well organized are the gangs, and do they have strong leaders?
- Are gang members migrating to our jurisdiction from other cities?
- Do prison and jail gangs have an influence on our street gang activity?
- Are gang members involved in drug and gun sales and markets?

Analysis

The second step in the SARA problem-solving process, analysis, is a crucial one. A good way to begin an analysis is by considering how specific gang problems are being dealt with locally and the successes and shortcomings of each approach. It is also helpful to try to identify and understand the events and conditions that precede and accompany the problem. Then, a working hypothesis can be developed concerning why the problem is occurring.

The problem analysis triangle can be useful as well, which forces police to consider the characteristics of *offenders,* *places,* and *victims* or targets as they analyze the gang problem and develop tailor-made responses. This triangle is based on the theory that a crime occurs when a motivated offender and suitable target come together at a particular time and place, and there is no suitable guardian (e.g., police officer, security officer, parent, custodian) present to prevent it. Therefore, in order for a crime to be committed, all three sides of the triangle—offender, target, location—must be in place; if one of these three elements is removed, or a capable guardian is involved, the crime will not occur. The task for the police, then, is to analyze the three sides of the triangle, as well as guardianship, to see what might be done to prevent crimes from occurring.

During the analysis it is helpful to identify the data to be used. Possible sources of information and data can include, but are not be limited to, the following sources:

- Police computer-aided dispatch system, especially for determining hot spots, calls for service relating to gang activities, shots fired, and so on
- School personnel—teachers, administrators—and students, who can provide information about gang-related incidents in schools
- Emergency room personnel, who can provide evidence of gang-related gunshot and other wounds and the presence of gang tattoos

- Juvenile court records of gang membership
- Jails and prisons (especially the gang status of returning offenders)
- The Firearms Trace Data maintained by the Bureau of Alcohol, Tobacco, Firearms and Explosives
- Findings of the annual National Youth Gang Survey of police agencies concerning the extent of youth gang problems
- Interviews with gang members and associates

Organizing and analyzing the information is the next step. A variety of analytical tools can be used. Advanced statistical analysis can depict the strength of relationships between variables. In addition to the conventional methods and technologies (e.g., CompStat, geographic information systems, crime mapping), social networking sites are also making it easier for the police to analyze gang activities, as gang members may use such sites to recruit members, set up narcotics transactions, intimidate people, and other activities.

Responses

After the gang problem has been clearly defined and analyzed, the police confront the challenge of developing effective responses for dealing with it. During this stage, actions to be considered include the following:

- Reviewing their findings from their analysis of the three sides of the crime triangle—victim, offender, and location
- Developing creative solutions that will address at least two sides of the triangle
- Overcoming the temptation to implement a response prematurely
- Being creative—seeking responses that go beyond traditional ones like arrests
- Seeking solutions that will remove the underlying causes of the problems

Responses can be focused and closely associated with the source of the problem as revealed in the analysis phase, but they can also be wide ranging and include arrests. Regardless of the scope of responses, in general, responses should include prevention, intervention, and suppression.

Prevention

As with any type of crime, proactively preventing a criminal act from taking place is better than having it occur and law enforcement having to reactively devote time, effort, and resources to investigate, prosecute, and incarcerate the offender. With regard to this discussion of gangs, the goal of prevention is to stop youths from joining gangs, so prevention responses should target the largest segment of the problem: youths at risk for gang membership. Prevention programs, therefore, include a broad potential audience and are typically aimed at groups that pose some risk. For example, a prevention program may focus on preschool children who reside in gang neighborhoods before they show any symptoms of having joined the gang life. Perhaps the best-known gang prevention program is Gang Resistance Education and Training (G.R.E.A.T.), which attempts to reduce the probability of school-age persons joining a street gang. Developed by the Bureau of Alcohol, Tobacco, Firearms and Explosives in conjunction with local police, the program consists of a series of lessons for students that attempts to help them resist gangs and gang membership, avoid involvement in crime, and learn of the dangers associated with crime and gangs.

Prevention efforts are both *primary* and *secondary* in nature. Primary refers to those efforts that target the whole community, particularly communities that have high rates of gang membership or violence. Secondary prevention targets those most at risk, such as the youths who display early signs of gang membership or have other problem behaviors that indicate high risk for involvement in gangs or gang crime. Secondary prevention efforts may include the following elements: (1) meaningful alternatives to gang membership; (2) effective support systems like family, community, and school; and (3) accountability on the part of the juvenile for personal behavior.

Intervention

Oftentimes, police agencies use the term *intervention* to mean—and *gang intervention unit* to perform—such activities as gathering intelligence information, tracking gang members, and maintaining files with pictures—activities that are suppression oriented in nature. Although gang intervention certainly can include coordinated enforcement and prosecution, intervention in this context involves a broader approach, targeting youths who are at risk of becoming a gang member, in the early stages of membership, or at some stage of membership where they can be pushed out of the gang. The primary aim is to persuade these youths to abandon the gang lifestyle or to reduce their gang-related crime.

The National Crime Prevention Council provides an overview of gang intervention: It is a coordinated effort that involves both the community and the police for reducing the likelihood that high-risk youth with become involved in gangs. This coordinated effort can also involve educators, job-training resources, parents, and community groups, and can combine efforts by those agencies with other community efforts such as neighborhood mobilization and job training for youth. For such a coordinated intervention approach to be successful, it is important that the type of gang be identified (no two gangs being alike) as well as the level of the individual's involvement in the gang. Then, police, probation personnel, and prosecutors share information about gang activity, diffuse crises that arise from gang conflict, and refer the individual to community-based services. Street outreach through community organizations and parents can also be used to supplement partnerships among agencies to make well-integrated services available to at-risk youth.

Intervention is most effective when it paired with the aforementioned prevention strategies.

Suppression

Although most police agencies understand that suppression alone is not effective as a long-term gang prevention and intervention strategy, suppression tactics have a part to play in addressing gang problems. Suppression programs revolve around the goal of reducing or eliminating gang activities, typically relying on the criminal law and the collaboration of several criminal justice agencies for their success. However, deterrence that is both general (population-at-large) and specific (individual offender) is often included as a goal, and police will often deploy specialized gang units or task forces. Other suppression approaches are vertical prosecution (i.e., taking cases into higher—state or federal— courts) and sentencing enhancements.

Use of focused deterrence. One approach to reducing high rates of gang and youth gun violence that has demonstrated success and rapidly spread across the country is modeled on one that began in Boston,

Massachusetts, in May 1996 and was known as Operation Ceasefire, which entailed a problem-oriented policing approach and focused on specific places that were crime hot spots. This approach— involving local, state, and federal criminal justice agencies as well as community leaders, gang outreach workers, and public and private social service agencies—has been implemented in Chicago, Illinois; Cincinnati, Ohio; Indianapolis, Indiana; and, recently, in five California cities.

After performing an in-depth analysis of the problem (e.g., geographic location of violent incidents, demographic information on individuals involved in gun violence, and patterns of gang violence), a working group is then organized for designing and implementing the local strategy. This process of implementation typically includes such activities as communicating directly with gang members a violence prevention message, linking these gang members and youth to training and employment opportunities, and coordinating law enforcement efforts. Law enforcement efforts include a strategy of focused deterrence that embraces a tactic termed *pulling levers;* in other words, if a youth or gang member is engaged in violent behavior and is caught with a gun during his or her time on probation or parole, every available resource would be brought to bear, such as more stringent bail, swift prosecution, and enhanced penalties. Meanwhile, as indicated above, social services are made available to gang members to support an alternative to life in the gang.

This comprehensive, focused approach to deterrence has resulted in declines in youth homicides, firearm assaults, and shots-fired calls for service. In addition, typical outcomes include the gangs' drug markets being disrupted, arrests being made for outstanding warrants, and strict enforcement of probation and federal sanctions.

Gang units. Gang units as a suppression tool were created as part of a larger trend toward police specialization that began in the 1980s for dealing with certain crimes (e.g., repeat offenders, domestic violence, and hate crimes). Forming such units allowed officers to develop knowledge, skills, and abilities in those areas that otherwise would not have been possible.

Today about 365 of the nation's large (employing more than 100 sworn officers) police departments and sheriff's offices have specialized gang units; about one-third (35%) of these units were formed between 2004 and 2007. Furthermore, about 6 out of 10 gang units (63%) participate in a local or regional gang task force.

There is much that can be done by gang units with respect to community policing and problem solving: A 2004 federally funded study by Charles Katz and Vincent Webb examined four major southwestern cities' gang units and their responses to gangs. One of their findings, with regard to community policing and problem solving, was that the units rarely sought citizen input, rarely formed partnerships with community groups or businesses, did not believe that it was their responsibility to address underlying problems related to gang crime, and did not engage in formal problem solving. Indeed, most gang unit officers were untrained to use the SARA problem-solving process, and some were only vaguely aware that it even existed. In sum, these units were reactive, did not consider formal problem-solving strategies as a means to address their local gang problems, and typically were not assigned to permanent geographic areas in order to become more knowledgeable of their areas, get to know the citizens, and therefore be better positioned to hear of citizens' concerns and glean their insights pertaining to crime and neighborhood disorder.

Civil gang injunctions. In addition to using the criminal law to address gang-related issues, another problem-solving approach (or response) used by the police in some jurisdictions is to work with prosecutors' offices to obtain civil gang injunctions as a response to their gang problems. A civil gang injunction is a court-ordered instrument used for such things as barring gang members from congregating in specified public areas, engaging in specified criminal and nuisance-type behaviors (such as selling drugs), driving through certain neighborhoods, loitering, cursing, making certain hand gestures, listening to loud music, and even talking on cell phones. This strategy has legal implications and often requires a considerable standard of proof, with law enforcement and prosecutors bearing the legal burden of developing probable cause, collecting evidence, and documenting gang membership and activity. Once such information has been presented to a judge, the injunction may be granted forbidding the above types of acts.

Assessment

Finally, in the assessment phase of the SARA problem-solving process, the police evaluate the effectiveness of their responses. In addition to looking at such indicators as numbers of arrests, levels of reported crime and citizen complaints, clearance rates, and calls for service (CFS), and depending on the nature of problems that were present, some types of questions that might be posed for determining whether or not the responses were effective are as follows (some questions require citizen surveys):

- Were reduced calls for police service concerning gang activities realized?
- Were reduced acts of and costs for repairs of damages from gang-related vandalism noted?
- Was the amount of gang-related graffiti reduced?
- Were fears and perceptions reduced concerning gangs and related graffiti?
- Was open-air drug-related activity by gang members visibly reduced?
- Did youth gun homicides involving gang members decrease?
- Were youth gun assaults by gang members decreased?

Some additional measures may also shed light on whether the gang problem was reduced or eliminated (again, citizen surveys may be required):

- Reduced instances of repeat victimization
- Neighborhood indicators (increases in profits for businesses in the target area, usage of the area, property values, and less loitering, truancy, abandoned cars)
- Citizen satisfaction regarding the handling of the problem

Kenneth J. Peak

See also Broken Windows Theory; Building Partnerships and Stakeholders; Citizen Surveys; CompStat; Computer-Aided Dispatch; Crime Analysis; Crime Mapping; Crime Prevention Through Environmental Design; Gangs and Their Crimes, Characteristics of; Global Positioning Systems/Geographic Information Systems; Hot Spots; Problem, Definition of; Problem-Solving Initiatives, Assessment and Evaluation; Problem-Solving Process (SARA); Tipping Points of Neighborhoods

Further Readings

Decker, S. (2008, April). *Strategies to address gang crime: A guidebook for local law enforcement*. Washington, DC: U.S Department of Justice, Office of Community Oriented Policing Services. Retrieved from http://www.cops.usdoj.gov/Publications/e060810142Gang-book-web.pdf

Howell, J. C., & Curry, G. D. (2009, January). *Mobilizing communities to address gang problems*. Washington, DC: U.S. Department of Justice, Office of Juvenile Justice and Delinquency Prevention. Retrieved from http://www.nationalgangcenter.gov/Content/Documents/NYGC-bulletin-4.pdf

Katz, C. M., & Webb, V. J. (2004). *Police response to gangs: A multi-site study*. Washington, DC: U.S. Department of Justice, National Criminal Justice Reference Service. Retrieved from https://www.ncjrs.gov/pdffiles1/nij/grants/205003.pdf

Kennedy, D. M. (2006). Old wine in new bottles: Policing and the lessons of pulling levers. In D. L. Weisburd & A. A. Braga (Eds.), *Police innovation: Contrasting perspectives* (pp. 155–170). New York, NY: Cambridge University Press.

Langdon, L. (2010, October). *Gang units in large local law enforcement agencies, 2007*. NCJ 230071. Washington, DC: U.S. Department of Justice, Bureau of Justice Statistics. Retrieved from http://bjs.ojp.usdoj.gov/content/pub/pdf/gulllea07.pdf

McGloin, J. M. (2005, September). *Street gangs and interventions: Innovative problem solving with network analysis*. Washington, DC: U.S. Department of Justice, Office of Community Oriented Policing Services. Retrieved from http://www.cops.usdoj.gov/pdf/innovations/e09050001.pdf

National Crime Prevention Council. (2012). *Strategy: Gang prevention through community intervention with high-risk youth*. Retrieved from http://www.ncpc.org/topics/violent-crime-and-personal-safety/strategies/strategy-gang-prevention-through-community-intervention-with-high-risk-youth

National Gang Center. *National Youth Gang Survey Analysis*. Tallahassee, FL: Author. Retrieved from http://www.nationalgangcenter.gov/Survey-Analysis

Police Executive Research Forum. (1999, May). *Addressing community gang problems: A practical guide*. NCJ 164273. Washington, DC: Author. Retrieved from https://www.ncjrs.gov/pdffiles/164273.pdf

U.S. Bureau of Alcohol, Tobacco, Firearms and Explosives. (n.d.). *Firearms trace data*. Washington, DC: Author. Retrieved from http://www.atf.gov/statistics/trace-data

Weisel, D. L., & Painter, E. (1997). *The police response to gangs: Case studies of five cities*. Washington, DC: Police Executive Research Forum.

Websites

Gang Resistance Education and Training (G.R.E.A.T); http://www.great-online.org

National Gang Center; http://www.nationalgangcenter.gov

Gangs and Their Crimes, Characteristics of

The first challenge one might theoretically confront when discussing gangs is trying to arrive at a suitable definition for what constitutes a gang. In fact, if a jurisdiction fails to exercise due care in defining gangs in its municipal ordinances, it may well deem as gang members a collection of weekend poker players or some other relatively crime-free assemblage and—as some cities have learned—find itself being sued.

Perhaps a good approach when seeking to characterize what constitutes gang behavior is to adopt the definition provided in Title 18, Sec. 521 of the United States Code, where "criminal street gangs" are defined for federal purposes as "ongoing groups, clubs, organizations, or associations of five or more individuals that have as one of their primary purposes the commission of one or more criminal offenses." This section then defines *criminal offenses,* for purposes of this Code, as follows: (1) a federal felony involving a controlled substance; (2) a federal felony crime of violence (involving the use or attempted use of force against the person); and/or (3) a conspiracy to commit an offense described in (1) or (2). If this definition is liberally construed, a sizeable number of organized groups or syndicates of criminals could be defined as gangs, including a wide assortment of ethnic and racial gangs as well as outlaw motorcycle gangs, prison gangs, White supremacists, militias, and Mafia organizations (although several of these are not "street gangs" in the usual sense of the term).

This entry focuses on street gangs, which are typically composed of individuals who share a gang name, symbols or "signs," geographic territory, a regular meeting pattern, and an organized course of ongoing criminal activities.

There are many incorrect myths, stereotypes, and beliefs surrounding the problem of street gangs, largely because most people and much of the media tend to glean an understanding of gangs from what they have heard about longtime gangs such as the Bloods and Crips in Los Angeles, California. Times have changed and gangs have evolved, so this entry discusses what research has revealed to be the nature and extent of today's gangs as well as the crimes in which gang members are engaged.

Evolution

Street gang activities in the United States may be traced back to the early 1900s in southern California, where most gangs were small (six to 20 members) and generally formed in socially disorganized neighborhoods. Gangs were generally agreed to be the result of disintegration of family life, low-wage occupations, unemployment, a lack of wholesome recreational opportunities, and other socioeconomic factors.

Now, however, the gang problem in the United States has increased in size and in operations. Since the 1980s, they have grown in membership, with estimates of approximately 1.4 million active street, prison, and motorcycle gang members comprising more than 33,000 gangs in the United States. This growth coincides in large measure with gang cultures melding with crack cocaine dealing and consumption in the African American neighborhoods as well as the expansion of new Asian and non–Puerto Rican Latino immigrant gangs. Ethnic-based and nontraditional gangs have also expanded and now include African, Asian, Eurasian, Caribbean, and Middle Eastern gangs. The northeast and southeast regions of the United States have seen the greatest increases in gang memberships since the 1980s, but the West and the Great Lakes regions now hold the greatest numbers of gang members.

Street gangs can significantly damage a community, inciting fear in citizens and dictating where they will and will not travel. Gangs also play a role in homicides, graffiti, intimidation, firearms transactions and violence, drug sales and use, burglaries, car thefts, vandalism, and a number of other crime problems.

Nature of Gangs in Communities

To determine whether or not a community has an actual gang problem, police and citizens must be aware of what Marcus Felson termed the *big gang theory*, wherein small groups of individuals mimic the signals, symbols, colors, graffiti, clothing, and language of truly violent big-city gangs. The media can unwittingly foster this mimicry as well, speculating that certain criminal acts were likely performed by a gang and thus perpetuating the frightening image of street gangs. Some police departments have even refused—often to the detriment of their public relations—to provide the media with the names and crime information that might have actually involved gang members so as to avoid the public anxiety that can ensue.

Research indicates that there are basically three groupings or levels of gang problems that exist today in the United States. First, the more persistent and serious gang problems exist in cities and suburban areas with populations greater than 100,000. In fact, all cities in this population category perennially report gang problems. Second are those cities that have populations of 25,000 to 100,000. These communities are the most difficult to categorize in terms of the severity of their gang problems because many such communities will have a gang problem at some point, but it may not be permanent or serious in nature. Last are those communities having fewer than 25,000 citizens that do not have the population base to sustain gangs and have either never experienced gang problems or, if they have, they are not a persistent problem. The majority of crimes problems in this nation are in the first category.

In contrast to popular belief, gangs do not tend to migrate across the country to set up satellite operations; in reality, most, if migrating at all, typically form other gang operations within 100 miles of their city of origin. Possibly for this reason, gangs are basically loose-knit in nature and there tends to be little homogeneity among them; thus there is no single model of gangs—rather, there is a wide variety of forms. However, as a general rule, the more structured the gang, the more dangerous the gang tends to be.

Nature of Gang Membership

The term *gang* implies that there is a high degree of structure involved in the organization. However, several studies have found that gangs are far less organized than one might expect. In fact, street gangs are typically loosely structured with transient leadership and membership, codes of loyalty that are frequently overlooked or not observed, and informal rather than formal roles for their membership.

Of course, gang members can be of any age, but participation in gangs tends to be a young person's enterprise: about 70% of gang members are between the ages of 15 and 24 years, while only about 13% are older than 24 years. As a result, many jurisdictions report a growing problem involving juvenile gangs and violence. This problem is often attributed to the increased incarceration of older gang members as well as aggressive recruiting of juveniles in schools; young prospects have historically been highly sought after due to a belief that there is less likelihood that they will receive a harsh sentence if arrested, as well as their willingness to perform acts of violence. Several jurisdictions are also attributing the increase in gang membership to the gangster rap culture and the use of communication and recruitment through the Internet and social media to extol the gang culture and spread its message.

As indicated above, gangs have evolved tremendously since the 1980s, and stereotypes of gangs that are based on such longtime gangs as Los Angeles's Bloods and Crips (founded in the 1960s)—that a gang member is typically an African American male who lives in a lower-class, inner-city ghetto (or barrio), and belongs to a racially and ethnically homogeneous and highly organized gang—are often wholly inaccurate today.

First, although understudied and trivialized until recently, the percentage of gang members who are female is ranges 8% to 22% (and even 38%, according to some criminologists) of all gang members.

Another widely held myth, that gangs typically "prey" on younger people, actively recruiting new members under threat of force and through offers of protection, is also largely untrue. Studies show that gangs rarely use strong-arm tactics for recruiting, that members typically can leave a gang without suffering serious consequences, and that most youths do not remain in gangs for long periods of time. In sum, it is not as difficult for youths to resist gang pressures as is commonly believed. Furthermore, gang membership and gang problems tend to ebb and flow, particularly in cities with populations of 50,000 or less.

Since around 2000, a number of "hybrid" gangs have also developed. Hybrid gangs are those whose members may have diverse characteristics, represent different racial and ethnic groups, and hold membership in multiple gangs; adhere to unclear rules or codes of conduct; have more than one symbolic association with a gang (e.g., different colors and graffiti from multiple gangs); or cooperate with rival gangs in criminal activity.

Modern gangs are also becoming more institutionalized; they are not only found in communities and prisons but also in schools and on Indian reservations. About one-third of all students surveyed in one study reported a gang presence in their schools. Prisons and military units are also witnessing increases in gang problems. Regarding the former, estimating the actual number of prison gang members, like that of female gang members, is quite difficult. However, surveys indicate that there are approximately 230,000 gang members incarcerated in federal and state prisons nationwide; their activities include bribery, intimidation, and violence to exert influence and control over many correctional facilities. Also, more than 50 gangs have been identified on both foreign and domestic military installations. The greatest concerns here are with the gang members' ability to learn tactics involving advanced weaponry and combat deployment and then using those same tactics on the streets once they leave military service. Indeed, gangs have already acquired high-powered, military-style weapons and equipment.

Criminal Activities

Gang membership fosters criminal behavior. Studies show that youths living in high-crime areas and who belong to gangs are responsible for far more criminal acts than their non–gang member counterparts; more specifically, research indicates that gang members are responsible for four times as many offenses as their total population share would suggest, while gang members' violent offense rates are about seven times higher than those of youths who are not members of gangs.

Research has also shown that gang members who belong to older (or early-onset) gangs are far more likely to be involved in violent crimes (e.g., homicide, aggravated assault, robbery) and property crimes than those gangs in localities that were late-onset (i.e., forming in the last decade); the same holds true with drug distribution, where trafficking activities were far less likely to be significant problems in jurisdictions with late-onset gangs.

Considering gang members of all ages and in all locations, even considering that gangs' criminal activities are often overstated and wax and wane, it is clear that gangs represent a significant crime problem. According to a federal report:

- Criminal gangs commit as much as 80% of all crimes in many communities, and typical gang-related crimes include alien smuggling, armed robbery, assault, auto theft, drug trafficking, extortion, fraud, home invasions, identity theft, murder, and weapons trafficking.
- Gang members are the primary retail-level distributors of most illicit drugs. U.S. gangs also are banding together with Central American and Mexican gangs to establish far-reaching drug networks as well as for smuggling of guns and illegal immigrants.

Of particular concern with the drug trade is the gangs' tendency to move into suburban and rural communities to recruit new members, form new alliances, and even collaborate with rival gangs. Two gangs that are known to be exceptionally violent include the Mexican drug cartel known as La Familia Michoacan, a gang that is heavily armed and heavily engaged in drug smuggling, money laundering, and weapons trafficking across the border into the United States; and MS-13 (or Mara Salvatrucha), which is composed of Central Americans and known for its highly violent crimes as well as its variety of illegal activities that include drugs, robbery, extortion, weapons trafficking, and murder. Concerns are also being raised in a number of jurisdictions with increases of violence involving outlaw motorcycle gangs, which now have approximately 44,000 members in about 3,000 gangs; their increases in membership leads to greater potential for turf wars.

In the West, street gangs have diversified their criminal activities to include identity theft, while continuing to supply narcotics, mostly methamphetamines and marijuana; gangs in the West, furthermore, are partnering with organized crime figures, particularly the Mexican drug cartels and the Asian Mafia. Gangs are also now turning to computers and the Internet, posting their own photographs, gang signs, colors, and tattoos; federal authorities have thus found social networking sites like MySpace and YouTube to become helpful in gathering gang intelligence.

Gang involvement in alien smuggling, human trafficking, and prostitution have also increased, largely due to these crimes' higher profitability and lower risks of detection and punishment in relation to drug and weapons trafficking. Federal, state, and local law enforcement officials in at least 35 states and U.S. territories report that gangs in their jurisdictions are involved in these three types of criminal enterprises.

In the past few years numerous federal, state, and local law enforcement agencies nationwide have reported gang involvement in incidents of alien smuggling. In some instances this involves gang members themselves being smuggled across the border following deportation. In other cases, gang members facilitate the smuggling of illegal immigrants across the U.S.–Mexico border. Human trafficking is also lucrative for some gangs, with victims—typically women and children—being forced into prostitution and forced labor. Some gangs in the New England area are also combining human and drug trafficking operations, with female victims used as couriers for delivering drugs and to participate in prostitution. Finally, prostitution can involve gang members working as pimps and luring or forcing young females to engage in acts of prostitution.

Kenneth J. Peak

See also Gang Crimes, Community Policing Strategies for; Hot Spots; Immigration: Issues, Law and Police Training; Problem, Definition of; Problem Analysis Triangle; Youthful Offenders, Characteristics of; Youthful Offenders, Community Policing Strategies for

Further Readings

Decker, S., & Pyrooz, D. (2011, Winter). Gangs, terrorism, and radicalization. *Journal of Strategic Security, 4*(4), 151–166.

Felson, M. (2006). *Crime and nature.* Thousand Oaks, CA: Sage.

Howell, J. C. (2006, August). *The impact of gangs on communities.* Washington, DC: U.S. Department of Justice, Office of Juvenile Justice and Delinquency Prevention. Retrieved from http://www.nationalgangcenter.gov/Content/Documents/Impact-of-Gangs-on-Communities.pdf

Howell, J. C. (2007, Spring). Menacing or mimicking? Realities of youth gangs. *Juvenile and Family Court Journal, 58*(2), 39–46. doi: 10.1111/j.1755–6988.2007.tb00137

Howell, J. C., & Egley, A., Jr. (2005, June). *Gangs in small towns and rural counties.* Washington, DC: U.S. Department of Justice, Office of Juvenile Justice and

Delinquency Prevention. Retrieved from http://www
.nationalgangcenter.gov/Content/Documents/Gangs-in
-Small-Towns-and-Rural-Counties.pdf

Katz, C. M., & Webb, V. J. (2004). *Police response to
gangs: A multi-site study.* Washington, DC: U.S.
Department of Justice, National Criminal Justice
Reference Service. Retrieved from https://www.ncjrs.gov/
pdffiles1/nij/grants/205003.pdf

Moore, J., & Hagedorn, J. (2001, March). *Female gangs:
A focus on research.* Washington, DC: U.S. Department
of Justice, Office of Juvenile Justice and Delinquency
Prevention. Retrieved from https://www.ncjrs.gov/
pdffiles1/ojjdp/186159.pdf

National Gang Intelligence Center. (2012). *National gang
threat assessment 2011: Emerging trends* (NGIC-VA
#405).Washington, DC: U.S. Department of Justice,
Federal Bureau of Investigation. Retrieved from http://
www.fbi.gov/stats-services/publications/2011-national-
gang-threat-assessment/2011-national-gang-threat-
assessment-emerging-trends

Starbuck, D., Howell, J. C., & Lindquist, D. J. (2001,
December). *Hybrid and other modern gangs.* NCJ
189916. Washington, DC: U.S. Department of Justice,
Office of Juvenile Justice and Delinquency Prevention.
Retrieved from http://www.nationalgangcenter.gov/
Content/Documents/Hybrid-and-Other-Modern-
Gangs.pdf

GENERATIONS (THREE) OF COMMUNITY POLICING

Policing historians have identified three eras of U.S.
policing. They consist of the political, reform, and
community eras. The last era, in which community
policing became a prominent policing approach, is
said to span the years 1980 to present day. As this is
a span of over 30 years, it tends to mask the subtle
changes that have occurred during the community
era. Policing in 2010 is assuredly different from
policing in the 1990, despite both falling within the
community policing era. Thus, police historians have
further asserted that within the community era there
have been three generations of community policing.
They consist of the *innovation* generation covering
1980 to 1986, the *diffusion* generation spanning the
years 1987 to 1994, and the *institutionalization* generation running from 1995 to the present. There is
the possibility that U.S. policing has moved into a
fourth generation or possibly even a fourth era, as

the concepts of homeland security have become so
pervasive in modern times.

The basis for categorizing policing history in the
United States into eras was based on the changes
seen in policing's authorization, function, organizational design, relationship to the environment,
the demand for its services, changes in tactics and
technology, and the outcomes desired by both politicians and citizens. The first era, the political era,
spans from 1838 and the creation of the Boston
(Massachusetts) Police Department through the
1920s. Policing during the political era was marked
by the political machines and their control over the
police. Policing during this time period was ineffective, inefficient, mostly corrupt, and often brutal.
That began to change in the 1920s with the movement to professionalize the police by such visionaries
as August Vollmer and O. W. Wilson, thus moving
policing into the reform era, which spanned the
decades the 1930s through the 1970s. By the 1970s,
however, policing had become so professionalized
that it tended to disassociate itself from the community, and in the 1970s there was a movement to
reunite the ties between the police and the public.
The community era began in 1980 and continues to
modern times.

While these three eras of policing are broad time
periods for categorizing changes in U.S. policing,
they tend to ignore the minor changes and developments that occurred within each era. There is an
understanding among police historians that within
the community era there has been a progression
of community policing. This progression has been
called the generations of community policing, and
three have been distinguished: innovation, diffusion,
and institutionalization. This entry discusses these
three generations and examine whether community
policing has evolved into the next generation.

First Generation: Innovation

The first generation of community policing com-
menced about 1980 and ran through 1986, and is
known as the innovation generation. While there
were some early pioneers working on the concepts
of community policing in the late 1960s and 1970s,
most of the early work fell under similar but differing concepts, such as police-community relations
and team policing. Two major works influenced
the innovation toward community policing during

this generation. The first was James Q. Wilson and George L. Kelling's broken windows theory in 1982, which posited that minor crimes and public disorder, if left unfixed, communicate that the community is not concerned about the problems, and thus attracts further crime in the community. The second was Herman Goldstein's (1979) problem-oriented policing, which argued that police officers, wrongly, treat all calls as isolated incidents and that in reality many are of the crimes and disturbances to which they respond are linked by an underlying problem. By identifying the problem and developing possible solutions, police can implement a response to solve the problem.

The innovation generation was marked by early concepts of community policing being tested on a small scale. Often labeled *experiments, test sites*, and *demonstration projects*, these limited-in-scope attempts toward implementing community policing concepts, ranging from broken windows to problem solving, and incorporating community collaboration, were the early innovations upon which community policing would be developed. Many of these experiments were conducted in large metropolitan cities, such as Flint, Michigan; Newark, New Jersey; and Newport News, Virginia. They were often funded through state grants and foundation support, and were carried out by progressive police chiefs. The type of community policing innovation was typically limited to one style of policing, such as implementing foot patrols (e.g., Flint, Michigan), problem-solving methods (e.g., Newport News, Virginia), and establishing community substations (e.g., Boston, Massachusetts). The majority of the assessments of these innovations were through case studies, nonequivalent comparison pretest and posttest surveys, and one-group pretest and posttest designs.

The benefit to the innovation generation of community policing was the fact that the small scale testing of specific police styles allowed for an understanding of which techniques worked in reducing crime and fear and improving police-community relationships. The testing of these new ideas allowed for the diffusion of these programs across U.S. police departments.

Second Generation: Diffusion

The second generation of community policing spans the years 1987 through 1994, and is known as the diffusion generation. The concepts and philosophy of community policing began to spread across U.S. police departments during this time frame, and police departments began implementing many of the innovations from the earlier generation. No longer was community policing limited to only major metropolitan police departments, but it began to see greater implementation among medium-size police agencies and some smaller departments. It has been estimated that slightly over 300 police departments had implemented community policing at the beginning of this generation. By the end, it is estimated that over 8,000 agencies had adopted at least some of the tenets and programs of community policing.

Community policing during the diffusion generation was largely organized through various programs that consisted of newly created units or the reorganization of previously existed units (e.g., police-community relations units). Examples of these types of programs include the Community Patrol Officer Program (CPOP) in New York City and Citizen Oriented Police Enforcement (COPE) in Baltimore County, Maryland. Many of these programs were implemented through federal and state grants such as the Innovative Neighborhood Oriented Policing (INOP) initiative sponsored by the Bureau of Justice Assistance. The style of community policing tended to be much broader during this generation, focusing more on ways in which police and citizens could collaborate to improve quality of life rather than on one method. The concepts typically entailed targeting the problem of drugs, reducing fear of crime, improving police-community relationships, and assisting in organizing and involving the community in order maintenance. It could include police and neighborhood collaborations through problem solving that may then require the implementation of foot and bicycle patrols, local code-enforcement, and neighborhood cleanups. The means for assessing this more holistic approach to community policing became more sophisticated and included research methodologies such as longitudinal, comparative, and quantitative studies.

The benefits to the diffusion generation is that community policing became a broader use of different styles and programs of policing, focused on a philosophy of police and citizen collaboration to improve quality of life. In addition, the rapid diffusion of community policing across the United States brought an enormous amount of attention to this new approach to policing and opened up new opportunities for sharing which methods worked for reducing crime and fear and improving police-citizen relationships.

Third Generation: Institutionalization

The third generation of community policing began in 1995 and runs, potentially, to the 2010s, and is considered the institutionalization generation. This specific term is used to denote the fact that community policing, after seeing widespread diffusion across the United States during the second generation, has now become the most common form of police services in the United States. This is evidenced by the fact that over 13,000 police agencies have claimed to be involved in some level of implementation of community policing practices. In addition, it is used to denote the importance of intergovernmental relationships among federal, state, and local governments that have also contributed to this process. Since the passage of the federal crime bill—The Violent Crime and Law Enforcement Act of 1994—community policing has become deeply entrenched within the national political process, a strong sign that a public policy, in this case community policing, has become institutionalized. Although community policing had a pronounced grassroots quality about it in the first generation, with the election of President Bill Clinton in 1992 and the passage of the Crime Bill, it became a high-visibility national public policy.

During the presidential campaign of 1992, Arkansas Governor Bill Clinton spoke about his policy of adding "100,000 cops" to the streets of America under the concepts of community policing. Nine months into his presidency, it became the centerpiece of his legislative efforts. Once passed, the bill dedicated $8.8 billion to hiring 100,000 police officers in the United States, through grants that would provide 75% of an officer's pay and benefits for three years. These grants were originally divided into monetary allocations for small towns under the COPS Funding Accelerated for Small Towns (FAST) program and for large metropolitan police departments under COPS Accelerated Hiring Education and Deployment (AHEAD). Eventually the grants would become known jointly as the Universal Hiring Program (UHP) program, and in 2000, additional funding was allocated by Congress to hire and additional 50,000 police officers. Still further, grants to

employ technology and equipment and enhance the community policing experience were put into place under the COPS Making Officer Redeployment Effective (MORE) program, and training and education of these new community policing officers were funded through the creation of Regional Community Policing Institutes (RCPIs). This federal intervention in community policing, namely in terms of grant dollars, dramatically changed the widespread adoption of community policing and allowed it to become more institutionalized and fixed within police departments and sheriff's offices across the country.

The third generation has witnessed the advancement of community policing in a number of police agencies in the United States. No longer were the majority of departments implementing demonstration projects. They were adopting a wider approach to implementing community policing, often incorporating concepts of enhanced police-citizen contacts, problem-solving methods, and special programs aimed at addressing neighborhood-specific issues through such methods as hot spot policing and crime prevention through environmental design (CPTED). While there were and continue to be agencies that have adopted the practices of community policing for the first time in the institutionalization era, this has been often driven by the availability of federal funding because community policing became an institutionalized federal-state public policy. One other factor that is evidence for the institutionalization of community policing comes in the form of the routinization of evaluations on the adoption of community policing. Again, in many ways the result of the federal funding, but many of the grants during this era began to routinely include funding or requirements for assessments to be conducted on the success of the community policing programs, and analysis has moved beyond simple case studies to quantified statistical analysis and meta-analysis of community policing programs.

The benefits to the institutionalization generation of community policing is that the philosophy, practices, and programs of this new approach to policing have become fixed in policing across the United States. While this has been lauded by many and often equated with one of the reasons for the crime drop beginning in 1994, there is a noted drawback to the increased funding, and that is the evidence that many agencies only adopted the tenets of community policing for the federal grant dollars. While this may have changed the intent and implementation of community policing, regardless, it has secured its institutionalization in U.S. policing.

Next Generation?

In the public policy field and its innovation, diffusion, and institutionalization literature, it is generally noted that after a policy is deemed as institutionalization, it has only a finite set of possible futures. First, it could evolve into a fourth generation. Second, it could decline and disappear as a public policy. Or third, it could be replaced by a new public policy. There is enough present evidence to suggest that community policing has not declined and disappeared. It is still a part of U.S. policing and there are no indicators that it will disappear anytime soon. That leaves the two other alternatives: that it is evolving into a fourth generation or being replaced by a new era of policing. There is evidence to suggest that the events of September 11, 2001, and the concept of homeland security have impacted community policing, but it may be too soon to tell whether this is in fact the fourth generation of community policing or a new era of U.S. policing.

In the wake of 9/11, there has been much discussion of conducting homeland security through community policing. Programs, grant dollars, and academic discussion have raised this as a distinct possibility. It is argued that the police-community relationships developed during the previous three generations has established a means of protecting our communities and neighborhoods from potential terrorists and that these measures would help to prevent future terrorist attacks. Others have argued, however, that terrorists strive to blend into a community, hence they become good neighbors while they await orders to carry out an attack, and that regardless of how strong police-citizen relationships are, it will not be effective enough to identify would-be terrorists. Still further, the style of policing under the concepts of homeland security would be vastly different then it is under community policing, raising the question of whether it is possible to institutionalize both styles of policing in any one department. The adoption of police intelligence units, incident command structures, and interagency task forces is a very different style of policing when compared to community policing. Again, it is probably too soon

to tell whether U.S. policing has entered a fourth generation of community policing or rather a fourth era (strategy) of U.S. policing, but homeland security has contributed to some change in contemporary U.S. policing.

Willard M. Oliver

See also Broken Windows Theory; Community Policing, Evolution of; Community Policing and Problem Solving, Definition of; Foot Patrols; Policing, Three Eras of; Problem-Oriented Policing, Goldstein's Development of

Further Readings

Angell, J. (1971). Toward an alternate to the classic police organizational arrangement: A democratic model. *Criminology, 8,* 185–206. doi: 10.1111/j.1745–9125.1971.tb00766

Germann, A. C. (1969). Community policing: An assessment. *Journal of Criminal Law, Criminology, and Police Science, 60*(1), 89–96.

Goldstein, H. (1979). Improving policing: A problem-oriented approach. *Crime and Delinquency, 25*(2), 236–258. doi: 10.1177/001112877902500207

Kelling, G. L., & Moore, M. H. (1988). The evolving strategy of police. *Perspectives on Policing, 4.* Washington, DC: U.S. Department of Justice, National Institute of Justice.

Trojanowicz, R. C., & Bucqueroux, B. (1990). *Community policing: A contemporary perspective.* Cincinnati, OH: Anderson.

Wilson, J. Q., & Kelling, G. L. (1982, March). Broken windows: The police and neighborhood safety. *Atlantic Monthly, 249*(3), 29–38.

Yin, R. (1979). *Changing in urban bureaucracies: How new practices become routinized.* Lanham, MD: Lexington Books.

Zhao, J., & Thurman, Q. C. (1997). Community policing: Where are we now? *Crime and Delinquency, 43,* 345–357.

GLOBAL POSITIONING SYSTEMS/ GEOGRAPHIC INFORMATION SYSTEMS

Global positioning systems (GPS) and geographic information systems (GIS) have become key tools used by police departments in recent years. Both of these technologies focus on examining the geographic information that is associated with tasks performed by the police. Many consider GPS and GIS to be separate yet related technologies; however, new information suggests that police departments around the world are using blended versions of the technologies to more intelligently address the tasks of the modern police department. This entry introduces the technological development of GPS and GIS systems separately, focusing on the use of the technologies by the police. The entry concludes with a discussion of how the technologies are currently being blended together and the future potential uses of the hybrid GPS and GIS technologies.

Technological Development

The use of geographic information within police departments has become more common since the transition to community policing. While the technology associated with both GPS and GIS systems originated in the late 1950s with the nation's "Space Race," the technologies were not implemented in most police departments until late in the 20th century. The reason for the delay in implementation of these systems was not due to lack of desire, but rather due to the high costs of computing power and software packages. As costs of computers and software have declined in the past 30 years, more and more police departments have implemented some form of GPS or GIS to their tool box. Although the two technologies are interrelated, both using geographic data, they have followed different progressions of usage in police departments and so the technological developments of each are discussed independently.

GPS

Global positioning systems (GPS) are systems that allow for the determination of an exact location on the planet by triangulating a user's position. The user's position is displayed as a latitude (depicting relative position north and south) and longitude (depicting relative position east and west) in degree, hours, minutes, and seconds. Currently there are approximately 30 satellites in orbit of Earth that are used for triangulating user's positions across the globe. Although there is a large degree of variation in the precision of the location estimate, GPS can estimate

position with between 1 centimeter and 100 meters of error. Originally GPS was designed to aid in the precise location of military equipment, which frequently operates in locations that cannot be easily described without the use of GPS.

As a technology, GPS became readily available and began implementation in law enforcement agencies in the early 1990s. Since the introduction of the technology in law enforcement agencies, the uses for the technology have grown at a seemingly exponential rate. Currently law enforcement agencies use GPS technology for locating people, places, and things. Some law enforcement agencies have incorporated GPS technology into patrol cars and into officers' uniforms to allow an exact location to be determined in real time or to guide the officer to a specific destination. Additionally, many law enforcement agencies are now using GPS technology to aid in the collection of evidence for major investigations. For instance, in the past officers would often have to draw complex diagrams for major crime events and traffic accidents. With the advent of GPS, officers are now able to take a GPS reading depicting the physical location of evidence that is later converted to a diagram with relative ease. Last, law enforcement agencies have found the use of GPS technology helpful for getting information about complex crime problems. Many police departments around the United States now plant—after obtaining a warrant issued by a court allowing them to do so—GPS devices on vehicles hoping to learn about the travel patterns of the driver. This has been helpful in breaking up car theft rings responsible for large numbers of vehicle thefts. With the transition to community policing, the desire for and use of GPS technology has increased. Law enforcement agencies now recognize the potential benefits associated with obtaining precise geographical information about problems they are tasked to resolve. Oftentimes in the problem-solving process, it is useful to have more precise information on the location of an event than simply the address. Many agencies now use GPS to create a data point that represents the exact location where a crime occurred, especially in settings covering a large amount of area with one address (e.g., apartment complexes and shopping malls). Additionally, obtaining specific locations of crime events with GPS signals speeds the job of crime analysts who no longer have to geocode data and removes the errors associated with geocoding. The process of geocoding is fully addressed in the following section.

GIS

Geographic information systems (GIS) allow geographic information to be depicted on a map as a visual interpretation. GIS maps are produced by converting data into an electronic format that can be graphed using an x- and y-based coordinate system. The base maps, depicting streets or police beats, are produced by telling the computer to draw a line from a certain set of x and y coordinates to another. After the base map is produced, data points or dots can then be added to the map relatively easily by providing the computer with the exact address or intersection where the dot is to be placed. The computer, through a process of geocoding, locates the approximate location of the address and provides the point with x and y coordinates to be depicted on the map. Geocoding has two primary drawbacks: imprecise estimates and data loss. The visual depiction of data points is an estimate based on the characteristics of the maps used in the process. While the imprecision is typically not a problem when looking at large units of aggregation (e.g., neighborhoods) it can be potentially problematic when looking at smaller units of analysis (e.g., block faces, or one side of a street). Additionally, geocoding is based on being able to match the characteristics of the reported address with a location on the map. However, this can be problematic due to spelling errors, out-of-date maps, and sites that cannot be located. When the points are geocoded, points that cannot be reliably matched to a location on the map become lost data, which introduces potential for incorrect conclusions to be made.

The earliest GIS software in the United States was produced by researchers at Harvard University in the late 1960s. These systems were used to create modern version of the traditional pin map that depicts the location of specific crime incidents. The next step in the development of GIS technologies for police departments in the United States came with the work of researchers and police officers in St. Louis, Missouri, in the 1970s. Here the researchers were concerned with examining the efficiency of patrol operations in the city. In order to equally distribute work according to crime and calls for service, the researchers were the first to create designated mapping areas that would subsequently become new beats for the officers. In essence, the researchers developed the ability to spatially join data to artificially created geographic boundaries and compare workloads in these geographically defined areas. This work was largely responsible for creating the *layers* that are a crucial component of GIS. Layers represent various fields of data that can be laid over the top of each other, like slides on an overhead projector, to allow for analysis and manipulation of data based on their physical location (e.g., street address) or spatial location (e.g., within a polygon depicting police beats).

Since the original development of the software in the 1960s, the power of GIS systems has rapidly increased and the price rapidly decreased, beginning in the 1980s and continuing to the present day. Dated estimates from the late 1990s suggest the prevalence of GIS systems in police departments was approximately 40%, although indications from the Law Enforcement Management and Statistics (LEMAS) survey suggest these numbers have likely grown substantially since then. Presently there are a number of GIS programs available for purchase by police departments that allow them to depict and analyze geo-crime data. The most popular programs currently on the market include MapInfo and ArcGIS, each selling for approximately $1,000 per user license.

Geographic crime data is typically analyzed by crime analysts within the police department, although some departments have trained officers how to develop their own maps. The transition to community policing has led to an increased need for GIS systems within police departments. Currently GIS systems are used to produce maps depicting the location of incidents, calls for service, arrests, identifying hot spots, CompStat programs, and other intelligence-led policing initiatives. With the transition to community policing, and specifically for problem-solving activities, GIS has become imperative for police departments. GIS assists police agencies in all stages of the problem-solving process by compiling and depicting vast amounts of data. Although these data are often already collected by the department, GIS assists in making the vast amount of data manageable and interpretable.

Blending GPS and GIS

While there has always been a well-established relationship between GPS and GIS technologies (e.g., GPS requires GIS to interpret the data), the potential uses of the two has largely remained untapped. The demand for geographic information has long lagged behind the needs of law enforcement agencies. Recently, law enforcement agencies have begun to realize the full potential of both GPS and GIS technologies together, especially since the transition to community policing with its focus on problem solving. The precise information required for the problem-solving process exceeds the abilities of either technology independently because of the problems highlighted above.

One of the first integrated uses of GPS and GIS technologies stems from the imprecise estimates associated with traditional geocoding processes. During the problem-solving process, it is no longer informative to have an approximate location of a crime incident or call for service; rather, implementing effective problem solving requires the knowledge of the exact location of the problem. Previously, geocoding data points alone would indicate a rash of car burglaries at a major shopping center. This pattern of vehicle burglaries could have been dismissed as a problem associated with large numbers of patrons visiting the shopping center or presented a more complex problem for police to solve. By blending the GPS and GIS information, law enforcement agencies can locate the exact location of each burglary and then determine if there is indeed a more localized pattern that can be addressed by officers. The blended use of the technologies could be the difference between the problem being dismissed or remaining unsolved versus a relatively simple fix (e.g., increasing lighting) to the problem.

Additionally, the blended use of GPS and GIS has served to improve the response time to potential problems that are located by the police. Instead of archival data that is at least one day old being geocoded and then depicted by trained crime analysts, data can now be depicted on maps almost instantaneously. This is advantageous for law enforcement personnel who can potentially identify and address problems at near real-time speed, allowing for proactive responses instead of the traditional reactive responses. Law enforcement agencies in the United States (e.g., Charlotte-Mecklenburg, [North Carolina] Police Department) are already using this blended version of the technologies to identify and solve problems in the community with a great deal of success.

The Future of Blended GPS and GIS Technologies

As indicated above, a number of law enforcement agencies are tapping into the creative resources of people both inside and outside law enforcement to develop blended technology solutions to crime problems. These solutions are on the cutting edge of research, technology, and policing around the world. Many law enforcement agencies are now using CompStat-type programs to address identified crime problems; however, some agencies are working to refine technology to allow problems to be identified *before* they occur. This process is known as *predictive policing*.

The Los Angeles (California) Police Department is using this technology to identify potential problem areas in response to gang violence. Analysts enter information concerning violent attacks involving suspected gang members, and the computer produces locations where retaliatory violence is likely. In addition to focusing on rare instances of gang violence, the department is using predictive policing technology to combat property crime, which accounts for more than half of all crimes reported. The predictive model uses information about reported offenses to predict areas where additional crimes may occur. Predictive policing thus shows signs of success in reducing crime throughout the city.

Other law enforcement agencies in the United States are looking at combining GPS and GIS technologies with a new twist that will allow officers to proactively target crime. Currently, the Tampa (Florida) Police Department is developing technology to assist officers in reducing the most prevalent crimes in the city; such technology will allow officers to quickly access information about reported crimes in the area immediately surrounding their present location. As the officers move throughout their patrol area, the map will change to display those incidents that are closest to their present location. This information then permits officers to access details of the crime and what has already been done in the investigation—and thus minimize unnecessary repeated contacts with citizens about the same crime event. Additionally, this also allows officers to look for patterns of cases that match the case they are currently working and to identify potential suspects based on known behavioral traits.

Jon Maskaly

See also Computer-Aided Dispatch; Crime Analysis; Crime Displacement; Crime Mapping; Place-Based Policing; Predictive Policing

Further Readings

Anderson, M. (1996). GPS used to track criminals. *GIS World, 9,* 15.

Beck, C., & McCue, C. (2009). Predictive policing: What can we learn from Wal-Mart and Amazon about fighting crime in a recession? *The Police Chief, 76,* 11.

Boba, R. (2009). *Crime analysis with crime mapping.* Thousand Oaks, CA: Sage.

Harries, K. (1999). *Mapping crime: Principles and practices.* Washington, DC: U.S. Department of Justice, National Institute of Justice.

Kemp, K. K. (2008). *Encyclopedia of geographic information science.* Thousand Oaks, CA: Sage.

Leipnik, M., Bottelli, J., Von Essen, I., Schmidt, A., Anderson, L., & Copper, T. (2003). Apprehending murderers in Spokane, Washington using GIS and GPS. In M. Leipnik & D. Alpert (Eds.), *GIS in law enforcement: Implementation issues and case studies* (pp.167–183). London, England: Taylor & Francis.

Paulsen, D. J., & Robinson, M. B. (2009). *Crime mapping and spatial aspects of crime.* Upper Saddle River, NJ: Prentice Hall.

Siuru, B. (1999). Tracking "down": Space-age GPS technology is here. *Corrections Technology and Management, 3*(5), 12–14.

Sorensen, S. L. (1997). Smart mapping for law enforcement settings: Integrating GIS and GPS for dynamic, near-real time applications and analysis. In D. L. Weisburd & J. T. McEwen (Eds.), *Crime mapping and crime prevention* (pp. 349–378). Monsey, NY: Criminal Justice Press.

Tampa Police Department. (2010). *Focus on four: Crime reduction plan.* Retrieved from http://www.tampagov.net/dept_police/Files/publications/FocusOnFour10print.pdf

Weisburd, D. L., Bernasco, W., & Bruinsma, G. J. N. (2009). *Putting crime in its place: Units of analysis in geographic criminology.* New York, NY: Springer-Verlag.

HOMELAND SECURITY

Homeland security as a domestic defense strategy became a national priority after the September 11, 2001, attacks on the World Trade Center in New York City, the Pentagon in northern Virginia, and United Airlines Flight 93 that crashed in Pennsylvania. The attacks, conducted by the terrorist group, al Qaeda, resulted in nearly 3,000 deaths, including 343 firefighters and 60 police officers who responded to the attacks. Those attacks led to changes in how government bodies in the United States respond to terrorist threats.

The attacks and the new emphasis on homeland security resulted in changes in government at all levels, particularly the federal government. It created new thinking in the Department of Defense. Rather than focusing primarily on traditional warfare involving wars with nation-states, the U.S. military began using unconventional warfare tactics and engaging in military operations designed to combat terrorist groups and terrorist threats. In 2002, as mandated in the Homeland Security Act of 2002 (P.L. 107–296), the Department of Homeland Security (DHS) was created by reorganizing many departments and agencies in the federal government. Agencies such as the U.S. Customs and Border Protection, Secret Service, the Federal Emergency Management Agency (FEMA), the Transportation Security Administration, and the National Domestic Preparedness Office became part of the newly organized Department of Homeland Security, creating the third largest department in the federal government.

This entry begins by defining *homeland security* and then details government efforts involving homeland security since 9/11. Last, this entry explains how the strategies involved in community policing fit into a homeland security strategy.

Homeland Security Defined

Homeland security refers to efforts to protect a nation against terrorism and other hazards that may threaten it. The U.S. Department of Homeland Security (DHS) has identified five core mission areas of the nation's homeland security strategy: (1) preventing terrorism and enhancing security, (2) securing and managing the nation's border, (3) enforcing and administering the nation's immigration laws, (4) safeguarding and securing cyberspace, and (5) ensuring resilience to disasters. As can be seen from the DHS's missions, homeland security not only applies to terrorist attacks but also encompasses natural disasters (e.g., fires, earthquakes, tornados, and hurricanes) and man-made disasters (e.g., chemical fires or transportation accidents involving hazardous materials).

When terrorist attacks, natural disasters, or other events involving homeland security occur in a local community, the initial response comes from local public safety and disaster response personnel, including police officers, firefighters, medical personnel, and other disaster agency officials. If the situation requires greater resources than the local authorities can provide, state agencies may become involved. States have disaster relief and response agencies, and personnel from these agencies often assist local first responders in the event of a disaster. Finally, if the state does not have adequate resources to respond effectively, the federal government is available to assist. The primary federal agency is the Federal Emergency Management Agency (FEMA), but other agencies may be called in depending on the nature and severity of the event. This layered response places considerable responsibility on local authorities, especially the police, who very likely are first on the scene. Because of this tiered response strategy, local law enforcement has to develop critical homeland security capabilities, including substantially increasing the number and types of skills that police officers possess.

National Response Framework

The National Response Framework (NRF), developed in 2008 by DHS, lays out guidance for how communities and agencies should respond to incidents, including disasters and terrorist attacks. The framework consists of four goals. The first is to prevent and disrupt terrorist attacks. This involves surveying the community to identify possible terrorist targets or critical infrastructure such as (1) physical assets, including transportation and manufacturing facilities; (2) human assets, or large concentrations of people such as those at sporting events or shopping venues; and (3) cyber assets such as physical structures and software that can be manipulated to cause significant damage to cyber networks.

After surveying the community, the second goal of the NRF is to protect the American people and the aforementioned critical infrastructure and key resources. This phase requires that local authorities develop response and protection plans for each type of critical infrastructure in terms of responding, providing aid, and facilitating evacuations. It also means that police personnel must be trained in how to respond and access proper equipment, including equipment that enables them to respond to a chemical or biological event. The NRF requires that local officials conduct exercises to practice responses and to evaluate where there are shortfalls and identify improvements.

The third goal is ensuring that local authorities and their communities can respond to and recover from incidents that do occur. This phase requires the National Incident Management System (discussed below) to be implemented, which is an organizational system that has existed since 2005 and is well understood by the emergency management community at the local, state, and federal levels. It is the foundation of the NRF.

Finally, the fourth goal of the NRF is to continue to strengthen the foundation to ensure our long-term success. This requires that adequate resources in terms of training, equipment, and personnel be devoted to maintaining the capabilities of the NRF at a high level.

Police Organization

The threat of terrorism may not be equally distributed across U.S. cities and communities. Because terrorists generally plan their attacks to generate the greatest amount of damage and loss of life, large, densely populated cities are more likely to be attacked. The primary terrorism targets in the United States have been major cities such as New York City, Washington, D.C., Chicago, and Los Angeles. Cities attempt to gauge their likelihood of terrorist attacks and plan accordingly. For example, because New York City has experienced terrorist attacks, including the bombing of the World Trade Center in 1993 and the attacks on the World Trade Center on September 11, 2001, the New York City Police Department has instituted a complex homeland security defense plan to indentify, prevent, and respond to terrorist attacks. Other large cities have taken similar steps.

Many large cities have altered their organizational chart to include homeland security units, sections, or bureaus. For example, the Washington Metropolitan Police Department in Washington, D.C., has a Homeland Security Bureau commanded by an assistant chief. The bureau contains several units, such as a tactical patrol, special events, traffic safety, domestic security operations, and intelligence units. The tactical patrol branch includes an emergency response team and an explosive-ordinance disposal unit as well as several tactical patrol units, such as air support, horse-mounted, and canine units. These units can assist in the initial response to an event. The special events branch plans for and coordinates security for special events, such as political gatherings and dignitaries, which are possible terrorist targets. The traffic safety-specialized environmental branch contains a number of units that are involved in traffic. These units, which can provide security and divert traffic patterns, are of critical importance should there be an incident. The domestic security operations branch contains two squads that can be quickly deployed should there be a problem or event. Finally, the intelligence fusion division contains a number of units including a joint operations command center, command information center, the joint terrorism task force, a fusion center, and an intelligence unit. The intelligence fusion division is actively involved in collecting intelligence information about potential terrorists, possible terrorist plots, and criminal activities.

In addition to having homeland security responsibilities, units in Washington Metropolitan Police Department's Homeland Security Bureau are involved in many activities that are more in line with traditional police work. A policing strategy that maintains a proper mixture of activities can result in an effective and rapid response to incidents. Washington Metropolitan Police Department's model of having units pay attention to traditional responsibilities while at the same time being prepared to respond to a terrorist attack or disaster provides a model for other cities when implementing homeland security.

The National Incident Management System

When a significant event occurs, the response is guided by the National Incident Management System. The U.S. Department of Homeland Security developed the system to provide a uniform and consistent response to incidents. A standard event response system helps to ensure that the response is effective. This is particularly true in large events that involve local, state, federal, and community-based organizations. A consistent format ensures that all resources are assigned tasks and the tasks are reasonably coordinated. These tasks or responsibilities include communication among various agencies and the general public; resource management, including the acquisition of equipment, food, water, and temporary shelter; and managing ongoing activities.

An important part of the National Incident Management System is the establishment of an incident command system. The incident command system is the equivalent of police departments' command posts that are established at the scenes of barricaded persons, natural disasters, chemical spills, and other significant incidents. The incident command system consists of a command center composed of local, state, and federal agencies and may include police and firefighter personnel, emergency medical personnel, state and local disaster relief personnel, representatives from FEMA, and representatives from other state and federal agencies, depending on the nature of the disaster. The incident command system allows for better coordination among the many agencies because all orders are coordinated and dispatched from a central location. This also ensures less confusion as mitigation and recovery efforts unfold.

Role of Police Officers and Community Policing Officers

Police officers play an important role when there is a homeland security incident, as their assessment of situations is vital to an effective response. As first responders, they evaluate the severity of the incident. This assessment often determines which other first responders should be called to the scene and the equipment necessary for responding to the incident. For example, a chemical spill or fire at a chemical plant may require firefighter personnel and special protective equipment. If this need is not immediately recognized, it may result in officers, other first responders, or civilians being exposed to hazardous materials. The primary objective is to protect life and prevent additional injuries.

Officers also identify the injured and provide immediate assistance. This may require administering first aid and summoning medical personnel. When medical personnel are called, officers must manage traffic into the area, including establishing roadblocks, if necessary, to ensure a quick response. In some cases, officers may assist in coordinating evacuations. Police notify people of the evacuation, which can involve officers going door-to-door, and identify people who need assistance, such as those who are elderly or disabled. Police also identify evacuation facilities or a safe place for evacuees to congregate. By doing so, police not only remove people from danger but also facilitate the work of other emergency personnel. If needed, police officers also secure the area to prevent looters from removing items from vacant homes and businesses. Similarly, police need to keep curious citizens from entering the area to see what has happened, as they can often impede disaster relief personnel who are working in the area or expose themselves to dangerous conditions.

Police officers who have been trained in community policing often are the best qualified for these duties. Community policing requires officers who can be firm but at the same time show empathy toward victims. Community policing training often instills the communications skills and attitudes necessary for these tasks. A major problem that occurs when dealing with people at the scene of events is a lack of effective communications. People often want to cooperate with the police, but some police officers do not communicate effectively, including not providing clear direction and rationale for commands or orders. Moreover, community policing officers often have better working relationships with citizens. When citizens know their police officers, they may be more likely to comply with requests and orders.

Community policing can also play an important role in the gathering of terrorist-related intelligence. Because a hallmark of community policing is community building and community relationships, community policing officers have good relations with the people in a neighborhood, which may result in people being more willing to talk with officers about problems and provide information about suspicious activities and persons. Developing positive, working relationships with people is an extremely important part of community policing because terrorists and terrorist cells generally try to "hide in plain sight," that is, they try to integrate themselves in a neighborhood, making discovery difficult. Good police relations with the community are an effective manner by which to discover possible terrorist operations.

The skills and community contacts that community policing officers possess can also be important when attempting to discover additional information about an incident. Talking with citizens and victims often leads to the identification of nonevident problems or the identification of undiscovered victims. People residing in a disaster area often have useful information that is not known to the police or other disaster personnel. Even in homeland security incidents, such as terrorist events and disasters, police officers must take the time to listen to citizens' concerns and problems. Community policing training enhances officers' ability to work effectively with people and obtain important information.

Homeland security involves complex problems, and strategies to ensure homeland security require police officers to work with a variety of agencies and citizens. To do so, police officers must develop and maintain the skills necessary to mitigate homeland security events, including community policing skills.

In sum, community policing can play an important role in the gathering of terrorist-related intelligence. A hallmark of community policing is community building and community relationships. When police officers have good relations with the people in a neighborhood, people may be more willing to talk with officers about problems and may often provide information about suspicious activities and persons. Developing positive working relationships with people is an extremely important part of community policing because terrorists and terrorist cells generally try to "hide in plain sight," that is, they try to integrate themselves in a neighborhood, making discovery difficult. Good police relations with the community are an effective manner by which to discover possible terrorist operations.

Larry K. Gaines

See also Terrorism, Future Impact of Community Policing on

Further Readings

Gaines, L. K., & Kappeler, V. E. (2012). *Homeland security.* Upper Saddle River, NJ: Prentice Hall.

Shemella, P. (Ed.). (2011). *Fighting back: What governments can do about terrorism.* Stanford, CA: Stanford University Press.

U.S. Department of Homeland Security. (2008). *National response framework.* Retrieved from http://www.fema .gov/pdf/emergency/nrf/nrf-core.pdf

U.S. Department of Homeland Security. (2011). *Implementing 9/11 Commission recommendations: Progress report 2011.* Washington, DC: Author.

Website

U.S. Department of Homeland Security; http://www.dhs.gov

Hot Spots

Hot spots is a term used to describe places that experience a large number of crimes or places where there is a higher than average risk of crime victimization. Crime tends to cluster in small areas such as street blocks or addresses. These clusters of crime are commonly referred to as hot spots.

It has long been known that crime is not randomly distributed across space. Some of the earliest writers on criminology acknowledged this, including

Adolphe Quetelet in the 1800s. Much early research focused on cities or neighborhoods within cities. In a 1989 work that spoke of hot spots, Lawrence Sherman, Patrick Gartin, and Michael Buerger found that "crime is both rare and concentrated," with 50% of all crime occurring at just 3% of all places. Other researchers have found that not only is crime geographically concentrated but also that the hot spots of crime are stable over time.

The knowledge that crime clusters in small areas is useful for community policing and problem solving. First, it is not that entire neighborhoods are crime prone. Instead, some places within neighborhoods, such as a single park or a handful of street blocks or even a single address, have high levels of crime. Most other places are either low crime or have no crime. This is true even in high-crime neighborhoods—only a relative handful of places within each neighborhood are high crime. Second, various policing interventions at hot spots have been found to reduce crime at the hot spot locations without displacing crime to other nearby locations. Identifying the location and nature of hot spots is therefore often an important step in the problem-solving process. This entry looks at how hot spots are identified, why crime clusters at certain locations, and why it tends to involve certain times of day and types of goods.

The Definition of Place and Identifying Hot Spots

The exact definition of *place* can vary depending on the focus of the analysis. Sherman and colleagues described a place as a "fixed physical environment that can be seen completely and simultaneously, at least on its surface, by one's naked eyes." Examples of places include a single address, an apartment building, a street block, a strip shopping center, or a park. The important distinction is that a place is not as large as a census tract or an entire neighborhood. Places are small discrete areas; hot spots are places with higher than average crime.

Just as there is no consensus definition of a place, there is no consensus mathematical definition of exactly what constitutes a hot spot. Most authors, however, agree that hot spots are "hot" compared to the local distribution of crime. This means that places considered high crime in one jurisdiction may not be high crime in another jurisdiction. It also means that hot spots for different crime problems could be defined differently within the same jurisdiction.

Hot spot identification methods vary by the problem type, the data available, and the purpose of the analysis. The most commonly used hot spot identification method is also the most simple: a visual inspection of crime locations plotted on a map. While pins have long been inserted in paper maps for this purpose, computer-based mapping technology became available in the mid-1990s and spurred analysis of hot spots by police. There are many options for displaying crime information in a way that demonstrates the concentration of crime across space. For example, graduated symbols can be used, where the size of the dots on the map is proportional to the number of crimes at that place. A color gradient can also be used, often with darker dots representing higher levels of crime.

Other techniques rely on complex computations and spatial statistics. For example, quartic kernel density maps overlay a grid of cells on a study area. Point locations of crime are plotted against this grid. Points within each grid cell are weighted according to their distance from the center of the grid. Final grid values are calculated by summing the weighted values. Kernel density maps produce a smooth surface showing the concentration of crime but generally cannot determine whether a cluster of points is statistically significant. Various local indicators of spatial association (LISA) statistics have been developed to solve this problem. These include the Local Moran's I, Local Geary's C, Gi, and Gi* statistics.

Still other methods exist for identifying hot spots. Computer software has been developed for this purpose. CrimeStat III is one such application. Developed by the research and evaluation firm Ned Levine & Associates and funded by the National Institute of Justice, CrimeStat III offers analysts several different methods for identifying clusters of crimes. Each method has its own strengths and weaknesses and there is no technique that is clearly superior in every circumstance.

The variety of technical implementations and output types among these differing hot spot identification methods underscores the importance of the analyst conducting the analysis. The analyst's decisions often have a material impact on the end product. Maps created from the same base data can have differing numbers of an intensity of hot spots. For example, quartic kernel density maps are sensitive to the grid size and search radius from the center of the grid, often with dramatically different output. Even simple decisions, such as the colors used on a map, can have dramatic consequences for how the map is interpreted.

Why Are Hot Spots Hot?

Three criminological theories inform the study of crime concentrations at places: rational choice, routine activities, and crime pattern. *Rational choice theory* suggests that offenders choose to engage in crime after a consideration of cost and benefits of doing do. Crime is more likely when the benefits are considered to outweigh the costs. Costs and benefits are both defined broadly. Costs of crime include formal costs such as legal punishments. Informal costs are assessed as well, such as disapproval from parents or friends. Benefits include monetary gain and satisfaction. Benefits could also include inherent benefits such as the pharmacological effect of drugs. Modern conceptions of rational choice theory recognize that decision making is bounded by the availability of relevant information, the ability to assess that information, and the time available to make the decision. Rational choice theory is useful because it suggests that manipulating the environment in which decisions are made could change the outcomes of those decisions. A subfield of criminology, situational crime prevention, is rooted in these concepts.

While rational choice theory focuses entirely on offenders and their environment, *routine activities theory* recognizes the importance of targets and places. According to routine activities theory, crime is a confluence in space and time of motivated offenders, suitable targets, and a lack of capable guardians at a place. Suitable targets can be individuals, such as victims of assault, or homes that are burglarized, or a specific product that is stolen. Capable guardians prevent crime and could include friends of an intended assault victim or a stay-at-home parent. Characteristics of the place are important as well, with place management structuring decisions of persons who use the place. For example, a bar owner may decide to market her bar as a dance club or as a neighborhood bar. Due to variations in target availability, guardianship, and place management, some places are more likely to result in a successful crime than others, even when the population of offenders is the same.

Crime pattern theory combines rational choice and routine activities theory to explain the spatial patterning of crime. Crime pattern theory suggests that targets come to the attention of offenders as offenders move through an area engaging in the routine activities of life. Moreover, criminal offenders can only exploit the opportunities they are aware of. This helps to explain crime concentrations because the distribution of offenders, targets, guardianship, and therefore criminal opportunities is neither random nor uniform across space. As an extreme example, the number of potential robbery targets is greater at a busy bus depot than along a rural road due to the greater number of people traveling through the bus depot. Using official data and interviews with offenders, criminologists have also found that most offenders search for criminal opportunities near the places that are part of their noncriminal lives, such as work, shopping, and recreation. Offenders rarely travel long distances solely for the purpose of committing crimes—the average journey to crime is less than three miles.

As this discussion makes clear, criminological theory suggests multiple reasons that hot spots could be hot. It could be that there are a large number of targets in a particular area, a large number of offenders, or inadequate guardianship. Due to this variety of causes, hot spots analysis for the purpose of problem solving often requires a crime-specific focus. The hot spots of burglary, for example, are likely to be different than the hot spots of robbery. In fact, the statutory definitions of crime are often not specific enough. For example, residential burglary usually follows a different pattern than commercial burglary. Similarly, bank robbery and street robbery hot spots are unlikely to show the same pattern.

Knowing why a spot is hot helps to tailor intervention strategies to the problem. Interventions based on situational prevention that target why the hot spot is occurring are the most likely to produce crime reductions. Merely increasing traditional police patrol presence in hot spots can also yield a small crime prevention benefit depending on the nature of the problem. Understanding why a hot spot occurs also helps to understand possible crime displacement from geographically focused interventions.

Other Concentrations of Crime

The basic idea of hot spots is that crime is not randomly distributed in space but instead is concentrated at a small number of places. Crime tends to concentrate along other dimensions as well. A purely geographic focus would therefore ignore important aspects of crime that are relevant for community problem solvers. One such dimension is by facility type. A facility is a place used for a particular purpose. Examples of facility types include bars, parking lots, hotels, apartments, and bus depots. Crime concentrates in a small number of these types of places. The majority of facilities will not have crime problems. Most bars in a city, for example, will not be high crime. Only a handful of bars have crime problems. These high-crime bars are high-risk places, or risky facilities.

The concentration of crime at risky facilities is so pronounced that it is often useful for analysts and police when devising interventions and building community trust. For example, in Chula Vista, California, police analysts found that out of all 26 motels in the city, the top five motels contributed 51.1% of all police calls for service to motels. The concentration of crime among a few motels allowed the police to focus their interventions on the motels with the highest levels of crime and allowed the police to explain why particular motels were chosen for intervention.

Crime is also not randomly distributed across time of day and days of the week. Some crime problems tend to occur on certain days of the week and at certain times. These are often referred to as "hot times." Determining the time of day and days of the week a crime problem occurs can help determine the cause of the problem and guide community policing toward solutions. For example, disorder problems at bus stops may cluster around school pick-up and drop-off times, or assault problems at bars may cluster around closing time on the weekend.

Just as all places are not at equal risk of crime, not all goods are at equal risk of theft. "Hot products" are items that are more likely than others to be stolen. Jewelry and consumer electronics, for example, are more likely than other goods to be stolen. Ronald Clarke has developed an acronym for the key attributes of hot products: CRAVED. Items that are concealable, removable, available, valuable, enjoyable, and disposable are more likely to be stolen than goods that are not. The key element is often disposal. For example, heavy metal theft is more likely when thieves can sell the metal to scrap dealers with no record of the transaction.

It is not just places, times, and products that show concentration. Crime is also concentrated among certain people. Both offenders and victims often show repeat patterns. These patterns can be scrutinized for possible points of intervention in a community problem-solving framework. Marvin Wolfgang, Robert Figlio, and Sellin Thorsten conducted pioneering research on chronic offending, finding that 6% of their sample was responsible for over half of the offenses committed by their sample. Research since has found similar concentrations among offenders, with a small number of chronic offenders committing a large proportion of crimes. Police agencies frequently find that a hot spot of crime is due to a small number of offenders. In fact, some hot spots are created by a single prolific offender.

Crime is also concentrated among victims, with some victims experiencing multiple victimizations. Repeat victimization extends to places as well, with burglars often returning to the burgled site and other nearby sites ("near repeat" victimization).

Troy C. Payne

See also Crime Analysis; Crime Displacement; Crime Mapping; Directed Patrol, Studies of; Place-Based Policing; Repeat Victimization, Community Policing Strategies for

Further Readings

Braga, A. A. (2001). The effects of hot spots policing on crime. *Annals of the American Academy of Political and Social Science, 578*(1), 104–125. doi: 10.1177/0002716201578001007578

Braga, A. A., & Bond, B. J. (2008). Policing crime and disorder hot spots: A randomized controlled trial. *Criminology, 46*(3), 577–607. doi: 10.1111/j.1745–9125.2008.00124

Braga, A. A., Papachristos, A. V., & Hureau, D. M. (2012). The effects of hot spots policing on crime: An updated systematic review and meta-analysis. *Justice Quarterly,* 1–31.

Braga, A. A., & Weisburd, D. L. (2010). *Policing problem places: Crime hot spots and effective prevention.* New York, NY: Oxford University Press.

Chainey, S., & Ratcliffe, J. (2005). *GIS and crime mapping.* West Chester, England: Wiley.

Clarke, R. V. (1999). *Hot products: Understanding, anticipating and reducing demand for stolen goods.* (Police Research Series, Paper 112. Policing and Reducing Crime Unit). London, England: Home Office.

Guerette, R. T., & Bowers, K. J. (2009). Assessing the extent of crime displacement and diffusion of benefits: A review of situational crime prevention evaluations. *Criminology, 47*(4), 1331–1368. doi: 10.1111/j.1745–9125.2009.00177

Koper, C. S. (1995, December). Just enough police presence: Reducing crime and disorderly behavior by optimizing patrol time in crime hot spots. *Justice Quarterly, 12*(4), 649–672.

Santos, R. B. (2012). *Crime analysis with crime mapping* (3rd ed.). Thousand Oaks, CA: Sage.

Sherman, L. W., Gartin, P. R., & Buerger, M. E. (1989). Hot spots of predatory crime: Routine activities and the criminology of place. *Criminology, 27*(1), 27–55.

Sherman, L. W., & Rogan, D. P. (1995, December). Effects of gun seizures on gun violence: Hot spots patrol in Kansas City. *Justice Quarterly, 12*(4), 673–693.

Sherman, L. W., & Weisburd, D. L. (1995). General deterrent effects of police patrol in crime "hot spots": A randomized, controlled trial. *Justice Quarterly, 12*(4), 625–648.

Wolfgang, M. E., Figlio, R. M., & Sellin, T. (1972). *Delinquency in a birth cohort.* Chicago, IL: University of Chicago Press.

Website

Center for Problem-Oriented Policing; http://www.popcenter.org

Immigrant Populations, Community Policing Strategies for

As first responders, law enforcement officers must be able to interact with all communities and communicate with suspects, victims, and witnesses effectively and without delay. This is even more critical for those operating within a community policing framework, which focuses on engaging community members in problem-solving partnerships to address crime and social disorder.

In the United States, police often have to navigate unfamiliar cultures and languages to engage community members as partners in ensuring public safety. Nearly 40 million foreign-born individuals now live in the United States and 7 million of these persons have arrived since 2003. Thus, it is critical for police officers to have positive relations with immigrants. Doing so, however, requires overcoming significant challenges posed by language barriers, cultural biases and differences, and immigrants' fear and mistrust of law enforcement. This entry discusses these challenges in policing multicultural populations and describes some effective strategies for providing community policing in multicultural neighborhoods and communities.

Challenges

To effectively serve and protect multicultural communities, law enforcement must first address and overcome a number of challenges resulting from language barriers, cultural differences and biases, and immigrants' fear and mistrust of police.

Language Barriers

Almost 20% of Americans, both foreign- and native-born, speak a language other than English at home. About 9% can be categorized as limited English proficient (LEP)—they have a limited ability to read, write, speak, or understand English. With large numbers of LEP individuals living in the United States, it is likely that many of the nation's 18,000 law enforcement agencies will have some level of contact with people who do not speak English.

Police have reported that these interactions can be frustrating if they do not have the tools or resources to overcome the language barrier. In responding to calls for service involving LEP individuals, police cannot know what to do or how to help if language barriers prevent them from understanding what has happened. When LEP individuals cannot communicate with police personnel, they may not be able to fully explain to police what happened to them as victims or what they observed as witnesses. If police respond to a domestic violence call and cannot communicate with anyone on the scene, they may not be able to make an arrest or, in jurisdictions that have mandatory arrest policies, they may have to arrest both the victim and perpetrator because they cannot determine who is culpable.

Community policing crime prevention initiatives such as neighborhood watch programs and crime reporting hotlines cannot be utilized by LEP individuals if language assistance is not provided to overcome the language barrier.

Cultural Differences and Biases

Both police and immigrant communities have distinct cultural beliefs and practices that govern how they perceive and interact with each other. Misunderstandings between law enforcement and community members based on cultural differences can lead to frustrations and unnecessary escalation of routine police-civilian interactions.

Many immigrants come from countries that have vastly different criminal justice systems where the role of police is drastically different from what is commonly understood in the United States. In some parts of the world, particularly those with oppressive regimes, law enforcement officials actively target and terrorize civilians and can extort money from anyone they stop. In these locations, when stopped by a police officer while driving, for example, it is a normal cultural practice for immigrants to not make eye contact and to offer the officer cash. In other parts of the world, where law enforcement may be less threatening, it may be customary for drivers to walk out of their vehicles toward a police car during a traffic stop, which is not customary in the United States and can be understood by police to be an aggressive act. For these and more serious police-community interactions, it is foreseeable that misunderstandings about the role of police and how to behave during encounters could lead to miscalculations of each other's intentions and incorrect responses.

Limited police understanding about cultural practices and beliefs among people of different cultures can lead to inaccurate perceptions of who within a community is at risk of perpetrating or being victimized by crime. For example, in some parts of Asia, there are health care practices such as "coining" and "cupping," which are done to treat illness and can leave bruises. This could be misinterpreted by law enforcement as a sign of physical abuse, and parents who practice this treatment on their children could be deemed child abusers. Likewise, the cultural and religious practice of women covering their hair and bodies within Muslim communities may be erroneously interpreted as signs of oppression and precursors of domestic violence by non-Muslim law enforcement.

Immigrants' Mistrust and Fear of Law Enforcement

Many immigrants—refugees especially—come from places where police are corrupt and abusive.

People who have fled to the United States from places with civil war, genocide, or martial law may have difficulty trusting that police in the United States are here to help. Likewise, immigrants who lack legal immigration status or have family members who are undocumented may be reluctant to take any risk in making their immigration status, or the status of their family members or neighbors, known to authorities. A robbery victim who does not have legal permission to remain in the country, for example, may not call police for fear that he or a family member will be deported.

Even in situations where the local law enforcement agency has a strict policy against sharing information with immigration authorities, immigrants may be reluctant to report crime. One reason is that there currently is no consistent policy or practice among local law enforcement agencies regarding immigration enforcement. In a number of jurisdictions, the city, town, or village law enforcement agency deals with undocumented immigrants differently than does the county sheriff's office. Many county jails share detainees' demographic information, including country of birth, with the Immigration and Customs Enforcement (ICE) agency, which then has the capability to determine the inmates' immigration status and initiate deportation proceedings against those who do not have legal immigration status.

Impacts of Challenges on the Policing Profession

Underreporting of Crime

In addition to leaving criminal activities unaddressed by the criminal justice system, immigrants' underreporting of crime makes them a prime target for criminals. There has been a growing crime trend of opportunistic crimes, in which criminals actively seek out immigrants for robberies and other crimes because they know that there is little chance they will be later identified and punished. Similarly, it has been found that some unscrupulous employers take advantage of undocumented immigrants' labor and refuse to pay wages, knowing that the workers are not likely to report them to police or other authorities.

Heightened Dangers for Police

Law enforcement officers are trained to deal tactically with a whole host of possible threats they may encounter when out in the field. Police are continuously looking for possible hazards and bracing themselves for a number of risks. When law enforcement officers do not understand what is being spoken due to a language barrier, or they do not understand the purpose or motives behind a particular cultural practice, their ability to protect themselves is impaired. As such, they may not understand when there is a danger present and may unknowingly put themselves in a precarious situation.

Impaired Investigations and Prosecutions

When police cannot communicate with a victim or witness because of language barriers, they are unable to properly document the circumstances of an incident, which in turn threatens the success of an investigation. As the case proceeds, prosecutors cannot communicate as effectively with LEP victims and witnesses if they do not have adequate language resources. In addition, should a case be litigated in court, law enforcement may also struggle in ensuring complete processing and service of court documents if the recipient of the documents cannot understand what the officer is saying or what is written in the court papers.

Effective Strategies for Policing Multicultural Communities

Across the country, some police agencies have been able to minimize cultural and language gaps through practical approaches. These approaches include becoming a familiar face in the community, teaching the immigrant community about policing, training officers on tactics for effective interactions with immigrants, equipping officers and civilian staff with access to language assistance, translating key documents, and seeking feedback from immigrant community leaders. This section discusses each of these approaches and the different ways police agencies have carried them out.

Become a Familiar Face in the Community

A common way for government officials to obtain feedback from constituents is by hosting community forums. Law enforcement personnel who conduct these forums often find themselves addressing a wide variety of questions and concerns of community members, on topics that touch upon many aspects of policing. While these forums can be efficient avenues for sharing information with large numbers of people and dispelling pervasive misconceptions among the community, they can sometimes devolve into a situation where police representatives feel as though they are standing before a firing squad and have little control over the situation. It can also be difficult to get immigrants to attend these public events because of their fear of law enforcement. Despite these shortcomings, community forums, particularly those that are ongoing, can be an effective way for law enforcement to have dialogue with community members and then craft appropriate responses to the community's needs, interests, and concerns.

Some agencies have sought to maximize opportunities for face-to-face dialogue between immigrant residents and police personnel by designating one or more liaisons to the immigrant community. Larger agencies have created specialized units with a team of liaisons covering different districts within the jurisdiction or different immigrant communities. The liaisons can be either civilian personnel or sworn officers; while civilian liaisons may be easier to hire, sworn officers may have a more nuanced understanding of crime trends. What is often more important is the language proficiency of the liaisons. Liaisons who are multilingual and speak one of the predominant languages spoken among local immigrants are initially better poised to build rapport with, and gain the trust of, immigrants in their community.

In providing a community-based "home" for its liaisons, some police departments have placed substations in the heart of immigrant neighborhoods or commercial districts that are heavily frequented by these community members. By locating these substations within an immigrant community, law enforcement agencies are able to have daily, routine contact with immigrants and be easily accessible to victims or witnesses who want to report crime or other public safety concerns and may fear going to police headquarters.

Virtually all immigrant communities in the United States have cultivated ethnic media outlets, both print and broadcast. Law enforcement agencies seeking to reach immigrant community members, both in their locale and in bordering towns and cities, have done so by writing and submitting articles to ethnic print media and appearing on ethnic radio and television programs. Ethnic print media outlets often are able to translate articles written in English into the readers' language. On broadcast programs, law enforcement officials can come on as guests to address listener or viewer questions about a variety of policing topics. The challenge of these sorts of media outreach approaches is ensuring that law enforcement officials are able to maintain control of the message that is delivered.

Teach the Community About Policing

As noted above, many immigrants come from places where the laws and role of law enforcement are completely different. Likewise, notions of community policing and quality-of-life concerns are unknown to large segments of the immigrant population, particularly those who have recently settled in the United States. Some police organizations have recognized the importance of taking the lead on educating community members, particularly immigrants, about local laws and ordinances and the role of police in enforcing them. Such education has been delivered through one-off presentations in English-as-a-second-language classes and other community settings to more extensive citizen police academies that are 8- to 10-week-long classes led by police for local residents. Citizen police academies that are specifically targeted to immigrants are often taught in the immigrants' primary languages or provide onsite interpreters for LEP participants.

Train Officers on Tactics for Effective Interactions With Immigrants

Law enforcement is a heavily trained profession; all police officers must graduate from a police academy, pass a number of tests, and receive hundreds of hours of training each year to maintain their rank and positions. While diversity training has been offered to law enforcement agencies for numerous years, the success of these trainings has been questioned because they have typically been more theoretical and have not often been tailored to the realities of law enforcement.

More successful approaches for training law enforcement officers on how to effectively interact with immigrants have focused on tactics. For example, tactical training could involve teaching officers about culturally specific ways certain immigrants behave when questioned by law enforcement

or other authority figures, or simulating situations where police may have to respond to a crime situation involving people who only speak Spanish. Tactical training can happen in the police agency's training center or out in the immigrant community. Greater opportunities for viewing and understanding how immigrants respond to law enforcement officers will exist with trainings conducted in the community.

A number of training resources have been developed that teach police how to say greetings, commands, and a few other phrases in other languages. Learning these key phrases can be very useful to police when they are trying to control a situation or elicit a quick response from someone. However, this limited language knowledge can sometimes lead officers into more complicated dialogues in a language they do not know. As stated above, a language barrier can pose numerous challenges to police; police should know when they can and cannot communicate effectively. Some agencies have benefitted from investing time and resources into foreign language instruction for officers through in-house training, college courses, or online language training programs.

Equip Officers and Civilian Staff With Access to Language Assistance

As noted above, language barriers can severely hamper and even prevent critical responses to crime and other safety concerns by civilian and sworn police personnel. Having multilingual personnel is the best way to overcome such barriers; however, this is neither practical nor possible in the United States, where hundreds of languages are spoken each day and law enforcement agencies are operating within tight budgets. Agencies that are fortunate enough to have such personnel have encouraged them to assist monolingual personnel, particularly in high-stakes situations such as interrogations. In some departments, bilingual civilian personnel and volunteers have been grouped together to systematically assist officers as interpreters. For those agencies that are not able to fully cover the language gap with in-house resources, there are number of telephonic interpreter companies that are available to provide on-demand interpretation over the phone for law enforcement and other professionals. These services can assist with communications in many different languages and dialects and charge a fee for each minute of the conversation. The best way to work with a telephonic interpreter is for the people whose conversation is being interpreted to use a speakerphone or a dual handset phone that allows two people on the same phone to use separate handsets. Calls conducted over a speakerphone can be less private. Speakers should only say one to two phrases at a time to ensure that the interpreter is able to interpret everything that is said accurately and completely. Thus, conversations that are conducted through an interpreter are usually twice as long in duration.

Translate Key Documents

While interpreters can assist with oral communications, translations must be conducted with written communications. It is often impossible and expensive to ensure that every piece of paper produced within a law enforcement agency is translated into the various languages spoken and read in a community. Thus, an effective way for law enforcement to communicate in writing with LEP individuals is to translate signage and documents that communicate vital information to the public into the most prevalent languages spoken by immigrant community members. Examples of such signage and documents are notices of rights, signs that state how to request police assistance (911), written Miranda warnings, consent and waiver forms, and internal affairs complaint forms. Prevalent languages spoken by LEP community members can be determined by reviewing U.S. Census data and data collected by local departments of education and health and municipal courts.

Involve Community Leaders in Decision Making

Agency executives who have trusted confidants in the immigrant community are best able to learn of community concerns and receive informed and appropriate feedback on the agency's policies and practices. Some agencies have developed formal advisory committees that are made up of civilians who pass a background check and who represent different perspectives of the jurisdiction's immigrant communities. Such committees meet regularly with agency decision makers to discuss the public safety needs of their communities and guide the department in appropriately addressing the needs. Members

of these committees can advise on the community impact of pending police policies and programs and educate community members about the role of law enforcement agencies. Community members of advisory committees may also be able to defend justifiable police responses, when appropriate.

Recognizing that police officer recruitment is a pervasive challenge for the law enforcement profession, particularly when ensuring a diverse police force, immigrant community leaders can serve on recruitment councils, which specifically focus on increasing the pool of qualified applicants who represent the jurisdiction's diversity.

The above-described practices have been quite effective in fostering positive law enforcement relations with many multicultural communities in the United States. This being said, feasibility, cost, and local politics can prevent some of these approaches from being adopted in certain police agencies. Yet all police practitioners have the ability to think about how the challenges discussed early in this chapter affect their work and to develop local solutions. In doing so, law enforcement agencies across the nation can move closer to their common goal: improving public safety for all.

Susan M. Shah

See also Building Partnerships and Stakeholders; Demographics, Future Impact on Community Policing; Immigrant Populations, Community Policing Strategies for; Immigration: Issues, Law, and Police Training; Police-Community Relations

Further Readings

Curtis, N. (2006). *Language assistance for law enforcement.* Seattle, WA: National Association of Judiciary Interpreters and Translators. Retrieved from http://www.carlamathers.net/attachments/File/Resources/LawEnforcement200609.pdf

Gambetta, R., & Burgess, M. (2011). *Public safety programs for the immigrant community: 17 good practices in U.S. cities.* Washington, DC: National League of Cities and Municipal Action for Immigrant Integration. Retrieved from http://www.nlc.org/find-city-solutions/research-innovation/immigrant-integration

Guerette, R. T. (2006). *Disorder at day labor sites.* (Problem-Oriented Guides for Police Problem Specific Guide Series No. 44). Washington, DC: U.S. Department of Justice, Office of Community Oriented

Policing Services. Retrieved from http://www.popcenter .org/Problems/problem-disorder_daylabor.htm

Khashu, A. (2009). *The role of local police: Striking a balance between immigration enforcement and civil liberties.* Washington DC: Police Foundation. Retrieved from http://www.policefoundation.org/strikingabalance/ strikingabalance.html

Khashu, A., Busch, R., Latif, Z., & Levy, F. (2005). *Building strong police-immigrant community relations: Lessons from a New York City project.* New York, NY: Vera Institute of Justice. Retrieved from http://www .vera.org/download?file=83/300_564.pdf

Lysakowski, M., Pearsall, A. A., III, & Pope, J. (2009). *Policing in new immigrant communities.* Washington, DC: U.S. Department of Justice, Office of Community Oriented Policing Services. Retrieved from http://www .cops.usdoj.gov/RIC/ResourceDetail.aspx?RID=526

Moy, J., & Archibald, B. (2005, June). Reaching English-as-a-second-language communities. *The Police Chief, 72*(6). Retrieved from http://policechiefmagazine.org/ magazine/index.cfm?fuseaction=display&article_ id=614&issue_id=62005

Police Executive Research Forum. (2010). *Police and immigration: How chiefs are leading their communities through the challenge.* Washington, DC: Author. Retrieved from http://policeforum.org/library/ immigration/PERFImmigrationReportMarch2011.pdf

Police Executive Research Forum. (2012). *Voices from across the country: Local law enforcement officials discuss the challenge of immigration enforcement.* Washington, DC: Author. Retrieved from http:// policeforum.org/library/immigration/ VoicesfromAcrosstheCountryonImmigration Enforcement.pdf

Schofield, R., & Alston, M. (2006, February). Accommodating limited English proficiency in law enforcement. *CALEA Update, 90.* Retrieved from http://onlineresources.wnylc.net/pb/orcdocs/ LARC_Resources/LEPTopics/LE/LEPinLE/limited english.htm

Shah, S., & Estrada, R. (2009). *Bridging the language divide: Promising practices for law enforcement.* New York, NY: Vera Institute of Justice. Retrieved from http://www.vera.org/content/bridging-language-divide-promising-practices-law-enforcement

Shah, S., Rahman, I., & Khashu, A. (2007). *Overcoming language barriers: Solutions for law enforcement.* New York, NY: Vera Institute of Justice. Retrieved from http://www.vera.org/content/overcoming-language-barriers-solutions-law-enforcement

Venkatraman, B. A. (2006, April). Lost in translation: Limited English proficient populations and the police.

The Police Chief, 73(4). Retrieved from http:// policechiefmagazine.org/magazine/index .cfm?fuseaction=display&article_id=861&issue_ id=42006

Immigration: Issues, Law, and Police Training

The general increase of the immigrant population in the late 20th century and early 21st century in the United States has caused an increase in local, state, and tribal law enforcement encounters with both legal and illegal immigrants during routine police duties; accordingly, the need for law enforcement officers to have a working knowledge of immigration law and policy has increased concurrently as well. In response to these demands, the federal Office of Community Oriented Policing Services (COPS) sought a single, national officer training program, rather than each state or local police agency spending valuable time and training funds trying to develop individual programs. In 2007, the COPS Office provided funding for a private corporation and public university to develop and implement a pilot web-based Basic Immigration Enforcement Training (BIET) program, which was available for free to the first 500 law enforcement officers and later offered at a nominal charge through a private web-based provider. The COPS Office's funding and continued support for the BIET program evidences the extent of and concern for immigration issues in the community policing arena.

This entry examines the policing issues that surround immigration and some of the related laws that govern law enforcement at all levels, including police problems in dealing with immigrants, the specifics of BIET training, and the nexus of a 2012 U.S. Supreme Court decision specifying what police actions are permitted when dealing with suspected illegal immigrants.

Illegal Immigration

According to the Pew Hispanic Center, there are now an estimated 11.5 million illegal immigrants in the United States—the lowest number in a decade, and still declining. From 2000 to 2005, an average of 800,000 illegal immigrants entered the United States annually, and since then, an average of 500,000 arrive per year. This decline is the result of several factors. Increased patrolling and enforcement have had an impact. The federal Immigration and Customs Enforcement (ICE) has stepped up the frequency of its raids on U.S. businesses that employ illegal immigrants. Furthermore, the U.S. economic recession of the mid- and late 2000s resulted in fewer immigrants coming here because jobs were disappearing.

The reasons for immigrants wishing to come to the United States are varied. Some want to relocate here primarily in order to live a productive and more comfortable life. Conversely, there are some who enter the United States in order to plan, facilitate, and commit terrorist acts on U.S. soil. Whatever the reasons for illegal immigration, it presents significant challenges for federal and local law enforcement.

How the United States should address illegal immigration is controversial politically, economically, and socially, affecting policymakers, business owners, police, and private citizens. Politicians—conservatives and liberals alike—have had to balance the need for favorable business conditions with national security concerns and the rising costs of providing public assistance.

For example, President George W. Bush signed into law the Secure Fence Act of 2006, which allocated $1.2 billion for a "double-layer," nearly 650-mile system of physical barriers between the United States and Mexico. Included were 299 miles of vehicle barriers, 350 miles of pedestrian fencing, checkpoints, lighting, cameras, satellites, and unmanned aerial vehicles along the southwestern border in areas of California, Arizona, New Mexico, and Texas, where more than 95% of all illegal border crossings occur.

State and local lawmakers have also sought to control the illegal immigrants who make it through the federal government's border protections by limiting their opportunities to obtain work, housing, and even driver's licenses. In 2008, more than 200 state laws were enacted relating to immigration, the majority of which focused on restrictions aimed at illegal immigrants and their employers. In 2011, Georgia lawmakers introduced a bill to make the written driver's license test English-only. The bill was tabled, but the action opened fierce national debate over offering driving tests in foreign languages. And in 2010, the city of Fremont, Nebraska, passed a municipal ordinance prohibiting business owners and landlords from hiring and renting to illegal immigrants, sparking a national conflict over municipal power to control immigrants in their own backyard. Similar ordinances were passed in Pennsylvania and Texas, but federal judges struck down all of the ordinances in whole or in part.

Law and a U.S. Supreme Court Decision

In April 2010, the Arizona legislature enacted Senate Bill 1070 (Support Our Law Enforcement and Safe Neighborhoods Act), the most stringent immigration enforcement law in U.S. history. Intruding on what had historically been almost exclusive federal jurisdiction over immigration issues, Arizona lawmakers passed the first-ever state "trespassing" law that criminalized the mere status of being in the country illegally. The law also prescribed jail time for immigrants who fail to carry their federal registration documents and who seek work in Arizona. But the most controversial aspect of the law, and indeed the most critical for community policing, was the requirement that police officers make a "reasonable attempt" to determine the immigration status of a person if the officer has "reasonable suspicion" that such person is an illegal immigrant.

Critics charged that the provision—known as the "show me your papers law"—required officers to engage in state-mandated racial profiling, so the legislature ultimately passed an amendment providing that race, color, or national origin alone could not trigger reasonable suspicion and that officers could determine the immigration status of a person only while in the process of a lawful stop, detention, or arrest (the original language referred only to "lawful contact"). Despite the compromise amendment, several immigrants' rights groups and other organizations challenged the law, ultimately taking their fight to the U.S. Supreme Court. The Court issued its 5–3 decision in June 2012 (*Arizona v. United States*, 567 U.S. ___ [2012]). All of the law's provisions were struck down except the one that most affected police officers: requiring them to act on reasonable suspicion to check a person's immigration status while enforcing other laws.

Many police officials had hoped the Court's decision would settle the long-running debate about what role officers should play in immigration enforcement. Instead, the Court's decision raised additional questions. For example, how long must officers wait for federal authorities to respond when they question someone concerning their immigration status? (The workload placed on federal agencies to handle such inquiries is anticipated to be immense.) If the police release a person too soon, are they exposing themselves to a lawsuit for failing to enforce the law? How do they avoid being sued for racial profiling? What justifies reasonable suspicion that someone is in the country illegally? The answers to such questions are still being formulated by individual officers, agencies, and lawmakers.

Training in Immigration Law

The Supreme Court's decision on the Arizona law made immigration enforcement an even more challenging legal arena for the police, triggering the need for formal training to ensure fair and just enforcement of immigration laws. The COPS-funded BIET program was designed to respond to that need for local, state, and tribal law enforcement officers by addressing topics such as the following:

- *Identifying false identification:* Federal law prohibits the production "without lawful authority an identification document or a false identification document" (18 U.S.C. § 1028). But technology now allows counterfeiters to make false documents appear legitimate—to include the state hologram, watermarks, even bar codes. The police dilemma is daunting: How can they keep citizens safe if they do not know the true identity of the people they arrest? Some federal, state, and local authorities have developed a plan whereby each person who is arrested is fingerprinted using a fingerprint apparatus connected to a computerized database, which then relays the person's identity (from known fingerprints) to the local police within 30 minutes. If that person is an illegal immigrant, U.S. Immigration and Customs Enforcement (ICE) agents will interview the immigrant, detain as necessary, and if warranted, begin the deportation process.

Local law enforcement officers also have technology to authenticate passports, driver's licenses, and ID cards, and validate employee and visitor identification. In addition, officers can process magnetic stripes and bar-coded data from licenses and ID cards to calculate age and record document transactions in a local network and save images of each document along with a cropped facial image from photo IDs. Such technologies allow officers to perform cross-checks against information contained in other documents and datasets, and can verify data contained in electronic passports.

- *Consular notification:* If foreign nationals in the United States are arrested or detained, officers must inform them that they can notify their country's embassy or consulate, and embassy or consulate officials must be allowed access upon request. In some cases, officers must notify the foreign embassy regardless of the individual's wishes. Notification is also required when a foreign national dies or is involved in an airplane crash or shipwreck, or a guardian is appointed for a foreign national who is a minor or an incompetent adult.

- *Nonimmigrant visas:* International visitors wishing to visit or reside in the United States temporarily for purposes of business, work, tourism, or study have to obtain nonimmigrant visas. These visas are effective for a limited time—from six months to several years—and can be extended. Most nonimmigrants can be accompanied or joined by spouses and unmarried minor (or dependent) children.

- Differences between immigrant and nonimmigrant status:

  o *Immigrant status* (also known as a Lawful Permanent Resident [LPR]) is granted to one who has the right by the U.S. Customs and Immigration Service to reside permanently in the United States and to work without restrictions. Such immigrants are issued a "green card" (USCIS Form I-551), which is evidence of their LPR status.

  o *Nonimmigrant* status is granted to one who has the right to reside temporarily in the United States. (e.g., foreign students) and who may enter the country on an F-1 visa; such persons may or may not be allowed to work in the United States, and some may or may not have rigid time limits for their stay. Specific rules apply to each nonimmigrant person, and if even one of these rules is violated for at least 180 days, the nonimmigrant can be deported and cannot reenter the United States for three years. Those who violates their conditions for more than one year are deportable and unable to reenter the United States for 10 years.

The ever-changing immigrant population in the United States poses a host of challenges to police officers. The COPS-funded BIET training program provides information about federally identified immigration laws and issues, and the U.S. Supreme Court has provided guidance on enforcing statutes like Arizona's "show me your papers" law. Training and knowledge of the law, together with fundamental community policing principles, helps to prepare local police agencies to address the changing face of illegal immigration.

Pamela M. Everett and Kenneth J. Peak

See also Community Oriented Policing Services, Office of; Counterterrorism and Community Policing; Cybercrime and Community Policing; Demographics, Future Impact on Community Policing; Homeland Security; Terrorism, Future Impact of Community Policing on

Further Readings

Johnson, K., & Biskupic, J. (2010, April 30). Arizona immigration crackdown raises flags. *USA TODAY*. Retrieved from http://www.usatoday.com/news/nation/2010–04–29-arizona-immigration_N.htm

Kelly, E. (2010, April 24). Arizona immigration law revives calls for federal action on reform. Retrieved from http://www.azcentral.com/news/articles/2010/04/24/20100424arizona-immigration-bill-federal-action.html?nclick_check=1#comments

Kleiman, M. A. R. (2002). The false ID problem. *Journal of Policy Analysis and Management, 21*(2), 283–286. doi: 10.1002/pam.10029

Miller, R., & Aguilar, D. (2009, May). *Basic immigration enforcement training (BIET). Final report.* Lawton, OK: Cameron University and Advanced Systems Technology.

Pacific Institute of Research and Evaluation, Myers, D., Willingham, M., & Stewart, K. (2001/2011). *Law enforcement guide to false identification and illegal ID use.* Calverton, MD: Author. Retrieved from http://www.udetc.org/documents/FalseIdentification.pdf

Sullivan, B. (2004, August). *9/11 report light on ID theft issues: Scant mention raises civil liberties concerns.* NBCNEWS.com. Retrieved from http://www.msnbc.msn.com/id/5594385/ns/us_news-security/t/report-light-id-theft-issues/

U.S. Department of State, Bureau of Diplomatic Security. (2011, July). *Diplomatic and consular immunity: Guidance for law enforcement and judicial authorities* (DOS Report 10524). Washington, DC: Author. Retrieved from http://www.state.gov/documents/organization/150546.pdf

IMPLEMENTATION OF COMMUNITY POLICING

The implementation of community policing is crucial to the eventual success and longevity of adopting the concept within a policing organization and the community it serves. When implementing community policing, one of the most important decisions police management make is the scope of change they want to undertake. If a more limited approach is preferred, implementation can be a simple, straightforward endeavor. However, if a more in-depth change is sought, implementation can become a complex three-stage process (pre-implementation, implementation, and post-implementation) involving many phases with concurrent internal and external foci. It requires an administrator who understands the department and the community it represents as well as the assets, strengths, weaknesses, limitations, and capacities of each entity. In essence, implementing community policing requires both strong management skills and well-honed leadership abilities. Furthermore, implementation requires specified knowledge of the phases of planned change, organizational behavior, underlying theoretical and conceptual principles, transformational leadership traits, and assessment of the process. In this entry, each of the three stages of implementation is discussed separately before being integrated to provide a complete picture of the complex community policing implementation process.

Pre-Implementation Stage

Successful implementation of organization-wide community policing begins far before the change is put into motion. The planning stage is crucial and time consuming, consisting of goal setting and the creation of a management foundation. While community policing in practice is often discussed as a bottom-up concept, implementation within a department is top-down, starting with an executive decision and the commitment to complete the process from inception to completion. Pre-implementation begins by training all sworn and non-sworn personnel in the organization on community policing and problem solving, focusing on the underlying philosophies as well as strategies and practices. Furthermore, it requires identifying stakeholders within the organization and community that are most likely to support the idea as well as those that are most likely to resist. In this phase, police executives define what community policing means in their organization and community. This is done through internal (other administrators within the department, officers, and staff) and external (administrators in other agencies, community stakeholders, policymakers whose decisions impact police operations, and previous literature) communication. This early communication informally begins the implementation phase and primes the organization for the change that will soon take place.

If the original scope decision is for an organization-wide version of community policing, further pre-implementation phases are required before the executives proceed. This is where theoretical and conceptual knowledge become paramount through reviewing previous literature and research, as does understanding the behavior of organizations going through change. In this phase, the executives must embrace the notion of innovation and beware of mimetic isomorphism (institutions in the same organizational field becoming similar through mimicking what other have done) without greater attention to their unique organizational history and community environment. Furthermore, research has found that community policing through the utilization of federal grants often becomes a form of coercive isomorphism—influencing departments that accept the grants to become the same in terms of structure or process. Thus, executives must be keenly aware of the pitfalls of isomorphism when planning the implementation of community policing and focus on innovative management methods to avoid the failures described and detailed in the community policing literature.

In this phase, budgeting issues are addressed through planning. The implementation of an organizationwide change to full community policing requires incurring costs (for planning, training, equipment, meetings, information systems, additional officers, and other needs to ensure success). Failure to allocate these resources through the budgeting process in the pre-implementation stage can hamper the implementation stage; thus, during this stage, budgeting becomes a management priority, especially in times of resource scarcity. Furthermore, the allocation of funds to the organizational change formalizes that the process will be moving forward and expresses that the organization values

the change. This approach also clearly delineates the monetary costs of the transition to community policing and has the potential to spur the search for grants to offset these costs, providing a benefit for the organization and its stakeholders.

Research has found that a participatory management style is often associated with successful implementation of community policing. Under this management style, the executive or executive team makes a conscientious effort to be open, inclusive, and available to all internal and external stakeholders. Within a formal, traditional police hierarchy, this type of management style requires transformative, not transactional, leadership. Transformational leaders get the community and officers to buy-in to the change taking place. Thus, community policing cannot be mandated within a department even though implementation is a top-down process because stakeholders may find ways to resist, defy, pacify, and bargain rather than comply or acquiesce to the pressures of change. To overcome this, transformational leaders enable others to accept, if not embrace, the change, bring them into the network, and permit their opinions to be heard while relinquishing some of the control and command of the traditional police structure.

As the pre-implementation stage progresses, police executives formalize a community network, assembling stakeholders with a commitment to change. They ask and answer questions such as

Who are our partners and what role do they play?

What changes to accountability and organizational decision making is being sought?

What citizen groups, school personnel, civic and business leaders, churches, nonprofits, and other entities need to be included in the process?

What is the past and current state of police-citizen relations in the jurisdiction?

All of these questions frame the structural community network through which the process of community policing will take place once fully implemented.

Once the avenues of communication are formally opened and transparent, the network formed and activated, the organizational pitfalls addressed, and the participatory management style embraced, police executives must put all those areas to work in defining the department's new values, focusing on the changes to structure and process that will accompany the philosophical change, and deciding on the outcomes sought as a result of implementation. These areas require considerable effort and time spent with internal and community stakeholders in the proper balance. Through consultation, discussion, and communication, the department reevaluates the values that will drive it toward new outcomes after community policing is implemented. While the department is still expected to maintain order, enforce the law, and control crime, the move toward community policing includes new values, such as citizen satisfaction, citizen participation, and a focus on disseminating and receiving information throughout all levels of the policing organization. These values determine what changes to structure and processes need to be undertaken to achieve new goals based on the new values. For example, if police response-to-calls times have been found to be a problem within the community, then the patrol division would need to value a more rapid response, with goals based on that value. Changes to patrol assignments or shifts can then be made or adjusted and the dispatch and response methods can be analyzed to formulate more rapid response and the community's reaction, which are measurable outcomes. Without this step, changes made would not be pertinent or purpose driven, undermining the adoption of community policing.

The final step of the pre-implementation process is the formal communication of values, goals, and changes through internal training sessions and community meetings to inform external stakeholders. While information about the organizational change taking place may be relayed informally (such as by rumor or word of mouth) in the department, police executives need to directly articulate the scope of changes to increase the understanding of all stakeholders. This can be done only after the community network is assembled and values, goals, and outcomes have been decided. As with any organization, changes not clearly articulated to the stakeholders may be met with resistance, and the line supervisors and officers as well as staff at all levels need to be informed of their expected roles and functions in the new policing philosophy being implemented. They need to be participants, not followers; active in the change, not passive; and they need to be enabled, not commanded. Similarly, community stakeholders need to understand the changes taking place as well

as their expected roles. Without such an approach, there may be confusion, misunderstanding, apprehension, and resistance, all issues which can impact the implementation stage.

Implementation Stage

While the pre-implementation stage is executive focused, the implementation stage is more leadership driven. During this stage, police administrators and supervisors utilize certain traits of leadership—motivation skills, communication, determination, commitment, and setting of examples—to ensure the desired change takes root within the organization as intended, researched, and designed.

Institutional organizations have been known to resist change, bargain to not fully enact the change sought, or exhibit outright defiance for various reasons. To guard against internal resistance, police administrators can go into the field with officers to monitor officers' actions and determine whether implementation has taken place. Further, rather than discipline or punish officers who are resisting, the administrators directly counsel them in the appropriate actions.

During the early stages of implementation, police executives must be in constant communication with the policing network: staff, officers, supervisors, policymakers, local politicians, community stakeholders, and local media. This informs the public at large of the changes that can be expected in the police services they receive and puts the pressure on the police personnel to adhere to the new roles and expectations placed upon them. As such, implementation cannot be an internally driven process, a major feature which separates community policing from the traditional professional model, which was closed from the public. In fact, the implementation process itself is intended to open up these formally closed hierarchies. Importantly, the police administrators and supervisors must be committed and dedicated to the changes taking place to truly implement their vision of community policing. It is a complex process to reorient an entrenched institution to a new and different way of viewing its mission, role, and function. Change may be slow, meaning implementation is an ongoing process that cannot have a definitive "start date" but is rather subtly enacted from conception to action over time. Such a transition can be difficult for some officers and supervisors, especially those who have been on the job for a significant amount of time. In this stage, police administrators and supervisors hold officers and the community accountable for performance and effort, but do so through enablement rather than command and control.

The implementation phase is also the time when the department, having actually enacted community policing, begins to seek grants, enhance community partnerships, build the community network, and undertake research on the outcomes sought. This final feature of community policing is often forgotten but is extremely important to measuring success of the pre-implementation and implementation phases. The administration can seek research partners to gauge the attitudes and thoughts of officers, supervisors, and citizens throughout the community with which to measure success or shortcomings after implementation. This knowledge informs police administrators of the organizational and community pulse for the changes that are being implemented so they can address the issues as they arise. Thus, during implementation, police administrators must be hands-on, evidence driven, available, and open, both internally and externally to motivate the change rather than mandate it.

This participatory management style combined with transformational and consistent leadership is important for implementing community policing throughout an entire policing organization. However, rather than deciding to implement an organization change that requires a new philosophy and management approach, structures, processes, and outcomes combined with enhanced leadership skills, many agencies defer to just adding a community policing office or a few community policing officers. Research has often found that community policing not implemented to its full potential in the organizational field is often resisted internally to a large degree.

Post-Implementation Stage

A final stage that is vital to the successful implementation of community policing but is often overlooked is that of post-implementation analysis, assessment, reflection, and adjustment. As stated earlier, implementing community policing on an organizational scale is an ongoing process of transitional phases. Simply stating that a policing agency's "community polices" does not make it so, and institutional resistance can often delay or deny the proper implementation as designed and envisioned. Thus, leadership and management are equally important in this stage for success and longevity.

A key component of successful implementation of community policing is communication, and this is crucial in each stage of the process for different reasons. After formal implementation, police administrators must allow feedback and information to come up through the chain of command and in from outside the organization in contrast to the top-down approach required during the pre-implementation phase. In this stage, leaders listen to other stakeholders critically to analyze the scope and impact of the change undertaken. This communication is informal (rumor and word of mouth) as well as formal (internal meetings, community meetings, survey research, e-mails, and letters) and provides the evidence to reflect and reassess.

After feedback from line officers, supervisors, staff, police executives, and community stakeholders is received, such feedback is assessed and analyzed to determine necessary adjustments. This is when questions should be asked:

What are the outcomes of the organizational change?

Are stakeholders reacting as expected?

Has buy-in been established?

Has resistance receded or expanded?

A multitude of other questions can also be asked during this stage to hone the approach taken within the organization to accommodate environmental influences and stakeholder input. This is accomplished through careful assessment of the approach taken, the effectiveness of leadership, the outcomes attained, the beliefs of the organization's personnel, and the state of police-community relations.

Further changes can then be made to the community policing process to accommodate what has been learned and enhance further implementation of new changes. This is why momentum is important. Police administrators assess and analyze while leaders reflect, adjust, and maintain positive momentum through renewed dedication and commitment, even if the department falls short in some areas.

Complete Picture

Properly implementing a complete, holistic, conceptually grounded, practical version of community policing within a largely closed institutional organization is a complex process. Implementation requires the skills of a strong police chief executive with the traits of a transformative leader. It requires someone with the ability to cede control and command within the organization while blurring the lines between *us* and *them* that is fundamental to the traditional model of policing. It requires the community to participate in the process of policing at greater levels than under the traditional model. It requires officers to accept and understand the change and its importance and to trust their leadership and supervision. It requires supervisors to bridge the gap between the conceptual notion of community policing and its practical application at the nexus of officer and citizen. It requires communicating vertically and horizontally, opening a closed system, building and maintaining action and exchange networks, creating new processes to reach new outcomes, and importantly, it requires all stakeholders to live up to new expectations.

Joseph Ferrandino

See also Community Policing: Resources, Time and Finances in Support of; Decentralizing the Organization/Organizational Change; Strategic Planning

Further Readings

Adams, R. E., Rohe, W. M., & Arcury, T. A. (2002). Implementing community-oriented policing: Organizational change and street officer attitudes. *Crime and Delinquency, 48*(3), 399–430. doi: 10.1177/0011128702048003003

Chappell, A. T. (2009). The philosophical versus actual adoption of community policing: A case study. *Criminal Justice Review, 34*(1), 5–28. doi:10.1177/0734016808324244

Cochran, J. K., Bromley, M. L., & Swando, M. J. (2002). Sheriff's deputies' receptivity to organizational change. *Policing: An International Journal of Police Strategies and Management, 25*(3), 507–529. doi: 10.1108/13639510210437014

Glensor, R. W., & Peak, K. J. (1996). Implementing change: Community-oriented policing and problem solving. *FBI Law Enforcement Bulletin, 65*(7), 14–21.

Redlinger, L. J. (1994). Community policing and changes in organizational structure. *Journal of Contemporary Criminal Justice, 10*(1), 36–58.

Sparrow, M. K. (1988). *Implementing community policing.* NCJ 114217. U.S. Department of Justice, National Institute of Justice. Retrieved from https://www.ncjrs.gov/pdffiles1/nij/114217.pdf

Williams, E. J. (2003). Structuring in community policing: Institutionalizing innovative change. *Police Practice and Research, 4*(2), 119–129. doi: 10.1080/1561426032000084909

IN-SERVICE TRAINING

In-service training provides police officers with the ongoing opportunity to develop, reinforce, and maintain important knowledge, skills, and abilities. In-service training also provides officers with a means for maintaining their police certification, which is required in many states. In-service training ensures that officers have access to the most current and relevant training topics needed in providing effective police services, including topics associated with the community policing approach and it strategies. Building upon the foundational training content found in basic police academy and field training programs, in-service training creates momentum for officers who are actively seeking to learn more effective ways of policing. This entry briefly discusses the background of in-service training, the important role it plays in an officer's career, and the need to continually provide community policing-related in-service training opportunities. The entry concludes with a discussion on the future trends and needs of in-service police training.

In-Service Police Training Programs

In-service training has become an essential part of a police officer's career. Over the course of the last three decades, police training has continued to become more professionalized and standardized, with many efforts being made to continually provide in-service training opportunities to keep officers current on their professional knowledge, skills, and abilities. Among the police leaders who were at the forefront of this development were Berkeley (California) Police Chief August Vollmer during the early 1900s through the 1920s, and Chicago

(Illinois) Superintendent of Police O. W. Wilson in the 1960s; both recognized the need to provide ongoing training for police officers. Today, all 50 states provide some type of either mandatory or nonmandatory in-service training for officers. This continual offering of in-service training of police officers not only enables officers to perform their duties more efficiently and safely, it limits potential liabilities from civil actions that may arise from an officer's actions and gives an officer documented expertise when having to support their actions or testify in court.

The delivery of in-service training generally occurs through formal classroom instruction ranging from 4- to 40-hour blocks of instruction. While classroom training may be the most prominent method of delivering in-service training, it is not the only option. Advancements in technology and shrinking agency training budgets have required more and more police departments to look for alternative delivery methods, including instruction provided online or in an electronic format, webinars, and during roll call or shift briefings. Private companies, universities, police academies, and local community colleges have also emerged as viable alternatives in developing and delivering specialized in-service police training programs. These providers offer a great deal of in-service training for officers, with 88% of all current police academies alone offering in-service training to police officers.

Topics for in-service training of police officers can include community policing and problem solving, ethics, law and legal updates, domestic violence, and firearms qualifications. While the topics listed above are examples of in-service training topics, not all are mandatory. Mandatory in-service training is generally directed toward high-risk and high-liability topics, or topics that are required to maintain an officer's certification. The high-risk and high-liability topics that most states have identified as mandatory include domestic violence, firearms, use of force, vehicular pursuit, law and legal updates, bloodborne pathogens, hazardous materials, and CPR and first aid. These mandatory topics are usually instructed by certified police instructors or subject matter experts (SMEs), and often occur within the individual officer's police agency.

In-service training allows officers to maintain their certification by providing documented learning. Certification requirements for officers can occur

at a number of different levels. For many, basic officer certification is the first level of certification required in order to meet state minimum standards. This certification process begins at the basic recruit academy and concludes with an officer successfully completing the field officer training program. Once officers complete basic certification requirements, they move to maintaining that certification, usually through in-service training. As officers advance in their careers, many move into supervisory, mid-management, and executive-level positions. In these positions, most states require annual training to maintain advanced officer certification levels. In-service training provides individuals in advanced positions with the training that is needed to support supervisory, mid-management, and executive-level responsibilities. Much of the advanced in-service training includes ethics, leadership, budget administration, risk management, critical thinking, and decision making. Although mandatory and certification maintenance training is often directed toward leadership and management-related topics, most states also recognize the need and importance of providing additional in-service training topics that are beneficial to all officers regardless of their positions or responsibilities.

One such topic that is often provided through in-service training is community policing. Community policing continues to play an important role in an officer's career. In-service training is an essential component in ensuring that officers receive ongoing community policing training.

The Role of Community Policing in In-Service Training

Increased demands and expectations on police officers are requiring many law enforcement agencies to rethink their approaches to policing. Many police agencies are experiencing tightened budgets and smaller work forces, making it more challenging to provide adequate police services.

One significant organization that has provided ongoing support for in-service community policing training is the U.S. Department of Justice's Office of Community Oriented Policing Services (COPS). In 1994, under the direction of the Clinton administration, the COPS office was formed to help hire, train, and equip newly hired police officers. In 1996, the COPS office created a national network of Regional

Community Policing Institutes (RCPIs) to help train officers in applying community policing strategies. Through the RCPIs and a number of additional training venues, including in-service training, the COPS has disseminated 5 million training and technical assistance publications to the law enforcement field and trained more than 600,000 law enforcement practitioners.

There remains an ongoing need for officers to receive in-service training on community policing. Police officers need to be able to find creative and innovative approaches to solving problems, leveraging resources, and promoting effective community partnerships. As officers continue in their careers, they will be challenged with complex problems that may often require them to use untraditional approaches. In-service community policing training can provide officers with effective strategies to help solve problems by using strategies such as the SARA (scanning, analyze, response, assessment) problem-solving model, whereby they take complex reoccurring problems and systematically work them to successful resolution. In-service training directed toward community policing can also help reinforce and remind officers of the philosophy of community policing, in which the police and community work together as they build trust, mutual respect, and commitment toward achieving common goals. Officers at all levels can benefit from in-service training in community policing, and a commitment to providing this training must remain a priority for police agencies.

Future Needs of In-Service Training

As a new generation of police officers enters policing, in-service training will have to expand and adapt to advancements in technology, increasing diversity and social changes, economic distress, and threats of terrorism. Thus, in-service training must continually seek to provide the most comprehensive and innovative ways to prepare officers in performing their duties. In-service training will continue to play a role in keeping officers safe by providing annual training in officer safety areas, such as firearms, defensive tactics, and emergency vehicle operations.

Other important training topics, including community policing, problem solving, critical thinking, diversity, and communications, will also likely remain essential training topics. In-service training must continue to build upon the proven principles and adult learning practices that create training opportunities that support an officer's role and responsibilities. With continued advancements in policing, more emphasis is being placed on the importance of in-service training and the expectation that this training will create more professional and prepared officers. In-service training remains a vital and active part of a police officer's ongoing career development.

Brian Kauffman

See also Citizen Police Academies; Community Oriented Policing Services, Office of; Mentoring; Model Curriculum; Police Training Officer (PTO) Program; Regional Community Policing Institutes

Further Readings

Bumbak, A. R. (2009). *Dynamic police training*. Boca Raton, FL: CRC Press.
Charles, M. T. (2000). *Police training—Breaking all the rules*. Springfield, IL: Charles C Thomas.
Neil, R. H., Sr. (2011). *Police instructor: Deliver dynamic presentations, create engaging slides, & increase active learning*. Cleveland, OH: CreateSpace.

INTELLIGENCE-LED POLICING

Intelligence-led policing (ILP) is a business model for managing policing resources that originated in Great Britain during the late 1990s. It allows police leadership to address crime problems and improve the allocation of resources through the use of crime analysis and criminal intelligence. Its purpose is to provide law enforcement executives with information to make communities safer.

ILP emphasizes the sharing of information and collaboration to address crime problems. As a result, ILP is viewed as congruent with current law enforcement philosophies and strategies exhibited in community policing and problem-oriented policing. This entry describes how ILP, adopted by law enforcement agencies in the United States during the early 2000s, was expanded to address the rapid spread of communications and technologies that increased the sophistication of organized criminal groups and threats of terrorism.

Definitions

Disagreements exist about the definition of ILP and its utility in policing. This is particularly the case with the word *intelligence*, which has several meanings in law enforcement vernacular and in the law. Jerry Ratcliffe, in his 2008 book *Intelligence-Led Policing*, provides this definition:

> Intelligence-led policing is a business model and managerial philosophy where data analysis and crime intelligence are pivotal to an objective, decision-making framework that facilitates crime and problem reduction, disruption and prevention through both strategic management and effective enforcement strategies that target prolific and serious offenders. (p. 89)

David Carter, in *Law Enforcement Intelligence: A Guide for State, Local and Tribal Law Enforcement Agencies* (2004), characterized ILP as an underlying organizational philosophy that fits into all areas of operations and the overall mission of the agency. He further argued that ILP cannot be simplified as an add-on function but must be integrated into an agency's goals and functions. There are many other articles published in academic and government journals and practitioner magazines that identify the utility of ILP in addressing threats of terrorism. Law enforcement agencies adapt ILP to meet their individual needs. Some agencies focus more on its use as a business model, whereas others may use it to enhance their community and problem-oriented policing efforts.

Origins and Emergence in the United States

ILP began as an outcome of the Kent Constabulary's efforts in the United Kingdom during the 1990s to manage law enforcement resources efficiently and to respond effectively to serious crime. There was concern that police were spending too much time responding to crime problems and too little time targeting offenders.

In 2000, the National Criminal Intelligence Service published the *National Intelligence Model* (NIM), which established the following priorities for British police service:

- Target prolific offenders through overt and covert means.
- Manage crime and disorder hot spots.

- Identify and investigate linked series of crime or incidents.
- Apply prevention measures that include working with a broad range of other disciplines.

The priorities for NIM were based on research and the experiences of law enforcement practitioners. Longitudinal studies in the United States and United Kingdom demonstrated that that a small percentage of offenders are responsible for a majority of crimes. Research has also identified that traditional policing strategies, such as random patrol, rapid response, and retrospective investigations have little impact on crime and neighborhood disorder. Research also shows that crimes and calls for service cluster at specific locations. It is also known that collaboration among law enforcement agencies is vital to crime control and prevention strategies and tactics.

It is important, however, to understand that the dynamics of law enforcement in the United States vary from the U.K. model and present limitations in adopting NIM for America's law enforcement agencies. Implementation in the United Kingdom simply required that the Association of Chiefs of Police Officers (ACPO) for the 43 constabularies in England and Wales agree to adopt NIMS. The smallest constabulary has 900 officers that support the hiring of analysts and personnel to perform ILP functions. The United States, conversely, boasts nearly 17,000 law enforcement agencies, many with fewer than 10 officers and lacking the budgets or trained personnel necessary to perform ILP functions.

What Is Intelligence?

Intelligence is often a misused word. For some, the word *intelligence* invokes a negative impression of police abuse of citizens' privacy rights. Others view *intelligence* as synonymous with *information*. However, information is not intelligence; rather, information plus analysis equals intelligence, and without analysis, there is no intelligence. Intelligence is what is produced after collected data are evaluated and analyzed by a trained intelligence professional.

In the United States, the use of the word *intelligence* in the context of policing continues to raise concerns. Law enforcement agencies during the 1950s and 1960s were required to reform their intelligence-gathering practices as a result of abuses and violations of privacy. Police, on the other hand, have argued that restrictive government legislation hampers the ability of agencies to gather intelligence and maintain intelligence files crucial for crime-fighting efforts. Federal guidelines for how law enforcement agencies must acquire, use and store intelligence information are found in 28 Code of Federal Regulations (CFR) Part 23. There is an additional concern that some police agencies' restrictive interpretation of 28 CFR Part 23 has denied them the use of criminal intelligence they may legally acquire in their crime control and prevention efforts.

ILP Features and Functions

Successful adoption of ILP generally involves the following practices:

- Information collection is part of the organizational culture—the chief executive, supervisors, and managers encourage line officers and investigators to regularly collect and forward intelligence.
- Analysis is indispensable to tactical and strategic planning—record management systems are robust, analysts are well trained and equipped, actionable intelligence products are regularly produced to inform both tactical and strategic decisions.
- Enforcement tactics are focused, prioritized by community harm assessments, and prevention oriented; operations are mounted against repeat or violent offenders; serious organized (gang, trafficking, etc.) groups are identified and dismantled; traffic violations are enforced at dangerous intersections or roadways.

To be successful, ILP must include police executives, officers, and analysts working together to address crime issues. Such executives must work closely with analysts and officers to better understand crime problems and allocate necessary resources. Officers become better at collecting data and information important to developing operational intelligence. For analysts, the development of tactical and strategic intelligence reports is key. This means that officers are provided timely, tactical intelligence about crime problems, persons, and crime trends. Police executives are provided strategic intelligence that gives them a clear picture of the crime environment. Automated computer-aided dispatch, records management systems, crime analysis, and crime mapping provide vital tools for the crime analyst to examine crime data and produce actionable intelligence for the strategic needs of police executives and tactical needs for officers in the field.

Organizational Change

While long-term evaluations of the implementation of ILP have yet to be conducted, studies have identified challenges related to technical, organizational, and cultural factors. ILP, like many other innovations in policing, requires significant organizational change, which is commonly met with resistance at all levels. The successful implementation of any organizational change requires that a leader provide a vision for the organization and convince employees of the necessity and benefits of change. ILP presents additional challenges for many organizations that lack the funding to provide the technologies and trained personnel to analyze intelligence data and information. This means that duplicate entry of data is necessary to accomplish analysis, which creates problems with agencies that lack staffing to perform such functions.

Civil Rights Concerns

The inclusion of threats and terrorism into the U.S. model of ILP presents a host of civil rights concerns. The ongoing, contentious debate about the USA PATRIOT Act, enacted in 2001, demonstrates people's sensitivity to privacy rights issues. The most common concerns about the Patriot Act relate to the type of information it allows law enforcement agencies to gain access to, such as individuals' e-mail, the Internet sites they have visited, and their library records. Indeed, these concerns are reminiscent of Big Brother concerns voiced by citizens during the 1950s and 1960s. While this debate may not be resolved soon, it is important that law enforcement agencies provide citizens with answers to their questions about intelligence and their ILP efforts.

The ILP process may identify individuals and organizations about which there is no more than a reasonable suspicion of criminal involvement. As such, and in accordance with the guidelines established in 28 CFR Part 23, this information must be classified as "criminal intelligence." The rules of collection, retention, and dissemination of criminal intelligence information are vastly different from those for criminal investigation information. This requires that law enforcement agencies develop separate record-keeping systems to protect and restrict access to criminal intelligence information. Failure to follow the guidelines of 28 CFR Part 23 may subject an agency to civil liability.

ILP in Action

ILP requires that law enforcement agencies develop trusted relationships with the public and with private organizations to share information. Over the past three decades, many police agencies reorganized under a community policing philosophy that encouraged officers to build close and productive relationships with citizens. The benefits of these relationships are improved communication and sharing of information vital to addressing crime and safety in communities. The benefits for ILP are that close relationships with the public may also serve as a gateway of local information vital to preventing terrorism as well as other crimes.

Crime and Intelligence Analysts

Many police agencies have both crime analysts and intelligence analysts. Crime analysts keep their fingers on the pulse of crime in the jurisdiction: which crime trends are up, which ones are down, where the hot spots are, what type of property is being stolen, and so on. Intelligence analysts, on the other hand, are likely to be more aware of the specific people responsible for crime in the jurisdiction—who they are, where they live, what they do, who they associate with, and so on. Integrating these two functions—crime analysis and intelligence analysis—is essential for obtaining a comprehensive grasp of the crime picture. In sum, crime analysis allows police to understand the "who, what, when, and where" of crime (the question of "why" is often related to financial gain, but crime can also involve other motives), intelligence analysis focuses on providing an understanding the "who"—crime networks and individuals.

Suspicious Activity Reporting

In 2007, the federal government established a National Strategy for Information Sharing, which called for the establishment of a unified process for reporting, tracking, and accessing suspicious activity

reports in a manner that protects citizens' civil liberties. This resulted in a Nationwide Suspicious Activity Reporting (SAR) initiative. The basis of SAR is to help the public understand "what is suspicious" and provide a system of reporting concerns to law enforcement.

Law enforcement agencies have educated the public about suspicious activities in a number of ways. Some agencies have adopted citizen police academies where the public learn about SAR along with the various functions of their local law enforcement agency. Many agencies have developed public service announcements and short training videos played on public television and at churches and business group meetings. Each of these methods provides an opportunity to educate the public and further develop the trust necessary for police and citizens to exchange information.

Fusion Centers

Fusion centers were created by the U.S. Department of Justice for the purpose of improving information and intelligence across all levels of law enforcement, government agencies, and the private sector. The goal of fusion centers is to stop immediate or emerging threats using sophisticated crime and intelligence analysis technologies. Fusion centers serve as a clearinghouse for suspicious activities reported by law enforcement agencies, such as repeated reports of persons taking pictures of a water treatment plant, bridges, or federal buildings.

Fusion centers involve a collaborative effort of two or more state or local police agencies to provide resources, expertise, and information and thus maximizing their ability to investigate and respond to criminal and terrorist activity. Such centers are staffed with intelligence officers (who often must first receive a security clearance) who perform such duties as: analyzing intelligence and information to develop a comprehensive threat picture; reviewing relevant homeland security information; disseminating intelligence information to state and local agencies, other fusion centers, and the federal government; assisting in the identification, investigation, and apprehension of people, weapons, and related contraband that pose a threat to homeland security.

Examples of ILP in Action

The New Jersey State Police instituted a comprehensive ILP architecture in the wake of the terrorist attacks of September 11, 2001, in which terrorists hijacked four planes, flying two into the World Trade Center in New York, one into the Pentagon in northern Virginia, and the fourth crashing into a field in Pennsylvania. The purpose of the NJSP's ILP efforts was to address the agency's new responsibilities for homeland security.

One of the NJSP's first successes involved the work of leadership, analysts, and intelligence flow to disrupt the Nine Trey gang, which is a subset of the Bloods gang. Operation Nine Connect, as it was termed, resulted in the arrest of 90 gang members in 2006. The successes of the NJSP's use of ILP were largely a result of its ability to identify, target, infiltrate, and disrupt the gang. ILP moved the New Jersey State Police's analysts from a criminal case support role toward a more tactical and strategic role of assessing criminal intelligence information.

Conclusion

Since the late 1990s, law enforcement agencies across the United States and abroad have adopted strategies to encourage closer relations with the public in an effort to enhance safety in communities. Problem solving (an element of problem-oriented policing) provided an additional method of analyzing and responding to a variety of different crime and quality of life issues. ILP allows law enforcement agencies to optimize resource allocation based on a situational analysis of crime and safety that uses tactical and strategic crime analysis methods.

Ronald W. Glensor

See also Broken Windows Theory; CompStat; Crime Analysis; Crime Analyst; Crime Mapping; Predictive Policing; Problem-Oriented Policing: Elements, Processes, Implications; Problem-Solving Process (SARA); Terrorism, Future Impact of Community Policing on

Further Readings

Carter, D. L. (2004). *Law enforcement intelligence: A guide for state, local and tribal law enforcement agencies.* Washington, DC: U.S. Department of Justice, Office of Community Oriented Policing Services.

Heaton, R. (2000). The prospects for intelligence-led policing: Some historical and quantitative considerations. *Policing and Society, 9*(4), 337–355. doi: 10.1080/10439463.2000.9964822

New Jersey State Police. (2006). *Practical guide to intelligence-led policing.* New York, NY: Center for Policing Terrorism at the Manhattan Institute.

Ratcliffe, J. H. (2008). *Intelligence-led policing.* Cullompton, England: Willan.

U.S. Department of Homeland Security. (2012). *National network of fusion centers fact sheet.* Retrieved from http://www.dhs.gov/national-network-fusion-centers-fact-sheet#0

U.S. Department of Justice. (2005). *Intelligence-led policing: The new intelligence-led architecture.* NCJ 210861. Washington, DC: U.S. Department of Justice, Office of Justice Programs. Retrieved from https://www.ncjrs.gov/pdffiles1/bja/210681.pdf

INTERNATIONAL COMMUNITY POLICING

Community policing and problem-solving strategies are not limited to police agencies in the United States. Rather, these strategies are now practiced in a wide array of countries. As examples of the kinds of activities being practiced and successes realized, this entry briefly reviews community policing and problem-solving strategies in seven selected venues: Canada, Japan, Australia, Great Britain, Israel, Sweden, and the Netherlands.

Canada

Community policing has long been practiced in Canada. In fact, in 1994 Edmonton's Police Service received the prestigious Herman Goldstein Award for Excellence in Problem-Oriented Policing for its demonstration project to reduce thefts from automobiles. Another example of this practice is the Ontario Provincial Police, which began its entry into community policing with its Community Policing Development Centre and a website that explained the advantages of its community policing strategy over traditional, reactive policing. It also developed what it termed *P.A.R.E.*, for problem identification, analysis, response, and evaluation. In fact, P.A.R.E. proved invaluable in the 2000s for solving a problem involving deer-vehicle collisions—more than 400 collisions occurring in one year at a single location. A group composed of police, citizens, government agencies, and insurance companies analyzed the problem and considered several viable responses, including the installation of deer whistles on vehicles, improved signage, fencing, the expansion of deer hunting season, and a roadside reflector system that reflected car headlights, causing the deer to become motionless and not enter the roadway. The results were impressive: While vehicle-deer collisions almost doubled in the control area, the test area saw collisions reduced from 24 to four in a year. In addition, results included reduced emotional trauma on vehicle occupants, injuries, health care costs, and the amount of time previously spent by police investigating vehicle-deer collisions.

In Burnaby, an area of about 38 square miles on the southwest coast of Canada, the Royal Canadian Mounted Police (RCMP) developed and implemented a problem-solving strategy that won the prestigious Herman Goldstein Award in the United States for decreasing crime and disorder in three apartment buildings and the surrounding area. Using the SARA (scanning, analysis, response, assessment) problem-solving process, crimes and calls for service (CFS) were reduced by 40%.

Another recipient of the Herman Goldstein Award was the city of Vancouver, for its work with a problem involving a neighborhood next to the downtown area that was plagued by drug use and dealing. Analysis of the problem was accomplished from several perspectives, including the social dynamics of the problem population, the park structure and its effect on criminal behavior, past police responses, and community meetings and surveys. A variety of responses was employed, including the use of plainclothes, or undercover, operations, observation points set up in homes offered by area citizens, and a volunteer foot patrol that provided police with information about drug-dealing activities. The park board and local youths assisted with controlling graffiti and litter, while university criminal justice students' suggestions helped horticulturists to understand crime prevention through environmental design (CPTED) and how a local park should be changed to eliminate obstructed views and places where dealers hid their drugs. Furthermore, the local animal control department increased its enforcement of unleashed dogs that were being used by drug dealers to intimidate residents.

Japan

Japan's Showa Constitution contains many articles that are similar to those found in the Fourth, Fifth, Sixth, and Eighth Amendments to the U.S. Constitution. This nation can also lay claim to possessing the oldest community policing system in the world. Japan initiated its system immediately after World War II out of a combination of traditional Japanese culture and American democratic ideals. According to authors Jerome Skolnick and David Bayley in 1988, several elements seem to be at the core of this philosophy: (1) community-based crime prevention, (2) increased accountability to the public, and (3) decentralization of command.

Each of Japan's 47 prefectures has its own autonomous police force, and all of which emphasize community policing and community-based crime prevention. Officers deal face-to-face with citizens and therefore are a part of the community. Also, Japanese neighborhood crime prevention associations have helped to provide closer relationships between people.

Even though the Japanese police are very closely involved with—and, by U.S. standards, probably very intrusive into—peoples' lives (see, e.g., the discussion of kobans, below), the people appear to be far more willing than Americans to accept a police presence. As a result, Japanese police place great emphasis on order maintenance and crime prevention, aiding the community to resolve problems that could lead to disorder. A major part of this effort are counseling services that are part of every Japanese police station. All police stations assign an experienced officer, usually a sergeant, to provide a wide range of general counseling, ranging from family disputes to questions about contracts and indebtedness. Trained in dispute resolution, the police are able to provide a helpful informal conciliation. Rural police officers are required to visit each household twice per year and to work with citizens to resolve area problems.

Urban police officers visit households and do police business in small neighborhood police stations known as *kobans*. Kobans consist of a reception room with a low counter or desk, telephone, radio, and wall maps; a resting room for personnel, often with a television set; a small kitchen or at least a hot plate and refrigerator; an interview room; a storeroom; and a toilet. A koban may be found every few blocks; there are about 15,000 kobans across the country, 8,000 of which are referred to as *chuzaisho* or "police substations," in which the officers actually live. Police officers generally stand watch at the doorway of the koban or at nearby traffic intersections to help minimize crimes and traffic accidents, direct traffic, and make arrests when necessary. Officers also use the kobans to prepare and disseminate crime bulletins and provide citizens with tips concerning crime prevention. There are also mobile police boxes, or wagons, that assist the koban as needed, and temporary kobans can be established if needed. The Japanese police try to keep the number of people for which a koban is responsible to fewer than 12,000 and the area to less than four-tenths of a square mile. However, no koban may be less than six-tenths of a mile away from another one.

Australia

Community policing exists across Australia. In one example of a problem where police used the problem-solving approach, data analysis by Queensland, Australia, police revealed that residential burglaries had increased 176% during the previous 20 years and 66% during a recent five-year period. Analysis revealed two contributing factors to the burglary problem: a lack of proper security measures, and the ease with which stolen goods could be fenced for profit. Furthermore, there were high rates of repeat victimization and low rates of offender apprehension.

A response termed *Stopbreak* was implemented to address the primary contributing factors. A community policing approach was adopted, police were trained in proper security audit techniques, and hot spots were examined to reduce repeat victimization and home burglaries in general. Citizens were advised concerning crime prevention and proper security measures, and victims were referred to support organizations; homes and businesses that had been targets of repeat burglaries had temporary portable silent burglar alarms installed. These alarms were linked to police headquarters. An assessment found that officers and victims alike indicated that the strategies were substantially positive in nature, and a majority of

victims implemented at least one of the security measures recommended by the police.

Great Britain

There are presently 43 police forces in England and Wales, 27 of which are county, eight are combined police areas, and six are metropolitan forces (two more are combined units). Almost all police forces in this region are introducing or are actively considering the introduction of community policing.

Community policing in Great Britain is established and practiced to such an extent that each year it recognizes winners of its prestigious Tilley Award, established in 1999 to acknowledge a police agency's excellence in problem-oriented partnership principles. Tilley was a professor at Nottingham Trent University, carried out a considerable body of work in community policing in the United Kingdom, and was often commissioned by the Home Office (the governmental department responsible for immigration, security, and law and order) to develop problem-oriented policing.

Indeed, community policing and problem solving has progressed to such a level in Great Britain that the Home Office in London has published dozens of monographs on the subject (termed *Brit POP*), including two that are highly significant in the field: the Police Research Group's *Problem-Oriented Policing: Brit POP*, which described the early stages of a development project implementing problem-oriented policing in one division in Leicestershire, and *Brit POP II: Problem-Oriented Policing in Practice*, which highlighted the lessons learned for introducing and maximizing the benefits from problem-oriented policing.

The philosophy of community-oriented policing in Britain, as well as several important aspects of its practice, such as neighborhood-based patrols, can be traced to the formation of professional policing in the 19th century and the ways in which the police mandate was established and legitimated. As students of Sir Robert Peel's early efforts are aware, early architects of British policing established the idea that effective policing can be achieved only with the consent of the community. From the 1970s onward, arguments in favor of greater use of foot patrol have assumed an increasingly important place in public debate about policing in Britain.

Community surveys have found that people want more foot patrol, so there has been a return to the bobby on the beat. Foot patrol remains a key feature of community-oriented policing in Britain.

Almost all of the 43 police authorities in Great Britain have established formal police-community consultative committees. Some of the issues addressed by the committees are maintaining mutual trust between the police and the public; maintaining community peacefulness and improving quality of life; promoting greater public understanding of policing issues, such as causes of crime and police procedures and policies; examining patterns of complaints against officers; fostering links with local beat officers; and developing victim support services. For Britain's police, Neighborhood Watch forms the most common and popular form of community-based crime prevention. Neighborhood Watch programs have grown immensely in Britain.

Israel

In the mid-1990s, Israeli police decided to transition from the traditional form of policing to community policing and problem solving. For the previous 20 years, the national police force had been engulfed in security duties to deal with terrorism and other emergency matters. Because of a shift of police resources to antiterrorist and bomb disposal units, efforts to reduce crime at the local station level had not been successful, and domestic violence and family abuse had become particularly problematic.

A strategic plan was developed to implement the strategy, and a new headquarters unit was established to implement the planned change, beginning with a bottom-up approach that would start with the station level and officers in the field, who best knew the communities' problems. In phase one, the local police and mayors of many communities were approached and asked if they were willing to undertake the change to community policing; their enthusiasm was usually high. Then the officers and selected community leaders were trained in the working principles of community policing, including explanations of the need for the police and the public to collaborate and the problem-solving approach to analyzing and addressing problems.

A three-day planning workshop was held with the police and with community and local organizations and associations. Each police station's mission statement was developed and local problems and needs were scanned, prioritized, and analyzed. The strategic plan, including timetables, responsible persons, and needed resources was then developed.

By the second year of its implementation across Israel, more than 50 communities had undergone the shift to community policing. Cities were rewarded by being allowed to send one person abroad to study community policing and problem solving in other countries. Planning workshops were provided and headquarters' objectives were developed, leading to greater acceptance of the new philosophy. Community policing centers were established in various neighborhoods to decentralize services, and a major organizational change occurred that resulted in a greater flattening of the force to empower patrol officers working on the street.

Recently, because of increases in crime, particularly racketeering and drug trafficking, and the influx of immigrant groups, a major crime prevention initiative was launched that incorporated community policing. Citizen contact was strongly encouraged and programs developed to address domestic violence, auto theft, and teen alcohol consumption.

Sweden

Sweden began laying its foundation for community policing and problem solving in 1972 with the establishment of a national center for research, development, and coordination of policing; this center's aim was to reduce crime at its foundation. Later, during the 1990s, initiatives were taken to establish a new community policing function, developing officers who were acquainted with their areas of responsibility and who work in partnership with the local community. The cornerstones of community policing for the Swedish police are being visible in the community and crime prevention. Each community police station is responsible for a specified community police area, which is basically a geographic area within a district. Police activities are centered on a problem-oriented approach, with a focus on the underlying and direct causes of crime and public disorder. The community police officers then engage in a routine exchange of information with other public agencies in their area, such as schools, social services agencies, and so forth.

As part of its emphasis on community policing, a U.S.-type of National Council for Crime Prevention was formed to work with police, social services, and youth groups. Soon this organization began publishing monographs consisting of the best crime prevention techniques and ideas developed among local police departments nationwide. Eventually, local crime prevention councils were established in 232 of the country's towns and cities. The council also facilitated the expansion of community policing as well as provided a forum for the community and the police to exchange ideas. Police, for their part, became more user-friendly and accountable for their actions. Simultaneously, the Swedish police became very involved in situational crime prevention, a strategy aimed at reducing actual crime rates in neighborhoods by removing selected persons and target opportunities, mapping crimes, and evaluating their problem-solving efforts, based on clear goals, in selected areas.

The Netherlands

The Netherlands is a small country with virtually open borders, a multicultural population, and a high standard of living. Its police are regionalized into 25 forces, and with only 5,600 officers, the policing style is generally considered to be laid back and quite tolerant. Police officers are normally well trained and speak several languages, while having a great deal of autonomy with a focus on crime prevention. The mayor in each police region oversees the development of policing policies, and the police chief is subordinate to the mayor.

A recent development in the Netherlands' community policing initiatives has been the introduction of the community beat officer. Under this philosophy, emphases are placed on the proximity to the public, citizen involvement in dealing with crime problems, and the police working with local public and private agencies. Also relatively new is the extensive cooperation being fostered with external partners and the strong involvement of citizens in determining what issues should be addressed. But perhaps most important is the shift in responsibility. In each designated area, the community officer is held responsible for what is termed *organizing security*. If the officer requires assistance from colleagues in specialized departments, those specialists are obliged to help. Responsibility is thus pushed down to a lower level in the organization.

Recently the capital city, Amsterdam, experienced increases in street crimes on busy streets and in public transport and nightspot areas. In addition, there were large numbers of youths who were intoxicated and noisy, motorists ignoring traffic regulations, numerous pickpockets targeting tourists, local drug addicts shooting up and dealing in drugs in the area, and homeless and mentally ill individuals being aggressive on the streets. The police established one police district for the entire inner-city area, with six neighborhood teams consisting of 700 officers. As part of this new inner-city district, a special support team of 75 officers was tasked with the responsibility of maintaining public order in the entire district. Officers in this team could be sent into places where temporary disruptions of public order were anticipated. This team was able to regain authority and bring back a sense of norms, with a low tolerance for small breaches of law. For instance, urinating in public was identified as a major problem to be solved, especially after such behavior was found to be undermining the foundations of the 16th-century buildings in the downtown area. This zero-tolerance approach to infractions contradicted a long tradition of leniency toward deviance in the social order.

Summary

Community policing and problem-solving strategies are now in use around the world. The concept of community policing is equated with people interacting face to face, and the SARA problem-solving process drives problem solving efforts.

Several common themes or practices are present in this discussion: taking the police from their "mechanized fortresses" and putting them in closer contact with the public (together engaging in the use of problem-solving methods), decentralizing the organization to areas and neighborhoods, developing a sense of community, sharing decision making (empowerment) with the public, and initiating a pilot project before implementing the concept departmentwide.

While there may be vast cross-cultural and geographical differences among countries, community policing and problem-solving practices are not that different in the United States and other countries where they have been adopted.

Kenneth J. Peak

See also Building Partnerships and Stakeholders; Community Cohesion and Empowerment; Metropolitan Police Act of 1829; National Crime Prevention Council; Problem-Solving Process (SARA)

Further Readings

Bayley, D. H. (1991). *Forces of order: Police behavior in Japan and the United States.* Berkeley: University of California Press.

Jones, A. A., & Wiseman, R. (2006). *Community policing in Europe: Structure and best practices—Sweden, France, Germany.* Los Angeles, CA: Los Angeles Community Policing. Retrieved from http://www.lacp .org/Articles%20-%20Expert%20-%200ur%20 0pinion/060908-CommunityPolicingInEurope-AJ.htm

Kalunta-Crumpton, A. (2009). Patterns of community policing in Britain. In D. Wisler & I. D. Onwudiwe (Eds.), *Community policing: International patterns and comparative perspectives* (pp. 149–164). Boca Raton, FL: CRC Press. Retrieved from http://www.crcnetbase .com/doi/abs/10.1201/9781420093599.ch7

Punch, M., van der Vijver, K. (2008). Community policing in the Netherlands: Four generations of redefinition. In T. Williamson (Ed.), *The handbook of knowledge based policing* (pp. 59–75). Chichester, England: Wiley.

Putt, J. (Ed.). (2010). *Community policing in Australia.* Canberra: Australian Institute of Criminology. Retrieved from http://www.aic.gov.au/publications/current%20 series/rpp/100–120/rpp111.html

Royal Canadian Mounted Police. (2012). *Community policing problem solving model.* Retrieved from http:// www.rcmp-grc.gc.ca/ccaps-spcca/capra-eng.htm

Skolnick, J. H., & Bayley, D. H. (1988). *Community policing: Issues and practices around the world.* Washington, DC: U.S. Department of Justice, National Institute of Justice.

Terrill, R. J. (2009). *World criminal justice systems: A comparative survey* (7th ed.). Cincinnati, OH: Anderson.

Weisburd, D., Shalev, O., & Amir, M. (2002). Community policing in Israel: Resistance and change. *Policing: An International Journal of Police Strategies and Management, 25*(1), 80–109. doi: 10.1108/ 13639510210417917

INVESTIGATIONS, COMMUNITY POLICING STRATEGIES FOR

Community policing strategies for investigations refers to systematically engaging in community partnerships and employing those partnerships to aid in solving crimes as well as preventing future criminality. While the overarching goal of community policing is preventive—to address and respond to conditions that give rise to criminal activity— community policing strategies for investigations use partnerships and problem-solving techniques that are both reactive (to respond to past crimes) and proactive (to prevent future crimes).

Detectives are encouraged to be generalists, rather than specialists, and to look for patterns of criminal activity. Chains of command may be adjusted to create better communication among patrol, investigative and administrative officers assigned to an area. Detectives will formally partner with patrol officers, community agencies, and civilians in the area they serve. Finally, case assignments will shift to be more responsive to the unique problems presented in the local community.

This entry briefly introduces the traditional method of police investigations and then discusses how community policing strategies differ from the traditional approach. The entry concludes with a discussion of some potential concerns about using community policing strategies for investigations.

Traditional Investigative Methods

Traditional investigations generally involve specialized teams, such as crime scene investigators, homicide investigators, pawnshop details, and vice units. Because of the high regard among officers for these units and the freedoms they entail (less shift work, the ability to wear street clothes, and greater autonomy) the "detective badge" is a coveted insignia. Experienced detectives may be steeped in institutional lore that supports a conservative approach to change and, frequently, strong resistance to notions of modernization.

Particularly in major urban areas, specialized detective units operate from a central location with little civilian or community interaction other than with victims or witnesses. As with officers in all traditional police operations, detectives are subject to a strict chain of command, with little formal direct contact between investigators from separate disciplines.

In larger departments, detectives may work together in teams, but the investigators do not routinely work directly with patrol units or community agencies. Where there is interagency activity, it is often a matter of the detective and the outside agency handing off responsibility from one to the other. For example, a social services worker may call in the police on suspicion of domestic violence, or the police may refer a complainant to social services for assistance. Where interagency collaboration exists, it is often ad hoc and informal.

Even in traditional departments, technology is rapidly changing the investigative function. The traditional detective structure grew, among other reasons, out of a need for greater sharing of information among investigators and the need to file reports at a central location. As technology relieves some of the communication burdens and logistical demands placed upon investigators, their ability to engage in community policing activities increases.

Community Policing Strategies for Criminal Investigations

Community policing strategies for investigations involve both structural and procedural changes to the traditional detective model. There are many organizational, administrative, and logistical adjustments that police departments adopt in moving their investigations teams to a community policing model. Some of the factors that are affected include physical location, chain of command, specialization, teamwork and citizen involvement, and case prioritization. Adjustments in each of these areas are considered in the following subsections.

Physical Location

To accomplish community policing goals, it is necessary to establish stable lines of communication among police, community agencies, and citizens by creating work assignments in police divisions that allow the same officers to be in the same place over time. Two key components are decentralization and area assignments, which take investigators and other police personnel out of a central headquarters and move them out to district substations or smaller local field offices. Assigning detectives to a specific geographic area accomplishes a number of goals. First, it gives the officers a sense of ownership and heightened responsibility over what occurs in their district. Second, it promotes a deeper awareness of the activities and rhythms of the community to which the investigators are assigned, and a greater familiarity with crime patterns. Finally, it allows the investigators to affiliate with the patrol officers in that locale, and to become acquainted with the business owners, community leaders, and others who are familiar with and have in-depth knowledge of the neighborhood.

Chain of Command

Community policing inevitably involves giving individual officers greater flexibility and responsibility for day-to-day decisions. Nevertheless, a chain of command needs to be in place. In a more decentralized setting, detectives will continue to report and receive direction either through an investigative chain of command or through an area command hierarchy based on geographic area. Sometimes area command will share responsibility at the mid-command, or sergeant, level. That is, one sergeant will oversee area patrol and another will oversee investigations, with the two working together out of the same office.

Specialization

As indicated, the traditional detective specializes in a particular type of crime, and is typically attached to a unit formed around that specialty (such as a homicide unit). Community policing takes the detective out of the role of specialist and into the role of searching for crime patterns. In the community policing model, a generalist is preferred. An emphasis on cross-training is logical, considering that most criminals are not specialists. It is not unusual for crimes of one type to be tied to crimes of another sort—for example, the sudden onset of vandalism and graffiti may be a sign that there is a new gang in the neighborhood, which may involve drug trafficking or other concerns. A detective who is knowledgeable and skilled in a variety of areas is preferable when the focus shifts from individual crimes by type to crime patterns by area.

Teamwork and Citizen Involvement

Teamwork and citizen involvement are central to the goals of community policing. In a community policing model, teamwork refers to police working in concert with community agencies, community leaders, and citizens in the community. Teamwork also refers to normally distinct police operations working together; for example, the patrol officer in an area having a cooperative relationship with the detective assigned there, even though they may continue to report through separate chains of command.

Teamwork among detectives, community agencies, businesses, and citizens means more than casual acquaintance or incidental contact. This process involves active participation of the team members in regular meetings and other activities in the community where they can share problems, concerns, and successes; identify crime patterns; and collaborate on solutions to community concerns. It also involves the use of citizen volunteers, who can be an invaluable resource that frees patrol, detective, and administrative personnel to spend more time in the active pursuit of their mission.

Case Prioritization

The traditional method of assigning cases depends upon two factors: seriousness and solvability. In a community-oriented investigative strategy, solvability factors are downgraded and the emphasis shifted to community concerns and patterns of criminal conduct. Rather than having a superior officer handing out cases based upon the likelihood of clearance by arrest, detectives are given responsibility for self-assignment and prioritization of their own cases. Each detective studies the crime reports for the assigned area and establishes case priorities based on trends and patterns. Civilian volunteers may also be involved in this process, in the role of record keeping, organization, and case management; they may also be used to take crime reports and even document the circumstances of high-frequency, low-severity crimes, such as car burglaries, vandalism, and petty theft.

Limitations and Further Considerations

The community policing model for investigations has some drawbacks. As suggested above, there may be some resistance on the part of both detectives and command staff to the changes a shift to community policing entails. However, there are now enough success stories among agencies that have made the change to overcome many of the objections on the part of officers and departments who are unfamiliar with the process.

Some investigators report feeling isolated in the move to area assignments and miss the camaraderie of working together as a team out of a central office, or feel that area assignments limit their opportunity to make the kind of professional linkages that lead to promotion. Computer technology and social media can serve as tools for resolving some of those worries.

Detectives who self-assign cases may have a tendency to take on too much initially, but over time, they learn to make adjustments. Doubts also have been raised about using citizen volunteers and citizen access to confidential information. Thus, a careful vetting process is necessary.

Finally, community policing strategies are easier to implement in smaller departments and more cohesive communities. In all cases, large departments or small, buy-in on the part of the stakeholders—police officers and command staff, agencies, and community partners—is the key to success.

Tom Cadwallader

See also Crime Analysis; Crime Mapping; Decentralizing the Organization/Organizational Change; Non-sworn Personnel and Volunteers, Use and Training of; Team Policing

Further Readings

Harfield, C., & Harfield, K. (2008). *Intelligence: Investigation, community and partnership.* New York, NY: Oxford University Press.

Miller, L. S., Hess, K. M., & Orthmann, C. M. H. (2010). *Community policing: Partnerships for problem-solving* (6th ed.). Clifton Park, NY: Delmar.

Ortmeier, P. J., & Davis, J. J. (2012). *Police administration: A leadership approach.* New York, NY: McGraw-Hill.

Peak, K. J., & Glensor, R. W. (2011). *Community policing and problem-solving: Strategies and practices* (6th ed.). Columbus, OH: Pearson.

Wycoff, M. A., & Cosgrove, C. (2001, August 6). *Investigations in the community policing context.* Retrieved from https://www.ncjrs.gov/pdffiles1/nij/grants/189569.pdf

INVOLVING LOCAL BUSINESSES

Just as a few people and a few places seem to require a lot of police attention, a few businesses make disproportionate demands on police resources. Nearly every community has at least one such place—the bar that always seems to have fights on weekend nights; the store whose clerks call several times a week to report thefts or shoplifting; the shopping mall that frequently needs help dealing with groups of unruly youth; the motel that often rents to drug dealers, prostitutes, and the like. Possibly the greatest cause of high crime and disorder levels at these businesses is poor management, such as routine overservice in bars, low staffing levels in retail establishments, and loose rental practices in motels. This entry discusses how community policing officers, working with these "risky facilities," that is, places such as bars, restaurants, stores, shopping malls, and motels with a high number of calls for service compared to places of the same type, can reduce such problems and reap large resource savings for police departments.

Reasons for Working With Local Businesses

An improved relationship with police can increase understanding about the nature and extent of crime against business. Compared to households, the risk of criminal victimization is much higher for businesses. Surveys of businesses also reveal high rates of revictimization, and low rates of reporting for crimes like employee theft and shoplifting. There are many reasons for not reporting, but it is usually because the business owner thinks the crime was not that serious or is an internal matter (such as employee theft), or that the police either cannot do anything to resolve the situation or are not interested. There seems to be a perception that the police do not take crime against business very seriously. But if business owners are treated respectfully by the police and are kept informed about the progress of the case (even if the case is unsolvable or few resources can be dedicated to it), this is likely to increase reporting in the future and improve perceptions of the legitimacy of the police. More accurate reporting can change perspectives on what are the most pressing problems faced by businesses. Just as police officers are often surprised to hear from neighborhood residents that their biggest problems are speeding cars and barking dogs, not the serious crimes that police expect would be of concern, they may be surprised to learn how often businesses are victimized, and that the nature of the victimization is not as expected. From an operational standpoint, business owners and their employees can be good sources of information about criminal activity and disorder in the area surrounding the business itself, as they often keep an eye out for suspicious behavior.

Another reason for police to work with businesses is access to resources beyond those available to the police department, such as donations of space or equipment. This is especially the case for private security, which, as discussed below, may have fewer fiscal constraints on the purchase of equipment (such as cameras and other surveillance devices).

Encouraging Businesses to Get Involved

Business owners make many decisions based on a cost-benefit analysis: Working with the police makes sense only if it benefits them more than it costs them. Fortunately, being involved with the police has many advantages for businesses. First, assuming other businesses are involved as well, there is the opportunity to learn from those others what works and what doesn't to prevent crime. Businesses can also benefit by pooling resources together, for things such as hiring a security company to patrol a number of businesses, or on a larger scale (as is the case with business improvement districts) providing services such as promotion and beautification. Second, because police have specialized knowledge about crime prevention, businesses can benefit from receiving training and information from the police. The police can also keep businesses advised about emerging crime patterns so that preventive action can be taken. Third, there can be benefits to businesses if they are seen to be engaging in good citizenship. Visibly supporting the police and other crime prevention activities, whether through donations or leadership, can build a business's reputation in the community.

Barriers to Business Involvement

There are a variety of barriers to business involvement in partnerships with the police. First, many people, business owners included, think the police do not need their help, either because the police cannot do much to solve the problem, or because the police are already dealing with the problem without the assistance of citizens. This first barrier affects reporting rates which, as discussed earlier, can impact police departments' resource allocation and officers' perceptions of the biggest crime problems facing businesses. Police can do much to change attitudes toward them by encouraging business owners to report victimization and providing feedback on the progress of the case. A related issue that is often grounded in ignorance concerns the effectiveness of the criminal justice system. As most practitioners in the system know, there is a vast amount of crime that is never reported at all, and the majority of reported crimes do not result in successful prosecutions and punishment of offenders. Exposure to this reality can help business people understand that they share some responsibility for preventing crime.

A second barrier to involvement is a lack of understanding of the costs of crime. For many businesses, costs associated with crime are part of their business model. For example, in retail, shoplifting is called "shrink," and is factored into budgets. Losses from more dramatic crimes, such as robbery or burglary, are typically covered by insurance. It can be hard to convince business owners that working with the police to reduce crime is in their best interests. But educating businesses about additional costs of crime, such as the impact of fear of crime on customers, the inability to attract good employees, expenses associated with security and security-strengthening measures, can encourage them to be more involved in crime prevention.

It is important to recognize that some businesses may be reluctant or outright opposed to becoming involved with police. Perhaps a business caters to those who engage in criminal behavior and the owner worries that cooperating with police will drive away customers or expose the business itself to liability. Neighboring businesses can be enlisted to encourage such businesses to get involved. Many jurisdictions have tools at their disposal to persuade recalcitrant businesses to get involved with the police, such as ordinances concerning excessive calls for police service or false alarms, or building, sanitary, and fire codes.

Types of Partnerships

Many police departments emphasize the importance of the business community in their overall community policing strategies. Specific tactics to involve businesses include regular meetings, distribution of newsletters, and the creation of communication networks to rapidly disseminate information. This sort of interaction ordinarily does not have a problem-solving focus; it is done primarily in the interests of police-community relations. However, if crime reduction is the goal, partnerships should be formed specifically for the task at hand.

The first form of police-business partnership entails police working directly with individual businesses to reduce their likelihood of victimization,

through mechanisms like security audits and crime prevention education. Given the high rate of repeat victimization experienced by some businesses, this approach has a good potential to reduce overall victimization, but it does little to harness the power of businesses working collectively to address crime problems in a larger area.

Partnerships involving multiple businesses or agencies can be area specific, issue specific, or business specific.

Area-Specific Partnerships

Area-specific partnerships focus on businesses in a set area, like a shopping district. All businesses could potentially be involved. This is a common variety of partnership between police and business; these partnerships are often formed as part of an overall community policing strategy with the goal of improving police-business relationships, and may not be focused on solving particular crime problems.

In Queensland, Australia, as part of a community policing strategy, police operate almost 50 "beat shopfronts" in shopping malls or central business districts, with the purpose of providing a physical police presence in these commercial areas. The presence of shopfronts (or, as they are more commonly called in the United States, storefronts or substations) seems to increase levels of reporting and reduce the actual incidence of victimization. In many commercial and retail areas, the local businesses organize themselves into business improvement districts (BIDs). Members agree to an assessment on top of regular property taxes; this extra revenue goes to supplement municipal services. Typical activities carried out by BIDs focus on advertising and promotion, beautification and cleaning, and security. The BID in downtown Philadelphia, Pennsylvania, known as the Center City District, coordinates a large-scale police-business partnership—the Philadelphia Crime Prevention Council. In bi-monthly meetings, about 300 people—law enforcement officials from federal, state, and local agencies, and high-ranking security personnel from numerous sectors (retail, office, banking, hospital, hotel, and utility) discuss emerging trends and current problems and develop strategies to address these issues. In addition, Center City District works with the Philadelphia Police Department to use geographic information systems technology to identify crime trends and allocate resources accordingly. The BID also conducts crime prevention seminars for businesses, employees, and police; does reviews of security policies and procedures; and works on crime prevention through environmental design (CPTED) initiatives. There is also an emergency notification system that was established in a collaborative process between the BID and the police.

Issue-Specific Partnerships

Issue-specific partnerships are formed in response to a problem and typically dissolve once the problem has been adequately addressed. An example of an issue-specific partnership comes from Surfer's Paradise, Australia. The downtown area was troubled by assaults and other disorderly behavior associated with excessive alcohol use. In a multiagency collaboration involving bar owners, the police, and others, including local politicians, community members, and the alcohol licensing authority, the licensees themselves devised and implemented "Model House" policies, procedures, and training for staff to limit overservice of alcohol. Assaults and disorderly behavior declined.

In Pinellas Park, Florida, the downtown area was adversely affected by concentrations of chronic public inebriates. Local liquor stores agreed to stop selling alcohol to individuals identified by the police as "habitual drunkards." This effectively displaced this group of chronic public inebriates from the area, as they were no longer able to obtain alcohol easily. This partnership had a number of benefits: an improvement in the police-business relationship, a tighter-knit business community, a reduction in crime and vagrancy, and more businesses opening up in the downtown area.

Business-Specific Partnerships

When a particular type of business experiences an increase in victimization, regardless of whether the businesses are located in the same area, a business-specific partnership is appropriate. Model programs that target specific types of businesses include the Taxi/Livery Robbery Inspection Program in New York City, where, under the law, the police are permitted to briefly stop an enrolled vehicle at any time of the day or night to verify the safety of the driver and riders.

The Retail Theft Program, in Seattle, Washington, is an example of collaboration between local police and about 120 stores. After a shoplifter has been apprehended, rather than the police responding to a call for service, the store contacts Seattle Police dispatch to obtain a case number and check if there are any warrants out for the shoplifter, completes a security incident report, issues a written trespass warning to the shoplifter, takes his or her photograph, and then releases the person. The security incident reports are sent to a detective assigned to the program and then passed on to the city attorney for review for charges. This alternative reporting procedure benefits stores, who can process shoplifters quickly without having to wait for the police to respond, and the police as well, who do not have to use resources attending to these calls.

Partnerships Between Local Police and Private Security

Traditionally, partnerships with private security have not been part of community policing, and until recently, few police departments had formal relationships with private security. But this is changing; a recent review documented a rapid growth in the number of formalized law enforcement-private security (LE-PS) partnerships.

There are barriers to LE-PS partnerships. Police may not always understand what private security does or what it can offer, and the same can be said about private security's understanding of the police. There is often a lack of trust, which impedes open sharing of information, thus making functional partnerships difficult.

However, working with private security offers many benefits to the police. The first is the role of private security as a "force multiplier." While there are fewer than 1 million full-time sworn law enforcement personnel, it's estimated that there are over 2 million people working private security in the United States, protecting over three-quarters of the country's critical infrastructure. Collaboration with private security increases the capacity of police to carry out their law enforcement functions and may even help reduce costs. Second, private security often has more resources and technology. Cybercrime and financial crime, in particular, are rapidly evolving, and it is difficult for the police to keep up with changes in offenders' tactics. But private industry employs people with specialized skills in these areas; involving them can help police investigate these crimes. Finally, both police and private security can offer expertise and information to the other.

Sharon Chamard

See also Building Partnerships and Stakeholders; Customer-Based Policing; Police-Community Relations

Further Readings

Chamard, S. (2006). *Partnering with businesses to address public safety problems.* (Problem-Oriented Guides for Police, Problem-Solving Tools Series, No. 5). Washington, DC: U.S. Department of Justice, Office of Community Oriented Policing Services.

Clarke, R. V., & Eck, J. E. (2007). *Understanding risky facilities.* (Problem-Oriented Guides for Police, Problem-solving Tools Series, No. 6). Washington, DC: U.S. Department of Justice, Office of Community Oriented Policing Services.

Connors, E. F., Cunningham, W. C., & Ohlhausen, P. E. (1999). *Operation cooperation: A literature review of cooperation and partnerships between law enforcement and private security organizations.* Washington, DC: U.S. Department of Justice, Bureau of Justice Assistance.

Taylor, N. (2003). Under-reporting of crime against small businesses: Attitudes toward police and reporting practices. *Policing and Society, 13*(1), 79–89.

Taylor, N., & Charlton, K. (2005). Police shopfronts and reporting to police by retailers. *Trends and Issues in Crime and Criminal Justice* (No. 295). Canberra: Australian Institute of Criminology.

The Law Enforcement–Private Security Consortium. (2009). *Operation partnership: Trends and practices in law enforcement and private security collaborations.* Washington, DC: U.S. Department of Justice, Office of Community Oriented Policing Services.

Kansas City Preventive Patrol Experiment

The Kansas City preventive patrol experiment was the first major study using an experimental design in law enforcement and is now considered a seminal policing study. It sought to test the effectiveness of routine preventive patrol, and the results showed that this form of patrolling, then considered a fundamental policing activity, was ineffective at achieving the desired effects, preventing crime. This conclusion and the subsequent debate ultimately resulted in police departments searching for other strategies to combat crime. Major strides were made in research and policy as a direct result of the study.

Prior to the study, patrol was seen as the most effective police tactic to prevent crime. Patrol, it was thought, prevented crime through omnipresence and apprehension. Omnipresence was achieved though random patrol where patrol units would give the impression of being everywhere all the time. This would give criminals the impression that there was no opportunity to commit a crime. If omnipresence failed to prevent a crime, patrol officers would be in a position to apprehend criminals. Although philosophically appealing, in actuality, police departments did not, nor do they today, have enough officers to accomplish these two objectives. The Kansas City experiment resulted in thinking beyond this ingrained strategy to other strategies, such as community policing and problem solving. This entry examines how the experiment was conducted,

its results, the reactions to the results, and how the experiment has continued to influence policing and policing research.

Overview of the Experiment

The inspiration for this study came from the Kansas City, Missouri, Police Department's review of the problems encountered by each district in the city. The department's southern district, where the experiment would later take place, provided a list of problems that was too long to address without making sacrifices in the manpower already dedicated to patrol in that district. A portion of the leadership in the southern district expressed skepticism about the need to maintain the current patrol levels and pressed for the district's problems to be addressed. Clarence M. Kelly, chief of the Kansas City Police Department, solicited the assistance of the Police Foundation, whose general mission is to help police be more effective in crime fighting. The Foundation was asked to research some of the basic assumptions of police work that had gone untested. Essentially, the traditional assumptions about patrol's role in reducing crime were tested.

The researchers conducted the patrol experiment using 15 of the 24 patrol beats making up the southern district. Nine beats were eliminated from the experiment because they did not have a residential population that was representative of the city. The experimental area consisted of 32 square miles with a population of 148,395. The beats' racial composition was heterogeneous and ranged from 78% African American in one area to 99% White in another. Officials from both the Police Department and the Police Foundation monitored the implementation of the study to ensure that the experimental conditions were not violated. This study tested the effects of police patrols by dividing the 15 beats in the experiment into three types: control beats, proactive beats, and reactive beats. In the control beats, officers patrolled beats at the same levels as before the experiment, which was one officer patrolling within a beat at any given time. In the proactive beats, two to three officers patrolled at any given time. The amount of patrolling in these beats was appreciably increased. The reactive beats had no police officers conducting preventive patrol within their borders. However, officers from the control and proactive beats responded to calls in the reactive beats, and upon completing the call immediately returned to their assigned beats. This experimental change in patrol levels began on July 19, 1972, and ended on September 30, 1973.

The purpose of the study was to gauge the impact of patrol on crime. Data were collected using a variety of techniques. There were several citizen surveys measuring perceptions about crime, fear of crime, and the quality of police services. Surveys were administered to businesses as well as residents. Police officers were queried about citizen reporting of crime, and official police reports about crime were examined. Participant observation was also used to collect and verify data. The study examined the effects of patrol on a wide range of criminal activities including burglary, larceny, robbery, sex offenses, assault, auto theft, vandalism, larceny, homicide, and traffic accidents.

Results

There were no significant differences found among the three types of beats using as dependent variables crimes committed and citizen perceptions. Many of the dependent variables were measured using multiple data sources. Each type of beat was compared to two other types of beats resulting in a total of 648 comparisons. Statistically significant differences were found for 40 of these comparisons (or 6% of all comparisons). There was no discernible pattern among the statistically significant comparisons. The researchers concluded that patrolling did not substantively influence the dependent variables. In other words, patrol was neither effective in influencing

crime nor in changing citizen perceptions of crime and police service.

Researchers examined those crimes that patrol officers should be particularly adept at preventing, such as burglary, auto theft, robbery, and street crimes. These crimes, theoretically, should be most susceptible to prevention through the use of preventive patrols. Crime was measured using a community survey to capture victimization and criminal activity not reported to the police as well as crime reported to police and arrests. The experimental conditions as a result of the study did not produce any changes across the three types of beats for these crimes.

Results from a community survey showed that both citizens' fear of crime, including the behaviors and measures they take to protect themselves from criminal victimization, and their opinions toward the police remained unchanged through the duration of the study. A commercial survey of business owners showed similar results with regard to fear of crime and opinions toward police. The amount of time required for officers to respond to calls within each type of beat was not significantly different, nor was citizens' satisfaction with those response times and their interactions with police. The researchers collected data to show that the experiment was implemented without error. They correlated the crime rates of beats adjacent to one another to account for what is known as *spillover* or *displacement theory*. This effect refers to the possibility that, in this experiment, the application of different levels of patrol in beats may cause individuals to change the location of where they commit crime. For example, criminals who, prior to the experiment, committed crime in proactive beats could move to commit crime in reactive beats, making it appear that higher levels of patrolling were decreasing crime when, in reality, they were merely displacing it. There was no evidence of displacement in the adjacent beats, with exception of auto thefts. Thus, it appeared that at most there was minimum displacement of crime.

There were other results not related to the experiment. Patrol officers worked 8-hour shifts. During their patrol shifts, they were working a call 40% of the time and officers were available to take calls for service during 60% of their time. Of the uncommitted time, roughly half was used for patrolling while the other half was spent on activities unrelated to police work. Officers did not substantively spend different portions of their time addressing calls for service based on the type of beat they were assigned. The researchers also surveyed officers to determine whether or not officers considered patrolling an integral part of their job. They found no evidence that officers supported the idea of patrol. Officers are generally told that patrolling is a primary function of police service. Nonetheless, officers appeared to not put into practice this belief to the degree that was ingrained in the police philosophy. Indeed, this was one of the first studies to examine how patrol officers spent their patrol time.

Preventive Patrol Today

Preventive patrol is conducted based on the assumptions that an officer's presence both inspires citizens to be less fearful of crime and deters individuals from committing criminal acts. To expand on the latter assumption, an officer's presence prevents crimes from occurring by removing the opportunity to commit crime. Based on this logic, the effects of preventive patrol may be increased by increasing the number of officers patrolling, which should lead to more individuals within beats being exposed to an officer's presence on a regular basis. However, it is without question that police departments do not have the resources to reach this tipping point. Patrol cannot be operationalized so that it as effective as envisioned.

Police departments have been resistant to change their patrolling routines despite the findings of this study. This resistance comes in part from officers' antiquated belief that reducing patrols would be a negligent act directly resulting in increases in crime. It is also the result of police departments continuing to be reactive; they must respond to calls for service. The allocation of patrol officers across beats allows officers to respond to calls with the shortest possible response time. It is difficult for departments to depart from routine patrol.

Although the authors believed that this study was evidence that the role police play in society is in need of reevaluation, they also stressed the need for caution in reaching conclusions based on the study. Patrol failed to influence crime and other variables; the study did not show whether an officer's presence influences citizens' and criminals' behavior. Patrol was the only activity studied and officers may conduct other activities that have valuable outcomes. The study does not prove that officers are ineffective

in their roles as police officers, and the study's results should not serve as a justification for cutting spending on law enforcement. The authors inferred from the study that in order to combat crime and reduce citizen fear of crime, the police should at least supplement patrol efforts with other strategies.

The study's results questioned the very foundation of American policing. As such, many questioned the study's validity with several criticisms. First, it was suggested that the increase in patrol officers in the proactive beats actually resulted in increases in the other beats as officers traveled to calls in the control and reactive beats. This called into question the actual number of officers in the three types of beats. Second, Kansas City may be unique, implying that the other jurisdictions may experience dissimilar results. In addition, police executives did not accept the legitimacy of the study or the researchers' conclusions, because if they were correct, it meant that police departments' primary anticrime strategy was called into question. Nonetheless, the results became accepted over time, and today are considered a basic principle of policing.

Acceptance of the Experiment in Its Aftermath

Richard C. Larson applauded the "seed effect" of the study, which has inspired other police departments and researchers to debate the merits of policing practices, to work together to craft new hypotheses, and to conduct their own field experiments. As George L. Kelling, one of the authors of the study, explained, the Kansas City preventive patrol study was a seminal work in the period from the mid-1970s through the 1980s and began a period where police increasingly opened up to and eventually collaborated with researchers.

One of the main reasons that the Kansas City preventive patrol experiment was so popular was the context in which it arose. Through the 1970s and 1980s, a general pessimism about the criminal justice system's ability to combat crime came into the mainstream as crime throughout the United States increased steadily. There was a belief that "nothing works" when attempting to prevent crime and rehabilitate criminals. David H. Bayley identified the Kansas City experiment as one of the three major works that have evaluated the staple of policing—patrol—and found it to be ineffective in achieving its desired ends. The Kansas City study was soon followed by the 1975 study *Response Time Analysis,* conducted in the same city, which found that officers' rapid response times to reports of crime were negligible in affecting crime.

These studies also inspired innovative styles of policing such as community policing and problem-oriented policing. Kelling argued for a change in the role of policing in society, beginning a discussion that would go on to inspire community policing. In his proposal to adopt the problem-oriented approach, Herman Goldstein noted the Kansas City experiment contributed to police having to abandon old practices to search for those that achieve their desired ends.

The Road to Community Policing

The Kansas City preventive patrol experiment was one of the first major studies in policing, and its results caused police administrators and policymakers to question the effectiveness of routine patrol preventive patrol. It also spawned future studies to examine how to improve police services and prevent crime. A precursor to community policing was team policing in the 1970s. Team policing was an experiment whereby authority and responsibilities were decentralized to small teams of police officers that were assigned to small geographical areas. The teams identified priorities and the strategies to deploy in their areas, which allowed officers to use tactics that went beyond routine patrolling. Although the team policing experiments devolved, they did set the stage for community policing.

Community policing has two primary components: community relationships and problem solving. Community partnerships were developed to identify neighborhood problems or priorities; to develop better relations with citizens to facilitate cooperation and the exchange of information; and to strengthen neighborhoods, enabling them to better combat crime and disorder. Problem solving is an important step beyond routine patrol and to some extent came about as a result of a realization that patrol is ineffective in dealing with some crime problems. In policing, problem solving involves applying the SARA (scanning, analysis, response, assessment) model. Police using the model analyze crime and disorder problems to determine their causes. Once

causes are determined, solutions are tailored to alleviate the problem. Solutions may involve preventive patrol, but frequently they involve other tactics, such as altering the environment, enforcing statutes such as alcohol-related laws, and dealing with disorder before problems grow into crime problems.

A recent innovation in policing is geographical policing whereby police focus on problems and their locations, rather than just examining calls individually. Crime mapping shows that crime and disorder are not equally dispersed across geography. There are concentrations of crime, or hot spots. Problem-solving tactics are used in these hot spots because these hot spots often involve complex problems requiring the police to use multiple interventions that go well beyond preventive patrol. Policing hot spots demonstrates how far policing has progressed from a dependence on preventive patrols to control crime.

In summary, the Kansas City preventive patrol experiment was one of the most important research studies in American policing. It represented the beginning of new thinking in policing and how to deal with crime. Policing today is viewed as a complex endeavor whereby police departments must have numerous tools in addition to preventive patrol when protecting and serving their communities.

D. Cody Gaines

See also Directed Patrol, Studies of; Evidence-Based Policing; Fear of Crime; Place-Based Policing; Police Foundation; Roles, Officers'

Further Readings

Kelling, G. L. (1978). Police field services and crime: The presumed effects of a capacity. *Crime & Delinquency, 24*(2), 173–184.

Kelling, G. L., Pate, L., Dieckman, D., & Brown, C. E. (1974). *The Kansas City preventive patrol experiment: A summary report.* Washington, DC: Police Foundation.

Larson, R. C. (1975). What happened to patrol operations in Kansas City? A review of the Kansas City preventive patrol experiment. *Journal of Criminal Justice, 3*(4), 267–297.

Pate, T., Kelling, G. L., & Brown, C. (1975). A response to "What happened to patrol operations in Kansas City?" *Journal of Criminal Justice, 3*(4), 299–320.

LEARNING ORGANIZATION

Adopting the "learning organization" philosophy can help police departments have the organizational capacity to carry out community policing and problem solving. Espoused by management expert Peter Senge, who popularized the concept of the learning organization in his 1990 book, *The Fifth Discipline,* this approach allows members of an organization to continually expand their capacity to nurture new and expansive patterns of thinking, pursue their collective aspirations, and continually learn to see the whole picture.

How does the concept of learning organizations relate to community policing and problem solving? The adoption of the community policing and problem-solving philosophy and practice involves a new way of thinking about and approaching policing as it attempts to embrace new means of addressing neighborhood crime and disorder. Therefore, as police organizations implement the community policing and problem-solving strategy and assess its efficacy, the need for them to become learning organizations is essential so that they may capitalize on their own and others' experiences—successes as well as failures—to continually hone strategies, tactics, and operations.

This entry describes what a learning organization is, some barriers to its creation, what it requires on the part of its leaders and employees, and how it might be sustained.

Five Key Disciplines for Learning Organizations

Prior to looking at the definition of a learning organization, it is important to first understand the five elements ("disciplines") that Senge envisioned as being central to learning organizations:

- *Personal mastery*—continually clarifying and deepening employees' personal vision, focusing their energies, developing patience, and seeing reality objectively
- *Mental models*—deeply ingrained assumptions, generalizations, or even pictures or images that influence how employees view the world and how they take action
- *Building shared vision*—suggests that if any one idea about leadership has inspired organizations for thousands of years, it's the capacity to hold a shared picture of the future the organization seeks to create
- *Team learning*—vital because teams, not individuals, are the fundamental learning unit in modern organizations
- *Systems thinking*—the "Fifth Discipline" that integrates the other four disciplines: essentially, the ability to understand how a system's constituent parts interrelate and how systems work over time and within larger systems

In addition, Senge saw the leader of the learning organization as occupying three key roles:

1. *Leader as Designer:* Senge likens this to being the designer of a ship rather than its captain. He defined it in three ways:

   o creating a common vision with shared values and purpose
   o determining the policies, strategies, and structures that translate guiding ideas into business decisions, and developing a culture that strategy is everyone's business
   o creating effective learning processes which will allow for continuous improvement of the policies, strategies, and structures

2. *Leader as Teacher:* The leader here is seen as a coach who works with the goals and objectives present in the organization. He or she must understand the usually tacit concepts of reality and restructure these views.

3. *Leader as Steward:* This refers largely to the attitude of the leader. Senge emphasizes the importance of a leader who feels a part of something greater; whose desire is first and foremost not to lead, but to serve the greater purpose of building better organizations and reshaping the way businesses operate.

The creation of a learning culture and environment acts as the foundation for a learning organization. This begins with a shift to employees' seeing themselves as integral components in the workplace, rather than as separate and unimportant cogs in a wheel. An environment that is conducive to learning, with a clearly stated outcome that inspires learners' physical and mental engagement, and activities that precipitate critical thinking and problem solving are important training processes as well.

Learning Organization Defined

Senge believes that learning organizations are those that allow their employees to continually expand their capacity to create the results that both the organization's leadership and employees desire. New patterns of thinking are nurtured and employees can see the whole together and work to solve problems more effectively. For an organization to be one that is "learning," it must possess the following characteristics:

- Staff members must have a clear view of the goals of the organization and their role in fulfilling those goals. For example, if at staff meetings they are concerned only with how decisions affect their area of responsibility, they are not part of a learning organization. Conversely, if they view their agency as a place where decisions affect all of its parts, a more strategic view, and are open to learning new methods, they are part of a learning organization.
- Employees in the organization must view their coworkers with a balance between expecting strong performance and cooperation. Without such a balance, there will be less dialogue. Without open dialogue, new ideas will not be raised and the views of the management staff will always prevail.
- Employees in the organization do not view the organization's change process with a "We've always done it this way" or an "If it ain't broke, don't fix it" mentality. Such viewpoints have no place in a learning organization, and employees must consider external as well as internal forces of change.

Leaders must establish an organization where people continually expand their capabilities to understand complexity, clarify vision, and improve shared goals and objectives. Leaders do not teach, but instead foster learning through problem solving and the vision to develop and build organizational capacity.

The first thing needed to create a learning organization is effective leadership, which is not based on a traditional hierarchy but rather on a mix of different people from all levels of the system, who lead in different ways. Second, there must be a realization that all employees have the ability to find solutions to the problems they are faced with, and that they can envision a future and forge ahead to create it. A learning culture, which is the culture that binds the organization together, is thus established. Such an organization is based on openness and trust, where employees are supported and rewarded for learning and innovating, employees are encouraged to promote experimentation and risk taking, and the organization values the well-being of all employees.

Obstacles to Learning

Many experts in education and adult learning believe that most people simply do not understand how to learn individually or in the context of an organization. The first requisite for learning is to have an active mind. One who does not learn does not think, either because that person is passive in nature or engages in active refusal to think. Furthermore, some people simply do not learn because they fail to conceptualize the meaning and implications of their experiences. This is a key aspect of learning, and the most effective learners are those who are the most mentally active, are able to conceptualize what has occurred in the past, and can anticipate the future.

A significant obstacle to developing a learning organization is leaders within who may be entrenched in traditional ways of thinking and leading. This must be overcome in order to foster the openness and confidence required for the organization to become a learning organization. Learning organizations require leaders to be open to challenges about their vision and behavior and to be prepared to change when necessary. In police organizations, leaders who are not open to change can impede the organization from implementing community policing and problem-solving principles. At the organizational level, learning and future growth in an organization can be limited by management practices that are grounded in routine methods, outmoded reward mechanisms that do not adhere to the organization's vision and goals, and an emphasis on organizational consensus—"groupthink." Other obstacles might include failure of the organization to transform new knowledge into more effective organizational policies and procedures. Taken together, such barriers can serve to undermine learning.

Sustaining the Learning Organization

Senge also knew the learning organization must be sustained, rather than being a mere short-term fad, as can be the tendency in organizational behavior. Therefore, a more recent book by Senge and colleagues, *The Dance of Change: The Challenges to Sustaining Momentum in Learning Organizations,* discussed how the challenges to sustaining momentum are mostly due to internal pulls to tradition.

To make the point, Senge and colleagues used nature as a metaphor, illustrating how an organization has a life cycle like any organism. They argued that biology, which shows that organisms are affected by both growth and limiting processes, can teach us much about the growth and premature death of organizational change initiatives. In biology, limiting processes are essential factors in the environment that control the growth or distribution of a certain organism in an ecosystem. Such factors include the availability of food, water, nutrients,

shelter, and predation—all of which can limit the growth of an organism's population size.

So it is with a learning organization. Senge and colleagues suggested that most learning organizations fail to deal with their limiting processes. By thinking of sustaining change in terms of the biological metaphor, the organization can overcome the challenges involved, such as concerns about the time required to be a learning organization. In the organization, such limiting processes can also include fear and anxiety, the failure to assess and measure, and leaders not believing in the ability of the organization to become a learning organization.

Forming a Learning Organization in Policing

Some police agencies have sent personnel to the MIT Sloan School of Management, where Senge is a senior lecturer, to learn more about learning organizations, in hopes that these personnel will guide their organization in becoming a learning organization. A strategic plan for developing police agencies into learning organizations should include the following components:

- Intelligence-led policing
- Community-oriented policing and problem solving
- Customer service and safety
- Innovation and technology
- Organizational culture and leadership
- Organizational enrichment

Each component is represented by a cross-sectional team of personnel in the organization. Each team is responsible for developing annual goals and reaching outcomes that support the cornerstones of developing a learning organization. Early analyses of the program indicate that personnel have focused on these six principle components and progress during these very difficult times and made significant progress in each area.

Steven Pitts

See also Mentoring; Police Foundation; Police Mission; Roles, Chief Executives'; Strategic Planning; Succession Planning

Further Readings

Argyris, C. (1991, May/June). Teaching smart people how to learn. *Harvard Business Review, 69*(3), 99–109.

Cartwright, G. (2008, September). A learning organization. *Law and Order,* 71–73.

Garvin, D. (1994, January). Building a learning organization. *Business Credit, 96*(1), 19–28.

Gephart, M. A., Marsick, V. J., Van Buren, M. E., & Spiro, M. S. (1996, December). Learning organizations come alive. *Training & Development, 50*(12), 35–45.

Johnson, K. W. (1993). The learning organization: What is it? Why become one? *Navran Associates' Newsletter.*

Senge, P. M. (1990). *The fifth discipline: The art and practice of the learning organization.* New York, NY: Doubleday.

Senge, P., Kleiner, A., Roberts, C., Ross, R., Roth, G., & Smith, B. (1990). *The dance of change: The challenges to sustaining momentum in learning organizations.* New York, NY: Doubleday.

M

MEASURING OFFICER PERFORMANCE

New approaches for evaluating police officer knowledge and performance are required under the community policing and problem-solving approach. Traditional measurements of officer performance—for example, numbers of citations issued, arrests made, calls for service handled, and other such outputs—are not appropriate under this problem-oriented strategy that focuses on addressing neighborhood crime and disorder. Furthermore, agencies need to know if their officers possess the proper skills, are looking for underlying causes of crime, and are applying appropriate responses to crime and disorder issues. An effective performance measurement system is characterized by three fundamental purposes: (1) It conveys the organization's philosophy; (2) It sets forth performance expectations; and (3) It facilitates the attainment of results. From a practical perspective, the fundamental goal of any measurement system is to develop an individual's capacity to perform and then determine if the effects of one's performance meets expectations. This entry describes the significant characteristics of such systems while simultaneously recognizing variances exist among different police agencies upon implementation.

Expectations and Assumptions

Inherent within any discussion regarding one's performance is clarifying what is meant by the phrase *measurement system*. For the purpose of this entry, a measurement system encompasses a series of interrelated processes that begins with assessing one's developmental progress and ends with documenting results in terms of linking outputs and outcomes to goals and objectives. Police executives make a substantial investment to ensure their employees are properly developed so that the organization can perform as the citizenry expects. Measuring officers' performance can help them determine the status of their employees' development and whether their investment has yielded expected returns.

The development of police officers begins with soliciting qualified applicants, requiring them to successfully complete a recruit training program, and mandating the successful completion of a field training program. At this point, management typically deems each person worthy of full-time employment as a police officer. The new officer, then, is given various job assignments to begin gaining experience.

Typically, this means a younger (in terms of tenure) officer is assigned to patrol and rides with a partner. Some agencies require young officers to participate in a structured mentoring program as a way of easing individuals into the rigors of police work before allowing them to ride solo. Irrespective of how young officers begin their experiences, there is one unilateral constant in almost all police agencies—the need to periodically assess how well an officer is performing.

Expectations

The framework governing the design and administration of a measurement system must be consistent with specific managerial expectations. Officers come to understand these expectations by virtue of operational implications associated with the types of criteria used to account for their performance, processes used to assess and measure that performance, and the measurement of specific types of outputs and outcomes. These expectations set the tone for guiding the development of officers over time. For example, do the elements of the measurement system convey to police officers

- What aspects of their work management deems most important?
- How they are expected to behave?
- The importance of attaining consensus about the nature of their work?
- How they are expected to use their duty time?
- The significance of producing results in accordance with specific goals and objectives?
- Management's sensitivity to their job satisfaction?
- The need to be aware of citizens' perceptions about police services?

These expectations (and others) provide officers with an understanding of important elements and nuances associated with their specific job assignments. Furthermore, as police work continues to become increasingly complex and specialized, police managers must recognize the unique demands certain job assignments place on officers. Successful performance in one job assignment does not necessarily translate to successful performance in another. As officers gravitate from one job assignment to another, it may take time for them to understand the full scope of management's expectations; thus, it is extremely important that management take time to measure what matters for every available job assignment.

Assumptions

Before any officer can produce significant and sufficient results, time must be spent developing that officer's capabilities. Furthermore, if management is serious about conveying to officers what aspects of their performance are important, then time must also be spent developing the appropriate assessment processes and criteria.

In many agencies, the traditional or standard assessment process is characterized by the following operating assumptions: (1) Performance will be assessed at least once or twice a year; (2) Performance

will be measured using the same criteria regardless of job assignment; (3) Performance documentation will be recorded on the same form regardless of job assignment; and (4) Rating scale descriptions will lack sufficient detail. The net effect of this type of approach over time is a malaise among employees because their capabilities will have exceeded management's ability to provide constructive developmental guidance. In other words, the assessment feedback may fail to provide any useful relevancy to officers—they are not learning anything new and are no longer being challenged to grow. The assessment process then becomes a token exercise in which officers and supervisors, more or less, just go through the motions.

A primary benefit of using this approach, however, is it breeds standardization, which helps ensure compliance with legal requirements. To avoid claims of favoritism or bias, even discrimination, any measurement system must be fair, valid, capable of producing interrater reliability, and meet the terms of labor contracts and agreements. It is in management's best interest to administer an assessment process that is simple to understand and painless to administer, thereby minimizing the difficulty of teaching supervisors how to maintain some semblance of accountability.

Methods of Assessing Performance

The most common method of assessing officer performance is use of a singular form, containing a specified number of criteria, and administered a set number of times during a calendar year. There is no allowance for adjusting for the uniqueness of one's job assignment, as the criteria is uniform across the agency. Supervisors are responsible for conducting the evaluation. The form may contain space for narrative comments, but is more apt to primarily consist of performance criteria each accompanied by a Likert rating scale with varying numeric ranges. In some instances, the rating scale may only require a distinction of "acceptable" or "unacceptable" assessments. The assessment process typically requires a meeting between the officer and supervisor to discuss all ratings, as well as the officer's signing a statement to the effect that the officer read and discussed the ratings. Generally, an appeals process exists allowing an officer to grieve a perceived or actual unfair rating.

A variation to this approach is designing instrumentation and criteria for specific job assignments.

For example, officers assigned to patrol versus investigations versus a support operation assignment are subjected to the application of function-specific performance criteria. The work of a patrol officer is essentially different from work performed by officers working in investigative assignments, so the performance criteria reflect those differences.

Another method of assessing performance involves the use of a 360-degree evaluation process. This method is more popular outside the police profession but has gained more support over time. This approach involves acquiring feedback about an officer's performance from multiple sources: coworkers, direct supervisor, customers, or the officer's direct supervisor's manager. This allows for the customization of performance criteria for a given job function or assignment and from the perspective of the rater. For example, a coworker can provide feedback from the perspective of being a team member, whereas a supervisor is expected to provide direct feedback on how well an officer behaves and performs certain tasks, activities, and responsibilities. While the supervisor's feedback is apt to be more instructive, feedback from other participants will likely focus on actions involving motivation, being a team player, communication effects, leadership implications, and so forth.

Measuring Results

While the term *results* is commonly defined in terms of accounting for outcomes, police organizations generally and frequently document levels of outputs. Whereas *outcomes* can be defined as the "results of actions taken," outputs focus on what is done (content), how much is done (quantity), and how well it is done (quality).

Traditionally, counting activities and determining how much is accomplished when performing them represented the most popular form of measuring outputs for officers. For example, it is not uncommon for patrol officers to account for the following types of outputs:

1. *The number of calls dispatched to during their tour of duty.* Management uses this output to determine the proportion of time an officer spends handling calls during his or her shift; the presence and number of repeat call locations; or linkages among certain types of calls to types of crime or disorder.

2. *The amount of time an officer spent handling activities other than responding to calls.* Management uses this output to account for how and where officers are spending their uncommitted time.

3. *The number of tickets written.* Management uses this output to determine the relationship between tickets written and the presence and types of accidents.

4. *The number of arrests made.* Management uses this output to discover what type of criminal activity is being addressed.

5. *The number of "self-initiated" activities performed.* Management uses this output to determine whether the location of activities performed corresponds with the location of crime problems.

These outputs collectively serve to provide supervisors with a gauge on how well officer activities are aligned with certain goals and objectives.

Because most police agencies do not conduct their own research using scientific methods, the legitimacy of outcomes is more likely to be "perceived" than scientifically valid. Furthermore, there is no guarantee outcomes perceived by the police will be consistent with outcomes desired by the public. Despite this potential inconsistency, the following examples of perceived outcomes can serve as a basis of collaboration between the police, the public, and educational institutions:

1. The use of red-light cameras in intersections with a high number of fatal or nonfatal accidents. The issuance of violations can be aligned against a reduction of accidents as well as a reduction in a proportion of accidents to number of vehicles traveling through an intersection.

2. The creation of specific regulatory local ordinances. Publicly accessible space in apartment community properties experiencing a high proportion of crimes can be affected (via local ordinances) by actions taken to improve conditions, minimizing opportunities for crime and disorder. Officers involved in liaising with apartment owners and property managers to institute these mandated improvements can measure the absence of crime occurring on property sites.

3. Officer response to problem areas with differing tactics over designated periods of time. This can

measure effects in terms of absence, displacement, or diffusion of crime, and the duration of each. The effect(s) can be influenced by varying the time and intensity of the interdiction.

4. Reduction in the number of specific repeat call locations. This is a significant outcome for the police. Rather than counting how many times one responds to the same location, steps can be taken to address the reasons citizens are repeatedly calling the police and then measure the reduction in service requests.

5. Redirection of suspects or offenders from jail detention to agencies capable of helping them alter their behavior. This may lead to a reduction in these types of calls for service. Placing chronic inebriates in sobering centers instead of jails increases the probability of a person's exposure to and willingness to pursue rehabilitation opportunities. Mental health consumers in crisis are more apt to effectively respond to assistance from specially trained officers and clinicians who in turn can redirect them to neuropsychological centers for assistance rather than placing them in a jail detention facility.

These are but a few of many examples management can use to demonstrate the perceived effects of using personnel wisely. The ability to increase the number of reported outcomes by an agency is incumbent upon management's willingness to focus on specific, legitimate, and manageable crime and disorder problems.

The identification of those problems rests on effective collection and analyses of information. The combination of using different analytic approaches (e.g., crime, strategic, link, traffic) with proven strategies (e.g., CompStat, intelligence-led, predictive) to develop tactical responses to an identified problem within a specific neighborhood serves as a basis from which both outputs and outcomes can be measured.

Additional Considerations

As seen above, the intent, nature, and methods of measuring officer performance are complex and dependent on several factors. First, an officer's capability to perform must be developed over time, giving credence to the notion that competency increases in accordance with experience and diversity of assignments. Second, accounting for what and how much officers do demonstrates the amount of effort being put forth within an organization. The amount of effort expended or needed is directly linked by management to budgetary needs, contending that more money can produce more effort.

Last, in the era of tight budgets and struggling local economies, elected officials are pushing hard for police chiefs to present consequences of efforts expended by their personnel. It is no longer a question of how much more can a department produce; the public wants to know what effects are being produced by the efforts of the current allotment of manpower, and what type of staying power will these effects have. This becomes a more challenging task in cities where budgets have been slashed, forcing police executives to lose significant portions of their personnel. The success of measuring officer performance under these conditions may even more difficult. Irrespective of these difficulties, management must continue to measure what matters and share their results with the public so they can maintain their confidence in the effectiveness of their police department.

Timothy N. Oettmeier

See also Community Policing: Resources, Time, and Finances in Support of; In-Service Training; Learning Organization; Mentoring; Officers' Job Satisfaction; Police Training Officer (PTO) Program; Problem-Solving Initiatives, Assessment and Evaluation; Roles, Officers'; Strategic Planning

Further Readings

Bynum, T. S. (2002). *Using analysis for problem-solving: A guidebook for law enforcement.* Washington, DC: U.S. Department of Justice, Office of Community Oriented Policing Services. Retrieved from http://www.cops.usdoj.gov/pdf/e08011230.pdf

Eck, J. E. (2002). *Assessing responses to problems: An introductory guide for police problem-solvers.* Washington, DC: U.S. Department of Justice, Office of Community Oriented Policing Services.

Oettmeier, T. N., & Wycoff, M. A. (1997). *Personnel performance evaluations in the community policing context.* Washington, DC: Community Policing Consortium. Retrieved from http://www.policeforum.org/library/human-resources

Quire, D. S. (1993). *Models for community policing evaluation: The St. Petersburg experience.* Tallahassee, FL: Florida Criminal Justice Executive Institute. Retrieved from http://www.fdle.state.fl.us/Content/

getdoc/3b38f54e-8fc3–467e-b90c-25264321d5db/Quire-Donald-abstract-Models-for-Community-Policin.aspx
Rosenbaum, D., Schuck, A, Graziano, L., & Stephens, C. (2008, January). *Measuring police and community performance using Web-based surveys: Findings from the Chicago Internet project.* NCJ221076. Chicago: University of Illinois, Center for Research in Law and Justice.

MENTORING

Mentor was the name of the man charged with providing wisdom, advice, and guidance to Odysseus's son in the ancient Greek epic *The Odyssey.* Today, mentoring is a process whereby one person (the mentor) shares experiences, wisdom, and advice with another (the protégé, sometimes termed a *mentee*) to assist and facilitate the protégé's development in specific roles. Certainly mentoring is essential for fostering understanding of community policing and problem solving, and three key assumptions are critical to the success of any mentoring effort. First, the process of mentoring is different in design, scope, and application from training. Second, a mentor must have an unwavering desire to impart information to help other people. Third, the protégé is a willing partner actively seeks to learn in furtherance of personal development.

The mentor-protégé relationship can take a variety of forms. A mentor may provide career guidance; offer suggestions or directions on work-related issues; provide feedback on the protégé's work quality; discuss educational opportunities; provide insight regarding management concerns; or work with the protégé in other ways agreed upon by both parties. The nature of this relationship is predicated on the type of mentoring application.

This entry describes various mentoring applications within police departments, identifies generic qualities for mentors, and concludes with brief descriptions of program components.

Applying Mentorship

New Hire Mentoring Programs

The most popular application of mentoring within police agencies is helping aspiring protégés succeed in becoming certified police officers. Mentors can work with protégés to ensure they properly follow processing requirements, which ultimately results in a decision to accept the protégé for entry into a recruit training program. New recruits often find the entry-level training program to be very challenging, particularly when it comes to learning various laws along with a myriad of policies and procedures. Having a mentor available to help guide them through these challenges is quite often a welcome benefit.

Field Training Officer and Police Training Officer Mentoring Programs

Men and women graduating from a recruit training program will, in most instances, be required to successfully complete a Field Training Officer (FTO) or Police Training Officer (PTO) program. The purpose of such programs is to train and assess each probationary officer's knowledge, skills, and attitudes as they relate to performance of responsibilities expected of a police officer working in a particular jurisdiction. Graduates of such programs are often thought to be ready for the rigors of police work; but in many instances, they need more refinement, coaching, and counseling before they have the degree of confidence needed to be successful.

This mentoring application focuses on working with young (in terms of tenure) protégés in the form of discussing a variety of true-life police scenarios, community issues and challenges, problem-solving situations, moral dilemmas, for example, over a period of several months. The intent of this mentoring application is to facilitate the psychological development and decision-making skills of an inexperienced protégé as a means of preventing, or at least reducing the probability, of mistakes being made that could jeopardize officer and citizen safety.

Succession Planning Mentoring Programs

Being promoted to a higher rank is a rewarding accomplishment and signifies an individual is ready to take on different types of challenges. Agencies without field training programs for officials of rank may require them to attend courses designed to help them prepare for their new job responsibilities. Upon completion of this education, assigning the promotee to work alongside a seasoned supervisor, manager, or executive allows the promotee to observe the application of knowledge and skills. Exposure helps build the appropriate mind-set and attitude needed to address the rigors of a new assignment. The mentoring experience also helps diminish the likelihood of making mistakes and facilitates the learning process.

Private Sector Mentoring Programs

Private sector mentoring can have different types of applications. One example occurs when police personnel work with community youth groups to encourage youths to become contributing members of society. Aspiring teenagers (serving as protégés) from local high schools meet for multiple weeks as a group to discuss a variety of issues and concerns with mentors from different police ranks. This informal type of interaction allows these young people a view of police personnel that is not strictly one of authority. Police mentors attempt to foster positive relationships based on the principles of integrity, dignity, trust, and mutual respect—all of which are basic building blocks to keeping a community safe.

Mentoring can also take the form of allowing police executives to work alongside their counterparts in the private sector or within other police agencies. There are many commonalities in terms of how work is performed and how problems are addressed between private and public sector organizations. Police chiefs mentoring new police chiefs, or police executives being allowed to accompany private sector counterparts for a period of time provides tremendous insight into different perspectives on how to deal with neighborhood and community issues, problems, and concerns. Exposure to these different perspectives can help public sector executives build a repertoire of tools with which to perform their responsibilities.

Generic Qualities of Mentors

Mentors' roles and responsibilities vary according to the purpose and design of an agency's program. The relationship between a mentor and protégé is highly dependent on both individuals' willingness to commit to a partnership in which both have a role to play. Protégés must be amenable to being exposed to different perspectives from their own, although their willingness to adopt what they have been exposed to is their decision. Mentors bring to the partnership stability for a protégé who is attempting to adjust to change. The success of any mentor is highly dependent on the qualities that person brings to the partnership. The ideal qualities that are essential in an effective mentor include but are not limited to the following:

- *A desire to help*—individuals who have demonstrated a willingness to help others
- *Exposures to positive experiences*—individuals who have had positive formal or informal experiences with a mentor or trainer tend to be good trainers or mentors themselves
- *A good reputation for developing others*—demonstrated ability to help improve another's job performance skills and attitudes toward work
- *Time and energy*—people who not only have the time but devote that time and mental energy to make meaningful contributions
- *Willingness to learn*—individuals who have maintained current skill sets or developed specialized skills which demonstrate a desire to improve their abilities
- *Positive attitude*—individuals who value learning and typically optimistic about life; motivation driven by a desire to encourage others and provide constructive guidance
- *Demonstrated effective mentoring skills*—individuals who have demonstrated effective coaching, counseling, facilitation, and networking skills apt to be effective mentors

Not everyone is capable of being a mentor. Thus, it becomes incumbent upon the organization to establish a screening process to identify those best suited to participate in a mentoring program.

The key to any mentoring effort is ensuring the relationship between a mentor and protégé is clear. First and foremost, both parties must understand the purpose of the mentoring program and the ensuing demands placed on them. Obtaining clarification to each of the following concerns will help shape the relationship between the mentor and protégé:

- *Mentoring programs have specific purposes*—It is critical that mentors and protégés understand the intent of the program and discuss up front what each hopes to gain from the relationship.
- *Mentoring programs have a definite life cycle*—It is essential that both parties have a realistic sense of the time commitment each expects from the other before working together. The time commitment may need to be adjusted as the

relationship develops, but both mentor and protégé must be willing to put in appropriate amounts of time and effort.

- *A successful relationship is based on mutual understanding*—Mentors and protégés must have a willingness to consider each other's viewpoints and communication styles. Mentoring is not a one-way street. Each partner in the relationship may have different ideas about how to approach a specific problem or task and should recognize mistakes, and disagreements are a part of learning. Both must accept that a protégé's decisions are ultimately a personal choice to make. Mentors and protégés will learn from each other.

Taken collectively, these considerations will strengthen the relationship between the mentor and protégé, thereby enhancing the learning environment and increasing the probability of attaining success.

Program Configuration

Given the diversity of reasons mentor programs are established, there is no standard protocol governing program configuration. However, there are a few program elements that are common to the design of any mentoring initiative:

- *Managerial accountability*—Programs should have structure and means of accounting for how the program is administered, managed, and measures successes and failures.
- *Selection process*—Criteria should be established to ensure qualified personnel are selected to participate as mentors.
- *Training*—A comprehensive training curriculum must be developed and administered to all program participants.
- *Measuring success*—Specific outputs or outcomes should be identified and tracked to gauge the success or failure of the program.

From an organizational perspective, mentoring initiatives are designed to supplement training programs. They provide protégés with opportunities to enrich their understanding of the work demands they are expected to tackle, enhance their awareness of different problem-solving strategies and tactics, and become more adept in avoiding missteps that can otherwise spoil one's ability to provide quality services to their respective customers.

Timothy N. Oettmeier

See also In-Service Training; Learning Organization; Measuring Officer Performance; Officers' Job Satisfaction; Police Training Officer (PTO) Program; Roles, Officers'; Succession Planning

Further Readings

Sprafka H., & Kranda, A. H. (2008, January). Institutionalizing mentoring in police departments. *The Police Chief, 75*(1), 46–49. Retrieved from http://www.policechiefmagazine.org/magazine/index.cfm?fuseaction=display_arch&article_id=1375&issue_id=12008

Uhl, J. (2010, June). Mentoring: Nourishing the organizational culture. *The Police Chief, 77*(6), 66–72. Retrieved from http://www.policechiefmagazine.org/magazine/index.cfm?fuseaction=display_arch&article_id=2115&issue_id=62010

METROPOLITAN POLICE ACT OF 1829

England's Metropolitan Police Act of 1829 (the "Police Act") resulted in a new police force and law enforcement practices that were revolutionary in the history of law enforcement. Sir Robert Peel drafted and introduced the Police Act in response to serious crime problems and social disorder in London in the early 1800s, and in doing so, he had to delicately balance the strong historical sense of English personal liberty with the need to prevent crime and enforce the criminal laws. Peel's Principles, as articulated in the Police Act, had an important historic effect on policing in the United States and, in particular, community policing as it was conceived and as we know it today. This entry provides information on the history of the Police Act, Peel's Principles, the act's implementation, its role as arguably the earliest form of community policing, and its effect on community policing in the United States then and now.

History of the Police Act

Necessity is often the mother of invention, and London in the early 1800s was in dire need of something to control runaway crime rates and related social disorder. But the historical context in which the Police Act was introduced and ultimately passed is more complex than simple crime rates of the day, and the broader historical backdrop explains why Peel sought such a revolutionary change in law enforcement and why the Police Act had such a profound effect on policing in England and later in the United States.

As far back as the late 13th century, policing in England had traditionally been a community responsibility, rooted in the concept of liberty and the subjects' obligation to keep the King's peace. Crown-appointed, unpaid justices of the peace maintained law and order by directing local city, parish, or borough constables, and even when those arrangements proved lacking or inefficient, as they were by the mid-18th century, Englishman of all classes were reluctant to consider further empowering government through a stronger police force. So the parish constable system would remain the English policing mainstay until events dictated otherwise; and with that system came significant problems, many of which are somewhat legendary.

Of particular relevance to community policing was the constables' lack of support from the citizens they policed; most viewed the officers as a dangerous representative of the Crown who surely intended to threaten personal liberties. As a result, when a constable put out the "hue and cry" to summon help with a criminal, people rarely offered assistance. In many cases, they vocally criticized the constable and almost cheered on the criminal suspect. Understandably, many constables preferred to turn a blind eye to criminal activity rather than incur the wrath of their fellow citizens.

Nightfall brought on a whole new set of problems. Criminals could move about more stealthily in the dark, but even if they had to operate in more visible locations, the night watchman was usually in a pub instead of out patrolling or maintaining his street lamps. And if the constables ever actually pursued a criminal, the lawbreaker found safe haven by simply crossing parish boundary lines. Constables did not assist their counterparts in adjoining jurisdictions and information did not flow across borders, so criminals safely moved to another section of town if and when a parish constable had discovered their operations.

As a result, wealthy citizens hired private guards and the poor turned to "thief takers," former constables who knew how to find stolen property and could work with thieves to get the property back. Inevitably, thief takers, like the infamous Jonathan Wild, capitalized and withheld some of the recovered property as profit for their services. Some even hired thieves to steal and then made a profit offering their services to recover the stolen goods.

But the citizens involved in law enforcement eventually changed before the whole of policing did. As the Industrial Revolution created more economic opportunities, the gentry (who were typically tapped to serve as justices of the peace) and men of lesser means simply could not afford to spend time maintaining law and order. Instead, it made much more economic sense for them to hire others to stand their posts and watches. Unfortunately, most of the men who were hired were available and willing because they were the least fit for the job. They were poor and susceptible to bribes and other criminal incentives. And as the poor became poorer, alcohol consumption increased and along with it, disorder and vice. Crime rates soared and the criminal law expanded to include more than 200 offenses punishable by death. But Londoners continued to fear increased government involvement and instead continued citizen police watches in their respective communities.

The first significant departure from this historical law enforcement model was in 1749 when the novelist Henry Fielding was appointed as magistrate for Bow Street in London. Fielding arrived just as crime rates were especially high and seemingly unstoppable. In response, he and his brother, Sir John Fielding, set up a modestly paid detective squad called the Bow Street Foot Patrol, also known as the Bow Street Runners (the Fieldings also established the Bow Street Horse Patrol to keep order on the highways leading into London). The Fieldings encouraged property owners to pay annual fees that could be used to fund the investigation and pursuit of robbers and other criminals. Through these privately paid fees (and continued government inaction), Londoners were still in control of local law enforcement, and despite efforts at reform in the ensuing years, the Bow Street Foot Patrol remained the only significant policing development until the early 1800s. While the Bow Street Police Office was a major improvement on the old parish-constable system, its administrators and officers could not possibly keep pace with the runaway crime rates of the day. Sir John Fielding saw yet another opportunity for police reform and he again led the call for change, most notably the proposed Act of 1773.

In response to a rash of burglaries and robberies in Westminster and London in late 1769 and early 1770, a committee was formed to investigate. Fielding presented the committee report to Parliament in 1770, explaining that there was an insufficient number of watchmen, who were inadequately paid but overburdened with duties. He noted that each parish answered to a separate director who defined local beats without consulting with neighboring parishes, leaving dangerous gaps in police coverage and confusion about jurisdiction. The committee also reported on how ineffective watchmen were often retained because it was too difficult to replace them.

Fielding's report included several important resolutions, including a call for a central authority to oversee all constables and watchmen; a new system of appointing and discharging constables; and specific regulations to govern constables, watchmen, and beadles. The Act of 1773 was passed but it failed to provide for central control and applied only to Westminster. While it provided for a night watchmen minimum wage and an apparently much-needed rule that prohibited watchmen from visiting alehouses while on duty, by all accounts it changed little in the field, and major reforms remained necessary while the status quo continued.

Lawmakers and citizens were jolted from their apathetic slumber in 1780 when the extremely destructive mob violence known as the anti-Catholic Gordon Riots took place in London. The police force was wholly ineffective and military troops had to be called in to avoid further destruction. The House of Commons and House of Lords even took up the issue, but ultimately, the effect of the riots would fade and people calling for criminal justice reform found few interested listeners.

Just five years later in 1785, Prime Minister William Pitt the Younger introduced a bill to establish a citywide police force in London. He cited the jurisdictional boundary problems with the parish system and explained how criminal activity moved through the city unchecked. Lawmakers defeated the bill, again fearing infringement on personal liberties and a military-type police presence. But Pitt had educated English statesmen on the need

for reform and his blueprint for a citywide force became the model for the Royal Irish Constabulary in Ireland, where Sir Robert Peel served as chief secretary from 1812 to 1818 (an experience that would influence his view on policing and his design of the Police Act).

The next major reformer on the London scene was Patrick Colquhoun, who aggressively called for improved police organization and criminal law reform. He was appointed a magistrate in London and immediately undertook a thorough study of law enforcement there. In 1795, Colquhoun anonymously published *A Treatise on the Police of the Metropolis*, in which he estimated that more than 50,000 London residents were habitual criminals. Colquhoun was primarily concerned with property protection at a time when crime was on a fast and furious rise in a city of 990,000, and with only 1,000 constables and watchmen to police 8,000 streets. He also noted that the police were under the direction of 70 different trusts, each operating in its own ward, parish, or borough, and most underpaid and often associated with known criminals. A centerpiece of Colquhoun's reform proposals was a central authority to oversee police operations.

Then in 1800, Colquhoun published another treatise calling for a specific law enforcement jurisdiction on the Thames. He posited that criminal activity would eventually destroy a metropolitan city that relies on trade and commerce for its livelihood. That same year, the Thames Police Act provided for a police jurisdiction that crossed parish boundaries and encompassed the river and its adjacent land. And for the first time, Londoners saw effective policing. But the Thames Police Act was extremely limited (geographically and legally), and Colquhoun's proposals for broader reform went nowhere.

History would repeat itself several times after Colquhoun's failed efforts. The Luddite riots beginning in 1811, the Corn Laws riots in 1815, and the Massacre at Peterloo in 1817 all brought the frightening inefficiencies of the police back into sharp relief. During and after each crisis, lawmakers, reformers, and concerned citizens called for change, but each time and for a variety of reasons, efforts fell short. The police's inability to keep order was again on full display during the funeral procession for Queen Caroline in 1821, and shortly thereafter, rather than consider legislation to reform policing, the chief magistrate at Bow Street was dismissed. But help was on the way. Later that same year, Sir Robert Peel was appointed to the Home Office, where he first tackled the criminal law, abolishing the death penalty for more than a hundred offenses, condensing more than 130 statutes dealing with larceny into one comprehensive law, and dispensing with the requirement that victims of sexual offenses offer certain proofs at trial.

But police reform was still a high priority for Peel, and as the economic and political situation in London began unraveling in 1825 (by 1828, one person in every 383 was a criminal and 12 of London's parishes with more than 20,000 residents had no night police whatsoever), Peel knew he could not delay his proposals any longer. In 1828, he commissioned a select study on policing and his report of its findings (which confirmed much of what he already knew and had previously proposed in Ireland) met with the usual opposition but also with some limited approval. This response, coupled with absolutely desperate times in terms of crime and social disorder, opened the door ever so slightly for Peel to move boldly—and he did.

In 1829, Peel introduced the Police Act—"A Bill for Improving the Police In and Near the Metropolis"—by noting that crime rates had increased 55% in London and Middlesex in the period between 1821 and 1828, and yet the population had increased by only 19%. He did not believe the increased crime rate was because of the depressed economic conditions but rather blamed a lax and inefficient police force. He pushed preventive policing—regular patrols by uniformed officers, gathering intelligence on criminal activities only, and centralization of all law enforcement operations within the London metropolitan area. (In a shrewd political move, Peel excluded the ancient City of London from the reach of the Police Act, which helped limit opposition—the City would later adopt the Police Act's provisions once their utility was proven outside the City.) Both houses of Parliament passed the Metropolitan Police Act and the Crown assented on June 19, 1829.

Peel succeeded where others had failed in large part because he understood that in pushing police reforms, he would have to assuage the fears of most countrymen as well as influential people like jurist William Blackstone and writer William Paley, all of whom still viewed a police force as a threat to constitutional liberties. Englishmen—statesmen and otherwise—constantly referred to the French police as a prime example of the dangerous ends to which police reform could lead. The French were notorious for using widespread intelligence networks not only for crime fighting but to spy on and apprehend government detractors. Peel knew he would have to distinguish his proposed reforms from the French model and to assure opponents that his plan was not perched atop a slippery slope that would inevitably lead to the French situation. Peel was masterful in finding middle ground and proposing moderate reforms based on fundamental principles that would change policing forever.

Peel's Principles

According to Peel, the basic mission for which the police exist was to prevent crime and disorder, and that mission could only be served by observing and complying with the following tenets:

- The ability of the police to perform their duties is dependent on public approval of police actions.
- Police must secure the willing cooperation of the public in voluntary observance of the law to be able to secure and maintain the respect of the public.
- The degree of cooperation of the public that can be secured diminishes proportionately to the necessity of the use of physical force.
- Police seek and preserve public favor not by catering to public opinion but by constantly demonstrating absolute impartial service to the law.
- Police use physical force to the extent necessary to secure observance of the law or to restore order only when the exercise of persuasion, advice, and warning is found to be insufficient.
- Police, at all times, should maintain a relationship with the public that gives reality to the historic tradition that the police are the public and the public are the police; the police being only members of the public who are paid to give full-time attention to duties which are incumbent on every citizen in the interests of community welfare and existence.

- Police should always direct their action strictly toward their functions and never appear to usurp the powers of the judiciary.
- The test of police efficiency is the absence of crime and disorder, not the visible evidence of police action in dealing with it.

Implementation of the Act

One thousand new police officers took to the streets of London on September 29, 1829. Their uniforms were the first indication that this police force was different, or at least intended to be different, and not just military troops in sheep's clothing. Officers wore top hats and a blue suit with brass buttons on the coat that said "Police." They were unarmed at first, but would later be allowed to carry birchwood clubs called *truncheons*.

Peel wanted more than window dressing though. He believed that retired noncommissioned army officers with good character certificates would make the best recruits, and he would demand men of the highest moral character. Still, to avoid temptations and keep officers from cozying up too closely with the residents on their beat, officers were drawn from areas outside their patrols. Those officers who were natives were assigned to patrols as far away as possible from their home neighborhoods. Peel wanted the bobbies to be viewed as representatives of the state and the police commissioners.

But even the right uniforms and strategic beat assignments could not convince the masses that this new arrangement would turn out well. The criticisms and complaints were immediate ("raw lobsters," "Peel's Bloody Gang," and "Blue Devils," were among just a few of the epithets of the day), and Peel knew his force would have to win public approval to succeed. Peel also knew that his officers could only win public approval with good character and civil conduct, both of which were closely supervised. Between 1829 and 1831, 8,000 men joined the force, and more than 3,000 of them were discharged for unfitness, incompetence, or drunkenness. As officers focused on preventing crime and maintaining civility with their communities, public opposition slowly but surely waned, and in 1834, a Select Committee reported that crime rates for violent offenses had declined and detection of more minor crimes had increased. Sir Robert Peel had finally brought meaningful police reform to England.

Influence on Community Policing in the United States

The Police Act and Peel's principles were bound to be popular and influential in the United States simply because they were so effective. But because American social conditions in the mid-1800s—disorder in the form of food riots, wage protests, for example—were so similar to the chaos in London that preceded Peel's reforms, the Police Act's influence was even greater and Peel's principles were an almost perfect fix for the law enforcement issues in the United States.

Those issues were most prevalent in the major U.S. cities, which were much like London in the early 1800s, limping along with the old constable-watch system, trying to retain a more informal approach to social control and avoiding any encroachment on civil liberties. Like Londoners, Americans were deeply suspicious and guarded against any government-directed law enforcement agency, and especially one that might bring a military presence to urban life.

But informal neighborhood controls like the constable-watch system simply could not keep pace with growing urban populations, and with the ever-increasing demarcation—geographically and otherwise—between the rich and poor. Those same social conditions were spawning more formal, bureaucratic responses to a variety of problems like health and welfare, so the time was ripe for municipalities to address the crime problem at the same time they were tackling issues like fire protection and sewage. Reformers urged lawmakers and bureaucrats to follow the London model in spirit and practice, while keeping ever-mindful of the differences in American and English life. As a result, newly established police departments in mid-1800 America adopted many of Peel's principles and practices but designed original innovations that were responsive to political and social conditions in their respective cities.

Like their English counterparts, the new American police officers were dedicated to preventing crime and disorder. They wore formal uniforms and set out on foot patrols to provide a professional presence in their communities, among the people.

Although officers here enjoyed broad discretion (rather than having their powers strictly codified and subject to the rule of law, as was the case in London), officers were expected to exercise their discretion consistently with the values and norms in the communities they patrolled. That discretion very often translated into physical force and a unique form of street justice for the lower classes and petty criminals. But the control and authority that patrol officers wielded was a welcome change to the middle and upper classes and municipal leaders, all of whom were desperate for order after the chaotic constable-watch years. Because municipalities were addressing social welfare issues at the same time, city leaders could support the police in their efforts by providing shelters for the homeless, ostensibly leaving only the more hardened and disorderly lower classes to be formally policed. That support and cooperation between the police and city leaders would ultimately get a bit too cozy, leading scholars to identify the period as the political era of policing, but the cooperative nature of the relationship had its foundations in Peel's principles and the Police Act.

When community policing was formally adopted in the United States in the 1970s to 1980s, Peel's influence was evident. Community policing programs around the country brought back foot patrols and the long-term beat assignments that fostered relationships between officers and the community. The community policing approach emphasized Peel's mission of maintaining order, with officers striving to be polite and respectful in their interactions with citizens, further enhancing the police-community relationship. Community policing proponents would also focus on falling crime rates as evidence of effective policing, just as Peel had done so many years before.

Pamela M. Everett

See also Broken Windows Theory; Citizen Patrols; Community Policing, Evolution of; Directed Patrol, Studies of; Foot Patrols; Generations (Three) of Community Policing; Police-Community Relations; Policing, Three Eras of

Further Readings

Brogden, M. (1987). The emergence of the police—The colonial dimension. *British Journal of Criminology, 27,* 4.

Lentz, S. A., & Chaires, R. H. (2007). The invention of Peel's principles: A study of policing "textbook" history. *Journal of Criminal Justice, 35*(1), 69–79.

Lyman, J. L. (1964). The Metropolitan Police Act of 1829: An analysis of certain events influencing the passage and character of the Metropolitan Police Act in England. *Journal of Criminal Law, Criminology, and Police Science, 55,* 141–154.

Reisig, M. D. (2010). Community and problem-oriented policing. *Crime and Justice, 39*(1), 1–44.

Reynolds, E. A. (1998). *Before the bobbies: The night watch and police reform in metropolitan London, 1720–1830.* Stanford, CA: Stanford University Press (original publisher, MacMillan Press Ltd., Hampshire, England).

Smith, P. T. (1985). *Policing Victorian London—Political policing public order, and the London metropolitan police.* Westport, CT: Praeger.

Uchida, C. D. (2010). The development of the American police: An historical overview. In R. G. Dunham & G. P. Alpert (Eds.), *Critical issues in policing: Contemporary readings* (pp. 17–36). Long Grove, IL: Waveland Press.

Walker, S. (1980). *Popular justice: A history of American criminal justice.* New York, NY: Oxford University Press.

Model Curriculum

In the 1970s and into the 1980s, police leaders, scholars, and other stakeholders started to think more strategically and analytically about the policing process. A series of research and evaluation efforts within the United States suggested that random patrol, criminal investigations, and rapid response were not particularly effective policing methods or strategies. It seemed clear that a different approach was necessary, that community policing had promise, and that systematic problem solving needed to occur. Herman Goldstein first published an article in 1979 that advocated for a problem-oriented policing approach. What followed was a series of early experiments in a variety of U.S. cities that suggested that a problem-oriented policing approach could yield benefits in crime prevention, community safety, and overall police effectiveness.

Since that time, many other police scholars have advanced our understanding regarding the importance of problem solving within the law enforcement process, and much has changed in policing. Specifically, community policing has been widely integrated and adopted within the United States and across several other countries. While some scholars might differentiate the nuances of community policing from problem-oriented policing, most agree that systematic problem solving and problem analysis remain central components of both approaches.

From a theoretical perspective, it seems clear that community policing and problem-oriented policing evolved from a myriad of criminological, environmental, and sociological theories. What was missing, perhaps, was a common understanding about what exactly is meant by *community policing*, *problem-oriented policing*, and *problem solving*. Even if such a common understanding was reached, one challenge moving forward was to develop a curriculum that could be taught within a variety of learning contexts and that would help to fully entrench community policing and problem-solving concepts and skills into academia, training academies, and law enforcement communities. This need was a particular concern in the United States, given its localized law enforcement process and the thousands of policing agencies that may or may not be capable of or interested in adopting community policing or problem solving.

This entry examines community policing curriculum development, provides a model curriculum, and outlines the various uses for same.

Problem-Oriented Policing Guides

The Office of Community Oriented Policing Services (COPS) recognized the need for research, training, and evaluation as a means of facilitating and sustaining community policing. In addition to the tens of thousands of grants made directly to local law enforcement agencies across the United States, COPS also established the POP Center, a nonprofit organization comprising affiliated police practitioners, researchers, and universities. The mission of the POP Center was to advance the concept and practice of problem-oriented policing in open and democratic societies by providing information, research, and training materials, which included a series of problem-oriented policing guides.

At the turn of the 21st century, a growing number of colleges, universities, police departments, and police training institutions were using the POP guides, an online interactive learning module, and other features of the POP Center website for teaching

and training purposes. In addition, police practitioners and crime analysts were pursuing undergraduate and graduate degrees to better prepare them for contemporary police functions, expectations, and challenges. Finally, problem-oriented policing and situational crime prevention were becoming essential knowledge for modern policing leaders and practitioners. To meet the emerging demand for knowledge about problem-oriented policing and situational crime prevention, the POP Center was tasked with developing a model academic curriculum that could be disseminated via the POP Center website.

The Model Curriculum

The model curriculum was designed primarily for undergraduate education, but with minor modifications it can and has been readily adopted and used in graduate courses, for preservice police and in-service police training, and community-based training. The curriculum has multiple components that are fairly flexible and which can be adapted for use in other courses or formats (e.g., online delivery). The complete curriculum, which is available online and for free to anyone, includes (1) the suggested course outline with active links to class readings; (2) 14 learning modules (in PowerPoint), developed for a standard 14- to 16-week college course or usable in other teaching and training settings; (3) suggestions and links for in-class and out-of-class exercises and assignments; (4) recommended class readings for each learning module; (5) suggestions for relevant videos, online resources, and exercises for a variety of instructional settings (e.g., graduate courses, in-service training). More specifically, the 14 learning modules cover the following topics: evolution of policing, community policing, problem-oriented policing, the SARA model, crime theories and crime opportunity, situational crime prevention, identifying and researching problems, problem-solving resources, crime analysis, responding to crime places, responding to offenders, responding to victims, evaluation and assessment of responses, and challenges.

Use of the Model Curriculum

The model curriculum has been used in college and university settings and in police departments in the United States and in other countries. The 14 individual modules can be used collectively (and were generally designed for that purpose) but can also be used independently as single teaching and training units or combined into specific parts depending on an agency's needs. In other words, the various components of the curriculum can be used to teach a one- or two-hour primer on community policing and problem solving, an entire course across a 17-week semester, or within a 16-week training academy. The choice is up to the instructor.

The entire model curriculum, which was carefully peer reviewed in multiple stages, can be found at the POP Center website and downloaded for free, in part or in its entirety. The curriculum does not include test questions, so individual instructors need to develop their own sets of exam materials. Otherwise, this complete course is ready to be used, easily adapted, and flexible so that it can be used in a wide variety of ways.

Joseph B. Kuhns

See also Center for Problem-Oriented Policing; Community Oriented Policing Services, Office of; Crime Analysis; Crime Displacement; Crime Mapping; Crime Prevention Through Environmental Design; Directed Patrol, Studies of; Foot Patrols; Problem, Definition of; Problem-Oriented Policing: Elements, Processes, Implications

Further Readings

Boba, R. (2003). *Problem analysis in policing*. Washington, DC: Police Foundation.

Braga, A. A. (2002). *Problem-oriented policing and crime prevention*. Monsey, NY: Criminal Justice Press.

Clarke, R. V. (Ed.). (1997). *Situational crime prevention: Successful case studies* (2nd ed.). Albany, NY: Harrow and Heston.

Clarke, R. V., & Eck, J. E. (2005). *Crime analysis for problem solvers in 60 small steps*. Washington, DC: U.S. Department of Justice, Office of Community Oriented Policing Services.

Goldstein, H. (1979, April). Improving policing: A problem-oriented approach. *Crime and Delinquency*, 25(2), 236–258. doi: 10.1177/001112877902500207

Kuhns, J. B., & Leach, N. R. (2012). *Model POP curriculum*. Retrieved from http://www.popcenter.org/learning/model_curriculum/

Scott, M. S. (2000). *Problem-oriented policing: Reflections on the first 20 years*. Washington, DC: U.S. Department of Justice, Office of Community Oriented Policing Services.

Website

Center for Problem-Oriented Policing, POP Center; http://www.popcenter.org

NATIONAL CENTER FOR COMMUNITY POLICING

The National Center for Community Policing (NCCP), originally named the National Neighborhood Foot Patrol Center, was created by the late Robert Trojanowicz, who was director of the School of Criminal Justice at Michigan State University (MSU). The NCCP performed some of the earliest conceptual development and research on community policing. In addition, the center provided some of the first training and technical assistance on community policing a decade before the Office of Community Oriented Policing Services (COPS) was created. This entry describes the foundation on which the NCCP was created, as well as its vision and its impact.

Origins

It is virtually impossible to separate a discussion of the NCCP from its founder, Robert Trojanowicz. The development and application of community policing drove Trojanowicz's work, and most of what is described in this entry is a firsthand accounting of the author's work and discussions with Trojanowicz over the 10 years preceding his death. While Trojanowicz was trained in both criminal justice and social work, his research and professional interests were significantly shaped by the respect and influence he had for his father, who was a foot patrol officer. Trojanowicz's vision was that the involvement of community members in defining and solving crime within their community in partnership with the police would be more effective in creating neighborhood safety than traditional police practices. The result would be lower crime, lower fear of crime, safer communities, less disorder, more efficient and effective police forces, and greater reciprocal respect between the police and community. The vision was pragmatic, not idealistic—that is, Trojanowicz did not believe this approach to policing would be universally successful, but that it would significantly increase the quality and productivity of the police-community relationship.

Trojanowicz's design and output for the NCCP was based in the ethos of MSU. Like the cultures of other Tier 1 research institutions, MSU's culture was for faculty to engage in high-quality scientific research, preferably with external funding. In addition, MSU's land grant philosophy was to translate scientific research into practice. These factors influenced Trojanowicz's work as he was contemplating his ideas about policing: He wanted to test his theories using rigorous scientific research, but he also wanted to translate the research findings into practice by developing policies and operational procedures that could actually be used by law enforcement agencies to battle crime. These factors served as core principles in both his research and the development of the NCCP.

Neighborhood foot patrol, as community policing was referred to in the early 1980s, had two key benefits. First, it would serve to stimulate the development of comprehensive anticrime neighborhood organizations with neighborhood foot patrol officers providing assistance and expert advice to community members and organizations. Second, through their patrolling activities the neighborhood officers would be in close day-to-day contact with community members. They would become familiar with the residents and problems of the community and then link them to appropriate governmental services and resources.

The question was, Would this concept work? To learn the answer, the concept needed to be field tested. The Charles Stewart Mott Foundation granted $2.6 million to the City of Flint, Michigan, to fund neighborhood foot patrols in experimental districts in the city, of which $251,932 was awarded to MSU to evaluate the program. This project and its subsequent publications were the factors that essentially created the NCCP. The Mott Foundation supported the NCCP to provide national training and technical assistance on community policing based on the lessons learned in Flint.

Community policing research, training, and technical assistance provided by the NCCP were all based in what Trojanowicz identified as the "Ten Principles of Community Policing":

1. *Change*—Organizational and individual behavior must change from the traditional "professional model" of policing (characterized by reactive, incident-driven methods and emphases on quantitative outcomes, such as number of calls for service, arrests, and so on) in order to enhance the way police services are delivered.

2. *Leadership*—There must be continual reinforcement of the community policing vision, values, and mission at all organizational levels.

3. *Vision*—Both police leaders and community members must have a clear understanding of desired outcomes for public safety and the quality of life.

4. *Partnership*—Police agencies must develop principles of equal partnerships among all groups within the community.

5. *Problem solving*—Police should use a comprehensive process for recognizing, pinpointing, and developing problem-solving solutions.

6. *Equity*—Citizens will receive valuable and respectful police service regardless of age, race,

gender, ethnicity, religious belief, sexual preference, or any other attribute.

7. *Trust*—The police must demonstrate integrity and follow through with promises.

8. *Empowerment*—The police agency must give greater authority to first-line personnel and the community.

9. *Service*—Police must commit to providing personal service directed toward the needs of the community.

10. *Accountability*—The police and the community must hold each other accountable for their actions.

Just as the Ten Principles articulated operational components of community policing, Trojanowicz, identified the "Big Six" entities that must work together in order for community policing to be a success:

1. *The law enforcement agency*—This includes the leadership of the agency, all sworn personnel regardless of assignment, and non-sworn staff.

2. *The community*—Not only formal entities such as community groups and churches are included, but also individuals who need to feel empowered through their relationship with the police.

3. *Elected officials*—Particularly at the local level, elected officials represent visible leadership within the community who need to be engaged and support the community policing initiative.

4. *The private sector*—Whether through a partnership with a major corporation or support from a local small business owner, a solid relationship with the private sector can provide important insights and remedies to neighborhood crime problems.

5. *Non–law enforcement public agencies*—Code enforcement, social services, the public health department, and nonprofit organizations all have a role in community safety and must be engaged.

6. *The media*—Members of the news media must understand the concept.

An important part of the NCCP's mission was to share the research and lessons learned with law enforcement agencies. This was accomplished in several ways. With support from the Mott Foundation, the NCCP held an annual conference on the MSU campus. Police officials from around the world attended the conference both as participants and presenters. The goal was to show diverse methodologies of implementing community policing and share experiences.

Another popular method of disseminating policy-based research on specific community policing issues was through what became known as the "green books." This was a series of monographs that explored topical issues, most of which were derived from discussions in the annual conference. The green books—available from the NCCP—became a popular tool to share cutting-edge community policing research and practice.

Based on the growth of the community policing philosophy, the NCCP partnered with the FBI Academy on two aspects of training and technical assistance. Between the sessions of the FBI National Academy, the FBI often sponsors special symposia and, on two occasions, the NCCP and FBI sponsored conferences for several hundred police leaders at the Quantico, Virginia, facility. Based on these experiences, the Behavioral Sciences Unit at the FBI Academy developed a new community policing course for police managers that embraced the research and concepts of the NCCP.

During this same time, the John F. Kennedy School of Government at Harvard University received funding from the National Institute of Justice (NIJ) for a series of Executive Sessions on policing. These sessions consisted of a small group of recognized police executives and scholars exploring critical policing issues. Trojanowicz, who also served as a research fellow at the Kennedy School, was not only a participant in the Executive Sessions but also a driving force on many of the community policing issues. Information contained in the papers relating to community policing that resulted from these sessions was also incorporated into the research, training, and technical assistance of the NCCP.

Trojanowicz, the driving force behind the NCCP, died of a heart attack in February 1994. A few months later, the U.S. Congress passed the Violent Crime Control and Law Enforcement Act, which created the COPS Office. In 1997, the COPS Office created the Regional Community Policing Institutes (RCPI) to provide nationwide training and technical assistance. As the recipient of one of the COPS RCPI grants, the work of the NCCP was largely continued by the MSU Regional Community Policing Institute.

David L. Carter

See also Center for Problem-Oriented Policing; Community Oriented Policing Services, Office of; Community Policing, Evolution of; Community Policing and Problem Solving, Definition of; Flint, Michigan, Experiment; Foot Patrols; Team Policing

Further Reading

Trojanowicz, R. C. (1982). *An evaluation of the neighborhood foot patrol program in Flint, Michigan.* East Lansing: Michigan State University, The National Neighborhood Foot Patrol Center. Retrieved from http://www.cj.msu.edu/~people/cp/evaluate.html

Website

National Center for Community Policing. *Publications*; http://www.cj.msu.edu/~people/cp/webpubs.html

NATIONAL CRIME PREVENTION COUNCIL

The National Crime Prevention Council (NCPC), a nonprofit organization headquartered in Arlington, Virginia, is committed to helping individuals, families, and communities prevent crime. NCPC focuses its efforts on teaching crime prevention strategies, engaging local communities, and partnering with law enforcement and other government agencies to enhance public safety. NCPC is perhaps best known as the organization responsible for McGruff the Crime Dog, whose purpose, as stated on the NCPC website, includes empowering people to help themselves and others to prevent crime, while also being respectful of police and community officials, teachers, parents, youth, senior citizens, businesses, and community organizations.

This entry examines the founding and history of the NCPC, focusing in particular on McGruff as a symbol for the organization over the past 30 years. The entry also examines the importance of NCPC efforts to promote community crime prevention and community policing.

Creation

The National Crime Prevention Council, founded in 1982, grew out of the efforts of 19 organizations that first joined together in 1979 in response to rising crime rates and a belief that citizens and communities could do more to aid crime prevention efforts. These 19 organizations founded the National Citizens' Crime Prevention Campaign, and through a collaboration with an advertising firm and the Advertising Council, the group released a television public service announcement in 1980. The announcement included a dog in a trench coat asking viewers to help "take a bite out of crime." This dog, unnamed at the time, would later become McGruff the Crime Dog in 1982 after a nationwide naming contest.

Also in 1980, the initial 19 organizations and other groups joined to form the Crime Prevention Coalition of America, designed to help citizens and communities work with the police to more effectively reduce crime. In 1982, in an effort to better coordinate crime prevention activities, the coalition created the NCPC to help oversee the coalition and campaign.

Today, the coalition has over 400 member organizations at the national, state, and local level, and McGruff the Crime Dog continues to be an important component of NCPC efforts to promote crime prevention. The NCPC conducts most of its activities with financial support from the federal government, particularly the Bureau of Justice Assistance and other units within the Office of Justice Programs in the U.S. Department of Justice.

Activities

NCPC is involved in a number of activities in efforts to advance their primary mission of crime prevention and keeping communities safe, some of which involve outreach efforts with community and law enforcement agencies. This section discusses some of those programs and activities.

Crime Prevention Coalition of America

As noted above, the Crime Prevention Coalition of America today consists of more than 400 member organizations. These include law enforcement agencies, government agencies, and community groups, but all are focused on promoting citizen efforts to reduce crime and promote public safety. These organizations are typically involved in training for law enforcement groups, policymakers, and citizens on the importance of prevention and how collaboration between groups can enhance the effectiveness of crime prevention efforts. NCPC provides services for member organizations, including training curricula, conference planning materials, and the opportunity to collaborate with NCPC to develop strategic prevention plans at the national level.

Coalition members are involved in a number of activities at both the national and local levels. Many of these fall under the Citizen Corps program, overseen by the Department of Homeland Security. Citizen Corps includes five programs designed to promote volunteering for community crime prevention and disaster preparedness efforts. These include Volunteers in Police Service (VIPS) and USAonWatch, the national organization that oversees neighborhood watch programs. VIPS is designed to encourage the use of civilian volunteers in police agencies. USAonWatch focuses on training neighborhood groups to be the "eyes and ears" for police and to use crime prevention tactics as target hardening (i.e., strengthening the security of a residence or building) to reduce opportunities for criminal activity to occur.

Celebrate Safe Communities

Celebrate Safe Communities helps promote innovative police-community partnerships in crime prevention. NCPC, through Celebrate Safe Communities, highlights successful partnerships as models for other local groups to follow. One major component of these efforts is Crime Prevention Month, which occurs each October and highlights public safety tips in a number of areas, including crime reporting, home safety, school safety, and drug abuse prevention.

Teens, Crime, and the Community Initiative

Teens, Crime, and the Community combines education and service experience to better prepare teenagers to prevent crime in their community. A major component of the program is the Community Works curriculum, which focuses on a series of interactive sessions in which teens learn about avoiding drugs and victimization and also how they can better work with police and community groups to promote public safety. The program also includes Community Resource People, a program designed to introduce teens to those involved in crime prevention in their communities. Finally, teens have a chance to apply what they have learned in service projects intended to provide direct experience with problem solving and crime prevention efforts in the community.

Be Safe and Sound in School

Be Safe and Sound in School is a comprehensive program administered to schools that involves a number of stakeholders coming together to enhance safety and security. Teachers, community members, parents, students, and police work together to identify security problems and develop and implement a detailed action plan that addresses both physical security in and around the school and social problems such as bullying that may be harming school safety.

Circle of Respect

Circle of Respect is one of NCPC's newest activities and is focused on efforts to reduce bullying and cyberbullying. The program is designed to refute the idea that bullying is an acceptable rite of passage. Circle of Respect promotes prosocial behavior and respect for all both inside and outside of school. NCPC has used a number of methods to promote respect, including YouTube videos, a monthly book club, and outreach events at malls.

McGruff the Crime Dog

Efforts by McGruff the Crime Dog are perhaps the most recognizable and well-known activities of the organization. McGruff the Crime Dog first appeared in 1980 as part of the National Citizens' Crime Prevention media campaign. The McGruff campaign has focused on both encouraging individuals to protect their property and self (i.e., "watch out") and to become more involved in community efforts to promote public safety (i.e., "help out"). The initial partnership with the Advertising Council (commonly known as the Ad Council) was crucial, because the Ad Council helps an agency produce public service announcements (PSAs) and works to obtain free advertising space in local and national markets. McGruff continues to appear today on television, radio, and in print, and the campaign is one of the Ad Council's longest running. McGruff

PSAs have also been among the most frequently appearing. For example, in 1994, McGruff the Crime Dog received about $92 million of donated television time and print space, making it the most prevalent campaign in the United States that year. To date, over $1.4 billion in advertising space has been donated to NCPC PSAs.

The McGruff campaign has changed its focus somewhat over time. The initial campaign was targeted toward adults and focused on "stop a crime." In these early ads, McGruff provided tips on making the home safer by taking steps such as locking doors and making the community safer through actions like starting neighborhood watch groups. More than 300,000 copies of the accompanying brochure, "Got a minute? You could stop a crime," were distributed in the first months after the ads began airing, and by 1981 more than 1 million were sent out. Over the course of the 1980s, McGruff also began to focus on children and teens, in particular providing tips for children to avoid becoming the victims of kidnapping and to resist peer pressure to use drugs. During this time, the campaign also encouraged residents to do more to clean up streets, parks, and playgrounds to make them less attractive locations for criminal activity. In the early 1990s, the campaign also began to discuss efforts to reduce gun-related violence. A toll-free number (1–800-WE-PREVENT) was introduced for people to call and request information on how to help prevent violent crime in their community. In 1992, McGruff's nephew, Scruff McGruff, first appeared in campaigns specifically targeted at younger children (ages 5 to 9). Additionally, children were reminded of the risks of playing with firearms. In the 2000s, the campaign has focused in large part on bullying, identity theft, and Internet safety. In recent years, new efforts have focused on cyberbullying and telemarketing scams that target senior citizens.

Today, McGruff remains one of the most popular and most recognized figures in crime prevention. He has his own website with a wealth of information targeted toward children and teenagers. The site includes games and videos, along with advice on a range of topics including bullying, online safety, home safety, school safety, guns, drugs, and gangs. According to the NCPC, there are about 4,000 McGruff the Crime Dog costumes in use across the United States, and McGruff appears annually at thousands of events ranging in size from school assemblies to the Macy's Thanksgiving Day Parade.

McGruff also has a club for children ages 6 to 10, known as the McGruff Club. The goal of this outreach effort is to provide children with information on crime prevention and get them involved at an early age in service projects that benefit their communities. Additionally, the club serves to introduce McGruff as a trusted voice on crime prevention and helps build connections between children, the police, and community groups. McGruff Clubs typically meet weekly for about 30 minutes and are overseen by trained adult facilitators.

Impact of McGruff the Crime Dog

Multiple studies have assessed the impact of the McGruff the Crime Dog campaign, although all of these studies are now at least 15 years old. A national survey funded by the National Institute of Justice from 1979 to 1982 found that the beginning of the McGruff campaign had made an impression on the American public. A majority of respondents were familiar with McGruff and among those who had seen at least one of the PSAs, over half had more positive views about citizen involvement in crime prevention as a result. About 25% of those seeing the PSAs responded that they had taken specific actions to help prevent crime. Subsequent focus group and survey research in the 1980s by Saatchi and Saatchi, the advertising firm that helped initiate the campaign, found that McGruff's name recognition and popularity continued to increase throughout the decade.

A second national survey of 1,500 adults to assess the impact of McGruff the Crime Dog was undertaken in the spring of 1992. About 80% of respondents were familiar with McGruff and reported seeing at least one PSA, a large increase from the 52% of respondents who were familiar with McGruff in 1982. Respondents were generally positive about the campaign; criticism, although rare, focused on the lack of realism of having a dog detective encouraging people to prevent crime. Similar to the prior survey, about half of respondents reported having improved attitudes toward crime prevention, about a quarter reported learning from the ad campaign, and about a fifth reported taking specific preventive actions as a result of the ads.

Media managers and community crime prevention practitioners were also separately surveyed to examine their views about the usefulness and effectiveness of McGruff. Overall, both groups were generally familiar with the campaign. Over half of media managers had run a McGruff PSA in the previous 12 months. The ads were generally viewed positively, and were seen as beneficial in promoting crime prevention, particularly among children. Similarly, practitioners reported frequent use of McGruff materials in their crime prevention activities, particularly in efforts to promote crime prevention among children.

The surveys were supplemented by a qualitative assessment of the content of McGruff PSAs. The ads typically fall in one of two categories: situational or experiential. The situational ads focus on real-life scenarios with concrete tips on addressing and preventing crime. These ads rely upon the viewers feeling a sense of ownership of their community and using collective action (e.g., starting a neighborhood watch group) to better the neighborhood and community. These ads stress the effect individual protective actions can have on improving the community. In contrast, the experiential ads rely more on emotion than on clear crime prevention guidance and focus more on individual action (e.g., requesting a brochure for more information) than building a stronger community.

Community Policing and the NCPC

As discussed above, much of the work of the NCPC is focused on greater involvement of individuals and communities in crime prevention efforts. A particular focus of the NCPC is instilling in young people the importance of community crime prevention efforts and partnering with law enforcement agencies in efforts to reduce crime. NCPC also offers training curricula and resources for community groups and crime prevention practitioners that are focused on the importance of community policing.

One training program is titled "Improving Police-Community Relations Through Community Policing" and focuses on VIPS and neighborhood watch as examples of ways that police and citizens can work together more collaboratively and productively. The training also stresses the benefits of community meetings and citizen police academies as ways to bring together citizens and police in nonconfrontational environments where both groups can recognize the benefits of working together. Training on crime prevention theory and practice also stresses the benefits of close police-community partnership. The NCPC guiding principles state that while police play a central role in crime prevention, without the cooperation of residents and community groups, prevention will be ineffective.

Cody W. Telep

See also Crime Prevention Through Environmental Design; Cybercrime and Community Policing; Neighborhood Associations; Publicity Campaigns; School Violence and Safety, Community Policing Strategies for

Further Readings

National Crime Prevention Council. (n.d.). Use of McGruff. Retrieved from http://www.ncpc.org/about/about-mcgruff/use-of-mcgruff

National Crime Prevention Council. (2008). *Mobilizing the nation to prevent crime, violence, and drug abuse: The 2007 report from the Crime Prevention Coalition of America.* Arlington, VA: Author. Retrieved from http://www.ncpc.org/programs/crime-prevention-coalition-of-america/publications/mobilizing.pdf

National Crime Prevention Council. (2009). *Protecting what matters to you: National Crime Prevention Council 2008 annual report.* Arlington, VA: Author. Retrieved from http://www.ncpc.org/about/annual-report/NCPC-webFinal%20-2.pdf

O'Keefe, G. J., Mendelson, H., Reid-Nash, K., Henry, E., Rosenzweig, B., & Spetnagel, H. T. (1984). *Taking a bite out of crime: The impact of a mass media crime prevention campaign.* Washington, DC: U.S. Department of Justice, National Institute of Justice.

O'Keefe, G. J., & Reid, K. (1989). The McGruff crime prevention campaign. In R. E. Rice & C. K. Atkin (Eds.), *Public communication campaigns* (pp. 210–211). Newbury Park, CA: Sage.

O'Keefe, G. J., Rosenbaum, D. P., Lavrakas, P. J., Reid, K., & Botta, R. A. (1996). *Taking a bite out of crime: The impact of the National Citizen's Crime Prevention media campaign.* Thousand Oaks, CA: Sage.

Website

National Crime Prevention Council; http://www.ncpc.org

NEIGHBORHOOD ASSOCIATIONS

Neighborhood associations are grassroots, voluntary, nonprofit organizations composed of people from a geographic area who work collectively and in a volunteer capacity to solve problems and pursue common goals. While this sort of organization is often called a neighborhood association, it also can be called a *neighborhood council, community council, neighborhood civic association, or block association.* This form of grassroots civic engagement can be traced back to the early town hall meetings in New England. In more recent times, formalized neighborhood associations emerged in the 1970s in some cities in response to fiscal constraints that led to coproduction of government services. *Coproduction* means that consumers of services, in this case residents, provide a public service jointly with the public agency, with the goals of reducing costs and increasing the quality of the service. Beyond helping to provide the service, citizens are involved in planning the service. In other cities, neighborhood associations have been created by local governments for the specific purpose of implementing community policing.

Typically, neighborhood associations develop organically. Neighbors get together to deal with problems in their communities, and sometimes this results in a more structured and formal organization that may become officially recognized. This building stage is occurring even today in many cities where parts of the community are not yet organized into neighborhood associations.

There are some organizations that appear on the surface to be similar to neighborhood associations but in fact are quite different. The first entails the appointment of community members by governmental officials or executives to serve as a formal conduit between government and the residents of a given geographical area. There is a considerable amount of governmental oversight of such bodies and little involvement on the part of community members who have not been appointed to the group.

Another organizational type that resembles the neighborhood association is a homeowners' association (HOA) or condominium association. These are actually corporations; their primary function is to promulgate and enforce, through power of law, covenants, conditions, and restrictions (CC&Rs). Therefore, homeowners' and condominium associations are not recognized by local governments in the same way that neighborhood associations are, even though they may also be concerned with public safety matters, such as safety, security, insurance, and so on. So while police departments may not have assigned roles with homeowners' or condo associations, as may be the case with officially recognized neighborhood associations, they can nonetheless be useful for community policing purposes.

Structure

In cities with formalized neighborhood associations, the general structure, functioning, and membership criteria is established by ordinance or policy, and there is little oversight if the groups meet these basic requirements. The local government usually ensures, through an application and certification process, that associations' boundaries do not overlap.

The size of geographic areas covered by neighborhood associations varies. The denser the community, the smaller the geographic scope of its associations, while less densely populated areas have neighborhood associations that are spatially larger. High-crime neighborhoods can be particularly susceptible to having very small neighborhood associations; the "bunker mentality" that exists in many of these communities can lead individuals' conceptions of their "neighborhood" to shrink to encompass only one block, or even just one building.

Neighborhood associations typically have elected officers (e.g., president, vice president, secretary, treasurer). There may also be additional people on the executive committee who are elected to at-large positions or to represent different areas within the boundaries of the neighborhood.

There may also be several committees that have specific functions like public safety, fund-raising, beautification, membership, special events, publicity and marketing, and land use and zoning. Each neighborhood association has a unique set of committees reflecting the needs and priorities of its members.

How often the neighborhood association meets is decided by the group itself, though municipal ordinance may specify a minimum number of meetings per year. How formal the meetings are is also decided by each neighborhood association. For some, adherence to Robert's Rules of Order is appropriate, while others prefer to operate more informally. Sources of revenue for neighborhood associations include dues, fund-raising activities, donations from individuals and businesses, regular grants from local government, and other grants from government or foundations for special projects. Many neighborhood associations are 501(c)(3) organizations; that is, they have been classified by the Internal Revenue Service as having tax-exempt status, which means donations to the associations are tax deductible.

One of the primary functions of neighborhood associations is to provide an opportunity for ordinary residents to have some influence over decision making by local government. For government, the advantage of this decentralized decision making is that it draws on local knowledge and fosters interest in and support for plans and projects. Neighborhood associations differ with respect to their role in municipal governance. Some are a recognized component of municipal government, with an official advisory role to play with respect to reviewing and commenting on zoning, land use and development issues, road projects, and other matters considered important to the livability and quality of the neighborhood. In other cases, the local government provides the neighborhood association with resources, such as meeting space, access to municipal staff, and help with mailing and spreading information, but the association has no formal role in governance. In many communities, there is a larger body that serves as an umbrella organization for all the neighborhood associations in the city.

Membership

Neighborhood associations' bylaws specify who can be a member. The bare minimum is that one be an adult residing in the particular geographic area. Many associations have expanded membership criteria to include property owners, business owners, and representatives of nonprofit organizations. Neighborhood associations are meant to represent the interests of all people in an area, regardless of whether they are active members, are rarely involved, or are not even aware that the association exists.

Research on the characteristics of members of neighborhood associations shows that in a given population, only a small number of people will get involved. Also, members tend to be older, better educated, more affluent, and more likely to be homeowners. They are more likely to be politically involved in other spheres, through participation in local and national electoral processes and voting, and attendance at city council, board, and commission meetings. In ethnically and socioeconomically diverse neighborhoods, not all groups will be equally represented. This raises the question of whether these groups, which are often officially seen by the local government as speaking on behalf of neighborhoods, are really representative of the other people who live, work, and own property there. This point is expanded upon in the next section.

The relationship between involvement in neighborhood associations and views about the neighborhood and neighbors is U-shaped; that is, the people most likely to be involved in neighborhood associations are those who have either positive or negative, as opposed to neutral, feelings about their neighborhood and their neighbors. Some research has found that the most active members of neighborhood associations are the most pessimistic about the likelihood of other people doing what needs to be done to address neighborhood issues. This explains their involvement—they doubt that other people will work toward the common good, so they are motivated to do it themselves. A common pattern seen among those who become involved with neighborhood associations is that they start out with naive views of working side-by-side with their neighbors to improve the quality of life in the community. They soon learn that community organizing is considerably more difficult than it appears, that many of their neighbors are not interested in helping out, and that change takes a long time. Pessimism (or perhaps realism) ensues, though it often has the effect of increased commitment to the neighborhood and to the association.

Those who start out with negative views may be attracted to neighborhood associations because they provide a forum to vent complaints. This negativity can fuel passion for improving the neighborhood, but managing such people at meetings is a challenge faced by many neighborhood groups. Constructive discussion can easily be sidetracked by endless complaining, and it may discourage others from continued involvement.

Much of what neighborhood associations do involves problem- and conflict-oriented activities over livability issues of concern to the entire community, such as transportation, parks, safety, and land-use density. People attend neighborhood association meetings in large numbers when contentious issues are on the agenda, as in a proposed road project or a significant change in land use. Fighting something can bring people together, but a lack of success (which is common) can deter all but the most stalwart activists from further involvement with the group.

Activities

Neighborhood associations are a forum for neighbors to come together and discuss issues of particular concern, and to work collectively toward a solution. Associations are also believed to build trust and friendship bonds between members, teach people to work together, and encourage them to look beyond their own self-interest to the broader interests of the group. Yet there is the reality that many neighborhood associations are not representative of their communities. The broader interests of the neighborhood may differ considerably from those of the few people on the association's executive board. There is also a potential for screening of issues presented to the leadership of the neighborhood association; not everything that comes to the attention of the leadership will be presented to the general membership.

Although the specific activities of neighborhood associations ordinarily focus on matters that directly impact the neighborhood, they are largely driven by the individual interests of active members. Many of these activities promote the development of social cohesion—large social gatherings like picnics, barbecues, or block parties; newsletters; and flea markets. Others are clear examples of coproduction of government services: beautification through flower planting, streetscape improvements, and residential rehabilitation; community gardens, neighborhood and park clean-ups; and community patrols and neighborhood watch.

Neighborhood Associations and the Police

The nature of interaction between the police and neighborhood associations is affected by departmental policy. In some places, the police department may appoint one or more officers to function as liaisons between the department and neighborhood groups. Officers attend meetings where they disseminate information about police policies, report crime statistics, answer residents' questions, pass on tips about crime prevention, solicit information about crime incidents, and listen to residents' comments and complaints. Most people who attend neighborhood meetings have positive attitudes toward police and like seeing uniformed officers there. Yet sometimes, these interactions can be derailed by angry citizens who use the forum to challenge police actions or authority in general. The open nature of discussion at neighborhood association meetings can attract people with an axe to grind toward government services.

Use of liaison officers is a good first step to building good police-community relationships, but just receiving input from citizens is quite different from the collaborative processes demanded of community policing. Absent any substantive response to community issues from the police, residents are likely to feel they are wasting their time. In problem-oriented policing, neighborhood associations are good sources of information on the crime in the area. When police go to community meetings and ask the residents what the biggest problems are, they are often surprised to hear complaints about speeding cars or barking dogs. Typically, quality-of-life issues, many of which do not involve criminal behavior, are what trouble people the most. Yet, there may be disagreement within the neighborhood association about what the police should focus on. More ethnically and economically heterogeneous neighborhoods have a wider array of issues. Self-interest of individual members, as in their own experiences or where they live in the neighborhood, can affect "issue representation." Someone who lives in an active prostitution area and is frequently hassled by sex workers will present a very different definition of the crime problem than someone who lives a couple of blocks away and has little direct experience with prostitutes. The more powerful or talkative members of the group should not give undue influence to problem definition during the scanning phase.

Neighborhood associations may be primarily insular, that is, mostly interested in serving their own members, and frequently involved with other neighborhood associations in disputes over resources and turf conflict, or likely to work cooperatively with other neighborhood associations. It cannot be assumed that just because different neighborhood associations have identified similar problems that they are interested in working together. There may be historical conflicts or personality clashes. A potential downside of working closely with one neighborhood association is that success there will very likely lead to demands for similar services from other neighborhoods, who may well lobby their elected officials for priority police attention. Few police departments have enough resources to help every neighborhood, and sometimes the most demanding communities are the least willing to engage collectively in coproduction of public safety.

Given the well-established difficulties of making a sustainable impact on crime in neighborhoods with low levels of collective efficacy and social cohesion, it is good to prioritize these demands. For example, it might be required that a neighborhood association establish a public safety committee to work closely with police, or that it take initial steps to show it can benefit from police assistance, perhaps through conducting a neighborhood survey. It could be argued that making these demands may disadvantage poor or socially disorganized neighborhoods. But realistically, if the people in the neighborhood are not prepared to do any work themselves, if there is widespread attitude of "it's the job of the police to deal with crime," then any long-term success is unlikely.

On the other hand, even in this type of neighborhood, there are likely to be a few active members of a neighborhood association; research has found that these people are more likely to work with the police toward the coproduction of public safety, through activities such as community or citizen patrols, neighborhood or block watches, bicycle registries, and school escort programs.

Sharon Chamard

See also Community Cohesion and Empowerment; Involving Local Businesses; Police-Community Relations; Tipping Points of Neighborhoods

Further Readings

Hawdon, J., & Ryan, J. (2011, December). Neighborhood organizations and resident assistance to police. *Sociological Forum, 26*(4), 897–920.

Hays, R. A., & Kogl, A. M. (2007, May). Neighborhood attachment, social capital building, and political participation: A case study of low- and moderate-income residents of Waterloo, Iowa. *Journal of Urban Affairs, 29*(2), 181–205.

Knickmeyer, L., Hopkins, K., & Meyer, M. (2003). Exploring collaboration among urban neighborhood associations. *Journal of Community Practice, 11*(2), 13–25.

Meyer, M., & Hyde. C. A. (2004). Too much of a "good" thing? Insular neighborhood associations, nonreciprocal civility, and the promotion of civic health. *Nonprofit and Voluntary Sector Quarterly, 33*(3), 77S–96S.

NON-SWORN PERSONNEL AND VOLUNTEERS, USE AND TRAINING OF

Non-sworn personnel and volunteers are easily confused concepts in policing. *Non-sworn personnel*—who number about 370,000 in U.S. state and local law enforcement agencies—are permanently and regularly employed, either full or part time, provide vital support services to the sworn officers, and typically have their workplace situated within the stationhouse. Conversely, *volunteers*, while also providing vital and helpful services to the sworn officers, generally work for little or no governmental pay or benefits and are not regular, permanent employees of the governmental unit. Because the two are distinguishable, this entry focuses on non-sworn personnel and another entry in this encyclopedia addresses police use of volunteers.

The term *non-sworn* should also be construed liberally herein, so as to include those police agency personnel who are also engaged in problem-solving efforts that involve other nongovernmental agencies and individuals (such as utility companies, business owners, and apartment managers), associations (e.g., neighborhood watch), and other governmental entities (e.g., the city council, the county commission, the prosecutor's office, the health department) that are also stakeholders in civic wellness and community policing. (Relationships involving police and such stakeholders are also discussed in another entry in this encyclopedia, entitled "Collaboration with Outside Agencies.") This entry explains the role of non-sworn personnel and why agencies must carefully hire and train these individuals to support community policing and problem-solving efforts.

Uses of Non-sworn Personnel

Every police agency, regardless of size, has a basic organizational structure. This structure can be vertical, as in a large agency, and contain a large number of specialized units, or it can be flat, or horizontal, as in the case of small agencies. These structures essentially establish the division of labor and lines of communication within the organization.

At their most basic levels, organizational structures are also composed of both line (operational) and non-line (staff or auxiliary) elements. Most people are familiar with the line elements that primarily involve field-level police work—for example, patrol (the "backbone" of policing) and investigative functions. Lesser known and visible, non-line functions involve non-sworn employees and generally take place out of the public's view—while also affording citizens a wealth of career opportunities. These non-line functions fall within two broad categories: *staff services* and *auxiliary services*. Staff services are usually geared more toward the agency's people or human resources needs and can include but are not limited to the recruitment, training, and promoting of personnel, and even planning and research, community relations, and public information services.

Auxiliary services involve the following functions, each of which has their own role in community policing and requires unique types of training and education:

- *Forensic/crime lab technicians:* The crime laboratory is probably the fastest-growing arena in criminal justice in terms of technological advancement, given recent advances in forensic analyses. Some agencies also employ civilian forensic technicians for fieldwork, to respond to crime scenes, take photographs, collect, and analyze evidence.
- *Crime analysts:* These individuals assist law enforcement agencies by looking for crime patterns and trends and sometimes analyze intelligence information, thereby enabling sworn personnel to better understand where to focus their efforts and to predict where crimes may occur in the future.
- *Intelligence/fusion center analysts:* With recent emphases on CompStat, intelligence-led policing, and predictive policing, many agencies now employ analysts who are specially trained to collate and interpret intelligence gathered by officers in the field.
- *Civilian investigators:* Some agencies now employ specialized civilian investigators for such incidents as traffic collisions, financial crimes, and crimes against property and persons.

- *Crime prevention officers:* Crime prevention has advanced tremendously from its early "lock it or lose it" days, and simply because it is far better for citizens and the criminal justice system to prevent crimes from occurring in the first place, it has become a much more complex and challenging discipline.
- *Dispatchers:* Communications personnel use high-tech communications equipment to answer calls for service and dispatch police, fire, medical, and other first-responder personnel to scenes.
- *Information technology specialists:* Technological advances including in-car computers, computerized mapping, and various forms of wireless communication now require police agencies to employ qualified IT professionals.
- *Budgeting/grants personnel/research and development:* These three areas require a set of skills that typically require law enforcement executives to seek specially trained (non-sworn) individuals. These positions can also entail maintaining all personnel, facility, and equipment records; billing and managing of all grants; ordering of all equipment and supplies; and publishing newsletters.
- *Property/evidence managers:* Storing and protecting property and the chain of evidence from crime scenes and other forms of seizures typically involve non-sworn personnel who manage and organize these inventories.
- *Public information officers:* Some jurisdictions employ specially trained non-sworn public information personnel who work with media and field requests from the public about crimes and other subjects.
- *Records managers:* Law enforcement agencies, like the courts, must manage innumerable records, from officers' field interviews to crime and arrest reports and investigations; even given the greater reliance on paperless technologies, there remains a need for specialists who can handle data entry and records management.
- *Webmasters:* Department websites now provide real time neighborhood crime statistics (including crime maps), crime prevention and safety tips, virtual tours of the department, and the ability of citizens to anonymously report crime or complaints about officer conduct.
- *Victim service providers/advocates:* Many police agencies use non-sworn personnel to help victims and witnesses keep abreast of their cases, offer support and assistance, and make referrals for counseling, victim compensation programs, and social services.

Add to these functions the fact that many police agencies also use non-sworn personnel for animal control, zoning and code enforcement, prisoner transportation, offender booking and photo imaging, and parking enforcement—and even for responding to burglar alarms, due to the amount of time officers are tied up with such calls for service—and it becomes readily apparent that there is a "shadow group" of employees in law enforcement that the public seldom or never sees.

Certainly the value of such employees is not lost on city and county managers and their governing boards; as budgets have shrunk, many jurisdictions have found it more cost-effective to turn to non-sworn personnel to handle those tasks that do not always require a sworn officer. Nationally, many states even allow their non-sworn personnel to have their own collective bargaining provisions. For example, in Michigan, a union is involved with wages, hours of employment, and several other conditions of employment for full-time, non-sworn employees.

Even college and university police departments are experiencing growth in the number of non-sworn personnel. In four-year colleges and universities with 2,500 or more students, about one-fourth of campus law enforcement agencies use non-sworn personnel. Non-sworn personnel are used to direct traffic, patrol student housing, escort students at night, educate students about crime prevention, and other tasks.

Community Policing and Non-sworn Personnel: Needs and Challenges

Certainly all personnel employed in those police agencies practicing community policing and problem solving—from top to bottom in rank, both sworn and non-sworn, and in all types of assignments—play key roles in this strategy and must be trained in its philosophy and methods. The contributions made to community policing and problem solving by such non-sworn personnel as crime analysts, forensic lab technicians, crime prevention officers, and civilian investigators are obvious: They have a direct bearing on citizens' quality of life and maintain linkages to citizens for solving and preventing crimes. Furthermore, as a result of the observations made in the course of their daily work, these personnel can inform police executives, street officers, and others about crime trends, neighborhood disorder, new offenders and types of offenses that have surfaced, and other conditions that contribute to community distress.

Other non-sworn personnel play a role in supporting the organization's mission and values as well. Therefore, when new non-sworn employees are hired into the organization, emphasis should be placed on orienting them toward the mission and role of the department. Furthermore, newly hired support and technical employees need to understand that the department is committed to community policing and problem solving, in order for them to see how their jobs can support efforts to implement this approach. Finally, they all play a role in customer service, possibly interacting each day with citizens as well as police officers.

Therefore, as noted above, care must be given to the recruiting, hiring, and training of all non-sworn employees. In fact, the federal Office of Community Oriented Policing Services (COPS) recommends that problem-solving training be provided to non-sworn personnel, as well as to sworn personnel, as early as possible when an agency adopts community policing and problem solving. COPS also recommends that this training take place even prior to the strategy's implementation and include sworn officers, crime analysts, and community partners; refresher courses should also be offered periodically.

Furthermore, any newly hired employee having direct contact with the public (to include report takers, dispatchers, records clerks, receptionists, property and evidence clerks, and so on) should be trained in customer service and have explained to them the concept of community policing and how citizens and officers are empowered in this strategy. It is essential that such non-sworn personnel understand the evolving, nontraditional role of the patrol officer in this, the community era of policing.

Community policing and problem solving can also be undermined by traditionalists (both sworn and non-sworn) within a police department who deal with the public often and for whom community policing and problem solving is akin to social work, is not a proper crime-fighting role for the police officer, affords too much discretion to the street officer, or is something for which officers don't have time. Or, on the other hand, it is not unheard of for

political leaders to oversell community policing as the panacea for all that plagues the city, announcing that it will eliminate crime, racism, homelessness, drugs, gangs, and other social ills. Or they might create a soft image of community policing, always showing officers hugging children, speaking to groups, throwing block parties, and so on. Investigative personnel may resist, or not understand, the new emphasis placed on working in concert with community agencies, community leaders, and citizens, and not comprehend the need to leave the role of specialist and become more of a generalist—shifting to community concerns and patterns of criminal conduct and establishing case priorities based on trends and patterns.

As another illustration, the "serve and protect" reputation of the entire department can easily be undermined by non-sworn dispatchers who fail to explain to citizens why the shift to community policing can mean a delay or even a nonresponse by sworn officers to nonemergency calls. Dispatchers and other non-sworn personnel, as well as citizens, must adapt and become accustomed to, say, officers going out of service for extended periods in order to engage in a problem-solving assignment and not handling nonemergency calls until returning to service.

In sum, the nearly 370,000 non-sworn law enforcement employees in state and local law enforcement agencies are a large and important component of the field. As such, the hiring, training, support, and general functions of non-sworn police personnel are all critical to the success of community policing and problem solving.

Kenneth J. Peak

See also Citizen Patrols; Citizen Police Academies; Citizen Surveys; Community, Definition of; Community Cohesion and Empowerment; Community Oriented Policing Services, Office of; Community Policing: What It Is Not; Crime Analysts, Role of; In-Service Training; Investigations, Community Policing Strategies for; Model Curriculum; Neighborhood Associations; Volunteers, Police Use of

Further Readings

Cohen, D. (2001, June). *Problem-solving partnerships: Including the community for a change.* Washington, DC: U.S. Department of Justice, Office of Community Oriented Policing Services. Retrieved from http://www.cops.usdoj.gov/pdf/e06011157.pdf

Colletti, J. L. (1996, October). Why not hire civilian commanders? *FBI Law Enforcement Bulletin, 65*(10), 8. Washington, DC: U.S. Department of Justice, Federal Bureau of Investigation.

Eck, J. E. (1992, June). Helpful hints for the tradition-bound chief. Washington, DC: Police Executive Research Forum. Retrieved from http://www.policeforum.org/library/police-management/Helpful%20Hints%20for%20the%20Tradition%20Bound%20Chief.pdf

Office of Community Oriented Policing Services. (2012). *Community policing training and technical assistance.* Retrieved from http://www.cops.usdoj.gov/default.asp?Item=1974

Reaves, B. A. (2008, February). *Campus law enforcement, 2004–05.* NCJ 219374. Washington, DC: U.S. Department of Justice, Bureau of Justice Statistics. Retrieved from http://bjs.ojp.usdoj.gov/content/pub/pdf/cle0405.pdf

Reaves, B. A. (2011, July). *Census of state and local law enforcement agencies, 2008.* Washington, DC: U.S. Department of Justice, Bureau of Justice Statistics. Retrieved from http://bjs.ojp.usdoj.gov/content/pub/pdf/csllea08.pdf

Wilkerson, B. D. (1994, November). Civilian services: Civilian employees for police departments. *FBI Law Enforcement Bulletin, 63*(11), 21–24.

OFFICERS' JOB SATISFACTION

Job satisfaction refers to the positive outlook or feelings an individual has regarding his or her job. This measure can be used to describe general feelings regarding the job, various aspects of the job, or work experiences. Variation in job satisfaction can affect health, individual work performance, and performance of the organization. Poor job satisfaction in policing can also impact police-community relations. The correlation between officer job satisfaction and police-community relations is particularly salient when law enforcement agencies attempt to employ a community policing model. A properly implemented community policing model can improve both officer and community satisfaction. This entry describes what researchers have learned about the job satisfaction of police officers and how the strategies of community policing influence officers' job satisfaction.

Job Satisfaction

Job satisfaction is a complex concept. A variety of individual and environmental factors are examined as predictors of job satisfaction, which can be measured by many methods. In policing research, job satisfaction is often examined in terms of officer demographic characteristics, agency characteristics, and work conditions.

Officer Characteristics

A majority of job satisfaction research is focused on the relationship between the characteristics of officers and their reported level of job satisfaction. The most commonly studied characteristics include gender, race and ethnicity, highest level of education, marital status, length of service, and rank. Research on race and ethnicity, marital status, and length of service demonstrate consistent relationships with job satisfaction. African American police officers consistently report being more satisfied with their work than White officers. This finding conflicts with research on the general population examining race and job satisfaction with racial minorities consistently reporting lower job satisfaction than White employees in nonpolicing jobs. Occupational research reports that married employees in nonpolicing jobs generally report being more satisfied with their work than single employees. However, the reverse is true in policing, with married officers generally reporting lower job satisfaction than single officers. This finding tends to be attributed to the unique nature of police work and the strain it places on officers' families. An inverse or curvilinear relationship between length of service and job satisfaction is consistently reported in the research. This means that levels of job satisfaction decrease the longer the officer serves in the department, or that there is a decline in job satisfaction from the beginning of law enforcement work as a rookie until some point midcareer when job satisfaction levels begin to improve. Gender, education, and officer rank have all demonstrated inconsistent relationships with job satisfaction.

Agency Characteristics and Work Conditions

Researchers expanded their analyses beyond officer demographics to include agency characteristics and work conditions and their relation to officer job satisfaction. The inclusion of environmental characteristics reflects an acknowledgement that context can play a role in the degree of satisfaction an officer possesses regarding his or her work. These variables include agency size, organizational culture, work assignment, and shift.

It is often assumed that officers in large-size departments will report lower job satisfaction, while their counterparts in small-size agencies will report a higher level of job satisfaction, with officers in medium-size departments falling somewhere in between. Some research provides partial support for this assumption. Specifically, officers in small agencies report higher job satisfaction than officers in medium and large agencies, but there is no difference in satisfaction levels between officers in medium and large agencies. Additional research suggests that the variation in satisfaction levels between agencies of different sizes may not be attributable to size alone. Rather, the variation in satisfaction may be due to other factors, such as organizational culture, that often, but not always, vary with agency size.

Organizational culture is a term used to describe the nature and quality of the work environment, and it can have a significant impact on job satisfaction. Organizational culture is often discussed in terms of the strictness of the organizational hierarchy and how the hierarchy affects communication and the formality of relations between the ranks. Other factors include management methods and administrative stress. Taken together, the nature of communication, social relations, management practices, and stress generate a particular culture within the agency that can be positive or negative; a negative culture can lead to officer isolation, alienation, and decreased job satisfaction.

Agency size and culture are agencywide conditions that generally affect all officers. Conversely, work and shift assignments are conditions that introduce more variation in satisfaction at the individual level. Assignments, such as patrol, investigation,

management, or specialized units entail different types of work, require different skills, and involve varying levels of discretion and autonomy. Shifts can be described by time of day (days, afternoons, or overnights), length (8-, 10-, and 12-hour shifts), and stability (rotating or semipermanent). Both the type of assignment and shift, individually and in concert with one another, can impact attitudes toward work and job satisfaction.

Effects of Poor Job Satisfaction

Officers who are satisfied with their jobs experience less stress and tend to engage in higher levels of organizational citizenship behavior (OCB): This is an employee's individual, discretionary behavior that tends to promote the effective functioning of the organization. Officers with poor job satisfaction report lower morale, more cynicism, and burnout; have higher rates of absenteeism and contribute to higher rates of employee turnover; and experience more alcoholism and drug use. The effects of poor job satisfaction lead to agency instability, reductions in individual and agency performance and productivity, and negatively impact relationships with the community.

Community Policing and Job Satisfaction

Community policing is characterized by community engagement, problem solving, and organizational transformation necessary to achieve the desired levels of community engagement and problem solving. Community policing is both a return to the community involvement in public safety, as described in Sir Robert Peel's principles of law enforcement, and a response to calls for reform resulting from the negative effects of the professional era of policing.

The professional model, characterized by reactive, incident-driven methods and emphases on quantitative outcomes such as number of calls for service, arrests, for example, was the predominant style of policing from roughly the early 20th century into the 1960s, when civil unrest and a significant deterioration in police-community relations led to calls for police reform. The policing methods that were employed as part of the professional model resulted in the isolation of police from the public they served, which was detrimental to the police, the community, and the public safety enterprise.

Community policing requires organizational transformation and a change in the dynamic of the police-community relationship. The community policing model necessitates the redistribution of initiative, decision-making power, responsibility, and accountability to lower ranks within the organization. Police must also modify their view of the community to see community members as partners in public safety efforts rather than being external to these efforts. These changes facilitate cooperative efforts between the police and the community to identify and solve community problems. However, these are significant changes and may meet with resistance in organizations typically described as averse to change. Some advocates have argued that, despite initial difficulties with implementation, community policing may be one of the most effective methods for helping officers remain interested in, engaged in, and satisfied with police work.

Research supports the assertion that properly implemented community policing strategies can improve officer job satisfaction. Studies in Madison, Wisconsin, and Chicago, Illinois; a sample of small- and medium-size agencies in North Carolina; and a three-wave panel study using a national sample have all reported that officers working within a community policing framework report higher levels of job satisfaction than officers employing traditional policing methods. Officers employing community policing strategies were also more satisfied with their specific work assignments, their work conditions, and their supervisors. They were more optimistic about the impact of their work in the community, and more accepting of different and diverse policing strategies. Research has also reported that traditional officers in some agencies have expressed support for community policing principles.

Organizational leadership seeking to implement a community policing model should ensure agency and community support, sufficient agency infrastructure and interagency cooperation, fair and impartial application of community policing strategies, and genuine community engagement. These are necessary elements for a proper and sustainable community policing model. The proper and complete implementation of community policing may result in increased officer and community satisfaction.

Jennifer L. Lanterman

See also Agency Mission and Values, Changes in; Community Policing, Evolution of; Community Policing: Resources, Time, and Finances in Support of; Implementation of Community Policing; Police-Community Relations

Further Readings

Adams, R. E., Rohe, W. M., & Arcury, T. A. (2002). Implementing community-oriented policing: Organizational change and street officer attitudes. *Crime and Delinquency, 48*(3), 399–430. doi: 10.1177/0011128702048003003

Community Policing Consortium. (1998). *Understanding community policing: A framework for action.* NCJ 148457. Washington, DC: U.S. Department of Justice, Bureau of Justice Assistance.

Dantzker, M. L. (1997). Police officer job satisfaction: Does agency size make a difference? *Criminal Justice Policy Review, 8*(2–3), 309–322.

Fridell, L., & Wycoff, M. A. (Eds.). (2004). *Community policing: The past, present, and future.* Washington, DC: Police Executive Research Forum.

Skogan, W. G., & Harnett, S. M. (1997). *Community policing, Chicago style.* New York, NY: Oxford University Press.

Skolnick, J. H., & Bayley, D. H. (1988). Theme and variation in community policing. *Crime and Justice, 10,* 1–37. Retrieved from http://www.jstor.org/discover/10.2307/1147401?uid=3739672&uid=2133&uid=2&uid=70&uid=4&uid=3739256&sid=21101585254297

Wycoff, M. A., & Skogan, W. G. (1994). Community policing in Madison: An analysis of implementation and impact. In D. P. Rosenbaum (Ed.), *The challenge of community policing: Testing the promises* (pp. 75–91). Thousand Oaks, CA: Sage.

OPERATION WEED AND SEED

Operation Weed and Seed was launched in 1991 as one of the key strategies of the U.S. Department of Justice's antiviolence, antigang, and antidrug community revitalization programs with primary focus on high-crime neighborhoods. The three original grant sites—Kansas City, Missouri; Trenton, New Jersey; and Omaha, Nebraska—grew to about 600 sites that received federal funding for Operation Weed and Seed for a specific period of time, up to five years for a maximum of $1 million. At each site, the U.S. Attorney's Office plays a central role in bringing together multiple agencies at all levels of government to effectively mobilize and coordinate resources in a community. Theoretically, such a coordinated approach should result in synergistic impact and be more effective than isolated service delivery. This entry examines Operation Weed and Seed's goals and implementation, and several assessments of its effectiveness.

Goals and Implementation

With the Weed and Seed strategy, enforcement is used first to "weed" out crime, violence, and gangs and to stabilize the conditions in high-crime communities; then resources are identified and mobilized to "seed" the revitalization of the communities. The long-term goal is for the communities to become resistant to future problems that would result in a return to high rates of crime. Rigorous required evaluations of programs provide detailed findings of their outcomes. Continued evaluation at the sites also is critical in assessing problems and unmet needs to sustain the community's progress.

The major concepts are coordination, weeding, community policing, seeding, and safe havens. The strength of the established coordination among the community-based organizations and governmental decision makers is an important variable in the success of most of the sites. Weeding involves concentrated law enforcement activities to identify, arrest, and prosecute violent offenders, drug dealers and traffickers, and other offenders. The importance of involving the communities' citizens early and giving them substantial voice is an important lesson from the first sites.

Community policing builds bridges between the weeding and seeding components and is particularly important in building community trust and encouraging citizen involvement. Dedicated officers assigned to the weed and seed target areas help improve the neighborhood environment by participating in such activities as neighborhood cleanups, graffiti eradication, and code enforcement. These officers also are important in engaging young people in activities and providing them with positive role models and improving communication between the residents and police. The weed and seed approach aims to mobilize residents to participate in local crime prevention with such activities as neighborhood watches and citizen advisory committees.

Seeding may be the greater challenge because it involves more participation and commitment from public and private sector organizations. Just as the weeding component operates more efficiently within established structures, many sites attempt to build their seeding programs by expanding existing resources. Community residents' voices are integral to the success of seeding efforts. The requirement of safe havens—an accessible multiservice center for youth and adults to be safe from drug trafficking and other criminal activity, to obtain services, improve skills, and develop positive relationships—may increase the prevalence of intervention programs for the youth, such as afterschool programs, recreation and sports programs, job training, and health and substance abuse programs.

To encourage local participation, the planning structure in most Operation Seed and Weed communities should include a weed and seed steering committee, a weeding committee, a seeding committee, and weed and seed program staff. The steering committee—comprising key public agency administrators, local governmental officials, social service organizations and community representatives—provides oversight on program design and implementation, establishes overall goals and objectives, and ensures sustainability of the coordinating efforts across agencies and between the community and organizations. Individual weeding committees plan and monitor the enforcement efforts that include police and prosecutorial efforts. Federal prosecution provides opportunities for stricter sentences, although evaluations of Operation Weed and Seed found prosecution to be the weakest area. Explanations given for lack of prosecution include lack of additional funding, prosecutors often serving multiple municipalities with competing political considerations, and federal prosecutors not being involved to the degree anticipated. Individual seeding committees plan and monitor the prevention, intervention, treatment, and restoration activities. The weed and seed program staff carries out the daily activities, and to be most effective, they should be based in the same facility and develop coordination between the two components of weeding and seeding from the planning stage onward.

Effectiveness

The largest early national evaluation of Operation Weed and Seed programs was conducted in 1999 by the National Institute of Justice at 12 sites across eight jurisdictions that were considered examples of the program's key components, which are as follows:

- Enhanced coordination (coordinated analysis and planning of local problems and strategies to address them)
- Weeding (concentrated and enhanced law enforcement efforts to identify, arrest, and prosecute violent offenders, drug traffickers, and other criminals)
- Community policing (proactive police-community engagement and problem solving)
- Seeding (human services—including afterschool, weekend, and summer youth activities)
- Adult literacy classes
- Parental counseling
- Neighborhood revitalization efforts to prevent and deter crime

Each site's evaluation included individual interviews with program decision makers, law enforcement managers, service providers, and community leaders; group interviews with seeding program participants; resident surveys; and analysis of crime and arrest records in the specific target areas. The evaluation proposed to determine successful and failed elements and lessons to be learned. Although the results were not highly significant statistically, they were consistently favorable.

Interviews with program participants showed the seeding programs provided services that would not have been available without the Operation Weed and Seed program and these services increased the participants' feelings of emotional and physical security. The evaluation determined that additional structure and discipline were provided to young people in the area, and because of the opportunities and assistance provided through the program, adults received additional personal and professional growth. By the second year of Operation Weed and Seed implementation, six of the sites showed declines in Part I crimes (homicide, rape, robbery, aggravated assault, burglary, larceny, and auto theft) when compared to the year before implementation. Similar results were found at these sites in drug arrests. Initially, there was an increase in all arrests during intense weeding activities, but this was then followed by declining arrest rates. Public perceptions on such issues as fear of crime

improved at most of the sites that also saw reduction in crime rates.

From this early evaluation, investigators were able to deduce factors that helped or hindered successful implementation of Operation Weed and Seed. Helpful factors included strong, established networks of community-based organizations and leaders who communicated well with service organizations, and geographical advantages that favored economic development. Severe crime problems and transient community populations hindered strong outcomes. Early seeding of programs and resources while sustaining the weeding of criminal activity along with highly visible task forces, community policing and an active prosecutorial team led to constructive outcomes. Those sites that concentrated their resources on narrowly targeted groups of residents in small geographical areas had the greatest impact on crime rates.

An evaluation in 2006, from researchers O'Connell, Perkins, and Zepp, examined 100 Operation Weed and Seed sites, allowing comparisons across the sites of community problems and solutions. The researchers reviewed sites' strategic statements, which included the original problems and activities proposed in their applications for federal funding, thereby determining the range of issues and relative complexity of strategies developed at the sites. They also collected data sources available to the different sites but had little success in finding uniformity in content or reporting capabilities. Homicide rates were one common indicator across jurisdictions. Rates were examined before program implementation and multiple years after implementation. The sites had an average decline of 1.4 homicides per year following implementation, compared to a decrease of 0.5 homicides for the remainder of their jurisdiction.

Operation Weed and Seed has been labeled a *strategy*, not a grant program, by the U.S. Department of Justice. Included in every funded site were long-range goals to develop self-sustaining community-based interventions. Although the programs demonstrated positive results, as noted above, federal funding decreased and sites were encouraged to pursue other public and private funding. Federal resource guides for communities and training guides for site coordinators were developed to assist communities in implementing the weed and seed strategy. Experienced sites were asked to provide training and technical support to new sites. Regional training sessions were encouraged to facilitate the coordination of partners and collaborations.

As of June 5, 2011, the federal office managing Operation Weed and Seed grants, the Community Capacity Development Office (CCDO), closed due to a lack of federal funding. The last year CCDO added new Operation Weed and Seed sites was fiscal year (FY) 2009, with no plans to fund new Weed and Seed sites. For FY 2012 Weed and Seed grants, the Bureau of Justice Assistance was assigned to manage existing Operation Weed and Seed grants until the end of their grant award periods.

Vivian Lord

See also Drug Crimes, Community Policing Strategies for; Gang Crimes, Community Policing Strategies for; Police-Community Relations

Further Readings

Dunworth, T., & Mills, G. (1999, June). *National evaluation of weed and seed.* NCJ 175685. Washington, DC: U.S. Department of Justice, Office of Justice Programs. Retrieved from https://www.ncjrs.gov/pdffiles 1/175685.pdf

O'Connell, J., Perkins, M., & Zepp, J. (2006). *Weed and seed performance measures: Analyzing and improving data resources final report.* Washington, DC: Justice Research and Statistics Association. Retrieved from http://www.jrsa.org/ws-eval/studies_other/jrsa-performance-measures-final.pdf

Trudeau, J., Barrick, K., Williams, J., & Roehl, J. (2010). *Independent evaluation of the national weed and seed strategy: Final report.* Washington DC: U.S. Department of Justice, Office of Justice Programs. Retrieved from http://www.jrsa.org/ws-eval/studies_national/ WnS_Final_Evaluation_Report.pdf

U.S. Department of Justice. (n.d.). *Find answers to frequently asked questions regarding the status of the Community Capacity Development Office.* Washington, DC: U.S. Department of Justice, Community Capacity Development Office. Retrieved from http://www.ojp .usdoj.gov/ccdo/faqs.html#q2

U.S. Department of Justice. (2005). *The weed and seed program.* Washington, DC: U.S. Department of Justice, Community Capacity Development Office. Retrieved from https://www.cfda.gov/?s=program&mode=form&t ab=step1&id=43cb0562aabe94ac552214a3b535ab8d

PEEL'S METROPOLITAN POLICE ACT

See Metropolitan Police Act of 1829

PLACE-BASED POLICING

For police, there are two key features of crime: people and places. The work of police has traditionally focused on people—predominately offenders. By 2000, the focus of police on people had increasingly given way to a focus on places—that is, the particular physical locations in which offenders act. The transition occurred because research demonstrated that crime does not occur randomly in space; instead, it is highly clustered in small geographic areas and this concentration tends to remain stable over time. Groundbreaking research by Larry Sherman and colleagues in the mid-1980s showed that a small fraction of addresses generated the majority of police workload in Minneapolis, Minnesota. Subsequent research reinforced this important finding: Crime is more predictable by location than by any other factor.

The predictability of crime at specific places initially provided guidance to police on where to conduct directed patrols or crackdowns. It now also provides police with leverage to interrupt or prevent crime by improving place management. A central tenet of community policing is resolving community problems through partnerships; place-based policing operationalizes this concept by requiring accountability at the causal point most proximal to the problem—the specific location. Evidence shows that place-based policing is more effective than other policing strategies—particularly those focused on offenders—and uses scarce police resources more efficiently. To be effective problem solvers, police must be aware of the significance of policing specific places and their relationship to what are termed *hot spots*. This entry defines and examines the significance of crime places within the context of hot spots.

Definition of Place

Place has a very specific definition in crime theory. A *place* is a geographic location that is often a specific street address, such as a residence, a business like a bar, or a school. In terms of size, a place may be a slightly larger geographic area like a street corner, intersection, or block; occasionally a place may be as large as an apartment complex or small shopping center. A place is not so large as a police beat or a neighborhood.

The precise specification and size of a problem place varies in different settings and for different problems; the appropriate size is the smallest geographic area in which crime is concentrated and ownership established. Thus, while the actual size of a crime place will vary, it is essential to understand that a crime place is a very distinct location representing a very small geographic area; it is sometimes known as a "micro" place.

Importance of Place

Most police are keenly aware of place. Patrol officers are dispatched to specific places; provided a physical street address by a dispatcher, they drive to that location and record it on an incident report. Indeed, a patrol officer who returns again and again to the same address has a heightened awareness of problem places.

In contrast to problem places, areas in which crime clusters are often known as *hot spots*. Like problem places, hot spots represent the geographic areas in which offenses occur, and occur repeatedly. But, while hot spots are often considered general areas such as a neighborhood, they contain specific locations or places in which crime is even more concentrated. It is the recurrence of crime at places—a phenomenon known as *repeat victimization*—that actually creates a hot spot. A specific house or business that is victimized once is likely to be victimized again; the resultant accumulation of crime at places transforms the larger area into a full-blown hot spot.

The concentrations of crime show why place is so important to police. Because police spend so much time in hot spots, focusing on places within hot spots helps them identify the underlying features that persistently give rise to crime. While police must use somewhat general tactics in hot spots, they can use very specific tactics in places.

Leveraging Place Through Place Managers

A critical feature of crime places is that most contain a key type of person: a place manager. A place manager is a person who owns, operates, or uses a specific place—someone who has a vested interest in the well-being of a place; they do not want it to be damaged, become run down, lose value, or give rise to harm. While the interests of place managers in safety may arise from good will, a fiduciary responsibility to maintain a safe premise, or an economic calculation of costs, place managers have a strong voice or role in the management of places and are thus an important ally to the police. By enlisting the assistance of place managers, police leverage resources at these locations and prevent crime.

Place managers vary from one setting to another. In commercial settings, place managers include store owners, managers, and clerks. In bars, bouncers and bartenders are managers of places. In schools, place managers are comprised of principals, teachers, and school staff. In residential settings, place managers are landlords or owners, apartment managers, and doormen.

Key place managers are usually people who work in the location—the bar bouncer or school principal or apartment manager—and have a direct responsibility for the well-being of the location. There are other place managers whose responsibility for the location is indirect but still important; these ancillary place managers include shoppers, neighbors, parents, and bus drivers—people who live in, move through, or use the location in one way or another. Place managers are distinct from other individuals in places who are known as guardians; guardians monitor likely targets of crime, while place managers have a broader role of discouraging crime in the overall physical setting.

A place has a disproportionate share of crime—relative to its neighbors or similar types of places elsewhere—because of absent or ineffective place management. When effective, place managers monitor and regulate behavior on their property. These techniques vary by location. In rental housing, effective place managers screen tenants and evict those who cause problems. In bars, effective place managers require identification, limit the amount of alcohol served, serve alcoholic beverages in glasses that are not breakable, and bounce customers causing trouble. In parking lots, effective place managers limit access, provide good lighting, and may use security cameras or patrols. In motels, effective place managers require identification and credit cards from lodgers and may attempt to exclude individuals who are, for example, local and wishing to rent the rooms short-term for purposes of prostitution. Effective place management reduces crime in places. Identifying the problem place and its place managers provides an avenue to police to reduce crime.

Identifying Problem Places

As geographic information systems (GIS) have become widespread in police agencies, crime mapping provides a way to identify problem places. Dot or point maps using specific addresses show exactly which locations generate a disproportionate share of problems. Maps that use symbols scaled in size to the number of events—calls for service or crimes—at a particular address provide a visual representation of problem places. Figure 1 displays a map of residential burglaries in an urban jurisdiction: the larger-size icons identify places in which multiple burglaries occurred within a year, whereas the smaller dots reflect locations with only one burglary. Point maps focus crime prevention efforts on locations where they are most needed. In contrast, hot spot maps that highlight general areas do not serve the same purpose.

Identifying crime places may require examining similar types of places across a jurisdiction rather than locations within a geographic area because problem places may be geographically separated. A specific parking lot with numerous break-ins may appear to reflect crime in the neighborhood; however, a comparison of all parking lots may reveal the disproportionate concentration of the crime problem. Such comparisons must make adjustments for differences in size between places. Common types of problem places include bars or entertainment venues, apartment complexes, schools, budget motels, convenience stores, parking lots, and parks.

Activating Place Managers

Once problem places are identified, police must identify key place managers and deficiencies in place management. Creating place managers improves police efficiency and effectiveness. The type of response needed will vary based on the type of place; for instance, a drug location will require a different response than a place that has domestic violence. There are numerous examples in which police have focused on problem places and reduced crime: Requiring two employees on duty reduced robbery of convenience stores; applying nuisance abatement and code enforcement reduced drug markets; providing crime prevention information to

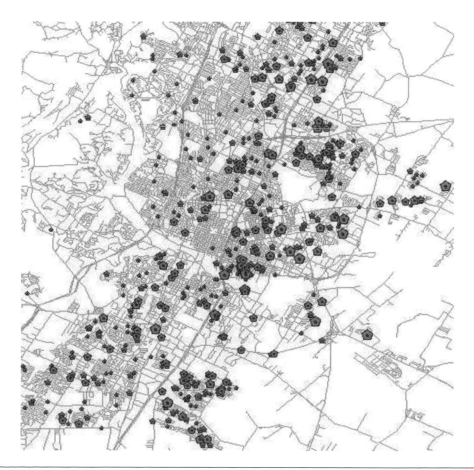

Figure 1   Residential Burglary Map
Source: Author.

burglary victims reduced residential burglaries; and altering traffic patterns reduced street prostitution in one location and drive-by shootings in another. Developing place-based strategies is considered an effective and efficient way for police to reduce and prevent crime.

Deborah Lamm Weisel

See also Crime Mapping; Directed Patrol, Studies of; Evidence-Based Policing; Global Positioning Systems/ Geographic Information Systems; Hot Spots; Repeat Victimization, Community Policing Strategies for

Further Readings

Braga, A. A., Weisburd, D. L., Waring, E. J., Green-Mazerolle, L., Spelman, W., & Gajewski, F. (1999). Problem-oriented policing in violent crime places: A randomized controlled experiment. *Criminology, 37,* 541–580. doi: 10.1111/j.1745–9125.1999.tb00496

Eck, J. E., & Wartell, J. (1996). *Reducing crime and drug dealing by improving place management: A randomized experiment.* Washington, DC: U.S. Department of Justice, National Institute of Justice.

Eck, J. E., & Weisburd, D. L. (1995). Crime places in crime theory. In J. E. Eck & D. L. Weisburd (Eds.), *Crime and place* (pp. 1–33). Monsey, NY: Criminal Justice Press.

Sherman, L. W. (1995). Hot spots of crime and criminal careers of place. In D. L. Weisburd & J. E. Eck (Eds.), *Crime and place, crime prevention studies* (Vol. 4; pp. 35–52). Monsey, NY: Criminal Justice Press.

Weisburd, D. L. (2008, January). Place-based policing. *Ideas in Policing No. 9.* Washington, DC: Police Foundation. Retrieved from http://www .policefoundation.org/pdf/placebasedpolicing.pdf

POLICE FOUNDATION

Established in 1970, the Police Foundation (also known as the National Police Foundation) is a private, nonpartisan, nonprofit organization with the mission of supporting innovation and enhancing effectiveness in policing through collaborative efforts in research, technical assistance, and communications programs. The foundation has supported research in police behavior, policy, administration, and procedure, and aims to diffuse contemporary knowledge and best practices to all levels of law enforcement—especially local municipalities. More importantly for present purposes, for many years the foundation has sponsored research that has greatly contributed to our breadth of knowledge concerning policing in general, and to the development and application of community policing and problem solving in specific. After briefly describing the origins of the foundation, this entry discusses the purposes and pillars of the foundation, including research and professional services.

Origins

As noted on the Police Foundation's website, the nonprofit Ford Foundation, through a $30 million fund, established the Police Foundation to "assist a limited number of police departments in experiments and demonstrations aimed at improving operations, and to support education and training projects." This fund originally supported projects for a five-year period and sought collaboration with federal, state, and local agencies in an effort to serve as a force multiplier for the issues at hand. As a result of the foundation's success in spearheading change within the law enforcement community during this five-year period, the Ford Foundation decided to continue its support of the Police Foundation. In 1993, the Ford Foundation provided an endowment fund in the form of a grant to the Third Decade Fund for Improving Public Safety to support the foundation's work and secure its permanency.

Purpose and Pillars

The purpose of the foundation is to assist the police in being more effective in a variety of areas, including patrol, calls for service, and community policing initiatives. As knowledge about effective policing is gained through research, police agencies may need assistance to integrate that knowledge into practice. Similarly, as society's demands increase, police agencies may need to revise their practices to not only meet these demands but also maintain an effective fit to protect and serve society. Thus, the foundation established the Institute for Integrity, Leadership, and Professionalism in Policing, which helps agencies address these issues.

Research

The advancement of scientific knowledge to best inform police practice is perhaps the strongest pillar of the foundation—knowledge that is both welcomed and unwelcomed by the community for which it is intended. The foundation strives to maintain an active research agenda by facilitating partnerships with law enforcement and the academic community. Such partnerships provide a means by which innovative ends can be identified. By bringing together professionals and academics, the foundation serves as a conduit for the two-way communication of new ideas and best practices. Leading scholars in the field of policing have presented their research and published their ideas through the foundation's Ideas in American Policing series.

At times, research findings from experiments sponsored by the foundation have challenged traditional police beliefs. Two such experiments were the Kansas City preventive patrol and the Washington, DC, Policewomen on Patrol. In Kansas City, it was found that routine preventive patrol with marked vehicles did not significantly affect crime rates. In Washington, D.C., female patrol officers mirrored performance levels of their male patrol colleagues at a time when police administrators were hesitant to place female officers into the patrol function.

A significant proportion of foundation research led to questioning the traditional model of professional law enforcement and toward a new view of policing—the community-oriented policing philosophy commonly adhered to today. Research programs on foot patrol, interactions with citizens, and satisfaction of communities and police have all helped to facilitate the movement toward this community-oriented model. As one of the partners in the Community Policing Consortium, along with four other leading national law enforcement organizations, the foundation played an integral role in the advancement of community policing within agencies in the United States. Since 1993, the foundation has provided community policing education, training, and technical assistance to more than 1,000 law enforcement agencies and communities.

Since the foundation's inception, its leadership has emphasized the role of the foundation as having a practical impact on the field of policing. More specifically, the foundation supports research that focuses on extending the knowledge base through empirical evaluations of police working in the field. This research, simply put, should inform police how to do their jobs more effectively and efficiently. For those working in the field, this information can

prove invaluable. For example, a police chief of a municipal police department may find himself having to identify ways of providing the same level of safety and service to the community with decreasing resources. Research supported by the foundation aims to inform a police chief in this position of how to accomplish this mission through best practices, emerging technologies that have been proven to streamline processes, or even collaborative programs with federal, state, or private partners.

The foundation has also facilitated comprehensive research on police use of force, which led the foundation to develop software to help police agencies monitor officers whose use of force places departments at risk by eroding public confidence, increasing civil liability, and undermining the agency's effectiveness. According to the foundation's website, "a widespread absence of any systemic approach for assessing risks that place municipal interests at risk can be faulted for the inability of officials to cope with this increasingly difficult problem." The Police Foundation's Risk Analysis Management System (RAMS) software centralizes key performance data, identifies critical risk areas, and allows for early intervention and strategic response to reduce the potential for liability, to assist officers, and to promote community confidence.

The foundation also developed a Quality of Service Indicator (QSI) for the collection, analysis, and comparison of a range of performance-related data associated with traffic stops. This QSI system enables police administrators to quantify performance over a specific date range and creates a base for comparisons among officers, between commanders, and for the entire department against department established standards. RAMS, according to the foundation's website, was designed as "a comprehensive approach to ensuring proper training, accountability, quality service, and community satisfaction with police services."

Professional Services

A more direct impact the foundation can have on the field of policing is through the professional services it provides. Going beyond conducting research to improve policing, the foundation offers a range of professional enhancement opportunities, such as training, technical assistance, and access to technology. Attempts are made to custom design training programs to meet the needs of the individual law enforcement agencies. For example, while many of the underlying concepts of community policing are generalizable across different communities, some police departments may face highly urban and heterogenic environments whereas others may be rural with similar demographics. The foundation's technical assistance capability is enhanced through its Crime Mapping and Problem Analysis Laboratory, which provides training and consulting services to law enforcement agencies. This assistance arm of the foundation also promotes the application of problem analysis, crime analysis, crime mapping, and works to progress the physical infrastructure necessary for further technological innovations in policing. While not just a technical assistance capability, this laboratory also assists agencies in learning the concept of problem solving and how to apply these cognitive skills to their day-to-day operations.

Contributions

As noted, decades ago the foundation began to sponsor studies that had a directly bearing on community policing and problem solving—areas of policing that were, at the time, largely unknown territory, such as crime mapping, evidence-based policing, integrating intelligence and crime analysis, and place-based policing (all of which are discussed in other entries). Through a host of internal avenues, the foundation has succeeded in advancing practice and research in policing. Despite such success, the foundation recognized the need to further develop outlets for contributing similar ideas to the field. For example, the foundation has helped to create independent organizations dedicated to the advancement of policing. These organizations include the Police Executive Research Forum (PERF), the National Organization of Black Law Enforcement Executives (NOBLE), and the Police Management Association. The foundation also funded *POLICE* magazine, which was published from 1978 until 1983. While these outlets no longer exist, it should be noted that special sections within the foundation were created throughout the years to address specific needs based on community concerns, political unease, and the progression diversity.

In 1976, the foundation created the Police Executive Institute for executive development training for police administrators. Through research, much of which was supported by the foundation, it was recognized that quality of policing and the advancement of new ideas within agencies was dictated by those atop the chain of command. The foundation also assembled the National Advisory Commission on Higher Education for Police Officers in 1976. In 1979, the National Information and Research Center on Women in Policing was established in response to a growing need for information directly affecting women in law enforcement.

Jeremy G. Carter

See also Community Policing Consortium; Crime Mapping; Executive Sessions on Policing; Kansas City Preventive Patrol Experiment

Further Readings

Kelling, G. L., Pate, T., Dieckman, D., & Brown, C. E. (1974). *The Kansas City preventive patrol experiment: A summary report*. Washington, DC: Police Foundation.

Pate, A. M, Wycoff, M. A., Skogan, W. G., & Sherman, L. W. (1986). *Reducing fear of crime in Houston and Newark: A summary report*. Washington, DC: Police Foundation.

Police Foundation. (1981). *The Newark foot patrol experiment*. Washington, DC: Author.

Website

Police Foundation; http://www.policefoundation.org

POLICE MISSION

To define the mission of the police, one can reflect upon the concepts and principles from which policing in modern democratic societies derive. The design and creation of the Metropolitan Police in London in the early part of the 19th century formed the basis for how Western society has sought to preserve the peace, control crime, and ultimately improve quality of life for the people living within those societies. The reforms during that time changed the fundamental principle of policing from suppression of crime and disorder through the application of military force to the concept of working with people throughout the community to prevent crime and disorder.

In the United States, police agencies have long embraced the notion that their ultimate mission is to keep the peace, protect the public, and preserve the civil liberties afforded through the Constitution.

Again that mission is carried out through strategies designed to work with communities to prevent crime and disorder, using the least amount of force necessary to enforce the law and preserve the peace.

The methods and strategies identified as convention by the institution of policing collectively, as well as how individual police organizations adopt and implement those strategies, can cause the perception that the basic mission of policing has changed from the foundation established in 19th-century England. This entry examines how policing in the United States has evolved and discusses how the mission of crime prevention, collaboration with the public, and the reduction of fear of crime has remained constant throughout that evolution. It concludes with a review of how the philosophy and practice of community policing and problem solving serves to dispel any notion that the mission of policing has changed.

Laying the Foundation

The roots of policing in a democracy rest in the dynamics of governance in the United Kingdom early in the 1800s. Upon the end of the Napoleonic Wars in 1815, England was in the throes of famine and chronic unemployment. Groups within the country were clamoring for parliamentary reform to address the poor economic condition. On August 16, 1819, a crowd of 60,000 to 80,000 people gathered at Peter's Field in Manchester, England, to demonstrate and demand reform. The demonstration was inflamed by the rhetoric of masterful orators speaking on behalf of the Manchester Patriotic Union, a group agitating for parliamentary reform.

Shortly after the demonstration began, local officials ordered the speakers arrested and the crowd dispersed. Acting upon those orders, the British Cavalry charged into the crowd with sabers drawn, killing 15 people and injuring up to 700. The 1819 Peterloo Massacre, as it was later dubbed in comparison to the massacre at Waterloo four years earlier, set in motion profound reform within the United Kingdom. One of those reforms was the basis for a new formulation of principles for policing in civil society.

In 1822, Home Secretary Sir Robert Peel was commissioned to review the current state of affairs within the United Kingdom regarding the provision of police services. Attributed to Peel, working in part to address the lessons learned from the Peterloo Massacre, are nine principles for policing that became the underpinnings for the establishment of the Metropolitan Police. Those principles sought to reject the notion that to maintain a peaceful and law-abiding civil society, government must use force, or the threat thereof, in order to ensure compliance by the people who comprised the community.

Peel's first principle clearly stated that the basic mission of the police is to prevent crime and disorder. This fundamental concept was further reinforced by the first Commissioner of the Metropolitan Police, Sir Richard Mayne, as the idea of the police first preventing crime and disorder was juxtaposed with the previously prevailing practice of achieving those objectives through repression by military force and severity of legal punishment.

The Peelian Principles, as they have become known, build upon the premise that the police must first seek to prevent crime and disorder, and in doing so, engage the public in an attempt to achieve that basic mission through cooperation and approval by the public, of actions taken by the police toward those ends. Then, and only then, should physical force be utilized to enforce the law or restore order, and then only the minimum force necessary to restore order. The police are defined most eloquently in the seventh principle:

> Police, at all times, should maintain a relationship with the public that gives reality to the historic tradition that the police are the public and the public are the police; the police being only members of the public who are paid to give full time attention to the duties that are incumbent upon every citizen in the interests of community welfare and existence.

The mission of the police is then firmly grounded with a statement that the measure of success for the police is the absence of crime and disorder, as opposed to the visible evidence of police attempts to control crime and keep the public order.

The application of Peel's nine principles in the establishment of the Metropolitan Police became the underpinning of policing in the United Kingdom from that point on. Those same principles were soundly embraced in the United States as police agencies were organized on the eastern seaboard and then spread westward across the country. The stark departure from the use of military force and unilateral threat of punishment to enforce civil law and bring order to civil society redefined the mission of policing.

Policing in the United States

The fundamental mission of modern policing, as it derives from 19th-century England, has endured for close to two centuries. The ideals of crime prevention, approval of the public for the strategies and practices of the police as well as the cooperation of people within the community, and the use of force by the police at the lowest level necessary and only after seeking compliance are the hallmarks of policing throughout the country. Although the manner in which police organizations have been structured and the practices they employ have evolved over time, those founding principles have remained constant and at the very core of the police mission.

Policing in the United States began in large urban areas along the eastern seaboard. These early police departments derived their power and authority from local elected officials and were directly controlled by the most politically powerful elected officials. This era of policing in the United States has been characterized as the political era, as the patronage system that was prevalent throughout government was mirrored in their police departments.

The ills of rampant corruption in government brought about by inordinately powerful politicians, and those who did their bidding, were offset by the actions of the beat cop whose basic role was one of broad social control within the local community. It was not uncommon for the local police officer on the beat to have face-to-face interaction with the people who lived, worked, and played within the community in which the police officer walked every day. That interaction was catalyst to the beat cop intervening with juveniles and families in a fashion that was the model for delinquency and crime prevention strategies embraced over 100 years later. Beat cops of the day were known to help immigrant families assimilate into the community, directing them toward employment, housing, and schools, and helping them steer clear of the crime-ridden areas of the community. The mission of the police was embedded in the daily activities of the police culture during the political era, and although the institution was evolving in many ways, those fundamental principles remained at the core of policing in a free society.

Policing in the United States began to evolve as the country rejected the ills of patronage in government, and as the Industrial Revolution brought efficiencies to industry that could be used to bring efficiencies to the public sector. Merit systems of hiring, promotion, and control in police departments sought to control for the undue influence of the politically powerful. By embracing the bureaucratic reforms of centralization and hierarchy of control, centralization of records, and the proliferation of rules and regulations, police agencies began to look very different from their predecessors. These elements combined with the ever-marching advance of technology, set in motion the elements of what became known as the reform era of policing. The advent of the two-way radio, combined with the use of cars to rapidly move police officers to where they were needed, changed the look and feel of the beat cop that everyone in the community knew and trusted. Face-to-face interaction with the police now most often occurred only when one made a telephone call to a police dispatcher to request police assistance and any one of many police officers working at the time arrived to handle the call for service. The fundamental strategies of the police during the reform era of policing were rapid response, visibility, and follow-up criminal investigation after a crime had been committed.

Although this crime control model in effect de-emphasized the importance of crime prevention and engagement of the people in the community, the strategies that were embraced were intentioned to ultimately prevent crime by being more efficient and effective through the use of technology and progressive human resource management. The police departments of the reform era reined in the rampant corruption of their predecessors, and became much more efficient in addressing the pressing crime and disorder problems facing their cities and towns. These same departments also became reactive in nature and removed from the community. The social unrest of the 1960s and 1970s gave way to a reexamination of the strategies that were designed to prevent crime and disorder and to include people in the community as partners with the police in those goals.

Community Policing and Problem Solving

As large cities throughout the United States experienced major social disorder in the late 1960s and early 1970s, many scholars and police leaders began to explore strategies that would again reflect the fundamental notion that the police are the people and the people are the police. The record on controlling crime was not improving by using a model which valued the image of the police as the anonymous professional crime fighter, at the expense of building mutual trust through involving members of the community to first prevent crime and disorder.

At the same time that the mission of the police was still acknowledged as it had been set centuries ago, scholars and practitioners were in agreement that the strategies of reactive patrol, rapid response, and remaining professionally remote from the very people who were being served were not likely to achieve the ultimate goals of controlling crime and disorder and reducing fear of crime. The emergence of community policing and problem-oriented policing was a direct response to the effort to refocus the institution of policing on the fundamental mission of preventing crime, preventing disorder, and reducing the fear of crime.

Community policing is characterized as using strategies that engage the people in the community to assist in identifying problems and in playing a role in the resolution to those elements that give rise to crime and disorder. Departments that have adopted community policing as a foundation for policing seek to marshal the efforts of all the unique elements of the community through decentralization of police resources to facilitate community self-help. This approach has been very effective in establishing ownership, identification, and trust between the police and the community, and in local communities has resulted in a dramatic reduction in the incidence of crime and disorder.

Problem-oriented policing, or "problem solving" as it has also been termed, seeks to focus first on what problems exist, use a model to fully assess what the underlying basis for the problem is, and then work with the community to build responses or strategies that can truly impact the problem and reduce crime and disorder. Both in philosophy and in practice, community policing and problem solving correspond directly with the founding tenets of modern policing.

The mission of the police employing community policing and problem solving, as well as the roles of the men and women in policing who strive to carry out that mission, are in direct alignment with the principles of preventing crime, engaging the people who are being policed, gaining approval and compliance of the community for police actions, and using only that force necessary to gain compliance. The success of the mission of policing in this fashion is measured by the absence of crime and disorder as opposed to the visible actions of the police dealing with those problems.

Ronald C. Sloan

See also Agency Mission and Values, Changes in; Broken Windows Theory; Community Policing and Problem Solving, Definition of; Metropolitan Police Act of 1829; Policing, Three Eras of; Problem-Oriented Policing, Goldstein's Development of; Problem-Solving Process (SARA)

Further Readings

Bittner, E. (1979). *The functions of police in modern society.* Cambridge, MA: Oelgeschlager, Gunn, & Hain.

Goldstein, H. (1990). *Problem-oriented policing.* New York, NY: McGraw-Hill.

Johnson, D. R. (1981). *American law enforcement: A history.* St. Louis, MO: Forum Press.

Kelling, G. L., & Moore, M. H. (1988). The evolving strategy of policing. NCJ 114213. *Perspectives on Policing, 4.* Washington, DC: U.S. Department of Justice, National Institute of Justice.

Mason, G. (2004). *The official history of the metropolitan police.* London, England: Carlton.

Trojanowicz, R. C., & Bucqueroux, B. (1990). *Community policing: A contemporary perspective.* Cincinnati, OH: Anderson.

Trojanowicz, R. C., & Carter, D. (1988). *The philosophy and role of community policing.* East Lansing: Michigan State University, National Center for Community Policing. Retrieved from http://www.cj.msu.edu/~people/cp/cpphil.html

POLICE TRAINING OFFICER (PTO) PROGRAM

In recent years, many law enforcement executives have expressed concerns with traditional recruit training, specifically its overemphasis on evaluation of new officers and a lack of attention to creating a learning environment that promotes critical thinking and problem solving. Many agencies attempted to include contemporary issues (e.g., community policing, problem solving, and leadership) in their Field Training Officer (FTO) program. The FTO program, which began in the San Jose (California) Police Department in 1972, assists recruits in their transition from the academy to the streets. Most FTO programs consist of an introductory phase (the recruit learns agency policies and local laws), training and evaluation phases (the recruit is introduced to more complicated tasks confronted by patrol officers), and a final phase (the FTO may act strictly as an observer and evaluator while the recruit performs all the functions of a patrol officer). This last phase of the recruit's training can have a profound effect on an officer's later career based on whether or not the neophyte officer is allowed to learn and put this strategy into practice.

To address concerns that the FTO program was not relevant to the community era of policing, in 1999 the U.S. Department of Justice's Office of Community Oriented Policing Services (COPS) provided a $300,000 grant for the Reno (Nevada) Police Department (RPD) to collaborate with the Police Executive Research Forum (PERF) to examine police training methods in general, and specifically to develop a new training program for the postacademy phase of the recruit's career. During a period of two years, the RPD consulted experts in the United States and Canada in order to determine what they believed was needed in a field training program under the community policing philosophy. These efforts ultimately resulted in the development of the Reno Police Training Officer (PTO) program.

In 2001, the RPD was awarded another grant in the amount of $200,000 for program implementation, and PTO was deployed within the RPD; subsequently, police agencies in five other cities (Savannah, Georgia; Lowell, Massachusetts; Colorado Springs, Colorado; Richmond, California; and Charlotte-Mecklenburg, North Carolina) were selected as test sites for the new program. Evaluations of PTO initiatives in each of those cities were collected and results were submitted to the COPS office in April 2003.

This entry discusses the development of the PTO program, its rationale and components, and the results of its use based on a survey of police practitioners.

Rationale for the Shift to PTO

The PTO approach, from the outset, was designed to provide police recruits a foundation for lifelong learning and to prepare them for the complexities of policing. Although the traditional police training methods emphasized task-based skills and rote memory capabilities, PTO focuses on developing an officer's learning capacity, leadership, and problem-solving skills. While task-based, applied skills are essential, they are merely one set of skills required for contemporary policing. The PTO approach is also highly flexible and takes into consideration the unique needs of police agencies.

Standardized training is an integral part of the law enforcement profession in the 21st century, but it has not always been so. In the United States, national training standards for policing were not developed until the 1960s. When it comes to training new police officers, policing continues to use teacher-centered, behavioral and cognitive instruction techniques and methods. This type of training consists mostly of lecture by the training officer, behavioral modeling, simulations, skills drills, and positive reinforcement, followed by subsequent evaluation of the trainee.

As indicated above, traditional police training is less focused on learning and more focused on making sure trainees prove themselves. In the traditional field training model, it is the trainers' responsibility to screen out those who are not up to the task of policing. The traditional model is becoming less congruent with the evolving police strategies used in today's community-oriented policing model of law enforcement. In many cases, traditional models follow a top-down chain of command structure and philosophy of conventional law enforcement hierarchy. This is similar to teacher-centered methods where students are not part of the decision-making process in identifying what is to be learned.

Application to Community Policing and Problem Solving

In contrast, law enforcement organizations that foster community policing and problem solving are often less hierarchical; the decision-making authority is shifted to the lowest organizational level, the police officer, who is involved in the decision-making process, determines what is needed to solve community problems, and is held accountable for the outcomes. This approach is similar to learner-centered methods utilized in adult and problem-based learning, where learners are included as decision makers in identifying what is to be learned, and held accountable to recreate the learning content that is useful.

Given the vast amount of information police officers must now possess in order to address society's problems of crime and disorder, as well as the omnipresent specter of civil liability, recruit training is an extremely vital part of the learning process. And so, the most important part of this process is the learning environment created in the field training process while under the tutelage and supervision of a qualified field training officer. To accomplish this transition, police agencies are increasingly using the PTO program.

Elements

Substantive Topics and Core Competencies

Two primary training areas—substantive topics (the most common activities in policing) and core competencies (the required, common skills in which officers engage and are required to utilize in daily performance of their duties)—are addressed in the PTO program.

Substantive Topics

The four substantive topics that define the key phases of training are (1) nonemergency incident response, (2) emergency incident response, (3) patrol activities, and (4) criminal investigation.

Core Competencies

There are 15 core competencies that must be met under the PTO approach; these are specific skills, knowledge, and abilities that have been identified as essential for good policing. Core competencies represent commonly encountered skill sets, which include the following:

- Police vehicle operations
- Conflict resolution
- Use of force
- Local procedures, policies, laws, and organizational philosophies
- Report writing
- Leadership
- Problem-solving skills
- Community-specific problems
- Cultural diversity and special needs groups
- Legal authority
- Individual rights
- Officer safety
- Communication skills
- Ethics
- Lifestyle stressors/self-awareness and self-regulation

The Learning Matrix

To guide both the trainees and trainers during the period of training, a learning matrix demonstrates the interrelationships between the core competencies and daily policing activities. The matrix also serves to inform trainees about what they have learned, what they need to learn to improve their performance, and which performance outcomes will be utilized to evaluate their performance.

Program Phases

Following is an overview of the eight phases of the PTO program:

Orientation Phase (length determined by the agency)

The orientation phase is intended to provide this necessary training and information prior to the trainee entering the field training experience.

Integration Phase

This period of time—normally one week in duration—is for the trainee to acclimate to the program and to the training officer. Areas of instruction during this phase may include learning how to acquire necessary equipment; familiarizing the trainee with the various department resources; understanding services rendered by other governmental organizations, administrative procedures, and the PTO learning processes.

Phase A

Phase A, of three-weeks duration, is the initial training and learning experience for the trainee and emphasizes nonemergency incident responses.

Phase B

Phase B, also three-weeks duration, is the second training and learning experience for the trainee and emphasizes emergency incident responses.

Mid-Term Evaluation

Following the successful completion of Phases A and B, the trainee transfers to a police training evaluator and participates in a midterm evaluation that is normally of one-week's duration. Police training evaluators utilize the learning matrix to assess the trainee's performance during the course of the week's activities. If the trainee has experienced difficulties and cannot successfully complete the midterm evaluation, the trainee may be rotated back to a prior phase for prescriptive training to correct the problem. Prescriptive training is unique to the needs of the trainee, but lasts approximately two weeks.

Phase C

This third training phase, lasting three weeks, is a learning experience for the trainee and emphasizes patrol activities.

Phase D

This is the final phase of actual training and learning, lasting three weeks and emphasizing criminal investigation.

Final Phase Evaluation and the Board of Evaluators

This phase lasts one to two weeks, depending on agency-specific needs and requirements. The trainee transfers from the PTO to a police training evaluator and is deployed on patrol in single-officer status. Again, the learning matrix is used as an evaluation tool to assess the trainee's performance during this final evaluation. If the trainee experiences difficulties or does not successfully complete the final phase evaluation, the trainee may be rotated back to an earlier phase of training. If a trainee still does not respond to training and is recommended for termination, all materials and documentation will be forwarded to the board of evaluators, which conducts a review of the trainee's performance. This board of evaluators consists of managers, supervisors, and trainers in the PTO program. The boards of evaluators' duties include evaluating trainee and trainer performance, conducting PTO program audits to ensure consistency and accuracy, and providing recommendations for program adjustments to agency executives.

Problem-Based Learning Exercises

At the core of the PTO program are problem-based learning exercises (PBLEs), which are used to familiarize trainees in the problem-solving process and to evaluate their knowledge of required subject material. Police officers work in a multitasking environment but are often trained using a building block method of doing one thing at a time. Because they will not be working that way in actual situations, new officers should not be trained in that same manner. PBLEs are designed to guide trainees through the problem-solving process and to expose them to handling more than one task at a time. These exercises are also a means to ensure that trainees will access resources available to them such as policies, maps, legal briefs, and articles.

Ill-Structured Problems

At times, trainees will be given PBLEs that are ill-structured problems and lend themselves to learning problem-solving methods. An ill-structured problem is a problem that is not easily solved, provides the trainee with a limited amount of information and a desired outcome, perhaps a task that needs to be completed or a presentation by the trainee. The trainee is required to gather resources and create a support group typically called a cohort group. By requiring the trainee to find answers through personal research, the learning experience is greatly enhanced. The cohort group helps the trainee by guiding and focusing the research efforts. Trainees will also find that the cohorts are good resources after graduation from the PTO program.

Evaluation

To evaluate PTO, a survey instrument to measure the effectiveness or ineffectiveness of the PTO program was designed in 2008 and administered to a Western police department. The survey instrument included a total of 16 questions, 11 of which utilized a 6-point Likert scale and five questions requiring qualitative summaries. The survey was presented as voluntary to 110 patrol personnel and specifically included administrators, police supervisors, and police officers. The purpose of the survey instrument was to elicit information regarding the following:

- The effectiveness and ineffectiveness of FTO and PTO programs
- The improvement or decline of policing skills, critical thinking, and problem solving with the PTO program
- The PTO program's impact on improving organizational performance

General Observations and Findings

PTO Program Selected as Most Effective Model

The PTO program was selected as the most effective training model by 39 (81.3%) of the participants who returned the survey. Participants commented that the PTO program is developed specifically as a training and teaching model and not an evaluation model. The PTO program provides flexibility and allows the trainee to personally participate in training and learning. The role of the trainer in the PTO program creates a relationship between the trainer and trainee of a coach, mentor, and facilitator. The PTO program appears to produce officers who are more focused on learning, problem solving, and interacting with the community they serve.

PTO Programs Improve Policing Skills

Eighteen (37.5%) of participants commented that the PTO program has significantly improved policing skills and 21 (43.8%) participants somewhat agree that the PTO program has improved policing skills. Comments of participants include the following: The PTO program creates an environment for free thinking and problem solving; the trainee becomes more responsible for his neighborhood and beat; trainees learn the importance of problem solving and being creative early in their careers, and trainees are able to rapidly adapt to the ever-changing environments in policing.

The inclusion of problem-based learning has allowed trainees to identify crime trends, community problems, and to develop the appropriate resources to address those problems within the community.

Only three (6.3%) participants commented that the PTO program has not impacted policing skills. These participants commented that due to personnel shortages and increases in calls for service, there seems to be no time for officers to perform proactive policing efforts. One participant

suggested that officers need at least 15 years of experience before their effectiveness can truly be measured; three (6.3%) participants commented that they somewhat disagree that the PTO program has improved policing skills. These participants commented that it is not the program, but the person, that is individually responsible for improving policing skills.

PTO Improves Problem Solving

Twenty-eight (58.3%) participants commented that the PTO program has significantly improved problem-solving skills and 16 (33.3%) commented that they somewhat agree that the PTO program has improved problem-solving skills. Observations included that the PTO program's flexibility allows for problem solving while developing individual policing skills. The PTO program is based upon life-long learning and adaptation. This provides trainees with a philosophy and method for assessing the challenges facing policing in the future. The PTO program develops trainees who have a more in-depth knowledge of community policing and who utilize a variety of available resources to solve community problems.

Principles Taught in PTO Improve Organizational Performance

Twenty-three (47.9%) participants strongly agreed and 17 (35.4%) somewhat agreed that the PTO principles have improved organizational performance. Participant comments suggesting PTO program effectiveness in organizational performance point to development of officers who are critical thinkers and more effective at problem solving. The PTO program also encourages interaction and discussion in a variety of environments (e.g., the community, governmental meetings, and agency programs). The capacity of trainees in the PTO is much larger than that of traditionally trained officers. PTO trainees identify and utilize outside resources more often and more effectively.

Steven Pitts

See also In-Service Training; Learning Organization; Mentoring; Model Curriculum; Recruit Academy Training

Further Readings

Barrows, H., & Tamblyn, R. M. (1980). *Problem based learning*. New York, NY: Springer-Verlag.

Buerger, M. E. (1998). Police training as a Pentecost: Using tools singularly ill-suited to the purpose of reform. *Police Quarterly, 1*, 32.

Delisle, R. (1997). *How-to use problem-based learning in the classroom*. Alexandria, VA: ASCD.

Dewey, J. (1916). *Democracy and education: An introduction to the philosophy of education*. New York, NY: Macmillan.

Dewey, J. (1929). *Experience and nature*. New York, NY: W.W. Norton.

Knowles, M. (1984). *Andragogy in action: Applying modern principles of adult learning*. San Francisco, CA: Jossey-Bass.

Reno Police Department, & Police Executive Research Forum. (2012). *Police training officer program*. Washington, DC: U.S. Department of Justice, Office of Community Oriented Policing Services. Retrieved from http://www.cops.usdoj.gov/default.asp?Item=461

POLICE-COMMUNITY RELATIONS

The topic of police-community relations became part of the police lexicon well before the advent of community policing. The meaning of the terminology has evolved as policing itself has. This entry first describes the term under a traditional policing environment, and then updates it within the context of community policing.

Origins of Police-Community Relations

The tumult of the United States during the 1960s, including violence between police and citizens during civil rights and antiwar protests, spurred discussions about police-community relations. During this time, crime increased, tensions rose, and police were recognizing that they did not enjoy strong support from throughout the community.

Louis Radelet, an academician at Michigan State University (MSU), had tremendous influence in the field of police-community relations. Radelet had served on the executive staff of the National Conference of Christians and Jews (NCCJ) from 1951 to 1963. In 1963, Radelet became a professor in what was then the School of Police Administration and Public Safety at MSU. In 1955, he founded the National Institute on Police and Community Relations (NIPCR) at MSU; he served as institute director from 1955 to 1969 and was also coordinator of the university's National Center on Police and Community Relations, created to conduct a national survey on police-community relations, from 1965 to 1973.

The institute held five-day conferences each May during its 15-year existence, bringing together teams of police officers and other community leaders to discuss common problems. In peak years, more than 600 participants came from as many as 165 communities and 30 states as well as several foreign countries. As a result of the institute's work, such programs proliferated rapidly across the nation, all of which had similar core purposes:

- To foster and improve communications and mutual understanding between the police and the community and to enhance cooperation among the police, the prosecution, the courts, and corrections
- To assist the police and other community leaders to achieve an understanding of the nature and causes of complex problems in people-to-people relations (and especially to improve police-minority relationships)
- To strengthen implementation of equal protection under the law for all persons

The NIPCR was discontinued in 1969.

The idea of "selling" police departments in the community resulted in a small number of officers given special assignments, some called *crime prevention officers*, and some called *community affairs officers or community relations officers*. Their goal was to describe the good work that the police did, and identify obviously disconnected portions of the community to which they could focus attention. Police-community relations in this early form involved mostly one-way information exchange; the police provided a flow of information to the community but were not seeking an abundance of information back. The information tended to reflect what the police thought was important, and in general, the messages were designed to be mostly complimentary to the police.

The Crime Prevention Genre of Programs

An accompanying movement in policing that grew throughout the 1970s was the crime prevention genre of programs. Officers specializing in crime prevention became police departments' front line in educating and informing the community on how citizens and businesses could better protect themselves from victimization. Training and academic programs evolved quickly, and in 1982 the National Crime Prevention Council, the home of the McGruff the Crime Dog character, was formed to administer the growing body of crime prevention materials and training. Police departments varied in the degree to which they combined or separated the officers working in community relations and crime prevention programs.

Many programs were developed throughout the 1970s and 1980s reflecting the desire to improve police-community relations. A prime example is the popular Citizen Police Academies. Often conducted on evenings or weekends, these programs are designed for community members to gain an overview of how and why their local police operate the way they do. Citizen academies grew through the 1990s in the United States, and as communities began to diversify, non-English-language sessions were developed by agencies seeking to connect with burgeoning immigrant populations. This level of outreach for non-English speakers reflected a strong commitment to build better police-community relations with nontraditional residents.

Another example of programming that strengthened police-community relations was the D.A.R.E. (Drug Abuse Resistance Education) program. Implemented in 1983 by then–Los Angeles Police Chief Darryl Gates, the program was designed to teach elementary and middle school children about the dangers of drug abuse. The program was often viewed as one of the most effective ways for police officers to reach out to community members previously disconnected from the police. Officers who were trained as D.A.R.E. instructors enjoyed a newfound level of support from both students and their parents. While D.A.R.E. has declined significantly, because of reduced funding and an absence of evidence of its long-term prevention value, during its peak years it was widely thought to have improved police-community relations in many communities.

As the boundaries between police-community relations and crime prevention blurred, the number and scope of crime prevention programming grew. Often, officers assigned in a community affairs section actively presented crime prevention programs such as burglary awareness and target hardening (strengthening a residence's or building's security), avoiding car burglaries, registering valuable property, and maintaining an inventory of one's home. New specialties emerged such as Crime Prevention Through Environmental Design (CPTED). Officers trained in CPTED provide thorough analysis of building plans and conduct on-site inspections, resulting in design recommendations to minimize victimization risk. CPTED has expanded over time, with city planners and private architectural firms employing this level of analysis.

Neighborhood watch is another enduring program that arose out of the crime prevention movement. This interactive program remains a staple in police departments' outreach efforts, and often contributes to a positive police-community relations atmosphere. Neighborhood watch is a tool that is used by police departments around the globe. It provides an opportunity to heighten community awareness, which usually strengthens police-community relations, and to provide crime prevention training and awareness directly to residents. Neighborhood watch groups are often the outcome of a property crime spree within a defined area, motivating the residents to study crime prevention techniques and keep a watchful eye out for their neighbor's property as well. The challenge of sustaining Neighborhood watch is the mobile nature of today's society. People are living busier lives and spending less time with groups of any kind, a social phenomenon analyzed in a 2000 book by political scientist Robert Putnam called *Bowling Alone: The Collapse and Revival of American Community*. Most successful neighborhood watch groups share the key ingredient of strong, neighborhood based advocacy active in a leadership role for the watch group. The use of e-mail and social media has reinvigorated some stalled watch groups, and police agencies subscribing to the philosophy of community policing have built communication networks (like e-mail lists) around the neighborhood watch groups in their cities.

An outgrowth of the popular Neighborhood Watch program is a version of it tailored for commercial areas. Often referred to as *Business Watch,* the crime prevention focus here may be more on antitheft, specifically shoplifting and employee theft. Another type of watch program is Fleet Watch, in which vehicle operators from a company's fleet (e.g., a public utilities company, bus system, or highway department) are trained to be observant and taught when and how best to contact the police. Even taxicab companies have shown interest, implementing Cabs on Patrol (COP). Police communication centers can phone taxi dispatchers and share be-on-the-lookout (BOLO) information for taxi drivers to serve as an adjunct to the patrol officers on duty.

In some cities where there are police accountability concerns, oversight committees comprised of community advocates developed under the mantle of police-community relations. While such efforts fall under many different names, a committee of citizens who gather to hear input from the community and offer advice and direction to the police remains in many cities. The range of responsibilities for these community affairs review committees varies widely; some have evolved into citizen watchdog groups that review cases where discipline may be warranted, or review the outcomes of internal affairs investigations. Some may even recommend discipline or in rare cases may implement the discipline. Others may be purely advisory in nature and stick to themes of crime prevention and police programming of services.

Police-Community Relations in the Community Policing Era

With the evolution of community policing and one of its key characteristics being community partnerships, police-community relations took on a different focus. Clearly, police agencies adopting the philosophy of community policing could not anticipate forging strong community partnerships without a requisite positive state of police-community relations. Community policing departments are quicker to develop crime prevention programming to sustain healthy police-community relations. Sometimes the programming seeks to overcome historic deficiencies under traditional policing. A nationwide effort to use broadcast media and roadside signage to alert drivers to watch for vehicles possibly used in

a child abduction case is an example. These alerts, known as *Amber Alerts,* were developed to expedite the police's ability to get vital information out to the public for purposes of aiding in the recovery of abducted children. Following on the successes of Amber Alert, many states have now adopted Silver Alert programs to disseminate rapidly information about missing senior citizens, many of whom may have dementia. A few states are even implementing Blue Alert to be used to alert the public about suspects involved in the killing of a police officer.

Police-community relations become a way of life rather than programming within the philosophy of community policing. Many programs have been implemented, with many more in development, to strengthen the bond between the police and the population they serve. Police agencies work with private sector companies as Nixle and CitizenObserver.com to provide services for sharing crime alerts through various means, such as e-mail, SMS text, Twitter, and Facebook. Citizens are able to access more information about crimes in the neighborhoods through either a police agency's website or third-party services.

With the advent of social media, some police departments concerned about the accuracy of their activities in traditional news sources have become their own source of news. Departments that recognize that younger generations receive an increasing percentage of news from nontraditional news sources are disseminating information using Facebook, YouTube, and other popular websites. The advantage of these outlets over newspapers and broadcast news is the ability to make the story interactive, with police representatives answering questions or clarifying facts that may be unclear to the audience. Even traditional news sources post content on their websites, and some police departments are actively using the blog comment space following articles to clarify and distribute the department's perspective on incidents or news stories.

In its most generic sense, the term *police-community relations* may refer to the current state of relationship between a community and its police agency within an interval of time. In community policing, one of the key characteristics is fostering community partnerships, which requires a trusting relationship. In policing, both high-profile events and the manner in which they are managed can impact the state of relations between the police and their communities served.

One of the more notable and infamous incidents in contemporary policing was the 1991 beating of Rodney King by police officers after a high-speed pursuit. While the Los Angeles (California) Police Department (LAPD) had occasional controversies arising from incidents of police misconduct, at the time of the King incident LAPD was still considered a model police department for its training and policing methods. The loss of public trust arising from the video of King being beaten and the subsequent trials significantly eroded police-community relations in Los Angeles. After more than two decades, the LAPD has instituted organizational change in an effort to improve its police-community relations.

While the videotape of King's beating was an early example of citizens holding the police accountable through video evidence, the ubiquitous nature of video capability in many smartphones and the evolution of handheld digital video recorders make recording the actions of street police officers commonplace. There is a contrast between departments operating under the philosophy of community policing and more traditional departments in how they react to obvious recording of the police.

Traditional police agencies may have a culture that is threatened by the presence of video cameras, and litigation has emerged to halt the practice of seizing cameras or phones from citizens simply because they were recording officers. Alternatively, some community-oriented police departments have provided training and guidance to officers that support citizens' right to record public acts.

The technology of mobile video has evolved so that many police squad cars have sophisticated digital video recording equipment that captures picture and sound in the vicinity in front of a police vehicle, while recent developments included body-worn devices to record an officer's actions and conversations. Community-oriented agencies that are active in collecting the work of their officers on video often will release video segments to demonstrate to the public that their officers are acting professionally, protecting the rights of all persons, and even sustaining injuries in the course of serving.

Police agencies that periodically release videotaped activities are demonstrating a quality that is increasingly critical to police-community relationships: transparency. Transparency refers to the openness with which an organization shares its activities, practices, and decisions. A transparent leader is one who is open and freely shares information about decisions, values, and actions. Transparency is a necessary precursor to trust for both individuals and organizations. Any perceptions of secrecy or withholding information can be detrimental to a foundation of trust upon which relationships are created. It is partly to meet the goal of transparency that police departments are using some of the technologies described previously to push information out to the community.

To strengthen police-community relations, some police leaders convene various citizens' groups to exchange information and address rumors. Those chiefs who practice transparency and are not afraid to provide honest answers in spite of the unpopularity of the facts are more likely to hold the respect and trust of the public.

Police-community relations may be viewed in an entirely different context when the primary agency providing police service is a sheriff's office. Because sheriffs are, by and large, elected to their position and are considered a constitutional officer under state law, their agencies are commonly referred to as sheriff's *office*, rather than *department*. Elected sheriffs must count on positive police-community relations for purposes beyond the effectiveness of their policing. If they are unable to secure the popular vote majority, their term in office will be short-lived. Accordingly, the employees of a sheriff's office are given high expectations of strong customer service and problem solving. Long-term sheriffs understand the importance of selling their "brand" to the community and backing it up with services and a strong customer orientation. While police chiefs who are strongly supported by their city officials may have more latitude in speaking out on unpopular matters, sheriffs can ill afford to jeopardize the police-community relations needed for reelection.

The growth of the use of volunteers by police agencies coincided with the growth of agencies practicing community policing. As departments developed stronger community partnerships and better engaged citizens into the planning and problem identification and solving processes, the involved citizens often desired to do more. The kind of volunteering that can arise out of a neighborhood watch experience opens up new relationships between residents and the police. Prominent use of volunteers by police departments is a positive and productive investment in police-community relations. What often began with volunteers being assigned basic clerical support functions as mailings and filing grew to where few elements of a police department are not touched by volunteers in some agencies. Some volunteers are recruited for their professional expertise; for example, information technology (IT) experts with either extra work capacity, or retired with ample time, may assist an agency with their IT needs. Some agencies have formed cold case squads to reopen and examine old, inactive investigations, usually homicides. Retired investigators from policing, the military, or the private sector can form the nucleus of such a cold case unit. Public education and crime prevention programs are readily taught by trained community volunteers, and serve to further engage common citizens through their example. Some cities even provide advanced training for Citizens on Patrol–type activities, and long-term legacy programs like police reserve officers take volunteerism all the way to the status of a sworn officer. Integrating citizen volunteers among police career professionals accelerates the ability of the police to form genuine community partnerships, one of the key community policing characteristics.

At times, seemingly minor police decisions or policies end up making a significant impact on police-community relations. With the advent of trunked, digital radio communication networks, some police agencies implemented encryption technologies that allow for more secure communication. While some agencies restrict their use of encryption to sensitive or undercover radio transactions, others have turned on the encryption for all communications. The proliferation of smartphone applications that bring a web-based police communication monitor right to the user's phone have increased police interest in restricting access to their messaging. Some agencies have thus chosen to encrypt all of their communications; however, such an action has created controversy, given that many citizens enjoy following local police activities via police scanner radios, and media outlets rely on monitoring communications to rapidly deploy to scenes of interest.

Political pressure and critical news articles have resulted in some police agencies backing down from the "always-on" mode of encryption. In some cities, the police have provided listen-only portable police radios to media outlets so that they can hear approved communication channels. The response by the police, showing understanding of the concerns of citizens and the media, seek to strike a balance between fostering positive police-community relations and ensuring operational security and officer safety. The radio encryption

example can be substituted with any number of policies that the police may implement with little concern about unanticipated consequences, which ultimately resulted in a decline in police-community relationships.

This illustrates the high value of all three of the key characteristics of community policing (community partnerships, focus on problem solving, organizational transformation); when a police department enjoys an authentic partnership with its community, public engagement and input helps prevent significant tension from arising. When concerns *do* arise, the problem-solving process is a natural path for the police and the community to follow toward resolution.

Richard W. Myers

See also Citizen Police Academies; Community Policing Consortium; Crime Mapping; Crime Prevention Through Environmental Design; Customer-Based Policing; Involving Local Businesses; National Crime Prevention Council; Neighborhood Associations; Non-sworn Personnel and Volunteers, Use and Training of

Further Reading

Putnam, R. D. (2000). *Bowling alone: The collapse and revival of the American community*. New York, NY: Simon & Schuster.

Websites

Citizens Observer.com; http://www.citizenobserver.com

CrimeMapping, the Omega Group; http://www.crimemapping.com

D.A.R.E. America; http://www.dare.com

The National Citizens Police Academy Association; http://www.nationalcpaa.org

Nixle; http://www.nixle.com

USA on Watch, National Sheriffs Association; http://www.usaonwatch.org

U.S. Department of Justice, Office of Justice Programs; http://www.amberalert.gov

Volunteers in Police Service (VIPS), the International Association of Chiefs of Police; http://www.policevolunteers.org

POLICING, THREE ERAS OF

The development of policing in the United States may be traced to England. Robert Peel, a member of Parliament, was concerned about population growth, industrialization, and crime in London. Peel introduced a bill in Parliament seeking to establish a police force in London. Peel succeeded in 1829 when Parliament enacted the Metropolitan Police Act. Peel established a full-time, paid police force, and the constables wore uniforms, patrolled beats, and focused on the prevention of crime. Peel's policing model in London was watched in America.

Policing has evolved in the United States and the history of policing may be divided into three different eras based on the philosophical basis of policing that was dominant in each era. The first era was the political era that encompassed the period from the 1840s to the 1930s. The second era was the reform era that lasted from the 1930s to the 1980s. The third era was the community era that began in the 1980s. There are no clear lines of demarcation between the eras of policing. U.S. society is complex, and social, economic, and political forces led to reform movements. The reform movements resulted in the evolution of policing from one era to another and represented the transition from one dominant philosophy of policing to a different dominant philosophy of policing. This entry explains the three eras of policing—the political era, the reform era, and the community era—and looks at whether the United States is entering a fourth era of homeland security.

The Political Era

The political era of policing began in the 1840s in New York State. New York City experienced population growth, industrialization growth, and the occurrence of crime. In 1844, the New York State Legislature enacted a statute establishing a full-time police force for New York City. State governments and state legislatures represented the basis of political power in the U.S. federal system of government, and the establishment of city police departments rested in the hands of state and city elected officials. The New York City Police Department served as a model, and other cities in the United States established police departments on the basis of the New York City model.

By the late 1800s, almost all large U.S. cities had police departments constructed on the basis of the New York City model. Cities during the political era were operated by elected city council members and elected mayors. City council members represented

geographic subdivisions of the city called *wards*. Political machines had local political leaders that were responsible for turning out the vote. Political machines provided citizens with material benefits in return for citizens' votes. Elected officials and the police developed a reciprocal relationship. The police relied on local elected officials for authority and resources, and local elected officials relied on the police to serve the citizens and help the local elected officials remain in office.

Police departments were organized on a decentralized basis. Wards were divided geographically into precincts, which were essentially mini–police departments. Police personnel were hired, assigned, and fired at the precinct level. Police officers were recruited from those citizens who lived in the precinct neighborhoods and were closely connected to the citizens and political leaders. Police officers worked in the precinct neighborhood where they lived. Police provided a wide range of services to citizens. The police were responsible for crime prevention and the maintenance of order. The police also performed many social services for citizens, understanding that there were really no government social service agencies in existence. Police departments operated soup kitchens, assisted newly arrived immigrants in becoming settled in the neighborhood, and assisted immigrants in finding employment. The primary tactic employed by the police was foot patrol, whereby officers walked a beat in their neighborhood. Police officers had a great degree of discretion in handling problems, crimes, and disorder on their beats. Demand for police services came from ward political leaders as well as citizens making requests directly to the officers on foot patrol. Police supervision and management existed mainly at the precinct level where precinct commanders worked in concert with ward political leaders.

Citizen and political satisfaction with police services were a primary goal of police departments. Police were fully integrated into neighborhoods and established close ties with citizens. The citizens interacted often with police officers and effective police-community communications that aided police in performing their duties existed. The integration of police, local political leaders, and citizens in the community provided citizen satisfaction with police services. The philosophical foundation of the political era was the establishment of a close and personal relationship between the police and the citizens. A downside of the close police, local political leader, and citizen relationship was police corruption. The decentralized nature of policing at the precinct level allowed police officers a great deal of discretion, and the discretion was used in a discriminatory manner against certain ethnic and racial minorities as well as against strangers who did not live in the neighborhood. Physical abuse and the rousting of people were activities engaged in by the police.

Corruption also resulted from the local political leader and police relationship. Political patronage resulted in people being hired as police officers on the basis of political connections as opposed to being the most qualified people to perform policing functions. Police encouraged citizens to vote for certain candidates and discouraged them from voting for other candidates. Police also interfered in elections, even assisting local political leaders in rigging elections. Corruption also resulted from the close citizen-police relationship. Police officers were vulnerable to bribes and kickbacks regarding the nonenforcement of laws. The political era encompassed the period from the 1840s to the 1930s.

The Reform Era

The political machines and political corruption came under fire by municipal reformers during the late 1800s and into the early 1900s. The progressive reformers desired to end the power and political rule in the cities. The progressive reformers believed that city government should be operated on the basis of corporate business principles that entailed the efficient and cost-effective delivery of city services to citizens. The progressive reformers believed in good government, and they defined good government as a city government that was operated like a private sector business entity. The progressive reformers advocated for nonpartisan city elections and for professional managers, known as *city managers,* to be responsible for the administration of city business. The progressive reformers were allied with police reformers. Police reformers rejected local politics as the basis of police organization and operation. Police reformers viewed politics and political involvement as the problem in policing in the United States. The 1920s and 1930s represented a transition from the dominant political philosophy of policing to a new dominant professionalism philosophy of policing.

August Vollmer was the police chief in Berkeley, California, from 1909 through 1923. Vollmer was a progressive police chief who advocated for police reform and put forth the proposition that policing should be a profession. Reform was instituted on the federal as well as state and local levels. During his tenure as director of the Federal Bureau of Investigation, J. Edgar Hoover (1935–1972) raised eligibility standards for hiring and implemented changes in training to achieve professional competence among agents. President Calvin Coolidge appointed the first National Crime Commission in 1925, known as the Wickersham Commission. The Wickersham Commission recommended that the corrupting influence of politics be removed from policing. The Wickersham Commission further recommended professionalism for policing: that police executives be selected on the basis of merit, that officers be tested, and that officers receive adequate training.

Policing in the reform era was based on professionalism and the criminal law, characterized by reactive, incident-driven methods and emphases on quantitative outcomes such as number of calls for service, arrests, and so on. Police departments became law enforcement agencies, and the focus of the policing function was based on the criminal law. Their goal was to control crime, deter offenders, and apprehend offenders. The police-citizen relationship was redefined during the reform era. The intimate, close relationship and interaction of citizens and police officers was replaced by police officers being neutral and distant.

There was little interaction between citizens and police officers. The citizens' responsibility in crime control was limited to calling the police. The police provided professional crime control services. The police were only responsible for crime problems; social problems were addressed by social workers. The structure and organization of police departments changed during the reform era. Police reformers structured their organizations in accordance with the principles of the scientific theory of administration. Frederick Taylor's scientific theory of administration was based on division of labor and hierarchical control.

The goal of the scientific theory of administration was to increase workers' productivity and the quality of the workers' work product. Division of labor entailed breaking tasks into components and allowing workers to become highly skilled in particular components and more efficient in completing their tasks. Hierarchical control was emphasized in police departments with centralized control over officers achieved by a chain of command, supervision, information flow, and record keeping.

Police administrators routinized and standardized police work. Technology facilitated the standardization and efficiency of police work. Automobiles allowed police officers to more efficiently perform their crime-fighting duties, rendering foot patrol an outdated tactic. Preventive patrol by automobile was viewed as an anticrime tactic and allowed officers to patrol larger geographic areas. Police automobiles also increased police efficiency because police could respond in a rapid fashion to calls for service. The reform era emphasized crime control and the apprehension of criminals. Police reformers engaged in record keeping and developed a system of crime classification and reporting. This system ultimately became the Uniform Crime Reports system, administered by the Federal Bureau of Investigation. Crime statistics and the crime rate as reported in the Uniform Crime Reports became measures of police effectiveness regarding crime control and the apprehension of criminals.

Difficulties with the reform era arose during the 1960s and 1970s. Although the focus of police work during the reform era was crime control and the apprehension of criminals, crime rates began to rise during the 1960s. Additionally research conducted during the 1970s suggested that preventive automobile patrol and rapid response to calls for service did not constitute effective tactics regarding crime control and the apprehension of criminals. Fear rose rapidly during the 1960s and 1970s. Subsequent research revealed that fear was more closely correlated with disorder than with crime. Many minority citizens, especially African Americans, complained of police mistreatment as well as receiving inadequate and insufficient police services. The antiwar and civil rights movements of the 1960s and 1970s presented many difficulties for police departments. The ideal of police professionalism was not fully achieved, and many of the scientific theory management practices had a negative impact on police professionalism. Additionally, cities experienced fiscal difficulties and many police departments experienced financial cutbacks while attempting to deal with the challenging

political and social changes and environment of the 1960s and 1970s. The reform era encompassed the period from the 1930s to the 1980s.

The Community Era

The 1960s and 1970s represented a transition from the dominant professionalism philosophy of policing to a new dominant community philosophy of policing. In the late 1970s and early 1980s, some city police departments reinstituted foot patrols. Foot patrols proved to be popular with citizens, and political and citizen demands for foot patrols resulted in the tactic once again becoming popular throughout the United States. Foot patrols increased citizen satisfaction with the police and helped reduce citizen fear. Additionally, police officers experienced an increase in job satisfaction and morale when involved in foot patrols. Police departments also discovered that they could more effectively deal with crime when they obtained information from citizens regarding crimes and criminals. Citizens also seemed to appreciate working with the police and communicating about community problems.

The community era encompasses a community policing approach. The criminal law continues to serve as the basis for the functioning of police as well as professionalism. However, the community era focuses more heavily on community. Community policing broadens the definition of the functions of the police. Crime control remains an important function under community policing. Community policing emphasizes crime prevention as well as crime control. Community policing entails conflict resolution, the provision of services, problem solving, and order maintenance. Community policing involves the police consulting with groups in the community and results in a decentralized organizational operation. Police officers are actively involved in diagnosing and responding to community problems and neighborhood concerns. The net result is that decision making occurs at the lower levels of the police department, as at the beat level. Decentralized decision making has resulted in participative management where officers at all levels plan, organize, and implement programs.

Community policing is premised upon an intimate relationship between police and citizens. Relationship building is accomplished in a variety of ways. Officers are assigned to beats on a long-term basis, knock on doors in the neighborhood to get to know citizens, consult with citizens, gather information, and conduct educational classes. Community policing also involves the police establishing and building relationships with neighborhood and community crime control groups. The goals of community are broad and citizen based. Community policing seeks to improve the quality of life in neighborhoods and citizen satisfaction with police services. Community policing also seeks to solve problems, reduce fear, increase order, and control crime.

Community policing has moved through three generations. The first generation is the *innovation* generation, which encompassed the period from 1979 through 1986. During this time, there was a search for alternatives to the professionalism philosophy of the reform era. Early community policing approaches were called *experiments, test sites,* and *demonstration projects.* Small and limited approaches such as neighborhood substations and foot patrols were employed. The community policing initiatives generally occurred in larger metropolitan cities.

The second generation is the *diffusion* generation, which encompasses the period from 1987 through 1994. The philosophy and principles of community policing and problem solving spread rapidly among law enforcement agencies throughout the United States. During the second generation, community policing was adopted in mostly large- and medium-size cities. The nature of community policing was broader than a specific program like a foot patrol program. Community policing approaches addressed neighborhood and quality-of-life matters. Emphasis was placed on improving police-community relationships. The emphasis of community policing became one of extending the philosophy and concepts of community policing throughout the police department and throughout the community. The community policing approach was more systematic and holistic.

The third generation is the *institutionalization* generation; this encompasses the period from 1995 to the present. Institutionalization refers to the fact there has been widespread implementation of community policing throughout the United States. Community policing has become the most common form of organizing police services. The federal government has embraced the community policing

philosophy. Congress enacted the Violent Crime Control and Law Enforcement Act of 1994. This act established federal grant money for community policing and created the Office of Community Oriented Policing Services in the U.S. Department of Justice. Community policing has evolved from a singular program within a police department to having become the culture of the police department. Presently, the dominant philosophy of policing is the community philosophy of policing.

A Fourth Era of Policing?

The question of whether U.S. policing is in a period of transition from the dominant community philosophy of policing to a new dominant philosophy of policing has recently been posed. Willard Oliver has argued that we are witnessing a fourth era of policing and that a new era has begun in U.S. policing that he has labeled the *era of homeland security.* On September 11, 2001, al Qaeda terrorists hijacked airplanes and attacked the World Trade Center in New York City, the Pentagon in northern Virginia, and United Airlines Flight 93 that crashed in Pennsylvania. The horrific events of 9/11 prompted the United States to focus on international terrorism and domestic security. Homeland security rapidly became a top public policy concern for the federal government as well as state and local governments. The terrorist attacks of 9/11 may well serve as one of those social, political, or economic factors that result in the transition from one era of policing to a different era of policing.

Oliver argues that the transition to the era of homeland security in policing has already occurred. The authority for police departments to adopt a dominant homeland security philosophy of policing comes from the national and international terrorism threat. Further, the events of 9/11 have prompted citizens to expect that government target terrorism and protect the United States. According to the Pew Center, since 9/11 the economy and terrorism defense have been tied atop the public's priority list, along with jobs. The functions and operations of police departments have been altered because of this concern for homeland security. Antiterrorism measures are centralized in terms of control by the federal government. Homeland security entails intergovernmental cooperation. Police departments assume responsibility for local threat assessments, intelligence gathering, and intergovernmental information sharing. Police departments must also adjust to their antiterrorism role by engaging in preparedness training, crisis intervention, and special team training. The federal government has provided federal grant money for homeland security efforts undertaken by police departments. The community policing elements of crime control, citizen satisfaction, and quality of life continue to be present, but whether the dominant community philosophy of policing will evolve to address homeland security or whether policing will experience a transition to a fourth era of homeland security has yet to be determined.

Robert Morin

See also Community Policing, Evolution of; Counterterrorism and Community Policing; Generations (Three) of Community Policing; Metropolitan Police Act of 1829

Further Readings

Alpert, G. P., & Piquero, A. (Eds.). (1998). *Community policing: Contemporary readings*. Prospect Heights, IL: Waveland Press.

Fogelson, R. M. (1977). *Big-city police: An Urban Institute study*. Cambridge, MA: Harvard University Press.

Gaines, L. K., & Kappeler, V. E. (2011). *Policing in America* (7th ed.). Waltham, MA: Anderson.

Johnson, D. R. (1981). *American law enforcement: A history*. St. Louis, MO: Forum Press.

Kappeler, V. E., & Gaines, L. K. (2008). *Community policing: A contemporary perspective* (5th ed.). Cincinnati, OH: Anderson.

Kelling, G. L., & Moore, M. H. (1988). The evolving strategy of policing. NCJ 114213. *Perspectives on Policing, 4*. Washington, DC: U.S. Department of Justice, National Institute of Justice.

Monkkonen, E. H. (1981). *Police in urban America, 1860–1920*. Cambridge, England: Cambridge University Press.

Oliver, W. M. (2004). The homeland security juggernaut: The end of the community policing era? *Crime & Justice International, 20*(79), 4–10.

Oliver, W. M. (2006). The fourth era of policing: Homeland security. *International Review of Law Computers & Technology, 20*(1–2), 49–62. doi: 10.1080/13600860600579696

Peak, K. J. (2012). *Policing America: Challenges and best practices* (7th ed.). Upper Saddle River, NJ: Pearson.

Pew Research Center. *Public's priorities for 2010: Economy, jobs, terrorism*. Retrieved from http://www.people-press.org/2010/01/25/publics-priorities-for-2010-economy-jobs-terrorism

Thurman, Q. C., & Zhao, J. (2004). *Contemporary policing: Controversies, challenges and solutions*. Los Angeles, CA: Roxbury.

Walker, S. (1977). *A critical history of police reform: The emergence of professionalism*. Lanham, MD: Lexington Books.

Walker, S., & Katz, C. M. (2008). *The police in America* (6th ed.). New York, NY: McGraw-Hill.

PREDICTIVE POLICING

The term *predictive policing* is a relatively new law enforcement concept that employs leading-edge crime analysis technologies to assist and improve crime control and prevention strategies. As such, it is viewed as advancing current policing strategies such as community policing and problem-oriented policing to include intelligence-led policing and hot spots policing. Private businesses have utilized predictive analysis to anticipate market conditions and trends in various industries for years. Technological advances have now provided law enforcement agencies the ability to employ predictive analytics to crime problems. This entry describes this tool as well as how it may have a significant impact on agencies' crime control and prevention efforts.

Defining Predictive Policing

In its simplest meaning, predictive policing helps law enforcement agencies respond more effectively to future crime by anticipating problems before they occur. In some ways, it is similar to how private businesses use social science to determine what customers might want to buy, and then offer these items to customers online. The methods of predicting shoppers' behaviors are similar to methodologies used to determine criminal behavior. The differences lie only in datasets used. However, because of security and privacy laws and court decisions governing the public sector, private industry may be able to utilize more personal data than is available to law enforcement.

The next generation of police problem solving could combine existing technologies like computers, crime analysis, geographic information systems, crime mapping, and police reports with a few emerging technologies such as artificial intelligence. The future may well bring a system that can predict crimes before they happen. Of course, high-tech tools alone cannot solve crimes, but when trained crime analysts and police management combine the tools with their ingenuity, anything is possible in this high-tech world.

How Predictive Policing Works

The police know that strong-arm robberies near check-cashing businesses increase at the end of the month, that domestic and violent crime soars on hot days and drops during rainy days, that residential burglaries often occur on Sunday mornings while people are attending church services, and that Super Bowl Sunday is usually the slowest crime day of the year. But officers' minds can store and remember only a limited amount of data. So when the police monitor crime data and query a computer system for historical and real-time patterns, they can predict, more systematically, over a bigger area, and across shifts and time spans, where crimes are likely to occur. More importantly, the crime-analysis software does not forget details, get sick, take vacation, or transfer to a different precinct (although it is susceptible to the usual kinds of technical problems). If commercial robberies were high in March 2010, crime analysis software may predict another spike in March 2011, and the police can then look at the types of businesses that were hit, their locations, and time of day. Such software can even analyze a robber's modus operandi—what was said, type of weapon used, and so on.

The following are a few examples of how predictive policing (e.g., looking specifically at patterns of behavior) can be applied by patrol officers and crime analysts. Consider the example of a domestic dispute involving a man and woman. The officer arrives at the home, knocks on the door, is escorted into the living room, and all goes as it has gone on such calls 1,000 times—but now the officer is engaged in a struggle for his life. Had the officer's mobile computer relayed information that the male subject was previously arrested for assaulting officers in another jurisdiction and recently arrested for driving under the influence, the officer might have approached this call differently and avoided such a struggle. In another example, there have been numerous copper thefts from construction sites in the city. With knowledge of the patterns of such thefts, the police can predict when and where similar thefts are likely to happen, rather than having to rely on parking a patrol car in various areas and hoping for blind luck. These are just a few simple examples of how predictive policing can be useful—simply by looking at patterns of behavior—to the patrol officer.

The Role of Crime Mapping and Geographic Information Systems

Geographic information systems (GIS) are computer programs that capture data so analysts can visualize, question, analyze, and interpret data in a variety of ways to reveal patterns, relationships, and trends in the form of charts, graphs, and maps. Data sources are limitless and may include crime reports, computer-aided dispatch incidents, schools, transportation, and public housing and code violations.

Crime analysts can use a variety of maps to display the location and density of crimes. Maps can provide officers with a visual display of hot spots. These are geographic locations where crimes cluster. A number of problem-solving techniques including predictive policing analytics may be utilized to analyze hot spots and provide officers with the best responses to organize resources to address crime problems.

Critics' View and Challenges

Some police executives and academics question whether predictive policing is a new paradigm. They argue that crime analysis has been around in policing for more than 40 years and predictive policing simply combines concepts already available to the field. The critics' arguments are based on the notion that nothing new is being done with data, but police are simply analyzing it more quickly and effectively. Critics also point out that the amount of information and data available to policing for analysis is far greater today than in the recent past and contributes to analysts' ability to apply predictive models and analytics to a crime issue.

Concerns about privacy and civil liberties also emerge in discussion about predictive policing. Similar arguments are seen in the implementation of intelligence-led policing and CompStat programs. The National Institute of Justice held the first National Symposium on Predictive Policing comprised of researchers and practitioners in Los Angeles, California, from November 18 to 20, 2009. At a plenary session concerning privacy and legal issues, recommendations for law enforcement agencies included developing privacy policies, educating officers about privacy and intelligence guidelines, and educating the public about predictive policing practices. Smaller and medium-size law enforcement agencies raise concern about the high cost of technology and lack of interoperability of their information technology systems to implement predictive analysis. The complicated software and trained personnel needed to conduct predictive policing is beyond the funding capacity of smaller agencies as well. Some assistance to these challenges may lie in smaller agencies utilizing volunteers with the needed skill sets to conduct analysis or university students with data analysis training as interns. Regionalization of smaller agencies to share resources may also lower the costs to individual agencies. Some agencies may be located in close proximity to a fusion center capable of providing predictive analysis crime data.

Examples of Successes

The Santa Cruz, California, Police Department implemented a six-month pilot project in an effort to predict certain crimes. A mathematical algorithm similar to that used in predicting earthquakes was adapted by crime analysts for the project. A Santa Clara University math professor offered technical assistance on the project. The algorithm was used in the analysis of crime data from the department's records management system and resulted in 10 hot spot maps where officers concentrated their crime control efforts. Results indicated the model predicted 40% of targeted crimes. Significant reductions in burglaries were also realized as a result of the pilot project.

In Arlington, Texas, the police department analyzed a residential burglary problem in its city by comparing hot spots and mapping data with locations where building code violations were occurring. Officers' analysis revealed that units with an increase in physical decay and code violations suffered six more residential burglaries than similar locations in the city. The Arlington police department developed a formula to identify the characteristics of units at risk so they could work more effectively with other city agencies and neighborhoods to prevent burglary crimes from occurring.

Ronald W. Glensor

See also CompStat; Crime Analysis; Crime Analysts, Roles of; Crime Mapping; Global Positioning Systems/Geographic Information Systems; Hot Spots; Intelligence-Led Policing; Problem-Oriented Policing: Elements, Processes, Implications

Further Readings

Mills, E. (2009). An ounce of prevention. *Law Enforcement Technology, 9,* 60–63

Pearsall, B. (2010) Predictive policing: The future of law enforcement? *National Institute of Justice* (NIJ) *Journal.* Retrieved from http://www.nij.gov/journals/266/predictive.htm

Rich, S. (2011, August 19). Predictive policing project reduces crime in Santa Cruz, CA. *Government technology.* Retrieved from http://www.govtech.com/public-safety/Predictive-Policing-Project-Reduces-Crime-Santa-Cruz-Calif.html

Russo, T. (2009). *Predictive policing: A national discussion.* Retrieved from http://blogs.justice.gov/main/archives/385

U.S. Department of Justice, National Institute of Justice. *Predictive policing symposium: The future of prediction in criminal justice.* Washington, DC: Office of Justice Programs, National Institute of Justice. Retrieved from http://www.ojp.usdoj.gov/nij/topics/law-enforcement/predictive-policing/symposium/future.htm

PROBLEM, DEFINITION OF

Definitions are important. They guide behavior, influence actions, and provide the context and scope for all activities that follow. Effective problem-solving projects, which are central to community policing efforts, require clearly defined and prioritized public safety problems that agencies seek to address. Clear problem definitions set the stage for improved analysis, response and evaluation efforts, as the absence of a clearly defined problem can result in wasted time and effort because of a lack of focus. This entry describes the ways that problems are defined in a policing context and emphasizes the importance of proper definition to maximize problem-solving efforts.

Problems in the policing context have been defined as a cluster of similar, related, or recurring incidents; a substantive community concern; or a unit of police business. Problems can also be defined by their characteristics including a type of behavior (graffiti, burglary); a place where they occur (a local convenience store, bar); a person or persons who are involved (repeat burglary victims, a repeat perpetrator of domestic violence); or time they take place (immediately after school). A problem may also be defined as a combination of the above. For example, a problem may be defined as the robbery of single-family homes, the burglary of convenience stores, or gun violence by youthful offenders. In its most basic form, a problem can be thought of as two or more incidents similar in one or more ways that is of concern to the police and a concern for the community.

Agencies use a variety of methods to identify and prioritize problems to determine if they warrant the investment of police resources that may be driven by those responsible for the specific problem-solving effort, including officers, crime or problem analysts, and sergeants. These efforts may include analyzing police data to look for patterns and trends regarding repeat offenders, victims, and locations. They can involve using crime mapping to look for clustering of certain types of problems or types of offenders, interviewing officers who may recognize recurring problems, and examining police reports. Problems can also be initially identified by feedback from community members through surveys of business owners and residents or participating in community meetings. Community feedback may be especially important, because agencies often find that the problems that they prioritize may not be the same problems that are of most concern to the citizens they serve.

After an initial problem is selected, agencies typically have to redefine the problem in order to ensure that it is properly focused. Frequently, agencies need to further specify the problem as the initial definition may be too broad. For example, "illegal drugs" is not a clearly defined problem. Defining drug-related problems so broadly reduces the effectiveness of responses as illegal drugs represent a compilation of a variety of other problems. The illegal drug problem in any community is exceedingly complex to analyze and understand, and potential responses would likely be much too broad to achieve clearly defined outcomes. Analysis and response efforts will be much more effective with a more clearly defined problem related to illegal drugs that identifies specific aspects of the problem, as the type of illegal drug, or the behaviors, offenders, victims, or locations involved or the specific times that it occurs most frequently. For example, an improved definition may begin

with identifying locations such as street corners or apartment complexes; specifying the offenders like unemployed youth or high school students; the type of substances like alcohol or marijuana; or the kinds of behaviors involved such as impaired driving or street-level selling. Specifying the problem increases the chances for success, because it results in more refined analysis and an improved understanding of the problem that produces more focused responses.

After agencies have settled on a definition, they should validate this against what Ronald Clarke and John Eck have specified as the six essential elements of any public safety problem, with the acronym CHEERS:

Community: A portion of the community must experience the harmful consequences of the problem. Who is affected by the problem?

Harmful: People or institutions must suffer harm from the problem. What are the harms created?

Expectation: Some members of the community must have an expectation that police are responsible for the problem. What are the expectations for the police response?

Events: The discrete events that combine to make up the problem must be able to be described. What are the events that contribute to the problem?

Recurring: The events must recur. How often do they recur?

Similarity: The discrete events must share an indefinable characteristic in common. How are the events similar to one another?

If agencies are unable to satisfactorily answer all of these questions, then their identified problem may not be appropriate for a problem-solving project. It is important to point out that under this framework, specific neighborhoods are not considered problems as such. Although neighborhoods can develop reputations for being problematic, usually these areas contain several discrete problems within them that can be addressed individually. This approach is likely to be more effective than a broad public safety response to the myriad issues that may be occurring within these neighborhoods.

Even if agencies carefully consider and define their problem, as they move through the problem-solving process, they may find it necessary to redefine the problem as they learn more about it. Agencies may determine that the problem they selected is merely a symptom of a different problem that should be the primary focus of their efforts. It is also important to recognize that illegality is not a defining characteristic of a problem, as some problems may involve legal behavior but still rise to a level of importance for the police. For example, community members may by concerned about speeding in residential areas and complain frequently about this to the police. However, in the process of analyzing this problem, the police may determine that drivers in residential neighborhoods are actually obeying the speed limit. This problem, which involves legal behavior, has now been redefined to the *perception* of speeding in residential areas, but it may still require a police response. Of course, this type of problem requires completely different solutions than an actual speeding problem, perhaps informing residents that drivers are not speeding or working with legislators and other stakeholders to lower speed limits to match citizen expectations and concerns.

Clarke and Eck also developed a useful way that agencies can classify all public safety problems that come to their attention in order to look for similarities between problems and to organize problem-solving efforts. They classify the range of problems that agencies are often called upon to address along two dimensions: the environment that they take place in and the behaviors of the offenders. Clarke and Eck specify 11 distinct environments where problems can occur: residential, recreational, offices, retail, industrial, agricultural, educational, human services, public ways, transport, and open/transitional. They then cross-reference this with six types of problem behaviors that individuals may engage in at these locations. These include predatory, consensual, conflicts, incivilities, endangerment, and misuse of police. This 11-by-6 matrix produces 66 discrete cells by which agencies can classify their problems and look for commonalities among them.

A final point on the proper definition of problems is that the best problem definitions begin with the end in mind. Agencies should be able to effectively articulate and specify the measures and indicators that will be used to gauge success. A properly defined problem will have clear measurable indicators that police can use to determine when the harms associated with the problem, the frequency of the problem, or its severity have been reduced. An inability to develop such measures may be evidence of a poorly defined problem.

Clearly defining and properly specifying problems are essential for effective police problem solving. Properly defined problems help focus analysis, response, and evaluation efforts and greatly increase the chances for successful public safety outcomes.

Matthew C. Scheider

See also Community Policing and Problem Solving, Definition of; Problem Analysis Triangle; Problem-Solving Initiatives, Assessment and Evaluation; Problem-Solving Initiatives, Examples of Assessment and Evaluation of; Problem-Solving Process (SARA)

Further Readings

Braga, A. A. (2008). *Problem-oriented policing and crime prevention.* Monsey, NY: Criminal Justice Press.

Clarke, R. V., & Eck, J. E. (2005). *Crime analysis for problem solvers in 60 small steps.* Washington, DC: U.S. Department of Justice, Office of Community Oriented Policing Services.

Eck, J. E., & Clarke, R. V. (2003). Classifying common police problems: A routine activity approach. In M. J. Smith & D. B. Cornish, *Theory for practice in situational crime prevention: Crime prevention studies, 16.* New York, NY: Criminal Justice Press. Retrieved from http://www.popcenter.org/library/crimeprevention/volume_16/TitlePages.pdf

Goldstein, H. (1990). *Problem-oriented policing.* New York, NY: McGraw-Hill.

Schmerler, K., Perkins, M., Philips, S., Rinehart, T., & Townsend, M. (2011). *Problem-solving tips: A guide to reducing crime and disorder through problem-solving partnerships* (2nd ed.). Washington, DC: U.S. Department of Justice, Office of Community Oriented Policing Services. Retrieved from http://cops.usdoj.gov/files/RIC/Publications/05060069_ProbSolvTips_0711_FIN.pdf

Scott, M. S. (2000). *Problem-oriented policing: Reflections on the first 20 years.* Washington, DC: U.S. Department of Justice, Office of Community Oriented Policing Services. Retrieved from http://www.cops.usdoj.gov/Publications/e03011022.txt

PROBLEM ANALYSIS TRIANGLE

The problem analysis triangle identifies the basic elements that facilitate or impede crime in order to guide how crime is examined and ultimately addressed (see Figure 1). Also known as the "crime triangle," it treats *problems* as the unit of analysis in crime prevention and therefore provides the foundation for the SARA problem-solving process (scanning, analysis, response, assessment) that underlies problem-oriented policing, which informs situational crime prevention.

Although it is referred to as a single triangle, the problem analysis triangle has been adapted over time and now consists of several embedded, complementary triangles—with the arms of each triangle representing a different intervention point that can aid analysis and crime prevention. This entry summarizes the theoretical foundation and evolution of the problem analysis triangle, its components, and its use in practice.

Theoretical Foundations

The problem analysis triangle is rooted in routine activity theory, a key theory of environmental criminology developed by Marcus Felson and Lawrence E. Cohen. In 1979, routine activity theory was formulated as a macro-level theory of crime to explain why U.S. crime was increasing despite improved social and economic conditions—a circumstance contradictory to sociological explanations of crime. According to Felson and Cohen, mundane, everyday activities that people "routinely" engage in (e.g., traveling to work or participating in leisure) offer important insights for explaining crime. They argued that such activities create opportunities

for crime when they bring together a *motivated offender* and a *suitable victim* at a time and location when *capable guardianship* is weak or absent. This arrangement has become known as the "chemistry of crime."

By identifying the minimal elements required for crime, routine activity theory offered a simple yet powerful premise for crime prevention: Crime cannot occur if any *one* of these factors is absent. Thus, in 2003, John Eck used these factors to create the original inner triangle of the problem analysis triangle with the three sides representing the offender, the victim or target, and the location or place. Later work from other criminologists led Eck to add another outer triangle representing crime "controllers" who can monitor each original element and disrupt its role in facilitating crime. The three sides of this triangle correspond with those of the inner triangle: handlers have been added to oversee offenders, managers for places, and guardians for targets or victims. In sum, the inner triangle identifies that factors needed for crime to occur while the outer controller triangle represents the factors that can prevent it.

In 2010, Rana Sampson, Jon Eck, and Jessica Dunham added a third (outer) triangle to account for super controllers. Super controllers are various types of entities that influence the actions of handlers, managers, and guardians, which offer an explanation of why crime controllers either facilitate or disrupt crime. Thus, super controllers do not have a direct effect on the necessary elements of crime from the inner triangle—they instead regulate the controllers that do.

Components

As described above, the problem analysis triangle focuses attention on the multiple factors that create or impede crime. The arms of each triangle introduce a different intervention point that must be considered in order to fully understand a particular crime problem. Numerous studies have demonstrated the value of considering these factors, which are discussed in more detail below and organized in sections according to each triangle.

The Inner Triangle: Offenders, Victims, and Places

In the context of the problem analysis triangle, offenders are seen as rational, decision-making actors. According to routine activity theory, the

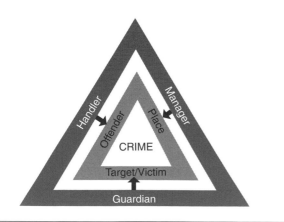

Figure 1   Problem Analysis Triangle

Source: Center for Problem Oriented Policing. (2013). Problem analysis triangle. Retrieved from http://www.popcenter.org/learning/60steps/index.cfm?stepNum=8. Reprinted by permission.

presence of motivated offenders is a given, which means that problem analysis should focus on understanding *how* offenders commit crime, not *why*. Research suggests it is important to examine the choices and actions of offenders before, during, and after the crime because this information can reveal insights about repeat offending, preferred techniques, and changes in their behavior.

Likewise, victims are not passive elements in the problem analysis triangle. It emphasizes understanding the factors that make some targets (which can be either individuals or inanimate items) appear more or less attractive to offenders, which can help explain repeat victimization and the appeal of what Ron Clarke calls "hot products" (i.e., material goods most preferred by offenders due to certain characteristics like being valuable or easily disposable).

Finally, the problem analysis triangle draws attention to the importance of understanding crime places, or the discrete locations where offenses occur (e.g., a particular bar, street block, apartment complex). Studies show that certain places are prone to a disproportionate number of offenses, resulting in geographic concentrations of crime or hot spots. Problem analysis can help determine if hot spots are the locations that generate, attract, or enable crime—each of which presents a different type of problem with different implications for prevention.

The Outer Triangle: Controllers

When crime does not occur because an offender, victim, or place is absent from the chemistry of crime, it could be due to the influence of a crime controller. Controllers are exactly what the name implies: They are entities capable of exerting control over one of the factors that facilitate crime. When controllers are effective, they essentially remove an arm of the inner triangle, making the occurrence of crime not possible. Controllers were an important addition to the problem analysis triangle because they help explain why offenders and victims *do not meet* at the same time and place, which directly informs crime prevention. A full analysis includes understanding how different controllers facilitate or impede these factors from coming together so that strategies can be developed to better mobilize them.

As mentioned above, the problem analysis triangle organizes each of the three controllers to correspond with one of the necessary elements of crime from the inner triangle. First, a *handler* is someone who interacts with potential offenders and can potentially change their actions or discourage them from committing crime. There are a variety of handlers, which may vary depending on the potential offender. For younger persons, an effective handler might be a parent or teacher, whereas for an adult, an effective handler might be a spouse or coworker.

Place managers, the second type of controller, are responsible for controlling what happens at specific locations. For example, bartenders are in charge of how much alcohol patrons are served at drinking establishments and residence hall advisors are responsible for controlling noise levels at university dormitories.

Finally, capable *guardians* from routine activity theory become controllers in the problem analysis triangle, and are responsible for protecting potential victims and targets. Individuals can act as their own guardians when they take measures to protect themselves and their property from crime. However, individuals like the police or a neighbor can provide guardianship to others. When the crime target is an inanimate object, a guardian could be a security device (e.g., a lock for an unattended bicycle).

The Outermost Triangle: Super Controllers

Super controllers were introduced in a later version of the problem analysis triangle to answer the question why crime prevention fails or succeeds. Super controllers are entities that provide incentives that influence the actions of controllers, so they help explain why controllers are either effective or ineffective at disrupting crime. Because super controllers control controllers, they impact the chemistry of crime indirectly through controllers. The various types of super controllers are broadly categorized as formal, diffuse, or personal.

An example of a formal super controller is a game authority that reduces poaching by regulating those who manage hunting reserves. By contrast, a diffuse super controller is unlikely a single, discrete entity. The news media could be an example of a diffuse super controller. Negative or positive publicity could mobilize certain controllers to prevent crime (e.g., news coverage of repeat offenses occurring at a particular bar could hurt its business and prompt owners to improve place management). Finally, groups or family members can act as personal super controllers, which attempt to control behavior more informally. For example, a neighborhood group could pressure its local transportation authority to install speed bumps in order to reduce pedestrian injuries and fatalities.

The Problem Analysis Triangle and Environmental Criminology

As an applied crime prevention framework, the problem analysis triangle encompasses several key tenets of environmental criminology—a set of theories that describes crime events (which is distinct from traditional criminology that tries to explain offender motivation). First, it emphasizes the importance of addressing *specific* types of crime. Even seemingly similar crime events will involve different types of offenders, targets, and places, and effective controllers and super controllers may also differ and play different roles. For example, a broad class of crime like "theft" actually takes multiple forms that are unique types of problems (e.g., auto theft, bicycle theft, and theft at construction sites are very different from each other), and the problem analysis triangle directs us to consider the varied elements of each form.

Second, the problem analysis triangle treats crime *problems* as the unit of analysis, an approach rooted in Herman Goldstein's work on problem-oriented policing. The idea is that police and other stakeholders should be problem solvers and try to understand and change the conditions that create recurring crime problems (rather than focusing on single incidents or cases). The problem-solving approach is fundamentally different from the standard (or traditional) model of policing, which relies on reactive law enforcement and uses a limited set of more general tactics like rapid response to calls for service, follow-up investigations, and preventive patrol. By identifying problems as the unit of police work, the problem analysis triangle prompts analysts to consider an array of underlying causal factors, which expands the number of potential interventions.

Third, the chemistry of crime, the foundation of the problem analysis triangle, is based on the idea that *opportunity* makes crime possible. The convergence of offenders and victims in time and space increases the chance of crime occurring simply because it creates an opportunity to commit it. Thus, the problem analysis triangle points the analyst to the factors necessary to either produce or disrupt criminal opportunities. In sum, the problem analysis triangle encapsulates environmental criminology's aim to better understand the opportunity structures that underlie specific crime problems.

The Problem Analysis Triangle in Practice

The problem analysis triangle provides the basis for several interrelated crime prevention approaches. As mentioned above, Goldstein introduced the *problem* as a unit of police work, which provided the foundation for his concept of problem-oriented policing. Toward this approach, Goldstein described a systematic process to solve problems sequentially by first defining them specifically, then conducting in-depth analyses and, finally, using the information gained from previous steps to create a tailor-made, practical response to address the immediate, direct causes of a problem. Today, the acronym SARA is used to abbreviate the four steps of problem-solving process that characterize problem-oriented policing: scanning, analysis, response, and assessment. The problem analysis triangle is critical to problem solving and problem-oriented policing because it identifies the elements that should be examined to aid SARA.

Once the SARA process is used to reveal the criminal opportunity structure of a particular problem, analysts can turn to situational crime prevention to identify potential opportunity-reducing techniques. Initially developed by Ron Clarke and elaborated by others, situational crime prevention is the application component of environmental criminology and is thus interconnected with the problem analysis triangle (i.e., it translates the triangle into interventions). Its goal is to manipulate specific, immediate situations in a way that makes committing crime look unfavorable to would-be offenders.

In its most recent form, situational crime prevention tries to achieve this through 25 techniques based on five main factors: effort, risk, rewards, provocations, and excuses. The main premise is that crime is best prevented when interventions increase its effort and risk, reduce its anticipated rewards and provocations (i.e., precipitating factors that induce crime), and remove the excuses that justify it. The problem analysis triangle fuels the SARA problem-solving process that underlies problem-oriented policing, which ultimately leads to responses informed by situational crime prevention.

Interventions Using the Problem Analysis Triangle

Early examples of effective crime prevention strategies consistent with the problem analysis triangle exist, although it was not formally represented as a "triangle" at the time. For example, in the 1980s, the Newport News (Virginia) Police Department was selected as a pilot agency to test problem-oriented policing and engaged in the analysis of a variety of crime problems. As a result of responses developed from the problem-solving process, the city experienced considerable reductions in thefts from vehicles in a parking lot, burglaries at an apartment complex, and personal robberies in the central business district. This first demonstrated success of problem-oriented policing spurred further work on problem solving and the development of tools that aid its use like the problem analysis triangle.

Today, the image of the problem analysis triangle is widely recognized and consulted directly by police agencies and communities across the world trying to reduce crime and disorder. Like Newport News, other jurisdictions have used problem solving to reduce traditional offenses, including various forms of theft, burglary, and robbery, but also drug- and alcohol-related crime and street prostitution. In addition, however, it has been used to address other less recognized types of crime, as graffiti on subway trains in New York City and prescription fraud in San Diego, California.

Finally, as its name implies, the problem analysis triangle is not limited to preventing only crime but is also useful for addressing other (noncrime) public safety problems. For example, problem-solving principles were used in Shawnee, Kansas, to address pedestrian-vehicle crashes, as well as in Illinois to address false alarms and in San Francisco, California, with regard to homeless encampments. Because of its practical yet theoretical basis, wide application across jurisdictions and types of problem, and potential effectiveness, the problem analysis triangle has a prominent role in policing, criminology, and crime prevention.

Justin A. Heinonen

See also Crime Analysis; Crime Analysts, Roles of; Problem, Definition of; Problem-Oriented Policing: Elements, Processes, Implications; Problem-Oriented Policing, Goldstein's Development of; Problem-Solving Initiatives, Examples of Assessment and Evaluation of; Problem-Solving Process (SARA); Situational Crime Prevention

Further Readings

Cohen, L. E., & Felson, M. (1979). Social change and crime rate trends: A routine activities approach. *American Sociological Review, 44,* 588–608.

Clarke, R. V. (1980). "Situational" crime prevention: Theory and practice. *British Journal of Criminology, 20,* 136–147.

Clarke, R. V., & Eck, J. E. (2005). *Crime analysis for problem solvers in 60 small steps.* Washington, DC: US Department of Justice, Office of Community Oriented Policing Services.

Goldstein, H. (1979). Improving policing: A problem-oriented approach. *Crime and Delinquency, 25*(2), 236–258. doi: 10.1177/001112877902500207

Goldstein, H. (1990). *Problem-oriented policing.* New York, NY: McGraw-Hill.

Sampson, R., & Scott, M. S. (2000). *Tackling crime and other public-safety problems: Case studies in problem-solving.* Washington, DC: US Department of Justice, Office of Community Oriented Policing Services. Retrieved from http://www.cops.usdoj.gov/html/cd_rom/inaction1/Problem_Solving_Case_Study_toc_f.htm

Tilley, N. (Ed.). (2005). *Handbook of crime prevention and community safety.* Portland, OR: Willan.

Wortley, R. (2001). A classification of techniques for controlling situational precipitators of crime. *Security Journal, 14*(4), 63–82. doi: 10.1057/palgrave.sj.8340098

PROBLEM-ORIENTED POLICING: ELEMENTS, PROCESSES, IMPLICATIONS

In the early 1980s, the notion of community policing emerged as the dominant direction for thinking about policing. It was designed to reunite the police with the community. It is a philosophy and not a specific tactic; a proactive, decentralized approach, designed to reduce crime, disorder, and fear of crime. Later, problem-oriented policing evolved (being first articulated by Herman Goldstein in 1979), which was grounded in principles different from but complementary to community policing. Problem-oriented policing is a strategy that puts the community policing philosophy into practice. It advocates that police examine the underlying causes of recurring incidents of crime and disorder. The problem-solving process, SARA, helps officers to identify problems, analyze them completely, develop response strategies, and assess the results.

This entry discusses problem-oriented policing: its elements, processes, and implications for the future.

Basic Elements

The basic elements of problem-oriented policing are as follows:

1. Police business is understood as clusters of crime or disorder incidents, similar in one or more ways. These clusters of incidents are referred to as "problems."

2. Problems are carefully analyzed, drawing on the knowledge and skills of crime analysts as well as field personnel.

3. The ultimate purpose of problem analysis is to discover new and more effective responses to problems.

4. Responses that work to prevent crime and disorder incidents, and not merely to react to them after they have occurred, are given high priority.

5. Response strategies that are not entirely dependent on the operations of the criminal justice system are encouraged.

6. Response strategies that engage the community, other public agencies, and the private sector in reducing the problem are emphasized.

7. New response strategies are implemented as fully as possible.

8. The impact that new response strategies have on the problem is carefully evaluated.

9. The results of the analysis, response implementation, and evaluation are reported so that others can benefit from the newly acquired knowledge.

10. The accumulated knowledge gained through this process contributes to the development of a larger body of knowledge that enhances professional policing.

Basic Premises

Problem-oriented policing builds upon some basic lessons learned about policing over the past several decades. The following paragraphs describe some of the most critical of these lessons.

The function of the police is, and always has been, much broader than merely enforcing criminal laws. Police are expected to address a wide range of community problems that threaten public safety and order. Enforcement of the criminal law, often thought to be the basic purpose of the police, is better understood as but one means to achieving the ends of public safety and order.

The police exercise a tremendous amount of discretion, at all levels of their hierarchy, in carrying out their function. Problem-oriented policing represents a significant effort to harness and guide that discretion toward more effective and fair policing.

The police, as an institution, operate not merely as the front end of the criminal justice system, but as a key institution in a web of social institutions that share responsibility for providing for public safety and order. Problem-oriented policing encourages police to collaborate both within and outside the criminal justice system to address public safety problems.

The police have, for various reasons, been compelled to rely excessively on the criminal justice system as a means for addressing crime and disorder. The overuse and misuse of the criminal law has contributed to major problems in policing. Problem-oriented policing promotes the use of alternatives to arrest as means of addressing problems.

Police have long used formal and informal alternatives to criminal arrest to address problems, but the use of those alternatives has not always been officially sanctioned or even acknowledged. Police officers have long been left to improvise in situations where use of the criminal law is inadequate. Problem-oriented policing stresses the importance of giving formal sanction to legitimate, alternative methods of dealing with problems.

The main strategies employed by the police—rapid response to citizen calls for service, criminal investigation, and random preventive patrol—have proven far more limited in their capacity to provide for the public's safety than commonly believed. Consequently, while these strategies remain important aspects of police service, they are insufficient for achieving the entire police mission. Problem-oriented policing acknowledges the practical limitations of these main strategies while capitalizing on their benefits. It urges police to explore a much wider range of responses to problems beyond the conventional strategies.

Police managers and others who shape police policy and practice have become preoccupied with the administration of police organizations, to the exclusion of focusing on how police organizations can best deliver services to address public safety problems and meet community needs. Problem-oriented policing serves as a corrective to this "means over ends" syndrome.

Line-level police officers, as well as community members, have a reservoir of knowledge, talent, and resources that can be better tapped by police managers for understanding and responding to public safety problems. Problem-oriented policing promotes new styles of working relationships between the police and the public, and between police management and line officers—relationships that can make better use of line officers and community members than have conventional police management approaches.

These and other conclusions helped form a much more realistic understanding of the police institution, with all its flaws and limits, than existed before. It was upon this foundation of knowledge that problem-oriented policing was built.

Looking at Problems and Patterns

Problem-oriented policing introduces a new basic unit to police work: the problem. In conventional policing, a call for police service, or a case, is the basic unit of police work. Each call and each case is handled separately. Once handled, each call or case is considered closed, and attention turned to the next call or case. Problem-oriented policing looks for patterns among individual calls and cases, patterns that may be formed by a common set of offenders, victims, locations, times, or behaviors. It clusters calls and cases into new basic units known as problems. The enterprise of policing is thereby transformed from one of merely handling individual calls and cases to one of addressing problems.

Some examples of problems commonly faced by police are assaults in and around bars, retail theft in shopping malls, cruising along commercial strips, traffic control during large public gatherings and demonstrations, street prostitution, disorder at budget motels, speeding in residential areas, homicide among intimate partners, sexual abuse of children, drug dealing on street corners, illicit sexual activity in public parks, loud parties, and street robbery, to name but a few.

These sorts of problems constitute the business of policing. These problems can be experienced and addressed at various levels of aggregation. That is, problems may be experienced at particular locations, at multiple locations throughout a jurisdiction, or across multiple jurisdictions.

To address problems, police must first understand the conditions that contribute to these problems. Developing this understanding requires that police carefully and completely examine and analyze the factors that are contributing to or causing the problems. Doing so requires the police to go well beyond merely proving the elements of a crime or filling in the boxes on a standard police incident report. It calls for blending social science research principles with practical police experience to explore answers to important questions:

How big and how serious is the problem? Who is harmed by the problem, and how? How concerned is the community about the problem?

What conditions and factors contribute to the problem? Where does the problem exist, and, conversely, where does it not exist? What explains the difference?

How do police currently handle the problem, and with what effect? Is the current police response helpful, ineffectual, or does it perhaps create more serious problems?

What other groups, organizations, and individuals share responsibility for addressing the problem, and how are they currently addressing the problem? What is the police interest in seeing this problem addressed, and what is the proper role for police in addressing it?

How are similar problems handled elsewhere? What alternatives are there to handling the problem that might improve upon the current response? Are those alternatives currently feasible, and if not, what needs to be done to make them so?

With new insights into the problems gained from careful problem analysis, police are encouraged to develop new responses to problems, responses that are tailored to the problem and to the particular conditions of the local setting in which it occurs. Police are encouraged to develop responses, or more typically, combinations of responses, beyond the conventional. They are especially encouraged to consider responses that minimize the need for police to use force, that have community support and engagement, and that have potential to prevent future incidents or minimize the harm caused by them. Alternatives to the conventional responses of arrest and preventive patrol might include the following: pressuring others who control the conditions that give rise to problems to alter those conditions; mediating conflicts; physically redesigning buildings, streets, and other structures; mobilizing the community; conveying information; or using civil laws to regulate problematic conduct or conditions.

Analyzing problems in this fashion has heretofore not been routine for police. To the extent police have analyzed crime problems, it has more typically been with an eye toward predicting the next crime in a series and trying to interrupt it and apprehend the offenders. The sort of problem analysis prescribed by problem-oriented policing goes well beyond conventional crime analysis. Thus, the concept will require police to develop a much greater capacity to analyze the problems that constitute their business, and a capacity to use that analysis to inform their policies and practices.

A problem-oriented approach to police work requires that police adopt an open posture with respect to their work; that they be willing to critique their own actions, to actively search for ways to improve their responses, and to rigorously assess their efforts to inform further improvements. It requires a new level of openness and candor with the public and other government officials about what is realistic to expect of the police with respect to various problems. It calls for a new level of engagement by various sectors of the community and the government to assist the police in addressing difficult public safety problems.

The overarching objective of problem-oriented policing is to make police more effective in addressing the wide range of public safety problems they routinely confront. Merely making police more efficient, and even better, liked and supported by the public, are subsidiary objectives to the ultimate set of objectives related to keeping society safe and orderly, consistent with the principles of a constitutional democracy.

Problem-Solving Processes

Problem-oriented policing makes use of any of a number of problem-solving methodologies, all rooted in the social scientific method of inquiry.

Perhaps the best-known problem-solving methodology associated with problem-oriented policing is the one known as the SARA model. SARA is an acronym that stands for *scanning, analysis, response,* and *assessment.* It was developed by researchers in an early experiment applying problem-oriented policing in Newport News, Virginia, in the 1980s. The SARA model, like other similar problem-solving models, is commonly portrayed as a linear or sequential model—that is, that it flows neatly from beginning to end. In fact, it is an iterative or cyclical model—inquiries lead to some answers and to more inquiries, and all the while the inquiry is underway, police and others may be taking interim action to address the problem. Assessment, or evaluation, of the effort may well lead to the development or refinement of responses or to new lines of inquiry.

Each stage of the SARA model calls for the following specific steps to be taken:

Scanning

The scanning phase involves identifying recurring problems of concern to the public and the police, identifying the consequences of the problem for the community and the police, prioritizing those problems, developing broad goals, confirming that the problems exist, determining how frequently the problem occurs and how long it has been taking place, and selecting problems for closer examination.

Analysis

The analysis phase involves identifying and understanding the events and conditions that precede and accompany the problem, identifying relevant data to be collected, researching what is known about the problem type, taking inventory of how the problem is currently addressed and the strengths and limitations of the current response, narrowing the scope of the problem as specifically as possible, identifying a variety of resources that may be of assistance in developing a deeper understanding of the problem, and developing a working hypothesis about why the problem is occurring.

Response

The response phase involves brainstorming for new interventions, searching for what other communities with similar problems have done, choosing among the alternative interventions, outlining a response plan and identifying responsible parties, stating the specific objectives for the response plan, and carrying out the planned activities.

Assessment

The assessment phase involves determining whether the plan was implemented (a process evaluation), collecting pre- and post-response qualitative and quantitative data, determining whether broad goals and specific objectives were attained, identifying any new strategies needed to augment the original plan, and conducting an ongoing assessment to ensure continued effectiveness.

Relation to Community Policing and Other Police Reform Ideas

Problem-oriented policing shares common features with several other movements in police reform and crime prevention, among them community policing, team policing, and situational crime prevention. It also draws upon other conceptual frameworks for analyzing and responding to crime problems, including crime prevention through environmental design (CPTED), crime analysis, the CompStat method, hot spot policing, and crime mapping. Problem-oriented policing rejects, however, the premises underlying such concepts as zero-tolerance policing because those concepts imply that police discretion will be suspended, and that the widespread use of criminal arrest is a viable solution to many public safety problems.

Certain innovations in prosecution and court management run parallel to problem-oriented policing. They recognize that the roles of prosecutors and courts, too, are broader than merely processing cases through the legal system and that public safety problems require changes in the conditions that cause them, and a more preventive perspective in addressing them. Concepts such as community prosecution and restorative justice are generally considered compatible with problem-oriented policing.

Implications for the Management of Police Organizations

Full incorporation of the basic elements of problem-oriented policing into the mainstream of policing requires substantial changes in the ways that police organizations are managed and supported. The most profound changes necessary for problem-oriented policing to exploit its full potential are described below.

Developing a New Capacity for Analyzing Police Business

Police organizations, either with internal resources or with assistance from outside research institutions, will need to improve their capacity to organize and analyze information about the demands made upon them in order to be able to improve their responses to public safety problems.

Building a Body of Knowledge About Policing

In contrast to most other professions and trades, police have long lacked an organized, accessible, well-researched body of knowledge about how they ought to respond to the many public safety problems they confront. Problem-oriented policing represents a commitment to learning what works, under what conditions, for what kinds of problems. Building this body of knowledge will require contributions from police agencies, research institutions, and government funding agencies. The *Problem-Oriented Guides for Police,* produced by the Center for Problem-Oriented Policing with funding from the U.S. Department of Justice's Office of Community Oriented Policing Services, represents one effort to build this sort of body of knowledge.

Training and Educating Police

The shift away from an incident-driven style of policing in which police merely respond to emergencies, handle calls for service, and investigate crimes, to a problem-oriented style of policing will require that police officials, at all levels of the hierarchy, learn new knowledge and new skills. They will need to learn more about the dynamics that give rise to many public safety problems, and the skills necessary to identify and analyze problems and to manage problem-oriented police operations. New educational and training methodologies will be in order as well. Problem-based learning methodologies will need to replace conventional police training methodologies.

Supporting Police

For police organizations to become more effective in controlling public safety problems, they will require a different level of support than simple funding for police officers and police equipment. The respective governments under which police organizations exist, and the public at large, must come to view public safety in broader terms—to see public safety not as the sole province of police, but as the joint responsibility of police, other government agencies, nongovernmental organizations, and the various sectors of the community. It will require greater recognition of the interrelationship of crime and such other realms as land use planning, architecture, urban design, civil code regulation, mental health and substance abuse treatment, youth services, product design, and business policies and practices. It will require that the ownership of and responsibility for addressing various public safety problems be negotiated among the various sectors of society, police included, that have stakes and interests in those problems.

Problem-oriented policing implicates nearly every aspect of police management. In addition to the changes described above, it calls for rethinking how police officers are recruited and selected, how police officers' and police agencies' performance is measured, how police agencies are organized and staffed, and how public expectations for police service are managed.

Michael S. Scott

See also Community-Oriented Policing; CompStat; Crime Mapping; Hot Spots; Restorative Justice

Further Readings

Braga, A. A. (2002). *Problem-oriented policing and crime prevention.* Monsey, NY: Criminal Justice Press.

Goldstein, H. (1977). *Policing a free society.* Cambridge, MA: Ballinger.

Goldstein, H. (1979). Improving policing: A problem-oriented approach. *Crime & Delinquency, 25*(2), 236–258. doi: 10.1177/001112877902500207

Goldstein, H. (1990). *Problem-oriented policing.* New York, NY: McGraw-Hill.

Center for Problem-Oriented Policing. (2000 et seq.). *Problem-oriented guides for police.* Washington, DC: U.S. Department of Justice, Office of Community Oriented Policing Services. Retrieved from http://www.popcenter.org

Sampson, R., & Scott, M. S. (2000). *Tackling crime and other public-safety problems: Case studies in problem-solving.* Washington, DC: US Department of Justice, Office of Community Oriented Policing Services. Retrieved from http://www.cops.usdoj.gov/html/cd_rom/inaction1/Problem_Solving_Case_Study_toc_f.htm

Scott, M. S. (2000). *Problem-oriented policing: Reflections on the first 20 years.* Washington, DC: U.S. Department of Justice, Office of Community Oriented Policing Services. Retrieved from http://www.cops.usdoj.gov/Publications/e03011022.txt

Problem-Oriented Policing, Goldstein's Development of

When Herman Goldstein, a law professor at the University of Wisconsin–Milwaukee (UWM), was designing new methods of thought processes for the criminal law course curriculum to challenge his students, he came to understand the broader application this approach could have for policing. With regard to this method of thinking in the criminal law class, Goldstein noted that the police had a generic response to everything they did: Enforce the law. This was without regard to its appropriateness or effectiveness and frequently resulted in their overuse of the authority to search and to arrest when some other less intrusive action could be more effective for dealing with the problem.

This realization led to Goldstein's 1979 seminal work, "Improving Policing: A Problem-Oriented Approach." This method of thinking began to lay a foundation upon which not only an innovative policing philosophy would be fashioned, but also a basic tenet of policing would be identified: *Problems* are at the heart of policing. Enhanced through continued conceptualization throughout a career of scholarly productivity, Goldstein's problem-oriented policing philosophy is a specific approach for improving the processes by which police provide service and enforce laws. This approach challenges police to improve their understanding of the causal and correlate factors related to community problems and to provide solutions to these problems through a more comprehensive method than traditionally utilized. This entry explains the rationale underlying Goldstein's call for reform in police philosophy, priorities, and methods.

The "Means Over Ends" Syndrome

Throughout the bulk of the 20th century, Goldstein argued that police scholars, such as August Vollmer, Bruce Smith, and O. W. Wilson, emphasized the importance of the organization, function, and operations of police departments—an issue he coined as the *means over ends syndrome*. He believed police at this time were overlooking the substantive nature of their work, which was to resolve or remove a variety of problems within the communities they serve. For example, police were focused on improving the time it took to respond to a call for service and not on the quality of service provided once they arrived. Goldstein (1979) acknowledged the importance of the work put forth on efficient police management, as he notes, "The first priority was putting the police house in order . . . without a minimum level of order and accountability, an agency cannot redirect its administrators to address more substantive matters."(p. 239).

More specifically, police should focus on the outputs of their organizations—that is, the substantive issues their organization is tasked to have an impact upon. With respect to policing, a focus on substantive issues would be the attention of police on the recurring problems police must respond to, mitigate, or prevent (e.g., burglary and assaults). In an attempt to develop appropriate solutions for desired outcomes to the problems they face, police should ask questions such as what is the specific nature of the problem, what are the police doing about it, and how effective are their efforts. The key to this process is recognizing that problems, not formal criminal codes, should be the focus of police efforts.

The Problems

Goldstein's work certainly did not set out to make the claim that police did not address problems in their communities—he redefined how police literally defined the problems they faced. Through the process of making basic deductions from common occurrences police encounter and by providing examples of these encounters, he illustrated the pitfall of how police generally categorize problems. Consistent with their traditional roles as enforcers of the law, Goldstein noted police defined their problems by following criminal codes. Such an approach yields a gap in effective outcomes as police are responsible for not only enforcing laws, but maintaining order and providing service.

In an attempt to improve effectiveness, Goldstein posited that police must gather information about recurring incidents and develop an appropriate solution based on the nature of the underlying conditions that cause the problem. John Eck and William Spelman (1987) noted, for example, that social and physical conditions in a deteriorated apartment complex may generate burglaries, acts of vandalism, intimidation of pedestrians by rowdy teenagers, and other incidents. These incidents, some of which come to police attention, are symptoms of the problem, and the incidents will continue as long as the problem that creates them persists.

Furthermore, Eck identified a problem classification scheme that begins with a distinction between what he refers to as *common problems and system problems*. Common problems occur when an offender comes into contact with his or her intended victim. These common problems comprise the bulk of problems local police must address. Two factors are salient with respect to common problems. The first is behaviors of the people involved and the second is the environment in which these encounters take place. When perpetrators do not have to come into contact with their would-be victim in order to engage in crime, a system problem is identified. While system problems are commonly the responsibility of state, federal, and special unit law enforcement, it is important to note that the system which facilitates the criminal behavior is substituted for the environment found in common problems. For example, a case of identity theft using a computer system would be considered a system problem.

Regarding the process of specifying problems in policing, Goldstein himself noted in 1979 that problem-solving requires "identifying problems in more precise terms, researching each problem, documenting the nature of the current police response, assessing its adequacy and the adequacy of existing authority and resources, engaging in a broad exploration of alternatives to present responses, weighing the merits of alternatives, and choosing among them" (p. 243). Michael S. Scott (2000) puts forth a tangible method of thinking for police tasked with specifying problems in that they should present their problems in a grammatical form that always includes a verb—the verb being the specific problem. For example, rather than generalizing (or writing in shorthand) that the problem is "juveniles skipping school," it should be more specific as in "juveniles vandalizing foreclosed homes while skipping school." Such a grammatical approach brings clarity to the identification of problems.

Problem-Oriented Policing in Practice

With the notion in hand that police could be more successful in their efforts to provide effective outcomes to crime and disorder, a more tangible method of translating this philosophy into practice was needed. In Newport News, Virginia, one of the first locations in the United States to implement problem-oriented policing, a tangible method for police to put this philosophy into practice was identified. This problem-oriented policing philosophy challenged officers to specifically identify problems within their communities by scanning their patrol beats and through analysis identify critical causal factors that allowed the problem to rise. Once attributes of the problem have been identified, officers are tasked to develop solutions to achieve a desired impact and thus remedy the problem—which is the response to the problem. Last, to gauge the extent to which the response is having a desired impact, police must do an assessment of the problem and the response. As a result, this process has become known as the SARA model (for scanning, analysis, response, assessment). While other problem-oriented thought processes have been put forth, the SARA model has continued as a pillar of the philosophy Goldstein established. Such a pillar that allows for the philosophy to be translated to practice deserves further discussion.

The SARA model begins by identifying a recurring problem by officers scanning their patrol beats and communities. Key to this scanning stage to identify problems is broadening the recognition of problems beyond a single incident or crime classification. For example, all arsons are not the same. Teenagers committing arson as an act of property damage on a condemned home is much different than a small business owner burning down his or her struggling business in order to collect insurance money. Police are required to recognize the interconnectedness of multiple problems and to understand what behaviors and conditions require a directed response. Once the problem is identified, it is followed by an analysis of the underlying conditions of the problem. Police need to collect data from disparate sources (e.g., open source, community members, and/or investigations) that might best inform officers of

the problem. The police want to identify individuals involved in the problem, under what circumstances the problem occurs, and what approaches have been used in the past to address the problem. These disparate pieces of information are then analyzed for the purpose of developing effective responses.

Relying on the knowledge gained from the previous steps, police develop and implement a response or set of responses to impact the problem. Any, and all, implemented responses should consider and encompass all possible remedies that could impact the problem. Such a response may include traditional enforcement functions as well as other alternative responses, like environmental design or educational awareness programs. Last, once responses have been implemented, it is imperative on behalf of the police to assess the impact the selected responses had on the problem. To determine this effectiveness, police should measure indicators of the problem. Such an assessment provides direction for future actions. If the interventions have not achieved the desired impact, more time may be needed or additional analysis and responses may be required. It could perhaps also be the case that the implemented responses were effective and the problem no longer requires focused resources— though this is unlikely as many problems police face will never truly be solved, simply mitigated. This model is arguably the first application of the scientific method to daily police functions. The SARA model is a policy-based approach to research which Goldstein suggested officers could use as a fundamental part of their daily routines.

However, despite yielding promise, it is important to recognize that in practice the development and implementation of problem-oriented responses do not always follow the succinct steps of the SARA model. Rather, depending on the complexity of the problems, the process can be characterized as a series of disjointed and often simultaneous activities. A range of issues can cause diversions from the SARA model—such as problems requiring further analysis due to ineffective initial responses as well as implemented responses that occasionally uncover new problems. The SARA model is perhaps best described as an available model for integrating problem-oriented policing into police organizations. A commitment to the problem-oriented philosophy is paramount while the means by which problems are specifically, and correctly, identified is flexible.

Problem-Oriented Policing and Community Policing

During the late 1980s and throughout the 1990s, problem-oriented policing and community policing were largely considered to be alternatives to the traditionally held professional model (whereby police relied on incident-driven methods and quantitative outcomes). Despite a litany of research works on both approaches, scholars have questioned if they simply mirror one another or if they are distinctly different concepts. Problem-oriented policing has consistently been conceptualized as a process of directing police efforts toward underlying causes of problems related to crime incidents, whereas a focus on strong community and police partnerships for reducing actual and perceived crime is the emphasis community policing.

This is not to assert that overlap does not exist. During the course of their efforts to improve communities, community-oriented police officers use problem solving as a means to reach their desired ends while problem-oriented departments must form partnerships with their communities to learn of the problems they face. As Gary Cordner and Elizabeth Biebel (2005) describe, *problem solving* is often conceptualized as what officers do to respond to recurring problems within their jurisdiction. The key distinction between problem solving and *problem oriented* is that problem-oriented policing is based on its analysis of the problem—whatever that problem may be—and making a determination as to the inherent nature, or root cause, of the problem. Such an approach should provide officers with perspectives to better inform their efforts to remedy problems and remove generalizations often made of crimes as they relate to formal criminal codes. Michael Scott, the Director of the Center for Problem-Oriented Policing, alludes to the notion that Goldstein felt *problem solving* was not an appropriate term for police efforts to address problems in their communities as the majority of problems police face are highly complex and lack an absolute solution.

Evaluation of Problem-Oriented Policing

Goldstein's problem-oriented policing philosophy was first implemented in his backyard of Madison, Wisconsin, in 1981. Through his already established rapport with the Madison Police Department as a result of his collaborative efforts to improve responses to sex offenders and drunk driving, a promising opportunity to test problem-oriented policing presented itself. The Madison experience yielded anecdotal successes in police thought processes regarding the problems they face. These anecdotal findings were later confirmed with rigor and empirical support—a task far outside the capability of research at the time of the Madison experience, as the problem-oriented model was in its infancy. Contemporary findings will be discussed briefly to follow.

Immediately following the Madison experience, in 1982, the problem-oriented philosophy gained traction in the United Kingdom when police organizations in London and Surrey implemented an experiment of their own. In London, it was found that problem-oriented policing reduced robberies and fear of crime on the London underground transportation system. In Surrey, citizen fear of crime was reduced through initiatives to target street behaviors as a result of the problem-oriented approach. In the United States, the new philosophy was also gaining momentum. The Baltimore County (Maryland) Police Department introduced Goldstein's problem-oriented policing model into its Community-Oriented Police Enforcement (COPE) unit in 1983 followed shortly by the Newport News (Virginia) Police Department in 1984. In both domestic instances, problem-oriented policing proved fruitful for improving police effectiveness in responding to community problems. While these experiences noted above provided invaluable insights as to the implementation and process of implementing a problem-oriented approach, evaluations of rigor to assess impacts did not reach the policing literature until the early 1990s.

Academicians have found support for problem-oriented policing to have an effect on a variety of crime and disorder problems such as fear of crime, violent and property crime, alcohol-related violence, firearm-related homicide, store robberies, and prostitution. Lawrence Sherman and colleagues' 1997 review of problem-oriented policing posits the approach is promising. In a more rigorous review, David Weisburd and colleagues' (2010) systematic review of the problem-oriented policing literature suggests the approach deserves a worthwhile commitment on behalf of police administrators, but also suggests police—and researchers—should not necessarily expect large decreases or improvement in crime and disorder control from this approach. A central conclusion of the Weisburd and colleagues' review was that problem-oriented policing as an approach to mitigate crime and disorder problems has significant promise. Their review concluded that the most successful studies of this problem-oriented approach included parolee recidivism, violence in hot spots, and drug markets. The authors caution these findings as modest given the diversity of programs and approaches also simultaneously active during the evaluations. Such overlapping interventions are common across police departments, yet it proves difficult to isolate the impact of any one aspect of the desired approach.

Continued Relevance of Problem-Oriented Policing

The continued relevance of problem-oriented policing demonstrates itself through a litany of current programs, initiatives, and concepts that remain in demand of contemporary law enforcement. While perhaps not specifically titled "problem oriented," the concept and thought processes envisioned by Goldstein remain at the forefront of policing effectiveness. Through the community policing movement and now into newer emphases on homeland security and intelligence-led policing, critical thinking on behalf of police personnel to identify specific problems and develop appropriate responses resonates throughout all levels of contemporary law enforcement. Whether the daily task be related to crime analysis, intelligence analysis, awareness programs, or even town hall meetings with community members, attention to details and holistic thought processes continue to play a vital role of policing.

Implementing change with organizations is never easy, especially when the change challenges preconceived notions of what constitutes "how business is done." At the time he wrote his seminal piece in 1979, Goldstein argued there were a number of societal factors that would sway police administrators to shift their focus from organizational functions to the quality of police outcomes. He noted an increased accountability for financial allocations within departments, emerging research that questioned the value of police operations, a growing awareness among citizens for police to have an impact, and the logic behind why well-managed police departments face the same problems as do less advanced departments. While scholars have found problem-oriented policing to be more rhetoric than practice, and even Goldstein himself acknowledges not every police department will adopt this way of thinking, the societal factors noted by Goldstein over 30 years ago mirror those faced by present law enforcement organizations—arguably more pressing than ever before.

Jeremy G. Carter

See also Broken Windows Theory; Fear of Crime; Homeland Security; Intelligence-Led Policing; Policing, Three Eras of; Problem-Oriented Policing: Elements, Processes, Implications; Problem-Solving Process (SARA)

Further Readings

Cordner, G. W., & Biebel, E. P. (2005). Problem-oriented policing in practice. *Criminology & Public Policy, 4*(2), 155–180. doi: 10.1111/j.1745–9133.2005.00013

Eck, J. E., & Spelman, W. (1987). *Problem solving: Problem-oriented policing in Newport News.* Washington, DC: U.S. Department of Justice, National Institute of Justice, Police Executive Research Forum.

Goldstein, H. (1977). *Policing a free society.* Cambridge, MA: Ballinger.

Goldstein, H. (1979). Improving policing: A problem-oriented approach. *Crime and Delinquency, 25*(2), 236–258. doi: 10.1177/001112877902500207

Goldstein, H. (1987). Toward community-oriented policing: Potential, basic requirements, and threshold questions. *Crime and Delinquency, 33*(1), 6–30. doi: 10.1177/0011128787033001002

Goldstein, H. (1990). *Problem-oriented policing.* New York, NY: McGraw-Hill.

Goldstein, H. (2003). On further developing problem-oriented policing: The most critical need, the major impediments, and a proposal. *Crime Prevention Studies, 15,* 13–47.

Goldstein, H., & Susmilch, C. E. (1981). *The problem-oriented approach to improving police service: A description of the project and an elaboration of the concept.* Madison: University of Wisconsin Law School.

Scott, M. S. (2000). *Problem-oriented policing: Reflections on the first 20 years.* Washington DC: U.S. Department of Justice. Office of Community Oriented Policing Services. Retrieved from http://www.cops.usdoj.gov/Publications/e03011022.txt

Sherman, L. W., Gottfredson, D., MacKenzie, D. Eck, J. E., Reuter, P. & Bushway, S. (1997). *Preventing crime: What works, what doesn't, what's promising: A report to the*

Attorney General of the United States. Washington, DC: U.S. Department of Justice, Office of Justice Programs.

Weisburd, D. L., Telep, C. W., Hinkle, J. C., & Eck, J. E. (2010). Is problem-oriented policing effective in reducing crime and disorder? Findings from a Campbell systematic review. *Criminology & Public Policy, 9*(1), 139–172. doi: 10.1111/j.1745–9133.2010.00617

PROBLEM-SOLVING COURTS

Problem-solving courts are designed to serve individuals who have a particular problem that underlies their criminal behavior (e.g., substance dependence or mental illness), have committed a certain type of offense (such as domestic violence), or have committed an offense that is detrimental to a community's quality of life. Whereas the traditional court process is adversarial—the court serves as a forum where the prosecution and defense spar over the facts of a case—problem-solving courts employ a non-adversarial approach to decision making. In contrast to the emphasis of traditional courts on case processing—speeding cases through the system and efficiently meting out penalties—problem-solving courts focus on outcomes, aiming to ameliorate the problems on which they focus.

Problem-solving courts emphasize addressing the underlying issues that bring individual offenders into contact with the criminal justice system, instead of focusing on an offender's specific offense. To do so, they incorporate judicial oversight of treatment, integration of social services, and extensive interaction between defendants and the judge. Problem-solving courts originated more than two decades ago, and are now widespread: In 2012, there were more than 3,000 nationwide, with drug courts being the original and most prevalent type. This entry begins by discussing the origins and characteristics of problem-solving courts. It then gives a brief overview of some of the main types of problem-solving courts, including drug courts, mental health courts, community courts, and domestic violence courts. This entry concludes with a discussion of some of the issues and challenges that problem-solving courts face.

Origins and Characteristics

Problem-solving courts originated in 1989 with advent of the nation's first drug court in Dade County (Miami), Florida. It was a product of efforts to develop strategies of addressing significant court caseloads and backlogs resulting from the drug epidemic of the 1980s and intensive law enforcement policies and more severe sanctions that emanated from the War on Drugs. In the face of increased numbers of drug cases, traditional courts could merely attempt to expedite case processing, so as to reduce the time from arrest to conviction. By contrast, drug courts' objective is to break the cycle of drug use, dependence, and crime among substance-involved offenders by linking them to judicially monitored treatment. This first drug court was a harbinger of significant change in the nation's courts—a shift from the traditional emphasis on speedy case processing and efficiently meting out penalties to practices designed to reduce recidivism by addressing problems that bring about defendants' criminal behavior.

In the 1990s, the accomplishments of drug courts across the nation led to the development of other types of problem-solving courts. While problem-solving courts vary in terms of their specific missions and procedures, they have a shared purpose of offering innovative responses to criminal acts committed by individuals with problems that underlie their offending behavior. Whereas in the traditional court setting, the task of monitoring defendants is relegated to probation departments or community-based organizations, in the setting of the problem-solving court, judicial personnel, including judges and attorneys, take an active role in monitoring defendants. An overarching characteristic of problem-solving courts is their focus on outcomes—that is, meaningfully addressing the problems that they are designed to take on. These outcomes can include reducing offenders' recidivism (by addressing the issues, such as drug addiction, underlying their criminality), enhancing victims' safety (in the case of domestic violence courts), and improving community conditions (by offering a meaningful judicial response to offenses that harm a community's quality of life).

Other elements of problem-solving courts emanate from this focus. For example, they use improved information to facilitate enhanced decision making. Improved information—in the form of evidence-based needs and risk assessment tools—assists court practitioners in making better-informed decisions about offenders' risk levels and treatment needs, thereby helping to ensure that defendants receive appropriate levels of supervision and types of support. Moreover, problem-solving courts continuously collect and analyze information on operations—such as length of participation and defendants' records of compliance—to provide their personnel with feedback regarding court programming and outcomes.

Problem-solving courts also place an emphasis on holding defendants accountable by implementing systematic rigorous compliance monitoring (e.g., a drug court regularly testing its clients) and meting out sanctions (e.g., a restricted curfew time as the result of a positive drug test) for noncompliance. Despite this emphasis on accountability, research shows that defendants in problem-solving courts have an enhanced perception of procedural fairness—the sense that they have been treated humanely and with respect—relative to defendants in traditional courts. Finally, in lieu of the traditional adversarial court process, problem-solving courts promote collaboration, both among court personnel (such as judges, prosecutors, and defense attorneys) and other criminal justice actors (such as probation officers and police officers), as well as with potential stakeholders outside of the traditional court setting (such as drug counselors, other social service providers, and victims' groups).

Today in the United States, there are more than a dozen different types of problem-solving courts, including reentry, truancy, child support, and homeless courts. The following sections describe four of the most prominent types: drug courts, mental health courts, community courts, and domestic violence courts.

Drug Courts

The goal of drug courts is to address the problems of nonviolent drug-abusing offenders, who would otherwise be at high risk of recidivating, and provide them with treatment services paired with ongoing judicial monitoring and community supervision. Drug courts sentence substance-dependent defendants to long-term, judicially supervised substance abuse treatment in lieu of incarceration. Although criminal courts have long mandated defendants to substance abuse treatment, drug courts are distinguished by their active involvement in participants' cases, including frequent status hearings before a

judge, direct interaction between defendants and judges, graduated rewards and sanctions in response to behavior, and active involvement by case managers. When an offender successfully completes treatment, the courts typically reduce or dismiss the original charges.

Since their advent in 1989, drug courts have proliferated. Today there are more than 2,500 drug courts in the United States, located in every state and the District of Columbia. While the majority of these target adults from the general population, others have specific target populations, including juveniles, Indian tribes, military veterans, and college students. Across jurisdictions, these courts alternatively receive cases preplea (diversionary) or postplea. Also included in this number are more than 150 postplea driving-while-intoxicated (DWI) courts.

Research documents the effectiveness of drug courts. A 2005 report by the U.S. Government Accountability Office summarized findings from almost two dozen program evaluations, confirming that drug courts reduce crime. Although drug courts are more expensive than traditional court or probation services, this report also highlighted their long-term cost-effectiveness upon accounting for savings resulting from decreased criminal activity, including reduced law enforcement efforts, judicial case processing, and victimization.

Mental Health Courts

Just as drug courts address the substance problems that underlie defendants' criminal behavior, the mission of mental health courts is to address the mental illness that contributes to offenders' involvement in the criminal justice system. Mental health courts divert offenders with mental illnesses, who are overrepresented among criminal defendants, to court-supervised treatment instead of incarceration. Linking mentally ill offenders with community-based treatment also has the benefit of reducing the burden on states' departments of corrections that is caused by mentally ill inmates.

Assessment and careful case management play important roles. Defendants who are assessed to be eligible for a mental health court's programming are given the option of choosing it. Those who opt for it are quickly linked to community-based, individualized treatment plans, which are based in part on the relationship between defendants' mental illness and their criminal behavior. They are designed to take into account both their needs and the risks they pose to the community. As much as any type of problem-solving court, mental health courts operate based on the notion of therapeutic jurisprudence—linking defendants with mental illness to judicially supervised, mandatory treatment toward the objective of facilitating positive life changes for them. In mental health courts, the adversarial nature of the traditional court system is supplanted with a less formal team approach, with judicial personnel working with service providers to follow defendants through the program. Today there are more than 200 mental health courts operating in more than 30 states.

Community Courts

Community courts are designed to offer meaningful responses to offenses and offenders that contribute to disorderly conditions, thereby improving the quality of life in the neighborhoods they serve. Community courts represent an extension of the principles of community policing. Many community policing programs employ a collaborative problem-solving approach that consults with neighborhood residents, analyzes community problems, takes steps to address these problems, and then assesses the effects of the measures employed. Community courts are based on the notion that, like community policing initiatives, courts could constructively address disorderly conditions in communities. Behaviors targeted by community courts typically include low-level offenses such as petty theft, prostitution, drug possession, and vandalism.

In 1993, the nation's first community court, New York City's Midtown Community Court, opened. The court is designed to address quality-of-life crimes in Midtown Manhattan, an area that includes the Times Square entertainment district. A primary reason for the creation of community courts is the sense that the traditional centralized court response to low-level crime is neither meaningful nor constructive for the community, victims, or offenders. Standard criminal courts usually focus their resources on more serious crimes at the expense of substantively addressing quality-of-life offenses. Sentences such as time served in jail and bench warrants for nonappearance are common responses to misdemeanors, making the criminal justice system process the punishment. Community courts have several qualities and capacities that standard criminal courts lack. For example, they make heavy use of intermediate sanctions that simultaneously hold defendants accountable for their acts and pay back the community, and they can readily link defendants with underlying problems to meaningful social services. Other distinctive features of community courts include close monitoring of offenders' compliance with sentence conditions and strict sanctions for noncompliance. Evaluations of community courts show that, compared to conventional courts, they have higher rates of case disposition at arraignment, higher rates of compliance with intermediate sanctions, and cases are typically concluded more quickly. Moreover, repeat offenders view community courts as more burdensome, because the intermediate sanctions they receive are more time consuming than traditional courts' punishments of a relatively short time detained in jail, or a fine, or both. Today there are approximately 30 community courts operating in about a dozen different states.

Domestic Violence Courts

Whereas most problem-solving courts are focused on helping offenders, the primary emphasis of domestic violence courts is assisting and protecting the *victims* of domestic violence. Specifically, these courts are designed to deal with problems associated with domestic violence such as withdrawn charges, low victim reporting, threats to the victim, lack of defendant accountability, and high recidivism. While domestic violence courts are like other types of problem-solving courts in that they place an emphasis on using enhanced information to make educated and informed judicial decisions, they are distinct in that they arose from the increased criminal justice system focus on the issue of domestic violence over the last three decades.

In contrast to the handling of domestic violence cases in the traditional courts, where jurisdiction over such cases and the individuals involved in them is unsystematic, domestic violence courts use close judicial oversight of the defendant and careful coordination between the judiciary and social services. A designated judge works with other court actors such as prosecuting and defense attorneys, victim advocates, and representatives of social service agencies to guard against any form of intimidation by the defendant, family, or other associates toward the victim throughout the course of the judicial process. The courts also serve as a resource for victims with needs such as job training and housing. Finally, they monitor defendants for compliance with legally stipulated substance abuse treatment and compliance with protective orders, while defense attorneys work to make sure that defendants' rights and due process safeguards are not violated. Today there are more than 180 domestic violence courts, handling either felony or misdemeanor domestic violence cases, operating in approximately 15 states.

Issues and Challenges

The problem-solving court model has been subject to several criticisms. Some detractors are uneasy about the nonadversarial courtroom dynamic that pervades problem-solving courts. They doubt, for example, whether it is advisable for a judge to be the leader of a problem-solving team rather than a neutral arbiter. Whereas judges in the traditional court setting normally hear only what opposing attorneys choose to present about a case in the courtroom setting, in the problem-solving setting judges regularly consider information about offenders that is perhaps only tangentially related to the law or facts of a case. Related concerns include whether the structure of problem-solving courts provides judges with too much discretion to make decisions based not on the law but on their personal worldviews, and whether judges' impartiality is compromised by becoming intimately involved with and especially knowledgeable about the specialized class of cases on which their court focuses.

Other criticisms pertain to the altered roles of defense and prosecuting attorneys. Some are concerned that defense attorneys' close relationships with prosecutors and treatment professionals can lead to a less ardent defense of their client. In a similar vein, some view problem-solving courts as coercive to defendants, in that there are inadequate procedures in place to ensure that an individual's consent to be a defendant in a problem-solving court is freely and fairly given. On the other hand, some submit that prosecutors who are involved in problem-solving courts may be less inclined to argue for incarceration as a result; this would comprise their role as sentinels for public safety.

Problem-solving courts also face challenges regarding resources. Despite findings from evaluation research on the effectiveness of problem-solving courts, they can be vulnerable to cuts in funding, as they tend to have higher assessment and treatment costs relative to traditional adjudication. Their enhanced services—a key element that sets them apart from traditional courts—typically contribute to lost economies of scale. Yet, this more labor-intensive and expensive case processing potentially can lead to significant savings in prison and jail costs, as well as other justice system expenditures, by facilitating offenders' desistance from criminal behavior. Other potential fiscal benefits of problem-solving courts, such as improved quality of life in neighborhoods, are more difficult to determine.

Robert R. Weidner

See also Community Justice; Decentralizing the Organization/Organizational Change; Problem, Definition of; Problem-Solving Initiatives, Assessment and Evaluation; Problem-Solving Initiatives, Examples of Assessment and Evaluation of; Restorative Justice

Further Readings

American University. (2008). *Challenges and solutions to implementing problem solving courts from the traditional court management perspective.* Washington, DC: U.S. Department of Justice, Bureau of Justice Assistance.

Berman, G., Rempel, M., & Wolf, R. V. (Eds.). (2007). *Documenting results: Research on problem-solving justice.* New York, NY: Center for Court Innovation.

Casey, P. M., & Rottman, D. B. (2005). Problem-solving courts: Models and trends. *The Justice System Journal, 26*(1), 35–56.

Folkemer, N. T. W. (2008, March). *Problem solving courts* (Road Map Series). Chicago, IL: American Bar Association, Coalition for Justice.

Huddleston, C. W., III, Marlowe, D. B., & Casebolt, R. (2008). *Painting the current picture: A national report card on drug courts and other problem-solving court programs in the United States.* Alexandria, VA: National Drug Court Institute.

Labriola, M., Bradley, S., O'Sullivan, C. S., Rempel, M., & Moore, S. (2009). *A national portrait of domestic violence courts.* New York, NY: Center for Court Innovation.

National Association of Drug Court Professionals. (2004). *Defining drug courts: The key components.* NCJ

205621. Washington, DC: U.S. Department of Justice, Bureau of Justice Assistance. Retrieved from https://www.ncjrs.gov/pdffiles1/bja/205621.pdf

Sviridoff, M., Rottman, D., & Weidner, R. (2005). *Dispensing justice locally: The impacts, costs and benefits of the Midtown Community Court.* New York, NY: Center for Court Innovation.

Thompson, M., Osher, F. C., & Tomasini-Joshi, D. (2008). *Improving responses to people with mental illness: The essential elements of a mental health treatment court.* New York, NY: Council of State Governments Justice Center.

Wolf, R. V. (2007). *Principles of problem-solving justice.* New York, NY: Center for Court Innovation. Retrieved from http://www.courtinnovation.org/sites/default/files/Principles.pdf

PROBLEM-SOLVING INITIATIVES, ASSESSMENT AND EVALUATION

During the past several decades, the United States' criminal justice system has invested billions of dollars in policies and initiatives that were found not to have accomplished their goals. In times of fiscal crisis, such as the global recession of 2008 to 2012, there is a greater need for accountability and evidence-based initiatives that will succeed and be cost-effective.

To determine whether one approach is better than another, different approaches must be subjected to careful and skeptical scrutiny. It is important to know if a particular practice in criminal justice is worth the investment, is effective in terms of accomplishing its intended purpose, and is the better of competing options (or better than not having the practice at all). Furthermore, policymakers and politicians may require that the implementation and continuation of a community-oriented policing and problem-solving (COPPS) initiative involve an impact evaluation. This is necessary for comparing *actual* outcomes to *desired* outcomes (objectives). Indeed, the U.S. Congress mandates evaluations of state and local crime prevention programs that are funded by the U.S. Department of Justice.

This entry discusses the rationale behind and the challenges associated with performing assessment and evaluation of community policing and problem solving.

Rationale

Despite the widespread use and popularity of the community policing and problem-solving strategy, little empirical research exists concerning whether or not those initiatives are cost-efficient and reduce the public fear and incidence of crime and disorder. A long-standing criticism of such initiatives has concerned this lack of rigorous examination and evaluation. As a 1994 federal report, *Understanding Community Policing: A Framework for Action,* observed, ongoing input, evaluation, and feedback from both inside and outside the police organization are essential to making community policing work.

A strength of the SARA problem-solving model (scanning, analysis, response, assessment) is that it demands that police perform an assessment of their problem-solving initiatives, such as tabulating the number of calls for service, arrests made, noise complaints addressed, shots fired reported, and so forth. However, an assessment does not provide a complete measure of whether or not a particular problem-oriented policing initiative made a difference. For that to be determined, an impact evaluation of the initiative is required. There are several challenges to performing an evaluation, including the requisite specialized knowledge, skills, and abilities as well as the time necessary to perform sophisticated statistical analyses. The federal Center for Problem-Oriented Policing has collected more than 240 scientifically designed studies that evaluated interventions to reduce or prevent specific crime problems. The problems evaluated include violence, burglary, vehicle-related crime, alcohol and drug violations, disorder, robbery, and fraud.

Evaluating What Works

In policing, the need to know what works exists both for strategies dealing with existing crime and neighborhood disorder as well as strategies for crime prevention. At its root, addressing a research question such as "What works?" involves the use of proper means of obtaining data and then examining that data. Research questions involving policing strategies number in the thousands, but following are a few examples—all of which have been subjected to rigorous empirical analysis and have in some way changed the way police conduct business:

- Does the arrest of the primary aggressor at scenes of domestic violence significantly reduce or prevent such violence in the future?
- Do gun buy-back programs reduce street crimes committed with weapons?
- Are programs like Scared Straight, D.A.R.E., Neighborhood Watch, and jail or prison boot camps successful in reducing crime?
- Do after-school recreation programs reduce vandalism in public housing?
- Will strategies such as increasing the numbers of officers in a jurisdiction, the use of two-person patrol cars, or random patrolling reduce crime?
- Are therapeutic programs for drug-using offenders in prisons effective in reducing drug offenses?

In the early 21st century, technologies and other management tools provide real-time and trend data access for reported crime, arrests, repeat calls for service, and other information. However, many researchers are concerned that more attention is given to evaluating the planning and implementation of a strategy than what effects the program actually has on crime. While process evaluations can produce much valuable data on the implementation of programs and the logic of their strategies, they cannot offer evidence as to whether the programs work to prevent or reduce crime.

Critical Questions

To better understand the complementary but different nature of both assessment and impact evaluation, the following is a comparison of the critical questions to be asked for both; questions for the SARA problem-solving stages are on the left, and questions to address for impact evaluations are on the right.

It should also be noted that problem-solving responses and their assessment or impact evaluation should not be viewed as one-shot, short-term activities. In a year following a police department's concentrated responses, conditions in the area can begin to worsen considerably; drug and gang problems tend to resurface. Without ongoing maintenance in troubled neighborhoods, conditions can quickly deteriorate, requiring a new round of responses and assessment or impact evaluation for them, and doing so should be part of the agency's strategic plan.

Challenges

One explanation for the relatively small number of evaluations of problem-oriented policing is that ineffective research designs have been used. For example, it is difficult to identify comparison groups for problem-oriented policing programs because problems by their nature are often different and unique. Accordingly, many problem-oriented policing programs are evaluated using before-and-after research designs. The absence of a control group makes it difficult to differentiate between general trends in crime and trends produced by the intervention.

Another major challenge is that few sworn agents or officers in federal, state, or local law enforcement agencies possess the kinds of knowledge, skills, and abilities that are required to perform sophisticated impact evaluations of their efforts. In the social sciences, quantitative research typically involves the use of empirical investigations, concepts, and variables to test hypotheses in the search for relationships. More specifically, the researcher must typically obtain a dataset for a designated time frame as well as employ independent and dependent variables, while using the appropriate statistical techniques to test the data. Then, interpretation of the findings is required—which is when hypotheses are accepted or rejected. This is a broad and sophisticated undertaking that requires in-depth study of research methodology and statistics. To perform empirical studies of community policing and problem solving, police agencies often hire or obtain pro bono the assistance of a trained social scientist in a

Assessment (Under SARA)	Impact Evaluation
Did the response occur as planned?	Did the response occur as planned? (This involves what is known as a process evaluation—a thorough look at how the response was planned, staffed, implemented, and monitored.)
Did the problem decline?	Did the problem decline?
What should be done next?	If the problem declined, should alternative explanations be ruled out?

nearby college or university to set up and perform an impact evaluation.

Another legitimate consideration concerns time: even if police personnel were to be well steeped in empirical research, efforts such as these are labor intensive. It is doubtful that sworn personnel would be able to forego their other duties in favor of engaging in such analyses.

For the above reasons, the evaluation of initiatives is an area where police agencies may wish to take advantage of the "town-gown" relationship, calling on university and college academics to assist in their evaluation and assessment efforts, to bridge the gap between theory and practice. Typically, a person cannot be awarded a graduate degree in social sciences without first demonstrating (in the form of a written master's thesis or doctoral dissertation) the requisite skills in both research methodology and statistics. Colleges and universities are therefore prime resources for locating individuals who have the ability to assist police agencies in accomplishing evaluations.

Assessment vis-à-vis Impact Evaluation

Assessments and evaluations are different from but complementary to one another. *Assessments*—which can also be termed *outcome evaluations*—occur at the final stage of SARA. Assessments ask the following kinds of descriptive questions: Did the response occur as planned? Did all the response components work? Did the response result in fewer calls for service to the area? More arrests? Fewer reported gang activities?

An example is as follows: After performing a careful analysis, problem-solving officers determine that in order to curb a street prostitution problem, they will heighten patrols in the area, change several streets to one-way thus creating several dead-end streets to thwart cruising "johns," and work with courts and social services so that convicted prostitutes receive probation and assistance to gain the necessary skills for legitimate employment. An assessment under SARA determines whether the crackdown occurred, and if so, how many arrests police made, whether the street patterns were altered as planned, and how many prostitutes received job skills assistance.

Note, however, that an assessment does *not* answer the question, "What happened to the problem?" Assessments do not determine if the COPPS

initiative actually *caused* the outcome. That is where impact evaluations come into play.

Impact evaluations thus go a step farther by establishing not only whether a COPPS initiative is associated with the outcomes but also whether the initiative actually produced or caused them. Impact evaluation is an empirical process for determining whether a problem declined and whether the implemented initiative caused the decline. Evaluation begins at the moment the SARA problem-solving process begins and continues through the completion of the effort. To determine what did in fact happen to the problem, an impact evaluation is needed. An impact evaluation asks such questions as: Did the problem decline? If so, did the *response* cause the decline?

Consider the prostitution example above. During the analysis stage, vice detectives conducted a census of prostitutes operating in the target area. They also asked the traffic engineering department to install traffic counters on the major thoroughfare and critical side streets to measure traffic flow and to determine how customers move through the area. The vice squad made covert video recordings of the target area to document how prostitutes interact with potential customers. Then, after the response was implemented, the team repeated these measures to see if the problem declined. As a result of these measures, they discover that instead of the 23 prostitutes counted in the first census, only eight can be found. They also find that there has been a slight decline in traffic on the major thoroughfare on the weekends, but not at other times; however, there has been a substantial decline in side street traffic on Saturday nights. New covert video recordings show that prostitutes in the area have changed how they approach vehicles. In short, the team has evidence that the problem has declined after response implementation. As this example shows, an impact evaluation has two parts: measuring the problem and systematically comparing changes in measures by using an evaluation design to determine whether or not the response was the primary cause of the change in the measure.

Two other important aspects of performing an impact evaluation are

- Objectives must be clearly defined and measurable (e.g., in the prostitution example above, objectives for addressing the problem included installing traffic counters to measure traffic flow and making covert video recordings of the target area)

- Confounding factors must be identified (e.g., did a rash of violent crimes against prostitutes during the time the problem-solving initiatives were put into place contribute heavily to their leaving the streets?)

Kenneth J. Peak

See also Citizen Surveys; Community Policing: Resources, Time, and Finances in Support of; Crime Analysis; Problem-Solving Process (SARA)

Further Readings

Bureau of Justice Assistance. (1994, August). *Understanding community policing: A framework for action.* NCJ 148457. Washington, DC: U.S. Department of Justice.

Center for Problem-Oriented Policing. (n.d.). *Situational crime prevention evaluation database.* Retrieved from http://www.popcenter.org/library/scp

Connell, N. M., Miggans, K., & McGloin, J. M. (2008). Can a community policing initiative reduce serious crime? A local evaluation. *Police Quarterly, 11*(2), 127–150. doi: 10.1177/1098611107306276

Eck, J. E. (2002). *Assessing responses to problems: An introductory guide for police problem-solvers.* Washington, DC: U.S. Department of Justice, Office of Community Oriented Policing Services.

Mears, D. P. (2010). *American criminal justice policy: An approach to increasing accountability and effectiveness.* New York, NY: Cambridge University Press.

Quire, D. S. (1993). *Models for community policing evaluation: The St. Petersburg experience.* Tallahassee: Florida Criminal Justice Executive Institute. Retrieved from http://www.fdle.state.fl.us/Content/getdoc/3b38f54e-8fc3–467e-b90c-25264321d5db/Quire-Donald-abstract-Models-for-Community-Policin.aspx

Worrall, J. L., & Kovandzic, T. V. (2007). COPS grants and crime revisited. *Criminology, 45*(1), 159–190. doi: 10.1111/j.1745–9125.2007.00076

PROBLEM-SOLVING INITIATIVES, EXAMPLES OF ASSESSMENT AND EVALUATION OF

The September 11, 2001, terrorist attacks in the United States led to the emergence of homeland security policing. Some suggest this paradigm shift has altered police operations and philosophy. Although there has been little research so far on the shift of policing strategies after 9/11, it has been suggested that most components of community-oriented policing and problem solving remains a central strategy that has not only been retained but has increased.

The centrality and persistence of problem solving in the current era of policing suggests that the police continue to perceive the utility of the approach. Problem-oriented policing was a precursor to community-oriented policing. In community policing, the identification of the problem emanates from the public, and the problem-solving strategy is arrived at through collaborative efforts of the police and the public. In a problem-oriented model, the public may not necessarily have any input in the process. Hence, police agencies with a homeland security emphasis could use both internal and external sources for identification of and solutions to problems, particularly on homeland security and prevention and preemption of terrorist attacks.

Community policing involves three key components: organizational transformation, community partnerships, and problem solving. Furthermore, community policing involves collaboration between the police and the community that identifies and solves community problems. In addition, the police are no longer the sole guardians of law and order; all members of the community become active allies in the effort to enhance the safety and quality of neighborhoods. Given the centrality of problem solving in contemporary policing, it is important to understand how this process could be evaluated and its impact assessed. Examples of the range of problem solving initiatives and the assessments of the strategy are presented in this entry.

Problem-Solving Initiatives

Problem-oriented policing was first introduced by Herman Goldstein (1979) as an operational strategy to address the root causes of crime. Later, the fundamental problem-solving strategy called SARA (scanning, analysis, response, assessment) was developed by John Eck and William Spelman (1987). Eventually, other scholars and practitioners advanced the notion that problem solving is a component of or absorbed in the overall community-oriented policing philosophy.

Examples of Proactive Problem-Solving Initiatives

Problem-solving policing is a proactive initiative, where the police department relies heavily on its traditional police response operations such as stings, interdictions, undercover work, and hot spot policing. Citizens' inputs are rarely solicited and, if proposed, are rarely utilized in these forms of initiatives. In these police-initiated problem-solving initiatives, the departments are found to be mostly involved in creating special units.

For example, the Neighborhood Enforcement Services Team (NEST) of South Bend, Indiana, identifies law-and-order problem issues that that may need attention. Based solely on the unit's information gathering and analysis, the NEST employs different interventions involving mostly saturation drives, curfew enforcements, stings, and the like. In some instances, the police might seek assistance from academic experts to devise solutions to problems. However, the process remains internal to the department. For example, in experiments on deterrence, Lawrence Sherman (1984) used the police to develop responses to problems involving domestic violence and desistance of serious repeat offenders. In his experiments, Sherman showed how repeat incidences of domestic violence could be avoided through the use of arrests. In Washington, D.C., Sherman (1997) found that hot spot policing had an immediate effect on repeat occurrences of drugs and other serious crimes. The published results of these experiments have inspired other departments to proactively adopt these police operational responses.

At a higher level, law enforcement–initiated problem-solving initiatives could happen through the cooperative endeavors of different law enforcement organizations at the local, county, and federal levels. Several of these collaborative problem-solving initiatives involve the reduction of street violence, as with Project Safe Neighborhood. In this project, different law enforcement agencies at various levels collaborate to eliminate the proliferation of unauthorized firearms in the streets. Several cities in the United States have employed such intervention programs. Recently, with the intensified efforts to prevent terrorist attacks, fusion centers and intelligence centers were established. These centers have been instituted to analyze events and incidents and unravel their connections to potential terrorist threats or attacks. Thus, fusion centers and intelligence centers were problem-solving initiatives to address terrorism threats.

Examples of Problem-Solving Initiatives

Problem solving as a central strategy for community policing involves more intricate, collaborative efforts between law enforcement agencies and communities in which police listen to community concerns and solicit solutions or participation from community members. Notable initiatives established along these lines include the popular weed and seed programs, in which enforcement is used first to "weed" out crime, violence, and gangs and then stabilize the conditions in high-crime communities. Resources are identified and mobilized to "seed" the revitalization of the communities. The long-term goal is for the communities to become resistant to any future problems that could result in a return to high crime rates. Other initiatives have been based on James Q. Wilson and George Kelling's (1982) broken windows theory and Ronald Clarke and Marcus Felson's (1993) routine activities theory.

In response to these theories, several programs were instituted such as graffiti-paint over, foot patrol, night watches, citizen academies, and other neighborhood improvement programs. Likewise, crime prevention through environmental design (CPTED) also was adopted by most departments. CPTED programs may include such initiatives as giving away locks to homes or redesigning bus shelters in order to prevent loitering and pandering.

Evaluations of Problem-Solving Initiatives

Police scholars have long suggested that evaluations of problem solving should involve both process and outcomes. This means that in problem-solving evaluations, not only are results important but also whether or not problem solving is an institutionalized departmental operation. Additionally, other scholars argue that any evaluation should also differentiate outcomes from outputs. Outcomes are the ultimate results desired and outputs are the tangible immediate results of the process. Thus, reduction of fear of crime is the outcome but fewer complaints or calls for service is the output. In this regard, problem-solving initiatives should be evaluated on the attainment of these aspects.

The problem-solving approach aims to effect changes in the environment as well as changes in the operational protocols of the police organization. Some scholars suggest that community policing and problem solving and its components should be evaluated in terms of its effects in promoting positive views among officers about their jobs and the organization. Cynical perceptions and attitudes about policing and their superiors are some of the most frequent findings about police officers. Indeed, several studies have found that street-level officers have a more cynical perception of their jobs because of internal policies and organizational stressors. Problem solving could also potentially influence these perceptions. However, it has been hypothesized that since police innovations and problem solving emanate from the street-level officers, police cynicism will be lessened. Community policing may eliminate some stressors that emanate from the organization.

Process Evaluations

Process evaluations are conducted on three levels, namely, (1) individual level, (2) organizational level, and (3) social level. At the individual level, process evaluation looks at what each individual officer does in terms of problem solving. At the organizational level, process evaluation examines what processes and approaches the organization has instituted for solving problems. Finally, process evaluation at the social levels examines what the community does in solving problems.

Individual Level

A process evaluation at the individual level is mostly evaluated on the manner by which police officers spend their time during their shifts. This type of evaluation was done in Cincinnati, Ohio; Indianapolis, Indiana; and St. Petersburg, Florida. Scholars who conducted these evaluations participated in ride-alongs with police officers and recorded the officers' activities and interactions with the public. In addition, the researchers in these studies documented the problem-solving methods that officers employed during their shifts. One of the shortcomings of these studies is that most departments do not allow their officers to do problem solving (i.e., community policing) during their regular shifts.

Another means of evaluating problem solving is through individual interviews or focus groups with police officers or supervisors and asking them about the amount of time that officers are engaged in problem solving. In some studies, the researcher taps into these individual problem-solving efforts by asking officers how much they have collaborated with the community members of their beats. Familiarity with community members, civic leaders, and business were also used to examine the extent of problem solving engaged in by individual officers.

Organizational Level

At the organizational level, problem solving is assessed through the establishment of problem-solving processes. In this regard, departments are evaluated on their achievements of two benchmarks—SARA and CompStat.

SARA. John Eck and William Spelman introduced a model for police problem solving now commonly known as SARA (scanning, analysis, response, assessment). The Center for Problem-Oriented Policing (2012) outlines the important elements of the SARA model as

Scanning

- Identifying recurring problems of concern to the public and the police.
- Identifying the consequences of the problem for the community and the police.
- Prioritizing those problems.
- Developing broad goals.
- Confirming that the problems exist.
- Determining how frequently the problem occurs and how long it has been taking place.
- Selecting problems for closer examination.

Analysis

- Identifying and understanding the events and conditions that precede and accompany the problem.
- Identifying relevant data to be collected.
- Researching what is known about the problem type.
- Taking inventory of how the problem is currently addressed and the strengths and limitations of the current response.

- Narrowing the scope of the problem as specifically as possible.
- Identifying a variety of resources that may be of assistance in developing a deeper understanding of the problem.
- Developing a working hypothesis about why the problem is occurring.

Response

- Brainstorming for new interventions.
- Searching for what other communities with similar problems have done.
- Choosing among the alternative interventions.
- Outlining a response plan and identifying responsible parties.
- Stating the specific objectives for the response plan.
- Carrying out the planned activities.

Assessment

- Determining whether the plan was implemented (a process evaluation).
- Collecting pre- and post-response qualitative and quantitative data.
- Determining whether broad goals and specific objectives were attained.
- Identifying any new strategies needed to augment the original plan.
- Conducting ongoing assessment to ensure continued effectiveness.

SARA has become a dominant model for problem solving. The periodic surveys of the Bureau of Justice Statistics Law Enforcement Management and Administrative Statistics (LEMAS) now have a specific question addressing whether or not the police department employs SARA.

CompStat. A comprehensive model of problem solving has emerged from the New York Transit Police called the CompStat (Computer Statistics) model. The innovation in this model is not the use of computers, as police departments have begun to use computers to analyze crime patterns and aid them in their crime prevention programs (e.g., geographic information systems, crime analysis, intelligence centers, and crime prevention through environmental design or CPTED). Rather, the CompStat process involves information gathering and problem solving from the ground up. In this process, police precincts are required to solicit information from their beats. The beat officers discuss problems and solutions with community members. Beat commanders bring up this information to the central office for discussions with different stakeholders such as government officials, business leaders, and community leaders. Analyses are then conducted through the use of computers. From these, responses are instituted and their effectiveness is evaluated. This process has become a benchmark strategy for metropolitan police departments in places as New York City; Nashville, Tennessee; and Houston, Texas, among others. Coupled with SARA, CompStat became another benchmark for evaluating the problem-solving efforts of police departments.

Social Level

Process evaluation at the social level takes the form of community policing councils or the conduct of formal meetings that involve the community and the public. Most of the evaluations at this level have involved the level of community participation in meetings. For example, Wesley Skogan's long-term evaluations of the Chicago Alternative Policing System (CAPS) involved the examination of participation of community members with community policing initiatives. Sustained levels of community participation were used as the indicator for the success of the program. In some evaluations, creation or initiation of police-community relations programs either by the police or the members of the community were used as evaluation criteria. Evaluations in Cincinnati, Ohio; Indianapolis, Indiana; South Bend, Indiana; and St. Petersburg, Florida, were jurisdictions whose process evaluation includes the establishment of these community partnership initiatives.

Impact Assessments

Different benchmarks have been used to assess or evaluate the impact of community policing. The utility of problem solving initiatives could be based on (a) the impact of problem solving at the individual level, (b) the impact of problem solving at the organizational level, and (c) the impact of problem solving at the social level. This approach provides a holistic approach in evaluating program interventions.

Individual Level

Police officers have been documented to develop cynicism with their job and the public. Subsequently, police officers develop an "us versus them" mentality. These psychological states have been touted as having affected the morale of officers. Since problem solving is a collaborative effort between the police and the public, it was expected that, as a result of participating in problem-solving initiatives, police officers would develop a more positive attitude toward the public. Thus, most evaluations of community policing involve a measure of police officers' perceptions about their job and the public they serve. Specifically, the impact of problem solving was assessed based on how police officers have reduced their own cynicism about their job. Some impact assessments involve the change in attitude among police officers about the neighborhood that they serve.

Problem solving encourages communication and provides officers with an understanding of the working environment of other officers and their contributions to solving problems. The development of mutual respect, thus, becomes one of the key indicators for impact assessment.

Organizational Level

At the organizational level, assessment of problem solving efforts includes three indicators: (1) improved public relations, (2) number of complaints against the police, and (3) reduction in calls for service. These indicators assess how much police departments benefit from the use of problem solving. As Goldstein and other scholars have suggested, large volumes of calls for service, especially relating to the same incidents, suggest that police are not addressing the root causes of problems. Consequently, the police may be inundated with complaints against certain police officers, which can ultimately result in strained police-community relations. Problem solving is intended to reduce a police-community schism and therefore become the cornerstone for impact evaluation and benefits of problem solving.

Social Level

Several benchmarks have been established to evaluate the impact of problem solving in the community. These include crime prevention and reduction, fear of crime, quality of life, and citizen satisfaction with the police.

The premise behind problem solving is to address the root causes of crime and go beyond responding to incidents. Hence, the reduction of incidents becomes an indicator of an effective problem-solving initiative. Several studies have examined this effect of problem solving with crime or incident recurrences.

Some scholars believe that police have little impact on crime. One of the major outcome measures for police effectiveness in community policing is the fear of crime. Thus, fear of crime has been used as a benchmark for measuring the success of a problem-solving initiative. Fear of crime is normally evaluated through a survey of community members on how fearful they are about such activities as walking alone at night or with regard to living or being victimized in a particular neighborhood.

Quality of life involves the assessment of how the neighborhood has improved. As an alternative measure, this is assessed in terms of social capital invested by community members as well as a prospective view of the community members' expectations about their neighborhood in the future. These evaluation approaches were used in Cincinnati, Ohio; South Bend, Indiana; Chicago, Illinois; St. Petersburg, Florida; and Indianapolis, Indiana, to name a few. These quality-of-life measures are normally assessed through the use of a survey, but focus groups of community leaders have also been used as a means of assessing this impact.

Surveys can measure quality of life by asking respondents how familiar they are with their police and the length of time that they have lived in their neighborhood as well as their future plans of moving to another community. Other prospective questions such as the conditions of the neighborhood in the next five years are used to measure quality of life.

Citizen satisfaction with the police is normally assessed through community surveys and focus group discussions involving key stakeholders or leaders in the community. Assessment of this factor normally involves global questions as, "How satisfied are you with the police?" as well as specific questions such as, "How satisfied are you with the police in your neighborhood?" or "How satisfied are you with the police officer who responded to your request for service?"

In some assessments, the degree and level of collaboration for problem solving are benchmarks for evaluation. Thus, the establishment of regular community meetings, the number and expanse of participation in COP meetings, and the establishments of programs like night watch, citizen police academies, and even social events are considered collaborative efforts that are necessary for problem solving.

Melchor C. de Guzman

See also Broken Windows Theory; Citizen Surveys; Community Policing Consortium; Community Policing Self-Assessment Tool (CP-SAT); CompStat; Hot Spots; Problem-Solving Initiatives, Assessment and Evaluation; Problem-Solving Process (SARA)

Further Readings

Clarke, R. V., & Felson, M. (1993). *Routine activity and rational choice*. Advances in Theoretical Criminology (Vol. 5). Piscataway, NJ: Transaction.

Eck, J. E., & Spelman, W. (1993). Who ya gonna call? The police as problem-busters. *Crime and Delinquency, 33*(1), 31–52.

Goldstein, H. (1990). *Problem-oriented policing*. New York, NY: McGraw-Hill.

Peak, K. J., & Glensor, R. W. (2004). *Community policing and problem solving: Strategies and practices* (4th ed.). Upper Saddle River, NJ: Prentice Hall.

Sherman, L. W., & Berk, R. A. (1984). The specific deterrent effects of arrest for domestic assault. *American Sociological Review, 49*(2), 261–272.

Sherman, L. W., Gottfredson, D. C., MacKenzie, D. L., Eck, J. E., Reuter, P., & Bushway, S. D. (1997). *Preventing crime: What works, what doesn't, what's promising: A report to the Attorney General of the United States*. Washington, DC: U.S. Department of Justice, Office of Justice Programs.

Skogan, W. G., Hartnett, S. M., Dubois, J., Comey, J. T., Kaiser, M., & Lovig, J. H. (1999). *On the beat: Community and problem solving*. Boulder, CO: Westview.

Skolnick, J. H., & Bayley, D. H. (1986). *The new blue line: Police innovation in six American cities*. New York, NY: Free Press.

Wilson, J. Q., & Kelling, G. L. (1982, March). Broken windows: The police and neighborhood safety. *Atlantic Monthly, 249*(3), 29–38.

Problem-Solving Process (SARA)

The problem-solving process, often referred to as the SARA (scanning, analysis, response, assessment) model, is a systematic policing approach used to reduce recurring problems that cause harm in neighborhoods and communities. Problem solving is the defining characteristic of any problem-oriented policing project. This entry describes the origins of the problem-solving process, the development of the SARA model, the types of activities associated with each of the four SARA model steps (scanning, analysis, response, assessment), and the benefits and challenges of adopting a problem-solving approach within a police organization.

Origins

The problem-solving process is a method of addressing problems commonly faced by police. The process allows police to reduce or eliminate conditions that facilitate crime. Opportunities for specific types of crime incidents are identified, examined, and blocked in a systematic manner. This process was first proposed as part of a policing approach introduced in 1979: problem-oriented policing.

Herman Goldstein developed the concept of problem-oriented policing. Goldstein noted that police were overly concerned with the "means" of conducting police work and should instead focus on achieving the "ends," or desired outcomes. In other words, he suggested that police place too much emphasis on finding and chasing criminals, rather than finding ways to prevent crime from occurring in the first place.

Common police strategies prior to the advent of problem-oriented policing included random preventive patrol, rapid response to calls for police service, and follow-up criminal investigations. Yet, research consistently demonstrates that these strategies are largely ineffective. Preventive patrol does not prevent crime since police are unlikely to stumble across a crime in progress. Rapid response to calls for service rarely results in an arrest since many crimes are discovered long after they are committed.

Goldstein suggested that police could deal more effectively with crime and other problems that they were called upon to handle if they improved their operations. Specifically, Goldstein suggested that police adopt a "problem-solving" approach to police business. To do this, police must clearly define problems that generate repeat calls for service, study these problems in detail, search for solutions, and focus on outcomes. This problem-solving process requires police to shift from reactive incident-driven tactics to proactive crime prevention strategies. Problem-oriented policing necessitates that police direct more resources toward structured and systematic activities that address the root causes of crime problems and reduce emphasis and reliance on traditional enforcement tactics.

SARA is the most commonly used problem-solving framework. Although SARA was the first model developed, a number of countries have developed either a stand-alone variant of SARA or a complementary approach to guide police problem-solving activities. Most models like SARA suggest that the process should be carried out in a series of sequenced stages and are often presented in the form of acronyms. Examples of such associated models, or variations on SARA, include the following:

- ID PARTNERS: developed and used in England; it stands for identify, drivers of behavior, problem definition, aim, research and analysis, think creatively, negotiate/initiate responses, evaluate, review, celebrate success
- 9 Stage Model: a precursor to ID PARTNERS; it included the following phases: demand, problem, aim, research, analysis, options, response, evaluate, and review
- EPIC: used sporadically in the United Kingdom; it stands for enforcement, prevention, intelligence, and communication and is designed to encourage police to think about organizations and individuals that could help to foster crime prevention
- CAPRA: developed by the Royal Canadian Mounted Police to serve as their community policing problem-solving model; it stands for clients, acquire/analyze information, partnerships, response, assessment of action
- The 5Is: used in a number of European countries as well as Australia; it stands for intelligence, intervention, implementation, involvement, and impact
- PRIME: standing for problem resolution in multiagency environments; this model was created by the Hampshire Constabulary in England as a substitute term for problem-oriented policing; however, it is suggested that SARA be used in conjunction with its principles

Many of these models were developed to address perceived limitations of the SARA model. However, SARA continues to be the most widely used police problem-solving framework in the world.

Development

John Eck and William Spelman proposed the SARA model in 1987 as a framework for the problem-solving process. The inspiration for the model's development came from a joint collaboration between Eck and Spelman, who worked at the Police Executive Research Forum, and the Newport News Police Department (NNPD) in Virginia. The researchers were part of a committee that worked to introduce problem-oriented policing principles into the police department's organizational structure and everyday activities. The NNPD used the problem-solving approach advocated by Goldstein to tackle a wide variety of problems, including theft from vehicles in parking lots, burglaries in apartment complexes, robberies stemming from prostitution transactions, and homicides resulting from domestic violence incidents. The purpose of this National Institute of Justice–funded initiative was to determine whether problem-oriented policing could be adopted as a departmentwide approach to reducing crime.

Eck and Spelman combined insights gathered through regular NNPD committee meetings with basic management and strategic planning principles to develop a general problem-solving framework. Their goal was to create a problem-solving process that others could follow. To this end, they summarized and categorized the complex sequence of police activities observed throughout the initiative into the four-stage problem-solving process now known as the SARA model.

As noted above, SARA is the acronym used to denote the four steps that define the problem-solving process: (1) *scanning*—problems contributing to crime and disorder are identified and prioritized; (2) *analysis*—the underlying conditions, scope, and nature of a selected problem are investigated; (3) *response*—interventions that modify or eliminate facilitating conditions are developed and implemented; and (4) *assessment*—the implementation of the strategy and the interventions' impact on the problem are evaluated and the responses are modified, if necessary. Each of these steps is discussed more fully in the next section.

These four problem-solving stages and associated activities are presented in a sequential and linear fashion, but application of the SARA model typically requires a nonlinear approach. This is especially true when dealing with highly complex problems. As additional information about a particular problem is discovered during later stages of the problem-solving process, prior stages may be revisited to help redirect or refocus the project. As such, the problem-solving process is best conceptualized as a reiterative and dynamic process. Nevertheless, all four stages must be completed at least once during the problem-solving process.

While the purpose of each stage has been clearly defined by the model, the types of activities carried out at each stage tend to differ across problem-oriented policing projects. As mentioned previously, more complex problems may require additional steps or greater in-depth analysis. Recommended activities at each stage may also change as technological and theoretical advancements offer new insights into common problems. The following section provides detailed descriptions of the four SARA model stages and outlines some of the activities and theoretical frameworks that current research and practice suggest are useful at each stage.

Four Stages

Scanning

The first stage of the SARA model of problem solving is the scanning stage. The primary purpose of the scanning stage is to identify and prioritize problems. The overarching goal of the scanning stage is to find problems that are causing the most harm or are consuming the most police resources. Police can then focus their efforts and resources on eliminating these problems. To identify such problems, the CHEERS (community, harm, expectation, events, recurring, similarity) test and the 80–20 rule are often used in the scanning stage.

The CHEERS test requires a problem to meet specific criteria before it can be addressed through a problem-oriented policing project. First, the problem must negatively affect people, businesses, government agencies, or other societal institutions within a *community*. Second, the problem must cause *harm*. Problems are not simply equated with illegal activities; specific and measureable harm must result from these activities. Third, the public must *expect* the police to handle the problem and associated harms. Finally, the problem must consist of discrete *events* that are both *recurring* and *similar*. The recurring nature of the events suggests that efforts to address the problem will help to reduce harm in the future. To attempt prevention of events that are not expected to recur would be a futile exercise and waste of resources. Similarity among the events is also necessary to develop focused and effective solutions. The problem-solving process is only effective if applied to highly specific harms. This is because

different types of events will likely require different responses. For example, assaults resulting from domestic disputes and assaults that occur at soccer matches likely have different causes and facilitating conditions that will require a different set of interventions. An issue must meet all of the criteria of the CHEERS test to be classified as a police problem.

The 80–20 rule suggests that 20% of some things are responsible for 80% of observed outcomes. This rule highlights the fact that crime is highly concentrated. Research shows, for example, that the majority of all crimes are committed by a small percentage of all offenders (repeat offenders), are perpetrated against a small percentage of all victims (repeat victims), or are focused on only a small proportion of all available targets (i.e., highly attractive targets); furthermore, such crimes tend to occur in a small proportion of all possible places (hot spots and risky facilities). The 80–20 rule suggests that police should look at how crime is concentrated and distributed across offenders, victims or targets, and places in order to identify and define potential harms that require problem solving.

Analysis

The second stage of the SARA model of problem solving is the analysis stage. Once a specific problem has been identified in the scanning stage, police must determine the root causes or conditions that facilitate the problem. Data are collected to learn as much as possible about the problem and the facilitating conditions. The data are then analyzed to test competing hypotheses. A wide variety of analytical techniques can be used to examine the spatial and temporal distributions of the data. These techniques allow police to determine the extent of hot spot boundaries and identify the characteristics of the people and places that are generating crime. Two tools that are often used to guide analyses during this stage are the problem analysis triangle and crime scripts.

The problem analysis triangle stems from routine activity theory. Marcus Felson and Lawrence Cohen first proposed this theory in 1979. Additions to the theory were made in the 1980s and 1990s, and the most recent version is depicted in the form of a dual-layered problem analysis triangle. The "inner" layer of the triangle contains the three elements necessary for a crime to occur: an offender, a victim or target, and a place—which may take the form of either a physical or virtual setting—in which the offender and victim come together. The "outer" layer consists of three controllers, one for each of the necessary elements: a handler for the offender, a guardian for the victim, and a manager for the place. The presence of only one effective controller is sufficient to prevent a crime from occurring, even if all three inner elements are present. In the analysis stage, police use the triangle to guide their investigations. It is used to focus attention on the need to learn more about the elements involved in the problem, as well as the characteristics of controllers that are absent or ineffective.

Crime scripts are used to uncover the sequence of steps that are involved in the commission of a particular crime. For example, if a person decides to steal a car to sell to a chop shop, he must obtain tools to break into the vehicle, travel to a place where cars are available, find a suitable car to steal without being noticed, break into the car and start it, drive away from the area, and then find a shop that will buy the vehicle for an acceptable price. Each of the steps described in this scenario represents a "scene." Each scene represents a potential point of intervention. Police can block opportunities for the crime at any or all of these stages. Police may place restrictions on the selling of tools used by offenders, secure parking lots to prevent unauthorized entry or exit, conduct undercover stings to shut down chop shops, and so forth.

Response

The third stage of the SARA model of problem solving is the response stage. While the problem-oriented policing approach advocates the use of SARA or other problem-solving models to address problems in a scientific manner, it does not offer a theory of how problems are created, how they should be classified, or what solutions should be considered. Therefore, situational crime prevention is used in the response stage to identify and develop potential interventions.

Ronald Clarke developed situational crime prevention, a theory that offers a systematic and scientific framework for reducing crime opportunities. Situational crime prevention states that the attractiveness of any crime opportunity is dependent on five characteristics: the effort needed to carry out the offense, the risk of being detected, the rewards associated with the crime, feelings of provocation to commit the crime, and the ability for offenders to

excuse or justify their behavior. An attractive crime opportunity is one that requires little effort, poses little risk, offers high rewards, is instigated through strong feelings of provocation, and is easy to excuse. Situational crime prevention suggests that opportunities can be blocked by making crime harder, more risky, and less rewarding, and by removing provocations and eliminating excuses.

Situational crime prevention provides a list of 25 different opportunity-blocking techniques, five techniques for each of the five opportunity characteristics (effort, risk, rewards, provocations, and excuses). Situational crime prevention techniques have proven effective in reducing all types of crime problems, including property crimes, child abuse and pornography, domestic violence, organized crime, cyber crime, and violent crime. Findings gathered during the analysis stage of the SARA model are used in conjunction with the list of techniques to inform the selection or development of interventions. Research has shown that the most successful crime reduction strategies target multiple opportunity characteristics. The list of techniques allows police to systematically consider each of these characteristics and suggests various ways to make crime opportunities less attractive to potential offenders. It also allows them to identify potential community partners who can help implement proactive responses.

Assessment

The fourth and final stage of the SARA model of problem solving is the assessment stage. Two types of assessment should occur at this stage: a process evaluation and an impact evaluation. A process evaluation determines whether the interventions designed and implemented in the response stage were put into place as planned. An impact evaluation determines whether the problem declined as a result of implemented interventions. Both types of evaluations are necessary to assess the effectiveness of a problem-oriented policing project.

Impact evaluations also uncover unanticipated consequences of crime reduction efforts. These can include negative consequences, most notably crime displacement. Blocking crime opportunities may lead offenders to displace their activities to other locations, targets, or times. Offenders may also use different tactics or switch from one crime type to another. Research on displacement, however, demonstrates that displacement is never a certain outcome. Furthermore, when displacement does occur, it is usually limited in scope and complete displacement is extraordinarily rare. Instead, the most common unanticipated consequences are positive, such as anticipatory benefits and diffusion of benefits. Anticipatory benefits are declines in crime prior to the implementation of interventions. These tend to occur when offenders believe that interventions are in place before actual implementation. Diffusion of benefits describes crime declines that extend beyond the targeted problem. These benefits mirror the potential forms of displacement. Interventions may reduce crime in adjacent areas (geographical), during nontargeted times (temporal), or against other victims (target). They may also reduce the use of other methods (tactical) or other types of victimization (crime type). Comprehensive impact evaluations collect data to measure these outcomes as well as the project's impact on the specific crime opportunities targeted.

Benefits and Challenges

The benefits of adopting a problem-solving approach to address community problems are well established. Research consistently shows that the SARA model, when coupled with the problem-solving tools and frameworks associated with each stage, can be a highly effective method of reducing all types of crime and disorder. Rigorous evaluations of problem-oriented policing projects have been found to provide at least modest reductions in crime and disorder, and many quasi-experimental studies report significant positive impacts on targeted problems.

The SARA model is currently the most popular and well-known police problem-solving framework in the world. It has gained tremendous popularity over the past several decades. The model and basic principles of problem-oriented policing have been incorporated into U.S. police academy curriculum, as well as promotional examinations. Additionally, the U.S. government has taken steps to recognize excellence in police problem-solving efforts. Each year, the Center for Problem-Oriented Policing holds an international competition for the Herman Goldstein Award. Police agencies submit summaries of their work using the SARA model as a template. The center receives approximately 50 to 70 submissions each year, and five to 10 are typically selected as finalists. A panel of researchers and practitioners

judges and select the winner. The Home Office in the United Kingdom holds a similar competition to recognize innovative crime fighting projects.

While practice and research consistently find that problem solving effectively reduces crime and disorder, the adoption of this process within police agencies has proven challenging. When first introduced, many police officers and administrators did not believe problem-oriented policing would work. Some police argued that departments lacked the necessary resources, officers did not have sufficient analytical skills, and that problem solving did not represent "real" police work. Although these concerns still linger, most police agencies have overcome these perceived limitations.

Police departments are less resistant to problem-oriented policing projects than in the past, but substance and implementation issues remain. These issues have been documented at each SARA stage:

- *Scanning:* Some projects are not clearly defined. They fail to meet the basic CHEERS criteria and are too small or too broad in scope.
- *Analysis:* This phase tends to suffer from inadequate data collection and lack of thorough analysis. Existing officer knowledge replaces systematic use of the problem analysis triangle and detailed investigations into crime scripts.
- *Response:* Many projects fail to systematically consider all possible situational prevention techniques. An overreliance on traditional police tactics (patrol, rapid response, investigative follow up) is still problematic.
- *Assessment:* This is the step most often skipped. Critical evaluations are replaced by simple anecdotal evidence and officers' personal observations. Evidence of displacement, anticipatory benefits, and diffusion of benefits is often not properly collected or examined.

Despite these challenges, the problem-solving process moves police beyond simply handling discrete crime incidents. Research has established its ability to increase police effectiveness and provide long-term solutions to crime problems.

Tamara D. Madensen

See also Community Policing and Problem Solving, Definition of; Crime Analysis; Crime Analysts, Roles of;

Problem Analysis Triangle; Problem-Oriented Policing, Goldstein's Development of; Problem-Solving Initiatives, Assessment and Evaluation; Situational Crime Prevention

Further Readings

Braga, A. A. (2008). *Problem-oriented policing and crime prevention* (2nd ed). Monsey, NY: Criminal Justice Press.

Clarke, R. V., & Eck, J. E. (2005). *Crime analysis for problem solvers in 60 small steps*. Washington, DC: U.S. Department of Justice, Office of Community Oriented Policing Services.

Eck, J. E., & Spelman, W. (1987) *Problem-solving: Problem-oriented policing in Newport News*. Washington, DC: U.S. Department of Justice, National Institute of Justice, Police Executive Research Forum.

Felson, M., & Cohen, L. (1979). Social change and crime rate trends: A routine activity approach. *American Sociological Review, 44*(4), 588–608.

Goldstein, H. (1979). Improving policing: A problem-oriented approach. *Crime and Delinquency, 25*(2), 236–258. doi: 10.1177/001112877902500207

Goldstein, H. (1990). *Problem-oriented policing*. New York, NY: McGraw-Hill.

Scott, M. S. (2000). *Problem-oriented policing: Reflections of the first 20 years*. Washington, DC: U.S. Department of Justice, Office of Community-Oriented Policing Services. Retrieved from http://www.cops.usdoj.gov/Publications/e03011022.txt

Scott, M. S. (2006). Implementing crime prevention: Lessons learned from problem- oriented policing projects. In J. Knutsson & R. V. Clarke (Eds.), *Putting theory to work: Implementing situational prevention and problem-oriented policing*. Crime Prevention Studies (Vol. 20) (pp. 9–36). Monsey, NY: Criminal Justice Press.

Sidebottom, A., & Tilley, N. (2011, May). Improving problem-oriented policing: The need for a new model? *Crime Prevention and Community Safety, 13*, 79–101. doi: 10.1057/cpcs.2010.21

Weisburd, D. L., Telep, C. W., Hinkle, J. C., & Eck, J. E. (2010). Is problem-oriented policing effective in reducing crime and disorder? Findings from a Campbell systematic review. *Criminology & Public Policy, 9*(1), 139–172. doi: 10.1111/j.1745–9133.2010.00617

PUBLIC HOUSING, COMMUNITY POLICING STRATEGIES FOR

The 1937 Housing Act provided federal funding for publicly owned and managed housing for low-income families. During the 1970s, many cities throughout the United States were plagued by crime and disorder. Often federally subsidized public housing developments in those cities were significantly impacted by the increase in crime due to a number of factors. The traditional law enforcement response was reactive and had a short-term impact. Community policing, with a problem-solving focus, was introduced as a proactive response with long-term results. This entry describes two key components of an effective community policing program in public housing—partnership and problem solving— and presents a case study of a successful program.

Partnership

At the heart of a successful community policing program in public housing is the philosophy of shared responsibility and accountability among law enforcement, the public housing authority, and residents. The philosophy is based on trust and relationships, with the result being law enforcement, public housing, and the community working more closely in a formal partnership to address crime. This philosophy has a theoretical basis in social cohesion as it supports relationships between organizations and individuals to ensure public safety.

Inherently, the law enforcement and public housing agencies operate with different missions. Police and public housing professionals may have experiences or perceptions that have led to mistrust among staff, residents, and law enforcement personnel. A partnership begins with both agencies gaining knowledge of each other's mission, policies, and operations that will support interagency cooperation. Ultimately, the two agencies must agree on a shared goal, which is to reduce crime and fear for public housing residents and to improve the quality of life in those communities.

In many jurisdictions, police and public housing authorities do not have an established working relationship. A formal agreement between law enforcement and the public housing authority, which details the scope of the relationship and the partners' responsibilities, is needed to ensure collaboration and accountability. A formal agreement is an important step in ensuring a long-term commitment to addressing crime in public housing regardless of change in organizational leadership.

A successful community policing program in public housing must promote community involvement and ownership in the solutions to crime. Historically, communities put the responsibility for solving crime solely on law enforcement. Community policing encourages dialogue with law enforcement and action by public housing management, community leaders, and concerned residents. If community leaders are few, then leadership development and training by law enforcement and other agencies is necessary. Without sustained community involvement, crime in public housing will return to previous levels.

Another critical component is the selection and training of the community policing personnel. Those selected to work with public housing management and residents need to make a long-term commitment. Since the success of the program is based on relationship and trust, it may take time to build. The personnel must have the interest and capacity to work not only enforcement, but prevention and intervention strategies as well. The community policing personnel who are selected often report higher job satisfaction due to the positive relationship that develops with the public housing residents, the impact they have utilizing a proactive, problem-solving approach, and a sense of ownership.

Problem Solving

An effective community policing program in public housing must be grounded in problem solving. Together law enforcement, public housing management, and residents need to engage in the SARA process (scanning, analysis, response, assessment) to find long-term solutions to the crime and fear that has plagued their communities.

Scanning begins with a review of calls for service and reported crime in the public housing community. Knowing the frequency and impact of crime problems provides a way to prioritize crimes for further analysis. If police rely only on reported crime to solve problems, it will not be effective in high-crime public housing areas known for underreporting to law enforcement. The analysis explores additional ways to gather the information needed to design the most appropriate response to the identified crime problem.

The analysis stage gathers more details about the victim, suspect, crime, location, and the motivation. Community victimization surveys and focus groups with public housing staff and residents are an effective way to gain a more thorough understanding of community crime. Law enforcement needs detailed demographic information about the public housing community and the larger societal issues need to be analyzed as part of a long-term solution. These issues include but are not limited to education, employment, health, and level of social cohesion through neighborhood organization. Without the aforementioned information, effective enforcement, prevention, and intervention strategies cannot be implemented.

The potential law enforcement responses derived from the analysis are replete throughout crime reduction literature. As part of the planning process, law enforcement and public housing agency staff should review what strategies have been previously implemented at the site and look to other agencies that have reduced crime in public housing.

The assessment assists in determining if the response was appropriately implemented and if the crime reduction goals were achieved. Assessment data can be used to inform the continuation or modification of the community policing and public housing strategies. If the crime and fear is reduced and the quality of life is improved at the public housing site, then ongoing monitoring can ensure prompt law enforcement and public housing agency response to any crime that occurs.

The Maravilla Case Study

In 1993, the Housing Authority of the County of Los Angeles (HACoLA) in California entered into a contract with the Los Angeles County Sheriff's Department (LASD) to initiate a Community Policing Program (CPP) at the Maravilla public housing site in unincorporated East Los Angeles. Part I felony violent, property, and drug crimes committed were significant problems impacting the site based on calls for service and crime reports. This also resulted in increased fear experienced by community residents.

The Maravilla public housing site had 504 units of housing with 150 units dedicated for senior and disabled residents. Approximately 1,500 residents lived at the site and 46% of the resident population was made up of children. The housing site and surrounding community had a long history of crime and related gang violence. Within the larger community, there were 17 gangs with approximately 1,500 members. Maravilla housing had three primary gangs with more than 100 members. Gang members committed the majority of crimes.

The informal methods used to analyze Maravilla crime included observations and documentation by LASD area patrol deputies, HACoLA management and maintenance staff, and public housing residents. The formal method used to analyze data was from LASD crime reports for three previous years that identified high levels of personal, property, and drug-related crime by location. Data was also derived from the CPP team surveying residents and HACoLA's ongoing 20-year *Resident Satisfaction and Safety Survey.*

The motivation behind the drug sales and other crimes was economic. Tied to that was intimidation by the Maravilla gangs to control the site. The extensive graffiti and vandalism were a way for the gangs to establish their turf and control the community. The end result was a high level of crime and a community in fear of retaliation if they reported any information to HACoLA management or LASD.

Additional analysis of the suspects involved identified them as Maravilla residents or guests. The CPP team identified those who were on probation or parole and checked their conditions. Any probationers or parolees who used Maravilla apartments as their residence of record but were not on the lease, were unauthorized. Probation or parole agencies addressed those violations.

The analysis revealed that other factors contributed to the crime problems in Maravilla. Approximately 75% of the families were single female heads of households. More than 80% of the households earned less than $30,000 a year to support a family of four. Many residents had not completed high school, which contributed to limited employment opportunities for residents. For some residents, the illegal income through drug sales and other crimes helped to sustain their families. The multigenerational and familial ties within the gangs were other underlying causes that contributed to the crime problems at the site.

The primary goal for the LASD/CPP and HACoLA response was an overall reduction in violent, property, and drug crimes. Both agencies recognized the need to engage the district attorney's office, probation and parole departments, and other local law enforcement agencies to address the crime. It was evident that HACoLA's property management and eviction policies and procedures needed to be revised as part of the overall crime reduction strategy.

The CPP at the site was guided by a dedicated, full-time team of two deputies selected by LASD and HACoLA. They were immediately trained in problem-oriented policing (POP) and became familiar with the HACoLA lease conditions, civil procedures, crime prevention and intervention programs, and community engagement. The CPP team developed a sense of ownership and responsibility for crime at the Maravilla site.

A Maravilla Task Force was formed that included the CPP team, LASD narcotics and gang units, station patrol, the district attorney's office, probation and parole departments, HACoLA management, and the HACoLA eviction attorney. The group met monthly to exchange information about the previous month's crime incidents (reported and unreported) with details regarding the victims, suspects, locations, and other data to determine any pattern. HACoLA reported on eviction actions following LASD/CPP operations. With the combined information, specific strategies were planned, including arrests, surveillance operations, investigations, search warrants, and probation and parole searches.

To address the problem of two agencies that operated with different missions, weekly meetings between the CPP team and HACoLA site management were initiated to ensure a constant flow of crime information which included all LASD calls for services and arrests in Maravilla and HACoLA information from residents about crimes, suspects, and locations. The CPP team also attended the monthly resident council meetings and was always available to meet with any concerned residents and community leaders. An anonymous hotline was also promoted to encourage resident reporting.

HACoLA management responded by revising the public housing lease to include additional sections for violent crime, assaults, and drug crime. A major revision stipulated that a resident or guest engaged in violent or drug crime would receive a three-day eviction notice for such activity and not be able to appeal the eviction. HACoLA and the CPP team also developed a Housing Violation Form (HVF) that was used to document the most frequently observed lease offenders and offenses. When an HVF was issued, the resident was advised of the offense and told that HACoLA management would be in contact. The HVF remains one of the most effective tools the CPP team has used to impact crime at Maravilla because it holds residents accountable.

After the initial impact of the CPP, many problem residents were evicted and nonresident suspects were arrested. Even after eviction or arrest, nonresidents returned to Maravilla due to family and gang ties. They continued to engage in criminal activity, so the CPP team and HACoLA instituted two policies and procedures. A HACoLA policy prevented the criminal from returning to Maravilla for a year, but the residents inviting or harboring the banned nonresident were also warned that they were subject to eviction if the banned individual returned. A curfew policy was added to the lease. It stated that no minor under the age of 18 could be in the common areas of Maravilla between 10 p.m. and 6 a.m. and from 8:30 a.m. to 1:30 p.m. when school was in session. This policy had a direct effect on the young gang members and others loitering at the site to engage in drug sales or drug use.

Three other law enforcement tools were developed to support the efforts of the CPP. A permanent trespass enforcement authorization was included in the LASD contract with HACoLA, and a trespass warning form was prepared to bolster documentation for prosecutions. Probation and parole "stay-away" conditions were also used to keep nonresident criminals away from Maravilla.

HACoLA management also addressed the need for improved security at the site. Crime prevention through environmental design (CPTED) principles guided all public housing rehabilitation and target hardening (building security) improvements were made. A closed-circuit television (CCTV) system was also strategically installed throughout the Maravilla housing site and the CPP team used a laptop for remote surveillance operations.

Finally, the CPP team engaged youth, adults, and seniors through crime prevention and intervention activities. The events built relationships and trust between law enforcement and the public housing community. The sharing of crime information increased, as did resident ownership for solving community crime problems.

The assessment suggested a strong association between the implementation of the CPP and HACoLA and the reduction of criminal activities at the Maravilla public housing site over a significant period of time.

Crime analysis over an 18-year period revealed that there were 225 incidents of crime reported in 1992 before the CPP and HACoLA partnership was implemented, compared to 35 incidents in 2010. There was a direct relationship between the level of crime, the number of residents who were victims, the level to which they reported crime, and their perceived level of safety. With regards to the level of crime and the number of victims of crime, the analysis illustrated that when crime at Maravilla was at its highest level in 1992, the percentage of residents who were victims of crime were also at its highest point (42%). Furthermore, when crime was at its lowest point in 2010, primarily as a result of the partnership, the percentage of residents who were victims of crime was also at a low point (11%).

Regarding crime and the level of reporting, when reporting of crime by victims increased, criminal activity was reduced. Data also revealed that when criminal activity was reduced, residents' sense of safety increased. When criminal activity at the Maravilla housing development was at its highest point in 1992, the percentage of residents reporting that they felt safe was at its lowest point (47%). Conversely, when criminal activity was at its lowest point in 2010, the percentage of residents reporting that they felt safe was at its highest point (94%).

The primary goal for LASD and HACoLA was an overall reduction in violent, property, and drug crimes based on the response. Ultimately, the strong partnership between LASD/CPP and HACoLA resulted in a reduction in crime that improved the overall quality of life for Maravilla residents.

This case study demonstrates the array of activities that can be performed, types of strategies and programs initiated, and level of success achieved when a community policing and problem-solving strategy is employed with a public housing type of problem.

Betsy Lindsay

See also Community Policing and Problem Solving, Definition of; Fear of Crime; Gang Crimes, Community Policing Strategies for; Problem-Oriented Policing, Goldstein's Development of

Further Readings

Avila, C., Lindsay, B., & Baker, K. (2011). *Reducing crime in Maravilla public housing site*. Retrieved from http://

www.popcenter.org/conference/conferencepapers/2011/
avilaReducingCrimeinMaravillaPublicHousing.pdf

Dunworth, T., & Saiger, A. (1993, July). *Drugs and crime in public housing: A three-city analysis, final report.* Washington, DC: U.S. Department of Justice, National Institute of Justice. Retrieved from http://www.icpsr .umich.edu/icpsrweb/ICPSR/studies/6235

Goldstein, H. (1990). *Problem-oriented policing.* New York, NY: McGraw-Hill.

Mazerolle, L. G., Ready, J., Terrill, W., & Gajewski, F. (1999). *Problem-oriented policing in public housing: Final report of the Jersey City project.* Retrieved from http://www.ncjrs.gov/pdffiles1/nij/grants/179985.pdf

Ready, J., Mazerolle, L. G., & Revere, E. (1998). Getting evicted from public housing: An analysis of the factors influencing eviction decisions in six public housing sites. *Crime Prevention Studies, 9,* 307–327.

Stoloff, J. A. (2004). *A brief history of public housing.* Washington, DC: U.S. Department of Housing and Urban Development.

Weisburd, D. L., Telep, C. W., & Hinkle, J. C., &. Eck, J. E. (2008). *Effects of problem-oriented policing on crime and disorder.* Retrieved from http://www.ncjrs.gov/ pdffiles1/nij/grants/224990.pdf

Weisel, D. L. (1990). *Tackling drug problems in public housing: A guide for police.* Washington, DC: Police Executive Research Forum.

PUBLICITY CAMPAIGNS

If the heart and soul of problem-oriented policing is the development of innovative efforts to reduce crime and social disorder, then police agencies that undertake such interventions may consider advertising their work and ideas to their public. Departments can spread the word about their problem-solving philosophy and initiatives while encouraging citizens to help remove crime opportunities and to adopt better self-protection measures (while also warning potential and actual offenders of increased police vigilance or improved police practices).

When designed properly, publicity campaigns can offer police departments another problem-solving tool in the fight against crime. This entry discusses the various methods by which citizens—and media—can be reached, educated, and brought to bear in addressing neighborhood crime and disorder.

Target Audience

Before undertaking any publicity campaign effort, law enforcement agencies need to determine the exact target of their message. This will be based on a careful analysis of the crime problem at hand. If car break-ins are to be addressed, for example, the police agency needs to determine what population (offenders or victims) is most likely to respond to the crime prevention message. A victim-oriented campaign designed to reduce car break-ins by mailing flyers to local residences is not appropriate if most of the victims are commuters, visitors, or tourists from out of town. Of course, a publicity campaign can target both offenders and victims.

Victims

Publicity campaigns directed to victims usually take one of two forms. Police agencies can use publicity campaigns to advertise a particular intervention in their jurisdiction. The purpose of this type of campaign is not only to reduce eventual victimization but also to increase police-community contact in the hope of improving the agency's relationship with the public. The other type of publicity campaign is broader in nature and is designed to advertise general crime prevention principles, such as "lock your car" campaigns. This is campaign is not necessarily tied to the jurisdiction itself and can be part of a broader, even national crime prevention effort.

A problem concerning victim-oriented publicity campaigns is that most residents simply ignore the message and adopt an "it won't happen to me" attitude. Research on crime prevention publicity shows that many crime prevention messages go unheeded by the general public, even though the public has been exposed to the messages numerous times. Publicity campaigns seem to have a limited impact on actually changing resident behaviors in terms of implementing crime prevention practices. Residents routinely report that while they see the publicity message, they find the crime prevention theme irrelevant and not worthwhile.

What seem to have an effect on residents are campaigns that are carried out in small geographic regions and campaigns that address a specific crime that is occurring in the neighborhood. Therefore, while general car-locking campaigns are relatively ineffective, a police publicity campaign aimed at educating residents on how to reduce the theft of specific cars in a given neighborhood is much more likely to be seen as relevant by residents. Once again, the campaign's success is inextricably tied to the careful analysis of the crime problem by the local police agency. Victim-oriented campaigns can be carried through radio, television, newspapers, flyers, and even billboards.

Offenders

Publicity campaigns aimed at offenders seek to reduce criminal behavior by giving offenders information about the risks and legal ramifications of crime. Campaigns can inform on the risk of crime by advertising increased police presence in an area, thereby increasing the threat level of apprehension. Campaigns can also inform on risk by demonstrating the dangers of a given activity. For example, showing a catastrophic car accident after a car theft may deter young people thinking about stealing a car and joyriding in it.

In the same vein, publicity campaigns can warn potential offenders about the legal consequences of criminal behavior. Research has shown that oftentimes young offenders do not know the legal consequences of their actions. A billboard near a local high school reminding students that vandalism or tagging can incur a certain fine or jail sentence may prove instrumental in reducing the incidence of those activities.

When it comes to legal information, research has shown that legal penalties are much less salient to offenders than the knowledge that there is a high risk of apprehension at stake. It is as if offenders fear not the effect of an arrest, but the probability of an arrest. Therefore, publicity campaigns to reduce vandalism should advertise the presence of cameras and security guards (which increase the probability of apprehension) instead of the potential fine and jail sentence if one is apprehended.

Like victim-oriented campaigns, publicity aimed at offenders is more efficient when it targets a specific crime type and focuses on a specific area. Broad and general threats are much less likely to have an impact on crime reduction than prevention messages that delineate the scope and boundaries of a particular police intervention on a given crime type. For

example, "panhandlers caught at the farmers market are subject to arrest" is a much more salient message than "no panhandling." This targeted approach allows personalization of the message, making it more believable and pertinent to the local audience.

The publicity directed at offenders to reduce criminal behavior does not always have the desired effect. The lack of effect has been attributed to the moral appeal or finger-pointing aspect of numerous campaigns. Such campaigns rarely resonate with the offending population and they are usually dismissed or ignored because the offenders deem them irrelevant. Furthermore, crime prevention publicity campaigns directed at offenders rarely reach their intended audience during the immediate moment before crime occurs. Research has shown that publicity messages that are visible to offenders as they ponder their crime have a greater impact at reducing offending rates. For example, tags on clothing that remind customers that there are specific antitheft protection measures in the store are more likely to have an impact on shoplifting rates than a billboard on the side of a building reminding citizens that "shoplifting is wrong." Like victim-oriented campaigns, publicity directed at offenders can be diffused through radio, television, newspapers, flyers, and billboards.

Benefits of Publicity Campaigns

Low Cost and Ease of Implementation

Publicity campaigns are an efficient and inexpensive way for police agencies to reach potential victims or offenders in their jurisdiction. With the advent of cell phone technology, desktop publishing, and video editing software, law enforcement agencies have numerous media options to promote their message. Some methods are more active (e.g., text messages to local residents) than others (e.g., flyers or posters displayed in large impersonal businesses), but all remain within the reach of even cash-strapped agencies. Many localities may also provide free airtime or television spots for public service announcements (PSAs) from local agencies. Similarly, these PSAs can also be shown in local movie theaters prior to the main feature. Local businesses such as print shops can also be a resource upon which law enforcement agencies can rely for customized and sometimes free or donated work. If the publicity message is a printed one that needs to be distributed or disseminated within the community, volunteers, community activists, or social groups can be called upon to help distribute these flyers to the public.

Public Relations

Most publicity campaigns have an indirect benefit of improving police-community relations. This benefit is linked to the public perception that the law enforcement agency is concerned about a local crime problem. Citizens appreciate that the police are proactively working toward crime solutions, and police officers become agents of crime prevention as opposed to being solely responsible for crime repression. Publicity campaigns can change the perception of local police from crime control agents to public servants.

Increasing Message Adhesion

Like campaigns created to sell products for commercial purposes, publicity campaigns to reduce crime need to be well designed, the message needs to be clear and simple, and their appeal needs to be as broad as possible without losing their intended audience. Many municipal agencies, however, will not have the resources of the private sector. There are, however, certain tools that are available to increase the chances that a local publicity campaign will be successful. During the creation of the campaign, it is important to include all of the concerned stakeholders that are affected by the problem. Business leaders, for example, may have ideas and resources that they are willing to lend to the campaign. Including stakeholders and members of the community in the creation of the campaign may also prevent unanticipated problems with the dissemination of the campaign. For instance, a publicity campaign designed to reduce pickpocketing by telling residents to not carry cash on them when they venture out of the house may become problematic during the farmers market season when local growers are expecting to sell their produce to local residents. The campaign against carrying cash may have a direct impact on the farmers' economic outlook, something the police department may not have anticipated.

Another technique that may help the campaign's message is the inclusion of a local leader, or someone recognizable in the community. Impersonal publicity campaigns have less of a chance to make an intimate connection with their audience than campaigns that include students at the local high school or the local grocer. Appearances by local personalities increase the chances that the message will become more relevant to the target audience.

The content of the campaign should also be direct and easy to understand. Campaigns that are too verbose or complex in their detail tend to lose their audience and become useless. While refraining from overly simplistic and condescending messages, an effective campaign clearly highlights the problem at hand and offers its audience a simple message. If the message is directed at victims, the campaign should propose solutions that are easily implementable, cost-effective, and rational. If the message is directed at offenders, the campaign should attempt to steer the individual from the offense by offering immediate desistance measures the potential offender can relate to.

On a practical level, effective campaigns do not overstay their welcome. A campaign is more likely to be effective if it is administered in small but consistent doses. If an agency puts up a billboard that becomes deteriorated over time, people may not only become numb to the message, but they may also interpret the languishing poster as a sign of the level of attention devoted to the problem.

Evaluation of a Publicity Campaign

In a perfect world, publicity campaigns would be developed in front of focus groups and target audiences, much in the same way as they are carried out in the private sector. If a municipality has the budget to undertake these types of activities, then such focus groups may help refine the message and identify what works and what does not. However, most crime prevention publicity campaigns are created as a reaction to a social problem, and the urgency to get the message out often trumps the crucial pretesting phases.

What is more realistic is the post-publicity evaluation process. When evaluating a publicity campaign, resident surveys are usually the most direct and effective technique. It is important to know what percentage of the population was even aware of the campaign. And of those aware of the campaign, what specifically did they think of the message and the campaign format? Getting feedback from the residents may help in future campaign development and campaign dissemination, for example.

Issues Related to Publicity Campaigns

Heightened Anxiety

A salient problem with publicity campaigns is the issue of creating anxiety or moral panic with the audience. When it comes to victim campaigns to increase crime prevention activities, the underlying notion is that there is a constant threat of victimization in people's lives. Some people may not take well to this constant barrage of information reminding them that crime is just around the corner. Others may see all of this crime prevention information as overload, unnecessary, and simply distracting from their reality. In dismissing the information, these people may not adopt any of the measures and may put themselves at risk for victimization.

On a different note, campaigns that are directed to certain neighborhoods or areas in the city may become problematic for residents of those areas. Real estate values may suffer, visitors may no longer want to visit, and business owners may resent these "fear campaigns" as they keep potential customers away. Campaigns designed to deter offenders may also be responsible for a heightened sense of worry in a community as people may overestimate the actual offending rate. Generally, agencies linked to tourism, business development, and local area growth may consider such campaigns to be a deterrent to future business in the area. On one side of the coin, publicity campaigns can be seen as an effective tool to prevent crime, but on the other side, they can be seen as an admission that a crime problem exists and that it has yet to be under control.

Displacement

A common concern when it comes to publicity campaigns is that the problem may simply be shifted to another location or create an unanticipated crime problem as a result of displacement. Instituting a publicity campaign advertising closed-circuit television (CCTV) cameras in one housing site may cause concern for a neighboring site that crime will simply move around the corner and find a new home. Parking garages advertising increased police presence may be a source of worry for parking garages that cannot claim this extra protection. Publicity campaigns that illustrate the harm of a given illicit drug may be responsible for a shift to a different type of drug as people seek a different yet "safer" high. While some of these concerns are well founded, research on crime prevention efforts has shown that displacement is rare, and if it occurs it is minimal at best.

Geographic and Temporal Coverage

An effective publicity campaign delineates its geographic and temporal coverage. Temporal coverage refers to how long the campaign lasts, and as mentioned above, a good campaign is periodic in nature and does not languish so as not to lose its appeal. In terms of geographic coverage, law enforcement agencies need to determine if they want the coverage to be citywide, by district, or by neighborhood. Each level of coverage incurs differential costs, dissemination requirements, and evaluation concerns. For example, a printed citywide campaign may be more costly than a neighborhood-focused paper campaign. If posters are selected as the medium to disseminate the message, citywide coverage may be more demanding in terms of maintenance requirements, poster replacements, and basic upkeep.

When it comes to geographic coverage, there is also the issue of linguistics and neighborhoods with diverse populations. It is important for law enforcement agencies to be aware of their target audience's demographic composition. If coverage is to be extended to a non-English-speaking area, the materials of the campaign need to be translated into the appropriate language. This also adds to the cost of the campaign, but the rewards and benefits in terms of crime prevention may exceed this additional cost.

Emmanuel P. Barthe

See also Building Partnerships and Stakeholders; Fear of Crime; Problem-Oriented Policing: Elements, Processes, Implications; Situational Crime Prevention

Further Readings

Barthe, E. P. (2006). *Crime prevention publicity campaigns.* Response Guide No. 5. Washington, DC: Center for Problem-Oriented Policing. Retrieved from http://www.popcenter.org/responses/crime_prevention

Bowers, K. J., & Johnson, S. D. (2003). *The role of publicity in crime prevention: Findings from the reducing burglary initiative.* Home Office Research Study, No. 272. London, England: Home Office.

Clarke, R. V. (Ed.). (1993). *Crime prevention studies* (Vol. 1). Monsey, NY: Criminal Justice Press.

Hallahan, K. (2000, Winter). Enhancing motivation, ability, and opportunity to process public relations messages. *Public Relations Review, 26*(4), 463–480.

Poyner, B. (1993). What works in crime prevention: An overview of evaluations. In R. V. Clarke (Ed.), *Crime prevention studies* (Vol. 1). Monsey, NY: Criminal Justice Press.

Sacco, V., & Silverman, R. (1982). Crime prevention through mass media: Prospects and problems. *Journal of Criminal Justice, 10*(4), 257–269.

RECRUIT ACADEMY TRAINING

Recruit academy training provides a critical and important entry point for individuals entering the profession of policing. For many, recruit academy training—basic police training comprised of specialized courses that are designed to train and certify new recruits—offers the first step in learning how to deal with the complexities and challenges facing officers. Few training opportunities, such as academy training, have the ability to shape, form, and instill the values, principles, and community-oriented policing philosophy needed in providing effective community policing. The extensive length of time, comprehensive course content, and personal commitment in attending academy training creates a unique opportunity that is seldom replicated or achieved in an officer's career. This entry briefly discusses the history of recruit academy training, the structure and requirements of modern recruit academies, the role of community policing, and future trends and implications of recruit academy training.

History

Modern recruit academy training can trace part of its history back to the pioneering work and visionary leadership of Berkeley (California) Police Chief August Vollmer. Vollmer, considered by many to be the father of modern-day policing, made significant contributions to policing, including early efforts to advance formal police training. Although limited formal schools of police instruction were in place as early as the late 1800s, training provided in the form of recruit academies did not exist. With major reforms in policing beginning to take place in the early 1900s to address police corruption and to establish more professionalism within police organizations, Vollmer recognized the importance and need to provide more training to help advance professionalism within policing.

As early as 1907, Vollmer established the world's first police school where officers could learn about the laws of evidence. In 1916, Vollmer vigorously pursued training for his police officers through the application of a scientific-methods approach to police work. In his scientific-methods approach, Vollmer pioneered the teaching of criminal justice, creating a police training program within the Berkeley Police Department and a summer program at the University of California, Berkeley. After his retirement from the Berkeley Police Department in 1932, the University of California extended Vollmer's training program, offering it to students throughout the regular school year. These efforts were quickly recognized and adapted by other academic institutions that began similar programs including the University of Southern California, San Jose State College (California), and Michigan State College. Vollmer's vision and early efforts to improve and increase training opportunities for police officers greatly contributed to future advancements in both basic and advanced police training programs that would occur over the next several decades.

Continuing throughout the 1950s, 1960s and 1970s, several professional police organizations and presidential appointed commissions—the

International Association of Chiefs of Police (IACP); the International Association of Directors of Law Enforcement Standards and Training (IADLST); the Katzenbach Commission (1960); the Kerner Commission (1967); and the National Advisory Commission (1971)—continued to advance efforts and provide direction in standardizing police training.

As a result of these and other individual efforts, in 1959 New York became the first state in the nation to establish basic training for newly hired officers. By 1981, every state had formed Police Officer Standards and Training (POST) programs, which provided minimum standards for recruit academy training. While many of the early recruit training programs focused on basic knowledge and skills in areas such as investigations, defensive tactics, firearms, patrol procedures, and legal topics, new and emerging topics required recruit academies to expand and increase training, raising the current national average for academy training to 720 hours for individual recruits.

Modern Recruit Academy Training

Today's recruit academies continue to play a pivotal and important role in developing newly hired police officers. From traditional firearms and defensive tactics training to more complex and advanced technology, critical thinking, and scenario-based training, recruit academies are creating more prepared, educated, and professional police officers. The road to completing recruit academy training can be long and challenging for many individuals who aspire to become police officers. To become certified police officers, individuals must first successfully complete recruit academy training, which will place mental and physical demands on them over an extended period of time. Gaining entry into current recruit academy training can be accomplished in three primary ways.

The approach most widely accepted by states is the requirement that an individual be hired as a full-time police officer. While this approach is the most common, individuals in some states like California, Florida, Georgia, and Washington can also opt for self-sponsorship or sponsorship by a local police department. Self-sponsorship does not require that the recruit be hired and can be advantageous to both the individual and prospective hiring police agency. This option allows individuals who have not yet been hired as police officers to become more qualified and competitive in future hiring opportunities. This option also offers potential hiring agencies the opportunity to view a recruit's conduct and performance while at the academy. Choosing self-sponsorship, however, can be a costly endeavor. Recruits who have been hired full-time pay no costs for attending the academy and often receive a salary for their time; individuals who choose self-sponsorship can expect to pay all costs associated with attending the academy. Cost for attending recruit academy training averages between $3,000 and $6,000. Costs can increase depending on additional expenses such as uniforms, equipment, supplies, and books. Regardless of how individuals enter recruit academy training, all recruits must meet minimum requirements. Minimum requirements can differ in each state but most include minimum age requirements (18 to 21 years of age), passing physical fitness and written examinations, and passing a criminal history background.

Once accepted into academy training, recruits may encounter different approaches in how training is administered. Many states provide different options for attending recruit training, ranging from commuter academies provided by institutions of higher education or law enforcement agencies where individuals are not required to stay overnight, to mandatory on-site attendance where recruits are not allowed to leave during the week. While the national average for recruit training is 720 hours, many academies exceed this amount (e.g., Sacramento, California, Police Academy: 952 hours; Los Angeles, California, Police Academy: 960 hours; and the Miami, Florida, Police Training Center: 960 hours). During their attendance at the academy, recruits can expect to experience challenging training both mentally and physically.

During the training academy experience, recruits attend a wide range of classroom courses, including ethics and integrity, community policing, law and legal, patrol procedures, cultural diversity, interview and interrogation, report writing, and numerous other course topics. Recruits also spend a great deal of time outside the classroom. This training includes physical fitness and exercise time, training in defensive tactics where recruits learn how to apply control holds and take defensive actions to address threats, firearms and weapons training where recruits learn how to handle and use firearms and other weapons, and time driving at an emergency vehicle operations course. In addition, recruits may also experience real-life scenarios and activities where they are placed in situations that require them to apply their classroom instruction. Attending state-mandated recruit training (POST programs) may not be the end of a recruit's basic training experience.

In addition to the state-mandated training requirements, several police organizations have required additional, agency-specific training for their newly hired recruits. This additional training includes agency-specific policies and procedures, city or county rules, ordinances, regulations, agency protocols, and information on unique operations within the hiring jurisdiction. The successful completion of academy training by recruit officers is only the first step in becoming a police officer. The next step is in field or police officer training (PTO) where recruits apply what they have learned, being coached, mentored, and evaluated by a field training officer (FTO).

Implementing Community Policing in Recruit Academy Training

Since the early 1980s, community policing has played an active and important role for many law enforcement agencies that are looking for better ways to build and strengthen healthy community and police relationships. To prepare new recruits for their role in working with the community, recruit academy training provides one of the first venues for providing community policing training.

Community policing is generally placed in the first or second week of academy training to ensure that recruits can use this information throughout their academy experience. Providing such training early in recruits' academy experience is important as it begins to lay the foundation for other important knowledge and skills needed in other training experiences. In community policing training, recruits receive structured instruction that is designed to build critical knowledge and skills around the core principles of problem solving, developing partnerships, and organizational transformation. As recruits progress through academy training, they will be challenged with complex problems that often require them to use multiple approaches. In community policing training, recruits are taught how to use specific problem-solving approaches, such as the SARA (scanning, analyze, response, assessment)

problem-solving model, where they take complex reoccurring problems and systematically work them to successful resolution.

Recruits also learn how to incorporate the philosophy of community policing in all aspects of their training experiences. The philosophy of community policing instills the concept of the police and community working together to build trust, mutual respect, and commitment toward working on achieving common goals. Community policing in a recruit academy setting serves as a foundational guiding theme that continually reoccurs within the recruits' learning experience. It is a theme that provides balance between the needs of both the police and the community. While the subject of community policing is often taught in a single 4- to 8-hour block of instruction, many recruit academies have made efforts to incorporate the elements of community policing throughout the entire academy training experience.

By the end of academy training, new recruits have experienced several training situations that require them to incorporate community policing approaches. These situations range from basic field interviews to complex use of force situations where recruits must make critical decisions to resolve the issue.

A Case Study

As Henry Miller stated, "Example moves the world more than doctrine." So following is a description of how the recruit academy in Somerset County, New Jersey, was modified so that community policing was the underlying foundation.

In the classroom, police recruits learn the fundamentals of community policing. However, the centerpiece of the six-month program is a capstone project, which requires the recruits to work with members of the community to identify a problem or community concern. Senior citizens, educators, community members, business leaders, and representatives of the faith community are invited to the academy to participate in the project. Community members, referred to as "community facilitators" are recommended by their local police chiefs and agency heads and then paired with recruits based on either common interests or jurisdictions. These community facilitators work with recruits as they implement the SARA process to identify and develop responses to actual community problems.

Part of the project involves recruits writing a detailed analysis of the identified issue, which often results in a 25- to 40-page paper. Many capstone projects lead to the development of handbooks, curriculum, or strategic plans that recruits can take with them when they embark on their new careers. At the end of the academy, each capstone team gives an oral presentation, sharing how they addressed their community problem. Since the program was established, approximately 800 recruits have successfully completed capstone projects and received their community policing certifications.

Trends and Future of Recruit Academy Training

The future of policing continues to be complex, challenging, and demanding, requiring police officers who are professional, prepared, and equipped. As a new generation of individuals who have grown up in the age of advanced technology, increasing diversity and social changes, and increasing threats of terrorism enter recruit academy training, comprehensive and innovative ways may be needed to prepare these new recruits. However, training will likely continue to be directed toward officer safety (firearms, defensive tactics, and emergency vehicle operations) and other important training topics (community policing, problem solving, critical thinking, diversity, and communications) while building on sound principles and educational practices to create training environments that support adult learning principles. With advancements in technology, changes in law and legal issues, continued threats of terrorism, and changes in our social fabric, recruit academy training will need to adapt and change to meet these needs. However, when training content and learning experiences are integrated, desired outcomes of the training goals can be achieved.

Brian Kauffman

See also Citizen Police Academies; In-Service Training; Mentoring; Model Curriculum; Police Training Officer (PTO) Program

Further Readings

Bumbak, A. R. (2011). *Dynamic police training*. Boca Raton, FL: CRC Press.

Gaines, L. K., & Worrall, J. L. (2012*). Police administration* (3rd ed.). Clifton Park, NY: Delmar Books.

Peak, K. J., & Glensor, R. W. (2012*). Community policing and problem solving: Strategies & practice* (6th ed.). Upper Saddle River, NJ: Prentice Hall.

Wadman, R. C. (2009). *Police theory in America: Old traditions and new opportunities*. Springfield, IL: Charles C Thomas.

RECRUITING FOR QUALITY AND DIVERSITY

Beginning in the 1990s, some law enforcement agencies experienced decreasing numbers of applicants, largely felt to be due to the growing competition of the job market and the less-than-creative and stagnant recruiting strategies of law enforcement agencies. Although the bleak national financial picture of the first two decades of the 21st century may have increased the applicant pools again, negative media coverage, inflexible working schedules, long hours, and perceived dangers and hardships of the profession continue to impact the quality and diversity of law enforcement applicants and recruits. This entry examines the issues associated with recruiting quality and diverse persons for law enforcement positions and how community policing further affects these issues and necessitates additional requirements for quality and diversity in recruiting.

Skills

As law enforcement departments turn to community-oriented, problem-solving (COPS) policing that emphasizes the formation of community partnerships and the use of a systematic model to solve problems, administrators have realized that officers needed to possess traits and skills different from past traditional officers. Although training in the new skills could increase existing abilities, they began to recognize the importance of recruiting individuals with aptitudes of service orientation, of sufficient analytical minds to be creative and good problem solvers, and with excellent interpersonal communication skills.

A job-task analysis can identify the traits, skills, and aptitude of effective COPS officers. Comprehensive job analysis has been used for decades by many professions and was introduced to most law enforcement agencies after the enactment of Americans with Disabilities Act (ADA) in 1990. The ADA required the hiring of individuals with disabilities and the accommodation of them in the working environment as long as they could demonstrate their ability to complete the tasks; therefore, it became crucial that professions including law enforcement be able to clearly define what critical tasks each job entailed. Through states' training and standard criminal justice divisions, police agencies compiled specific lists of critical and frequent tasks, as well as the knowledge, skills, and abilities required to carry out the tasks of line officers and throughout the ranks. Applicants for law enforcement positions must demonstrate a certain entry level of competency for the listed tasks.

This need to systematically establish job-related responsibilities has evolved as law enforcement departments shift their line officers from the narrow role of crime fighting to the empowering responsibilities of identifying and analyzing problems, building trust, and interacting with diverse neighborhoods to help solve these problems. It became important also to expand job-task analysis to personal attributes that are measured in other ways than observable physical standards.

For example, the Sacramento (California) Police Department identified the following as core attributes: adaptability, commitment to service, communication skills, compassion, empathy, flexibility, integrity, objectivity, patience, respect, social concern, strong work ethic, tolerance, and intelligence. Other agencies have included independence; ability to make decisions; ability to receive, evaluate, and act on information from people of different cultures, values, and standards without bias; courage; and accountability. Law enforcement agencies often use psychological evaluations to measure these and other emotional and mental characteristics; however, they also include questions related to these attributes during background investigations and interview panels. These attributes are more difficult to evaluate and are more subjective than traditional, primarily physical traits and so require multiple assessment modalities. Questions to applicants' family members, employers, friends, and neighbors during background investigations provide specific examples of individuals' ability to cope with stress and anger, accountability, interactions with different types of people, and experience working independently among other attributes and behaviors. Many law enforcement agencies include a panel of ranking law enforcement officers who ask candidates a set of questions that help assess many of these same characteristics, as well as the candidates' ability to articulate and "think on their feet." Ethical dilemmas often are included in the questions to assess candidates' comfort in ambiguous areas.

Diversity

Although it is important for recruits to possess the qualities described above, it is also important for the applicant pool to be diverse and represent the community in which these recruits will be policing. Potential candidates from diverse communities may not perceive law enforcement as an attractive profession because of the history of police officers' interactions with specific communities. They also may fear the disapproval of their peers if they choose a profession the peers consider their adversary. It also has become critical to include recruits from the growing numbers of immigrant citizens who speak a variety of languages. Hiring individuals from different cultures helps reduce opportunities for misunderstanding and dispel fear of crime and of law enforcement officers within these communities. Officers who are fluent in specific communities' languages and can communicate with neighborhood leaders are very useful in teaching non-English-speaking residents what issues are considered urgent police matters, how to report emergencies, and alternative means to obtain nonemergency, but relevant services.

Also these officers from the immigrant communities can often emotionally support victims and their families, thereby reducing victims' reluctance to talk to police officers and increasing their probability of testifying later in court. Often first-generation immigrants have memories of corrupt and brutal law enforcement officers from their native countries. They may have problems viewing the criminal justice system in the United States as fair and as a service for them. After observing police officers from their own ethnic background in their new U.S. community, many new citizens may be persuaded to consider becoming law enforcement officers or allowing their children to consider the profession. Overcoming different communities' negative perceptions of law enforcement officers or the perception that the law enforcement profession is a "man's job" is a major obstacle. Trust must be established, and these new citizens need to be supported through the demanding recruiting, hiring, and training process.

Hiring officers from a variety of different ethnic groups in a community provides additional intangible benefits of enriched multicultural understanding to all law enforcement officers that cannot be replicated in formal diversity workshops. Working side-by-side with officers from different backgrounds can open the thoughts and ideas of officers who often were born, grew up, and never left their old neighborhood. Additional training is most valuable when it provides officers with specific points of communication-related issues and how these issues can be understood. Some of these specific areas include concepts of authority inside and outside the family, the concept of time, and approaches to managing differences between cultures.

Programs to Ensure Quality and Diversity

Law enforcement agencies throughout the nation have implemented a variety of different recruiting strategies to increase the size and diversity of their applicant pools. A number of studies have evaluated the strengths and weaknesses of these strategies.

One program, called Hiring in the Spirit of Service (HSS) and funded by the U.S. Department of Justice's Office of Community Oriented Police Services, examined the best practices of law enforcement agencies across the nation. They ranged from small departments in the Northeast to a large urban midwestern city and two sheriff's agencies. Lessons learned from their evaluation included the importance of a comprehensive job analysis that includes the identification of the knowledge, skills, and abilities (KSAs) inherent to community policing; the involvement of the community early, fully, and with assurances that their input is valued and utilized in the recruitment practices of the agency; and balance of community involvement with experienced officers' participation in the recruitment process. In efforts to overcome barriers to some minority groups, the studied agencies carefully examined the components of their selection criteria and assessments. For example, one agency provided tutoring for candidates who had problems with the written examination because English was their second

language. Other agencies found that mentoring candidates to help them adjust to the police culture and become aware of how to succeed in policing was particularly beneficial. Mentoring was perceived as a form of professional development that conveyed respect for the candidates and the candidates' value to the organization rather than just helping them to adjust. In return, the candidates see the mentors as people similar to themselves who help them explore unknown territory. Mentoring relationships often last a lifetime.

The researchers also discussed the importance of web-based recruitment that was citizen-user-friendly. Because potential applicants may be those citizens who have recently mastered English and also are not familiar with police jargon, the webmasters must think like the public rather than the police. Building the recruiting website is a critical area for community input. The community should see itself reflected in the officers portrayed and should be able to easily navigate the website. Piloting and providing feedback before the website goes "live" allows the law enforcement agency to understand clearly what attracts potential recruits and if they will be able to access necessary information.

Recruiting early with young people also has been found to be an investment that is especially important in breaking barriers. Children's experiences with law enforcement revolve around their family and neighborhood encounters and the media. For children to obtain a true image of a police officer as somebody who is there to help them and in a profession that they would enjoy and could do, current officers must foster relationships through such activities as sponsorship of sports teams and church youth groups. School resource officers, who children regularly see in school in uniform, can model helping behaviors and portray a trusting, helping authority rather than another authoritarian figure to be avoided. One study conducted by faculty at the University of North Carolina at Charlotte and funded by the Charlotte-Mecklenburg Police Department surveyed juniors in two large high schools. The questionnaire listed the major tasks of police officers as described in community coordinators' and line officers' performance evaluations. The students were not told they were police responsibilities, but rather the children were asked if they thought they would find the activities interesting and whether they could achieve the tasks (self-efficacy).

The majority of students, boys and girls, stated that they would find the activities interesting, and they could achieve them. Interestingly when asked in a simple question if they would consider a career in law enforcement, the majority of students, boys and girls, rejected the idea. The researchers and police administrators concluded that children beginning in elementary, and certainly by high school, should be better educated in the emerging community-oriented, problem-solving roles of police officers. There are excellent opportunities to recruit diverse pools of candidates if children learn early the progressive service-oriented responsibilities of today's law enforcement officers. Also because many potentially valuable candidates often are rejected due to early mistakes surrounding use of drugs or minor offenses, attracting these candidates' interest early in such programs as Police Athletic League, Explorers, and cadet programs can prevent such mistakes and keep them in the applicant pool as viable candidates.

RAND, with funding from the Office of Community Oriented Policing Services and the National Institute of Justice, convened a National Summit on Police Recruitment and Retention in the Contemporary Urban Environment in 2008. The participants came from a variety of different agencies of different sizes and geographical areas. In general, they agreed that recruitment was a problem, to which they did not devote sufficient resources. Traditional advertising and marketing was found to be out of date and out of touch with little knowledge of what attracts women and minorities to a career. The importance of social media to attract young applicants who might not otherwise be seeking a job could not be overemphasized. One participating agency distributes a video/podcast that depicts women officers from different ranks and assignments talking about what their professions had been before joining the police department. Most participants found their own employees to be important resources for recruiting; most applicants had heard about the agency through a friend or relative who worked at the law enforcement agency. Agencies awarded a bonus to current officers if they convinced a friend or family member to apply and mentored him or her throughout the selection process.

Accompanying the importance of their own employees as recruiters was the reputation of the agency especially around its treatment of women and minorities. There is no sufficient amount of publicity that can erase poor police-community relationships. Other recruitment tips included the importance of personalizing and streamlining the selection process. Many quality applicants are lost if police recruiters do not remain in touch with their candidates or take too long to complete the selection process. Local recruiting also proved to be the most cost-effective; most applicants do not want to move far just to become a police officer. Top recruit-producing neighborhoods and communities should be targeted with personal attention from recruiting officers. Applicants also should be classified according to their viability. Highly attractive candidates should be processed as quickly as possible with recruiters remaining in touch. This practice helps to keep the recruiting process moving smoothly rather than becoming congested at certain junctures for all candidates and potentially losing highly qualified candidates to other professions or departments.

Equally important, after identifying those processes that become bottlenecks, is for police administrators to develop performance measures that encourage and reward top recruiting performance and smooth out the logjams. For example, background investigations are time consuming, so those investigators who are particularly capable should be rewarded and used to help train other investigators. The participants concluded that retention can eliminate much of the need for recruiting. Focusing on and eliminating internal problems that might drive away effective officers can also improve the reputation of the agency and enhance the recruitment of the agency.

One means of introducing nonnative residents to policing is hiring them as non-sworn community service officers. Their responsibilities are molded to meet the needs of the community, including providing liaison between the community and department; translating and interpreting interactions between citizens and police officers; conducting classes on the criminal justice system, police procedures, and services for their community members; working with the youth, their parents and local businesses about drug and crime prevention; supporting victims as advocates; and providing nonpolice services such as means to report animal and noise complaints. These services as well as recruitment offices should be situated in satellite police stations within the ethnic communities. Also, encouraging leaders within ethnic communities to attend citizen police academies is ideal to break down barriers and allay concerns. Citizen police academies not only convey information, but also allow the leaders to ride along with officers and observe officers in a variety of activities.

Pressure from within newly settled ethnic groups, self-doubt about proficiency in the English language and knowledge of U.S. laws and police procedures, as well as competing opportunities of other professions make the recruiting of individuals from the many different ethnic groups represented in our communities a challenge. Building trust with members in ethnic communities through developing meaningful relationships, helping these citizens learn to perceive the police profession as a helping profession, and learning as much as possible about the communities' culture, practices, and norms can help police officers attract excellent second-generation and other minority groups into the pool of police applicants. Retention of officers also is a primary way for agencies to maintain an excellent reputation, which can also attract female and other minority recruits.

Vivian Lord

See also Immigrant Populations, Community Policing Strategies for; Model Curriculum; Police-Community Relations; Recruit Academy Training

Further Readings

Crime and Violence Prevention Center. (1999). Lengthening the stride: Recognizing diversity as an asset. In *Community oriented policing and problem solving: Now and beyond* (pp. 129–139). Sacramento: California Department of Justice.

Scrivner, E. (2006). *Innovations in police recruitment and hiring: Hiring in the spirit of service.* Washington, DC: U.S. Department of Justice, Office of Community Oriented Policing Services.

Wilson, J. M., & Grammich, C. A. (2008). *Police recruitment and retention in the contemporary urban environment: Conference proceedings.* Santa Monica, CA: RAND.

REGIONAL COMMUNITY POLICING INSTITUTES

Following passage of the Violent Crime Control and Law Enforcement Act of 1994, a unique community policing training program was required to address the changes in policing that were occurring with the transition to community policing. These training needs were met through the development of a national network of Regional Community Policing Institutes (RCPIs) designed to build capacity for law enforcement agencies across the country to engage in community policing. This entry traces the development of the dynamic and innovative training model unique to community policing, the specific activities required to sustain the model, findings specific to the evaluation of the model, and the lessons learned through the RCPI experience—lessons that are critical to the history of community policing and problem solving.

History

The passage of the Violent Crime Control and Law Enforcement Act created the Office of Community Oriented Policing (COPS Office) within the U.S. Department of Justice. It was a time when many law enforcement and criminal justice professionals alike, in response to spiraling crime rates of the late 1980s and early 1990s, were saying that traditional police practices were failing to curb rises in violent crime. In fact, they went so far as to advocate for a new model of policing—community policing—which presented an alternative to the traditional professional policing model (during which police officers were expected to patrol the streets randomly, reactively responding to calls for service, and be typically evaluated by such measures as the numbers of arrests made, calls handled, and even the number of miles driven during a shift), and which would require a far different emphasis in police training.

When the legislation passed, the new COPS Office was charged with managing $8.8 billion in grant funding, specifically designated for law enforcement. The primary goal of the COPS Office was to increase the numbers of officers on the beat by 100,000 in order to respond to increases in violent crime but, importantly, to further their engagement in this new way of policing that was beginning to evolve and was capturing widespread attention. Preceded by other attempts to change policing, such as neighborhood or team policing, the community-focused model was identified with the problem-solving model developed by Herman Goldstein, it emphasized police engagement in proactive problem-solving partnerships with the community as a basic foundational core.

Further, it called for implementing an array of law enforcement agency organizational changes that would be necessary to make this model work. Finally, the unprecedented levels of grant funding, more easily accessible through the COPS Office in comparison to other grant opportunities, provided an incentive for transitioning to community policing.

Despite these incentives, it was recognized that community policing would require a different orientation in police training. That realization emerged at about the same time that many were recognizing that traditional police training models were becoming dated and somewhat complacent. Although there were some examples of new and creative training programs in police academies across the country, for the most part police training in 1994 had not adopted contemporary techniques of adult learning or learner-centered delivery methods. Further, while many of the 17,000 chiefs and sheriffs across the country concurred with the basic tenets of community policing, their 600,000 officers were asking, "What are we supposed to do and how do we do it?" Accordingly, if community policing was to become a reality, something far different and more innovative than earlier reforms would be needed for training law enforcement departments across the country.

Creating a New Training Model

Clearly the police training landscape was ripe for innovation, but equally important was the fact that the COPS Office was legislatively authorized to allot 3% of the overall budget—$35 million—for training and technical assistance. From the outset, however, the COPS Office was interested in more than change for change sake or establishing a training that would evolve as just one more program. Rather, a foundation that incorporated vision, mission, and strategy compatible with basic tenets of community policing was needed to make sure that the vision became a reality. In essence, a training program was needed that could be implemented quickly, that embraced the strategies of community policing, that would introduce innovation into a new paradigm for national training, and one that would be built upon the types of collaborative partnerships espoused by community policing. This paradigm would introduce ways to change police mind-sets and to develop officers to interact in

their communities in very different ways. Further, it would support cutting-edge curricula based on principles of community policing that addressed emerging issues in law enforcement and criminal justice. Finally, it would help law enforcement agencies make the organizational changes that would be required to implement a community policing philosophy and attendant strategies.

Because there was no time to complete a thorough needs assessment, informal stakeholder input was solicited. Soon the vision for a network of regional training institutes began to emerge that would be charged with not only focusing on the basic tenets of community policing but also practicing what they preached. Within that context, the centerpiece of each institute in the regional network would be an individual governing body comprised of a threefold partnership that included equal representation from law enforcement, criminal justice academics, and community members.

This multidisciplinary partnership group would be responsible for an institute from its very inception. Starting with the grant proposal stage and through the acceptance of the award, the governing partnership would then be responsible for organizing the basic foundational core of the institute and the processes that would provide for innovative community policing training across a respective region. Further, the partnership was encouraged to think outside the box in developing training that would change mindsets from those of the traditional policing models. In 1997, the vision became a reality and culminated in the awarding of thirty-five $1 million grants which created and launched the national network of the 35 RCPIs, designed to serve all 50 states and Puerto Rico, and to provide a national platform for training designed to change how police functioned both at the individual and organizational levels.

Developmental Requirements

Each institute had a governing board that would organize and manage the institute, including hiring a director; facilitating the implementation of community policing training; showcasing how the creation of a collaborative partnership was unique to this training model and reflected the core of community policing; and continuing to seek out partnerships with other local government agencies. Each governing board was also required to develop a core community policing curriculum that, with the exception of minor variations to account for regional differences, would be fairly similar across all institutes. Each institute was also responsible for developing a specialty area related to community policing, such as ethics and integrity; collaborative problem solving; rural community policing; community partnerships; technology innovations; organizational change; strategic implementation and management; and the problem-solving process SARA (scanning, analysis, response, assessment). Finally, the institutes were funded through cooperative agreements rather than grants, allowing the COPS Office to have some say in ensuring that these requirements were met.

Assessing Institute Performance

Over time, a range of criteria were developed to assess each RCPI and to make recommendations for continued funding. Beyond traditional monitoring for compliance issues, the criteria were as follows:

- Creating the ability to develop new or original curricula, utilizing different delivery formats, and continuing to seek new audiences for training
- Developing new initiatives or programs in response to emerging issues in law enforcement and community policing
- Maintaining a diverse, functioning governing board that would make programmatic and finance decisions; show leadership in decision making, problem solving, and/or personnel selection; and be able to guide the institute through time of change
- Ensuring equal and integral citizen participation in the products, services, and governance of the RCPI that was representative of the demographics of the region and engaging other local government agencies and community organizations as partners
- Making a significant impact on the implementation and institutionalization of community policing among law enforcement agencies and communities within its region
- Moving beyond the initial three-tiered partnership to engage new partners, expanding reach and programming, developing new networks, and taking innovative steps to increase their funding base

Program Evaluation

The RCPI network sustained a national evaluation conducted by Circle Solutions, Inc., at the request of the COPS Office. Following are the findings, based on 10 on-site assessments and case studies:

- The impact of RCPI training was greater in larger law enforcement organizations with mission and value statements that reflected community policing philosophy and practices, and where recruitment and promotional practices supported community policing principles and community collaboration.
- There was a need for supervisory roles and responsibilities to be clarified in agencies that were attempting to implement community policing, and the roles of first-line supervisors had not received enough focus in the training and technical assistance efforts.
- Civilian employees (especially dispatchers) were vital to an agency's community policing practices but frequently received no training.
- Labor unions and police associations needed to be engaged in the community policing planning and implementation processes, or else the training may not be accepted.

The on-site assessments and case studies also found that the RCPIs had accomplished the following:

- Enhanced the national community policing efforts
- Expanded the partnerships between law enforcement organizations and the communities they served in order to address the most difficult crime and disorder problems facing the community
- Developed and delivered community policing training programs that enhanced problem-solving and critical-thinking skills of patrol officers, their supervisors, and citizens
- Created learning environments that fostered multidisciplinary training with law enforcement officers, community leaders, and citizens
- Fostered integration of community policing into recruit training curricula
- Created the capacity to nurture the next generation of law enforcement leaders by

providing supervisory and midmanagement training that would not have been otherwise available

- Addressed emerging and critical issues facing law enforcement such as issues related to ethics and integrity, or those related to specific groups such as tribal policing

In 2003, the COPS Office reported that since the RCPIs were created, more than 280,000 law enforcement personnel, community members, and government leaders had been trained in the RCPIs that were strategically located throughout the country.

Current Status

In 2012, 16 institutes remain as viable training entities. However, their journey has not been easy given diminished budget resources and the events of 9/11, which shifted the law enforcement emphasis to intelligence-led policing. Within that context, the COPS Office worked with the Federal Bureau of Investigation and the Bureau of Justice Assistance to deliver state and local antiterrorism training through the RCPI structure. Reportedly, upward of 5,000 participants were trained in less than a year in that effort, suggesting that the RCPI network could shift gears and provide a platform for other training. In fact, there was some advocacy for using a model similar to the RCPI network for general training in homeland security issues, but that idea gained traction on a more limited basis.

Clearly, those institutes that survived were those that managed to continue to meet and grow the assessment criteria. Further, those that turned out to be more successful also found ways to expand their funding base. Those institutes that had relied solely on federal funding were the most vulnerable when the other changes started to occur.

Lessons Learned

The question could be asked: How much impact can any training have on changing an organization? Even when substantive management trainings are provided, we have come to learn that true organizational change comes from internal leadership as the driver of organizational transformation. Accordingly, dynamic and innovative training

provides a good foundation, but sustaining change needs to occur at all levels of the organization through institutionalized policy and practices. Further, these changes cannot be connected only to one individual, such as a charismatic chief or sheriff, or to one training initiative such as the RCPI network. In essence, changes in many variables have to be institutionalized in order for transformational organizational change to occur and dynamic and innovative training is a significant part of that process.

While policing was changing from the reactive to proactive status, which also incorporated prevention, the community policing and collaborative problem solving partnerships message needed to be shaped early on in order to change police mind-sets. The RCPIs became a network for distributing that message. However, though RCPI messaging raised the level of awareness of community policing, training that was different had to be delivered or else the COPS Office could lose credibility.

Through the many training sessions and the governing board meetings, it became clear that collaborative partnerships were about more than sitting in the same room together. Rather, the partners needed to view their collaboration as a dynamic process that accommodated changing roles and responsibilities.

A 2006 COPS Office Fact Sheet contended that when renowned universities, forward-thinking law enforcement organizations, and nationally focused community groups come together in a unique partnership focused on public safety, they can accelerate the growth of community policing as a law enforcement management philosophy throughout the nation. That same Fact Sheet indicated that by 2006, the RCPI network was reaching more than 70,000 individuals each year.

Conclusions

The advent of the regional network of community policing institutes was an outgrowth of the development of the national movement to engage in community policing and was supported by the passage of the Violent Crime Control and Law Enforcement Act of 1994. The legislation provided for the infusion of federal dollars to law enforcement agencies across the county and enabled the hiring of 100,000 community policing officers. But with that mission, came the need to find new and innovative ways to train officers across the country to ensure that they had the core competencies to engage in this type of policing and to literally change the mind-set of policing from "respond, control and back in service" to that of "work with the community to solve the problem and continually evaluate to assess what is being sustained or what may need to be modified."

The RCPI network made innovative training available to law enforcement personnel and their agencies throughout the country and 16 of the institutes continue to provide a wide range of training. The question remains, however, as to how that training led to institutionalization of community policing. Beyond training, there are a number of other variables that affect institutionalization and there are events that could not be predicted, such as 9/11 and the threats of terrorism, which altered the law enforcement portfolio. Despite such, some form of community policing seems to have held ground over these years, particularly where collaborative partnerships and community engagement predominated and where the RCPI leadership engaged in creative and innovative approaches to training as well as funding. Though currently it is a smaller network, 16 RCPIs remain open for business.

Ellen Scrivner

See also Community Oriented Policing Services, Office of; Implementation of Community Policing; Learning Organization; Police Training Officer (PTO) Program; Recruit Academy Training; Violent Crime Control and Law Enforcement Act of 1994

Further Readings

Goldstein, H. (1977). *Policing a free society*. Cambridge, MA: Ballinger.

Goldstein, H. (1990). *Problem-oriented policing*. New York, NY: McGraw-Hill.

Laszlo, A. T., Garner, J. H., Briscoe, G. O., Crute, D. G., McCampbell, M. S., & Rinehart, T. A. (2000). *Regional community policing institutes: National evaluation*. Washington, DC: U.S. Department of Justice, Office of Community Oriented Policing Services.

Roth, J. A., Ryan, J., & Koper, C. S. (2000, August). *National evaluation of the COPS program—Title 1 of the 1994 Crime Act*. Washington, DC: The Urban Institute.

Scrivner, E. (2005, October). Building training capacity for homeland security: Lessons learned from community policing. *The Police Chief, 72*(10), 26–30.

REPEAT VICTIMIZATION, COMMUNITY POLICING STRATEGIES FOR

Recurring, or repeat, victimization of the same targets constitutes a large proportion of total crime victimization. Reducing inequality of crime victimization among people and places by reducing repeat victimization makes for an efficient use of limited policing resources and a service to equity in the distribution of victimization amongst citizens. A developing research base suggests that, implemented intelligently, prevention of repeat victimization can be a viable and effective strategy in community policing. A lack of knowledge about and systematic undercounting of chronic victimization stand in the way of recognition of the value of the strategy. This entry explains what repeat victimization is and how that knowledge can provide myriad advantages to officers who are engaged in community policing and problem solving.

Repeat Victimization Defined

There are several essential facts about repeat victimization. In general, crime victimization is the best readily available predictor of subsequent victimization. Areas differ in amount of crime suffered in large measure because of their rates of repeat victimization, making repeat victimization important at both individual and area levels. The risk of repeat victimization tends to be highest in the days and weeks after an earlier victimization, making prompt police identification and response necessary to maximize prevention and detection opportunities.

There are two components that determine the extent of repeat victimization: the flag and boost components. The *flag element* refers to the features which predated the first victimization (e.g., poor home security flags a burglary opportunity). Thus, repeat victimization occurred because a first victimization occurred because of enduring features of the person or place at risk. One can think of school bullying and hate crimes as having a large flag component. The *boost element* reflects the fact that the experience of a first successful offense yields information (e.g., goods remaining to be stolen), which boosts the chances of a repeat by the same offender.

Broken windows theory is based upon a presumed boost element in repetition.

Recorded crime understates the number of repeat victimizations. Even victimization surveys do so, especially in regard to series of offenses committed by the same people in the same circumstances.

Knowing these facts can help police officers to protect their communities from crime, and may persuade police managers that the effort is worth making.

Repeat Victimization as Targeting Tool

Sting operations are attractive to the police because they identify precisely where and when a crime is going to take place. The Center for Problem-Oriented Policing specifies the elements of the sting as

- an opportunity or enticement to commit a crime, either created or exploited by police;
- a targeted likely offender or group of offenders for a particular crime type;
- an undercover or hidden police officer or surrogate, or some form of deception; and
- a "gotcha" climax when the operation ends with arrests.

Sting operations are controversial, particularly when carried out by media organizations, because they are considered entrapment by some and because they result in the commission of crimes that may not have taken place without the inducement to offend provided by the sting. They also by definition bypass prevention. All successful stings end with an offense being committed. The prevention element (if it exists) is indirect, operating only through the incapacitation or deterrence of those caught in the sting who would otherwise remain criminally active.

The starting point for sting operations is predictability of offending, usually manufactured by the police and hence liable to charges of entrapment. The prediction of offending, albeit imperfect, can be arrived at by other, less controversial means. Grossly unequal risk of victimization by crime is ubiquitous. Its most accessible index is prior victimization of the same victim or of nearby places or people. The role of repeat (and near-repeat) victimization in policing strategy is to take advantage of this rough predictor by dispensing policing and other preventive effort in proportion to presenting risk. One can think of the prevention of repeat victimization as a sort of mirror image of sting operations, both approaches being concerned with targeting police resources at the optimal time and place. The points of contrast are thus:

- Sting operations end with an arrest; repeat victimization strategies end with the prevention of chronic victimization.
- Sting operations *elicit* crime; repeat victimization strategies utilize variations in risk to *prevent* crime.

Three questions may suggest themselves to the pragmatic police officer:

1. How good is prior victimization as a predictor of repeat and near-repeat victimization?
2. Is there any evidence that the prevention of repeat and near-repeat victimizations can reduce crime overall?
3. Are there current police practices that would cease to be viable under a repeat victimization prevention strategy?

It may be prudent to deal with the third point first, since if there is a substantial downside, a repeat victimization strategy is doomed to failure unless the necessary practice changes are put in place. The examples in what follows are taken mostly from work on domestic burglary as the most researched offense type, with more general applicability discussed toward the end of this entry.

In an attempt to reassure and in the absence of relevant analyses, police officers attending a domestic burglary may assert that targeting of homes by burglars is random, and that "lightning doesn't strike twice." The advantage of such advice in the case of burglary is that when no subsequent burglary is suffered, anxiety is not felt by the resident family. However, burglary victims may indeed worry about repetition despite reassurance, and telling them that their risk of being burgled is temporarily elevated but that taking security measures will reduce the risk can be empowering. Their "locus of control" becomes more internal. British criminologist Mandy Shaw's interviews with crime victims leads her to draw a parallel between crime victimization and the experience of bereavement, with the sequence of stages toward recovery being disrupted in the event of repeat crimes suffered, engendering a sense of helplessness and dismay in the repeat victim.

A second change in practice that follows from an emphasis on repeat victimizations concerns information technology (IT) systems. As matters stand, it is often difficult for a police officer attending a call for service to become acquainted with the history of events at the address before arriving. This is particularly crucial in cases of possible domestic violence, where police action may be influenced by knowledge of the relevant history of a place or person. To be prescriptive, the necessary enabling IT conditions for a repeat victimization reduction strategy are as follows:

1. Names and addresses of complainants need to be uniquely specified so that attending officers are aware of relevant histories across crime types (e.g., not just burglary histories are relevant to an officer attending a burglary). Precise geocoding of incidents facilitates this.

2. A stringent data validation process is necessary after each call for service has been responded to.

3. Actions taken after previous victimizations, including legal orders currently in place, must be recorded and available to attending officers.

The change of mind-set that underpins the changes in procedure noted above is that recording a crime is seen as the start of a proactive process rather than the end of a reactive process. An analogy may be drawn with how medicine deals with heart attacks. Suffering a heart attack is a function of genetic and lifestyle factors and their interactions, most of which factors lie beyond the scope of the medical profession to change. A first heart attack having been suffered, the persuasive power of medical practitioners and their capacity to intervene is much greater. Likewise, a first burglary is a function of location and lifestyle, but marks out a time, person, and place at high risk that justifies action. Heart attacks are more common among those who have survived a first. Burglaries (and other offenses apart from murder) are more common in the aftermath of earlier offenses.

Crime Concentration

If crime is concentrated on people and places to only a modest extent, community policing to reduce repeat victimization would not be especially powerful. While precision is impossible because of the problems surrounding the data sources, a frequently recurring figure is that some 4% of the population suffers some 40% of crime. Only in the areas with the smallest crime is it the case that preventing repeat crimes would make little impact on total crime. There is also the issue of distributive justice to consider. Just as there is a moral case for good things to be equitably distributed among places and people, so one could argue a moral case for bad things, like crime victimization, to be distributed equitably among people and places. Attending to repeat victimization serves distributive justice at the individual level and at the area level, the latter because of the large contribution that chronic victimization makes to area inequalities in crime.

The conventional way of expressing economic or other inequality is by means of Lorenz curves and Gini coefficients, and these have been calculated to represent the degree of inequality in victimization by different crime types. These vary according to policing area, but the essential advice to those wishing to reduce crime in a community by reducing the suffering of those most chronically victimized is separately to measure crime incidence, crime prevalence, and crime concentration. Incidence (i) is a product of prevalence (p), being the proportion of people/places available to be victimized that are victimized, and concentration (c), which is the number of victimizations per victimized person or place, with

$$i = p^*c.$$

The need to separate prevalence and concentration in understanding crime trends and policing impacts can be illustrated by the study of domestic violence. Domestic violence is notoriously poorly reported. Thus an increase in the *prevalence* of reports of domestic violence is welcome. It generally means that more of those suffering the problem bring it to police attention. One study showed that the introduction of an improved service for victims of domestic violence was associated with an *increase* in the number of women reporting to the police (p). Because a decent service was now being offered, there was also a desirable *decrease* in *concentration (c)*, that is, the average number of calls made per complainant. However, the *increase* in prevalence alongside the *decrease* in concentration cancelled each other out when incidence was considered. The total volume of calls (i) remained the same, giving the impression that the initiative had no effect. In fact, that conclusion had been reached before the study showed otherwise.

While there may be skepticism about the extent of repeat victimization among police officers and policymakers, there seems to be no shortage of offender willingness to give reasons for repeating crimes against the same target. As noted in Ulrica Ericsson's 1995 article "Straight from the Horse's Mouth,"

> 76% said they had gone back to a number of houses after a varying period of time to burgle them between two and five times. The reasons given for returning to burgle a house were because the house was associated with low risk . . . they were familiar with the features of the house . . . the target was easily accessible . . . or to steal more goods in general. . . . The reasons for going back for goods were things they had left behind . . . replaced goods . . . and unhidden cash.

According to Ashton, Brown, Senior, and Pease in 1998, burglars contended:

> The house would be targeted again "a few weeks later" when the stuff had been replaced and because the first time had been easy. . . . It was a chance to get things which you had seen the first time and now had a buyer for.

> Once you have been into a place it is easier to burgle because you are then familiar with the layout, and you can get out much quicker.

> Keys to the door were usually hanging round, either on a shelf or the top of furniture near to the door in empty houses, so they used the keys to unlock the doors to get out and to use for the next time they broke in.

> X burgled his father's business three nights in a row. X had left home because he could not put up with the rules his father set. . . . X also burgled his parents' home. He bore a grudge against his parents. . . . X said he had burgled his parents' home four times.

In 1998, Ashton and colleagues further noted that car thieves also had fairly obvious reasons to offend repeatedly against the same target:

> X had stolen the stereo from the same car more than once. He would return to the same street and if he spotted the same car parked on the street he would take the stereo again if it had been replaced. . . . You get more money for brand new things.

And with armed robbers, Gill and Pease in 1998 found similar reasoning:

> It was so easy I went back ten days later.

> If you get a good result, you go back a second time.

> (I did) a factory and shop twice. It is easy. It's about twenty-five minutes before the alarm goes off, and the shop didn't have one. They didn't learn.

> It was easy. I knew the woman, and she helped me, so I did it twice.

The concentration of crimes across victims is typically underestimated, for reasons that are discussed later. Detailed national comparisons in rates of repetition are given in Figure 1, which shows the proportion of all crime captured by the International Crime Victimization Survey 2000 that were repeats. Thus, even with conservative estimates of rates of repeat victimization, the savings in crime potentially available are substantial, as are the distributive justice implications mentioned earlier.

Understanding Why Repeat Victimizations Are Underestimated

Perhaps the most central reason why repeat victimizations are underestimated is that police see engagement with the community as a whole rather than with crime victims as central in community policing. In a large survey by the U.S. Police Foundation and the National Center for Victims of Crime, the result was that while a majority of police executives believe there are benefits in involving the victim in community policing, most also report that when it comes to problem solving and crime prevention, it is more useful for officers to interact with community members without special attention to who has been a crime victim. This section details the obstacles facing a community policing innovator in garnering the information that would justify a focus on repeat victims.

It has been contended that the extent of repeat victimization is understated in official data and police perceptions. There are some general reasons why this is so, and there is a particular issue around

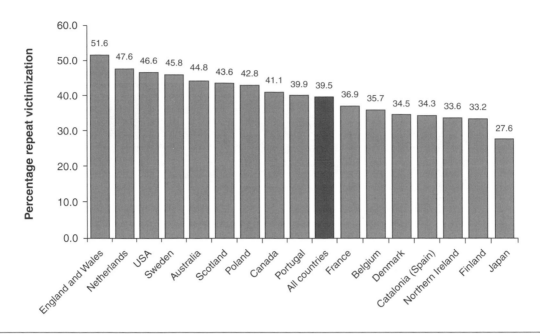

Figure I   Repeat Victimization by Country: ICVS 2000 Percentage of All Crimes That Are Repeats

Source: Farrell, G., Tseloni, A., & Pease, K. (2005). Repeat victimization in the ICVS and the NCVS. *Crime Prevention and Community Safety, 7(3),* 7–18.

Note: Switzerland excluded due to frequent absence of incidence rates.

"series" crimes (i.e., crimes of the same type believed to be the work of the same offender). While even conservative estimates in official data are enough to make crime reduction via the prevention of repeat victimizations an attractive strategy in community policing, it is important to spell out the reasons why police officers, both management and front-line personnel, may be misled into an underestimation of the extent of repeat victimization. General reasons include the following:

1. There can be inadequacies in police recording conventions, as in one case where the same hospital location had been entered in the crime information system in 17 different ways.

2. Conventionally, crime data is presented for a limited period, constituting a "time window." Repeat victimizations outside the time window are ignored, and the shorter the time window the greater the degree of underestimation.

3. The fragmentation of police work means that repeat victimization, however common, is rare in the experience of individual officers, who may be on different shifts or duties when repeats occur.

4. Repeat crimes against the same target by different means tend to be excluded from published reports (e.g., in reports of the British Crime Survey). This excludes targeting of the same people by different crimes, as, for example, in feuds and hate crimes.

Another issue is police treatment of series crimes (i.e., those reported in victimization surveys as being the same offense in similar circumstances, probably by the same offender). The prominence of these in the reports of victimization surveys is understated by devices such as limiting the number of events "permissible." So someone victimized in a series of 50 crimes may have the number of crimes they suffer truncated at five. The probable reason for this is the need to yield stable time trends that can be compared with trends in police recorded crime. This stability would be reduced by inclusion of a few chronically victimized respondents. While the benefit of this tactic is statistical convenience, the cost is the misrepresentation of the population's victimization profile. Table 1 shows the difference that would be made by including series crimes as respondents reported

Table 1   Crime in England and Wales in Thousands (BCS 2005–2006, crimes in last 12 months)

Crime Category	"Official" Crime Count (000's)	Actual Crime Count (000's)	% Difference When All Series Crimes Included
PROPERTY CRIME			
Vandalism	**2,731**	**3,376**	**23.6**
Vehicle vandalism	1,697	1,846	8.8
Other vandalism	1,034	1,528	47.8
Burglary	**733**	**877**	**19.7**
With entry	440	515	17
Attempts	293	362	23.6
With loss	315	342	8.7
No loss (incl. attempts)	418	535	27.9
All vehicle thefts	**1,731**	**1,779**	**2.8**
Theft from vehicle	1,121	1,159	3.4
Theft of vehicles	185	185	0
Attempts of and from	425	436	2.7
Bicycle theft	**439**	**446**	**1.7**
Other household theft	**1,158**	**1,361**	**17.5**
Theft from the person	**576**	**584**	**1.4**
Snatch theft from person	71	71	0
Stealth theft from person	504	512	1.6
Other theft	**1,196**	**1,213**	**1.4**
VIOLENCE			
Common assault	**1,490**	**2,956**	**98.4**
Wounding	**547**	**1,060**	**93.8**
Robbery	**311**	**333**	**7.2**
All BCS violence*	**2,420**	**4,421**	**82.7**
Domestic violence	357	857	140
Acquaintance	817	2,093	156.2
Stranger	863	1,067	23.6
Mugging	382	404	5.8
ALL HOUSEHOLD CRIME	**6,792**	**7,838**	**15.4**
ALL PERSONAL CRIME	**4,120**	**6,250**	**51.7**

Source: Farrell, G., & Pease, K (2007). Crime in England and Wales: More violence and more chronic victims. *Civitas Review,* 4, 1–4.

Note: *All BCS Violence includes common assault, wounding, robbery, and snatch theft.

them to British Crime Survey interviewers. Similarly major differences are made in the U.S. national victimization survey by adopting restrictive conventions on how series crimes are dealt with.

The proper representation of series crimes in the official depiction of victimization strengthens the case for community policing strategies centered on the prevention of repeat victimization. Before moving on to the key question about whether such a strategy is likely to be effective, a few final considerations are presented here:

- There is some suggestion that, at least for burglars and bank robbers, offenders who return are more prolific or commit more serious offenses than those who do not. This means that detection efforts directed at those who commit repeat crimes will automatically target priority offenders.
- Historically, victim support and crime prevention advice have been separated. The repeat victimization literature suggests that the same people need both and at the same time. Community policing centered on repeat victimization reconciles the two policing strands.
- The notion of repeat victimization can be extended to consideration of virtual repeats, (i.e., offenses against targets with the same salient features). Stores with identical layouts invite the same tactics so that victimization of one store is equivalent to victimization of any other. A computer operating system with a security weakness when installed in many homes and businesses affords the opportunity for virtual repeat crimes. In short, the notion of virtual repeat crimes is helpful in establishing and responding to accurate risk landscapes.
- A substantial literature has developed on *near-repeat victimizations*. It is now clear that risk spreads across a limited area for a limited time. This spatio-temporal risk transmission invites optimized predictive patrolling and community policing effort proportional to risk across areas. Space precludes attention to the near-repeat literature, but it has contributed greatly to repeat victimization research. The literature on near-repeat victimizations represents the offender as optimal forager (a term meaning that the offender will attempt to maximize benefit and minimize risk by keeping time spent searching

for victims or places to burglarize to a minimum), an important heuristic device in considering near-repeat crime patterns and how to disrupt them.

Preventing Repeat Victimizations

All the above would be irrelevant if the prevention of repeat victimization were not realizable in practice. A recent systematic review concludes that the evidence shows that repeat victimization can be prevented and crime can be reduced. Over all the evaluations, crimes decreased by one-sixth in the prevention condition compared with the control condition. Appropriately tailored and implemented situational crime prevention measures, such as target hardening (strengthening security of buildings) and neighborhood watch programs, appear to be the most effective. The effectiveness of these crime prevention measures increased as the degree of implementation increased. There were many problems of implementation, including poor tailoring of interventions to crime problems, difficulty of recruiting, training, and retaining staff, breakdown in communications, data problems, and resistance to tactics by potential recipients or implementers. The caveats about implementation are not surprising, and the scope for reduction certainly exceeds what has been achieved to date. The expansion of repeat victimization research and prevention measures to deal with near-repeat victimizations, and the achievements to date even when the scale of the repeat victimization problem has not been properly recognized, give cause for optimism with regard to preventing repeat victimization and preventing crime.

Ken Pease

See also Broken Windows Theory; Crime Displacement; Crime Mapping; Domestic Violence, Community Policing Strategies for; Hot Spots

Further Readings

Ashton, J., Brown, I., Senior, B., & Pease, K. (1998). Repeat victimisation: Offender accounts. *International Journal of Risk, Security and Crime Prevention, 3,* 269–280.

Ericsson, U. (1995). Straight from the horse's mouth. *Forensic Update, 43,* 23–25.

Farrell, G., & Buckley, A. (1999, February). Evaluation of a UK police domestic violence unit using repeat victimisation as a performance indicator. *Howard*

Journal of Criminal Justice and Crime Prevention, 38(1), 42–53.

Gill, M., & Pease, K. (1998). Repeat robbers: How are they different? In M. Gill (Ed.), *Crime at work: Studies in security and crime prevention.* Leicester, England: Perpetuity Press.

Grove, L. E., Farrell, G., Farrington, D. P., & Johnson, S. D. (2012, June 11). *Preventing repeat victimization: A systematic review.* Stockholm: Swedish National Council for Crime Prevention.

Johnson, S. D., Summers, L., & Pease, K. (2009). Offender as forager? A direct test of the boost account of victimization. *Journal of Quantitative Criminology, 25*(2), 181–200.

Pease, K. (1998). *Repeat victimisation: Taking stock.* Crime Detection and Prevention Paper 90. London, England: Home Office.

Shaw, M. (2001). Time heals all wounds. *Crime Prevention Studies, 12,* 165–197. Retrieved from http://www .popcenter.org/library/crimeprevention/volume_12/10-Shaw.pdf

Tseloni, A., & Pease, K. (2005). Population inequality: The case of repeat crime victimization. *International Review of Victimology, 12*(1), 75–90. doi: 10.1177 /026975800501200105

RESTORATIVE JUSTICE

Restorative justice is a philosophy that places emphasis on the harm caused by crime. It promotes responses to crime that seek to address these harms and hold offenders accountable for their actions by imposing sanctions drafted in a collaboration that includes the victim, community members, and the justice system. A restorative approach seeks to identify what needs to be done to correct problems caused by crime through recognition and understanding between the offender, the victim, and the community. Rather than utilizing the justice system for the sole purpose of punishing the offender, a restorative approach suggests that the justice system should impose sanctions on the offender that address the overall harm to the victim and the community caused by crime. This entry discusses the basic tenets of restorative justice, including the values and principles promoted by this model, provides examples of restorative sanctions, and concludes with a discussion addressing the role of community policing in the implementation of restorative justice at the community level.

Understanding the Restorative Justice Model

As opposed to a retributive model, in which crime is viewed only as a violation of the law and justice for the victim is achieved through the punishment of the offender, a restorative model considers crime in a more comprehensive manner. This theory recognizes that crime causes harm not only to the victim, but also to the offender and the community in which the crime took place. Restorative justice aims to identify the harm caused by crime, how this harm can be repaired, and how it can be prevented in the future.

A growing interest in the philosophy of restorative justice coincides with increasing interests in community building, concerns regarding overcriminalization and increasing levels of incarceration, and an increased focus on victims' rights. Rather than focusing on the determination of guilt of the offender, handing down punitive sanctions, and forcing the victim to be a passive participant in the justice process, the restorative approach advocates viewing crime in terms of harms, thus encouraging the punishment of the offender to be the repair of the harms that were caused. Although some believe this approach can be used only to remedy minor crimes, restorative justice techniques have been successfully applied to violent crimes as well as cases of domestic violence, sexual abuse, and child abuse.

For restorative justice to be successful, the victim and the community must play active roles in the restoration process. Crime can foment harm in many different ways, including physical, financial, emotional, and psychological. Therefore, it is necessary that all those who have been harmed by the crime or will be involved in the reparation of harm participate in the restoration process. Restorative justice recognizes that the harms caused by crime are often overlooked by the justice system or unable to be addressed by the system alone. By engaging the offender, the victim, and the community, the restorative justice model acknowledges that crime is more than just an act of violating the law; it is the violation of people.

Values and Principles of Restorative Justice

Advocates of the restorative philosophy have outlined various values and principles that have been widely accepted as key to the successful implementation of restorative justice. First, it is imperative that crime be viewed as a source of harm to the victim, as well as the general public, rather than just as a violation against criminal law. Crime should be handled as a threat to community safety. Second, the chosen response to crime should be one grounded on the reparation of harm that was done to the victim and the community and must be victim centered. By promoting a victim-centered approach, the restorative justice model seeks to eliminate feelings of alienation from the justice process on the part of the victim. In addition, it also provides an opportunity to help the victim gain a sense of empowerment that may have otherwise been taken from them by the offender.

Restorative justice promotes an equal concern for the offender as well as for the victim. This model encourages the condemnation of criminal behavior, but not of the offender. The restorative model seeks to educate the offender about the consequences associated with the crime that has been committed and hold the offender accountable to the victim, community, and to self. It is also important that the offender understands and acknowledges the wrongdoing during this process and must accept responsibility for committing the offense, as well as accept the costs associated with it. Once obligations have been agreed to by the parties involved, the offender should be encouraged by others to carry out and fulfill these obligations. It is important that the offender not view these obligations as harm to self, but rather as reparations for the wrongdoing and an opportunity to make good for the deviant behavior.

The community plays a large role in the success of the restorative justice model. It is important that community members recognize that they are also victims of the crimes perpetrated by offenders in their community. Crime may cause community members to feel unsafe in their surroundings and fearful of others in the community. These fears can negatively impact the overall quality of life in the community. Therefore, community members are encouraged to participate in the restoration process by supporting the victim in the recovery process, as well as in assisting the offender in repairing the harm done. By remaining active in this process, community members can voice their concerns and ensure they are addressed when proposing restorative sanctions for the offender.

Restorative justice requires the collaboration of the victim, the offender, and the community to help reintegrate the offender into the community rather than engage in behavior that encourages the isolation of the offender. This requires that both the victim and the community trust the offender to recognize the offense, to do the best possible to repair the damaged sustained, and to make a significant life change toward an anticrime lifestyle. The obligations given to the offender as a means of repairing the harm caused should be realistic and achievable and aim to restore trust in the individual. Through this collective effort, the restorative justice model is a means through which the victim and the community can once against trust the offender and successfully facilitate reintegration into society.

When agreeing to the terms of the reparations, those involved in the restorative process should remember that justice in this model is grounded in harm reduction, peacemaking, and the promotion of a safe community, not revenge. It is also important to keep in mind that the goal of restorative justice is to repair the harm of the crime. This is very different from many of the traditional goals upheld by criminal justice system, such as deterrence, incapacitation, and rehabilitation. What separates restorative justice from other philosophies is not the application of justice, but rather its intent. The purpose of this process is to recognize and address the harm caused by the crime and foster recovery through conflict resolution and communication involving the victim, the offender, and the community.

Restorative Justice in Action

Restorative justice encourages a balanced approach when drafting the obligations the offender must complete in the aftermath of the crime. These obligations must reflect a form of restoration toward the victim and the community, improve the competency of the offender, encourage reintegration, and promote community safety. By addressing these issues, restorative justice attempts to find a balance between the rights, responsibilities, and needs of the victim, the offender, the community, and the government.

Three common practices found under the restorative justice model are victim-offender mediation, family group conferencing, and community restorative boards. Victim-offender mediation provides the victim with an opportunity to communicate with the offender directly regarding the harm experienced as a result of the crime. It also affords an opportunity for the offender to understand the extent of the damage caused by the crime. The mediation process can be extremely emotional for all parties involved, but it provides an environment in which communication can be made between the victim and the offender. This interaction may also serve as a time when an agreement can be made between the two parties regarding the consequences of the crime the offender must repair.

Family group conferencing is an environment similar to victim-offender mediation, but allows for the participation of family members of both the victim and the offender, as well as members of the community. With the assistance of a mediator, participants are provided with the opportunity to discuss the direct and indirect effects of the crime they experienced personally and participate in the negotiation of consequences for the offender to accept in order to repair the damage caused by the crime. Family group counseling concludes when participants agree to accept the offender back into the community and assist in the reintegration process.

Community restorative boards provide community members with another opportunity to participate in the restorative process. This board generally comprises selected members of the community. The board listens to feedback provided by the victim and the offender and, after doing so, creates a list of proposed sanctions that the offender must complete. The offender is asked to report back to the board regarding progress on a regular basis.

Restorative Justice and Community Policing

There are many parallels between restorative justice and community policing, a significant one being that both restorative justice and community policing challenge philosophies that have been widely accepted and adopted in the criminal justice system for years. Both movements seek to provide the system with alternatives to crime control that emphasize citizen engagement, community support, collaboration, and problem-solving techniques. Restorative justice and community policing encourage the public to view crime in terms of individual and community needs and seek to ensure that these needs are met in a collaborative manner.

Police departments that have adopted a community policing framework are equipped with problem-solving techniques and communication skills that lend themselves to restorative justice sanctions. The occupational requirements of police officers allows them the opportunity to view how crime affects all those involved: They see victims who feels helpless and ignored; offenders who enter the system, only to exit with the same deviant thoughts with which they entered; and a community that is fearful and frustrated by the influence of crime on their surroundings and overall quality of life. Insight into these varied perspectives gives police officers the opportunity to play a key role in the implementation of restorative justice through the use of community policing techniques.

For police to find success in the adoption of restorative justice sanctions, they must establish a positive relationship with the community and its members. A strong relationship between the community and the police is also encouraged in the community policing philosophy. A sense of trust in the police must be fostered within the community in order for members to feel comfortable reporting crime, accepting the assistance of the police, and participating in such restorative activities as victim-offender mediation, family conferencing, or community restorative boards. It is important that community members trust in law enforcement to make decisions that are best for all parties involved, and it is imperative that the police make these decisions while simultaneously attending to the interests of the victim, the offender, and the community as a whole.

The involvement of the police in restorative sanctions has the ability to strengthen the relationship between law enforcement and the community. Victims, offenders, and community members that see police participation in such activities may think more highly of the police and view police officers as true problem solvers. Police departments and individual officers can benefit from the information obtained during group reparation activities. For example, by participating in a family group conferencing session, a police officer has the opportunity to learn about the harm caused by the crime from the victim, potential reasons for committing the crime from the offender, and community safety concerns from the general public. Active participation in restorative justice techniques provides officers with a chance to interact with community members, listen to their needs, and address their concerns accordingly. Officers must view themselves as more than enforcers of the law; they too are members of the community they serve.

Collaboration is a principle found in both restorative justice and community policing philosophies.

In addition to working with the community, a restorative approach to crime encourages all areas of the criminal justice system to work together, including the police, prosecutors, courts, and corrections. No one individual or group has all of the answers needed to solve every problem encountered in the criminal justice system. This collaborative effort among agencies has the ability to yield a diverse collection of problem-solving techniques, measures, and proposed solutions that can then be tailored to meet the needs of each individual case.

Restorative justice and community policing share the common belief that community involvement and organized community groups have the ability to positively impact crime control and the success of restorative sanctions. Police officers and community members must work together to identify problems and propose solutions through collaborative problem solving. They must also come together to ensure that the needs of the victim, the offender, and the community are met throughout the restorative process. The philosophies of restorative justice and community policing can come together to encourage action, change, and solutions that seek to prevent crime and repair the damage it causes at the local level.

Jordan C. Pickering

See also Community, Definition of; Community Cohesion and Empowerment; Community Justice; Neighborhood Associations; Police-Community Relations; Youthful Offenders, Community Policing Strategies for

Further Readings

Braithwaite, J. (1999). Restorative justice. In M. Tonry (Ed.), *The handbook of crime and punishment* (pp. 323–344). New York, NY: Oxford University Press.

Braithwaite, J. (2002). *Restorative justice and responsive regulation.* New York, NY: Cambridge University Press.

Braithwaite, J. (2007). Encourage restorative justice. *Criminology and Public Policy, 6*(4), 689–696. doi: 10.1111/j.1745–9133.2007.00459

London, R. (2003). The restoration of trust: Bringing restorative justice from the margins to the mainstream. *Criminal Justice Studies, 16*(3), 175–195.

London, R. (2011). *Crime, punishment, and restorative justice.* Boulder, CO: First Forum Press.

Martin, M. E. (2006). Restoring justice through community policing. *Criminal Justice Policy Review, 17*(3), 314–329. doi: 10.1177/0887403405284736

Nicholl, C. G. (1999). *Community policing, community justice, and restorative justice: Exploring the links for the delivery of a balanced approach to public safety.* Washington, DC: U.S. Department of Justice, Office of Community Oriented Policing Services.

Umbreit, M. S. (2001). *The handbook of victim-offender mediation: An essential guide for practice and research.* San Francisco, CA: Jossey-Bass.

ROLES, CHIEF EXECUTIVES'

The chief executive in law enforcement has many titles. In most municipalities, the title is *chief of police* and the position is usually appointed by a city manager or mayor with the concurrence of the city council; in counties, it is *sheriff* and is an elected position; in state organizations such as highway patrols, it may be *colonel* and appointed by the governor. Other titles such as *commissioner* or *superintendent* may be used, mostly in large organizations. Irrespective of which title is used, the chief executive officer is responsible for the total operation of a law enforcement agency. This entry examines the indispensable role of the police chief executive in developing, implementing, and maintaining community policing and problem solving, some impediments police chief executives may encounter in this process, and structural changes in the organization that may have to be put in place in order to accommodate this policing strategy.

The Traditional Role of the Chief Executive

Law enforcement executives are responsible to many factions and their roles change depending on to which faction they are responding. The most obvious faction is the law enforcement agency in which they work. The chief executive is expected to protect the organization and employees from inappropriate influences, develop future leaders for succession, create a career path for employees, maintain ethical standards for all employees at all levels, and provide resources and leadership that allows the agency to meet community expectations and to progress forward so that it may meet the unforeseen challenges of the future.

Chief executives are also responsible to the communities served by their agencies. They are expected to communicate with the community in a timely fashion and to be open and honest regarding all topics. The community expects to work with the police in a partnership and for the police to understand community needs. Chief executives must also mediate differences between what the community expects and what the agency can or should offer in the way of services.

Another faction is the responsibility to the municipal, county, or state government of which the agency is a part. The governing entity expects the chief executive to deliver quality service to the community, be realistic in resource needs, and be responsive to concerns of other department members as well as the political leaders' requests and inquiries. This is not an easy task, as the government entity usually consists of several elected and appointed public officials with diverse agendas. Chief executives must navigate these political waters yet still function in an ethical and professional manner.

Chief executives are ultimately responsible to the law enforcement profession itself. Executives in law enforcement are expected to provide leadership to the profession as a whole, develop leaders in their organizations, maintain or raise professional standards and training, and add to professional knowledge of the field.

While the traditional role of the chief executive remains essentially the same, it has added responsibilities in a community-oriented policing and problem-solving (COPPS) model.

The Role of Chief Executive in Community Policing

The role of the chief executive in community policing is extremely diverse. It begins with a specific and consistent vision of what community policing and problem solving means to the organization. While the chief executive is responsible for providing a vision, the formulation of the vision will include a broad spectrum of stakeholders from within and without the organization. The vision may not be an exact roadmap, but represents the ultimate goal. It also takes into consideration the extreme changes to the organization as a result of the new philosophy as well as the time required to implement change.

Community policing is a complex process that can take years to fully accomplish.

A clear mandate to the organization that outlines the responsibilities of all employees will help to avoid many mistakes. Employees may believe that community policing is not their responsibility because they are not part of the patrol division, which is often the primary focus for community policing efforts. The chief executive can prevent confusion by communicating the specific as well as the general responsibilities to the entire organization. Written instructions, formal and informal meetings, and regular updates of progress can enhance successful implementation. Chief executives and upper management who are consistent in their application of the model will also help ensure successful implementation.

A COPPS planning process is structured, yet still allows flexibility in design as issues arise. The chief executive is involved in all stages of planning. At first, the executive selects the right people to be involved in the process, people who are knowledgeable about the COPPS model and are dedicated to a successful outcome. Next, resources are acquired for adequate planning. A pilot program is then tested, which may result in redesigning the concept, followed by an assessment of the impact community policing may have on the organization. It is important that the chief executive be willing to admit mistakes if something does not work and make changes. Not everything will work the first time, nor does something that works elsewhere always work locally. If mistakes are not corrected and faulty procedures replaced, the model may lack credibility with employees as well as the community.

The chief executive's relationship with middle managers is a key issue in implementing a successful COPPS model. Middle managers in any organization are often resistant to change. The change to a community policing philosophy has many potential setbacks, the most common of which is the lack of support by middle managers. The chief executive can turn this liability into an asset by defining the role of the middle manager as a key component of community policing. Providing middle managers with ample training gives them the skills and knowledge to do the job. Likewise, involving middle managers in the planning, development, implementation, and assessment processes increases buy-in to the new philosophy as well as their credibility with subordinates. The relationship between upper and middle management will ultimately take on the format of consultative relationships, which supports a problem-solving approach to community policing.

Impediments to Innovation

There are always impediments to any innovation that is being considered for adoption. To successfully implement a community policing model, the chief executive must remain aware of certain impediments to it.

The definition of *community policing and problem solving* may be a source of confusion. Thus, it is imperative that the definition be established from the very beginning in a clear and specific fashion that precludes employees and others from finding a reason to reject the model. Including in-depth descriptions of the model rather than popular phrases or buzz terms can be helpful. Community policing is often mistaken with public relations. If this happens, then the model may fail.

Some terms found in community policing may also need to be defined, such as *partnership* and *problem solving*. Partnership is sometimes thought of as an unnecessary influence by the community rather than the idea of working together to solve problems. The chief executive can point out that having a partnership with the community does not involve having citizens direct police operations. Rather, it refers to engaging the community in deciding which problems to work on and how resources should be deployed. The community does not make the final decision but acts in a consultative mode for the police. It can also be advantageous to avoid defining community policing as something that is opposed to "traditional" policing. Community policing can be integrated with the traditional policing roles as much as practicable, but there may be conflicts that need to be mediated. After successful implementation, though, there will be one model of policing: community policing and problem solving.

The chief executive determines whether the community policing effort will be generalized to the entire department or specific to a community policing function. The latter is often difficult to maintain and can lead to noncommunity policing personnel to disregard the model and continue to operate the way they always have. A general model may take more work and consume more time for planning and implementation, but may ultimately solve many problems, such as deployment of personnel and material resources. In the general model, all employees are part of the community policing effort.

A major impediment to the adoption of the COPPS model is middle management resistance or indifference. Under the community policing model, upper management, at one end of the rank spectrum, see the benefits from the positive image generated by partnerships and problem-solving activities. At the other end of the rank spectrum, the first-line personnel see that they have additional power and authority. Middle managers, however, may focus on the loss of authority and the added responsibilities that seem to come with implementation of the new philosophy. The chief executive will need to work vigorously to dispel these notions and replace them with the positive outlook necessary to overcome resistance. Traditionally, middle management roles have been undefined compared to upper management, supervision, and first-line officers. They have also been in a unique position of controlling the delegation of authority from upper management and deciphering policies and procedures for the line-level personnel. In a community policing environment, chief executives are positioned well to redefine middle management roles so that they become an integral part of the process and become a positive tool for executive oversight of the organization.

There may also be a problem of employee resistance at all levels. This may stem from loyalty to the present image of the agency, a misunderstanding of what community policing is, conflict between management and line personnel, or labor issues. Another factor that may initiate employee resistance is the failure to treat internal employees as "customers." Whatever the issue may be, the chief executive will need to constantly monitor the situation both inside the agency and outside. Resistance to innovation can be caused by various factors, many of which are determined by local conditions, history of the agency, and political situations. This is an additional reason why proper communications is important. If chief executives are talking to everyone, they will not be surprised by resistance from any group.

A lack of team focus can obscure the vision and goals the chief executive is trying to accomplish. It is sometimes easier to give huge responsibilities to a few individuals who can be trusted to do the work. By doing this, conflicts can occur, which may lead to substandard results and even sabotage, intended or otherwise. Planning, developing, implementing, and assessing the COPPS model is a tremendous amount of work. Chief executives are responsible for ensuring that the work is distributed throughout the organization and monitored by middle and upper management personnel who have received proper training and are dedicated to making the changes work.

Leadership

Leadership has diverse meanings depending on its application to specific situations. Generally, though, *to lead* also means to influence others to solve problems. The chief executive provides leadership for the COPPS process, but also creates an environment that facilitates the development of leaders who will move the process of innovation forward by their own initiatives. This may be encouraged by linking rewards to those who engage in innovative activities that enhance the desired changes, treating well-intentioned mistakes as learning opportunities, developing external support groups for resources and support, and institutionalizing long-term partnerships so that they are sustained during the political changes that tend to affect law enforcement agencies.

Developing leaders at all levels of the organization is of paramount importance to successful innovation. If leadership is considered to be influencing others rather than command and control, then it is possible for any employee in the organization to be a leader. By increasing the number of leaders, the number of resources available to the chief executive to accomplish the mission is increased significantly. The chief executive should consider how leadership in the line, supervisor, and middle management ranks would serve as a multiplying effect that increases the opportunities for success.

Linking rewards refers more to recognition and delegated authority than to monetary compensation. The chief executive is in a position to publicly recognize the work of those who support and further the organization's ability to engage in community policing. This may include individual and group meetings with these employees on a regular basis, announcements in department newsletters of their accomplishments, having employees make presentations in town hall meetings and appear before governmental bodies.

Failing forward is a process that allows people to make mistakes and learn from them rather than be chastised over the results of honest intentions. This concept is a key element of the community policing–based Police Training Officer (PTO) Program. For employees to take chances and engage in innovative activities, they must believe that upper management will support their efforts and react to mistakes in a positive and constructive manner.

External entities such as the media, the general population, and community special interest groups may influence the outcomes of any change that is being considered. The chief executive can develop relationships with these groups to minimize potential barriers to organizational change. Early in the planning stages, the chief executive can make efforts to meet with these groups and explain what community policing is, how it will impact the community, and what the process will be to implement the philosophy, taking care to specifically address crime, response to calls for service, resources needed, and opportunities that are available to the community as a result of their partnerships with the police.

An important external influence that the chief executive may face is the pressure brought by elected political officials. Community policing and problem solving is a long-term strategy that takes time to be completely accepted by the police and the community they serve. Political agendas tend to have much shorter timetables; consequently, they may interfere with the successful outcomes desired. The chief executive can meet with elected officials regularly and actively recruit governmental officials such as city or county managers and department directors to become part of the change process as well. These people may act as ambassadors for the community policing model once they understand that it will positively affect their areas of responsibility.

The Structural Change of the Organization

As preparation for the change to community policing, the chief executive may find it necessary to assess the structure of the organization. In such an assessment, every aspect of the organization should be considered, beginning with the entrance requirements for new officers to reflect changes in the police role. Community policing requires officers who are educated problem solvers, with the ability to work with community groups and form partnerships, analyze issues to determine proper solutions to problems, communicate intelligently, and be self-motivated to actively pursue issues that impact quality of life in the community. A job-task analysis of the new police role can help identify those characteristics that will be needed by successful police applicants. The chief executive works with civil service and human resources personnel to establish the proper selection process necessary for community policing. As part of this assessment, the performance evaluation process must reflect the new job description, which will also facilitate the progression of the community policing philosophy in the rest of the organization.

Once new officers are hired, they undergo recruit training in the police academy. Police academies often employ traditional military-style training techniques in their curriculum. The community policing model demands a curriculum that is more in tune with the new role of a police officer. The chief executive may need to work with other executive officers in neighboring agencies to change the curriculum if the police academy functions as a joint operation. The state agency that oversees police certification must also be included in the process of change.

The next step, and perhaps the most critical in the training environment, is the field training program. The field training program is that step in which the trainee is exposed to the community and operates as a beat officer under the tutelage of a senior officer. A relatively new approach to field training that incorporates community policing and problem solving is known as the Police Training Officer (PTO) Program. This program is responsible for mentoring the trainee and facilitating the application of the skills, knowledge, and abilities learned in the academy to the real world. The chief executive is responsible for ensuring that the field training program is one that is suited to community policing. Many field training programs are modifications of the original field training officer (FTO) model and include community policing as a key element; however, many are still using the original program that was created in the late 1960s. Chief executives may elect to modify the field training program to reflect the needs of a community policing agency or they may decide to adopt a model such as the PTO program, which was designed specifically for the COPPS model.

Chief executives may find that they also need to analyze the shape of the organization. Law enforcement agencies tend to be hierarchical organizations that have numerous rank levels such as chief, assistant chief, deputy chief, major, captain, lieutenant, sergeant, corporal, senior officer, and officer. While these offer career advancement opportunities in many cases, they also provide numerous bottlenecks to communications efforts. The trend with community policing departments is to flatten the organizational pyramid. This is accomplished by melding some rank levels together and redefining the roles of those positions. The goal is to delegate more of the decision making to the beat officers and facilitate communications both upward and downward through the hierarchy.

Management and leadership styles should reflect the values and philosophy of community policing. In community policing, beat officers have more than just responsibility for community policing efforts at the line level; they also have the power and authority to make decisions. This "inverting of the power pyramid" is necessary to deliver service in a timely manner, activate the partnership between the police and the community, and operationalize the community policing model as it was originally intended.

Structural change may go farther than just that of the police agency. Because community policing will affect any governmental agency that interacts with the police, it is wise for the chief executive to brief all department heads on the community policing model and how it may impact their operations.

While organizational culture may not be structural, it is certainly affected by structure and, consequently, affects the total organization. As the philosophy of community policing is expressed in the behavior of the employees, the culture of the organization will change. Culture is the sum of the behavioral and material aspects of the organization and evolves as an outcome of numerous factors. The chief executive cannot direct culture to be a specific thing, but rather can guide its evolution with proper leadership, policies, training, and discipline. The most important thing is for the chief executive to be aware of organizational culture and how it is either changing to accommodate the model or remaining the same and blocking the changes.

Important Questions

Chief executives will be judged by their actions and whether they adhere to the same principles of community policing when they are performing their jobs.

Do they communicate with all parties involved? Do they adhere to a strict chain of command? Are they participative in their approach to problem solving? Do they delegate authority? Do they accept honest mistakes? Are they team players? These and other questions may be answered if chief executives practice community policing as administrators.

Community policing and problem solving is not only a philosophy or model, it is a way of thinking and doing police work that is encompassed laterally and vertically throughout the organization and intimately in the culture of the agency. Policies, procedures, rules and regulations, training, promotion, performance evaluations all entail community policing as a framework. The ultimate decision that chief executives need to make is whether or not they are going to personally practice what they are asking others to do. If they consider their role as a community policing agent, then community policing will become a pervasive belief throughout the organization.

Jerry Hoover

See also Agency Mission and Values, Changes in; Community Policing, Discretionary Authority Under; Community Policing and Problem Solving, Definition of; Decentralizing the Organization/Organizational Change; Directed Patrol, Studies of; Implementation of Community Policing; Measuring Officer Performance; Mentoring; Police Training Officer (PTO) Program; Roles, First-Line Supervisors'; Roles, Middle Managers'; Roles, Officers'

Further Readings

Ellison, J. (2006, April). Community policing: Implementation issues. *FBI Law Enforcement Bulletin, 75*(4), 12–16.

Gaines, L. K. (1994). Community-oriented policing: Management issues, concerns, and problems. *Journal of Contemporary Criminal Justice, 10*(1), 17–35.

Geller, W. A., & Swanger, G. (1995). *Managing innovation in policing: The untapped potential of the middle manager.* Washington, DC: U.S. Department of Justice, National Institute of Justice, Police Executive Research Forum.

Greene, J. R., Bergman, W. T., & McLaughlin, E. J. (1994). Implementing community policing: Cultural and structural change in police organizations. In D. P. Rosenbaum (Ed.), *The challenge of community policing: Testing the promises* (pp. 92–109). Thousand Oaks, CA: Sage.

Hill, C. E. (2005, September). How to build a culture. *Law & Order,* 142–146.

Kelling, G. L., & Bratton, W. J. (1993, July). Implementing community policing: The administrative problem. NCJ 141236. *Perspectives on Policing, 17,* 1–11. Washington, DC: U.S. Department of Justice, National Institute of Justice.

Morash, M., & Ford, J. K. (Eds.). (2002). *The move to community policing: Making change happen.* Thousand Oaks, CA: Sage.

Robin, G. D. (2000) *Community policing: Origins, elements, implementation, assessment.* Lewiston, NY: Mellen Press.

Schafer, J. A. (2001). *Community policing: The challenges of successful organizational change.* New York, NY: LFB Scholarly.

Trojanowicz, R. C., & Bucqueroux, B. (1998). *Community policing: How to get started.* Cincinnati, OH: Anderson.

Vito, G. F., Walsh, W. F., & Kunselman, J. (2004). Community policing: The middle manager's perspective. *Police Quarterly, 6,* 1–22. Thousand Oaks, CA: Sage.

ROLES, FIRST-LINE SUPERVISORS'

Police supervisors make up the important link between a police organization's managerial layers and the layer of the organization that operates on the street and directly enforces the law. Supervisors are often referred to as *first-line* or *field* supervisors because they must supervise their subordinates while they are in the field and also conducting police fieldwork themselves. Thus, supervisors operate on a thin line between manager and street-level practitioner and, as discussed in this entry, can lead to shifts in how supervisors approach their role depending on the conflicting interests of managers and street-level officers. After briefly discussing the role of the first-line supervisor in general, this entry more specifically describes how first-line supervisors further the training for and implementation and function of the community policing and problem-solving strategy.

Supervisors' Tasks

The job title of first-line supervisor is reminiscent of the view that supervisors are the first line of defense against officer misconduct, from slacking off on the job to the abusive use of police powers. Supervisors act as the primary agent in translating policy implementation directives from the administrators to the street-level policy enactors. Such directives may include the implementation of policies that lower-ranking officers have no desire to follow. Because supervisors face many difficulties in actively monitoring officers who conduct various activities throughout any given police district or beat, it is important for them to maintain positive relations with their subordinates. This entry provides an overview of the notion of leadership and its relevance for supervisors, how supervisors influence officer behavior, and where supervisors fit in the context of community policing.

In addition to their policing tasks, supervisors are required to perform several other tasks associated with their supervisory role. How these supervisory tasks are conducted has been a topic of interest in the literature. Activities that first-line supervisors perform often include the following:

- Directing officers to conduct necessary activities for the department
- Communicating to subordinates information that is pertinent to police work
- Ensuring that departmental guidelines are followed in conducting police activities
- Monitoring officers as they conduct activities to ensure that those tasks are completed timely and properly
- Reviewing officers' reports to ensure accuracy in their reporting
- Listening to and discussing problems expressed by officers
- Backing up officers on dangerous or high-profile calls for service
- Communicating the problems faced by street-level officers up to department administrators
- Taking the lead in directing and guiding officers' actions at high-risk calls for service or dangerous situations
- Translating department policies for subordinates in a manner befitting each officer's circumstances or the novel situations they face

Although this list is not exhaustive, it shows that supervisors must have an understanding of the department's policies and bureaucracy, a working relationship with both subordinate and superior officers, and the ability to both supervise other officers and conduct police operations properly in a field context.

Leadership and Police Supervisors

Most police supervisors hold the rank of sergeant, but this is not always the case. In some departments first-line supervisors are corporals and in small departments they may be lieutenants. Regardless of rank, all supervisors have similar responsibilities and must be able to lead. *Leadership* may be defined as the accomplishment of goals through the use of oneself and one's subordinates efficiently and without risk for failure. These goals are defined by the assignments provided to supervisors from their superiors.

Research examining leadership and supervisors finds that there are different styles of leadership. The apt term being *style,* as the determining of which style is often dependent on long-standing qualities of the supervisors themselves. These leadership styles may be imprinted by supervisors onto their subordinates, who would go on to lead in the same style. Some researchers have examined supervision and leadership using the amount of control supervisors exerts over subordinates. Authoritarian supervisors conduct all decision making and do not allow subordinates to have input on their job responsibilities. Others allow subordinates to provide input that supervisors will consider in making the final decision. Finally, supervisors may adhere to a participatory style, whereby officers are able to actually make decisions. These differences in leadership can affect officers' commitment to the department by including them in decision-making processes.

Other researchers have examined police supervisors based on their bureaucratic inclinations or those on which they place the most importance. For example, in 2002, Robin Engel developed a supervisory taxonomy from surveying police supervisors. The first type of supervisor identified was *traditional supervisors.* Traditional supervisors are concerned with traditional law enforcement. They expect their subordinates to write large numbers of traffic citations and make numerous arrests. These officers define performance based on the number of offenses processed with no consideration for long-term gains or losses and are resistant to alternative roles for officers. The second form of supervision identified was the *active supervisor.* These supervisors also write large numbers of tickets and make numerous arrests, but they do little to deviate from working as officers, making them weaker supervisors. They believe that conducting so much police work guarantees the strongest relations with their subordinates. Third are the *supportive supervisors*. These supervisors, like the group before them, have difficulty properly supervising their subordinates out of a refusal to side with administration on many issues. Finally, there are *innovative supervisors*. Innovative supervisors are the supervisors who are most likely to commit themselves to implementing community policing. They see the police role as one defined by the community. They aren't as concerned with patrol officers having to rack up their arrest and citation counts. They define performance more by the accomplishments of the police with the community as a whole. Engel examined one department and found that the four types of supervisors were evenly distributed throughout the department.

Moreover, although counterintuitive, active supervisors' subordinates engaged in more community policing activities as compared to the other types of supervisors. One may surmise that innovative supervisors' subordinates would be the officers most likely to be involved in community policing. However, these officers tended to emphasize administrative tasks such as completing paperwork. They operationalized their commitment to the community bureaucratically. It appears that supervisors who are active tend to be active in a variety of areas including community policing. These supervisors seem to be driven and dedicated to getting all sorts of work done.

It is important that the supervisor's leadership style matches the job or his or her assignment within the department. For example, supervising a records unit requires a different type of leader as compared to a patrol supervisor. The records supervisor must be more detailed oriented and possess technical knowledge, ensuring that all reports are filed and recorded accordingly. The records supervisor is very task oriented. On the other hand, a patrol supervisor must be task oriented to ensure that officers complete their assigned duties, but at the same time, must be more people oriented as compared to the records supervisor. Patrol supervisors must have good working relationships with their subordinates, a prerequisite to greater commitment.

How Supervisors Influence Officers' Behavior

Of critical importance in police supervision is the degree to which supervisors are able to influence subordinates' behavior. Police officers have a great deal of discretion. It is difficult for supervisors to monitor officers' activities while the officers are in the field, unless the supervisors specifically contact the officers in person or over the radio. In 2009, Richard Johnson studied the effects of supervisors' monitoring their subordinates' activities by examining the time officers spend on duty to conduct personal business. He found that supervisors could best get officers to reduce the amount of time spent conducting personal business by making face-to-face contact with them in the field and by the supervisors themselves not spending too much of their own time conducting personal business and setting a poor example for their subordinates. However, when supervisors made more contacts with their subordinates by radio, as opposed to in-person contacts, patrol officers were found to spend more time conducting personal business. This implies that radio contact is an ineffective tool for supervision. Face-to-face communications seem to be more effective in gaining compliance, implying that supervisors must endeavor to meet and see their subordinates as much as possible.

Johnson conducted another study examining supervisory influence. He examined supervisors' influences on officer behavior in writing traffic tickets. He found that supervisors who wrote more traffic tickets had subordinates who wrote larger numbers of traffic citations. However, supervisors who believed that it was a priority to enforce traffic law but did not write large numbers of tickets themselves had subordinates who wrote significantly fewer citations. This research shows that supervisors must go beyond merely setting priorities. They must demonstrate a commitment to subordinates. Such commitment may include performing these duties themselves or actively encouraging the officers to do so.

A number of studies, beginning with the Kansas City preventive patrol experiment, found that a large percentage of officers' time is uncommitted—in other words, they are not addressing calls for service or completing reports. In many cases, about half of officers' time is uncommitted. This means that they have opportunities to participate in community policing activities. Studies show that officers do not get involved in these types of activities even when they have the time. They tend to patrol or back up officers on other calls. This likely is due to supervisors not making community policing assignments or not having a commitment to them. Research shows that supervisors can influence subordinates' behavior, but efforts to do so must be made.

Moving Toward Community Policing

One of the challenges facing departments in their attempts to implement modern styles of policing that call for the department to switch from the reactive crime-fighter model to more proactive models, such as community and problem-oriented policing, is that these policies are implemented through the street-level ranks often in a top-down implementation style. Many police departments voice a commitment to community policing, but they fail to adopt policies, and in some cases, when they do, they fail to emphasize them to the rank-and-file officers. Police administrators must effectively communicate these policies to subordinates. This involves providing direction and setting priorities. In many cases, officers and lower-level managers and supervisors have their own ideas about how police work should be conducted, so administrators must make extraordinary efforts to change subordinates' attitudes and behavior. Once clear policies have been articulated, subordinates' compliant behaviors must be rewarded or at least recognized so that their commitment and behaviors do not become extinguished. This is an ongoing process that is required to move a department.

One of the problems in implementing community policing is that many officers, at all ranks, may not fully understand community policing. They may see it as a gimmick or extra work. They may not see the benefits from better community relations or problem solving, and in some cases, they may understand the benefits but remain committed to traditional law enforcement. In other words, the department's culture may be antithetic to community policing. In terms of culture, administrators can perform an inventory of the department's culture, norms, and values to inform the department and its officers where they are relative to community policing or other innovative practices while also identifying obstacles to implementing those practices. It can provide insights on how change should be implemented and who should be targeted. Once this occurs, implementation planning can begin. This includes examining all aspects of the department and detailing tactics by which to move the department in the desired direction. It is also important to inventory supervisors, as they are the key players when implementing new policies.

An important aspect of community policing and problem solving is training. Officers may be provided information particularly in the areas of problem-solving procedures and implementing the SARA (scanning, analysis, response, assessment) problem-solving model. This training is intended to impart a comprehensive understanding of these procedures so that officers become incapable of implementing community policing.

Officer training is not the only training problem. Supervisors and managers may not have adequate training. Supervisory and managerial training often focuses only on topics such as leadership, motivation, and other managerial and supervisory skills. Community policing supervisors and managers need community policing training, as well as training on its support services. This includes crime mapping, crime trends, victimization, and so on. They must understand the context of crime and disorder if they are going to develop and implement workable solutions.

Another problem with implementing community policing is that some departments may treat it as a specialized function or unit. If this is the case, officers are assigned to community policing and have exclusive domain over the function. This means that many officers in the department are detached from it, as they do not have a vested interest in its being successful. In some cases, these officers may view the community policing officers as not being "real" police officers. Rivalry may develop between police units. Even when a department uses specialists to implement community policing, it is important for the department to take measures to involve other officers in the program.

If community policing is to be implemented successfully, these problems must be overcome, and supervisors play an important role in accomplishing this task. To do so, supervisors must possess human, technical, and conceptual skills. *Human skills* refer to those skills that are used to motivate subordinates. Again, good relationships are a key ingredient here. *Technical skills* refer to a thorough understanding of departmental policies and procedures as well as the mechanics of community relations and problem solving. Perhaps the most important skill when implementing community policing is conceptual skills. *Conceptual skills* refer to supervisors' ability to monitor the environment or areas of responsibilities, understand problems, and conceptualize effective solutions or countermeasures. Too often when solving problems, police officers depend too much on traditional measures, limiting their range of responses. Conceptually, officers must think outside the box and consider alterative measures. Police officers working in the area where the problem exists often can provide insights to these solutions. They are exposed to it on a daily basis, often answering calls or providing additional information to people at the location in question. These officers become an excellent information resource.

In summary, supervisors play a key role in community policing. Their primary responsibility is ensuring that subordinate officers comply with departmental policies and procedures including the dictates associated with community policing. In order to implement and supervise community policing, they must be effective leaders and be able to develop good relations with their subordinates. They must understand the mechanics of community policing.

D. Cody Gaines

See also CompStat; Decentralizing the Organization/ Organizational Change; Directed Patrol, Studies of; In-Service Training; Kansas City Preventive Patrol Experiment; Mentoring

Further Readings

Engel, R. S. (2002). Police supervision in the community policing era. *Journal of Criminal Justice, 30,* 51–64.

Johnson, R. R. (2009). Field supervisor behavior and officer on-duty personal business. *International Journal of Police Science and Management, 11*(3), 205–217.

Kappeler, V. E., & Gaines, L. K. (2011). *Community policing.* Cincinnati, OH: Anderson.

Peak, K. J., Gaines, L. K., & Glensor, R. W. (2010). *Police supervision and management: In an era of community policing* (3rd ed.). Upper Saddle River, NJ: Prentice Hall.

ROLES, MIDDLE MANAGERS'

The role of the middle manager in community policing and problem solving is instrumental to the successful implementation of that philosophy in any police agency. Middle management in law enforcement agencies typically includes lieutenants, captains, and their civilian employee counterparts in administration, dispatch, and records divisions. Middle managers are normally responsible for commanding such functions as patrol watches, tactical units, detective units or divisions, and some that are sensitive or specialized, such as internal affairs. Middle managers report directly to upper management personnel, such as deputy chiefs, majors, and lieutenant colonels. They immediately supervise first-line supervisors such as sergeants and corporals and have direct contact with beat officers and detectives. This entry discusses the redefined roles of middle managers under community policing.

The Middle Manager and Change

Middle managers became increasingly responsible for developing and controlling departmental policing philosophy during the early eras of policing. This continued into the professional era (characterized by reactive, incident-driven methods with emphases on qualitative outcomes such as number of calls for service, arrests, and so on), where they became the principal managers who developed policies and procedures for their organizations, interpreted communications efforts between upper management and supervisors and beat officers, and provided operational leadership for the various functions.

These characteristics put middle managers in a unique circumstance of influencing innovation and change, both positively and negatively. The negative influences have been documented in police literature quite well because of the obvious impact to organizational innovation. The problem that middle managers have with organizational change is that they often perceive threats to their jobs, whether real or imagined. It is not the specific innovation that they resist so much as the potential for loss to their power base and a decrease in the amount of discretion they have in performing their various roles. As a result, they tend to filter information from the top and resist new ideas. In doing so, they manage to limit the implementation of different police philosophies, strategies, and other techniques that would change the status quo of the organization and, consequently, their jobs.

The process of change, while originating at the top, must be an inclusive effort that engages all employees of the department as well as stakeholders in the community. Innovative practices, such as community policing and problem solving, need to be developed at the local level, include the input and feedback of all employees, and be implemented in a manner that is least influenced by those who would resist it. However, it is precisely the middle managers' unique circumstance that allows them to be a positive influence on this implementation process. Instead of the middle managers becoming bottlenecks in the communications process, they have the strong potential to be conduits that allow information to flow freely. Lieutenants and captains work closely with first-line supervisors and beat officers, and because of this they have strong working relationships with the officers and may provide a positive view of the changes that come with community policing. Instead of filtering information, they become the information channel for the rest of the department to access for answers.

The New Role of the Middle Manager

Police corporate culture tends to identify police officers and supervisors as the employees who do the work, make the initial contacts with the community, carry out police agencies' law enforcement functions and as the visible entities to the community. Executives and upper management personnel are seen as those who provide the mission, vision, and funding resources for the organization, but are not operationally involved, often believed to be the political aspect of law enforcement. Consequently, the middle manager's role is rather nebulous and ill defined. This can be beneficial to an agency by establishing a positive role for the middle manager in the implementation of change, particularly community policing efforts. The police agency that is considering community policing has an opportunity to redefine the middle manager role and change what has historically been an oppositional force to innovation to a positive influencing force in support of change.

The new role of the middle manager may be defined as part of the development process of the community policing philosophy. First, middle managers can oversee the response to calls and ensure that the department's response is not affected negatively by community policing. By staying involved at the operational and procedural levels, middle managers may alleviate many concerns that beat officers may have about community policing, such as being soft on crime, focusing on public relations, or failing to respond quickly to calls for service. In this situation, the middle manager acts as the person who defines community policing for the beat officers. This demands a full understanding by the manager as well as a complete buy-in to the philosophy so that the officers know that community policing is not just a series of phrases or buzz words.

Second, middle managers actively identify the amount of authority delegated to first-line supervisors and beat officers. This involvement can lessen the fear of loss because it is the manager who delegates the necessary amount of authority to get the job done, thereby maintaining responsibility for that function. This requires that middle managers fully understand how community policing and problem solving is applied to law enforcement activities and become engaged from the very beginning of the planning, development, and implementation process.

Third, middle managers are the ones who can allocate time and resources to community policing activities, which allows them to be active partners in community policing rather than passive observers. Middle managers, such as watch commanders, traditionally control this aspect of the patrol function. Under the community policing model, this task is divided between managers and supervisors. The first-line supervisor is responsible for assigning officers to geographical areas and directly overseeing their activities. The manager is responsible for providing the necessary resources such as personnel, equipment, and expertise so that the beat officers can vary their duties to meet the needs of problem-solving efforts. The manager, supervisor, and beat officer tend to work more as a team than a hierarchy of roles.

Fourth, middle managers facilitate community policing efforts, mediate conflicts and problems, and act not only as conduits but also buffers when officers need protection to do their jobs. The manager is in a position to see a larger picture than supervisors and beat officers and can use this advantage to facilitate the overall process of community policing and problem solving. The manager is also positioned well to mediate conflicts between supervisors who are competing for a finite amount of resources. As officers begin to dedicate more time and effort to problem solving, they may become subject to criticism from those who may feel that other functions or duties are being ignored. The manager acts as a liaison between the beat officers and their critics.

Fifth, middle managers may use the rank and position of lieutenant and captain to provide a credible image of the department and its community policing and problem solving philosophy. The foundation of community policing is the development of a partnership between the community and the police. While it is of paramount importance that the beat officer engage the community directly and often, the manager must also be part of this partnership. Community members expect to have upper management's support and involvement in their area. This is not something that executives and upper managers can do on a regular basis, but lieutenants and captains can. They are also of a rank high enough that they can represent the chief of police in a credible manner.

Finally, middle managers are responsible for establishing the training of personnel in the philosophy of community policing and problem solving. Because middle managers typically command or oversee basic and advanced training functions, they are intimately involved in one of the most important aspects of implementing this philosophy. Middle managers may use their influence to include the community policing and problem solving philosophy in the academy as well as adopt a field training program such as the Police Training Officer (PTO) Program, which was specifically designed for police agencies engaged in community policing and problem solving.

Middle managers in law enforcement are often seen as resistant to change and lacking a focus in their duties. The implementation of community policing and problem solving requires that all personnel accept the philosophy and actively engage in its development and implementation. Middle managers provide the expertise, credibility, and unique relationships with field personnel and upper management to accomplish this goal. Their involvement in all phases of design, development, and implementation of the community policing and problem solving philosophy, as well as the subsequent ongoing training to support it, is critical. Instead of being the weak link in the organizational chain, the middle manager is the key to a successful effort.

Jerry Hoover

See also Agency Mission and Values, Changes in; Community Policing, Discretionary Authority Under; Community Policing and Problem Solving, Definition of; Decentralizing the Organization/Organizational Change; Directed Patrol, Studies of; Implementation of Community Policing; Measuring Officer Performance; Mentoring; Police Training Officer (PTO) Program; Roles, Chief Executives'; Roles, First-Line Supervisors'; Roles, Officers'

Further Readings

Gaines, L. K. (1994). Community-oriented policing: Management issues, concerns, and problems. *Journal of Contemporary Criminal Justice, 10*(1), 17–35.

Geller, W. A., & Swanger, G. (1995). *Managing innovation in policing: The untapped potential of the middle manager.* Washington, DC: U.S. Department of Justice, National Institute of Justice, Police Executive Research Forum.

Greene, J. R., Bergman, W. T., & McLaughlin, E. J. (1994). Implementing community policing: Cultural and structural change in police organizations. In D. P. Rosenbaum (Ed.), *The challenge of community policing: Testing the promises* (pp. 92–109). Thousand Oaks, CA: Sage.

Kelling, G. L., & Bratton, W. J. (1993, July). Implementing community policing: The administrative problem. NCJ 141236. *Perspectives on Policing, 17,* 1–11. Washington, DC: U.S. Department of Justice, National Institute of Justice.

Vito, G. F., Walsh, W. F., & Kunselman, J. (2004). Community policing: The middle manager's perspective. *Police Quarterly, 6,* 1–22. Thousand Oaks, CA: Sage.

ROLES, OFFICERS'

To understand the role of the police in the United States in general as well as in the practice of community policing and problem solving, one must first define what is meant by "the police." The police are an institution in the United States, firmly established and deeply rooted in the nation's history. The police are the agencies people call when they require assistance with crime or disorder. Finally, the police are people who work collaboratively with the community to address problems. Each of these three conceptualizations of the police has undergone dramatic change over time. Those changes have left them positioned as they are today. This entry discusses the roles of the police under the three conceptualizations in turn.

Roles for the Institution of American Police

The role of the police as an institution has changed considerably over the course of recorded history. Throughout much of that history, there has been little distinction between the military and the police. For millennia, armed guardians have been responsible for protecting us not only from others, but also from each other. Although the nature of those guardians (i.e., civilian or military) has varied along with the various other roles they have assumed, the police have always been responsible for law enforcement. This dates back to the earliest record of law and its enforcement, the Code of Hammurabi (composed about 1750 BCE and consisting of 282 laws).

U.S. policing is rooted in the practices of our English forebears. Under the frankpledge system in England, the constable and the shire-reeve (the forerunner of the modern-day sheriff) served the dual roles of law enforcers and tax collectors. As agents of an absolute sovereign monarch, they were often brutal and corrupt. Presumably, then, they were selected on the bases of their abilities to discharge these roles of collecting taxes and enforcing the king's will—by force, if necessary. These practices included active involvement of community members in the policing enterprise.

Policing in England took a huge leap forward when Sir Robert Peel successfully led Parliament to enact the Metropolitan Police Act of 1829. This act built on the ideas put forth by Patrick Colquhoun, a local magistrate, to establish a police force whose job would be to prevent crime, inform the public about their role in that regard, and record incidents of crime. Here, too, efforts were made to hire officers with skills and abilities that mapped onto these roles, such as being even tempered and maintaining a professional appearance. Indeed, in establishing the first modern police force, Peel specifically called for selection and training tied to demands of the role.

U.S. police practices were patterned largely after the English model. Community members took turns on night watches to maintain order and prevent escapes, respectively, but the law enforcement function was chiefly provided by the local sheriff. Here, too, the roles were law enforcement and tax collection. As with England, one would presume sheriffs were chosen according to their ability to perform these functions.

The policing function in the United States began to shift from sheriff's departments to municipal police departments in the mid-1800s. The early days of American policing were known as the political era because the police were largely both the product and the instruments of the prevailing political machines of the day. Their function was to maintain order and suppress crime. Order was maintained through harsh, sometimes brutal tactics, often employed against immigrants. In addition to selecting officers for their brute strength, they were also selected on the basis of their political loyalty.

As the political era of policing gave way to the reform era of professionalization, the law enforcement role of the police remained, but the criteria for selection and promotion improved. Not surprisingly, in this era of imposition of rules, policies, procedures, and other structures to limit police officers' discretion and hold them accountable for their actions, officers were selected on the basis of reading comprehension, knowledge of law and rules, and other objective criteria. This was so because, although the law enforcement role persisted, the political role was subsiding and the increased accountability rendered the heavy-handed approach undesirable if not altogether obsolete.

The advent of the community era formally and theoretically ushered in a more expansive role of the police. "Formally" because community policing explicitly embraced this broader role, which the police were known to have undertaken for some time; it has long been known that the overwhelming majority of time spent policing is spent in order maintenance activities, as opposed to law enforcement–related ones. "Theoretically" because the full extent to which community policing was implemented—and persists—is not entirely clear. Some agencies never bought into the philosophy. Others seem to have been "in it for the money," judging from their retrenchment from community-oriented policing principles once the federal funding began to be reduced. Still others have seemingly "moved on" to more homeland security–focused priorities—notwithstanding the fact that local problems are more likely to take their constituents' lives or affect the quality of those lives than are international ones. Still, most agencies claim to be community oriented in their approach, and the role of community-oriented police agencies expands to cover problem solving, prevention efforts, and quality-of-life issues more so than traditional policing.

Roles for Police Agencies

It is tempting to presume, from the foregoing march through the history of the institution of U.S. police, that agencies transitioned smoothly and completely from one era to the next, as if a memo went out from

Police Central informing each agency that effective 0800 Monday morning, the agency will formally become a "reform era" agency. Such is tempting, but would be inaccurate. U.S. policing has no Police Central. Instead there are nearly 20,000 different agencies operating on their own timelines, engaged in different styles of policing, according to local priorities. U.S. policing is fragmented and decentralized; it is at once a great strength and a profound weakness. It is a strength because it fosters local control, which is good for meeting community expectations; but it is a weakness because it relies heavily on local accountability, in the absence of which there is risk there will be no accountability.

Although each policing agency in the United States essentially charts its own path within certain legal constraints, common themes have emerged which allow one to categorize agencies. Whereas the preceding discussion shed light on macro-level evolution of the institution of U.S. policing, the discussion in this section includes a more microlevel analysis of what takes place in individual agencies.

Perhaps the most familiar typology of policing styles was advanced by James Q. Wilson in his 1968 classic *Varieties of Police Behavior*, in which he described three different policing styles that agencies follow: the legalistic, the watchman, and service orientations. An understanding of these styles informs and illumines our understanding of the roles of police in the United States.

Legalistic

The legalistic policing style involves enforcing the "letter of the law." Agencies employing this approach generally subscribe to the idea that fairness is maximized where laws, rules, and policies are applied uniformly. Discretion is regarded as a gateway to inequity at best and corruption at worst and, consequently, is not tolerated. Decision making in these agencies tends to be top-down. Officers in these agencies presumably are selected in order to apply the law and follow the rules in a consistent, routine way. Problem-solving abilities, judgment, and discretion are not especially important, while equal application of the law is important.

Watchman

The watchman style of policing is common in large agencies with high demand for police services.

Because of this demand, officers use problem-solving skills to resolve issues informally, if possible. Minor violations are overlooked and attempts are made to avoid engagement of other agencies and otherwise formally trigger official responses to problems. Because of this role, officers must use problem-solving skills to resolve problems informally, employ discretion to determine the solution that strikes the proper balance between effectiveness and efficiency, and good judgment overall.

Service

The final model discussed by Wilson is the service model, which is typically employed in middle- and upper-class communities. Under this style, the police protect the community against outsiders and serve the community by preserving property and privacy interests from offenses like theft, burglary, and robbery. Not surprisingly, then, officers who fill these roles should be selected based on their service orientation. They should be oriented toward meeting the needs of the community.

Conclusions About Policing Styles

Just as it would be hasty and erroneous to conclude that all agencies moved from one institutional era to the next, so it would be a mistake to conclude that every police agency fits neatly into one and only one of Wilson's categories. Every agency is some mix of features from these three styles. Moreover, Wilson's categories are not the only ones that have been advanced by scholars over the years. Nevertheless, they serve as a useful heuristic for understanding the roles that U.S. police agencies have served over the years.

Roles for Officers

As the foregoing cursory recounting of historical and other variations in policing approaches makes clear, police officers have been expected to undertake their jobs in very different ways. Because the police are no longer tasked primarily with tax collection and suppression of misbehavior by force, there is concurrently a lesser need for officers to fulfill the role of physical intimidation. Of course, force is still sometimes necessary. When it must be employed, there are many officers to come to a fellow officer's aid (as compared with staffing levels, say, a century ago). Moreover, technological advances in less lethal force techniques have also lessened the need for heavy reliance on physical prowess.

Another major role consideration has to do with the fundamental nature of police work. As noted above, we have long been aware that "law enforcement officers" spend only a fraction of their time engaged in law enforcement activity. Instead, the vast majority of their time is spent in maintaining order. In this way, the title "peace officer" is probably more accurate a description than that of "law enforcement officer."

Contemporary Roles

Today's police officer should be a technically proficient, community-oriented, service-minded, prevention-focused problem solver. This combines all of Wilson's agency styles described above: legalistic (technical proficiency), watchman (problem solving, prevention focused), and service (community oriented, service minded). Technical proficiency is demanded not only by the need for officers with substantive competence pertaining to law and policy (i.e., knowing what the law is), but also process competence, including, for example, the use of technology to accomplish the goals of the agency.

Problem Solvers

Contemporary policing needs problem solvers as opposed to incident resolvers. Just as the physician spins her wheels if she treats only the symptoms, but never gets to the underlying problem, so do police engage in a Sisyphean endeavor if they respond only to incidents. The people of the officers' communities deserve more and the police are capable of providing that service to them.

Being a problem solver means that officers have to listen. Just as a good diagnostician must listen carefully to his patient, so must police officers attend carefully to their constituents. They should listen to the description of the problem in a nonjudgmental way, not only to keep people opening up, but also by way of treating people with dignity and respect. This is not the only strategic reason for active listening, as listening—or, more precisely, allowing someone to be heard—is powerful in its own right.

Being heard is a robust component of the experience of justice. Until the 1960s, justice was thought of in distributive terms; that is, it was assumed people felt as though they had been treated justly if they saw a distribution of rewards and punishments that seemed fair. Then, John Thibaut and Laurens Walker (1975) posited that outcomes might not be the only thing that matters—that procedural justice may be important to the experience of justice as well.

Again and again, it has been found that people report greater experienced fairness when they are given a chance to be heard—irrespective of the ultimate outcome. People who have such experiences are more likely not only to comply with the law, but also, to cooperate with police. The traffic cop's old saying, "Tell it to the judge," may have it precisely backward; if the officer hears the complaint himself or herself, there may be no experienced need on the part of the alleged violator to take it to the judge. Not only does this conserve judicial resources but also saves in overtime costs.

The need to listen to people is not purely utilitarian. There are also deontological reasons for doing so. The police are the most conspicuous agents of a government that is supposed to be of the people, by the people, and for the people. As much as police might hate to hear the phrase, "I pay your salary," the fact of the matter is that the police do derive their powers from the consent of the governed.

Of course, it is not enough to listen clearly in order to be a good problem solver; one must think clearly as well. But to solve contemporary problems, much more is required. Police officers practicing community policing should know (a) how to approach problems, (b) how to find data or other information to solve the problem, (c) how to think critically about problems, and (d) how to evaluate the effectiveness of their solution to the problem.

The Wilson Analogy

Home Improvement was a situation comedy television series that aired throughout the 1990s. It featured the affable, but frequently misguided Tim "The Tool Man" Taylor, who was constantly creating problems because he misunderstood the world around him. Fortunately, Tim had a neighbor, Wilson, to whom he turned regularly for sage wisdom and advice—which were always forthcoming; Wilson would help Tim reason through the issue and come up with a solution. The world would be a better place if each of us had a neighbor like Wilson.

In his 2000 book entitled *Bowling Alone: The Collapse and Revival of American Community*, Robert Putnam detailed painstakingly the extent to which we are detached from one another as individuals and as communities. If there is no Wilson available, where are people to turn? For better or for worse, the answer is oftentimes "the police." Accordingly, if the police are going to be effective in addressing people's problems, they will have to engage in problem solving.

The Physician Analogy

The foregoing references to physicians as diagnosticians and nonjudgmental listeners are not the only direct analogies between police work and the practice of medicine. People's images of doctors include emergency room doctors treating people bitten by poisonous snakes or impaled on telephone poles. They might involve the equivalent of diagnostic rock stars, who are able to figure out the most complex medical cases and the most elusive diagnoses. But think about your *experience* with doctors. Those experiences are less likely to involve emergent issues, lights and sirens, helicopter rides and the like. They are more likely to involve quiet, controlled, orderly, low-key interactions.

Undoubtedly, those quiet, behind-the-scenes interactions save more lives than the trauma physicians do. The gentle nudge to lose a few pounds, the encouragement to take that screening test, the admonishment about smoking—all of them quietly save, extend, and improve the quality of countless lives every year. It may not be as thrilling, but ask yourself: Wouldn't you rather avoid the helicopter ride if you could?

Policing works the same way. The "real" work is not so exciting. It may not be the Hollywood view of lights and sirens, screeching tires, and spike strips; rather, it is the quiet nudge to try a little harder to get along with the neighbor, the encouragement to be proactive and install an alarm system, the admonishment about trespassing.

There is one way in which police have a real advantage over physicians, namely, the lack of a specialty area. It turns out that, for most people, the thrills and adventure that are so stimulating in their youth are somewhat less desirable as they age. Unfortunately, for the trauma surgeon, when the adrenaline no longer satisfies, it is too late to change over to dermatology, which has relatively few emergencies requiring a callout. Thus, physicians are stuck in ways police officers are not. Officers can—and do—choose to do things differently as they get older. The lights and sirens give way to a calmer approach that is probably more effective in most cases and better for all involved.

The Parent Analogy

A final analogy to police work as community oriented and problem solving in nature as offered here is that of parent. Parents set boundaries and impose consequences, but, ideally, they do so for good reasons: (a) to keep the child safe for whom the consequences are imposed, (b) to teach the child for whom the consequences are imposed, or (c) to protect another child or family member. The police do, or at least should, act similarly. Consequences are imposed to keep people safe, to teach them a lesson, or to protect others from harm. Like parents, the police should impose those consequences rationally and even-handedly, not out of personal frustration or vengeance.

Implications of Roles

Once the roles of the police as being an institution, agency, and officer are clarified, this discussion can move toward implications. Most of these implications relate directly to what is contemporarily known as Strategic Human Resource Management (SHRM). SHRM is an approach that dovetails the human resource function with the mission of the agency. Businesses work hard to bring into alignment their goals, roles, and procedures. Police agencies can do the same. Consistent with the SHRM philosophy, decisions about whom to recruit and hire should be made with an eye toward the roles which those individuals will fill. For example, given the degree of problem-solving skills that officers need to possess to be effective community policing officers, should officers be required to have a degree? If so, should it be in a particular substantive area?

Once hired or otherwise selected (e.g., through promotion), training and professional development focuses on building knowledge, skills, abilities, and other characteristics which will be important for the officers' roles. What makes a good D.A.R.E. officer is not necessarily what makes a good SWAT officer. Consequently, one might expect training for those positions to look quite different from one another. Likewise, performance assessment can map out the goals, roles, and procedures that have been brought into alignment. Many agencies report to be community oriented in their approach, yet continue to count officers' citations issued, arrests made, and cases cleared among their most important benchmarks for officer performance.

In his book *The Pursuit of Justice*, published in 1964, Robert Kennedy famously said, "Every society gets the kind of criminal it deserves. What is equally true is that every community gets the kind of law enforcement it insists on." At an institutional level, people in the United States have insisted that police be more than a collective of political hacks and cronies. They also have begun to insist that police take charge of public safety and manage it, rather than simply respond to crime after it occurs. Like the patient who would rather avoid getting the disease than fight it successfully, they want the police to keep them from harm in the first instance, rather than address the harm once it materializes.

Kennedy's point about the law enforcement people insist on also applies at the community level. Some communities have one style of policing, whereas others will have another. Each community is served by an agency with a mix of styles, but that mix presumably is dependent on the community itself. It is no coincidence that urban areas adopt similar styles; upper-class communities do the same, and so on.

Kennedy's point is perhaps most applicable to individual officers. Taking Kennedy to heart, communities can insist that their police officers be interpersonally skilled problem solvers, committed to serving others, while maintaining high ethical and professional norms. Whether the community thinks of them as professionals possessed of particularized expertise, or as parents caring for their children, or just as friendly neighbors, the community expects them to be there when they need them ready to serve capably, competently, and willingly.

Phillip M. Lyons Jr.

See also Agency Mission and Values, Changes in; Community Oriented Policing Services, Office of; Measuring Officer Performance; Metropolitan Police Act of 1829; Policing, Three Eras of

Further Readings

Kennedy, R. F. (1964). *The pursuit of justice*. New York, NY: Harper & Row.

Putnam, R. D. (2008). *Bowling alone: The collapse and revival of American community*. New York, NY: Simon & Schuster.

Thibaut, J. W., & Walker, L. (1975). *Procedural justice: A psychological analysis*. Hillsdale, NJ: Erlbaum.

Tyler, T. R. (2004, May). Enhancing police legitimacy. In W. G. Skogan (Ed.), *To better serve and protect: Improving police practices. Annals of the American Academy of Political and Social Science, 593*(1), 84–99. doi: 10.1177/0002716203262627

Tyler, T. R. (2006). *Why people obey the law*. Princeton, NJ: Princeton University Press.

Wilson, J. Q. (1968). *Varieties of police behavior*. Cambridge, MA: Harvard University Press.

Rural Areas, Community Policing in

Community policing research has tended to focus on how the community policing and problem-solving approach works in urban areas. Like many other aspects of U.S. policing research, less is known about police agencies and operations in rural environments. The social, demographic, economic, and cultural forces found in urban and rural areas can be profoundly different from urban centers. As a result, both the nature of crime problems and their responses are not necessarily the same. This entry discusses those unique aspects of rural areas that can enhance the viability of community policing as well as aspects of the culture of rural residents that can complicate the use of this policing approach.

Defining Rural Areas

The definition of what constitutes a *rural area* is not always clear. Though some areas are clearly rural, the exact dividing line between those areas and their urban and suburban counterparts remains hazy. What can be said is that rural areas almost always have small police departments, if they have any dedicated law enforcement function. The converse (that small agencies are necessarily rural) is not always true. Nearly half of all municipal agencies employ fewer than ten full-time sworn officers and many are situated in rural environments. It would be a mistake to presume homogeneity within the universe of small and rural agencies. There are potentially important and unexplored distinctions. All of these converging forces limit the understanding of community policing in rural areas.

What can be noted about community policing in rural areas is based on the limited available research, documented experiences, and reasonable inferences from what is known about the dynamics of crime and justice in small towns and rural communities. Survey data tend to suggest residents of rural areas and small towns have favorable views of community policing efforts, but they also prefer more traditional, law-and-order approaches to criminal justice. When residents of rural areas recognized community policing efforts were in place in their community, they were more likely to have more positive views of the police, to take more self-protection strategies, to report less fear of crime, and to have a greater sense of community integration. Unlike their counterparts in urban environments, residents of small jurisdictions have not demonstrated the same race, class, or gender influences on community policing attitudes and perceptions. Demographics have not shown a strong and consistent influence on community policing attitudes, which has normally been noted in urban studies.

All small and rural agencies should not be presumed to all be the same. Variation can be noted in the amount of time officers spend on commonly identified policing tasks. Even proximate agencies might vary considerably in their priorities, approaches, and styles of policing. Likewise, when considering community policing in particular, variation has been noted not only between large agencies but also between smaller agencies in terms of the adoption of a range of community policing activities. Variation has also been noted within rural police agencies. Officers who are primarily assigned to community policing duties have been found to offer stronger endorsements of policing styles consistent with the philosophy of community policing. Officers not assigned such duties tend to express stronger support for more traditional models of policing that emphasize motor patrol and the enforcement of the law.

Policing in Rural Environments

It has long been noted that there are important differences between policing urban communities and policing rural and small-town environments. Residents of rural communities have different expectations of and interactions with law enforcement personnel than residents of urban areas. This situation has important implications for community policing in rural areas. While the idea of rural policing may invoke images of sedate, quiet, service-oriented policing, many rural regions struggle with crime, poverty, drugs, and violence. Rural areas often experience forms of crime that are not normally seen in urban centers, including wildlife, agricultural, and environmental crime, as well as distinct forms of extremism.

In this way, policing in rural areas can present unique challenges for law enforcement personnel. Even where serious and violent crime is less prevalent than in urban centers, police personnel often confront problems with limited proximate backup and with limited means to implement crime reduction strategies. Officers may understand the "best practices" for solving persistent problems, but requisite social, economic, educational, and other resources may not be available. It may be difficult for an officer to set aside dedicated time to address persistent problems when she is the only responder on duty in her jurisdiction. Despite these challenges, police personnel in rural areas often enjoy a higher degree of social integration within the communities they serve. This can influence both the nature of police-community interactions and the styles of policing officers employ. Although the nature of rural policing can create circumstances amenable to community-oriented and collaborative policing styles, officers tend to report a working style more consistent with the professionalism-based traditional law enforcement orientation.

Small Police Agencies

U.S. policing is dominated by small agencies, many of which are situated in environments that would be fairly classified as rural. Popular images of policing often focus on high-crime, urban environments. Analogously, policing scholarship has disproportionately examined the nature of policing in large, urban agencies. Small agencies tend to exhibit far less organizational complexity than their large, urban counterparts. The majority of personnel, including supervisors and top executives, are assigned to the patrol function. Smaller jurisdictions struggle to recruit and retain a demographically diverse workforce, which can complicate community policing objectives. This can be compounded when most personnel are drawn from the local area, particularly if the jurisdiction is experiencing a rapid social transformation. The police may reflect the formerly homogeneous nature of the community, its values, and its culture, in a time of increasing heterogeneity.

Smaller agencies often lack the resources to develop and sustain strict hiring and training standards in relation to larger jurisdictions. Personnel typically have limited access to professional development and training experiences once they complete an entry-level academy. As new issues and ideas emerge within the policing profession, small agencies, particularly those in rural areas, face appreciable challenges providing personnel with access to cutting-edge ideas about policing and patrol operations. Limited training budgets and being situated in remote areas further isolate personnel in these jurisdictions from the broader policing profession, though emerging distance education and social networking technologies are ameliorating some aspects of this trend. Rural agencies make less use of specialized duty assignments and patrol methods. The smaller scale of the policing function, however, may mean that specialization is rarely needed.

Small jurisdictions tend to operate on budgets that are smaller, both in raw totality and when computed as a function of expenditures per officer or community resident. The overall smaller scale of fiscal operations results in lower salaries for personnel of all ranks. Smaller total budgets provide agencies with less flexibility when confronted with sudden fiscal crises, such as rising fuel costs. These observations are not universal truisms for large or small, nor urban or rural agencies. Yet there is a risk that less stringent and competitive hiring standards, lower pay, limited training opportunities, and isolation from progressive ideas about police professionalism might bring some fulfillment to the belief that small town police offers are inept. It may be difficult to advance less clearly defined initiatives, such as community policing, in such environments.

Despite the many critiques that might be issued about small agencies, there are aspects of small and rural work environments that can be favorable, particularly in advancing aspects of community policing. The typical small agency has less formality to its structure and less organizational complexity. This translates into employees enjoying more autonomy and fewer bureaucratic requirements. Where community policing is an objective, either for the organization or an individual officer, there are fewer forces working against the successful implementation of that style of policing. Individual officers enjoy more freedom to pursue community policing objectives on their own. Rural officers have more latitude in how they perform their duties, there is less culture and tradition emphasizing command-and-control supervisory systems, and the absence of cumbersome policies and dense bureaucratic requirements allow officers to exercise creativity, discretion, and situational responses in the pursuit of problem solving, community enhancement, and capacity building.

Looser organizational structures and restrictions contribute to closer social relations among coworkers, as well as between front-line and supervisory personnel. Having less formalized policies and procedures, as well as command personnel who are seen routinely performing the same tasks and functions as personnel assigned to patrol duties, can diminish the belief that supervisors and agency executives are out of touch with street-level policing operations. These internal dynamics would be expected to yield favorable outcomes in the external relationships between the police and the community. A more open and friendly set of internal social dynamics is likely to translate to stronger community relations. Members of the public may be more inclined to trust police personnel because they know officers on a personal level. When initiating a community policing effort in a small or rural agency, personnel may have to do less work to enhance relationships and trust with local citizens. Officers and citizens are likely to know each other and perhaps even have friendly, amicable, or positive relationships.

This situation creates both opportunities and challenges for police organizations and personnel. Strong and direct personal relationships between officers and citizens make it easier to ensure quality two-way communication between an agency and the public. Officers may have an easier time securing information about crime, disorder, and other community problems. Citizens may be far more willing to speak with the police. When resources are needed to further a problem-solving initiative, officers in small and rural agencies are more likely to personally know the business or individual that can provide the needed assistance. Officers and citizens have favorable relationships built on trust and respect because they have known each other for so long on a personal level.

All of these factors can also work against community policing efforts if circumstances are inverted. Because an officer seeking a citizen's assistance may not be an anonymous public official, but rather a former high school classmate, the nature of preexisting personal relationships will condition responses. An officer who was a bully or "stole" a citizen's girlfriend 20 years earlier might not receive a citizen's trust or support. Even where police personnel have favorable relations with the public, good communication and interpersonal relations can be both a blessing and a burden. Police officers are not simply representatives of the local government. They are friends, neighbors, Little League coaches, members of the same church congregation, or lower-ranking members of philanthropic organizations. An officer's personal and private roles with the public can become blurred. From a community policing perspective, the relationship between an officer and the public is of vital importance. From an officer well-being perspective, it can become challenging when officers do not have sufficient "down time" as normal residents. Problems can arise when personnel are treated as police officers, even in their personal lives, or are routinely called upon to act in an official capacity while off duty.

Modern Rural Community Policing

In many ways, community policing is an extension of what naturally emerges in many rural policing environments. Organizations emphasize ends over means and functionality over adherence to strict bureaucratic form. Interpersonal relationships (both internally and externally) are friendly, based on trust and respect, and facilitate getting things done. Citizens are more invested in their community and are willing to work to fight against the incursion of crime and disorder. This does not, however, suggest community policing is universally evident in rural areas. In reality, not all officers embrace a community policing ideology. Not all rural or small agencies engage in the same level of community policing activity.

Examining the adoption of community policing activities in the 1990s, Edward Maguire and colleagues found that among smaller agencies (serving 50,000 or fewer citizens) and nonurban agencies, community policing activities were more common among the larger agencies within these categories. This does not necessarily mean there is "more" community policing in midsize jurisdictions. Rather, it might mean those agencies engage in a broader form of community policing or simply engage in more formal community policing relative to smaller

jurisdictions. Stated differently, small-town and rural police agencies might still engage in community policing, but that style of community policing might be based more on interpersonal and informal relationships versus formal partnerships and established collaborations. Maguire and colleagues also noted that some of the variation in their study might have been an artifact of federal community policing funding efforts, which were quite robust in the 1990s.

William Pelfrey found variation among officers working in rural agencies. Specifically, not all officers expressed the same level of endorsement of community policing approaches. Community policing has presumed greater viability in rural areas because of the stronger relationship between the police and the public, as well as the lower level of organizational structure and formality (which tend to work against the success of community policing efforts). However, its success remains predicated on the predisposition of agencies to embrace this philosophy and the proclivity of officers to integrate community policing into the heart of their operational approaches.

Joseph A. Schafer

See also Building Partnerships and Stakeholders; Community, Definition of; Community Cohesion and Empowerment; Decentralizing the Organization/ Organizational Change; Involving Local Businesses; Police-Community Relations

Further Readings

Falcone, D. N., Wells, L. E., & Weisheit, R. A. (2002). The small-town police department. *Policing: An International Journal of Police Strategies & Management, 25,* 371–384.

Kuhns, J. B., III, Maguire, E. R., & Cox, S. M. (2007). Public-safety concerns among law enforcement agencies in suburban and rural America. *Police Quarterly, 10*(4), 429–454.

Liederbach, J., & Frank, J. (2003). Policing Mayberry: The work routines of small town and rural officers. *American Journal of Criminal Justice, 28*(1), 53–72.

Maguire, E. R., Kuhns, J. B., Uchida, U. D., & Cox, S. M. (1997). Patterns of community policing in nonurban America. *Journal of Research in Crime and Delinquency, 34*(3), 368–394.

Pelfrey, W. V., Jr. (2007). Style of policing adopted by rural police and deputies: An analysis of job satisfaction and community policing. NCJ 221488. *Policing: An International Journal of Police Strategies & Management, 30*(4), 620–636.

Reaves, B. A. (2010). *Local police departments, 2007.* NCJ 231174. Washington, DC: U.S. Department of Justice, Bureau of Justice Statistics. Retrieved from http://bjs.ojp .usdoj.gov/content/pub/pdf/lpd07.pdf

Weisheit, R. A., Falcone, D. N., & Wells, L. E. (1999). *Crime and policing in rural and small-town America* (2nd ed.). Prospect Heights, IL: Waveland.

S

SARA Problem-Solving Process

See Problem-Solving Process (SARA)

School Violence and Safety, Characteristics of

The horrific killings in December 2012 of 26 children and teachers at Sandy Hook Elementary School in Newtown, Connecticut, underscored once more the vulnerability of our nation's schools and the need for local police to be prepared for such critical incidents. Although one study found that *mass killings*—defined as incidents in which four or more people are killed by the attacker—only account for about 1% of all murders, on average such incidents occur about every two weeks; children (ages 12 and under) are frequently victims, representing about one-fifth of all victims.

Much has changed since the April 1999 mass killings of 13 people by two shooters at Columbine High School in Littleton, Colorado, where on-scene officers waited 45 minutes for an elite SWAT team to arrive. The most immediate change calls for police to react swiftly to an "active-shooter" situation, with responding officers being trained to rush toward gunfire and stop the active shooter before more lives are lost. (The approach prior to Columbine was for police to take a contain-and-wait strategy, to prevent officers and bystanders from getting killed; first responders would establish a perimeter to contain the situation, protect themselves, and then wait for the special-weapons team to go in and neutralize the shooters[s]).

The term *school violence* refers to both lethal and nonlethal incidents that occur within schools. Recent research, however, has also expanded the concept of school violence to include not only physical harm but also psychological harm and property damage. School violence can also include specific behavioral problems that occur on campus, such as bullying; intimidation; verbal threats; vandalism; fighting; sexual harassment; gang activity; the carrying of weapons on school property; and hate crimes or hate speech directed toward students of a specific race, ethnicity, or religion, or toward gay, lesbian, bisexual, or transgender students.

This entry provides an overview of the more common offenses associated with school violence. Lethal school violence most often involves school shootings that result in homicide or suicide. Nonlethal school violence encompasses a range of incidents occurring on school property, usually among students. These offenses include rape, weapon possession, gang-related activity, and various forms of bullying.

Schools have introduced several safety initiatives in response to incidents of violence. This entry briefly discusses the background of school-related violent crime and the research on the prevalence of the offenses. The entry then discusses school administration and the criminal justice system's response to address safety within schools. Given the unpredictable nature of and the recent problems involving acts of school violence, it is imperative that police officers, school personnel, and community stakeholders engage in problem-solving efforts if they are to address and prevent such problems.

Background

Victimization of schoolchildren is among the top concerns of policymakers and the general public, and violence directed toward schoolchildren receives extensive media coverage. Perhaps what drives a lot of this attention are the highly publicized incidents of school shootings in the United States and Canada during the past two decades, which have affected public perception of school security and student safety. The resulting fear has contributed to the clamor for increasing school security measures, such as installing metal detectors, securing entrances to buildings, strict disciplinary policies, and assigning police officers to patrol school corridors. Interestingly, whether or not any of these expenditures are justified based upon the threat to children's safety within the school is debatable. Similar heightened concern about school crime and violence in the 1970s led the U.S. Congress to commission a study on school crime, which found that schools are relatively safe places for children.

Despite these findings, the incidents of school shootings throughout the United States and Canada during the 1990s and 2000s significantly altered public perception of school safety. Sociologist Joel Best claims that heightened concern about school violence culminated with the shooting at Columbine High School, near Denver, Colorado, in April 1999. Immediately following the shooting—which resulted in the death of 12 students, one teacher, and the two gunmen—the media dedicated around-the-clock coverage to the event and its aftermath, which helped fuel increased attention to school safety. Despite these concerns about school shootings, however, data from the National Crime Victimization Survey suggest that children are safer in school than at home or elsewhere in terms of their becoming victims of homicide and other violent crimes.

Lethal School Violence

Lethal school violence involves homicides perpetrated by one or more students against their classmates or school staff. Following the shooting at Columbine, in 2002 the U.S. Department of Education and the U.S. Secret Service combined their resources to conduct an analysis of school violence

and safety. They result was the Safe School Initiative, which included publication of a guide, entitled *Threat Assessment in Schools: A Guide to Managing Threatening Situations and to Creating Safe School Climates*, which described incidents of "targeted violence" in school settings—school shootings and other school-based violent attacks. The Secret Service considers it an act of "targeted school violence" when a school is deliberately selected as the location for an attack, as opposed to when a school experiences random violence or opportunistic attacks. The term *targeted violence* is related to the Secret Service's five-year study of the behavior of individuals who have carried out, or attempted, lethal attacks on public officials. According to the Secret Service's study, warning signs were apparent prior to the attack in many cases of targeted school violence.

Despite the widespread public concern about school safety following a shooting on campus, these attacks are extremely rare events. According to FBI data, between 1999 and 2005, the number of children who were killed by family members was 15 times more than the number of students who were killed at school by their classmates. Nonetheless, these incidents have resulted in more stringent disciplinary policies and school safety initiatives.

Nonlethal School Violence

Weapon Possession

Survey data indicate that weapon carrying by students is a common practice regardless of student socioeconomic status or whether the school is urban, suburban, or rural. Weapons in school can also undermine feelings of safety among staff and students. While more students carry weapons to school than actually use them, data suggest that students who carry weapons display the following characteristics: substance abuse, depression, suicidal ideation, having had property stolen or deliberately damaged at school, having been threatened or injured with a weapon on school property, and having engaged in physical fighting.

Gangs in Schools

Gangs are contributors to school violence. Gangs and gang activity can increase the likelihood of weapon carrying in school. The risk of violence escalates when rival gangs attend the same school. Gang-related problems, though, tend to reflect problems within the communities surrounding the school. The school can also serve as a recruitment center for gangs, in addition to providing a location in which to sell drugs and rob students. Gang members may also vandalize school property and intimidate or assault teachers.

Bullying

According to bullying expert Dan Olweus, a student is being bullied when that student is exposed to repeated negative actions over time by one or more other students. The bullying can be physical, which includes hitting, kicking, pushing, spitting, or taking personal belongings by force; verbal, which includes threats; emotional, which includes intimidation or social exclusion; and sexual, which involves sexual abuse or harassment. Being both a victim and a perpetrator of bullying is correlated with school violence, such as the carrying of weapons, fighting, and substance abuse. Some school shooters as well as students who have committed suicide have been identified as being victims of persistent bullying by their classmates; indeed, this appears to be a consensus view now. Many perpetrators of school violence also exhibited poor coping skills.

Safety Initiatives to Prevent School Violence

There are often warning signs prior to incidents of school violence, particularly with shootings. The Safe Schools Initiative recommends that schools utilize a fact-based, threat-assessment approach in analyzing a student's behavior. School administrators should focus on preventing school violence by creating an atmosphere in which students feel comfortable reporting incidents and reports of threats to school staff.

Many policies address the possession of weapons on school property. School codes of conducts that explicitly detail what items are prohibited on school property and the consequences for violating the codes should be implemented.

Initiatives to prevent school violence can involve restructuring school policies, whereby bullying, intimidation, and sexual harassment are not tolerated. Individual interventions include holding meetings with students who bully and supporting and counseling the victims. School staff should also include the parents of the involved students.

The goals of community policing and problem solving include building closer ties between the police and the community, identifying and addressing the underlying problems within a community that contribute to neighborhood crime and disorder, and participating in crime prevention activities. Therefore, a major responsibility and priority of the police as they practice this strategy is to include the safety and protection of children who devote a large proportion of their young lives to school activities.

Jonathan M. Kremser

See also School Violence and Safety, Community Policing Strategies for

Further Readings

Benbenishty, R., & Astor, R. (2005). *School violence in context: Culture, neighborhood, family, school, and gender.* New York, NY: Oxford University Press.

Best, J. (2002). Monster hype: School violence, the media's phantom epidemic. *Education Next, 2*(2), 51–55. Retrieved from http://educationnext.org/monster-hype

Chastain, M. A. (2009, April 19). Shoot first: Columbine tragedy transformed police tactics. *USA TODAY.* Retrieved from http://usatoday30.usatoday.com/news/nation/2009–04–19-columbine-police-tactics_N.htm

Elliott, D. S., Hamburg, B. A., & Williams, K. R. (Eds.). (1998). *Violence in American schools: A new perspective.* New York, NY: Cambridge University Press.

Fein, R. A., Vossekuil, B., & Pollack, W. S. (2002). *Threat assessment in schools: A guide to managing threatening situations and to creating safe school climates.* Washington, DC: U.S. Department of Education & U.S. Secret Service. Retrieved from http://www.secretservice.gov/ntac/ssi_guide.pdf

Fox, J. A., & Burstein, H. (2010). *Violence and security on campus: From preschool through college.* Santa Barbara, CA: Praeger.

Hoyer, M., & Heath, B. (2012, December 19). Mass killings occur in USA once every two weeks. *USA TODAY.* Retrieved from http://www.usatoday.com/story/news/nation/2012/12/18/mass-killings-common/1778303

Jimerson, S., & Furlong, M. (Eds.). (2006). *The handbook of school violence and school safety: From research to practice.* Mahwah, NJ: Routledge.

Muula, A. S., Rudatsikira, E., & Siziya, S. (2008). Correlates of weapon carrying among high school students in the United States. *Annals of General*

Psychiatry, 7(8). doi: 10.1186/1744–859X-7–8. Retrieved from http://www.annals-general-psychiatry .com/content/7/1/8

Olweus, D. (1993). *Bullying at school: What we know and what we can do.* Oxford, England: Blackwell.

Vossekuil, B., Fein, R., Reddy, M., Borum, R., & Modzeleski, W. (2000). *Safe school initiative.* Washington, DC: U.S. Secret Service National Threat Assessment Center. Retrieved from http://cecp.air.org/ download/ntac_ssi_report.pdf

SCHOOL VIOLENCE AND SAFETY, COMMUNITY POLICING STRATEGIES FOR

The goals of community policing include building closer ties between the police and the community, identifying and addressing the underlying problems within a community that contribute to crime and delinquency, and involving the participation of the community in crime-prevention strategies. Community policing strategies for the prevention of school violence and safety encompass a number of approaches that build on these goals. This entry discusses the community policing approaches that are most widely used in addressing school violence and safety within U.S. schools, including the School-Based Partnerships (SBP) program, Child Development and Community Policing (CD-CP), the Drug Abuse Resistance Education (D.A.R.E.) program, the Gang Resistance and Education (G.R.E.A.T.) curriculum, and the School Resource Officer (SRO) program.

Community Policing Approaches to School Violence

School-Based Partnerships Program

Community policing encourages law enforcement officers to become more integrated within the life of the community and to form partnerships with the schools. In 1994, Congress passed the Violent Crime Control and Law Enforcement Act. The act led to the creation of the Office of Community-Oriented Policing Services (COPS). During 1998 to 1999, the COPS Office initiated—and provided nearly $30 million in funding

for—the School-Based Partnerships program, which formed partnerships between police and school administrators, faculty, bus drivers, parents, students, and local businesses to address bullying, threats, intimidation, drug dealing, victimization on the way to and from school, assault, sexual assault, vandalism and graffiti, loitering and disorderly conduct, disputes that could affect student safety, and larceny. No local match was required under School-Based Partnerships, although each agency was encouraged to contribute an in-kind match to its project. This program has not been funded in recent years.

Child Development and Community Policing

New Haven, Connecticut, has developed a community policing model that involves collaboration between the Yale Child Study Center and the New Haven Department of Police Services. According to the National Center for Children Exposed to Violence, the goal of the CD-CP is to heal the wounds that chronic exposure to violence inflicts on children and families. By working closely with mental health professionals, the police in New Haven CD-CP program emphasize early intervention with children who have witnessed and experienced violence, as well as with children who have committed serious violent acts. One of the mechanisms of the partnership between the police and mental health professionals involves working with parents or teachers to facilitate a discussion with schoolchildren within the classroom following an incidence of violence. Desired outcomes of the program's intervention among schoolchildren include reduced incidents of posttraumatic stress disorder symptoms over the short term, and a reduction in depression, social withdrawal, and aggressive behavior over the long term.

Drug Abuse Resistance Education Program

Another example of a community policing strategy to address school violence and safety is the D.A.R.E. program. The program was developed by the Los Angeles (California) Police Department in 1983, and has been implemented in more than half the school districts within the United States. The program targets children in kindergarten through high school, and its purpose is to equip children with the skills necessary to avoid drugs and gangs. Additionally, the D.A.R.E. program provides students with information about drugs, teaches decision-making skills, self-esteem building, and choosing healthy alternatives to using drugs. The curriculum utilizes lectures by police, group activities, question-and-answer sessions, audiovisual material, workbook exercises, and role-playing exercises.

Officers who teach the D.A.R.E. program receive a substantial amount of specialized training. The 80-hour curriculum focuses on classroom management skills, teaching strategies, communication skills, adolescent development, drug information, and curriculum instruction. Experienced D.A.R.E. officers undergo additional instruction to become instructors. The instructors make periodic classroom visits to ensure that the program is implemented with fidelity.

Numerous evaluations of the D.A.R.E. program have found no convincing evidence that the program is effective at long-term reduction in drug use among participating pupils. Susan Ennett, Christopher Ringwalt, Nancy Tobler, and Robert Flewelling from the Center for Social Research and Policy Analysis evaluated the D.A.R.E. program and found that D.A.R.E.'s short-term effectiveness in preventing or reducing drug use is small. Furthermore, the program did not appear to have any effect on reducing alcohol or tobacco use among D.A.R.E. participants in comparison with a control group.

Internationally, the D.A.R.E. program has been implemented in schools in Sweden. The Swedish version is a replica of the U.S. program, and similarly focuses on the prevention of drug use among schoolchildren, with the additional objectives of preventing violence and bullying among youths. Evaluations of the Swedish version have been as disappointing as the American counterpart. Results show no significant difference between pupils participating in the D.A.R.E. program and those in the control group. Furthermore, the portion of the program that focused on prevention of violence similarly showed no difference between the participants in the program and the control group.

Gang Resistance Education and Training Program

Similar to the D.A.R.E. program but targeting gang activity is the G.R.E.A.T. program. The G.R.E.A.T.

program was developed in 1991 through a collaborative effort between the U.S. Bureau of Alcohol, Tobacco, Firearms and Explosives (ATF) and the Phoenix (Arizona) Police Department. The program expanded nationally in 1992 after the Federal Law Enforcement Training Center (FLETC) provided the support to train the program's instructors. Since the beginning of the program, G.R.E.A.T. has certified more than 12,000 instructors, and nearly 6 million students have completed the program.

The program is aimed at middle-school pupils, and its objectives are to reduce their involvement in gang activity and delinquent behavior, teach the consequences of involvement in gangs, and build positive relationships with the police. The objectives are taught in schools by uniformed law enforcement officers during a 9-hour curriculum.

A multisite, multiyear evaluation of the G.R.E.A.T. program yielded mixed results. While there were some weak positive changes in the prosocial attitudes of the participants, there was a consistently absent effect on levels of delinquency and gang membership. These results have led to reviews and revisions of the program's curriculum. The current curriculum consists of 13 lessons designed to teach necessary life skills to prevent involvement in gangs and delinquency.

Findings from a 2012 study, commissioned by the National Institute of Justice and reported by the National Gang Center, indicate that G.R.E.A.T. has positive effects on youth gang membership and on a number of risk factors and social skills thought to be associated with gang membership. Further findings indicate the program resulted in more positive attitudes toward police, less positive attitudes about gangs, and less anger.

School Resource Officer Program

The community policing strategy of assigning police officers to individual schools was developed in Flint, Michigan, in 1958 as part of a delinquency prevention plan. This early police-school liaison program gradually became what is known today as the SRO program.

According to Title 1 of the Omnibus Crime Control and Safe Streets Act of 1968, Part Q, the SRO is defined as "a career law enforcement officer, with sworn authority, deployed in community-oriented policing, and assigned by the employing police department or agency to work in collaboration with school and community-based organizations." The SRO program has grown to more than 2,600 trained officers throughout the United States, and is represented by its own organization, the National Association of School Resource Officers (NASRO).

The goals of the SRO program generally involve preventing juvenile delinquency and improving relations within the community. In the delinquency prevention role, officers assigned to schools can investigate criminal activity, make arrests, and refer youths to court. Officers also act as instructors, provide counseling and mentoring to students, gather information on students with disciplinary problems or who exhibit threatening behavior, and collaborate with other law enforcement agencies within the community such as the juvenile probation office. Furthermore, they can consult with school administration on school security and law enforcement matters.

The SRO program also focuses on building community relations. Officers speak at parent-teacher events and youth clubs. Resource officers can contact parents of students who exhibit behavioral problems and work with the parents to prevent the escalation of the child's misbehavior into delinquency. The role of the SRO has also broadened to include educating youths about traffic safety, drug use, and gangs. Some SROs monitor social networking websites to gather information about youth involvement with illegal activity or plans to commit violent acts. Some studies suggest that a police presence within the school can deter crime, but this argument remains mostly inconclusive. According to Peter Finn, the benefits of the SRO program include improving the image of the police among youth, forming a collaborative relationship between the police department and the school district, and building a positive image of the police within the community.

A positive aspect of the SRO program is that administrators have a sworn police officer with full arrest powers on site. This could be beneficial in more rural communities that have a longer police response time. As a community policing strategy, SROs can provide counseling and mentoring to youth. The officers can also share information on problems occurring within the school and the community, as often these problems are interrelated.

Challenges between school resource officers and administrators can arise when responsibilities of the police in enforcing school codes of conduct are not clearly delineated. Confusion and miscommunication can occur when principals exercise discretion and do not involve the SRO in matters involving students who have violated the law and school policy. School districts need to establish clear guidelines on when to involve the SRO in matters involving student misconduct. Other difficulties involve budgeting for a full-time SRO. Districts are often responsible for funding full-time SROs, and budget shortfalls could result in the loss of the police presence within the school.

School-based policing programs have been implemented in school districts internationally. In Canada, school resource officers are members of the Royal Canadian Mounted Police (RCMP) or local police departments. The province of Alberta formed the Alberta Association of School Resource Officers (AASRO) in 1998, which is currently the only school resource officer organization in Canada. The AASRO provides school-based officers with resources, such as training opportunities, a networking system, and information on youth-related issues, to support the officers' work in the schools throughout the province.

The RCMP operates the National Youth Officer Program. This community policing initiative partners the police with the schools and communities, with the purpose of reducing offenses among youths and helping them become contributing members of the community. The RCMP provides services for approximately 5,000 schools across Canada.

In 2006, the RCMP formed the Youth Officer Resource Centre (YORC) as a component of its overall National Youth Services Program. Similar to the curriculum-based policing programs in the United States, the YORC delivers programs to youth in the schools and communities. Topics include anger management, bullying, dating violence, drugs, family violence, gangs, drunken driving, Internet safety, peer pressure, traffic safety, and law.

Similar community-based policing initiatives can be found in the Netherlands, where school safety initiatives are primarily the responsibility of the local municipalities and provinces, and a community-based approach for schools has been advanced. Local officials are generally responsible for the youth and safety policies. These authorities promote contact between the police and schools to prevent vandalism, minor crimes, and violence. Agreements are currently in place in many municipalities between the police and the municipality, the judicial authorities, and the schools. Important community policing aspects of the agreements include the following: enhanced communication between the police, schools, and social services through a permanent liaison; schools record incidents and report punishable behavioral problems to the police; the schools inform parents; and police and judicial officials quickly address problems and offer support to the schools where needed.

Jonathan M. Kremser

See also School Violence and Safety, Characteristics of

Further Readings

Bureau of Justice Assistance. (1995). *Drug abuse resistance education (D.A.R.E.).* NCJ FS000039. Washington, DC: U.S. Department of Justice.

Bureau of Justice Statistics. (2007). *School crime supplement to the National Crime Victimization Survey: 2007.* Washington, DC: U.S. Department of Justice. doi: 10.3886/ICPSR23041.v1

Dinkes, R., Kemp, J., Baum, K., & Snyder, T. (2009). *Indicators of school crime: 2008.* Washington, DC: U.S. Department of Justice, Bureau of Justice Programs. Retrieved from http://nces.ed.gov/pubsearch/pubsinfo.asp?pubid=2009022

Elliott, D. S., Hamburg, B. A., & Williams, K. R. (Eds.). (1998). *Violence in American schools: A new perspective.* New York, NY: Cambridge University Press.

Ennett, S. T., Tobler, N. S., Ringwalt, C. L., & Flewelling, R. L. (1994). *How effective is drug abuse resistance education? A meta-analysis of Project DARE outcome evaluations.* Research Triangle Park, NC: Center for Social Research and Policy Analysis. Retrieved from http://www.ncbi.nlm.nih.gov/pmc/articles/PMC1615171/

Esbensen, F-A. (2008). In-school victimization: Reflections of a researcher. *Journal of Contemporary Criminal Justice, 24*(2), 114–124.

Fein, R. A., Vossekuil, B., & Pollack, W. S. (2002). *Threat assessment in schools: A guide to managing threatening situations and to creating safe school climates.* Washington, DC: U.S. Department of Education & U.S. Secret Service. Retrieved from http://www.secretservice.gov/ntac/ssi_guide.pdf

Finn, P. (2006). School resource officer programs: Finding the funding, reaping the benefits. *FBI Law Enforcement Bulletin, 75*(8), 1–7.

National Gang Center. (2012). *Has G.R.E.A.T. proven effective?* Retrieved from http://www.great-online.org/faq/Default.Aspx

Rich, T., Finn, P., & Ward, S. (2001). *Guide to using School COP to address student discipline and crime problems.* Washington, DC: U.S. Department of Justice, Office of Community Oriented Policing Services.

Sampson, R. (2002). *Bullying in schools.* Washington, DC: U.S. Department of Justice, Office of Community Oriented Policing Services.

Verano, R., & Bezdikian, V. (2001). *Addressing school-related crime and disorder: Interim lessons from school-based problem-solving projects.* Washington, DC: U.S. Department of Justice.

SITUATIONAL CRIME PREVENTION

Situational crime prevention (SCP) is a crime prevention strategy that seeks to reduce the opportunities for disorder and criminal activity. It adopts changes to the physical environment to make it harder to commit criminal acts and for offenders to find less reward in their criminal endeavors. In addition to making crime more difficult, it attempts to create situations where there is an increased sense of the likelihood of apprehension, leading to offender desistance and deterrence. In short, SCP makes crime less attractive by reducing crime facilitators and removing the benefits of criminal activity. Situational crime prevention is also novel in its approach to crime reduction in that it focuses more on *crime* prevention than *criminality* prevention. In essence, situational crime prevention is less concerned with the social causes of crimes than it is with the elements that allow crime to occur. Situational crime prevention is crucial to community policing and problem solving because it is focused on the settings for and prevention of crimes rather than on persons committing them; it also seeks to forestall the occurrence of crime by making criminal action less attractive to offenders. This entry examines the theoretical underpinnings of this theory as well as its approach to the environment and specific types of crime. Included are examples of situational crime prevention in practice.

Theoretical Background

Situational crime prevention is based on several different assumptions and theories about criminal behavior, such as environmental criminology, rational choice theory, and routine activity theory.

Environmental Criminology

The first theoretical premise lies in the arena of environmental criminology. Environmental criminology examines the location of crime, focusing on elements like city layouts, street patterns, building designs, and the daily movements of offenders and victims. Environmental criminologists are interested in how the physical environment facilitates criminal endeavors and how offenders capitalize on these physical features to engage in their criminal activities.

Rational Choice Theory

The second theoretical perspective is the rational choice theory, which postulates that offenders commit crime because of the rewards they gain from it. Based on Jeremy Bentham's criminal calculus, rational choice theorists claim that when benefits outweigh the costs, offenders will choose to engage in crime. Low levels of apprehension, continued gains, and poor understanding of the criminal consequences are all key elements that enable offenders to perceive the criminal enterprise as beneficial. Rational choice theory does not imply that all offenders are making good decisions—rather, they are making decisions they perceive as rewarding, which is not always the objective reality.

Routine Activity Theory

The routine activity perspective takes the criminal event apart and examines the respective roles of the three required elements: the offender, the victim or target, and the lack of guardianship. Routine activity theory states that for a crime to occur, all three elements must be present concurrently, and that if only one element is removed or altered, the criminal act is thwarted. For example, while there may be a motivated offender interested in shoplifting from a clothing store, the presence of a security guard or closed-circuit television cameras (guardianship) will increase the probability that the crime will not take place. Routine activity theory focuses less on the offender's propensities (be these social, economical, or psychological) and puts the emphasis on the criminal act. Routine activity theory is a central component of the situational crime prevention approach as it requires police officials and researchers to understand the dynamics of crime or the conditions that make crime possible.

Focus on Offender Decision Making

As discussed above, situational crime prevention focuses on how offenders perceive the environment around them, calculating the risks and rewards of the criminal enterprise. In this respect, situational crime prevention relies heavily on offender decision-making models and attempts to alter the variables in the offender's surroundings to direct the decisions to noncriminal events. In effect, *perceptual deterrence* comes into play as situational crime prevention's goal is to not only establish actual crime-reducing strategies but to also create the illusion that such strategies exist. Offenders, therefore, are constantly wondering about the risk of apprehension, the threat of detection, and the reality that they may meet legal consequences. Perceptual deterrence is a central component of situational crime prevention as crime-reducing strategies are designed to impact the manner in which offenders process information and hopefully choose the path of desistance. According to the situational crime prevention approach, offenders go through two stages before they commit a criminal act: the involvement decision and the event decision.

Involvement Decision

The involvement decision refers to the processes that facilitate an offender's decision to become involved in crime. The involvement decision is linked to the offender's social characteristics, background factors, and the legitimate opportunities available to them. According to situational crime prevention, the involvement decision must occur before the event decision, which is the actual commission of a crime. In short, people do not simply wake up one day and decide to become professional car thieves. Rather, some people may possess certain psychological or demographic characteristics and when these are combined with delinquent peers, or a troubled social setting, there is an increased chance that they will decide to be involved in the world of car theft. The involvement decision is usually drawn out over a certain period of time, and the conditions responsible may not be entirely crime related. For instance, a youth that grows up in absolute poverty may decide to be part of the criminal underworld. However, the poverty itself is not a criminal notion nor is it necessarily a climate for that youth to be exposed to criminal behaviors. In sum, the involvement decision is made up of numerous sources of information that lead an individual to the decision to commit a criminal act.

Event Decision

The event decision, on the other hand, is much more time bound and immediate in nature. The event refers to the criminal act that the offender carries out after having gone through the involvement decision. It is during this offender decision-making process that situational crime prevention seeks to have the most impact, and the majority of crime-prevention techniques developed are instituted at this level of the criminal decision process. In order to impact or alter the event, situational crime prevention techniques play on the criminal calculus that offenders undergo when sizing up a criminal opportunity.

As mentioned above, it is assumed that offenders commit crime when the benefits outweigh the risk, and the role of crime prevention is to alter the cost of crime so that when it comes to the event decision, the offender will desist and pass on the criminal activity. In terms of car theft, if an offender is out looking to steal a car, a crime-prevention technique that may alter the event decision may be to make the offender aware that the car has vehicle identification number etching, an alarm system, a global positioning tracking device, and carries a sticker that allows the police to pull it over when it is driven during late-night hours. If the car owner is successful in relating all of this information to the offender through the use of stickers or placards, situational crime prevention would dictate that the car is less likely to be stolen. In that instance, the offender weighs the pros and cons of the event, and through a rational decision-making process, decides not to follow through with the event.

In terms of the event decision and trying to impact the offender's criminal calculus, situational crime prevention does highlight some limitations. When attempting to pass on information to help the offender make a more rational decision, it is assumed that the offender is receptive or capable of decoding this information. However, many offenders are in a state of arousal or under the influence of substances that cloud their judgment, and hence they suffer from what is referred to as *bounded rationality*. Bounded rationality is a state when offenders either do not have all of the information necessary to make a rational decision or they are incapable of seeing and absorbing the information that is provided for them because of an altered state due to drugs or alcohol.

A good example of this bounded rationality involves drunk drivers. Numerous publicity campaigns have extolled the dangers of drunk driving, and in a sober state, most drivers would never consider getting behind the wheel after a few drinks. However, after a few drinks and in their state of alcohol arousal, some drivers will suffer from bounded rationality and get behind the wheel as if they had never been exposed to any anti–drunk driving information. In essence, situational crime prevention's goal is to alter the event decision, but sometimes efforts to highlight the costs of crime are not always heeded by the offenders themselves. Of course, situational crime prevention also includes techniques that do not rely on offender rationality, but simply prohibit the act from occurring by changing the mechanics of the offense so that it is impossible to complete. For example, requiring hotel patrons to have a key card to access their floor from an elevator prevents even the most inebriated malfeasant from carrying out any type of disorder or crime.

Changing the Environment

One of the foundations of situational crime prevention is the idea that to alter the offender's criminal decision making, a specific change in the physical environment has to take place so that a criminal opportunity is altered or removed altogether. Changing the environment or altering the elements of potential criminal situations has the ultimate goal of affecting the assessment made by potential offenders about risks and rewards of criminal activity.

The situations conducive to crime need to be manipulated so that the criminal act is no longer viewed as attractive by the offender. Situational crime prevention uses the word *environment* in the broad sense. While it can refer to street layouts, it can also apply to the location of stairwells in a high-rise building, the amount of lighting in a store, or the protocol for guests to access their hotel room. In short, a criminal situation occurs within a specific environment, and through targeted techniques, crime-prevention approaches are applied to redesign criminogenic spaces.

Focusing on the physical aspects of crime and seeking to reduce criminal opportunities is a novel approach to crime reduction. Traditional approaches have involved the criminal justice system, law enforcement agencies, and routine police work. Offenders were chased by the police, sometimes apprehended, and then processed through the criminal justice system. Unfortunately, the police cannot be everywhere all the time, nor can they arrest every offender. Therefore, in terms of true crime prevention, there need to be systems in place that reduce crime without the requirement of a heavy police presence. Situational crime prevention theorists do not state that the police have no role in crime prevention or reduction, but that the reliance on police as the sole crime-prevention agents has not proven effective in terms of addressing the overall crime problem.

Many of the techniques used in situational crime prevention are drawn from basic prevention behaviors that people routinely engage in. The notion that one should lock the front door when leaving for work seems logical enough. Locking up one's bike with an antitheft bicycle lock is another commonsense behavior. The majority of these techniques have not been invented for situational crime prevention, but rather they have been tailored and refined so that they can be applied to specific crime problems. It has been said that situational crime-prevention techniques are the "scientific arm of routine precautions."

An important part of situational crime prevention is the idea of increasing guardianship. In essence, if there is a suitable target sought by a motivated offender, one change in the environment could be to increase the level of protection for that target to reduce victimization.

The idea of guardianship, however, is not limited to traditional security measures such as security guards, police officers, or any other uniformed entity. Guardianship can be created indirectly by creating situations whereby the offender is not alone but under the watchful eye of other members of the community. For example, elevators with clear doors that allow an unobstructed view of the passengers as they travel from floor to floor create guardianship against vandalism. Illegal behavior can be seen more quickly and reported to authorities. Similarly, individuals seeking to vandalize the elevator may not take such a risk as they would be quickly identified and apprehended. Older, more traditional elevators, where the passengers are isolated the minute the doors close, create instant anonymity and privacy—the perfect situation for vandalism to occur.

Finally, situational crime prevention supports the idea that any crime-prevention effort should be widespread, supported by the community, and be part of an integral probe to the problem at hand. This all-encompassing approach to crime reduction seeks to draw in law enforcement professionals, business leaders, researchers, victims, offenders, and other stakeholders affected by the problem. Only when all of these members agree to be part of the solution, can real progress be made. Of course, when implementing a situational crime prevention technique, there may be certain costs to the community—be these real or perceived. Situational crime prevention theorists state that this cost must be shared by all community members seeking the rewards of crime reduction. For example, while there has been a virtual elimination of aircraft hijackings due to increased baggage screening and other security measures, there is a cost which includes increased wait times for passengers, frustration, and a general annoyance with the screening process.

Crime Specificity

Before a situational crime prevention crime-reduction technique is implemented, officials need to have a detailed understanding of the dynamics of the crime problem being targeted. Simply expecting results by blindly adopting a crime-prevention measure is doomed to fail. The benefit of the situational crime prevention approach is that it tailors responses to very specific crime problems. For example, situational crime prevention does not address the general crime of burglary. Instead, it will focus on burglaries of electronics from large box stores by teenagers. Only after having broken down the crime into its different components can a situational crime prevention measure be effective as each individual element can be addressed in the crime-reduction response. This focus on crime specificity merges well with Herman Goldstein's problem-oriented policing approach. Goldstein proposed that for police interventions to be effective against crime problems, police officials needed to first understand the underlying or root causes of the problem. Only after understanding why a specific disorder problem occurred in an area can the police tailor and implement an efficient response. By incorporating Goldstein's problem-solving approach, situational crime prevention can now analyze crime problems with a defined methodology, an action research model, so that viable intervention or crime-prevention techniques can be developed.

Twenty-Five Techniques of Situational Crime Prevention

Over the last few years, situational crime prevention has developed 25 techniques which cover five major crime reduction strategies: (1) increasing the effort, (2) increasing the risks, (3) reducing the rewards, (4) reducing provocation, and (5) removing excuses. Under each one of these five categories, there are subsets of activities that can be implemented to reduce crime. For example, under increasing the risks, one of the proposed activities includes "reducing anonymity" which can, for example, be achieved by requiring taxi driver identification placards, "How's my driving" decals, or school uniforms.

Reactions to Situational Crime Prevention

Situational crime prevention's emphasis on changing the landscape of crime by tinkering with the dynamics of criminal situations has not been free of criticism. Some critics of this crime control measure claim that situational crime prevention increases the amount of state control over its citizenry in exchange for the promise of safety and well-being. The installation of cameras in public spaces, checkpoints, identification mechanisms, for example, are seen as infringing on personal liberties and an extension of the ominous symbol of George Orwell's "Big Brother."

Other critics state that situational crime prevention reduces the amount of personal responsibility found in society and that making crime harder to commit does not necessarily teach people the moral reasons why people should not be committing crimes. Finally, there are arguments that situational crime prevention's focus on the criminal act itself and its redesigning of the environment ignores the narrative about the true roots of crime that are found in social and economic inequality, discrimination, and other social ills.

Emmanuel P. Barthe

See also Hot Spots; Predictive Policing; Problem-Oriented Policing, Goldstein's Development of; Publicity Campaigns

Further Readings

Brantingham, P. L., &. Brantingham, P. J. (1990). Situational crime prevention in practice. *Canadian Journal of Criminology, 32,* 17–40.

Clarke, R. V. (1997). Introduction. In Clarke, R. V. (Ed.), *Situational crime prevention: Successful case studies* (2nd ed.; pp. 2–43). Albany, NY: Harrow and Heston.

Clarke, R. V. (2005). Seven misconceptions of situational crime prevention. In N. Tilley (Ed.), *Handbook of crime prevention and community safety* (pp. 39–50). Cullompton, England: Willan.

Cornish, D. B., & Clarke, R. V. (Eds.). (1986). *The reasoning criminal. Rational choice perspectives on offending.* New York, NY: Springer.

Lab, S. P. (1997). *Crime prevention: Approaches, practices and evaluations* (3rd ed.). Cincinnati, OH. Anderson.

SOCIAL CAPITAL

Two of the most fundamental and indispensable qualities of a thriving community are public safety and social order. Police cannot hope to be successful in addressing neighborhood crime and disorder without partnering with the community's members; this is the nexus of "community" and "policing." Building partnerships between citizens and police is part of a larger community-building movement which requires high levels of trust and engagement.

Having members of a community who are bonded together, looking out for one another, and willing to engage in collective action when threatened is key to the peaceful coexistence if not the very survival of an orderly society. This entry explains how social capital is defined and how the concept relates to community policing.

Social Capital Defined

The term *social capital* is believed to have first come into use in the early 1900s in the writing of Lyda Judson Hanifan, a Harvard graduate and West Virginia school reformer who often urged communities to become more involved in their schools—which, he believed, were places that cultivated good will, fellowship, and social intercourse.

Today, however, the term *social capital* has no clear, generally agreed-upon meaning but rather its definition depends on the discipline or context in which it is used.

Social capital concerns social networks and relationships, bonding people, and establishing bridges between them. Many people understand that having and fostering goodwill toward each other is a valuable resource. As such, social capital is a force or social structure that helps to bind people together (generating social cohesion) and is fundamentally about how people interact with each other. Social capital can concern people who are in close proximity to one another—neighbors—who share rootedness, and involves their social, psychological, and even economic dependence on one another. It also can refer to the institutions, relationships, and norms that help to shape social interactions.

Social capital exists in two contexts or domains: local and public. The local level of social capital is the most basic and concerns individual citizens who have trust and reciprocity with one another. It involves people's informal assumption of responsibility to take care of one another as well as to enforce informal rules of conduct. One is reminded of John Steinbeck's book, *The Grapes of Wrath,* with the Joad family leaving Oklahoma's dust bowl and heading west to California for a better life of farming. The migrant families stopped every night and created a little society in their roadside camps, governed by unwritten, unspoken rules that over time carried the force of law—don't flaunt good food in front of neighbors who are famished; don't foul the drinking water; don't intrude on the privacy of others. No one told the families these rules, but their survival depended on following them.

The public level of social capital involves networks that tie individuals together through the existence of broader social institutions: churches, schools, civic organizations (Elks, Rotary), volunteer groups (neighborhood watch groups, the Red Cross), social groups (softball leagues, veterans' organizations), employee groups (unions, bar associations), and so on. Such networks allow people to develop familiarity and trust among one another while also accomplishing shared goals. Other demonstrations of social capital are political participation, newspaper readership, donations of time and funds to nonprofit organizations, maintenance of public places so that they are safe and clean, work to advance both formal and informal education, and work to alleviate poverty and squalid living conditions.

Social Capital and Community Policing

Police who practice community policing and problem solving are aware of the underpinnings of social capital and its ability to bring people together for the common good. One of the reasons for the move away from the reform era of policing (also known as the *professional era of policing*) in recent years was that police had become isolated from the public as they reactively sped from call to call, accomplishing little in the way of long-term problem solving, emphasizing qualitative outcomes, while also witnessing increased crime. In the current community era of policing, the police take advantage of the benefits of social capital not only by generating informal partnerships and friendships with citizens, but also by developing such formal associations as citizen police academies and advisory boards, youth athletic leagues, and reserve or auxiliary units. Indeed, it might also be noted that the use of the SARA (scanning, analysis, response, assessment) problem-solving process, at its heart, involves collaboration between citizens and the community to identify community problems and then implement custom-made responses for addressing them.

The drive and tendency to form networks can have negative outcomes as well. Gangs, hate groups, vigilante groups, and citizen militia groups all represent destructive forces in our society that must be addressed.

Certain forms of social capital, however, are correlated with lower rates of serious crime. Neighborhood meetings, informal friendship and kinship networks, and organizations such as neighborhood watch groups have been formed in response to citizens seeking to increase the safety of their children and bring about a general reduction in property crimes. Social capital often comes into play in community policing and problem solving, as in the following:

- *Crime prevention:* The crime prevention field— which is key to community policing and problem solving—has found social capital to be useful for bringing together the collective, informal efforts of government and nongovernment stakeholders (to include businesses, community groups, police agencies) and work to help communities find solutions to local crime problems; such efforts also serve to promote public awareness of crime prevention and the root causes of crime and victimization, and to engage people in and educate them about crime prevention.

- *Schools:* Police school liaison officer programs bring together parents, police officers, and teachers who form informal networks to work with high-risk students, victims (of bullying, for example), and children and adolescents who are showing early signs of aggression and violence.

- *Restorative justice:* Restorative justice emphasizes repairing the harm to people, relationships, and the community caused by crime by bringing together victims, offenders, and community members to determine how to best address the harms.

- *Community meetings, social media, and websites:* Community policing and problem solving, as mentioned above, requires the ability of police officers to actively listen to the public in order to foster social capital within the community. Accordingly, mechanisms must exist that allow police to receive input from the public 24 hours a day through a combination of methods: the use of real-time, interactive websites as well as citywide, beat, and neighborhood meetings, social media, citizen surveys, and other such methods.

The strategic formation of social capital partnerships is essential for community policing and problem solving, and represents an effective means of responding to community needs.

Kenneth J. Peak

See also Broken Windows Theory; Building Partnerships and Stakeholders; Citizen Surveys; Collaboration With Outside Agencies; Community, Definition of; Community Cohesion and Empowerment; Community Policing, Evolution of; Customer-Based Policing; Problem-Solving Process (SARA)

Further Readings

Hanifan, L. J. (1916). The rural school community centre. *Annals of the American Academy of Political and Social Science, 67,* 130–138.

Pino, N. W. (2001). Community policing and social capital. *Policing: An International Journal of Police Strategies & Management, 24*(2), 200–215.

Policy Research Institute. (2005, September). *Social capital in action: Thematic policy studies.* Montreal, QC, Canada: Author. Retrieved from http://www.horizons .gc.ca/doclib/SC_Thematic_E.pdf

Sampson, R. J. (1999). What "community" supplies. In R. F. Ferguson & W. T. Dickens (Eds.), *Urban problems and community redevelopment* (pp. 241–292). Washington, DC: Brookings Institution.

Steinbeck, J. (1939). *The grapes of wrath.* New York: Viking Press.

STATE POLICE/PATROL, COMMUNITY POLICING STRATEGIES FOR

Primary state police agencies represent a relatively small slice of U.S. policing. Whereas local law enforcement agencies (municipal and county police departments and sheriff's offices) employ 72% of the sworn police personnel in the country, and the federal government employs 14%, primary state police agencies employ only 7% (special-purpose jurisdictions like colleges, parks, and transportation systems account for the remaining 7%). In part because they comprise a fairly small share of the overall policing industry, state police are often overlooked in police research and the policing literature.

Primary state law enforcement agencies generally fit into one of two categories: state police or highway patrol. Highway patrol agencies typically focus their efforts primarily on traffic enforcement and traffic safety, whereas state police usually have broader jurisdiction and are more likely to respond to calls for service and conduct criminal investigations in addition to handling traffic-related responsibilities. Of course, the precise jurisdiction of each of these agencies varies depending upon state law, and agency names also vary beyond just state police and highway patrol, to include state patrol, state troopers, and departments of public safety.

Community policing is not quite the natural fit for state law enforcement agencies that it is for city and town police departments and sheriff's offices. Part of the explanation is historical. Some of the earliest state police agencies were created in response to civil disorder and labor strife, and their role was clearly one of protecting the government and the means of production (mines, factories), not serving the needs of ordinary people. Later, in the early to mid-1900s when most state law enforcement agencies came into existence, their focus was mainly on regulating automobiles and their mission was predominantly enforcement. This entry describes some of the barriers that keep state police agencies from engaging in community policing, and details the ways in which a community policing and problem solving approach can be beneficial to these agencies.

Impediments to Community Policing

Today, state police agencies (and especially those in the highway patrol category) still focus on traffic enforcement to a much greater degree than local law enforcement agencies. More generally, state policing seems to reflect the enforcement style of policing, in contrast to the service and watchman styles that have a closer correspondence with community policing. In addition, state troopers are typically assigned to cover a very large geographic area, in some ways the antithesis of neighborhood policing. Related to this issue of geography, it is highly unlikely that state police can patrol on foot or on bicycle, modes of patrol that are sometimes associated with community policing.

Under community policing, local police officers are expected to be responsive to neighborhood needs and accountable to the community. State police accountability, however, flows through their chain of command back to headquarters in the state capitol, and ultimately to the governor. Basically, the role of the state police is to enforce the *state's* laws throughout the state, without concern for local pressures or issues. They are expected to be responsive to statewide needs and state-level priorities, not local needs. State police are part of a system of federalism and checks and balances, and their particular role in that system is to counterbalance local considerations, not defer to them.

A 2011 national survey of rural law enforcement police chief executive officers (CEOs), including heads of state police agencies, conducted for the Rural Policing Institute at the Federal Law Enforcement Training Center provided some results that illustrate the differing missions of state police and local police as they relate to community policing.

Compared to local police chiefs and sheriffs, state police directors were twice as likely to attach little or no significance to the task of "meeting with community residents about local problems." Similarly, they were three times as likely to ascribe low significance to "diagnose and solve local crime and disorder problems."

Application of Community Policing to State Police

Despite these specific impediments and the seeming incompatibility of state police and community policing, there is evidence that points in the other direction. In the study noted just above, one-third of state police CEOs reported that "meeting with community residents about local problems" was a very significant task for their personnel, and less than 30% rated "diagnose and solve local crime and disorder problems" as very significant. On a related item, nearly three-fourths said that "problem solving, critical thinking, and decision making skills" were very significant for their state police employees.

One important feature of state policing is that troopers almost always work alone and, because they are so widely dispersed geographically, must frequently rely on local police or even the public when they need back-up assistance. Consequently, there is a significant operational advantage to maintaining cordial relations with other law enforcement agents, other institutions such as volunteer fire departments, and community residents. These relationships may not always evolve into formal and official partnerships or collaborations, especially in rural areas, but nonetheless they are characteristic of community policing.

Those state police who have general policing responsibilities (as opposed to narrow highway patrol duties) have some of the same incentives as local police for developing positive community relations. A trooper's ability to resolve family and neighborhood conflicts may depend on familiarity with the people involved and on his or her reputation for fairness. The trooper will also need knowledge of locally available resources, such as domestic violence shelters or community mental health services. And the trooper's success in solving reported crimes will depend heavily, as it does for local police, on the public's willingness to provide information and serve as witnesses.

Since state police provide policing services primarily in rural areas, those forms of community policing that tend to be associated with urban policing are not likely to be relevant. Foot patrol and bike patrol are rarely feasible options for state police, and programs like Safe Houses and Neighborhood Watch may not fit situations in which houses are hundreds of yards or even miles apart. Monthly beat meetings are not likely to be appropriate and community meetings in general may not be popular. Troopers may find that community engagement works best in more informal settings as country stores, co-ops, and fire stations.

The very concept of "community" is at the heart of the issue regarding the applicability of community policing for state police. Some state police are in fact assigned to local communities, making the fit with community policing fairly straightforward. Connecticut, Illinois, and Maryland, for example, have (on occasion) assigned so-called resident troopers. This approach can simply be part of the state police deployment strategy, or it can be a contractual service for which local communities pay. In Pennsylvania, sheriff's departments do not provide police services, so the state police provide all police services for any town, township, borough, or village that does not have its own police department—as a result, many troopers patrol local areas, handle calls, and investigate crimes. In many other states, sheriff's departments and state police share the responsibility for policing both unincorporated areas and those local jurisdictions that choose not to fund their own police departments.

"Community" can also take nongeographic forms, though, some of which might make more sense for many state police and highway patrol agencies. In particular, motorists might be identified by a state police agency as their primary "community," or perhaps even subgroups such as truckers, motorcyclists, and teen drivers. These are groups with specific interests and issues related to roadway usage and traffic safety. A state police agency trying to increase its effectiveness in relation to traffic safety might want to develop formal connections and even partnerships with groups such as these.

In conjunction with these types of nongeographic partnerships, there is a natural fit for state police with the problem-solving component of community policing. For many decades, the standard approach to traffic safety has been to (1) analyze traffic accidents to determine when and where they happen and why; and then (2) design engineering, education, and enforcement responses based on the aforementioned analysis. This approach to traffic safety is consistent with problem-oriented policing, including the SARA (scanning, analysis, response, assessment) model. The Washington State Patrol and the California Highway Patrol are two state police agencies that have systematically adopted the problem-oriented approach to traffic safety, with highly successful initiatives focused on teen fatalities, motorcycle safety, migrant-labor transportation, uninsured motorists, dangerous roadway segments, and other similar issues. In carrying out these initiatives, the Washington State Patrol and the California Highway Patrol have often partnered with applicable interest groups and collaborated with other law enforcement and public safety agencies.

Community policing and problem solving have much to offer state police and highway patrol agencies. The fit may not be quite as natural as for a municipal police department or sheriff's office, and some of the typical components of community policing may need to be tweaked and adjusted, but in the end, even state agencies stand to benefit from community engagement, collaborative problem solving, and enhanced relations with the public.

Gary W. Cordner

See also Agency Mission and Values, Changes in; Colleges and Universities, Community Policing Strategies for; Community Policing: Resources, Time, and Finances in Support of; Community Policing Self-Assessment Tool (CP-SAT); Decentralizing the Organization/Organizational Change; Traffic Problems, Community Policing Strategies for

Further Readings

California Highway Patrol. (2002). *SAFE: A safety and farm vehicle education program reducing farm labor vehicle collisions.* Retrieved from http://www.popcenter .org/library/awards/goldstein/2002/02–07%28W%29.pdf

Cordner, G. W. (2011). The architecture of U.S. policing: Variations among the 50 states. *Police Practice & Research: An International Journal, 12,* 107–119.

Cordner, G. W., & Scarborough, K. S. (2003). Operationalizing community policing in rural America: Sense and nonsense. In Q. C. Thurman & E. F.

McGarrell (Eds.), *Community policing in a rural setting: Innovations and organizational change* (2nd ed.; pp. 11–20). Cincinnati, OH: Anderson.

Falcone, D. N. (2001). The Missouri State Highway Patrol as a representative model. *Policing: An International Journal of Police Strategies & Management, 24*(4), 585–595.

Johnson, D. R. (1981). *American law enforcement: A history.* St. Louis, MO: Forum Press.

Reaves, B. A. (2011, July). *Census of state and local law enforcement agencies, 2008.* NCJ 233982. Washington, DC: U.S. Department of Justice, Bureau of Justice Statistics. Retrieved from http://bjs.ojp.usdoj.gov/content/pub/pdf/csllea08.pdf

Reaves, B. A. (2012, June). *Federal law enforcement officers, 2008.* NCJ 238250.Washington, DC: U.S. Department of Justice, Bureau of Justice Statistics. Retrieved from http://bjs.ojp.usdoj.gov/content/pub/pdf/fle008.pdf

Washington State Patrol. (2012). *Community outreach: Problem oriented public safety.* Retrieved from http://www.wsp.wa.gov/community/pops.htm

Weisheit, R. A., Falcone, D. N., & Wells, L. E. (1999). *Crime and policing in rural and small-town America* (2nd ed.). Prospect Heights, IL: Waveland Press.

STRATEGIC PLANNING

Strategic planning has become a popular movement in the public sector since the U.S. Congress passed the Government Performance and Results Act in 1993. Section 3 of this act stipulated that all federal departments would have a strategic plan in place by September 30, 1997. Strategic planning has become a fixture of many publicly administered organizations, including law enforcement agencies. U.S. police departments have made significant strides in the past two decades in creating strategic plans for their organizations. In the context of police agencies, strategic planning is a process initiated by top managers that sets goals and identifies steps to achieve success, taking into account personnel and budgetary resources.

The community policing movement has incorporated strategic planning as a key element of its philosophy. Different from previous reforms in the history of U.S. policing, community policing represents an overhaul of almost every facet of an agency's public safety mission, including community mobilization, innovative programs, and philosophical change. A primary feature of this contemporary reform concerns the use of the concept of planned change, in the implementation and evaluation of innovative activities such as reorientation of patrol and managerial innovations (e.g., employee empowerment). CompStat, with its primary emphasis on controlling crime geographically, is another example of planning strategically in order to make the best use of limited organizational resources. In addition, police organizations across the United States have developed long-term plans for fighting terrorism and responding to crisis situations. Not surprisingly, law enforcement agencies across the nation claim that they have adopted a variety of strategic planning processes. This entry describes how police agencies have implemented strategic planning and the models they have used for employee participation.

What Is Strategic Planning?

Strategic planning is a future-oriented process that deliberately anticipates planned change for an organization over a period of time, usually within a span of two to five years. It also is understood that strategic planning must be responsive to the need to adapt to a change in the external environment, such as an increase in the crime rate.

There are at least three elements in the definition of strategic planning that deserve further clarification. First, strategic planning involves setting up goals for operations that will be implemented over an extended period of time. Each goal may have multiple objectives, and likewise, each objective may have multiple measures. Goals usually are set for the entire period of a strategic plan, but the objectives attached to a goal can differ each year (e.g., reduction in juvenile crime incidents by 5%).

Second, strategic planning is a process in which the achievement of an established goal is targeted for accomplishment during a given period of time (e.g., one year or 18 months). During that process, the effectiveness of goal achievement will be judged by meeting each objective. Finally, the strategic plan itself often is considered representative of a significant, systematic change in the process of planned change. Goals set in a strategic plan often are related to each other, and strategic planning can be viewed as a holistic approach for achieving goals.

Current Status of Strategic Planning and American Police Agencies

In 2008, Jihong Zhao, Quint Thurman, and Ling Ren conducted random and stratified telephone interviews with personnel in 289 law enforcement agencies. Results showed that respondents typically identified two primary reasons for developing a strategic plan. The first reason was to "meet community demands" (91.4% overall). Large- and medium-size agencies identified this as their top reason more than small-size agencies did (92.7% and 92.1% for large- and medium-size agencies, respectively, compared to 83.3% for small-size agencies), suggesting that the more employees a law enforcement agency has, the more responsive it perceives it must be to the external environment. The second reason identified in the survey results was "to serve as a management tool for upper and middle level managers" (identified by 87.6% overall). Among the agencies that responded, 49% invited community organizations to take part in the development of their strategic plan.

The most commonly used information to assess goal achievement is "jurisdiction-wide crime data" (80.6%), reflecting the priority of crime reduction in these plans. Also, the size of a department is positively associated with the use of crime data. For example, large agencies are more likely to use jurisdictionwide crime data (83.3%) than small agencies (66.7%). The next widely used data in goal assessment was "district-specific crime data" with 71.8% of all agencies reporting using it. Again, department size is closely correlated with the use of specific crime data among these agencies. In addition, citizen surveys were commonly used to examine whether a specific goal was achieved (47.6% overall).

As part of this study, researchers developed a theoretical model of strategic planning in U.S. law enforcement agencies based on seven site visits. Two dimensions of the implementation grid to differentiate strategic planning in law enforcement agencies (see Figure 1) can be identified based upon a Weberian view of organizational complexity that is primarily vertical (control and flow of information) versus horizontal (the complexity of the task). Each dimension can be conceived of as varying along a continuum where the left side represents the lowest level and the highest level is depicted to the far right.

The Extent of Coverage Under the Strategic Plan (Width)

The first dimension reflects the number of divisions or units that are included in a law enforcement agency's strategic plan. Some police agencies developed their plans inclusive of the entire organization. In such a case, specific goals and measures are identified for all major divisions or units (e.g., patrol division or precinct). Alternatively, other agencies implement plans that are limited with extent to

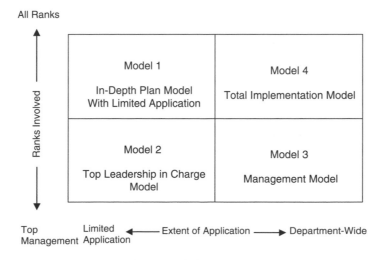

Figure 1 Implementation Grid: Four Models of Strategic Planning

Source: Zhao, J., Thurman, Q. T., & Ren, L. (2008). An examination of strategic planning in American law enforcement agencies: A national study. *Police Quarterly, 11*(19).

the involvement of the units that might participate. Only a few are expected to participate in the development and implementation of the plan. To a large extent, this dimension reflects the extent of horizontal involvement a law enforcement agency has in strategic planning.

The Extent of Hierarchical Involvement in Strategic Plan (Depth)

A second dimension refers to the number of ranks involved in the strategic planning process. In some departments, only top administrators (the chief or deputy chiefs) are involved in the plan. Alternatively, there are law enforcement agencies in which patrol officers are expected to fully participate in strategic planning. Hierarchical involvement reflects the extent of employee involvement. Thus, the key question that arises is, Does the agency want to create a plan primarily for management purposes, or is the intent to include rank-and-file officers and thereby hold them accountable for the plan that is created? Arranging these two dimensions on a continuum from limited involvement to full participation across divisions and ranks, four models of strategic planning in law enforcement agencies emerge. These models fit the profiles of strategic plans in the seven agencies we observed. Figure 1 shows the relationship between the two dimensions and four models.

In Model 1, the in-depth planning model with limited application, rank involvement is high and the extent of application is low. This model can be the beginning of a broader change with a relatively narrower focus involving strategic planning as applied to only one or two divisions or precincts in an agency. Goals and measures are set up for the relevant divisions, while other units may not be directly involved. In contrast to the strategic plan's limited horizontal complexity, the vertical dimension is expansive such that all employees from top administrators to line officers are involved in planning and implementation.

In Model 2, the top leadership in charge model, rank involvement is low and the extent of application is low. Befitting this model, there is limited involvement in planning below the executive level of management. Typically, the top two layers of the organization, usually the chief and immediate lieutenants are in charge of implementation and nearly exclusively are the ones with full knowledge of the plan's progress. Dissemination of the information on the strategic plan is infrequent, and thus, most employees have very limited knowledge concerning the status of the plan. Strictly speaking, law enforcement agencies that adopt this model do not fully comply with the essential principle of strategic planning: consensus building, employee participation, and dissemination of information.

In Model 3, the management model, rank involvement is low and the extent of application is high. Law enforcement agencies employing this model develop strategic plans that are usually departmentwide. Most divisions are included in the plan and, as a consequence, have specific goals and measures that apply uniquely to them. Updates are frequent and formal and measures are in place to assess goal attainment in each division. But in contrast to elevated horizontal complexity, this model features low hierarchical involvement, usually limited to the command-staff level, and as a result, line officers typically are not aware of the plan.

Model 4, the total implementation model, entails a fundamental change in the way law enforcement agencies set priorities and manage personnel and resources; thus, both rank involvement and the extent of application are high. Here implementation of the strategic plan is departmentwide, thus involving all divisions. Goals, objectives, and measures are formally set at each level. In addition, all employees from the executive level to rank-and-file officers are held accountable according to the strategic plan. In fact, the strategic plan becomes the agency's blueprint for daily operations and change. This model indicates a total transformation of a law enforcement agency from a reactive approach of management to a proactive approach with the participation of all the employees. This model reflects all the principles of strategic planning.

Jihong Zhao

See also Community Policing Self-Assessment Tool (CP-SAT); CompStat; Crime Analysis; Learning Organization; Problem Analysis Triangle; Problem-Solving Initiatives, Assessment and Evaluation; Roles, Chief Executives'; Succession Planning

Further Readings

Gordon, G. (1993). *Strategic planning for local government*. Washington, DC: International City/County Management Association.

Greene, J. (2000). Community policing in America: Changing the nature, structure, and function of the police. In J. Horney, R. Peterson, D. L. MacKenzie, J. Martin, & D. P. Rosenbaum (Eds.), *Policies, processes, and decisions of the criminal justice system* (Vol. 3; pp. 299–370). NCJ 182410. Washington, DC: U.S. Department of Justice, National Institute of Justice. Retrieved from https://www.ncjrs.gov/criminal_justice2000/vol_3/03front.pdf

Kotten, J. (1997). *Strategic management in public and nonprofit organizations* (2nd ed.). Westport, CT: Praeger.

Moore, M. H. (1995). *Creating public value: Strategic management in government.* Boston, MA: Harvard University Press.

Poister, T. H., Pitts, D., & Edwards, L. H. (2010). Strategic management research in the public sector: A review, synthesis, and future direction. *The American Review of Public Administration, 40*(5), 522–545. doi: 10.1177/0275074010370617

Ugboro, I. O., Obeng, K., & Spann, O. (2011, January). Strategic planning as an effective tool of strategic management in public sector organizations: Evidence from public transit organizations. *Administration and Society, 43*(1), 87–123. doi: 10.1177/0095399710386315

Zhao, J., Thurman, Q. C., & Ren, L. (2008). An examination of strategic planning in American law enforcement agencies: A national study. *Police Quarterly, 11*(1), 3–26. doi: 10.1177/1098611107309624

SUCCESSION PLANNING

Succession planning is a process whereby police organizations take affirmative steps to plan for filling vacancies they know will exist in key positions. Studied extensively by scholars, effective succession planning involves identifying the right people for the job and developing them in ways that will allow them to assume the mantle of leadership if and when the time comes.

Changes in both civil service and retirement benefits packages have disincentivized prospective applicants for leadership positions by making it more attractive for them to stay where they are. These factors have combined to make succession planning more important now than ever before, but it is still often overlooked. Through attention to the essential underpinnings of succession planning and by undertaking specific implementation steps, police organizations are able to ensure the leadership vitality of the agencies and nurture and develop

organizational culture in the desired direction. This entry describes the benefits of succession planning and explains the steps that can be taken to ensure that when key leaders step down, new leaders are ready to take their places.

Defining Succession Planning

Succession planning builds on the notion that some positions are critical to the mission of an organization and, therefore, must be filled by persons who are highly competent and qualified. It is a systematic way of ensuring that the filling of vacancies in key positions will not be left to chance. Just as the problem focus of community policing is an antidote to the reactivity of responding to random calls (e.g., the "tyranny" of the 911 system), so is succession planning an antidote to the reactivity of filling unexpected vacancies within an organization. Moreover, the failure to engage in succession planning is difficult to justify in light of the reality that all positions will become vacant eventually and require successors.

Succession planning has been the focus of scholarly attention for some time. Organizational strategists have examined how succession planning can be part of aligning goals, roles, and procedures in order to gain a competitive advantage. Sociologists have studied succession planning vis-à-vis the processes of bureaucratization and organizational adaptation to changing environments. Industrial and organizational psychologists and human resource management researchers have considered succession planning from the standpoint of individual employees. Each of these perspectives has yielded valuable insights and furthered our understanding of effective succession planning.

Effective succession planning requires active and intentional management of the flow of persons into (and out of) an organization, as well as the identification and development of persons who will occupy key roles in the organization in the future. To borrow a metaphor Jim Collins used in his description of how to make "good" organizations "great," effective succession planning will require organizations to (a) get the right people on the bus, (b) get the wrong people off of the bus, and (c) get the right people in the right seats. However, many managers in the public sector have not realized that succession planning involves substantially more than merely generating a pool of applicants as vacancies occur. Moreover, law enforcement agency administrators in particular need to be aware that succession planning should not be left only to the human resources department if organizational culture is to be nurtured, developed, and preserved.

Benefits of Succession Planning

Retirement benefits for some officers have reached levels never seen before, and some cities and counties are responding by reducing those benefits. The combination of high levels of benefits and threats to their retention has prompted some officers to retire early. This includes a substantial number of chiefs, which has resulted in a relative dearth of police leadership.

Gary Brown, a former police chief, has suggested that qualified chief candidates are difficult to recruit and retain for other reasons as well. He points out that the generous civil service protections and benefits afforded lower-ranking officers makes the job of chief less secure. Chiefs who were promoted up the ranks sometimes voluntarily demote back down the ranks, to their former position, in order to have contractual job protection that they do not enjoy as police chief executives who serve "at will," meaning they serve at the pleasure of the city council. This, he asserts, has led to shrinking numbers of qualified chief applicants.

Succession planning plays an important role in ensuring quality leadership, and the overwhelming majority of human resource professionals agree that leadership is an "extremely important management issue." One of the reasons it is so important is that it is instrumental in facilitating bureaucracies' adaptations to their changing external environments. This is because it is difficult to change organizational structures, policies, and procedures without also changing the people who institute and oversee them. Consequently, it is vitally important to develop new leaders with fresh ideas in order to ensure the organization can adapt. This is especially true where, as in the context of community-oriented policing, there is a fundamental change in conceptualization of the organizations' core services.

Despite its importance, succession planning is often overlooked because, as Rick Michelson (2006) noted in a magazine article in *Police Chief,* "it is not assigned, budgeted, organized, planned, scheduled, or evaluated." Indeed, succession inertia is perhaps the greatest challenge to succession planning and management. It is worth trying to overcome this inertia not only because of the need for succession planning to remediate organizational deficiencies, but also because of the benefits that accrue beyond meeting those needs, such as improving the quality of leadership overall throughout the organization, modernizing workers, enhancing training, and improving management and leadership skills at each level of the agency.

Elements of Succession Planning

As the foregoing discussion makes clear, succession planning is not wholly independent from other processes within the organization. Indeed, an understanding of several interrelated organizational concepts is useful in delineating the contours of succession planning. These include replacement planning, continuity planning, and talent management. Each is discussed in the following subsections.

Replacement Planning

Replacement planning is routinely undertaken by many organizations, including police agencies. It involves developing personnel so that someone is positioned to fill in for each key position in the event of an emergency or other circumstance rendering unavailable someone in a key position. Replacement planning differs from succession planning in that the former tends to involve limitations either on the scope of duties or duration as compared with the latter.

Continuity Planning

Planning for replacement of key personnel during times of disaster is a specific component of the broader approach known as continuity planning. Continuity planning involves preparing against internal and external threats in order to facilitate the continuous operation of the organization. It is intended to ensure the organization can continue its core mission in the event of some catastrophic event. Clearly, continuity in leadership is an important part of continuity planning.

Talent Management

Talent management is a term that was coined in the 1990s to describe approaches for increasing and leveraging human capital within organizations. It is a corollary to asset management, which focuses on ways of increasing and leveraging more traditional forms of capital. Talent management involves nurturing and developing personnel so they can be put to their highest and best use. More talented and competent personnel will improve the organization's capacity for developing successors from within.

Mentoring

Mentoring can serve as a particular type of talent management effort. Mentoring, though, is commonly employed for other purposes as well. Mentoring involves relationship building in the service of promoting professional growth and development, which in turn deepens the talent pool, thereby improving the organization. Mentoring programs may be formal or informal, but have the common characteristic of involving a senior, more experienced mentor providing friendship, motivation, and advice to a less experienced protégé.

Replacement planning, continuity planning, talent management, and mentoring all involve increasing the capacity of existing personnel. Good succession planning systems focus not only on passing along power to successors but passing along knowledge as well. In this way, all three of these approaches can be viewed as inextricably tied to succession planning.

Organizational Culture

Succession planning requires an honest and candid self-reflection on the part of management to determine what works and what needs improvement. At the same time, planners will have to look outward to work collaboratively with union leaders, human resources staff, and others. To be effective, succession plans must take account of the agency's culture, personality, union and budgetary issues, resources, and community concerns. As Michelson has observed, succession planning does not require a tremendous amount of funding, staffing, or resources. But it does require a change of thinking.

Steps in Succession Planning

Commitment From the Top

Perhaps the most important step in succession planning is to get unwavering support from the top of the organization. In this step, the chief executive communicates clearly and unambiguously the vital importance of succession planning throughout the organization and its employees.

Job Analyses

Job analyses are undertaken for the chief executive and command staff, and the knowledge, skills, abilities, and other characteristics (KSAOCs) associated with those jobs are identified. Moreover, these and other job analyses ought to be future-oriented job analyses (FOJA). That is, staff should seek to identify not only the KSAOCs associated with the job now, but also those KSAOCs that likely will be required for the future.

Gap Analyses

The FOJA will allow for a gap analysis to determine the kinds of education, training, or experience that is required to fill the gap in order to prepare someone for the position. Based on the results of the gap analyses, steps are then taken to fill the gaps and assessments are undertaken to evaluate the effectiveness of those approaches.

Performance Evaluation System Review

The FOJA has the added benefit of informing a review of the organization's performance evaluation system. As part of a strategic human resource management approach, existing performance evaluation systems are revised so as to assess contemporary job demands. Promotional processes, merit systems, and the like are all reviewed with an eye toward the current and future needs of the organization.

Perhaps the most significant departures of community policing from policing models of the past are its intentionality and emphasis on acting in anticipation of future problems. Community policing teaches police to be thoughtful about problems and their solutions, rather than react to them reflexively. Importantly, community policing teaches that reaction should not be the essence of police work, but rather, that police should identify problems and fashion solutions.

Succession planning aligns perfectly with this model. Losing police leaders is a problem, but not one that police agencies must passively accept. Consistent with the community policing philosophy, police leaders can anticipate the problem and implement solutions in the form of succession planning. Indeed, mindful that a change in leadership creates opportunity for organizational change for the better, agencies can turn one problem (the loss of a former leader) into the solution of a different problem (a need to change some facet of the organization). Moreover, through conscientious efforts at ensuring good leadership succession, organizations can improve their operations to the benefit of the communities they serve.

Phillip M. Lyons Jr.

See also Decentralizing the Organization/Organizational Change; Mentoring; Recruiting for Quality and Diversity; Roles, Chief Executives'; Strategic Planning

Further Readings

Collins, J. (2001). *Good to great: Why some companies make the leap . . . and others don't.* New York, NY: HarperCollins.

Drucker, P. F. (1995). *Managing in a time of great change.* New York, NY: Truman Talley.

Goldstein, H. (1990). *Problem-oriented policing.* New York, NY: McGraw-Hill.

Grusky, O. (1961). Corporate size, bureaucratization, and managerial succession. *American Journal of Sociology, 67*(3), 263–269.

Haveman, H. (1993). Ghosts of managers past: Managerial succession and organisational mortality. *Academy of Management Journal, 36*(4), 864–881.

Hughes, P. J. (2010, October). Increasing organizational leadership through the police promotional process. *FBI Law Enforcement Bulletin.* Retrieved from http://www .fbi.gov/stats-services/publications/law-enforcement-bulletin/October-2010/copy_of_confronting-science-and-market-positioning

Kelling, G. L., & Coles, C. (1996). *Fixing broken windows: Restoring order and reducing crime in our communities.* New York, NY: Touchstone.

Kesner, I. F., & Sebora, T. C. (1994, Summer). Executive succession: Past, present and future. *Journal of Management, 20*(2), 327–372. doi: 10.1016/0149–2063(94)90019–1

Michelson, R. (2006, June). Preparing future leaders for tomorrow: Succession planning for police leadership. *Police Chief, 73*(6).

Murphy, S. A. (2006). Executive development and succession planning: Qualitative evidence. *International Journal of Police Science and Management, 8*(4), 253–265.

Pascarella, P. (1997). Winners supply new leaders. *Management Review, 86,* 50–52.

Senge, P. (1990). *The fifth discipline: The art and practice of the learning organization.* New York, NY: Doubleday.

Sparrow, M. K., Moore, M. H., & Kennedy, D. B. (1990). *Beyond 911: A new era for policing.* New York, NY: Basic Books.

Walker, S. L. (1992). *The police in America: An introduction.* New York, NY: McGraw-Hill.

Wills, G. (1992). Enabling managerial growth and ownership succession. *Management Decision, 30*(1), 10–26. doi: 10.1108/00251749210008650

TEAM POLICING

Team policing was intended to improve police-community relations and police crime control effectiveness by permanently assigning a group of police officers to a particular small geographic area as a neighborhood. This team of officers was responsible for providing all police services, such as patrol and investigations, to that specific neighborhood and developing appropriate police strategies and programs for that neighborhood. Team policing represents an important early experience in reforming police work to be more focused on addressing community concerns and developing positive police-community relationships. This entry briefly reviews the development and implementation of team policing, summarizes the available evaluation evidence, and concludes by comparing community policing and team policing concepts.

Development and Implementation

Civil unrest during the 1960s led to a growing recognition that police departments were not responsive to community concerns and not well connected to community members, especially in disadvantaged minority neighborhoods. Drawing on some promising experiences in the United Kingdom, the U.S. President's Crime Commission endorsed the team policing concept in 1967. The Syracuse (New York) Police Department was the first to adopt the approach in 1968. Other progressive police leaders embraced the concept, and by 1974 as many as 60

U.S. police departments had adopted some form of team policing.

The Police Foundation, a police research and policy institution in Washington, D.C., produced an influential report on the implementation of team policing in seven U.S. cities in the early 1970s. Although team policing varied across these cities, these programs generally had three common operational elements: (1) permanent assignment of police teams to small neighborhoods, (2) close internal communications among police team members assigned to the neighborhood area, and (3) maximal communication between police team members and the community. The most successful teams also had one supervisor responsible for a particular area at all times, lower level flexibility in policymaking and program development, unified delivery of police services, and combined patrol and investigative functions.

The Police Foundation report also identified three obstacles to the successful implementation of team policing. First, team policing programs were greeted with a large amount of opposition from middle management police officers as captains and lieutenants. These mid-level managers were threatened by changes to the existing police command structure and their diminished ability to control the day-to-day decisions and actions of lower level officers. The Police Foundation report noted their resistance was manifested as failure to address organizational problems that arose as a result of implemented changes, "bad-mouthing" the program, and openly opposing their superior officers in the management and implementation of the program.

Second, in locations where the program was viewed as successful, the Police Foundation report found that team policing officers were resented by their peers who were not participating in the program. Police officers not participating in the team policing program perceived that they were working harder than their team policing counterparts. Indeed, a workload analysis confirmed that the team policing programs may have been overstaffed and the average workload was indeed slightly lighter. Resentment and jealousy over these inequities soon followed. In certain jurisdictions, this resentment was exacerbated due to a lack of communication between the police command staff and other officers. Apparently, police officers working in the same neighborhoods but not involved in the team policing program were not informed of its goals and procedures.

Third, decentralized team policing work conflicted with the established operations of the centralized radio dispatching system used by these seven police departments. During that time period, the available technology did not allow dispatchers to distinguish between particular officers and specific subareas of responsibility, such as specially designated team policing neighborhoods. As such, police dispatchers repeatedly requested that team police officers answer emergency calls for service outside of their designated neighborhood areas. The Police Foundation report observed that New York City team police officers spent as much as half of their time resolving calls outside their focus neighborhoods. In Detroit, Michigan, team police officers were observed spending as much as one third of their time outside their designated areas. The additional pressure and workload generated by these out-of-area emergency calls for service undermined the ability of team police officers to provide services in their focus neighborhoods and pulled them toward traditional policing activities.

Evaluation

Between 1971 and 1976, the Police Foundation and the Urban Institute collaborated on a formal evaluation of the Community Sector Team Policing (COMSEC) program in Cincinnati, Ohio. The findings of the evaluation were mixed. Relative to traditional policing, COMSEC was found to be more successful in reducing burglary and as effective in controlling other types of crime. The evaluation

also revealed that COMSEC increased citizen perceptions of safety while walking at night in their neighborhoods, improved citizen beliefs that police officers were likely to respond to calls for service, and increased the visibility of police on foot in the neighborhood. The police officers participating in the COMSEC program reported improved job satisfaction and morale. The evaluation showed that citizen satisfaction with police service and belief in police honesty remained high but did not change as a result of COMSEC. Moreover, the Cincinnati Police Department spent more on police officer salaries during the experiment when compared to previous expenditures. The final report also noted that mid- and upper-level managers in the police department were ambivalent toward the program. These police managers were generally not supportive of a central tenet of team policing—the decentralization of decision-making authority to line-level officers.

Coupled with the implementation difficulties noted in the Police Foundation case studies, these mixed evaluation findings suggested that the team policing approach may not be the most desirable way to control crime and improve police-community relations. Team policing came to be seen as a policing fad of the 1970s and eventually faded away. Team policing was replaced by new models of community policing in the 1980s that built upon some of the important ideas undergirding the original approach.

Team Policing and Community Policing

U.S. police departments have a long history of engaging centralized command-and-control structures to manage patrol, investigation, and other service functions. While these centralized management structures divide jurisdictions into larger police-defined units such as precincts and districts, the delivery of police services was rather standard across the varying neighborhoods that comprised these police units. Community policing and team policing programs share a focus on neighborhood problems. These initiatives attempt to tailor the delivery of police services to the problems and needs of specific neighborhoods or communities. The neighborhood focus of these programs was intended to improve police-community relations problems, better position the police to address crime and disorder problems, and improve police officer morale.

Decentralized decision-making authority is a key element of the neighborhood focus of community policing and team policing programs. The specific needs of a neighborhood are viewed as essential to shaping police policies, programs, and actions. Line-level officers are given the autonomy to make their own decisions about the crime and disorder problems to be dealt with and the strategies and tactics they will use to address them. This represents a radical departure from the traditional, hierarchical style of police management. Research conducted during the 1970s documents that team police officers were advised to ignore department policies and form their own standard operating procedures in Cincinnati, and the team policing initiative in the Venice section of Los Angeles, California, was described as operating like a separate small police department rather than a subunit of the Los Angeles Police Department.

An unfortunate consequence of police reform efforts between the 1920s and 1960s was the distance that was created between the police and the public they served. This separation was facilitated, in part, by the adoption of anticorruption policies to insulate the police from undue public influence and the increasing use of new technologies such as radio dispatch and the patrol car. Community policing and team policing programs both actively seek community input on neighborhood problems and encourage citizen involvement in the development and implementation of police strategies and programs. Neighborhood residents are engaged as collaborative partners who have an important role in maintaining public safety in neighborhoods.

While community policing and team policing programs share common ground as attempts to redefine traditional conceptions of the police role, there are some noteworthy differences. Team policing programs had the explicit goal of reducing crime through enhanced police-community relations and improved police organization. Community policing is often described as a philosophy that promotes community partnerships, organizational transformation, and problem-solving techniques to address a wide range of public safety, order, and fear of crime issues. This is clearly a much broader mandate than the very specific crime control goal of team policing programs. Equally important, community policing involves departmentwide changes in organization and the delivery of services. In contrast, the team policing programs of the 1970s represented small

groups of officers who operated in a radically different manner than the traditional workings of their larger police organizations.

Anthony A. Braga

See also Community Policing, Evolution of; Community Policing: Resources, Time, and Finances in Support of; Officers' Job Satisfaction; Police Foundation; Police-Community Relations; Strategic Planning

Further Readings

National Institute of Justice. (1973). *Neighborhood team policing.* Washington, DC: U.S. Government Printing Office.

Schwartz, A. I., & Clarren, S. N. (1977). *The Cincinnati team policing experiment: A summary report.* Washington, DC: Police Foundation.

Sherman, L. W., Milton, C. H., & Kelly, T. V. (1973). *Team policing: Seven case studies.* Washington, DC: Police Foundation.

Walker, S. (1993). Does anyone remember team policing? Lessons of the team policing experience for community policing. *American Journal of Police, 12*(1), 33–56.

TERRORISM, FUTURE IMPACT OF COMMUNITY POLICING ON

Community policing was the dominant law enforcement paradigm before the September 11, 2001, terrorist attacks in the United States. After the attacks, antiterrorism efforts gained prominence and ushered the emergence of an antiterrorism policing or homeland security policing philosophy. Policing scholars such as David Bayley and David Weisburd suggest that this new approach to policing seeks to enhance law enforcement capabilities to prevent and respond to terrorist activities. In light of these developments, this entry presents the incongruities and complementariness of the community policing approach with regard to terrorism as well as the emerging hybrid model of law enforcement philosophy.

Incongruities

One of the leading authors on community policing, Gary Cordner, suggests that there are four essential components or dimensions of community policing: namely, the philosophical, programmatic, strategic, and organizational dimensions. In brief, Cordner explains that community policing, as a department philosophy, should value citizen input and deliver more personalized service. Furthermore, he recommends that the police role should be broadened and not merely concerned about law enforcement. As a strategy, he recommends that police service be face-to-face and have geographic focus (i.e., permanency of assignment) and focused on preventing crime. For the tactical dimension, he recommends that police departments adopt problem solving, develop partnerships, and engage the community members in positive interactions. Cordner suggests that police organizations should reorient their structures, indoctrinate their personnel to community policing, and develop a new management style. The Community Oriented Policing Services (COPS) Office has reduced these components into three: (1) community partnerships, (2) organizational transformations, and (3) problem solving.

Preemption Versus Prevention

Community policing is a preventive strategy. This strategy means that it conducts interventions that may not necessarily directly address the actual crime phenomenon but are pursued to avoid the emergence of crime. On the other hand, a noted sociologist, Donald Black, suggests that antiterrorism should be preemptive. This means that actions pursued by antiterrorism law enforcement agents should identify a clear connection between the abated phenomena to terrorism. Failure to do so would pave the way for an attack. Thus, in prevention strategy, the abatement of a circumstance may or may not result in crime. Alternatively, a preemptive strategy is pursued because the nonabatement of the circumstance is certain to produce an attack. Because of these strategic differences, community policing and antiterrorism policing may not be compatible.

Service Versus Law Enforcement

The strategic distinction between prevention and preemption also influences the orientation of the police toward service and enforcement. In their insightful book about the policing in the United States, Lawrence F. Travis and Robert H. Langworthy (2008) suggest that police officers pursue all their essential roles—law enforcement, order maintenance, and service—but not emphasize them all equally. James Q. Wilson notes that departments will show a tendency toward one of these roles. In a community policing philosophy, service becomes that primary role of the police. However, with homeland security, law enforcement would become the primary role of the police. Thus, emphasis on antiterrorism would create a shift in this role orientation.

The Element of Public Trust

Several scholars have contended that community policing may not be compatible with an antiterrorism policing approach due to the element of public trust. In particular, Melchor C. de Guzman suggests that the clandestine nature of antiterrorism or homeland security policing could erode trust between the citizen and the public. Because of the perceived intrusive nature of antiterrorism policing and its potential to violate people's rights to privacy, critics have opined that public cooperation and trust with law enforcement agents could not be sustained in a homeland security era. While antiterrorism policies and practices tend to have to employ more "hard" police strategies—for example, surveillance, intelligence gathering, the use of informants, and the implementation of a number of antiterror laws—many authors feel that the public understands and supports this more hardcore approach. These authors therefore view public trust as not only a part of but also indispensable for both antiterrorism and community-oriented policing. However, trust building within an antiterrorism context may require police officers to have a sophisticated level of cultural intelligence in order to understand the complexities of the communities with which they are working.

Complementariness

Certain elements of community policing are compatible with and, perhaps, can coexist, with antiterrorism efforts. The first among these elements is the strategic requirement for geographic focus. Community policing requires police officers to have permanent beats to be familiar with the community members, identify problems, and find solutions to these problems. Antiterrorism activities also require familiarity with the territory. Such familiarity enables police officers to detect suspicious movements of goods and people. Hence, geographic assignment is a valuable component for both community policing and antiterrorism policing. In fact, geographic focus is considered necessary to develop another component of community policing and antiterrorism policing: community partnerships.

The second main component of community policing that may be compatible with antiterrorism is problem solving. As originally proposed in 1979 by Herman Goldstein, police departments need to detect and address the underlying causes of crime. Likewise, several terrorism scholars, including Jonathan White, have pointed out that the underlying causes of terrorism also need to be addressed. The skills that are developed under a community policing model, like problem solving, could also be useful for antiterrorism policing. For instance, the problem-solving model SARA (scanning, analyzing, response, assessment) that was propounded by John Eck and William Spelman could be used to analyze the events surrounding terrorism phenomena. Ordinary events or crime could be analyzed to unravel these events' connections to the preparations for terrorist attack or planning. In particular, skills in crime analysis, crime mapping, crime prevention through environmental design, and other crime prevention strategies that have been learned in community policing could become the intervention and analytical models for antiterrorism policing.

In a study by MoonSun Kim and de Guzman, problem-solving efforts were the only community policing strategies that have not been deescalated by U.S. local police departments. Instead, police departments after the 9/11 events have increased their pursuit of problem solving, particularly their use of the SARA model.

The third component of community policing that may be compatible with antiterrorism policing is community participation. The police can take advantage of the community members' inputs regarding intelligence information. Such participation can only emerge when trust between the community and the police exists. In the solution of ordinary crimes, it has been found that willingness and availability of witnesses are the keys to solving crimes and apprehending suspects. Similarly, community information is important in gathering information about terrorist plots and detecting terrorists. However, community trust can be volatile and fickle. Community mistrust and noncooperation between the community and the police may occur if police officers overstep their

boundaries. Thus, strengthening community relationships is important in both models of policing.

New Hybrid Model of Policing

The new hybrid model of policing combines community policing and homeland security concerns. In community policing, the goals of positive police-community relations, problem solving, and geographic focus are all compatible with homeland security policing. However, homeland security policing, in addition to the shared community policing components, includes the following components: emergency response, emergency preparedness, early warning devices, and community mobilization in cases of terrorist threats or attacks. All of these elements of homeland security can be appended to the current community policing models. Several police departments in the United States have started to incorporate homeland security policing components into their strategies. In the latest Law Enforcement Management and Administrative Statistics survey, U.S. police departments were asked about their preparedness and emergency response systems against terrorist attacks.

Melchor C. de Guzman

See also Community Oriented Policing Services, Office of; Counterterrorism and Community Policing; Homeland Security; Immigrant Populations, Community Policing Strategies for; Problem-Solving Process (SARA)

Further Readings

Bayley, D. H., & Weisburd, D. L. (2009). Cops and spooks: The role of the police in counterterrorism. In D. L. Weisburd, T. Feucht, I. Hakimi, L. Mock, & S. Perry (Eds.), *To protect and to serve: Policing in an age of terrorism* (pp. 81–100). New York, NY: Springer-Verlag.

Brown, B. (2007). Community policing in post-September 11 America: A comment on the concept of community-oriented counterterrorism. *Police Practice & Research, 8*(3), 239–251. doi: 10.1080/15614260701450716

Cordner, G. W. (1997). Community policing: Elements and effects. In R. G. Dunham & G. P. Alpert (Eds.), *Critical issues in policing: Contemporary readings* (3rd ed.; pp. 451–468). Prospect Heights, IL: Waveland Press.

de Guzman, M. C. (2002, September/October). The changing roles and strategies of the police in a time of terror. *ACJS Today, 22*(3), 8–13.

Eck, J. E., & Spelman, W. (1987). Who ya gonna call? The police as problem-busters. *Crime & Delinquency, 33*(1), 31–52.

Goldstein, H. (1979). Improving policing: A problem-oriented approach. *Crime & Delinquency, 25*(2), 236–258. doi: 10.1177/001112877902500207

Kim, M., & de Guzman, M. C. Police paradigm shift after the 9/11 terrorist attacks: The empirical evidence from the United States municipal police departments. *Criminal Justice Studies, 25*(4), 323–342.

Office of Community Oriented Policing Services. (2012). *What is community policing?* Retrieved from http://www.cops.usdoj.gov/default.asp?tiem=36

Skolnick, J. R., & Bayley, D. H. (1986). *The new blue line: Police innovation in six American cities.* New York, NY: Free Press.

Travis, L. F.,III, & Langworthy, R. H. (2008). *Policing in America: A balance of forces* (4th ed.). Upper Saddle River, NJ: Prentice Hall

TIPPING POINTS OF NEIGHBORHOODS

A neighborhood is a small geographic area defined by a combination of public service agencies, developers, planning agencies, people, and tradition. Neighborhoods are geographic places and are identified by houses, streets, parks, schools, retail establishments, and commercial business properties. Neighborhoods are also collections of people identified by age, race, ethnicity, education level, income level, and civic engagement. Each city or community represents a collection of many neighborhoods. Neighborhoods impact citizens' lives on a day-to-day basis, which, of course, affects community policing and problem solving. Neighborhoods are living, dynamic entities and may be classified as healthy or unhealthy. A number of factors may result in the decline of a neighborhood, eventually resulting in an unhealthy neighborhood. A number of factors may also result in the revitalization of a neighborhood, leading to a healthy neighborhood. These factors may place a neighborhood at the *tipping point*, a point where a neighborhood may either decline or revitalize. This entry defines this concept and discusses some factors determining whether or not neighborhoods will reach their tipping point.

Meaning of the Concept

The tipping point concept is based on a book about social change entitled *The Tipping Point: How Little Things Can Make a Big Difference,* written by Malcolm Gladwell (2000). The concept of social change, according to Gladwell, is similar to an epidemic. Ideas, messages, and behaviors act like outbreaks of infectious disease. The tipping point is that moment when an idea, trend, or social behavior crosses a threshold and then tips and spreads. The possibility of sudden change is at the center of the concept of the tipping point. Big changes occur as a result of small events. Things can happen all at once, and little changes can make a huge difference. According to Gladwell, social problems behave like infectious agents. Small changes in a neighborhood may result in a tipping point, and the neighborhood may then experience a large-scale change. Communities and neighborhoods need to be sensitive to and identify the early warning signs of decline and small changes in order to avoid a downward tipping point.

Factors Affecting Neighborhood Health

A number of factors impact the health of a neighborhood—factors that may compel the tipping point to either tip downward or tip upward. The first factor is the *appearance* of the neighborhood. Disrepair of structures, graffiti, abandoned vehicles, junk vehicles, litter, and overgrown weeds in vacant lots are indicative of a neighborhood in decline.

The second factor affecting neighborhoods is *civic engagement.* A healthy neighborhood is one where the residents connect and interact with each other. Civic engagement may take the form of participation in neighborhood events, religious organizations, recreational activities, and voting. The third factor is *commercial activity.* A healthy neighborhood is one where commercial activity, retail and industrial, benefit the neighborhood. Poorly maintained and vacant commercial properties have a negative impact on the neighborhood. The fourth factor concerns the *environmental* aspects of a neighborhood. Healthy neighborhoods have a healthy environment in terms of air, water, and soil quality.

The fifth factor is *housing.* Homes and apartments in healthy neighborhoods are safe, decent, and attractive. The rate of home ownership is important. Higher rates of home ownership are indicative of residents who maintain homes, care about home attractiveness, and protect their financial home investments. The sixth factor is *infrastructure,* elements of which include street lighting and pavement, curbs, gutters, sidewalks, ditches, and utility poles and wires. In a healthy neighborhood, infrastructure is in good repair and the residents are engaged in maintaining the infrastructure.

The seventh important neighborhood factor is *organizational capacity.* Organizational capacity refers to a neighborhood where the residents have a neighborhood organization, leadership, and active residents—all of which work collectively to make improvements to their neighborhood. There is collective action resulting in improving the neighborhood. The eighth factor is *parks and recreation.* Healthy neighborhoods possess parks and facilities for the recreational interests of the residents. The parks and recreational facilities in healthy neighborhoods are well maintained, attractive, safe, and regularly used by the residents.

The ninth factor is *safety.* A healthy neighborhood is a safe neighborhood, where residents feel safe—and are in fact safe. Crime rates, graffiti, building blight, and gang activity represent indicators of safety. The tenth factor is *schools.* A healthy neighborhood is one where schools are clean, attractive and integral to the functioning of the neighborhood. Learning and academic achievement are valued by the residents of the neighborhood. Residents are involved in parent-teacher association activities and the schools are the venue for neighborhood meetings, functions, and events.

These 10 factors may positively or negatively impact a neighborhood and represent potential tipping points of neighborhoods. It is important to note that no one factor or formula applying these factors mechanically identifies the tipping point of a neighborhood. The tipping point concept requires an ongoing monitoring and assessment of these factors in order to ascertain the health of a neighborhood.

Complementary Theories and Approaches

Broken Windows Theory

The broken windows theory complements the tipping point of neighborhoods concept. The broken windows theory asserts that physical deterioration and an increase in unrepaired and dilapidated structures leads to increased concerns for personal safety among the residents of an area. These concerns lead to further decreases in maintenance and repair resulting in an increase in vandalism, graffiti, and crime. Physical evidence of disorder leads to a feeling of social disorganization. If the physical disorder is not reversed, crime will increase because residents will not feel safe and will remain indoors. The physical evidence of disorder and blight represents a signal to criminals that the neighborhood is out of control and leads to an increase in criminal activities. The broken windows theory resulted in law enforcement agencies concentrating their efforts on quality-of-life offenses in order to address crime in neighborhoods. To reverse disorder, law enforcement agencies enforced quality-of-life offenses such as panhandling, graffiti, littering, prostitution, jaywalking, and public urination. The physical decline of a neighborhood is a tipping point that invites criminal activity.

Social Disorganization Theory

Social disorganization theory also complements the tipping point of neighborhoods concept. Social disorganization theory views the ecological conditions of a neighborhood as shaping crime rates over and above the characteristics of individual residents. The focus is on different types of neighborhoods creating conditions favorable or unfavorable to crime. According to social disorganization theory, poverty, residential mobility, ethnic heterogeneity, and weak social networks decrease the capacity of a neighborhood to control the behavior of individuals in public and increase the likelihood of criminal activity. Neighborhood structural factors impact the creation of informal social control. Informal social control may take the form of informal surveillance and the form of direct intervention. Informal surveillance entails residents of a neighborhood observing neighbors' homes and property, paying attention to strangers in the neighborhood. Observant neighbors then report problems to law enforcement. Direct intervention entails residents of a neighborhood directly addressing individuals engaging in suspicious or inappropriate behavior without reporting problems to law enforcement.

Complementary Approaches

Community policing is premised on two complementary approaches. The first is a community orientation, which maintains that the police cannot be successful without the cooperation of their citizens, and must form partnerships with citizens in order to address crime and neighborhood disorder. The second approach is problem-oriented policing, which provides that police should address the root causes of problems and spend time solving those problems. These two approaches form the basis of today's community era of policing, and must function in a proactive manner to monitor and address the various factors that constitute the tipping points of neighborhoods.

Robert Morin

See also Broken Windows Theory; Building Partnerships and Stakeholders; Community Cohesion and Empowerment; Community Policing, Evolution of; Community Policing and Problem Solving, Definition of; Hot Spots; Operation Weed and Seed; Place-Based Policing; Police-Community Relations; Situational Crime Prevention

Further Readings

Bursik, R. J., Jr., & Grasmick, H. (1993). *Neighborhoods and crime: The dimensions of effective community control.* New York, NY: Lexington Books.

Gladwell, M. (2000). *The tipping point: How little things can make a big difference.* Boston, MA: Little, Brown.

Harcourt, B. E., & Ludwig, J. (2006). Broken windows: New evidence from New York City and a five-city social experiment. *University of Chicago Law Review, 73,* 271–320.

Jacksonville Community Council Inc. (2003). *Neighborhoods at the tipping point.* Jacksonville, FL: Author. Retrieved from http://www.jcci.org

Kelling, G. L., & Coles, C. M. (1996). *Fixing broken windows: Restoring order and reducing crime in our communities.* New York, NY: Free Press.

Kubrin, C. E., & Weitzer, R. (2003). New directions in social disorganization theory. *Journal of Research in Crime and Delinquency, 40*(4), 374–402. doi: 10.1177/0022427803256238

Skogan, W. G. (1990). *Disorder and decline: Crime and the spiral of decay in American neighborhoods.* Berkeley: University of California Press.

Wilson, J. Q., & Kelling, G. L. (1982, March). Broken windows: The police and neighborhood safety. *Atlantic Monthly, 249*(3), 29–38.

Yang, S. M. (2010). Assessing the spatial-temporal relationship between disorder and violence. *Journal of Quantitative Criminology, 26*(1), 139–163.

TRAFFIC PROBLEMS, CHARACTERISTICS OF

Traffic-related problems historically have not been a primary concern for citizens, academic researchers, and law enforcement practitioners. Community policing and problem-solving efforts are routinely developed for and focused on violent crime or quality-of-life offenses in a particular neighborhood and then evaluated on their success or failure within those limited focus areas. Traffic problem responses, when thought of at all, are usually a reaction to a high-profile crash such as a child wandering into the street and being struck by a passing vehicle. When an incident of this sort occurs, police may be immediately directed to the area for a period of time and tasked with high-visibility enforcement of minor traffic violations, primarily those related to vehicle speed. After a short period of time, the police generally move back to other nontraffic duties and the problem is deemed successfully resolved.

According to the Centers for Disease Control and Prevention, every year in the United States nearly twice the number of people die as a result of traffic crashes as are killed in homicidal violence. A recent study commissioned by the American Automobile Association (AAA) and conducted by Cambridge Systematics estimated the annual economic cost of U.S. fatal and nonfatal traffic crashes at over $299 billion. In this same study, it was further determined that U.S. citizens annually spend 4.8 billion hours and consume 3.9 billion gallons of fuel sitting in traffic congestion in the course of their daily activities. This amounts to an additional cost of over $97 billion, bringing the total dollar cost of the two primary traffic problems—crashes and congestion—to almost $300 billion a year in the United States alone.

Ronald Clarke and John Eck define a *police problem* as "a recurring set of related harmful events in a community that members of the public expect the police to address." The sheer number of daily traffic crashes and traffic congestion and their associated human and economic costs obviously meets this problem definition. This entry looks at the common characteristics of the two primary traffic problems: traffic crashes and traffic congestion and the harms associated with them.

Traffic Crashes

In the United States, one fatal traffic crash occurs every 14 minutes. The National Highway Transportation Safety Administration (NHTSA) annually compiles the leading causative factors of traffic fatalities on America's roadways. Every year, the three primary factors are speed/aggressive driving; driving a vehicle while under the influence of alcohol and or drugs of abuse (DUI); and failure to wear a seatbelt when one is available.

For nonfatal traffic crashes, there are a wide variety of causative factors that range from failure to maintain assured clear distance to the car in front so as to be able to stop without striking the other vehicle when it stops, to running a red light and hitting a vehicle or pedestrian who had the right of way in the intersection. The wide array of causes for nonfatal crashes can be categorized under the general heading of failure to control the vehicle being operated. With the ever-increasing number of cellular telephones and other portable technology that can divert driver attention from the roadway, distracted driving will likely be listed as a primary crash cause in future studies.

The vast majority of both fatal and nonfatal crashes have the common cause of human error as the primary contributing factor to the crash. That is, the crashes are caused by the actions or inactions of a person, not because of defects in the vehicle itself or as a result of poor roadway design. Traffic crashes can be further broken down into three category types: vehicle versus vehicle, vehicle versus fixed object, and vehicle versus person.

Vehicle versus vehicle crashes are the most frequently occurring category of crash and are what one customarily thinks of when hearing the words *traffic crash*. In a vehicle versus vehicle crash, two or more vehicles come into direct contact with one another and damage is caused to at least one of the vehicles as a result of the contact. This crash type has both primary and secondary costs. Primary costs are for vehicle repair and, if there are injuries, medical costs, which the Federal Highway Administration in 2009 estimated at $126,000 per injury. Secondary costs include the use of public safety resources (police, fire, departments of transportation) to investigate the crash and clear the roadway; roadway congestion, which causes inconvenience to other motorists and commercial carriers who use the roadway where the crash takes place; secondary crashes, which are a direct result of either the congestion or of other motorists focusing their attention on the initial crash and public safety response and not their driving; increased insurance premiums for those at fault in the crash; and costly litigation if injuries are involved.

Vehicle versus fixed object crashes are the next most frequent category of traffic crash. In this type of crash, a motor vehicle comes into direct contact with a stationary object, such as a guardrail, barrier wall, light pole, tree, or building, and damage is caused to the striking vehicle, the object struck, or both. A preponderance of crashes of this type can be directly attributed to human error on the part of the person operating the motor vehicle involved. The human error can range from simple failure to control the vehicle to driving at excessive speed for conditions in inclement weather; operating a vehicle while impaired; or driving while distracted, primarily by a cellular telephone call or text message. Vehicle versus fixed object crashes have similar primary and secondary costs as those described in vehicle versus vehicle crashes.

Vehicle versus person crashes are the final crash category. In crashes of this type, a vehicle strikes a pedestrian or bicyclist and causes damage to the vehicle or injury to the person struck. The majority of crashes of this type involve drivers failing to yield right of way to pedestrians in crosswalks, pedestrians crossing the street not in a crosswalk, or children running into the street between parked cars. Recently, an increased number of distracted pedestrians have been struck by vehicles as they walk into the street, while looking down at a cellular telephone or sending a text message, and fail to account for roadway traffic. Vehicle versus person crashes are more likely to result in serious injuries than other crash types, as the person struck lacks the protective equipment provided by a vehicle. Vehicle versus fixed object crashes have similar primary and secondary costs as do vehicle versus vehicle crashes and vehicle versus fixed object crashes.

Traffic Congestion

Traffic congestion can be defined as vehicles travelling at a substantially slower speed than the roadway was designed for, vehicles repeatedly stopping and starting instead of flowing freely, or vehicles sitting in traffic and not moving. All of these are problematic. While traffic crashes generate three times as many economic costs as do traffic congestion, traffic congestion generates many more complaints to police and to other government officials, and more demands for something to be done to alleviate it than do traffic crashes.

There is a clear link between traffic congestion and traffic crashes. Traffic crashes have been proven to cause traffic congestion. On roadways that experience traffic congestion, a higher number of secondary traffic crashes—crashes not part of the original problem but that occur as a direct result of it—regularly take place and cause even more congestion.

Traffic congestion occurs for two primary reasons: too much traffic volume for roadway capacity, especially at peak periods as mornings and afternoons as motorists travel to and from places of employment; and some event on or near the roadway that negatively impacts traffic flow, such as a traffic crash, disabled motorist, or roadway construction. Traffic congestion can be further classified into three category types: predictable recurring, predictable nonrecurring, and unpredictable.

Predictable recurring traffic congestion occurs on a regular basis at the same times of day and at the same locations. These regularly congested areas are called *traffic chokepoints*. Chokepoints occur when traffic volume exceeds traffic capacity on a particular stretch of roadway. They are often located near interstate highway on-ramps as additional vehicles attempt to merge onto an already overcapacity roadway and as a result, traffic slows to a crawl for a period of time until the increased volume is absorbed. A unique feature of chokepoint-related congestion is there are no traffic crashes or other incidents that cause or contribute to the congestion.

To visualize how a chokepoint works, think of a funnel. Liquid comes rapidly into the wide-capacity top, progresses more slowly into the narrow bottom, and then flows rapidly again once it leaves the bottom of the funnel. Traffic flow in congested areas operates in the same manner. Vehicles will be traveling rapidly on a roadway and then encounter congestion. The congestion will occur for a period of time and then dissipate suddenly, leaving motorists puzzled as to why there was such a delay when there were no obvious roadway obstructions such as crashes that may have caused it.

Predictable recurring traffic congestion generates the majority of traffic congestion-related complaints and also the largest number of traffic crashes as the start-and-stop nature of it leads to rear-end collisions when vehicles are forced into closer proximity and cannot maintain the normal assured clear distance needed for safe stopping.

Predictable nonrecurring traffic congestion occurs for a short period of time, at a certain location, for a specific reason. The reasons include road construction that diminishes roadway capacity but does nothing to reduce the volume of vehicles traveling on the roadway, resulting in traffic back-ups; sporting events or other large-scale events in which large numbers of people are all attempting to arrive or exit a venue at a particular time and the increased traffic volume overwhelms existing roadway capacity; and other events such as parades or street festivals that result in street closures and condense existing roadway capacity for a short period, forcing the sometimes increased traffic volume to seek alternate routes in close proximity to those currently closed.

Predictable nonrecurring traffic congestion is the most easily managed of the three types of traffic congestion, as it occurs with advance notice and can be planned for and designated alternate travel routes can be identified prior to the expected congestion. Public education, through the traditional media and electronic signage, about expected delays and suggested alternate travel routes is the most popular method due to its relatively low cost. Increased police presence in the affected area, solely dedicated to maintaining traffic flow, is effective but can be cost-prohibitive depending upon the duration of the event.

With the increasing popularity of social media like Facebook and Twitter, especially among younger drivers, police agencies and governments are starting to partner with event venues and sports teams to send out instant traffic updates to those attending events in order to reduce expected traffic congestion. The team or event venue or police can send out a traffic update message, at scheduled times before and after the event, advising of designated alternate travel routes to avoid congestion. Although a relatively new idea, these instant messaging formats are proving to have success in educating drivers in their teens and twenties and will continue to evolve as technology changes.

Unpredictable traffic congestion, by its very nature, is the most difficult to plan for and resolve once it occurs. Unpredictable traffic congestion causes include traffic crashes; disabled vehicles; roadway failure, such as sinkholes or buckling pavement; weather; or other natural events like landslides or flash flooding. When sudden unexpected incidents occur on a roadway, especially one operating at or near capacity, two main problems quickly develop: how to get needed personnel and equipment to the scene to begin remedying the problem and what to do with the vehicles already on the road with nowhere to go.

When unexpected traffic congestion occurs on a roadway, motorists react in a variety of ways that can hinder the arrival of the personnel and equipment needed to resolve the situation. Drivers may pull vehicles onto roadway shoulders or berms, which can then block the only available travel route to an incident scene for emergency responders. More dangerously, drivers may attempt to back up, turn around, or drive the wrong way on entrance ramps to escape the congestion. Such actions, in addition to creating risk of serious injury to other motorists, can cause further hazards and congestion on the roadway. Another, usually safer, alternative action for drivers is to exercise patience, stay in their cars, and await emergency response. Once the responders are on scene and the initial situation is stabilized, responders take efforts to clear the congestion in a safe and orderly manner.

Reducing Crashes and Congestion

The two primary traffic problems encountered by those who travel in vehicles are traffic crashes and traffic congestion. Traffic crashes and traffic congestion have a mutual cause-and-effect relationship—traffic crashes cause traffic congestion and traffic congestion causes traffic crashes. Each incidence of a crash or congestion has both human and economic costs. When the costs of crashes and congestion are combined, they annually approach $300 billion in the United States.

Because of the extent of the cost of traffic crashes and congestion, police, departments of transportation, and academic researchers may want to focus attention on reducing both. Best practices in crash prevention and traffic incident management can be identified and then researched for empirical validation of their success in both identifying underlying causative factors of problems and their ability to remedy the problem once

identified. After validation, successful programs can be publicized to practitioners, implemented where possible and also used to better educate the public on how to prevent crashes and what to do when a crash or congestion occurs.

Formal social media efforts to inform and educate the driving public can be increased. When a crash or congestion occurs, people are frequently unsure what to do and often their well-intentioned efforts to help may place their own personal safety at risk and add to the problem.

When traffic crashes and congestion are looked are from a mutual cause-and-effect perspective, instead of as individual problems, better problem solving can occur and their cumulative harms reduced.

Daniel W. Gerard

See also Collaboration With Outside Agencies; Evidence-Based Policing; Hot Spots; Place-Based Policing; Problem-Solving Initiatives, Assessment and Evaluation; Publicity Campaigns; Traffic Problems, Community Policing Strategies for

Further Readings

Cambridge Systematics. (2011, November). *Crashes vs. congestion: What's the cost to society?* Bethesda, MD: Author. Retrieved from http://www.camsys.com/pubs/2011_AAA_CrashvCongUpd.pdf

Centers for Disease Control and Prevention. (2011). *Vehicle crash injury estimates.* Retrieved from http://www.cdc.gov/motorvehiclesafety/index.html

Clarke, R. V., & Eck, J. E. (2005). *Crime analysis for problem solvers in 60 small steps.* Washington, DC: U.S. Department of Justice, Office of Community Oriented Policing Services.

National Highway Traffic Safety Administration. (2011). *U.S. fatality and crash estimates.* Retrieved from http://www.nhtsa.gov/FARS

Texas Transportation Institute. (2011). *2011 Annual Urban Mobility Report.* Retrieved from http://mobility.tamu.edu/ums

TRAFFIC PROBLEMS, COMMUNITY POLICING STRATEGIES FOR

Unlike traditional police responses to community problems, which primarily consist of slight variations on the standard response model of policing, community policing problem-solving efforts are most often thought of as wide-ranging responses to criminal activity. These responses target specific place-based locations that as street corners, apartment buildings, businesses, or even entire neighborhoods. Response development includes both traditional and non-traditional police activities, which often require a change in police organizational thinking and outside partnerships with the community residents, other governmental agencies, private businesses, and the media. The goal of the outside partnerships is to mutually develop an actionable response to the problem. Once jointly developed, the targeted interventions focus on modifying the behaviors of certain individuals or groups of individuals who by their actions have reduced the overall quality of life for the other residents in a neighborhood.

Traffic problems are usually not what one thinks of when hearing the words *community policing.* When a citizen hears the word *traffic,* three images usually come to mind: receiving a citation for a traffic violation, being involved in or driving past the aftermath of a traffic crash, or sitting in traffic congestion and becoming ever more frustrated as traffic does not move. None of these three images are pleasant and the negative connotations from them are usually directed to the police or to departments of transportation. Poor driving behavior, traffic crashes, and traffic congestion are all traffic problems encountered by law enforcement every day.

In a considerable majority of police departments, traffic problems are normally relegated to secondary importance, behind crime-related problems. There are two clear reasons for this. First, crime problems receive more media coverage and generate more external pressure, from both citizens and politicians, for something to be done about them. Second, the effectiveness of police executives across the United States is typically evaluated, by both their employers and by citizens, in terms of their community's crime rates and not on traffic fatalities and traffic flow. This may be an important oversight, as studies by the National Highway Traffic Safety Administration (NHTSA) show that traffic crashes are the leading cause of death for all Americans between the ages of 3 to 34 years.

This entry looks at the application of community policing strategies for traffic problems and how harms from them can be reduced using the nontraditional community policing approaches of outside partnerships and a change in police organizational thinking.

Outside Partnerships

Outside partnerships to assist the police with traffic problems can be broken down into four main categories: community members and groups, other governmental agencies, private businesses, and the media.

The use of outside partnerships to solve traffic problems is often a difficult concept for police agencies to understand. After all, neither private businesses nor the members of a community investigate daily traffic crashes or write citations for traffic law violations, so how could they understand how to remedy traffic problems? In reality, though, every traffic crash investigated and traffic citation issued involves a member of the community as either a participant or a violator. The vast majority of vehicles that travel the roadways each day are not police vehicles but those operated by ordinary citizens and the business employees who populate an area. Collectively, those who live and work in a community possess tremendous institutional knowledge about local traffic patterns and traffic flow at all times of the day and are a largely untapped source of knowledge.

The police can ensure this knowledge is collected by the use of several methods. Surveys can be sent, either via e-mail or traditional mail, to licensed drivers in a certain area. The surveys can ask questions about driving patterns (e.g., whether the primary purpose of vehicle trips is business or pleasure), average trip length, duration, and time of day. The police can also request that citizens identify any problem areas for congestion that are routinely encountered. A more in-depth discussion with local community focus groups can be held to help better understand driving behaviors, patterns, and problems from the perspective of the users of the roadways.

Once the initial community-based results are tabulated, they can be analyzed along with existing police traffic data to identify problem areas for crashes and congestion. Follow-up contacts can be made with the initial survey participants and with the community at large both to share the survey results and to seek suggested responses to the problem areas identified. Responses that appear to have merit can then be implemented and assessed for success. If successful, public recognition given to the problem solver(s) who developed the response may generate even more ideas, as the public sees the police are serious about addressing their traffic-related concerns and are willing to listen to their ideas for solutions.

The next group in the outside partnerships category that can help the police impact traffic problems is other governmental agencies, which can be further broken down into two subcategories: law enforcement and non–law enforcement. Outside law enforcement partnerships provide additional resources and increase police visibility in an area, often at no additional costs to the local community. When one lives in, works, or travels through an area daily, the local police are an expected part of the landscape. As people go about their daily routine activities, local police fade into the background and much like trees or buildings, people see them but pay no particular notice of them. By partnering with an outside law enforcement agency, like a state highway patrol organization or a county sheriff's office, and patrolling in tandem, local police agencies can increase their visibility among their citizens. Area motorists who see a different law enforcement agency in their locale may be unsure of the new agency's tolerance for traffic violations and may modify their driving behavior, primarily by reducing vehicle speed and by increasing seat belt usage. Lower travel speeds have been empirically proven to reduce crash severity, and increased seatbelt usage has been empirically proven to increase occupant protection in the event of a crash. Thus, an outside law enforcement partnership may ultimately save lives among those who are involved in traffic crashes.

Non–law enforcement government partnerships can include local and state departments of transportation, state traffic safety offices including those affiliated with the Governor's Highway Safety Association, and the National Highway Traffic Safety Administration. Government partnerships are important for the police as these agencies provide ongoing assistance in the form of funding, data analysis, equipment, and other resources to help plan for and deal with both small- and large-scale traffic-related incidents.

Local and state departments of transportation are responsible for maintaining and improving both

roadways and interstate highways and also for managing the traffic flow by determining proper speeds and traffic control device placement such as red lights and stop signs. Although both police agencies and departments of transportation are in the business of maintaining safe and orderly traffic patterns, often they do not work closely together or regularly share information. Because both entities possess detailed and complementary knowledge about the causative factors of traffic crashes, traffic flow, and traffic congestion, they could have a far greater impact working together than by working individually. In addition, when a major traffic incident such as a fatal crash, long-term roadway construction, or a long-term road closure from a natural disaster or hazardous material spill occurs, both police and departments of transportation play major roles in shutting down the affected roadways so that the situation can be safely remedied.

Regular communications between both entities ensures a more efficient and effective joint response when traffic problems are encountered. For example, Cincinnati (Ohio) police host quarterly meetings of the Regional Incident Management Task Force (RIMTF), which brings together law enforcement, fire, communications, and department of transportation officials from Ohio and Kentucky to discuss ongoing traffic problems that affect both states. At each meeting, training in critical traffic-incident response, such as hazardous materials, is provided and recent major traffic-incident responses are presented and reviewed for both effectiveness and best practices development.

State traffic safety offices are tasked with analyses of statewide traffic crash patterns to determine causative factors and with development of traffic safety programs on a statewide basis. They partner with law enforcement agencies of all sizes in an individual state and provide training in areas like basic traffic crash investigation and advanced detection of drivers impaired by alcohol or drugs of abuse.

In addition, state traffic safety offices administer and award both state and federal funding to local agencies, for traffic safety programs that include driving while intoxicated (or driving under the influence) task forces; additional speed enforcement, especially in construction zones and high-crash locations; overtime for high-visibility patrols in crash hot spots and for special purpose programs such as motorcycle speed and license compliance enforcement. All of these training programs and additional funds allow law enforcement to dedicate additional resources to traffic problems without depleting existing street strength—which is a key concern as law enforcement budgets nationwide are being cut and many agencies no longer have the resources to dedicate officers full time to traffic safety.

The National Highway Traffic Safety Administration (NHTSA) develops nationwide traffic safety programs, funds them on a state level, assesses their effectiveness, and maintains traffic safety and crash data on a national level. The NHTSA coordinates yearly national enforcement programs such as Click It or Ticket, which is designed to increase seatbelt usage, and Drive Sober or Get Pulled Over, which focuses on the removal from highways drivers impaired by alcohol or drugs. NHTSA analysis, programs and funding assist law enforcement with traffic problems by providing a more in-depth analysis of traffic problems than most agencies are capable of and then by tailoring funding to programs designed to reduce the harms created by the problems.

Basically, NHTSA applies the SARA (scanning, analysis, response, assessment) problem-solving model to national traffic issues. NHTSA *scans* and *analyzes* nationwide traffic and crash data to identify traffic-related problems and their underlying causes; it then develops and funds law enforcement programs in *response* to the identified problems, and then *assesses* program effectiveness. If successful, the programs and funding are continued; if not, additional analysis is conducted to determine why so that new programs can be tried or existing ones modified.

Private businesses are the next outside partnership that can assist police with traffic problems. They can provide programs that supplement existing law enforcement traffic safety programs or finance public safety campaigns about problem driver behaviors like watching out for motorcycles in the spring, when their crash rates with other vehicles are higher than the rest of the year. Private businesses such as insurance companies often provide education programs for teens on topics like distracted driving and for older drivers on how to compensate for slower reflexes and reaction times when confronted with sudden changes in traffic, for example, being suddenly cut off by another driver. Automobile manufacturers offer a program for newly licensed teen

drivers, Driving Skills for Life, in which race car and stunt drivers ride along with teens in modified vehicles that randomly simulate real-life driving hazards, such as vehicle skids and lane changes, to improve new driver awareness and increase skill level and confidence. Bars, restaurants, and sports teams can also send out Twitter blasts or Facebook messages to their followers reminding them to drink responsibly or advising of alternate routes to their venue when traffic is congested.

Another example of using private businesses is the Cincinnati police and traffic engineering departments partnering with two of the area's largest paving contractors to develop a microgrid of roadway surfaces in high-crash residential locations. The result was that the new roadway was both rough enough to stop vehicles from sliding in wet conditions and quiet enough that nearby residents were not disturbed when a vehicle drove over it. No fatal or serious injury crashes have occurred in any of these problem locations since the intervention.

The media is an often-overlooked outside partner but one that plays a critical role in any public education campaign. Law enforcement and media partnerships can assist in traffic problem solving through the use of public education campaigns designed around traffic safety and congestion-related problems. Studies show that people accept change better when they both know about it ahead of time and the rationale for it is explained. This can be especially true for changes that may impact the public's driving habits like roadway construction or stepped up traffic enforcement as in the aforementioned Click It or Ticket program. Furthermore, highly publicized alternate travel routes, information about expected travel delays, and explanations of the reasons for increased traffic safety enforcement can alleviate much of the community's associated stresses, make motorists more inclined to alter their driving behavior and thus have a hand in problem alleviation.

Organizational Transformation

Traffic problems are traditionally a secondary priority behind crime problems for a considerable majority of law enforcement agencies. However, there are two reasons for traffic problems receiving increased law enforcement attention: First, the human and economic costs surrounding traffic crashes and traffic congestion are estimated at over $300 billion a year. Second, for a large segment of society, the primary contacts with the police occurs when they are involved in a traffic crash, when they receive a citation for a traffic violation, or when they observe the police dealing with an event that has caused traffic congestion such as a large sporting event. How these situations are handled by police helps shape public opinions of police effectiveness and the legitimacy of their actions.

Organizational transformation needs to occur in two areas for an agency to successfully implement a community-oriented strategy for traffic problems. First, the leadership of the agency has to make traffic safety a priority within the agency and ensure that both supervisors and line officers understand why it is important. Once traffic safety has been established as a priority, strategic planning and analysis must be completed on an ongoing basis to determine the precise traffic problems and their underlying causes. Ongoing planning and analysis are important, as traffic problems can develop with little to no warning and the early identification of potential problem patterns can ultimately reduce harms from them. After an analysis is completed and problems are identified, responses are developed. The purpose and importance of the response must be communicated to the field officers who will implement the response, and to the driving public impacted by it. The listing of precise measures and anticipated results at the onset of the response allows for easier assessment. Timely ongoing assessment of the response must be undertaken and modifications to the response made if assessment shows it to not be successful. The specific reasons for the lack of success—whether implementation related, operational, or theoretical—must be clearly identified at this point if the plan's new modifications are to be an improvement over the prior intervention. If the response is successful and has a positive impact on the targeted traffic problem, the accomplishment needs to be made known to the officers who implemented it and also used to educate the public as to what the impact was. By internally and externally sharing the results of a successful traffic problem response, an agency can reinforce the police and public behaviors that jointly contributed to the positive results. Positive behavior reinforcement makes it easier to gain buy-in for future traffic problem responses from both the police and the public.

The second organizational change area involves technology and data. For successful traffic problem analysis, accurate and timely data are a must. The data must be accessible and compiled in a useable format. Law enforcement agencies regularly compile large amounts of data on a wide variety of issues relating to their daily functions, including traffic. However, most of these data are neither seen by a majority of the officers who compile it nor shared with outside entities who may be able to use it to assist the law enforcement agency in its traffic problem-solving efforts. For example, law enforcement traffic crash and enforcement data may not be shared with departments of transportation; departments of transportation may compile their own data, often on some of the same traffic topics as do law enforcement, and not routinely share this outside data with the police. Regular data sharing and idea brainstorming about traffic problems among law enforcement, other government agencies, and private businesses—all of whom regularly deal with the aftermath of a traffic problem—can produce collaborative ideas and responses that are more effective than each entity working independently and trying to resolve the same issues.

Conclusion

The strategies of community-oriented policing and problem solving can be used to mediate the harms caused by traffic problems. The involvement of the public in the planning and problem-solving process gives the community ownership of both the problem and the intervention developed to respond to it. This outside partnership increases police legitimacy in the community in the event the response generates criticism from others in the community who may be negatively impacted by some part of it. The use of outside law enforcement partners, other governmental agencies, and private businesses can contribute detailed analysis, expertise, resources, and funding not generally available to law enforcement that can be dedicated to traffic problems. The media can also help, by educating the public on both traffic problems and intervention implementation. The use of social media by law enforcement must increase so as not to miss younger drivers who do not get their information from traditional media sources but instead rely upon social media.

Organizational changes also need to take place to increase the importance of both traffic safety and problem solving around traffic issues. Accurate, meaningful data must be compiled, accessed, analyzed, shared and specific responses to identify traffic problems developed based upon the data analysis. The responses must continually be assessed for success and modified or even abandoned in favor of other interventions if needed.

Daniel W. Gerard

See also Collaboration With Outside Agencies; Evidence-Based Policing; Hot Spots; Place-Based Policing; Problem-Solving Initiatives, Assessment and Evaluation; Publicity Campaigns, Traffic Problems, Characteristics of

Further Readings

Cambridge Systematics. (2011, November). *Crashes vs. congestion: What's the cost to society?* Bethesda, MD: Author. Retrieved from http://www.camsys.com/pubs/2011_AAA_CrashvCongUpd.pdf

Centers for Disease Control and Prevention. (2011). *Vehicle crash injury estimates.* Retrieved from http://www.cdc.gov/motorvehiclesafety/index.html

Clarke, R. V., & Eck, J. E. (2005). *Crime analysis for problem solvers in 60 small steps.* Washington, DC: U.S. Department of Justice, Office of Community Oriented Policing Services.

Gerard, D. W., Corsaro, N., Engel, R. S., & Eck, J. E. (2012, July). Cincinnati CARS: A crash analysis reduction strategy. *Police Chief, 79,* 24–31.

Skogan, W. G., & Frydl, K. (Eds.). (2004). *Fairness and effectiveness in police: The evidence.* Washington, DC: The National Academies Press.

Office of Community Oriented Policing Services. (2009). *Community policing defined.* Retrieved from http://www.cops.usdoj.gov/Publications/e030917193-CP-Defined.pdf

Website

National Highway Traffic Safety Administration; http://www.nhtsa.gov

V

VIOLENT CRIME CONTROL AND LAW ENFORCEMENT ACT OF 1994

The Violent Crime Control and Law Enforcement Act of 1994 (the Crime Act) was the largest federal crime bill in U.S. history, allocating nearly $16 billion for a variety of criminal justice programs. The Crime Act was particularly significant with respect to law enforcement, and specifically to community policing. The Crime Act's community policing competitive grant program (the COPS Program) provided funding for 100,000 new police officers in community policing programs nationwide during a five-year period and more than $6 billion for related crime prevention programs. The Crime Act also created the federal Office of Community Oriented Policing Services (the COPS Office) to distribute and monitor the COPS Program grant funds. This entry provides information on the history of the Crime Act, its implementation and use, and its effects on community policing and violent crime.

History of the Crime Act

In February 1993, agents with the Federal Bureau of Alcohol, Tobacco, and Firearms, which was investigating David Koresh and his Branch Davidian followers for illegal possession and stockpiling of weapons, attempted to serve a search warrant on the Branch Davidian Ranch, on the outskirts of Waco, Texas. A two-hour gun battle ensued, beginning the historic Waco siege, which lasted another 50 days until April 19, when FBI agents assaulted the compound and it was destroyed by fire.

Just a few months later, on July 1, 1993, the elevator doors opened on the 34th floor of the high-rise office building at 101 California Street in San Francisco. Fifty-five-year-old businessman Gian Luigi Ferri stepped out into the law offices of Pettit & Martin, put on a pair of ear protectors, and opened fire with three handguns. Ferri shot and killed eight people before he shot himself as police officers closed in.

These events occurred just as national violent crime rates were peaking after a consistent upward climb. According to the U.S. Government Accounting Office, from 1983 to 1992—the year before the nationwide rates of violent crime began to decline—the number of violent crimes known to the police increased from less than 1.3 million to more than 1.9 million (approximately 54%), and the violent crime rate per 100,000 population increased from 538 to 758 (approximately 41%).

At the same time, throughout the nation, there were calls for police reform. Aggressive police practices in predominantly African American neighborhoods were criticized for contributing to racial strife and an ever-increasing chasm between African Americans and the police. The increased crime rates tarnished police officers' crime-fighter image and seemed to be evidence that police strategies were ineffective. Meanwhile, a series of academic studies criticized the professional model of policing (characterized by reactive, incident-driven methods and emphases on quantitative outcomes such as number

417

of calls for service, arrests, and so on), and departments all over the country were experimenting with community crime prevention, foot patrols, and other innovative practices. By the end of the 1980s, interest from inside and outside police departments in community and problem-oriented policing was growing.

These events set the stage for major crime legislation, and when William Jefferson Clinton was elected president in 1992, he quickly announced that putting more police officers on America's streets would be one of his top anticrime goals. In 1993, Representative Jack Brooks of Texas sponsored the Violent Crime Control and Law Enforcement Act of 1994, as originally written by Senator Joseph Biden of Delaware. The Crime Act was the largest crime bill in U.S. history—literally—at more than 350 pages in its final form, and in economic terms, at nearly $16 billion in funding for a variety of criminal justice programs (the Crime Act was actually several amendments to the Omnibus Crime Control and Safe Streets Act of 1968). President Clinton signed the Crime Act into law on September 13, 1994. Congress reauthorized the COPS Program in 2005 and appropriated another $587 billion to the program in 2008.

The Crime Act triggered bipartisan battles over flashpoint issues like gun control and the death penalty, but it also demanded bipartisan cooperation on less divisive issues like crimes against the elderly and children, violence against women, and criminal street gangs. The version ultimately approved by Congress included such still-aggressive and controversial provisions as the Federal Assault Weapons Ban, an expanded list of federal death penalty crimes, and the Violence Against Women Act, which allocated $1.6 billion to prevent and investigate violent crimes against women.

The Crime Act was particularly significant with respect to law enforcement and community policing. The community policing competitive grant program—the COPS Program—provided $1.3 billion in 1995 and $7.5 billion in 1996 to 2000 to put 100,000 new police officers in community policing programs nationwide during a five-year period and more than $6 billion for crime prevention programs designed in large part with input to Congress from experienced police officers. The federal Office of Community Oriented Policing Services—the COPS Office—was created to distribute and monitor the COPS Program grant funds.

The Crime Act provided a federal incentive to municipal law enforcement agencies to change the way they police, especially in the inner cities where crime rates were, and have historically been, much higher than other areas. The Crime Act has been characterized as the Department of Justice's first opportunity to provide leadership in improving the basic methods of local policing and the first official federal recognition that the solution to violent crime in the United States must come from people in communities, and that the local police are uniquely positioned to mobilize citizens.

Indeed, the "Additional Grants" language of the Crime Act was very specific with regard to the community policing practices and goals that the Department of Justice was seeking to promote and implement. Specifically, the act sought to increase the number of officers involved in interactions with the public in matters of proactive crime control; provide specialized training to officers to enhance their skills in conflict resolution, mediation, and problem solving; develop new technologies to assist agencies in proactively preventing crime; develop programs to permit members of the community to better assist the police in the prevention of crime, such as a citizen police academies and decentralized satellite offices (including video facilities) in police stations and courts buildings.

Implementation and Effect on Community Policing

From 1995 to 2008, the COPS Program awarded more than $13 billion in grants to local police agencies to hire community policing officers and to further police-community problem-solving programs.

The COPS Program was designed to put 100,000 additional police officers on the streets during the five years between 1995 and 2000 through three-year hiring grants that paid up to 75% of the cost to hire new officers. The Government Accounting Office reported in 2005 that the number of sworn officers nationwide increased during that period by about 90,000, but historic growth rates could account for the same number of additional officers, so researchers have found it difficult to determine the precise effect the Crime Act may have had on police officer hiring and redeployment.

The COPS grants also allowed police departments to acquire new crime-fighting technology and to fund innovative police programs like the following:

Salt Lake City Methamphetamine Initiative: The Salt Lake City Police Department (Utah) used grant monies to create an Intelligence Unit under the COPS Meth Initiative, which assigns an intelligence analyst to assist in investigations and research. The analyst is also involved in the drug hotline, taking and responding to calls and leads.

School Campus Officers: In the wake of the Columbine High School (Colorado) shootings and other school violence in the late 1990s, COPS funds have helped local school districts to increase police presence on school campuses ($763 million in funding between 1998 and 2006, resulting in 6,453 officers nationwide).

Officer-Next-Door Programs: COPS grants have also been used to fund Officer-Next-Door Programs, such as the flagship program in Alexandria, Virginia, where police officers have moved into high–crime risk neighborhoods like public housing communities and federally subsidized Section 8 communities. The officers then become friends and neighbors to residents, and are active in mediating arguments, counseling community youth, and acting as liaisons between the community and the city.

Armed for Terrorists in Case Killing Them With Kindness Doesn't Work: In the early 1900s, Berkeley (California) Police Chief August Vollmer used to say "kill them with kindness" when referring to law enforcement's relationship to the community. But in 2004, using part of a $500,000 COPS grant, Alameda County (California) Sheriff Charles C. Plummer created an antiterrorist unit to protect the San Francisco Bay Area. The centerpiece of that effort was two German-made machine guns mounted on the bow and stern of a patrol boat and officers trained to operate them in and around the San Francisco Bay.

And on the national level, the COPS Office established a network of Regional Community Policing Institutes (RCPI) and supported the operation of the Center for Problem-Oriented Policing (POP Center). As of midyear 2009, the RCPI network had trained more than 600,000 police officers, government officials, and community members

By statistical accounts, the Crime Act and its COPS Program resulted in the hiring and redeployment of community policing police officers, and also funded a variety of community policing programs.

The Act's Effects on Crime

Less clear is whether the Crime Act and the COPS Program have affected crime rates. Generally speaking, crime rates dropped beginning in the early 1990s, and supporters of the Crime Act and the COPS Program believed that these initiatives had contributed to that drop. But the research and conclusions have been mixed and highly controversial.

In 2002, researchers Jihong "Solomon" Zhao, Matthew C. Scheider, and Quint Thurman concluded that COPS grants appeared to be an effective way to reduce crime in the United States. The researchers used panel data from 6,100 cities for the period 1995 to 1999 and found that the COPS Program's hiring and innovative police program grants significantly reduced violent and property crime rates in cities with more than 10,000 people.

But that same year, David Muhlhausen found among other things, it failed to account for a variety of factors known to affect crime rates and also failed to control for more traditional local law enforcement efforts. Muhlhausen used panel data from 752 counties from 1995 to 1998 and concluded that hiring and new technology grants had no appreciable effect on violent crime.

Understandably, the Government Accountability Office (GAO) sought its own answers to the crime rate question and performed research on the issue while attempting to control for variables and factors that had exposed the independent 2002 study to criticism. The GAO researchers concluded in a 2005 report that COPS grant expenditures reduced crime during the 1990s. In 2007, William M. Evans and Emily Owens likewise concluded that rates for four types of crime (auto theft, burglary, robbery, and aggravated assault) dropped in the years after police departments had received COPS hiring grants. But researchers John L. Worrall and Tomislav V. Kovandzic shortly thereafter concluded that COPS grants had no discernible effect on serious crime during the period studied.

The issue of whether the Crime Act and COPS Program have affected crime rates (as Congress intended or otherwise) remains unsettled with some researchers concluding that the increased number of community policing police officers contributed to the decrease in crime rates in the 1990s, while others maintain that COPS grants failed to reduce crime at all.

While the jury remains out on the crime rate issue, there is no question that the Crime Act was historic in its extensive funding and scope. It was also a major landmark in the history of community policing, with both the executive branch and Congress recognizing the invaluable role that this approach plays in modern law enforcement.

Pamela M. Everett

See also Community Oriented Policing Services, Office of; Executive Sessions on Policing; National Center for Community Policing; National Crime Prevention Council; Regional Community Policing Institutes

Further Readings

Evans, W. M., & Owens, E. (2007). COPS and crime. *Journal of Public Economics, 91*(1–2), 181–201. doi: 10.1016/j.jpubec0.2006.05.014

Government Accountability Office. (2005, October). *Community policing grants: COPS grants were a modest contributor to declines in crime in the 1990s.* GAO-06–104. Washington, DC: Author. Retrieved from http://www.gao.gov/new.items/d06104.pdf

Muhlhausen, D. B. (2001). *Do community oriented policing services grants affect violent crime rates?* (Report no. CDA01–05). Washington, DC: Heritage Foundation, Center for Data Analysis.

Murphy, P. V. (1995). Violent Crime Control and Law Enforcement Act of 1994: The impact of additional police. *University of Dayton Law Review, 20,* 745–748.

Worrall, J. L., & Kovandzic, T. V. (2007). COPS grants and crime revisited. *Criminology, 45*(1), 159–190. doi: 10.1111/j.1745–9125.2007.00076

Zhao, J., Scheider, M. C., & Thurman, Q. C. (2002). Funding community policing to reduce crime: Have COPS grants made a difference? *Criminology and Public Policy, 2*(1), 7–32. doi: 10.1111/j.1745–9133.2002.tb00104

Volunteers, Police Use of

In the 21st century, the demands on law enforcement are numerous and varied. Agencies struggle to protect their communities from the threat of global terrorism and also face increasingly sophisticated challenges from computer and cybercrimes, narcotics trafficking, identity theft, and other crimes. These efforts take place against a backdrop of shrinking budgets and limited resources.

Yet, one thing law enforcement agencies can do to leverage existing resources and at the same time enhance public safety is engage volunteers. Volunteer programs allow agencies and officers to focus on policing and enforcement functions by providing supplemental and support services. At the same time, such programs create valuable ties between law enforcement and the community.

The following are some of the many benefits police volunteers can offer:

- Affording access to a broader range of expertise and experience
- Increasing paid staff members' effectiveness by enabling them to focus their efforts where they are most needed or by providing additional services
- Providing support for tasks that would otherwise have to wait for additional resources
- Acting as community liaisons to gain support for agency activities
- Opening a direct line to private resources in the community
- Raising public awareness and program visibility

Volunteers participate in activities ranging from checking the security of vacationing residents' homes to assisting in solving cold cases. Volunteers serve as well-informed ambassadors in the community, gaining credibility with the community as they support law enforcement without monetary compensation. They serve as a bridge to law enforcement agencies and surrounding communities working toward a common mission: to promote the safety of the community.

Budgeting and Funding a Volunteer Program

One of the major tenets of police volunteering is that volunteers support rather than supplant officers and paid civilians. Volunteers offer law enforcement agencies the resources needed to assist in and expand public services and crime prevention efforts in communities. While volunteers are not compensated for their time and efforts, establishing and maintaining a volunteer program is not a cost-free endeavor; it does have associated costs. However, the returns can be substantial. The costs associated with establishing and maintaining a volunteer program depend on the scope of the opportunities offered and can include personnel (e.g., salary and benefits for a volunteer coordinator-manager), volunteer screening, training, work space requirements, supplies, equipment, uniforms, and recognition.

Law enforcement volunteer programs are funded through a variety of mechanisms, including donations, fund-raising, and grants. While traditional funding streams may be reduced at this time, law enforcement agencies have a host of other sources to look to for financial support. Funding can come from donations via local businesses and organizations. In-kind services or donations can range from gift cards for volunteer recognition to a vehicle for citizen patrols. Many volunteer programs engage in fund-raising to support their activities.

The policies and procedures for direct fund-raising by law enforcement agencies vary, so agencies should check with their legal departments for fund-raising guidelines and regulations. Local branches of civic and service organizations may be willing to provide support by raising funds on behalf of agencies that are prohibited from soliciting funds. Grants.gov is a central storehouse for information including more than 1,000 grant programs. The U.S. Department of Justice's Office of Justice Programs offers federal financial assistance to state and local governments and agencies. Their website also offers Grants 101, which contains information ranging from the life cycle of a grant to types of funding. Many volunteer programs also partner with existing local nonprofit associations or have been involved in creating associations that can raise funds and secure nonprofit status. Many agencies also form nonprofits through their citizen police academy alumni associations.

Building Program Infrastructure

The characteristics of a law enforcement agency and its community will influence the need for and acceptance and availability of volunteers. Including community members or organizations in the program development process is key to a successful program. Factors to consider are agency size, community size, demographics, and the presence of higher education institutions and philanthropic organizations. Support for the program begins with the top executive and filters down through the agency to paid employees, sworn and civilian. This buy-in is essential to maintaining a successful program. Agencies must involve labor groups, officers, and civilian employees in identifying activities that volunteers can perform.

The first step in establishing a volunteer program is to assess the needs of an agency. Comprehensive position descriptions detailing the duties and expectations of volunteer positions are also necessary. Such descriptions can be helpful in screening potential volunteers. Before a volunteer program is established, operational guidelines and policies about the governance and function of the program must be set. Having a set of policies provides the structure to manage the program equitably and can prevent future challenges. Agencies also need to make volunteers aware of agency policies and procedures. Liability concerns are common when implementing a volunteer program. Liability laws vary state by state, so agencies should consult with local government attorneys and state points of contact to determine what coverage may be provided. Other government departments may use volunteers and a policy may already exist. Some agencies classify their volunteers as unpaid employees or pay their volunteers $1 a year to provide coverage. Clearly outlining department policy with regard to volunteers is a fundamental step toward reducing risk.

Recruitment

To develop a successful law enforcement volunteer program, individuals who are qualified for the work they will perform must be sought out. Effective recruitment messages are inviting and encourage people to become involved with the program, with each message identifying specific needs of an agency, the ways volunteers can address those needs, and the benefits to the volunteer. Creating volunteer position descriptions is useful in forming the basis of recruitment efforts. Identifying activities performed by a volunteer is limited only by agency creativity and the ability to provide program structure, management, and guidance.

Many established volunteer programs grow out of citizen police academies, cultivating the participants' demonstrated interest in an agency into a long-term volunteer relationship. Brochures and flyers can be used in mailings or as takeaways at presentations and special events. Local media (television, radio, newspaper) can assist in advertising information about volunteer programs. These media organizations may also produce stories profiling volunteers and their accomplishments at a later date. Citizens are increasingly using the Internet to conduct research on volunteer opportunities, so agencies can publish information about a program, opportunities available, contact information, and an online downloadable application form on their websites. Other effective recruitment mechanisms are existing volunteer organizations. Community volunteer centers, Retired and Senior Volunteer Programs (RSVP), civic groups, educational institutions, and local Citizen Corps Councils are all excellent sources of potential volunteers.

Selection and Management

Agencies must screen individuals before bringing them on as volunteers. The level of screening depends on the role the volunteer will be serving. The screening process may include the following: completion of an application form, a criminal background check, a reference check, fingerprinting, drug testing, and polygraph. Candidate interviews can help to determine if a prospective volunteer is a good fit for a program, and also offer a chance to learn more about the applicant's interests, abilities, and experiences. Interviews can prevent future problems by ensuring that there is a clear understanding of the requirements of the volunteer position.

Effective management of a volunteer program is essential to a program's success. Selecting a person to coordinate the program is one of the most important keys to a successful program. A volunteer coordinator or manager can either be sworn or civilian. There may be several people responsible for the management of volunteers. Defining clear roles for the coordinator will help ensure a connection to the agency's mission and role of the volunteer department. The person responsible is expected to be committed and possess the skills and will to supervise volunteers, as well as provide support, feedback, and evaluation, just like regular paid employees.

Training

Before taking on any responsibilities, volunteers often receive an orientation to the police agency. The orientation may be supplemented with a handbook of policies and procedures for future reference. The following are customary elements of volunteer orientation:

- Welcome from the chief, sheriff, or other command staff
- Agency history
- Agency structure and organizational chart
- A glossary of language and abbreviations used by the agency
- Agency tour
- Emergency procedures
- Timesheets and other required forms
- A termination policy

Volunteer orientation may also include the issuance of proper credentials, introductions to supervisors and staff (paid and nonpaid) with whom volunteers will be working and a tour of the facilities, such as where to report and where to store personal belongings. Agencies may require additional training in such areas as sexual harassment, diversity, or ethics. Agencies may also consider asking volunteers to sign agreements acknowledging applicable policies and procedures and a commitment to a certain schedule or number of volunteer shifts.

Training for volunteers presents the specific information and skills they will need to perform their assignments in a manner that is appropriate to the complexity and demands of the positions and the capabilities of the volunteer. Training helps to increase volunteer job satisfaction and reduce liability risk. Volunteers can be trained through on-the-job demonstrations, lectures, written material, role playing, simulations, and case studies. Ongoing in-service training supplements initial training.

Recognition

Recognizing volunteers helps convey the important role they play in an agency and is a key to their retention. Recognition need not be time-consuming or expensive to be meaningful. Simple ways to recognize volunteers include conveying verbal expressions of thanks, writing letters of commendation, posting photos of volunteers on the job, giving gift certificates donated by local businesses, highlighting volunteers on an agency's website, asking staff to hold a potluck meal to honor volunteers, and recognizing volunteers' birthday and anniversary dates.

More formal recognition could include a volunteer of the month or year award, recognition banquets or events that allow volunteers to bring their families, and providing plaques, shirts, or bags with the agency's seal. Many states, local communities, and civic groups offer formal awards for volunteers and organizations. The state's volunteer commission, usually housed in the governor's office, or the local volunteer center may be able to provide information regarding what types of awards and recognition programs volunteers may be nominated for. There are also national award programs, through the International Association of Chiefs of Police and the National Sheriffs' Association, as well as the President's Volunteer Service Award. National Volunteer Week, held annually during the month of April, is another way to celebrate and recognize volunteers.

Assessing Cost, Benefits, and Performance

Assessing the costs and benefits of a volunteer program can assist decision makers in their budget and resource distribution decisions. It is important to document the resources required to manage, implement, and maintain a program. Collecting data before the implementation of the program can assist in measuring the growth and impact of a program. Commonly collected information includes the number of individuals volunteering, how many hours each volunteer contributes on a monthly basis, the types of activities volunteers are engaged in, and the number of activities completed.

Calculating the dollar value of volunteer contributions can be useful as well. Each year the Independent Sector sets the value of a volunteer hour, based on the average hourly wage for all nonmanagement, nonagricultural workers, as determined by the Bureau of Labor Statistics, with an increase to estimate for fringe benefits. Although the dollar amount may be helpful when making budgetary and programmatic decisions, the value of an increased presence in the community and the positive public relations generated by volunteers are not included. While difficult to measure, anecdotal information and feedback from the community are also important considerations.

Routinely assessing volunteers can provide valuable information about the volunteer and the volunteer program. Depending on the size and scope of the program, this assessment may be completed by the volunteer coordinator or the volunteer's supervisor. Many agencies choose to formally evaluate volunteers on an annual or biannual basis. The evaluation can be a useful tool to select a volunteer for formal recognition, identify and prevent a potential problem, determine what training would be helpful to the volunteer's performance of duties, determine whether the volunteer can and would like to take on a new or additional role, and obtain feedback and suggestions about the structure and management of the volunteer program. Talking to volunteers can also be helpful in determining what is and isn't working with the program.

While law enforcement agencies are designed and staffed to maximize services to the community, there is always more work to be done. As a result of the economic downturn that began in 2008, agencies are experiencing increased workload in a resource-constrained environment, so many use citizens to support and expand agency functions. The financial return on investment of a volunteer program can be substantial, amounting to hundreds of thousands of dollars worth of value added to agencies each year. While some agencies have been forced to cut staff and programs, the use of volunteers has remained consistent and, in some cases, increased. One program that provides information and resources on starting a volunteer program is the U.S. Department of Justice's Volunteers in Police Service, funded by the Bureau of Justice Assistance, Office of Justice Programs and managed by the International Association of Chiefs of Police.

Rosemary DeMenno

See also Citizen Patrols; Citizen Police Academies; Community Cohesion and Empowerment; Non-sworn Personnel and Volunteers, Use and Training of; Police-Community Relations

Further Readings

Connors, T. D. (Ed.). (2011). *The volunteer management handbook: Leadership strategies for success.* Hoboken, NJ: Wiley.

Ellis, S. J. (2004). *The volunteer recruitment (and membership development) book.* Philadelphia, PA: Energize.

Graff, L. L. (2004). *Beyond police checks: The definitive volunteer and employee screening guidebook.* Dundas, ON, Canada: Linda Graff and Associates.

Porter, P. G. (2009). *Volunteers: The volunteer experience with the retired senior volunteer program (RSVP).* Seattle, WA: CreateSpace.

Substance Abuse and Mental Health Services Administration. (2005). *Successful strategies for recruiting, training and utilizing volunteers: A guide for faith- and community-based service providers.* Washington DC: U.S. Department of Health and Human Services, Substance Abuse and Mental Health Services Administration. Retrieved from http://www.samhsa.gov/fbci/Volunteer_handbook.pdf

Volunteers in Police Service Program. (2009). *Volunteer programs: Enhancing public safety by leveraging resources—A resource guide for law enforcement agencies.* Alexandria, VA: Author. Retrieved from http://www.policevolunteers.org/resources/publications/?fa=leveraging_resources

Volunteers in Police Service Program. (2010). *Missing persons: Volunteers supporting law enforcement.* Alexandria, VA: Author. Retrieved from http://www.policevolunteers.org/pdf/IACP_MissingFINAL_web.pdf

Volunteers in Police Service Program. (2011). *Volunteers in police service add value while budgets decrease.* Alexandria, VA: Author. Retrieved from http://www.policevolunteers.org/resources/pdf/volunteers_police_service_add_value_while_budgets_decrease.pdf

Website Uses by Local Agencies

One of the fundamental components of community policing is having genuine partnerships with the community. In an effort to build such partnerships, many law enforcement agencies are going online to collaborate with members of the community. Police departments are finding that the ability to engage in positive interactions, solicit citizen input, and deliver services to citizens is made easier by using the World Wide Web. Community members may also find using the Internet a feasible method of interacting with their local police department, given that the Internet is available 24 hours a day and conveniently accessible via personal computers and handheld devices. Interacting electronically may be even more attractive to those citizens who wish their interaction to be anonymous or, at a minimum, confidential.

This entry briefly introduces the benefits and effectiveness of community policing using the web, discusses how agencies are using the Internet to provide information to the community as well as to solicit information from them, how agencies provide online services to the community, and how agencies go about engaging their citizenry utilizing the Internet.

Effectiveness of Community Policing Using the World Wide Web

Police agencies' use of the Internet has the potential to increase information sharing between police and the community, which may reduce crime by improving crime prevention behaviors and by supporting collaborative, proactive problem solving. Websites and social networking may be used to solicit information from the community about specific crimes, allowing police to solve more crimes faster. Social networking may help police identify unsafe conditions more quickly and help notify the public about problems and crises more effectively. Electronic media may also be useful for educating the community about crime and reassuring people that their neighborhoods are safer than they realize. Providing various police services electronically may increase client satisfaction with the police and prove to be the most efficient way to deliver some services, saving agencies precious financial resources.

Providing Information to the Community

Prior to the widespread use of the Internet, law enforcement agencies typically relied on printed brochures, newsletters, press releases, and community meetings to provide public information. Agencies were often at the mercy of print, radio, and television media to help publicize and disseminate information. While the media still play a role in assisting agencies to provide information to the public, police departments now have other options that may be quicker, cheaper, and more effective.

As ownership of computers and handheld devices increases in the U.S. population (with about 164 million computers and 293 million mobile phones in use), law enforcement agencies have and must continue developing methods for sending alerts and bulletins directly to peoples' computers, cell phones, and other digital devices. This has become an effective means for efficiently disseminating critical information to the public. How does an agency know which constituents are interested in receiving this information? Police agencies typically use their websites to invite people to sign up to receive alerts. Alert broadcasts that "push" information out to people's computers, phones, and other handheld devices can notify residents quickly about a serious or critical situation.

In addition, alerts and bulletins can be posted on a department's website. While this more passive method does not push the information out to people, it is another way of informing the public. One advantage to this approach is that extensive information can be provided, including additional text and pictures. Also, visitors to the website can search current and past bulletins if they are looking for specific information.

In the context of community policing, it is particularly important to convey relevant information that is geographically focused, for example, information tailored to a particular neighborhood. Some of the currently available alert systems have that capacity—people sign up for the alerts and enter their addresses or neighborhoods, and subsequently get alerts that are most pertinent to them. Other common features found on agency websites include information on current traffic conditions, crime prevention tips, and detailed (sometimes interactive) crime maps.

Furthermore, visitors to the website may find useful information about the department, such as contact information for various units, the agency's "10 Most Wanted," and how to contact an officer assigned to a particular neighborhood. In addition, educational information about the agency is often provided like annual reports, the agency's mission statement, a message from the chief, department organizational chart, and department history. These features provide a valuable service for the department and the community. In addition, many agencies make this information available in a variety of languages. Utilizing a department website to communicate this type of information to the community is not only more cost-effective than printing brochures but also more convenient, since community members can access the information at any time from their home or office computers and handheld devices.

Soliciting Information From the Community

Effective policing depends heavily on information from the public. Police need people to report crimes

so that investigations can commence. Information from the public about suspicious situations enables the police to respond and investigate. Information from witnesses is crucial in solving crimes after they occur. Tips from informants and the general public help the police find wanted persons and discover crimes that otherwise may not be reported.

Traditional crime control efforts can only succeed when people supply police with information. Police agencies need other types of information from the public too. For example, information about underlying and recurring neighborhood problems helps officers initiate problem-solving activities. Furthermore, information about citizens' fears and concerns alerts police to the need for reassurance efforts. Also, feedback from the public helps a law enforcement agency adjust its priorities and practices to better satisfy the community. This can include citizens' assessments of how they were treated in specific police contacts as well as overall opinions about police service and police protection. Web pages and other digital techniques provide many ways for police agencies to solicit information from the public. These techniques are generally efficient, inexpensive, and convenient for the public. Additionally, many of these systems provide a degree of confidentiality or even anonymity for those citizens who want to help but also want to limit their actual involvement.

These techniques hold great promise if people begin to use them routinely and responsibly. Presumably, for the time being, most people will continue to rely primarily on telephone calls to 911 to report emergencies, and calls to 311 or other nonemergency numbers to report less immediate problems. There are exceptions, though. Some people have trouble speaking and can communicate more effectively in written format; during some large-scale emergencies, voice telephone service may be interrupted or overwhelmed, but e-mails, texts, and social media outlets may still get through; and many situations are so minor that no immediate action is required, and a person might simply find it more convenient to report it by e-mail. It may also be true that some people who do not want to give their names feel that an e-mail or website comment is more anonymous than a telephone call.

Another common feature of law enforcement agency websites is soliciting information related to specific investigations. Web pages have a particular advantage for this function because photos, videos, and extensive text can be posted online for viewing by the public. In the past, a newspaper might publish one black-and-white photo of a bank robbery, for example, whereas multiple color photos can be provided on a web page. Similarly, television stations might agree to show a bank robbery video once or twice during their news programs, but the same video can be made available online for viewing at any time.

Another type of input that some law enforcement agencies seek from the public via the web is complaints or commendations pertaining to specific agency employees. Some departments provide forms on their websites to submit this kind of information, but the forms must be downloaded, completed, and then mailed or delivered. Other agencies make it possible to submit complaints and compliments online. Law enforcement agencies may also use their web pages to solicit general feedback from the public. This can take the form of a community survey, an issue poll, or simply encouragement to "contact us."

Providing Online Services

Another way that an agency can utilize its website to engage the community is by offering services online. Perhaps the most commonly available online police service today is the opportunity to file an official report of a crime or other incident. While this might be thought of as just another aspect of getting information from the public, it is also a direct service, since citizens often need to file reports for legal or insurance reasons. Technologically, administratively, and strategically, online crime reporting would have been unthinkable 30 years ago when the standard police response to any reported crime was to dispatch a patrol officer to the scene to conduct a preliminary investigation and complete a report.

Starting in the 1980s, however, many law enforcement agencies began adopting telephone reporting and other differential police response (DPR) alternatives. With these DPR alternatives as precedent, adding online reporting as one more option was a relatively small step once agencies had fully functional websites. Needless to say, there are advantages and disadvantages associated with taking crime reports over the Internet. On one hand, some degree of personal contact between the police and the public is sacrificed, and the chances of introducing inaccurate or even false information into official reports are increased. On the other hand, these forms of reporting may be the most convenient option for some citizens and they are undoubtedly labor-saving and cost-saving for police agencies. Some additional popular services offered include the following: providing citizens the ability to pay parking fines, apply for bicycle registration or alarm permits, or request police services such as extra patrol or vacation checks. In addition, a growing number of agencies make it possible for citizens to download job application materials or even apply for agency jobs electronically. This benefits both the agency and applicant because it widens the pool of applicants by limiting the number of visits a prospective employee might need to make.

Engaging the Community

Since community engagement is one of the principal components of community policing, it is important to consider how websites and social media might help a police department engage its community. Some agencies utilize the web to engage the community in discussions about crime and policing. Blogs, listservs, e-mail lists, discussion boards, and similar venues can give a law enforcement agency the opportunity to converse with many people who otherwise might not come in direct contact with the police.

While it is probably true that one-on-one personal contact is a more powerful tool, that method is limited in that it only reaches one person at a time. It may also be true that a face-to-face community meeting provides a qualitatively different opportunity to engage in dialogue, but not all community members attend or can attend community meetings. The greatest potential of social media is something more than just interaction, however, and lies in the realm of social networking. Twitter provides an efficient method of communicating electronically with citizens, 140 characters at a time. And a typical Facebook page may seem friendlier and more appealing to many constituents than a more formal agency website. But they each also have synergistic possibilities. For example, some people use their Facebook page as their personal home page on the Internet. If they have visited their local law enforcement agency's Facebook page and become a "fan" of that agency by clicking the "like" button, then whenever the agency issues an update to its Facebook page, that update will appear on their fans' Facebook newsfeeds. This can be a powerful communication tool for the agency specifically because so many people visit Facebook regularly, often leaving the site open while they are on their computer doing something else.

Another powerful aspect of Facebook, and especially Twitter, is that many people today access these sites from smartphones and other handheld devices. This means that information can reach people and people can send information, not just when they are sitting at home or at work in front of a computer, but also when they are out and about in the community (although hopefully not while they are driving). This creates an opportunity for police to engage a social network of mobile eyes and ears. An alert posted on Facebook or sent out by Twitter can reach people who are in a position to be watchful. A significant portion of the community can be instantly apprised of an emergency situation and, alternatively, notified that an emergency is over. These same people can send information to the police based on what they are seeing, and that information may be helpful to the police in assessing the situation and responding effectively. This kind of application might be especially powerful in well-defined settings like schools, college campuses, and sporting events.

Elizabeth B. Perkins

See also Building Partnerships and Stakeholders; Community Policing: Resources, Time, and Finances in Support of; Implementation of Community Policing; Investigations, Community Policing Strategies for; Police-Community Relations

Further Readings

Jude, D. (2011, July 29). KSP targets cyberspace to recruit new troopers [Press release]. Kentucky State Police. Retrieved from http://www.youtube.com/user/kentuckystatepolice

Givens, G. (1993). A concept to involve citizens in the provision of police services. *American Journal of Police, 12*(3), 1–9.

Parascandola, R. (2011, August 10). NYPD forms new social media unit to mine Facebook and Twitter for mayhem. *New York Daily News.* Retrieved from http://articles.nydailynews.com/2011–08–10/local/29887819_1_social-media-facebook-and-twitter-kamisha-richards

Price, C. (2001, December). The police web site as a community policing too. *Police Chief, 71*(12), 37–38.

Sipes, L. A., & Mentel, Z. (2009, April). Using social media to protect public safety. *Community Policing Dispatch, 2*(4). Retrieved from http://www.cops.usdoj.gov/html/dispatch/April_2009/social_media.htm

Wilkinson, E. (2011, July 20). How police forces are using Twitter to connect with the public. *The Wall.* Retrieved from http://wallblog.co.uk/2011/07/20/hastings-police-on-twitter

WEED AND SEED

See Operation Weed and Seed

WICKERSHAM COMMISSION

The Wickersham Commission's 1931 report on the criminal justice system was a landmark event in American policing. President Herbert Hoover appointed the commission to, among other things, address the many problems with Prohibition enforcement. But the commission's work led its members to explore other issues in the American criminal justice system, and some of their findings and recommendations shocked the nation and law enforcement professionals. Of particular importance were the commission's reports on policing and the lawlessness of law enforcement, the latter exposing primarily police brutality and corruption. While the commission's reports did not immediately result in reforms, some of the findings and recommendations provided philosophical and operational precursors for community policing as we know it today. This entry provides a history of the commission, information about its two reports on policing, and the effect of those reports on community policing.

History of the Commission

President Hoover appointed the National Commission on Law Observance and Enforcement in May 1929, not only when law enforcement agencies were failing at enforcing Prohibition, but also when the criminal laws regulating alcohol had created a whole host of new outlaws who were manufacturing and distributing forbidden beer and spirits. Law enforcement agencies were dealing with a broad spectrum of Prohibition-related criminals, from backyard moonshiners to sophisticated organized crime gangs in Chicago and New York. Overall crime rates were also on the rise and Hoover believed the time had come to scientifically study crime and the criminal justice system.

Hoover was likely influenced by the use of scientific commissions on the municipal level beginning in the early 1920s. Following the Chicago (Illinois) Crime Commission in 1919, the Cleveland (Ohio) Survey in 1922 was the first commission to apply a scientific approach to investigate all aspects of crime and the municipal criminal justice system (and would later provide the model for the Wickersham Commission's membership, scope of inquiry, and report generation). The Missouri Crime Survey did the same in 1926, broadening the review to include state corrections and county sheriff's departments. Then, beginning in 1929, the Wickersham Commission began examining an even broader scope of issues at the national level.

The commission was named for its chair, George W. Wickersham, former U.S. attorney general under President William Taft. Its 10 other appointees were all drawn from positions in law and politics: Roscoe Pound, dean of Harvard Law School; Newton D. Baker, former secretary of war under President Woodrow Wilson; Ada Comstock, president of Radcliffe College; Frank Loesch, Chicago attorney and leader of the Chicago Crime Commission (noted for his work in prosecuting Al Capone); attorney Henry W. Anderson; William I. Grubb, U.S. District Court judge (Northern Alabama); former U.S. senator and circuit court of appeals judge William S. Kenyon; New Orleans attorney Monte M. Lehman; former chief judge of the Washington Supreme Court, Kenneth Mackintosh; and Paul J. McCormick, U.S. District Court judge (Southern California).

The commission's scope of inquiry was unprecedented. It investigated the three major components of the criminal justice system—law enforcement, the courts, and corrections—but also examined issues like criminal statistics, prosecution, deportation enforcement, juvenile offenders, federal courts, criminal procedure, crime and the "foreign born," and the costs and causes of crime. In January 1931, the commission issued its findings in 14 volumes, with titles such as *Report on Prosecution, Report on Criminal Statistics,* and *Report on Penal Institutions, Probation and Parole.*

But by all accounts, the *Report on Lawlessness in Law Enforcement* (Volume 7) garnered the most attention and would have the most impact on public policy. This report heavily overshadowed the more general *Report on the Police* (Volume 14), but it was the latter volume that provided findings and recommendations that would prove most useful later in community policing models.

Report on Lawlessness in Law Enforcement

The *Report on Lawlessness in Law Enforcement* (the "Lawlessness Report") is unique in several ways. It is unclear who lobbied for the inquiry into this topic or why it was deserving of a separate report. Indeed, the Cleveland and Missouri crime surveys did not even address police corruption and abuse.

Further, the three consultants who prepared the Lawlessness Report—Zechariah Chafee Jr., Walter H. Pollak, and Carl S. Stern—were not law enforcement scholars or professionals. Instead, they had significant ties to civil liberties organizations and causes. Chafee published *Freedom of Speech* in 1920, Pollak was an attorney who argued the landmark First Amendment case of *Gitlow v. New York* before the U.S. Supreme Court in 1925, and Stern was an attorney who had represented civil libertarians in a variety of cases. Their backgrounds and experience led them to cast a discriminating eye on the issues of police power and corruption, for which the Lawlessness Report became most notable.

Whatever its origin, the Lawlessness Report detailed coercive interrogation practices, which came to be known as the "third degree." The Lawlessness Report indicated that use of those techniques was still rampant throughout the United States nearly 50 years later. The commission reported that suspects were hung out of windows; drugged; deprived of sleep and food and questioned for days on end; or were kept in a "sweatbox," a tiny room with a stove that burned coal, old bones, rubber, and garbage. The media seized on these stories and many in the nation were horrified, while police officials almost universally denied the practices existed.

For all its graphic detail about the issues, the Lawlessness Report did not recommend specific solutions. In fact, the authors did not write a separate section addressing potential reforms but, instead, concluded rather vaguely that the will of the community—presumably through the democratic process and less formally through citizen complaints—would dictate whether practices changed.

Nonetheless, the Lawlessness Report impacted U.S. policing primarily because it thrust the issue of abuse and corruption into the public spotlight. Police professionals, scholars, and jurists necessarily viewed postcommission policing events differently and changes occurred. For example, reformers like August Vollmer and O. W. Wilson pushed for the professional model of policing (characterized by reactive, incident-driven methods and emphases on quantitative outcomes such as number of calls for service, arrests, and so on) and, in particular, police chiefs with the strength and authority to keep misconduct in check. The professional model would dominate U.S. policing until community policing was ushered into place in the 1970s.

Report on the Police

The commission prefaced its *Report on the Police* (the "Police Report") with a rather matter-of-fact statement that police failures to combat runaway crime had caused the public to lose confidence in law enforcement and that the commission was seeking to find the universal underlying causes of those failures. The introduction to the Police Report also noted that the commission did not intend to add to the abundance of published material on the subject, but rather, it wanted to provide citizens with a plain-language, official report outlining the principal causes of the defects in police administration. The commission fulfilled its intentions by detailing a significant list of issues affecting policing in America, several of which would impact community policing years later.

First, the commission identified the short and politically driven terms of police chiefs as the major problem—the "chief evil"—in U.S. policing. The commission's survey of 747 municipal police departments revealed that the average term of service for a police chief was five years, and in 10 cities with populations of 500,000 or more, the average was 2.4 years. The commission found that not only was the executive position compromised by this revolving door, but also department shake-ups following a chief's departure invariably led to instability and caused all employees to be "restless, worried and inefficient." And no matter how long a chief served, he did so at the pleasure of politicians, which necessarily compromised his ability to make decisions. Further, politicians did not always appoint qualified chiefs but instead favored political allies and friends. The Police Report even noted one case where a mayor appointed his tailor as police chief simply because he had been a good tailor for 20 years.

To support the conclusion that politics and tenure were negatively affecting policing, the commission cited Milwaukee, Wisconsin, which had only two chiefs over a period of 46 years, both without political pressure or control; the city had consistently enjoyed low crime rates and high prosecution rates. The commission concluded that the corrupting influence of politics must be removed from America's police departments, and executives must stay in their positions longer to gain expertise and to earn the trust of their subordinates and the public.

The commission then moved down the chain of command and detailed the lack of competent, efficient, and honest patrolmen and subordinate officers. Patrolmen lacked training, education, and discipline, and civil service examinations were ineffective at identifying incompetents. The problem was further compounded when subordinate officers were tapped from the patrol ranks on the basis of seniority and political influences instead of merit. Politics dictated retention and promotion at every level, and officers and patrolmen ultimately reported to a politically motivated chief. Well-trained, disciplined, and honest (neutral) officers would be better able to resist political influences and the temptation for misconduct. Departments should secure such recruits through rigorous testing and then train and compensate them appropriately.

Crime fighting was the next focus of inquiry, and the commission found that a major reason police officers were unable to effectively investigate crimes and apprehend criminals was a lack of communication systems. The study revealed that no U.S. city with a population of 300,000 or more had an adequate communication system, but that Detroit, Michigan, where officers made more than 1,300 arrests in an average time of one minute and 42 seconds, frequently catching the criminal in the act, had an advanced system. The commission recommended call boxes, telephones, wireless radios, and teletype to ensure that officers could disseminate intelligence before the criminal had time to flee. Closely related to the communications issue was the need for centralized record keeping, including systematic recording of offenses, arrests, persons charged, and dispositions, and the commission called for such changes.

The Police Report also profiled how those who were being policed affected the work of law enforcement agencies—an issue that would later become critical in community policing. The influx of immigrants presented many challenges for police, including problems with communication and cooperation, because immigrants were often suspicious of people who did not speak their language or know their customs. And even if officers could connect with members of these diverse populations, immigrants were typically reluctant to cooperate with police and implicate one of their own. The commission called for police to hire officers who were familiar with foreign languages and culture.

Finally, the commission found that because the police were transitioning from rural to urban policing, officers and patrolmen were burdened with too many duties. The commission called for specialized units—divisions like today's vice squads, homicide divisions, and sex crime units. They advised that patrolmen should be segregated under designated officers who would be charged with preventing and detecting specific crimes (e.g., the commission recommended assigning women officers to juveniles and female offenders). The division of duties and coordinated responsibility would result in greater efficiencies at every level and officers would more easily establish meaningful relationships with citizens on their respective beats.

Impact of the Reports on Community Policing

Despite the comprehensive review of so many critical issues in criminal justice, the reports came during the second year of the Great Depression when the government and the nation had turned their attentions to economic issues. As a result, many have observed that the Wickersham reports did little more than collect dust on library shelves. Nonetheless, the reports had some immediate impact on police reform and the commission's findings were prescient with regard to several aspects of modern community policing.

Both the Lawlessness Report and the Police Report called for stronger, politically insulated police chiefs who could stop police abuses (thereby restoring public confidence) and, through longer terms, develop lasting relationships with the communities they served, including forging partnerships with individuals and groups who would cooperate with police crime-fighting efforts. Likewise, communities that looked beyond politics and retained competent executives would reap the benefit of a more efficient police department and a better quality of life. The commission's vision of the police chief and community as cooperative partners is a mainstay of modern community policing.

The commission's conclusions about police personnel would also find their way into community policing models. By recommending education, training, and discipline for police recruits, the commission recognized that police officers were no longer merely crime fighters—they were social workers for the community as well. The ability to understand a variety of people and cultures, with their respective values and norms, would be critical to garnering public trust and cooperation. The commission's identification of immigrant populations as requiring special police attention and handling was particularly forward looking. Community policing demands that officers respond to citizens' unique cultural needs and limitations as much as possible.

Further, by preventing police abuses—through a strong executive and a well-trained force—the public would be more willing to build partnerships with the police. Community policing requires beat officers to be respectful, to ask about citizens' problems, and to listen to their concerns. The commission's findings helped to set the stage for those changes.

The commission's recommendation for more motorized patrols would take officers off the streets and away from the people they served, the very antithesis of community policing, which requires officers to regularly seek personal interactions with the public, especially through foot and bike patrols. But the commission also recommended that officers work in specialized units, addressing specific crimes in specific areas, a practice recognized in community policing as critical to keeping officers on certain beats for extended periods during which they can cultivate trusting relationships with citizens.

Finally, the commission's call for centralized and organized record keeping is also a part of community policing, which requires police departments to actively seek and evaluate information and to share it within the organization, with other agencies, and the community. Keeping detailed records, as the commission then correctly noted, allows everyone to evaluate programs and crime patterns and, as such, police departments can be agents of important community change.

Pamela M. Everett

See also Broken Windows Theory; Community Policing, Evolution of; Generations (Three) of Community Policing; Immigrant Populations, Community Policing Strategies for; Metropolitan Police Act of 1829; Policing, Three Eras of

Further Readings

Cleveland Survey of Criminal Justice. (1922). *Criminal justice in Cleveland*. Cleveland, OH: The Cleveland Foundation.

Garrett, E. W., & Monroe, D. G. (1931, July/August). Wickersham report on police. *The American Journal of Police Science*, 2(4), 337–348.

Illinois Association for Criminal Justice. (1929). *Illinois crime survey*. Montclair, NJ: Patterson Smith.

Missouri Association for Criminal Justice. (1926). *The Missouri crime survey*. New York, NY: Macmillan.

National Commission on Law Observance and Enforcement. (1931). *Report on lawlessness in law enforcement* (Vol 7). Washington, DC: U.S. Government Printing Office.

National Commission on Law Observance and Enforcement. (1931). *Report on the police*. (Vol. 14). Washington, DC: U.S. Government Printing Office.

Vollmer, A. (1932). Abstract of the "Wickersham" police report. *Journal of Criminal Law and Criminology*, 22(5), 716–723.

Walker, S. (1980). *Popular justice: A history of American criminal justice*. New York, NY: Oxford University Press.

YOUTHFUL OFFENDERS, CHARACTERISTICS OF

A youthful offender is a person under the age of 18 years who has been accused of committing a delinquent or criminal offense and is being processed through the juvenile justice system. The types of offenses can range from status offenses—those acts deemed illegal based on the age of the offender, including running away from home or underage drinking—to violent criminal acts including rape, aggravated assault, or homicide. The developmental stage of the youth as well as certain risk factors can increase the likelihood of a child or adolescent becoming a youthful offender. This entry briefly addresses the types of crimes committed by children across developmental stages (child, preteen, and teen) and describes corresponding risk factors (individual, family, and peer or community) that can impact a child's probability of becoming a youthful offender.

Developmental Stages

There are changes in every developmental stage in a person's life, often influenced by family, peers, and other environmental factors. A child is taught what is right versus what is wrong through specific socialization within their culture. As a child goes through the developmental stages, there may be a greater desire for material things and when combined with peer pressure can lead to delinquent acts. When attempting to understand delinquency through a developmental approach, it is important to consider the biological development of the child's brain and its impact on rational thought processes. The National Institutes of Health maintains that the section of the brain that controls for risky behavior is not fully developed until the age of 25 years. This can significantly impact an adolescent's ability to focus attention, consider consequences, control impulses, consider multiple options, and exercise the best judgment in difficult situations.

Child (Ages 1 to 10 Years)

The average age that a youth comes into contact with the juvenile justice system is 14.5 years; however, signs of problem behaviors can be seen, on average, as early as 7 years of age. According to the U.S. Department of Justice's Office of Juvenile Justice and Delinquency Prevention (OJJDP), children between the ages of 7 and 12 years account for more than one-third of juvenile arrests for arson and one-fifth of juvenile arrests for sex-related offenses and vandalism. Children who are victimized at this early stage of development are more likely to develop maladaptive behaviors, particularly those who are exposed to multiple types of violence.

Exposure to numerous types of violence predicts negative outcomes beyond the effects of any specific type of exposure, including psychological distress, adjustment in adult relationships, college adjustment, school grades, physical health, teen pregnancy, delinquency, bullying, self-directed violence, physical fighting, teen dating violence perpetration, and adult intimate partner violence victimization and perpetration. Youth who engage in criminal or delinquent acts at such a young age are at the greatest risk of becoming chronic offenders, place the greatest financial strain on society, and are more likely to stay on a deviant path into preteen and teenage years.

Preteen (Ages 11 to 13 Years)

Status offenses commonly begin during the preteen years and are those behaviors that are considered violations of the law based solely on the offender's age, such as running away from home, truancy, and underage drinking. These may be in direct response to the child's family and social environment. Youth who are have poor parental relationships, use drugs, and associate with delinquent peers are more likely to have adjustment issues, experience behavior problems, and engage in juvenile delinquency and subsequent adult criminal activity. Children who are witnesses to violence in the home tend to become fearful, anxious, guilt ridden, shameful, depressed, and express feelings of powerlessness. These children are more likely to act out, perform poorly in school, have short attention spans, and use violence and aggression to express their emotions.

Preteen into the teen years are also when issues with bullying, depression, and aggression can impact a student's propensity to act out aggressively, and in some cases deadly, at school. Some early warning signals include a history of violent outbursts, threats of violence, bringing weapons to school, substance abuse, chronic truancy, cruelty to animals, obsessive interest in violent media and music, and suicidal attempts or threats. Also children with low tolerance for differences in others are more likely to bully; at particular risk for victimization are lesbian, gay, bisexual, and transgender youth.

Cyberbullying and sexting are two additional issues that often begin during this developmental stage. *Cyberbullying* is defined as bullying or harassing through the use of technology like cell phones, computers, or other electronic devices. The term *sexting* refers to production and distribution of nude or sexually explicit images of minors through the use of technology of cell phones, computers, or other electronic devices. These images can be considered child pornography even if they are self-produced and distributed. Sexting impacts the person in the image and others who receive and distribute the image. In some states, youth convicted of possessing these images have been required to register as sex offenders per the state's mandate.

The Federal Bureau of Investigation's *Uniform Crime Reports* provides data on the nature and type of crime committed in the United States and information on offenses committed by juveniles ages 18 years and under and 15 years and under. The top offenses committed by juveniles 15 years and under are generally property crime, arson, larceny-theft, other assaults, and disorderly conduct. Early aggression is a strong predictive factor for later criminal behavior, particularly if present during the preteen developmental stage.

Teen (Ages 14 to 17 Years)

Dating violence, including physical, sexual, and emotional abuse, is of particular concern for this age group. Nationally, a women's first experience with intimate partner violence occurs under the age of 24 years. However, teen dating violence is not gender specific; both boys and girls can be victims and perpetrators. Boys may be less likely to report abuse and girls may report more serious physical harm. Some common characteristics of teen dating violence perpetrators include anger management issues, depression, low self-esteem, being a direct victim of or witness to violence in the home or community, and association with delinquent peer groups. Teen abusers are also more likely to have difficulty having or maintaining healthy relationships into adulthood.

Teen drivers are at greater risk for speeding, driving without a seatbelt, driving while under the influence, or texting while driving. Because automobile accidents are the leading causes of death for teens, this is a significant issue facing communities nationwide. Teens' cognitive development can play a part in poor decision making while behind the wheel, and those who have an aggressive personality, are prone to risk-taking behavior, and have a disregard for rules are more likely to violate traffic laws and be involved in an accident. Prevention efforts to address teen driving incidents must address behavior, development, personality, demographics, and the youths' environment.

There is also a significant correlation between gang membership and delinquent behavior among adolescents, particularly gun violence and drug offenses. In some studies, gangs have been shown to account for up to 80% of serious and violent crime in a single community. Although most research focuses on the amount of crimes committed as a result of social normalization of delinquent behavior and associating with criminal peers, youth who join gangs are typically those who also engage in youthful offending when acting alone. Gang members are more likely to drop out of school, become teen parents, and have unsteady employment. Gang membership in adolescence also has greater impact as the youth transitions to adulthood.

Risk Factors

There is no prescribed set of risk factors for youthful offending that will predict with certainty a youth's propensity for criminal activity. The occurrence of the risk factor at various stages in a child's life, the child's developmental capabilities, the family and social circumstances, and the existence of protective factors all play a role in influencing a child's outcome. Risk is not causal but predictive, and no single risk factor leads to delinquency; however, the more risk factors a child is facing, the greater the probability of later offending.

Individual Risk Factors

Individual risk factors for youthful offenders include age, gender, substance use and abuse, and mental and behavioral factors. The age of the individual at the time of the initial illegal activity is a strong predictive factor for future criminal activity. Children with early involvement in the juvenile justice system have a greater likelihood of chronic offending throughout their adolescence and into the adult criminal justice system. Antisocial beliefs, low behavioral inhibitions, and negative attitudes toward law enforcement can also play a role in an adolescent's proclivity for violence. Other physical and physiological factors that may increase a child's risk of becoming a youthful offender include low IQ, delayed language development, poor cognitive development, and attention deficit and hyperactivity. The combination of aggression and hyperactivity has been shown to put children at the greatest risk for delinquency.

Experimentation with drugs, alcohol, and tobacco, particularly in younger children and preteens, has also been linked to antisocial attitudes and offending. There is a direct correlation with alcohol and drug use and truancy as well as a direct association with high school dropouts. These youth are more likely to be rejected by their peers, show signs of depression, and are at higher risk for mental health problems.

Family Risk Factors

Negative family risk factors can include poor parenting, family tension, family size, and most obviously child abuse, neglect, and maltreatment. Children of parents who have authoritarian, lax, or contradictory parenting practices are at greater risk for youthful offending. Other parental factors include the level of involvement in the child's life, emotional attachment with the child, conflict between parents, drug and substance use, and education and income. Poor parenting skills coupled with temperamental problems early in a child's life can greatly impact the level of positive interactions between children and parents. The lack of parental bonding and disengagement can lead to behavioral problems and youthful offending.

The size of the family can impact a child's risk of becoming a youthful offender, often as a result of inadequate supervision. Children living in households with lower incomes have higher exposure rates to sexual and physical assault than those children living in households with middle and high incomes. Children from lower-income families may be more likely to engage in adolescent risk behaviors, such as having premarital sex, joining gangs, and engaging in criminal activity.

Peer/Community Risk Factors

Social influences from peers and the community tend to occur later in a child's life, such as when a child enters school, than individual risk factors. Children and teenagers who associate with more deviant or delinquent peer groups are at greater risk to be exposed to and to engage in youthful offending. Juveniles involved in gangs are more likely to engage in delinquent behavior and have lower self-esteem and poor academic achievement. The impact of antisocial peers is amplified when there is a poor parental structure. Children who are isolated from peers are also at a greater risk of becoming youthful offenders and offending in early adulthood, particularly in the case of aggressive children who are rejected by their peers.

Children who have low educational aspirations or perform poorly in or have a low commitment to their schools are also at risk. Children living in areas of high crime, social disorganization, and poverty are at greater risk of youthful offending as very often these are the communities with limited economic opportunities, low levels of community ownership, and lack of community-based services and support systems. Other community risk factors include limited opportunities for prosocial recreational activities, job training, and employment, and often easy access to weapons including firearms.

While youth may face any number of risk factors for violence, there are many individual, family, peer, and social protective factors that help to safeguard them from engaging in crime and violence. Early intervention with at-risk youth is vital to counter the effects of violence, enhance resiliency, foster healthy child development, and prevent the generational cycle of violence into adulthood. Mentoring, counseling, and referral services are just a few intervention strategies for youthful offenders that target at-risk youthful offenders and coordinate services to the youth and their families. Mentoring programs that connect youth with compassionate role models and provide job skills training have a significant impact on a youth's path toward crime and violence. These protective factors increase the health and well-being of children and adolescents by providing resources, support and coping strategies to both the children and the families.

Cynthia E. Pappas

See also Domestic Violence, Characteristics of; Domestic Violence, Community Policing Strategies for; Drug Crimes, Characteristics of; Drug Crimes, Community Policing Strategies for; Gangs and Their Crimes, Characteristics of; Gang Crimes, Community Policing Strategies for; Mentoring; School Violence and Safety, Characteristics of; School Violence and Safety, Community Policing Strategies for; Youthful Offenders, Community Policing Strategies for

Further Readings

Centers for Disease Control and Prevention. (2010). *Fact sheet: Understanding teen dating violence.* Retrieved from http://www.cdc.gov/violenceprevention/pdf/TeenDatingViolence_2010-a.pdf

Child Welfare Information Gateway. (2009, November). *Understanding the effects of maltreatment on brain development.* Washington, DC: U.S. Department of Health and Human Services, Administration for Children and Families. Retrieved from http://www.childwelfare.gov/pubs/issue_briefs/brain_development/brain_development.pdf

Finkelhor, D., Turner, H., Ormrod, R., & Hamby, S. L. (2009). Violence, abuse, and crime exposure in a national sample of children and youth. *Pediatrics, 125*(5), 1–13. doi: 10.1542/peds.2009–0467

Lipsey, M. W., & Derzon, J. H. (1998). Predictors of violent and serious delinquency in adolescence and early adulthood: A synthesis of longitudinal research. In R. Loeber & D. P. Farrington (Eds.), *Serious and violent juvenile offenders: Risk factors and successful interventions* (pp. 86–105). Thousand Oaks, CA: Sage.

Thornberry, T., Huizinga, D., & Loeber, R. (2004). The causes and correlates studies: Findings and policy implications. *Juvenile Justice, 9*(1), 3–19. Washington, DC: U.S. Department of Justice, Office of Juvenile Justice and Delinquency Prevention. Retrieved from https://www.ncjrs.gov/pdffiles1/ojjdp/203555.pdf

U.S. Department of Health and Human Services. (2001). *Youth violence: A report of the Surgeon General.* Washington, DC: Author. Retrieved from http://www.surgeongeneral.gov/library/youthviolence/toc.html

Youthful Offenders, Community Policing Strategies for

Youthful offenders have a significant impact on a community's social and economic well-being as well as the individual's social, mental, and physical health. The term *youthful offender* typically refers to a person under the age of 18 years who has been accused of committing a crime and is being processed through the juvenile justice system or referred to some type of diversion program depending on the severity of the criminal act. Youthful offending can undeniably encompass a broad range of antisocial behaviors, criminal typologies, and motivations which can result in various criminal sanctions. The specific crimes committed by youthful offenders range from status offenses like truancy and underage drinking, to severe criminal offenses, such as aggravated assault, gun violence, and homicide.

Regardless of the type of criminal activity, however, proponents of a community policing philosophy maintain that law enforcement plays a crucial role in efforts to address the issues surrounding youthful offenders. This entry briefly introduces the role of community policing as it relates to youthful offenders across the main philosophical components of partnerships, organizational transformation, and problem solving. This entry also describes the role community policing strategies can play across the continuum of prevention, intervention, referral and treatment, and reentry of youthful offenders.

Community Policing Strategies

The U.S. Department of Justice's Office of Community Oriented Policing Services (COPS) defines *community policing* as a philosophy that promotes organizational strategies, which support the systematic use of partnerships and problem-solving techniques to proactively address the immediate conditions that give rise to public safety issues as crime, social disorder, and fear of crime. In its simplest form, community policing is about building relationships and solving problems. It is a way in which law enforcement agencies can focus on crime and social disorder through the delivery of police services that include aspects of traditional law enforcement as well as prevention, problem solving, community engagement, and partnerships. Unlike many traditional law enforcement approaches, community policing requires that police and the necessary stakeholders join together as partners in both identifying and effectively addressing the issues that are directly affecting the local community.

Community Partnerships and the Youthful Offender

To have successful community policing strategies for youthful offenders, there must be collaborative partnerships between law enforcement and the communities in which they serve. The partnerships can include: law enforcement; health and human services; social and child protective services; domestic violence services; mental health services; medical assistance providers; schools and early education; courts, prosecutors, probation and parole; forensic interviewers; and community and faith-based organizations. Child advocates, volunteers, residents, and formal and informal community leaders are valuable resources when developing a community-oriented strategy for dealing with youthful offenders. Strong role models and mentors within the community can help young children and teens to develop a genuine stake in their families, schools, and neighborhoods.

Advocacy and community-based organizations that provide services to child and teen victims, after-school programs, and reentry programs for returning youthful offenders should also play an integral part in prevention, intervention, treatment, and response to these issues. For example, child advocacy centers are located throughout the country and use multidisciplinary teams of professionals to provide services to sexually abused children and their families. These teams include law enforcement, mental health service providers, medical assistance providers, victim and family advocates, and resources to provide a continuum of care for child victims. Forensic interviews are provided by professionals in a safe and child-friendly setting to minimize the number of times the child has to repeat what happened; medical services are often available on site for a child requiring a medical exam; and mental health services are also made available to children and their families, including trauma-focused cognitive behavioral therapy, parent-child interaction therapy, and group therapy. These child-centered, multidisciplinary responses to child abuse, neglect, and trauma can have a great impact when developing early identification and treatment options for children and teens at risk of becoming youthful offenders.

Two additional partners when developing strategies for youthful offenders are private businesses and the media. Businesses can play a fundamental role in providing valuable resources for prevention, intervention, and reentry efforts. They can also identify such problems as shoplifting, truant youth, and gang-related violence and assist with response by providing resources such as additional security, video surveillance, and community outreach. The media can also play a significant role by promoting efforts to address youth-related violence or to address the public's perception or possible misconceptions about youth in the community. Media campaigns are a direct form of communication with the community to help community members understand the specific problem and enroll them in the appropriate response strategies. This targeted outreach can impact both the public and policymakers by raising awareness about the issues surrounding youthful offenders and promoting developmentally appropriate services for at-risk youth.

Organizational Transformation and the Youthful Offender

Successful community policing strategies to address youthful offenders are contingent on organizational support from within the law enforcement agency. This requires the alignment of management, structure, personnel, and information systems to support community partnership and proactive problem solving to address the myriad issues involving young people and youth-related crime and violence. Therefore, the climate and culture of the law enforcement agency must be one that first understands the social, emotional, and developmental needs of the youth in their community and then prioritizes addressing their needs in order to effectively prevent crime and respond to youthful offenders.

This begins with the leadership and engages the entire agency at the supervisor and line level. To be effective, an agency's policies, procedures, protocols, and training should include detailed information on

prevention efforts to help communities develop strategies to keep the youth on a healthy crime-free path;

early identification strategies to recognize youth at risk of engaging in criminal activity (understanding the risk factors);

referral processes to help provide necessary treatment and resources to at-risk youth; and

effective reentry and wraparound strategies designed to transition youth from the juvenile justice system back into their homes, schools, and communities.

As important as the written policy and procedures within an organization are, so is the caliber of officer who is hired. When seeking recruits, an agency should clearly articulate that it is seeking those applicants who have a spirit of service and who recognize the importance of community policing and problem solving in addressing youth-related offenses. Training at the beginning of an officer's career and throughout should support community policing tactics, analytical skills, problem solving, child development, and techniques for dealing with young status offenders as well as violent juvenile offenders. Officers should be taught the necessary strategies to engage the community in finding solutions to youth-related issues and learn from other jurisdictions that have dealt with similar issues.

Problem Solving and the Youthful Offender

The issues surrounding youthful offenders are broad in scope and require proactive and systemic examination of the specific problems within the local community. The use of a problem-oriented approach to crimes associated with youthful offenders is a vital component of a successful community-oriented strategy to address these issues. Any strategy to address a crime problem must be crafted in response to a solid, accurate, and complete picture of the local problem. The SARA problem-solving process is arguably the most highly recognized tool for law enforcement when developing a local response to problems. There is a large body of research available to law enforcement on this issue and essentially consists of *scanning* or identifying and prioritizing the local problem, conducting a thorough *analysis* of what is known about the problem, *responding* to the problem based on the detailed analysis, and *assessing* or evaluating the success of the response(s).

For example, addressing serious youth-related violence requires an understanding of the specific problem within the local community, analyzing the local problem (e.g., gang violence), and designing responses based on the analysis. The identification of the youth-related violence includes the experiences and observations of law enforcement, social service providers, formal and informal community leaders, and others in routine contact with the youthful offenders. A successful problem-solving process involves appropriate community stakeholders. Interviews and focus groups combined with official data like crime mapping provide insight into the victims, offenders, and locations of the specific crime problem being addressed (e.g., gang-controlled territory and hot spots for gang-related violence). Once the analysis of the local youth-related violence within a community has been conducted and a baseline for measuring the effectiveness of the response has been established, responses tailored to the local circumstances should be considered, implemented, and measured. Assessments based on qualitative and quantitative data help to determine if the specific objectives were obtained. Most important, however, is an understanding that problem solving is a dynamic process that requires constant assessment and revision, when necessary, to ensure continued effectiveness.

Prevention

There are three types of prevention efforts when developing strategies to address youthful offenders: primary, secondary, and tertiary. *Primary prevention* focuses on communitywide strategies and often involves education, outreach, and support for all children and teens. One example of a community-oriented prevention strategy is including youth in the problem-solving process and inviting the local youth community to meet to discuss the issues facing them and to brainstorm solutions. *Secondary prevention* focuses on those children and teens most at risk and intervening at the first sign. One example of a secondary prevention strategy is providing mentors to children and teens who are most at risk or have had initial contact with the juvenile justice system. *Tertiary prevention* efforts are focused on youth who have already committed crimes or acts of violence. Law enforcement officers have extensive interactions with youth in their homes, schools, and communities, and through the implementation of primary, secondary, and tertiary prevention strategies, they can play a significant role in identifying youth at risk of engaging in criminal activity.

Research shows that children who are direct victims or indirect witnesses to violence are at greater risk of negative psychological, behavioral, academic, and physical health outcomes than those children who were not exposed to violence. These children are likely to experience problems associated with substance abuse, depression, teen pregnancy, anxiety, aggression, posttraumatic stress disorder, bullying, low self-esteem, delinquency, and involvement with the child welfare and juvenile justice systems. With this understanding, law enforcement can play a central role of providing initial protection and support to children at risk of becoming youthful offenders by connecting them with an established network of social service providers. This community policing framework positions law enforcement at a crucial stage of identification to provide necessary support to children, families, and communities through collaborative relationships with local stakeholders.

The most effective prevention efforts include comprehensive risk assessments, interagency communication and information sharing across systems, community engagement, and the use of evidence-based community-oriented strategies that promote healthy youth development. A public health approach for the prevention of youth-related violence is one such example. This model identifies specific problems associated with youth-related crime and violence, uses data from multiple datasets, creates partnerships with necessary stakeholders, and engages in practical problem solving to create

a safer community. This approach views youth-related crime problems in the same manner as public health officials would approach a medical epidemic through primary, secondary, and tertiary prevention strategies. This approach has been successfully used in several larger cities through collaborative community efforts that include the mayor's office and the city council, the police department, the health department, the faith community, youth and social services, and outreach workers.

These collaborative community responses target at-risk youth and offer alternatives to a life of crime and violence. Cities that have implemented public health-focused youth violence prevention strategies are attempting to attack the root causes of violence while holding juvenile perpetrators accountable for their actions and offering rehabilitation where appropriate.

Intervention

Intervention is a key component of successful programs to address youthful offenders and can be effective in countering the effects of violence, enhancing resiliency, fostering healthy child development, and preventing the generational cycle of violence into adulthood. Law enforcement can play a crucial role of diverting at-risk children and youth by maintaining knowledge of protocols, procedures, and skills that enable effective intervention and by connecting them with an established network of social service providers. Law enforcement agencies that balance their traditional law enforcement role with interventions designed to divert at-risk children and youth toward the services they need have been shown to have improved public safety and better life outcomes for youth in the communities in which they serve.

Community policing intervention strategies for youthful offenders target at-risk youthful offenders and coordinate services, such as mentoring, counseling, and referral services, to the youth and their families. For example, home visiting programs have been shown to help strengthen at-risk youth's relationship with parents, provide support to pregnant and parenting teens, offer education and support to the parents of adolescents, and provide a trusting adult mentor for teen girls. Mentoring programs that connect youth with compassionate role models have also been shown to have a significant impact on a youth's path toward crime and violence, particularly programs that provide the youth with job skills training. School resource officers (SRO) can play a role in effective intervention programs by providing police with feedback on the concerns and fears of local youth, broadening departmental understanding about the educational concerns of community members, and encouraging young people to become involved in other police activities. Officers not only interact with all students in their assigned schools but also pay special attention to youth who have been involved with the juvenile justice system or are at risk of going down that path. SROs act as resource liaisons by referring students to professional services within both the school (guidance counselors, social workers) and the community (youth and family service organizations).

Probation and supervision also play a role in a community-oriented approach by providing assistance with referral of youth for education, employment, and training. These tertiary prevention efforts focus on youth who have already committed violence and are directed to the most appropriate response ranging from probation, juvenile diversion or detention, or counseling. Referring at-risk children and youth for services is one of the most important and potentially challenging roles to play for law enforcement. Law enforcement agencies that have an awareness of the different trauma-related services available have a greater likelihood to improve the chances of identification and treatment of vulnerable children and youth. A community policing strategy that is trauma informed as opposed to zero-tolerance focused can help to increase community trust and build relationships. Effective community-based strategies to address youthful offenders include alternatives that support comprehensive treatment of problems associated with violent behavior such as substance abuse and mental health issues.

Reentry

The comprehensive collaboration of family, community, and the criminal justice system is vital to the success of reentry programs for youthful offenders. From a law enforcement perspective, successful transition of youthful offenders back into their homes, schools, and communities is an issue of both officer and community safety. Reentry programs must balance building trust with the returning offender and reducing the community's fear of further criminal

activity from the youth in their neighborhood. Through a community policing framework, partnerships with parole agencies, probation offices, courts, and other stakeholders are vital to ease transition and to reduce recidivism of youthful offenders. Some of the most successful youthful offender reentry programs assist in teaching life skills and providing mentorship like police athletic leagues and restorative justice programs for juveniles.

Mentoring is an effective way to improve returning youthful offenders' behavior and self-esteem so that they may become productive, contributing members of society. Through athletic leagues and youth mentoring, many law enforcement agencies play a crucial role in the lives of returning juvenile offenders by connecting them with community programs and job opportunities. Through mentoring programs, the youth and law enforcement officers gain valuable insight about the concerns and issues facing one another. This can play a dual role in reducing the social distance between the two often opposing groups by providing the youth with powerful tools that will help them to make better decisions in their daily lives and giving the officers a greater appreciation of the social, emotional, and behavioral issues facing these young people. There are many national mentoring initiatives as well as local community and faith-based mentoring programs designed to build relationships and provide critical services to at-risk youth and youthful offender returning to their homes, schools, and communities.

Restorative justice programs provide an alternative to incarceration for juvenile offenders while still holding them accountable. The principles of a restorative justice model for youthful offenders are that crime committed by juveniles hurts the victims, the community, and the offenders and that there is an obligation on the part of the offenders to repair the harm. The primary goal of restorative justice programs is restoration through amends and the rebuilding of strained relationships between the offender and the community at large. These programs generally require that the youthful offender make amends directly to victim(s) or the community. The type of amends depends on the most appropriate course of action for the youthful offender and could include a letter of apology, restitution of funds or property, or neighborhood projects that reinforce the offenders' role in the greater community. These programs hold youth accountable while offering them an opportunity to make positive choices. The ultimate goal is that youthful offenders will accept accountability, take action to repair the harm, and become trusted and respected members of the communities in which they live.

Cynthia E. Pappas

See also Building Partnerships and Stakeholders; Community Cohesion and Empowerment; Community Justice; Community Policing and Problem Solving, Definition of; Community Prosecution; Gangs and Their Crimes, Characteristics of; Gang Crimes, Community Policing Strategies for; Implementation of Community Policing; Mentoring; Problem-Solving Initiatives, Assessment and Evaluation; Problem-Solving Initiatives, Examples of Assessment and Evaluation of; Problem Solving Process (SARA); Publicity Campaigns; Recruiting for Quality and Diversity; Restorative Justice; School Violence and Safety, Characteristics of; School Violence and Safety, Community Policing Strategies for; Youthful Offenders, Characteristics of

Further Readings

Altschuler, D., Stangler, G., Berkley, K., & Burton, L. (2009, April). *Supporting youth in transition to adulthood: Lessons learned from child welfare and juvenile justice.* Washington, DC: Center for Juvenile Justice Reform. Retrieved from http://cjjr.georgetown.edu/pdfs/TransitionPaperFinal.pdf

Butts, J. A., Bazemore, G., & Meroe, S. A. (2010). *Positive youth justice: Framing justice interventions using the concepts of positive youth development.* Washington, DC: Coalition for Juvenile Justice. Retrieved from http://juvjustice.org/media/resources/public/resource_390.pdf

Finkelhor, D., Turner, H., Ormrod, R., Hamby, S., & Kracke, K. (2009). *Children's exposure to violence: A comprehensive national survey.* Washington, DC: U.S. Department of Justice, Office of Juvenile Justice and Delinquency Prevention.

Nofziger, S., & Kurtz, D. (2005). Violent lives: A lifestyle model linking exposure to violence to juvenile violent offending. *Journal of Research in Crime and Delinquency, 42*(1), 3–26. doi: 10.1177/0022427803262061

Sedlak, A. J., & McPherson, K. (2010). *Nature of risk and victimization: Findings from the Survey of Youth in Residential Placement.* Washington, DC: U.S. Department of Justice, Office of Juvenile Justice and Delinquency Prevention.

Wasserman, G. A., Keenan, K., Tremblay, R. E., Coie, J. D., Herrenkohl, T. I., Loeber, R., & Petechuk, D. (2003). *Risk and protective factors of child delinquency.* Child Delinquency Bulletin Series. NCJ 193409. Washington, DC: U.S. Department of Justice, Office of Juvenile Justice and Delinquency Prevention. Retrieved from http://www.ncjrs.gov/pdffiles1/ojjdp/193409.pdf

Appendix

Community-Oriented Policing and Problem-Solving Case Studies

Following are brief descriptions of selected problem-solving initiatives throughout the United States. Several were adapted from submissions to the federal Center for Problem-Oriented Policing for the Herman Goldstein Award for Excellence in Problem-Oriented Policing, which is designated each year at the national conference of the Center for Problem-Oriented Policing. Others were adapted from joint publications of the U.S. Department of Justice and the Police Executive Research Forum.

Note for each case study the creative responses that were developed to address the problems, following a scanning and thorough analysis for each. Where information is available, assessment information of the response is given as well.

Following is a brief explanation of these four stages of the SARA (scanning, analysis, response, assessment) problem-solving model:

Scanning is where officers first look for a pattern or persistent, repeat incidents, and whether or not a problem exists and whether further analysis is needed.

Analysis is the heart of the problem-solving process; its purpose is to learn as much as possible about problems in order to identify their causes; information is gathered from sources inside and outside an officer's agency about the scope, nature, and causes of problems.

Response is implementing the most effective, tailored means of dealing with the problem; responses may be wide ranging and involve private and other government organizations (e.g., prosecutor's office for new ordinances, health

department to condemn an abandoned home being frequented by drug abusers).

Assessment determines whether the responses implemented were effective, and might include such criteria as numbers of arrests, levels of reported crime, response times, clearance rates, citizen complaints, and various workload indicators, such as calls for service and the number of field interviews conducted; if not effective, then new solutions must be developed and implemented.

Farm Laborer Traffic Problems: California's Central Valley

The following case study is based on a serious traffic problem in central California that persisted for several years during the mid- and late 1990s and was successfully addressed by the California Highway Patrol.

Scanning

One early morning in August 1999 during the peak of harvest season in California's Central Valley, 15 farm workers climbed into a 1983 van to go to work; soon thereafter the van slammed into a commercial vehicle making a U-turn on the road, killing 13 of the van's passengers. The van's driver, who had a lengthy record of driving violations, was arrested for operating the vehicle while under the influence.

Collisions of farm-labor vehicles were not uncommon in this area during the peak harvest season (May through September), when about 300,000 farm-labor jobs are available; with this influx comes increased traffic congestion, road infractions, and operation of unsafe vehicles.

Analysis

Analyzing farm-labor vehicle collisions proved to be challenging for the California Highway Patrol (CHP) due to discrepancies in how data were recorded. At a minimum, however, thorough data analysis showed an estimated 187 farm-labor collisions, with 20 fatalities and 121 injuries, during a recent three-year period. On average, traffic fatalities were 42% higher in the area during the peak harvest months. An examination of relevant statutes and regulatory laws showed room for improvement. For example, farm-labor vehicles were exempt from the state's mandatory seat belt law. Furthermore, language barriers and the farm-working culture affected outreach efforts and hindered efforts to improve farm worker safety.

Response

With the support of the CHP, the California State Legislature passed two bills to enhance the safety of farm workers and their vehicles. These laws made provisions for the following:

- Mandatory use of seat belts for farm workers in farm-labor vehicles
- Strengthening of safety and nonpunitive inspection and certification requirements for these vehicles
- Increase in CHP's personnel strength to work specifically with farm-labor vehicles
- Coordinated public education campaign, using town meetings and print and electronic media to announce inspection dates and places and to inform the farming community about licensing and safety requirements

Assessment

During the following year, for the first time in a decade, there were *no* farm-worker fatalities resulting from farm-labor collisions; in addition, collisions involving these vehicles decreased 73%. These positive results have continued to the present day.

Source: California Highway Patrol. (2001). Corridor Safety Program—A collaborative approach to traffic safety. *Excellence in Problem-Oriented Policing*, 5–14. Retrieved from http://www.popcenter.org/library/awards/goldstein/2001/01–09(W).pdf

Produce Market Problem: Miami, Florida

In 2000, several problems occurred in a produce market in Miami, Florida—a market that is a hub for the commercial shipping of fresh produce for the southeast United States. The following cases study describes how the police addressed these various problems.

Scanning

Miami's Allapattah Produce Market is the center for the commercial shipping of fresh produce for the southeastern United States. Local supermarkets, cruise ships, and mom-and-pop stores rely on the market for their daily produce as well. Over several years, the market area experienced an increase in the homeless population as well as in crime, causing the overall quality of life in the market to decline in this three-by-five-block area. Because of these problems, business operators allowed their facilities to deteriorate, and eventually garbage-strewn parking lots, vacant lots, improper disposal of rotted produce, and overflowing garbage bins became more prevalent and contributed to general pollution and sanitation and health hazards. Traffic problems also abounded.

Analysis

Officers analyzed calls for service and crime statistics for the market and surrounding neighborhoods, noting an average of 23 business burglaries per month in the market; they also interviewed patrol officers and code-enforcement personnel. They found that the location and layout of the market contributed to traffic congestion and noise problems. The fundamental problem at the market was that businesses had been allowed to operate with very little oversight by organizations charged with regulating health, sanitation, and pollution problems. The vendors' illegal disposal of unusable produce attracted homeless persons and drug dealers to the area. Nearby residents suffered from criminal victimization, traffic congestion, and decreasing property values.

Response

A response plan was designed to mitigate the problems, causes, and underlying conditions. The following five goals were established for the response plan:

1. Significantly reduce the pollution and improve sanitation and health standards.
2. Reduce traffic congestion and enhance the market's transportation infrastructure.
3. Reduce criminal activity in the area and fear of crime in the surrounding residential neighborhoods.
4. Reduce the homeless population in the area.
5. Promote a partnership between the commercial entities and Miami officials.

A key component of the plan was an increased presence of police and code-enforcement personnel, particularly to explain the response plan to business owners and vendors, who were urged to comply with code requirements by constructing locked, fenced enclosures around their individual trash bins.

A business owners' association was formed. To alleviate the traffic problems, officers worked with the commercial truck operators to develop improved parking, unloading, and turnaround facilities; a complete road redesign project was initiated for the market area.

As the project moved forward, homeless persons moved out of the area, and officers and business owners spearheaded a series of area beautification projects (with the assistance of a $600,000 state grant), including improvements in landscaping, lighting, and signage. Officers and business association owners also produced a video for vendors that explained proper disposal of garbage.

Assessment

The overall reported crime rate and calls for service in and around the target area declined during the following year, with reported business burglaries decreasing from an average of 23 per month to fewer than five per month. The transient population disappeared almost entirely, and traffic congestion was significantly reduced. Health and sanitation hazards were also reduced or eliminated; nearly all businesses were brought into compliance with codes and regulations. New businesses were attracted to the area, and annual sales of all businesses in the market increased.

Source: Columba, M. (2001). The roots of a problem: Miami's Allapattah produce market revitalization protect.

Problem Solving Quarterly, 14(2), 4–6. Retrieved from http://www.popcenter.org/library/psq/2001/Summer_2001_Vol_14_No_2.pdf

Domestic Violence: Charlotte–Mecklenburg, North Carolina

This case study of domestic violence in Charlotte–Mecklenburg, North Carolina, describes how a single officer's problem-solving efforts led to a more effective analysis approach and a reduction in domestic crime rates.

Scanning

For several years, the Charlotte–Mecklenburg Police Department had made domestic assaults a priority and worked to analyze those cases, intervene, and reduce their occurrence in the community. In October 2000, however, an officer working a particularly serious domestic assault case became concerned about the overall number of domestic assaults in his patrol district for that year: 305 domestic assaults, or 30% of the total assaults for that year. He began looking for previous reports involving the victim and suspect in this specific case and found a number of reports for such other "indicator" offenses as vandalism and threats. This examination of the case reports indicated that rather than a repeat call location being the "hot spot" for crime, the officer surmised that tracking the *participants* might be a better indicator of future violence.

Analysis

A more thorough analysis of domestic assault reports showed that the average victim had filed nine previous police reports, most involving the same suspect but sometimes crossing police district boundaries. Many of the prior reports were for other indicator crimes, such as trespassing, threatening, and stalking. Most repeat call locations were domestic situations. It became clear that it was best to regard the victim and suspect as hot spots instead of the traditional fixed geographic location.

Response

Officers developed a tailored response plan for each repeat offense case, including zero tolerance of criminal behavior by the suspect and use of other criminal justice and social service agencies. A Police Watch program was implemented in which systematic zone checks of the victim's residence and workplace were made when appropriate. A Domestic Violence Hotline voicemail system for victims was also initiated, which victims could use to report miscellaneous incidents involving a suspect. Officers developed detailed case files and created a separate database with victim and offender background data. The database tracks victims and offenders as hot spots moving from one address to another and across patrol district boundaries.

Assessment

Repeat calls for service were reduced by 98.9% during the following year at seven target locations. Domestic assaults decreased 7% in this targeted patrol district while increasing 29% in the rest of the city. Only 14.8% of domestic violence victims in the project reported repeat victimization as opposed to a benchmark figure of 35%. No complaints against officers were generated by officer contacts with residents.

Source: Charlotte–Mecklenburg Police Department. (2002). *Baker One domestic violence intervention project.* Retrieved from http://www.popcenter.org/library/awards/ goldstein/2002/02–09(F).pdf

Juvenile Drug Trafficking: Tulsa, Oklahoma

The following case study demonstrates the kinds of problems that can plague a residential neighborhood once the area has deteriorated over a period of two decades.

Scanning

During the late 1990s, North Tulsa experienced consistently higher crime rates than the rest of the city. Nearly half of the violent crimes reported occurred in this section of the city, which for a long time has been a depressed, low-income area, lacking in adequate services. The Tulsa Housing Authority (THA) was established to support the city's low-income public housing.

In an attempt to determine the nature of the crime problem in North Tulsa, a special management team of Tulsa police officials conducted a study and decided to concentrate on five public housing complexes where high crime rates and blatant street dealing existed.

Analysis

A resident survey, conducted by patrol officers in each of the public housing complexes, revealed that 86% of the occupants lived in households headed by single females. Officers assigned to the target area noticed in the housing complexes large groups of school-age youth who appeared to be selling drugs during school hours. A comparison of the dropout and suspension rates in North Tulsa schools with those in other areas of the city determined that the city's northernmost high school, serving most of the high school-age youth in the five complexes, had the highest suspension (4.4%) and dropout rates (10%) of any school in the city. It also reported the highest number of pregnant teenagers in the school system. Officers also knew that few of the juveniles observed in the complexes had legitimate jobs, and that several of them appeared to be lured into drug dealing because of the easy money. One youth commented, "Why should I work for minimum wage at McDonald's when I can make $400 to $1,400 a day selling dope?"

Supervisors at the Uniform Division North precinct arranged volunteers into two-officer foot teams, assigned to the complexes on 8-hour shifts. The teams were expected to visit and establish a rapport with residents to assure them that police were present to ensure their safety. Within a month, officers verified juvenile involvement in drug trafficking. As officers approached drug hangouts within the complexes, young lookouts (ages 12 to 16) would call out "Rollers!" to alert the dealers to discard their drugs and disperse. On those occasions when officers made an arrest, the youth often reappeared in the complex the next day. A strategy was needed to provide programs to deter youth from selling or using drugs.

Response

Officers S. and N., assigned to the foot patrol at one of the complexes, believed that the youth needed programs that would improve their self-esteem, teach them values, and impart decision-making skills. To provide positive role models for young men, the officers started a Boy Scout troop in the complex for boys between 11 and 17 years of age. In addition, they started a group called SHARE (stand, help, and rid evil), which worked to raise money for needy residents and police-sponsored youth activities. As a SHARE representative, Officer J. spoke at civic group meetings and local churches throughout the city to solicit donations and increase awareness of the needs of young people on the city's north side. Those receiving help from SHARE agreed to participate in programs geared to improving life and job skills. Volunteers came from the churches and the civic groups where Officer J. spoke.

Officers B. and F., foot patrol officers at another complex, developed plans for unemployed young people. Officer B. organized a group called The Young Ladies Awareness Group that hosted weekly guest speakers to instruct young women in how to dress for job interviews and employment, with role-playing officers demonstrating proper conduct during interviews. The women were also instructed in résumé writing and makeup, hair care, and personal hygiene.

Officer F. worked with a government program called the Private Industry Training Council (PITC) that sponsored sessions on goal setting and self-esteem building to prepare young people to enter job training programs, also offered by PITC. Officer F. also helped area youth apply for birth certificates, which were required to enter the PITC program, and he arranged for volunteers from the Oklahoma Highway Patrol and a local school to help teach driver's education. Officers even provided funds for some young people who were unable to pay the fees to obtain birth certificates or driver's licenses.

The foot patrol officers became involved in a day camp project conducted at the Ranch, a 20-acre northside property confiscated by police from a convicted drug dealer. The project used the property for a day camp for disadvantaged youth recruited from the target projects. Tulsa's mayor and chief of police came to the Ranch to meet with the youth, as did psychologists, teachers, ministers, and celebrities. Guests tried to convey the value of productive and drug-free lives, among other ethical values.

To combat dropout and suspension problems, a program called Adopt a School involved police officers patrolling schools during classes, not to make arrests but rather to establish rapport with the students. The program was intended to reduce the likelihood of student involvement in illegal activities.

Assessment

The police noted a decline in street sales of illegal drugs in the five target complexes. Youth reacted positively to the officers' efforts to help them, and the programs seemed to deter them from drug involvement. The police department continued to address the problems of poor youth in North Tulsa. Foot patrol officers met with the Task Force for Drug Free Public Housing to inform the different city, county, and statewide officials of the needs of youth in public housing. Other social service agencies began working with the police department, establishing satellite offices on the north side of the city, scheduling programs, and requesting police support in their efforts.

Source: Tulsa Police Department. (1989). *Problem-oriented approach to drug enforcement.* Retrieved from http://www.popcenter.org/library/unpublished/CaseStudies/131_Problem_Oriented_Approach_to_Drug_Enforcement_Four_Case_.pdf

Mobile Home Park Problems: Reno, Nevada

Mobile home parks, providing affordable living, often have very transient and dense populations and crime problems. The following case study concerns a park problem that began to develop over time in an area recently converted from a campground and successfully addressed by the Reno Police Department.

Scanning

Panther Valley is a small secluded community of approximately 3,500 residents located in a northeast section of Reno, Nevada. It comprises middle- to low-income single family residences, a small industrial park, and a KOA campground that was converted into a residential trailer park. The trailer park contains 150 trailer spaces that are rented on a weekly or monthly basis. Residents of the park represent the area's lowest socioeconomic status population.

A short time after the conversion of the KOA, there was a significant increase in calls for service in the trailer park that were related to disturbances, thefts, burglaries, and drug activity. Residents living outside the park also complained about its deteriorated condition and its residents, whom they suspected were responsible for the increased crime in the area. A swing shift supervisor for North

Patrol, approved a request to work on the problems in Panther Valley as a problem-oriented policing project.

Analysis

A crime analysis for the area found there were significant increases in the number of burglaries, vandalism, larcenies, assaults, and family disturbances. There were also increased calls for service related to speeding vehicles, juvenile disturbances, and drug activity.

Sgt. T. and Officer H. conducted an extensive environmental survey of the area and identified several factors that contributed to the park's deteriorated condition. Abandoned vehicles cluttered the narrow streets, creating hazardous conditions for children who used them as a playground. Most of the teenagers living in the park were unsupervised and suspected of being responsible for the majority of drug activity and vandalism. Trailer spaces were improperly marked or illegible, creating a slower response by police and fire. Poor lighting existed throughout the park, making it convenient for conducting drug transactions and other crimes. Public bathrooms were inoperable and had become "offices" for narcotic activity. Residents, afraid to use the public bathrooms, often urinated and defecated in the open spaces around the park. The park swimming pool was not used because of sanitation and filtering problems; it became a dumping ground for refuse because of the lack of garbage containers in the park. Residents also deposited garbage in the unrented trailer spaces throughout the park.

Response

Officer H. contacted the manager of the trailer park, learning that new owners were in the process of purchasing it. He discussed the problems with the manager and suggested they conduct a series of meetings with residents to discuss crime-related incidents and environmental factors contributing to the park's poor condition. The following responses ensued:

- New tenant rules were established for residents, including their responsibility to keep their spaces clean and uncluttered by abandoned vehicles.
- Several of the problem residents were evicted from the park.

- Ten abandoned vehicles were towed from the park. A local salvage company removed the vehicles for scrap metal.
- A general cleanup of trash and refuse was completed by park residents.
- The public bathroom was repaired and repainted, and proper lighting installed by the manager.
- Arrangements were made through the Job Corps vocational training program to use students to repair a number of plumbing and lighting problems that existed.
- The swimming pool was cleaned and repainted, and a new filtering system was installed. The pool was opened to the entire community.
- Speed bumps were installed to slow vehicles.

Assessment

These efforts resulted in a significant reduction in crime and calls for service. Neighborhood meetings greatly improved the relationship between the park manager and residents. Follow-up inspections conducted by the health department and city building inspector noted significant improvements. As a result of this collective effort, the overall environment and quality of life in Panther Valley improved.

Source: Adapted from Police Executive Research Forum. (1992, Summer). *Problem Solving Quarterly, 5*(3), 8. Retrieved from http://www.popcenter.org/library/psq/1992/ Summer_1992_Vol_5_No_3.pdf

Drugs and Guns: San Diego, California

A single building can pose many problems of crime and disorder—particularly where the building is operated under a transient motel-type license and apartments are rented by the night or for several weeks at a time. Such was the case in San Diego, where the problems grew to such a level they had to be confronted by the city's police department.

Scanning

Located in the southeast section of San Diego in a residential neighborhood of mostly apartment buildings, this privately owned, three-story complex contained more than 75 units. The complex was divided into four buildings with a small, grassy commons area between the buildings. An on-site manager, employed by the building management company, was responsible for maintenance. Shortly after the complex opened, in the late 1980s and early 1990s, serious drug using and dealing problems became evident.

Combating narcotics activity in this area proved difficult for patrol officers. Initially, officers focused on making arrests, but suspects often evaded police by running into the apartments or by running through a canyon on the north side, an open field on the east side, or a row of apartments on the west side. Police determined that drug users and dealers congregated in and around two complex laundry rooms because officers had found small plastic bags, glass pipes, and used matchbooks—all signs of crack cocaine use—in these rooms. Police considered each of the locations "an easy place to make an arrest" as there was usually someone around who was either in possession of drugs or under their influence.

Gunfire and gang-related violence became common occurrences at the complex during evening hours. Police learned that the complex had become a major supply source of crack cocaine for several area gangs. Two beat officers applied selective enforcement and converged on the area with large groups of officers at random intervals, making arrests. However, because this approach provided only temporary relief, the officers decided to implement community policing and problem-solving strategies.

Analysis

Officers A. and W. first determined that they needed additional information. Knowing that apartment managers sometimes were coerced into helping drug dealers or even volunteered to assist traffickers in exchange for money and drugs, the officers spoke with the apartment manager and suggested that he adopt the security measures of placing locks on the laundry room doors and installing additional lighting in the center of the complex. Two weeks later, the suggested improvements had not been made.

The officers next evaluated their arrest and field interview data. From this information, which included suspect interviews, they identified many dealers, gangs, and tenants collaborating with dealers. Evidence indicated that the manager had been dissuading residents from contacting police, saying he would deal with the problem.

The officers then contacted the complex's management company and requested a key to a vacant apartment so they could observe drug dealers. Noting that some dealers carried guns, the officers later uncovered a gun-running operation, and in a subsequent investigation seized a large weapons cache of mostly handguns, an Uzi machine gun, a MAC-10 automatic pistol, and several sawed-off shotguns.

Officers A. and W. sought search warrants for the apartments where they had observed drug dealing. When they informed the management company of their findings, its representatives offered to cooperate, agreeing to evict problem tenants and install security doors on the laundry room.

Response

With the assistance of the special weapons and tactics (SWAT) unit, five search warrants were executed simultaneously in the complex. Numerous guns and large quantities of drugs and drug paraphernalia were seized and numerous eviction notices were immediately served on the problem tenants. During the legal eviction process, Officers A. and W. continued to work with the private management company and maintain their surveillance, but drug users and sellers continued to congregate on the apartment grounds and in the general vicinity.

The patrol officers went directly to the owner of the complex and learned that he was unaware of the situation. Once informed, he fired the apartment manager and subsequently replaced the management company. The new company hired security guards, improved the apartment grounds, and initiated a new tenant screening process.

Assessment

During the year following these responses, the complex was virtually drug free. Residents were mostly families with children, and the security guards reported no drug or gang activity.

Source: U.S. Department of Justice, Office of Justice Programs, Bureau of Justice Assistance. (1993). *Problem-oriented drug enforcement: A community-based approach to effective policing.* Retrieved from https://www.ncjrs.gov/pdffiles/problem.pdf

Crime and Drugs: Queen Village, Philadelphia, Pennsylvania

The following case study describes the kinds of actions that can be taken when a larger (six-square-block) neighborhood is beset with several types of problems involving crime and disorder.

Scanning

Residents and police officers working in the Queen Village area of Philadelphia, with 7,200 residents, were concerned about the prevalence of crime and drug trafficking. Both agreed that the neighborhood's physical appearance and dilapidated housing were major contributing factors to the crime, drug trafficking, and fear in the community. Together, they decided to improve the physical environment and remove the drug dealers.

Analysis

Officers conducted an environmental survey of the neighborhood to identify and collect information on the physical conditions that were contributing to the problem. Officers also noted that six blocks had poor lighting due to the lights being broken or the overgrowth of trees. One vacant house in the area was the site of drug dealers operating and users congregating to smoke their crack cocaine (with police receiving nearly forty 911 call complaints concerning the property in two months' time); complaints also included problems relating to area sanitation, litter, trash, abandoned vehicles, disturbances, and loud noise during the night. In addition, there was increased concern for the potential of fire on the block due to smoking crack pipes.

Response

Officer B., an eight-year veteran, was placed in charge of addressing the problems identified in the environmental survey. The officer immediately began removing the abandoned vehicles, securing and demolishing abandoned or dilapidated buildings, and clearing up vacant lots. Vehicle owners were identified through state motor vehicle records and ordered to remove or repair the vehicles within 30 days. The officer coordinated the removal of unclaimed vehicles by working with several salvage companies in the city. In total, 32 vehicles were removed.

Officer B. then turned his attention to the problem of abandoned and dilapidated housing. Some houses had become litter strewn, drug infested, and crime ridden. Large crowds gathered daily to hang out, drink, and sell drugs. They also presented a hazard to children who were observed by patrol officers to be playing in the houses. Officer B. began working on the one house where there was obvious evidence of drug dealing. He coordinated his efforts with the city's licensing and inspection departments, responsible for inspecting buildings and enforcing building code violations. After an unsuccessful attempt at contacting the owner, it was discovered from records that $3,000 in real estate taxes were due.

Because the house had to be demolished, the situation was referred to the city's contractual services department, which hired wrecking companies. Officer B. contacted the director of contractual services and a bid was accepted and the building demolished. Officer B. worked with the city's building and inspections department and residents to clean up other abandoned lots in the area.

Assessment

Although no formal evaluation of the results was conducted, the community policing officer followed up the responses for six months and found that residents were pleased with the physical improvements of their neighborhood. He continued to monitor the problems during his patrol of the area.

Source: Adapted from Philadelphia Police Department. (1989, June). *Problem-oriented approach to drug enforcement: Case studies.* Retrieved from http://www.popcenter.org/library/unpublished/CaseStudies/144_Problem-Oriented_Approach_to_Drug_Enforcement_Case_Studi.pdf

Homeless Problems: Colorado Springs, Colorado

Homeless camps can present many public health and crime issues; such was the case in mid-2008 in Colorado Springs. This case study details how homeless problems can be addressed through the SARA problem-solving method.

Scanning

In mid-2008, an estimated 500 homeless individuals were living in tents on public land in Colorado Springs, Colorado. People in the camps began generating a tremendous amount of litter (including human waste). The public health hazard (and unsightliness) caused a citizen outcry for the police to do something about the camps. Others, however, supporting the individuals' right to be there, were concerned about the potential civil rights violations and wanted a hands-off approach. Law enforcement personnel were caught in the middle and forced to balance individual freedoms with the overall health, safety, and welfare of the community.

Analysis

The Colorado Springs Police Department (CSPD) formed a three-officer homeless outreach team (HOT). One of the HOT's first assignments was to research the local problem and evaluate the efforts of other cities that were dealing with similar issues. They also began meeting local service providers and local homeless people.

At the beginning of the project, there were an estimated 500 people found to be living in tents on public land. The CSPD crime analysis unit mapped calls for service typically associated with the transient population (e.g., intoxicated person, panhandling, trespass), and the highest density of these calls was found in locations also associated with homeless camps. It was also found that 21% of people living in the homeless camps were severely mentally ill and 23% had chronic substance abuse problems. Over 35% of the people counted in a police survey were unsheltered (not in transitional or emergency housing).

Surveying 100 homeless people over a one-month period in the summer of 2006, the HOT found the average time respondents had lived in Colorado Springs was 7.5 years, with an average of 3.3 years living on the street. Many reasons were given to explain why they were homeless, including lost jobs, family, alcohol or drug addiction, injuries, physical and mental health issues, and legal issues. There were also many reasons the people surveyed did not stay in one of the shelter beds available in Colorado Springs, including that the length of stay in the shelter was too short, some respondents having warrants outstanding against them and feared being arrested, the shelter felt like a prison, lack of freedom, and shelter does not accept pets. Most respondents did not know the extent of resources available in Colorado Springs.

Response

Collaborating with an agency charged with coordinating a strategic plan for homeless services in the region, the HOT was better able to understand the local homeless problem and the causes of homeless camps. A number of community forums were held to allow citizen input for possible solutions to homeless issues. Those in attendance included homeless people, Colorado Springs City Council members, advocates, and other citizens. The ideas expressed at the forums ranged from leaving the situation as it was to the immediate and forcible removal of all homeless individuals.

After visiting other jurisdictions concerning their homelessness problem, one of the major lessons learned was that any solution would have to be a communitywide effort. The CSPD also wanted to generate a permanent solution to the homeless problem, taking into account the welfare of the homeless individuals, the environment and overall aesthetics of the city, the safety of all citizens, and the civil rights of everyone involved.

The project began with the HOT patrolling the areas where homeless camps were located and officers introducing themselves to homeless individuals, building a foundation of trust. This trust was formed after repeated contacts with the same individuals who were able to see that the HOT was not there to harass them but to help them. The team used their contacts with area service providers to make referrals. People could get the services that they needed to help them get off the street. Success stories were frequent.

A number of response alternatives were considered, including adding a social worker to go to homeless camps with the HOT, developing an ordinance prohibiting camping on public land, a sanctioned homeless camp, and resuming homeless camp cleanups.

In addition to forming the HOT, the responses included the following key strategies:

- Developing a multiagency partnership to increase "street-level" collaboration of service providers
- Maintaining personal contact between the HOT officers and homeless people to increase trust and make referrals to service providers
- Prohibiting camping on public property and working collaboratively with involved advocacy groups, service providers, and homeless people to transition campers to housing

The HOT worked with nine shelter agencies, 11 food providers, six mental health care providers, and a number of other agencies providing medical treatment, drug and alcohol treatment, clothing, and other services. The HOT attends weekly meetings with local service providers, civil rights leaders, local homeless advocates, concerned community members, and the homeless themselves. These weekly meetings are attended by over 60 separate entities (when the HOT was initially formed two years earlier, fewer than 10 people attended the meetings).

Following the passage of a no-camping ordinance and a two-week voluntary compliance period, enforcement began. To accomplish effective enforcement, three additional officers and one sergeant were temporarily assigned to the team. The HOT began a methodical approach to enforcement, concentrating on one geographical area at a time. Many of the homeless campers had already found alternative housing and were gone. The remaining property was clearly abandoned or unusable and was cleaned up along with the other waste. The trails and adjacent areas were returned to their natural state. Since the passing of the ordinance in February 2010, the HOT has not had to make a single arrest for a camping violation.

Assessment

At the beginning of the project, there were an estimated 500 individuals living in tents on public land. With the help of the HOT, Homeward Pikes Peak (the agency charged with coordinating a strategic plan for homeless services in the region) has sheltered 229 families and returned 117 individuals to family out of state using the bus tickets funded by a foundation. They also documented 100 people becoming employed and self-sufficient. Many homeless camps have been cleaned following this effort, and the trails that citizens had been avoiding are again in use. From 2009 to 2010, the HOT made 2,301 outreach contacts and 872 referrals and participated in 40 cleanups of vacant camps; they also made 29 felony and 80 misdemeanor arrests.

Source: Colorado Springs Police Department. (2010). Homeless Outreach Team (HOT). Retrieved from http://www.popcenter.org/library/awards/goldstein/2010/10–37(W).pdf

Resources

Articles

The following journal articles should provide background information for all aspects of community policing and problem solving, from early development to contemporary practices.

Adams, R. E., Rohe, W. M., & Arcury, T. A. (2002). Implementing community-oriented policing: Organizational change and street officer attitudes. *Crime and Delinquency, 48*(3), 399–430. doi: 10.1177/0011128702048003003

Alpert, G. P., Flynn, D., & Piquero, A. (2001). Effective community policing performance measures. *Justice Research and Policy, 3*(2), 79–94.

Anderson, M. (1996). GPS used to track criminals. *GIS World, 9,* 15.

Angell, J. (1971). Toward an alternate to the classic police organizational arrangement: A democratic model. *Criminology, 8,* 185–206. doi: 10.1111/j.1745–9125.1971.tb00766

Argyris, C. (1991, May/June). Teaching smart people how to learn. *Harvard Business Review, 69*(3), 99–109.

Aryani, G. A., Garrett, T. D., & Alsabrook, C. L. (2000, May). The citizen police academy: Success through community partnerships. *FBI Law Enforcement Bulletin, 69*(5), 16–21.

Ashton, J., Brown, I., Senior, B., & Pease, K. (1998). Repeat victimisation: Offender accounts. *International Journal of Risk, Security and Crime Prevention, 3,* 269–280.

Barlow, S., Branch, J., & Close, G. (2009, March). Citizen police academies: A model for small agencies. *The Police Chief, 77*(3).

Beck, C., & McCue, C. (2009). Predictive policing: What can we learn from Wal-Mart and Amazon about fighting crime in a recession? *The Police Chief, 76*(11).

Bonello, E. M., & Schafer, J. A. (2002, November). Citizen police academies: Do they just entertain? *FBI Law Enforcement Bulletin, 71*(11).

Bowers, K. J., & Johnson, S. D. (2003). Measuring the geographical displacement and diffusion of benefit effects of crime prevention activity. *Journal of Quantitative Criminology, 19*(3), 275–301.

Bowers, K. J., Johnson, S. D., Guerette, R. T., Summers, L., & Poynton, S. (2011). Spatial displacement and diffusion of benefits among geographically focused policing initiatives. *Journal of Experimental Criminology, 7*(4), 347–374. doi: 10.4073/csr .2011.3

Braga, A. A. (2001). The effects of hot spots policing on crime. *Annals of the American Academy of Political and Social Science, 578*(1), 104–125. doi: 10.1177/0002716201578001007

Braga, A. A., & Bond, B. J. (2008). Policing crime and disorder hot spots: A randomized controlled trial. *Criminology, 46*(3), 577–607. doi: 10.1111/j.1745–9125.2008.00124

Braga, A. A., Papachristos, A. V., & Hureau, D. M. (2012). The effects of hot spots policing on crime: An updated systematic review and meta-analysis. *Justice Quarterly,* 1–31. doi: 10.1080/07418825.2012.673632

Braga, A. A., Weisburd, D. L., Waring, E. J., Green-Mazerolle, L., Spelman, W., & Gajewski, F. (1999). Problem-oriented policing in violent crime places: A randomized controlled experiment. *Criminology, 37,* 541–580. doi: 10.1111/j.1745–9125.1999.tb00496

Braithwaite, J. (2007). Encourage restorative justice. *Criminology and Public Policy, 6*(4), 689–696. doi: 10.1111/j.1745–9133.2007.00459

Brantingham, P. L., & Brantingham, P. J. (1990). Situational crime prevention in practice. *Canadian Journal of Criminology, 32,* 17–40.

Brogden, M. (1987). The emergence of the police—The colonial dimension. *British Journal of Criminology, 27,* 4.

Brown, B. (2007). Community policing in post-September 11 America: A comment on the concept of community-oriented counterterrorism. *Police Practice & Research, 8*(3), 239–251. doi: 10.1080/15614260701450716

Brown, L. P. (1991, September). Community policing: Its time has come. *The Police Chief, 62,* 10.

Buerger, M. E. (1998). Police training as a Pentecost: Using tools singularly ill-suited to the purpose of reform. *Police Quarterly, 1,* 32.

Buerger, M. E. (2005, January-February). COMPSTAT: A strategic vision. *The Associate,* 18–23.

Cartwright, G. (2008, September). A learning organization. *Law and Order,* 71–73.

Casey, P. M., & Rottman, D. B. (2005). Problem-solving courts: Models and trends. *The Justice System Journal,* 26(1), 35–56.

Cetron, M. J., & Davies, O. (2008, February). 55 trends now shaping the future of policing. *The Proteus Trends Series,* 1(1).

Chappell, A. T. (2009). The philosophical versus actual adoption of community policing: A case study. *Criminal Justice Review,* 34(1), 5–28. doi: 10.1177/0734016808324244

Clarke, R. V. (1980). "Situational" crime prevention: Theory and practice. *British Journal of Criminology,* 20, 136–147.

Cochran, J. K., Bromley, M. L., & Swando, M. J. (2002). Sheriff's deputies' receptivity to organizational change. *Policing: An International Journal of Police Strategies and Management,* 25(3), 507–529. doi: 10.1108/13639510210437014

Cohen, L. E., & Felson, M. (1979). Social change and crime rate trends: A routine activity approach. *American Sociological Review,* 44, 588–608.

Cohn, E. G. (1996). The citizen police academy: A recipe for improving police-community relations. *Journal of Criminal Justice,* 24(3), 265–271. doi: 10.1016/0047–2352(96)00011–6

Colletti, J. L. (1996, October). Why not hire civilian commanders? *Federal Law Enforcement Bulletin,* 65(10), 8.

Connell, N. M., Miggans, K., & McGloin, J. M. (2008). Can a community policing initiative reduce serious crime? A local evaluation. *Police Quarterly,* 11(2), 127–150. doi: 10.1177/1098611107306276

Cordner, G. W. (1986). Fear of crime and the police: An evaluation of a fear reduction strategy. *Journal of Police Science and Administration,* 14, 223–233.

Cordner, G. W. (2011). The architecture of US policing: Variations among the 50 states. *Police Practice & Research: An International Journal,* 12, 107–119. doi: 10.1080/15614263.2010.512135

Cordner, G. W., & Biebel, E. P. (2005). Problem-oriented policing in practice. *Criminology & Public Policy,* 4(2), 155–180. doi: 10.1111/j.1745–9133.2005.00013

de Guzman, M. C. (2002, September/October). The changing roles and strategies of the police in a time of terror. *ACJS Today,* 22(3), 8–13.

Decker, S., & Pyrooz, D. (2011, Winter). Gangs, terrorism, and radicalization. *Journal of Strategic Security,* 4(4), 151–166.

DeLorenzi, D., Shane, J. M., & Amendola, K. L. (2006) The CompStat process: Managing performance on the pathway to leadership. *The Police Chief,* 73(9).

Dickout, D. (2006). A community based approach for creating safer night-life spaces: 2nd Generation CPTED in action. *CPTED Journal,* 2, 25–32.

Eck, J. E. (1992, June). Helpful hints for the tradition-bound chief. *Fresh Perspectives,* 1–7. Washington, DC: Police Executive Research Forum.

Eck, J. E. (1993, Summer). The threat of crime displacement. *Problem Solving Quarterly,* 6(3), 1–2.

Eck, J. E., & Spelman, W. (1987). Who ya gonna call? The police as problem-busters. *Crime & Delinquency,* 33(1), 31–52.

Ellison, J. (2006, April). Community policing: Implementation issues. *FBI Law Enforcement Bulletin,* 75(4), 12–16.

Engel, R. S. (2002). Patrol officer supervision in the community policing era. *Journal of Criminal Justice,* 30, 51–64.

Ericsson, U. (1995). Straight from the horse's mouth. *Forensic Update,* 43, 23–25.

Esbensen, F-A. (2008). In-school victimization: Reflections of a researcher. *Journal of Contemporary Criminal Justice,* 24(2), 114–124.

Eterno, J., & Silverman, E. (2010, February 15). The trouble with CompStat: Pressure on NYPD commanders endangered the integrity of crime stats. *New York Daily News.* Retrieved from http://articles.nydailynews.com/2010–02–15/news/27056291_1_compstat-crime-reports-commanders

Evans, W. N., & Owens, E. (2007). COPS and crime. *Journal of Public Economics,* 91(1–2), 181–201. doi: 10.1016/j.jpubec0.2006.05.014

Falcone, D. N., Wells, L. E., & Weisheit, R. A. (2002). The small-town police department. *Policing: An International Journal of Police Strategies & Management,* 25, 371–384.

Farrell, G., & Buckley, A. (1999, February). Evaluation of a UK police domestic violence unit using repeat victimisation as a performance indicator. *Howard Journal of Criminal Justice and Crime Prevention,* 38(1), 42–53.

Finkelhor, D., Turner, H., Ormrod, R., & Hamby, S. L. (2009). Violence, abuse, and crime exposure in a national sample of children and youth. *Pediatrics,* 125(5), 1–13. doi: 10.1542/peds.2009–0467

Finn, P. (2006). School resource officer programs: Finding the funding, reaping the benefits. *FBI Law Enforcement Bulletin,* 75(8), 1–7.

Francisco, V. T., Fawcett, S. B., Schultz, J. A., Berkowitz, B., Wolff, T. J., & Nagy, G. (2001, April). Using Internet-based resources to build community capacity: The community tool box. *American Journal of Community Psychology,* 29(2), 293–301.

Fung, A. (2001, March). Accountable autonomy: Toward empowered deliberation in Chicago schools and policing. *Politics & Society, 29*(1), 73–103.

Gaines, L. K. (1994, February). Community-oriented policing: Management issues, concerns, and problems. *Journal of Contemporary Criminal Justice, 10*(1), 17–35.

Gardner, J. (1994, September). There is more than a ray of hope for America's future: Rebuilding America's sense of community. *Journal for Quality and Participation, 17*(5). Retrieved from http://www.worldtrans.org/qual/americancommunity.html

Garner, G. W. (2003, June). Exceptional customer service. *Law and Order,* 103–106.

Garrett, E. W., & Monroe, D. G. (1931, July/August). Wickersham report on police. *American Journal of Police Science, 2*(4), 337–348.

Garvin, D. (1994, January). Building a learning organization. *Business Credit, 96*(1), 19–28.

Gauna, K. (2011, April 4). Citizen group uses controversial methods to patrol the U.S.-Mexico border. *Cronkite News.* Retrieved from http://cronkitenewsonline.com/2011/04/citizen-group-uses-controversial-methods-to-patrol-the-u-s-mexico-border/

Gephart, M. A., Marsick, V. J., Van Buren, M. E., & Spiro, M. S. (1996, December). Learning organizations come alive. *Training & Development, 50*(12), 35–45.

Gerard, D. W., Corsaro, N., Engel, R. S., & Eck, J. E. (2012, July). Cincinnati CARS: A crash analysis reduction strategy. *The Police Chief, 79,* 24–31.

Germann, A. C. (1969, March). Community policing: An assessment. *Journal of Criminal Law, Criminology, and Police Science, 60*(1), 89–96.

Gianakis, G. A., & Davis, G. J., III. (1998). Re-inventing or re-packaging police services? The case of community-oriented policing. *Public Administration Review, 58*(6), 485–498.

Givens, G. (1993). A concept to involve citizens in the provision of police services. *American Journal of Police, 12*(3), 1–9.

Glensor, R. W., & Peak, K. J. (1996). Implementing change: Community-oriented policing and problem solving. *FBI Law Enforcement Bulletin, 65*(7), 14–21.

Glensor, R. W., & Peak, K. J. (1998, March). Lasting impact: Maintaining neighborhood order. *FBI Law Enforcement Bulletin, 67* (3), 1–7.

Goldstein, H. (1963, September). Police discretion: The ideal versus the real. *Public Administration Review, 23*(3), 140–148.

Goldstein, H. (1979). Improving policing: A problem-oriented approach. *Crime & Delinquency, 25*(2), 236–258. doi: 10.1177/001112877902500207

Goldstein, H. (1987). Toward community-oriented policing: Potential, basic requirements, and threshold questions. *Crime and Delinquency, 33*(1), 6–30. doi: 10.1177/0011128787033001002

Goldstein, H. (2003). On further developing problem-oriented policing: The most critical need, the major impediments, and a proposal. *Crime Prevention Studies, 15,* 13–47.

Goldstein, J. (1960). Police discretion not to invoke the criminal process: Low-visibility decisions in the administration of justice. *Yale Law Journal, 69,* 543–589.

Guerette, R. T., & Bowers, K. J. (2009). Assessing the extent of crime displacement and diffusion of benefits: A review of situational crime prevention evaluations. *Criminology, 47*(4), 1331–1368. doi: 10.1111/j.1745-9125.2009.00177

Gurwitt, R. (1993, August). Communitarianism: You can try it at home. *Governing, 6,* 33–39.

Hallahan, K. (2000, Winter). Enhancing motivation, ability, and opportunity to process public relations messages. *Public Relations Review, 26*(4), 463–480.

Hanifan, L. J. (1916). The rural school community centre. *Annals of the American Academy of Political and Social Science, 67,* 130–138.

Harcourt, B. E., & Ludwig, J. (2006). Broken windows: New evidence from New York City and a five-city social experiment. *University of Chicago Law Review, 73,* 271–320.

Haveman, H. (1993). Ghosts of managers past: Managerial succession and organisational mortality. *Academy of Management Journal, 36*(4), 864–881.

Heaton, R. (2000). The prospects for intelligence-led policing: Some historical and quantitative considerations. *Policing and Society, 9*(4), 337–355. doi: 10.1080/10439463.2000.9964822

Hill, C. E. (2005, September). How to build a culture. *Law & Order,* 142–146.

Hillery, G. A., Jr. (1955, June). Definitions of community: Areas of agreement. *Rural Sociology, 20*(4), 111–124.

Howell, J. C. (2007, Spring). Menacing or mimicking? Realities of youth gangs. *Juvenile and Family Court Journal, 58*(2), 39–46. doi: 10.1111/j.1755-6988.2007.tb00137

Hughes, P. J. (2010, October). Increasing organizational leadership through the police promotional process. *FBI Law Enforcement Bulletin.* Retrieved from http://www.fbi.gov/stats-services/publications/law-enforcement-bulletin/October-2010/copy_of_confronting-science-and-market-positioning

Jang, H., Hoover, L. T., & Joo, H-J. (2010). An evaluation of CompStat's effect on crime: The Fort Worth experience. *Police Quarterly, 13*(4), 387–412. doi: 10.1177/1098611110384085

Johnson, K., & Biskupic, J. (2010, April 30). Arizona immigration crackdown raises flags. *USA TODAY.* Retrieved from http://usatoday30.usatoday.com/news/nation/2010–04–29-arizona-immigration_N.htm

Johnson, K. W. (1993). The learning organization: What is it? Why become one? *Navran Associates' Newsletter.*

Johnson, S. D., Summers, L., & Pease, K. (2009, June). Offender as forager? A direct test of the boost account of victimization. *Journal of Quantitative Criminology, 25*(2), 181–200.

Jude, D. (2011, July 29). KSP targets cyberspace to recruit new troopers [Press release]. Kentucky State Police. Retrieved from http://www.youtube.com/user/kentuckystatepolice

Kelling, G. L., & Bratton, W. J. (1993, July). Implementing community policing: The administrative problem. NCJ 141236. *Perspectives on Policing, 17,* 1–11. Washington, DC: U.S. Department of Justice, National Institute of Justice.

Kelling, G. L., & Moore, M. H. (1988). The evolving strategy of policing. NCJ 114213. *Perspectives on Policing, 4.* Washington, DC: U.S. Department of Justice, National Institute of Justice.

Kenney, D. J. (1986). Crime on the subways: Measuring the effectiveness of the Guardian Angels. *Justice Quarterly, 3*(4), 481–496.

Kesner, I. F., & Sebora, T. C. (1994, Summer). Executive succession: Past, present, and future. *Journal of Management, 20*(2), 327–372. doi: 10.1016/0149–2063(94)90019–1

Koper, C. S. (1995, December). Just enough police presence: Reducing crime and disorderly behavior by optimizing patrol time in crime hot spots. *Justice Quarterly, 12*(4), 649–672.

Kuhns, J. B., III, Maguire, E. R., & Cox, S. M. (2007). Public-safety concerns among law enforcement agencies in suburban and rural America. *Police Quarterly, 10*(4), 429–454.

Larson, R. C. (1975, Winter). What happened to patrol operations in Kansas City? A review of the Kansas City preventive patrol experiment. *Journal of Criminal Justice, 3*(4), 267–297.

Lentz, S. A., & Chaires, R. H. (2007). The invention of Peel's principles: A study of policing "textbook" history. *Journal of Criminal Justice, 35*(1), 69–79.

Levitz, J. (2009, September 8). Volunteer 5–0: Civilian patrols grow as recession puts citizens on guard. *Wall Street Journal.* Retrieved from http://online.wsj.com/article/SB125235840966590631.html

Liederbach, J., & Frank, J. (2003). Policing Mayberry: The work routines of small town and rural officers. *American Journal of Criminal Justice, 28*(1), 53–72.

Litwin, H., & Zoabi, S. (2004). A multivariate examination of explanations for the occurrence of elder abuse. *Social Work Research, 28*(3), 133–142.

London, R. (2003). The restoration of trust: Bringing restorative justice from the margins to the mainstream. *Criminal Justice Studies, 16*(3), 175–195. doi: 10.1080/0888431032000151844

Lum, C., Koper, C., & Telep, C. W. (2011). The evidence-based policing matrix. *Journal of Experimental Criminology, 7,* 3–26. doi: 10.1007/s11292–010–9108–2

Lum, C., Telep, C., Koper, C., & Grieco, J. (2012). Receptivity to research in policing. *Justice Research and Policy, 14*(1), 61–96. doi: 10.3818/JRP.14.1.2012.61

Lurigio, A. J., & Skogan, W. G. (1994). Winning the hearts and minds of police officers: An assessment of staff perceptions of community policing in Chicago. *Crime & Delinquency, 40*(3), 315–330.

Lyman, J. L. (1964). The Metropolitan Police Act of 1829: An analysis of certain events influencing the passage and character of the Metropolitan Police Act in England. *Journal of Criminal Law, Criminology, and Police Science, 55,* 141–154.

Maguire, E. R., Kuhns, J. B., Uchida, U. D., & Cox, S. M. (1997). Patterns of community policing in nonurban America. *Journal of Research in Crime and Delinquency, 34*(3), 368–394.

March, N. C., & Margolis, G. J. (2008 May-June). Campus community policing: It all started with us. . . . *Campus Law Enforcement Journal, 38*(3), 22–23.

Martin, M. E. (2006). Restoring justice through community policing. *Criminal Justice Policy Review, 17*(3), 314–329. doi: 10.1177/0887403405284736

Mastrofski, S. D., Worden, R. E., & Snipes, J. B. (1995). Law enforcement in a time of community policing. *Criminology, 33*(4), 539–563.

Michelson, R. (2006, June). Preparing future leaders for tomorrow: Succession planning for police leadership. *The Police Chief, 73*(6). Retrieved from http://www.policechiefmagazine.org/magazine/index.cfm?fuseaction=display_arch&article_id=904&issue_id=62006

Michigan Regional Community Policing Institute. (1999). Transformational leadership and community policing: A road map for change. In *The Police Chief* (December 1999, pp. 14–22). Retrieved from http://www.cj.msu.edu/~people/cp/roadmaparticle.html

Mills, E. (2009). An ounce of prevention. *Law Enforcement Technology, 9,* 60–63.

Moore, M. H., & Kelling, G. L. (1983, Winter). "To serve and protect": Learning from police history. *Public Interest, 70*, 49–65.

Moy, J., & Archibald, B. (2005, June). Reaching English-as-a-second-language communities. *The Police Chief, 72*(6). Retrieved from http://www.policechiefmagazine.org/magazine/index.cfm?fuseaction=display&article_id=614&issue_id=62005

Murphy, P. V. (1995). Violent Crime Control and Law Enforcement Act of 1994: The impact of additional police. *University of Dayton Law Review, 20*, 745–748.

Murphy, S. A. (2006). Executive development and succession planning: Qualitative evidence. *International Journal of Police Science and Management, 8*(4), 253–265.

Muula, A. S., Rudatsikira, E., & Siziya, S. (2008). Correlates of weapon carrying among high school students in the United States. *Annals of General Psychiatry, 7*(8). Retrieved from http://www.annals-general-psychiatry.com/content/7/1/8. doi: 10.1186/1744–859X-7–8

Niven, R. (2011, December 8). The role of social media in community building and development. *The Guardian.* Retrieved from http://www.guardian.co.uk/voluntary-sector-network/community-action-blog/2011/dec/08/facebook-social-media-community-development

Nofziger, S., & Kurtz, D. (2005). Violent lives: A lifestyle model linking exposure to violence to juvenile violent offending. *Journal of Research in Crime and Delinquency, 42*(1), 3–26. doi: 10.1177/0022427803262061

Ohmer, M., & Beck, E. (2006) Citizen participation in neighborhood organizations in poor communities and its relationship to neighborhood and organizational collective efficacy. *Journal of Sociology and Social Welfare, 33*(1), 179–202.

Oliver, W. M. (2004, March/April). The homeland security juggernaut: The end of the community policing era? *Crime & Justice International, 20*(79), 4–10.

Oliver, W. M. (2006). The fourth era of policing: Homeland security. *International Review of Law Computers & Technology, 20*(1–2), 49–62. doi: 10.1080/13600860600579696

Palmiotto, M. J., & Unninthan, N. P. (2002, March-April). The impact of citizen police academies on participants: An exploratory study. *Journal of Criminal Justice, 30*(2), 101–106.

Parascandola, R. (2011, August 10). NYPD forms new social media unit to mine Facebook and Twitter for mayhem. *New York Daily News.* Retrieved from http://articles.nydailynews.com/2011-08-10/local/29887819_1_social-media-facebook-and-twitter-kamisha-richards

Pate, T., Kelling, G. L., & Brown, C. (1975). A response to "What happened to patrol operations in Kansas City?" *Journal of Criminal Justice, 3*(4), 299–320.

Peak, K. J., Bradshaw, R., & Glensor, R. W. (1992). Improving citizen perceptions of the police: "Back to the basics" with a community policing strategy. *Journal of Criminal Justice, 20*(1), 25–40.

Peak, K. J., Stitt, B. G., & Glensor, R. W. (1998). Ethical considerations in community policing and problem solving. *Police Quarterly, 1*(3), 19–34.

Pearsall, B. (2010, June). Predictive policing: The future of law enforcement? NCJ 230414. *National Institute of Justice Journal, 266.* Retrieved from http://www.nij.gov/journals/266/predictive.htm

Pelfrey, W. V., Jr. (2007). Style of policing adopted by rural police and deputies: An analysis of job satisfaction and community policing. NCJ 221488. *Policing: An International Journal of Police Strategies & Management, 30*, 620–636.

Pino, N. W. (2001). Community policing and social capital. *Policing: An International Journal of Police Strategies & Management, 24*(2), 200–215.

Pitts, S., Glensor, R. W., & Peak, K. J. (2007, August). The police training officer (PTO): A contemporary approach to post-academy recruit training. *The Police Chief, 74*(8), 114–121.

Piza, E. L., & O'Hara, B. A. (2012). Saturation foot-patrol in a high-violence area: A quasi-experimental evaluation. *Justice Quarterly, 29*, 1–26. doi: 10.1080/07418825.2012.668923

Poister, T. H., Pitts, D., & Edwards, L. H. (2010). Strategic management research in the public sector: A review, synthesis, and future direction. *American Review of Public Administration, 40*(5), 522–545. doi: 10.1177/0275074010370617

Price, C. (2001, December). The police web site as a community policing tool. *The Police Chief, 71*(12), 37–38.

Raffel, W. E. (2005). Citizen police academies: The importance of communication. *Policing: An International Journal of Police Strategies & Management, 28*(1), 84–97. doi: 10.1108/13639510510580995

Ratcliffe, J. H., Taniguchi, T., Groff, E. R., & Wood, J. D. (2011). The Philadelphia foot patrol experiment: A randomized controlled trial of police patrol effectiveness in violent crime hotspots. *Criminology, 49*(3), 795–831. doi: 10.1111/j.1745–9125.2011.00240

Redlinger, L. J. (1994). Community policing and changes in organizational structure. *Journal of Contemporary Criminal Justice, 10*(1), 36–58.

Reisig, M. D. (2010). Community and problem-oriented policing. *Crime and Justice, 39*(1), 1–44.

Rich, S. (2011, August 19). Predictive policing project reduces crime in Santa Cruz, CA. *Government Technology.* Retrieved from http://www.govtech.com/public-safety/Predictive-Policing-Project-Reduces-Crime-Santa-Cruz-Calif.html

Robertson, C., & Schwartz, J. (2012, March 22). Shooting focuses attention on a program that seeks to avoid guns. *New York Times.* Retrieved from http://www.nytimes.com/2012/03/23/us/trayvon-martin-death-spotlights-neighborhood-watch-groups.html?_r=2pagewanted=all&

Rosenbaum, D. P., Graziano, L. M., Stephens, C. D., & Schuck, A. M. (2011). Understanding community policing and legitimacy-seeking behavior in virtual reality: A national study of municipal police websites. *Police Quarterly, 14*(1), 25–47.

Rosenbaum, D. P., & Lurigio, A. J. (1994). An inside look at community policing reform: Definitions, organizational changes and evaluation findings. *Crime & Delinquency, 40*(3), 299–314.

Sacco, V., & Silverman, R. (1982). Crime prevention through mass media: Prospects and problems. *Journal of Criminal Justice, 10*(4), 257–269.

Saleem, O. (1996). Killing the proverbial two birds with one stone: Using environmental statutes and nuisance to combat the crime of illegal drug trafficking. *Dickinson Law Review, 100*(4), 685–732.

Sampson, R. J. (2004). Neighborhood and community: Collective efficacy and community safety. *New Economy, 11,* 106–113.

Sampson, R. J., & Raudenbush, S. W. (1999, November). Systematic social observation of public spaces: A new look at disorder in urban neighborhoods. *American Journal of Sociology, 105*(3), 603–651.

Sampson, R. J., Raudenbush, S.W., & Earls, F. (1997). Neighborhoods and violent crime: A multilevel study of collective efficacy. *Science, 277,* 918–924. doi: 10.1126/science.277.5328.918

Sarkissian, W. (2003). Stories in a park. Second-generation CPTED in practice: Reducing crime and stigma through community storytelling. *CPTED Journal, 2,* 34–45.

Schafer, J. A., & Bonello, E. M. (2001). The citizen police academy: Measuring outcomes. *Police Quarterly, 4*(4), 434–448.

Scheider, M. C., Rowell, T., & Bezdikian, V. (2003). The impact of citizen perceptions of community policing on fear of crime: Findings from twelve cities. *Police Quarterly, 6*(4), 363–386.

Schmerler, K,. & Velasco, M. (2002). Primary data collection: A problem-solving necessity. *Crime Mapping News, 4*(2), 4–8.

Schofield, R., & Alston, M. (2006, February). Accommodating limited English proficiency in law enforcement. *CALEA Update, 90.* Retrieved from http://onlineresources.wnylc.net/pb/orcdocs/LARC_Resources/LEPTopics/LE/LEPinLE/limitedenglish.htm

Scrivner, E. (2005, October). Building training capacity for homeland security: Lessons learned from community policing. *The Police Chief, 72*(10), 26–30.

Shane, J. M. (2004, May). CompStat design. *FBI Law Enforcement Bulletin, 73*(5), 12–19.

Sherman, L. W., & Berk, R. A. (1984, April). The specific deterrent effects of arrest for domestic assault. *American Sociological Review, 49*(2), 261–272.

Sherman, L. W., Gartin, P. R., & Buerger, M. E. (1989). Hot spots of predatory crime: Routine activities and the criminology of place. *Criminology, 27*(1), 27–55.

Sherman, L. W., & Rogan, D. P. (1995, December). Effects of gun seizures on gun violence: Hot spots patrol in Kansas City. *Justice Quarterly, 12*(4), 673–693.

Sherman, L. W., & Weisburd, D. L. (1995). General deterrent effects of police patrol in crime "hot spots": A randomized, controlled trial. *Justice Quarterly, 12*(4), 625–648. doi: 10.1080/07418829500096221

Sidebottom, A., & Tilley, N. (2011, May). Improving problem-oriented policing: The need for a new model? *Crime Prevention and Community Safety, 13,* 79–101. doi: 10.1057/cpcs.2010.21

Sipes, L. A., & Mentel, Z. (2009, April). Using social media to protect public safety. *Community Policing Dispatch, 2*(4). Retrieved from http://www.cops.usdoj.gov/html/dispatch/April_2009/social_media.htm

Siuru, B. (1999). Tracking "down": Space-age GPS technology is here. *Corrections Technology and Management, 3*(5), 12–14.

Skolnick, J. H., & Bayley, D. H. (1988). Theme and variation in community policing. *Crime and Justice, 10,* 1–37.

Sprafka, H., & Kranda, A. H. (2008, January). Institutionalizing mentoring in police departments. *The Police Chief, 75*(1), 46–49. Retrieved from http://www.policechiefmagazine.org/magazine/index.cfm?fuseaction=display_arch&article_id=1375&issue_id=12008

Taylor, N. (2003). Under-reporting of crime against small businesses: Attitudes toward police and reporting practices. *Policing and Society, 13*(1), 79–89.

Taylor, N., & Charlton, K. (2005). Police shopfronts and reporting to police by retailers. *Trends and Issues in*

Crime and Criminal Justice (No. 295). Canberra: Australian Institute of Criminology.

Thornberry, T., Huizinga, D., & Loeber, R. (2004). The causes and correlates studies: Findings and policy implications. *Juvenile Justice, 9*(1), 3–19. Washington, DC: U.S. Department of Justice, Office of Juvenile Justice and Delinquency Prevention. Retrieved from https://www.ncjrs.gov/pdffiles1/ojjdp/203555.pdf

Trojanowicz, R. C. (1983, December). An evaluation of a neighborhood foot patrol. *Journal of Police Science and Administration, 11*(4), 410–419.

Tseloni, A., & Pease, K. (2005). Population inequality: The case of repeat crime victimization. *International Review of Victimology, 12*(1), 75–90. doi: 10.1177/026975800501200105

Tyler, T. R. (2004, May). Enhancing police legitimacy. In W. G. Skogan (Ed.), To better serve and protect: Improving police practices. *Annals of the American Academy of Political and Social Science, 593*(1), 84–99. doi: 10.1177/0002716203262627

Ugboro, I. O., Obeng, K., & Spann, O. (2011, January). Strategic planning as an effective tool of strategic management in public sector organizations: Evidence from public transit organizations. *Administration and Society, 43*(1), 87–123. doi: 10.1177/0095399710386315

Uhl, J. (2010, June). Mentoring: Nourishing the organizational culture. *The Police Chief, 77*(6), 66–72. Retrieved from http://www.policechiefmagazine.org/magazine/index.cfm?fuseaction=display_arch&article_id=2115&issue_id=62010

Varga, A. (2011). CompStat: Too big for small department? *Law and Order, 3*, 34–37.

Venkatraman, B. A. (2006, April). Lost in translation: Limited English proficient populations and the police. *The Police Chief, 73*(4). Retrieved fromhttp://policechiefmagazine.org/magazine/index.cfm?fuseaction=display&article_id=861&issue_id=42006

Vito, G. F., Walsh, W. F., & Kunselman, J. (2004). Community policing: The middle manager's perspective. *Police Quarterly, 6*, 1–22. Thousand Oaks, CA: Sage.

Vollmer, A. (1932). Abstract of the "Wickersham" police report. *Journal of Criminal Law and Criminology, 22*(5), 716–723.

Walker, S. (1993). Does anyone remember team policing? Lessons of the team policing experience for community policing. *American Journal of Police, 12*(1), 33–56.

Wasserman, R., & Moore, M. H. (1988, November). Values in policing. *Perspectives on Policing, 8.* Washington, DC: U.S. Department of Justice, National

Institute of Justice. Retrieved from https://www.ncjrs.gov/pdffiles1/nij/114216.pdf

Weisburd, D. L., & Eck, J. E. (2004, May). What can police do to reduce crime, disorder, and fear? *Annals of the American Academy of Political and Social Science, 593*, 42–65. doi: 10.1177/0002716203262548

Weisburd, D. L., Mastrofski, S., McNally, A. M., Greenspan, R., & Willis, J. (2003). Reforming to preserve: CompStat and strategic problem solving in American policing. *Criminology and Public Policy, 2*(3), 421–456. doi: 10.1111/j.1745–9133.2003.tb00006

Weisburd, D. L., Shalev, O., & Amir, M. (2002). Community policing in Israel: Resistance and change. *Policing: An International Journal of Police Strategies and Management, 25*(1), 80–109. doi: 10.1108/13639510210417917

Weisburd, D. L., Telep, C. W., Hinkle, J. C., & Eck, J. E. (2010). Is problem-oriented policing effective in reducing crime and disorder? Findings from a Campbell systematic review. *Criminology & Public Policy, 9*(1), 139–172. doi: 10.1111/j.1745–9133.2010.00617

Wilkerson, B. D. (1994, November). Civilian services: Civilian employees for police departments. *FBI Law Enforcement Bulletin, 63*(11), 21–24.

Wilkinson, E. (2011, July 20). How police forces are using Twitter to connect with the public. *The Wall.* Retrieved from http://wallblog.co.uk/2011/07/20/hastings-police-on-twitter

Williams, E. J. (2003). Structuring in community policing: Institutionalizing innovative change. *Police Practice and Research, 4*(2), 119–129. doi: 10.1080/1561426032000084909

Wills, G. (1992). Enabling managerial growth and ownership succession. *Management Decision, 30*(1), 10–26. doi: 10.1108/00251749210008650

Wilson, J. M. (2004, Fall). A measurement model approach to estimating community policing implementation. *Justice Research and Policy, 6*(2), 24.

Wilson, J. Q., & Kelling, G. L. (1982, March). Broken windows: The police and neighborhood safety. *Atlantic Monthly, 249*(3), 29–38.

Wilson, L. J. (1995, April). Placing community-oriented policing in the broader realms of community cooperation. *The Police Chief, 62*(4), 127–128.

Worrall, J. L., & Kovandzic, T. V. (2007). COPS grants and crime revisited. *Criminology, 45*(1), 159–190. doi: 10.1111/j.1745–9125.2007.00076

Wortley, R. (2001). A classification of techniques for controlling situational precipitators of crime. *Security Journal, 14*(4), 63–82. doi: 10.1057/palgrave.sj.8340098

Yang, S. M. (2010). Assessing the spatial-temporal relationship between disorder and violence. *Journal of Quantitative Criminology, 26*(1), 139–163. doi: 10.1007/s10940–009–9085

Zahm, D. (2005, Winter). Learning, translating, and implementing CPTED. *Journal of Architectural and Planning Research, 22*(4), 284–293.

Zhao, J., Scheider, M. C., & Thurman, Q. C. (2002). Funding community policing to reduce crime: Have COPS grants made a difference? *Criminology and Public Policy, 2*(1), 7–32. doi: 10.1111/j.1745–9133.2002.tb00104

Zhao, J., & Thurman, Q. C. (1997). Community policing: Where are we now? *Crime and Delinquency, 43,* 345–357.

Zhao, J., Thurman, Q. C., & Ren, L. (2008). An examination of strategic planning in American law enforcement agencies: A national study. *Police Quarterly, 11*(1), 3–26. doi: 10.1177/1098611107309624

Books, Book Chapters, Monographs, and Reports

As with the above listing of journal articles, the following books, book chapters, monographs, and reports can contribute to one's understanding of community policing and problem solving by providing primary research (original research findings in the field) by noted scholars, as well as secondary research (publications that do not present new research but rather are a compilation or evaluation of material that had been published to that point in time).

Albrecht, J. F. (2011). Analyzing the implementation and evolution of community policing in the United States and Scandinavia. In M. de Guzman, A. M. Das, & D. K. Das (Eds.), *Strategic responses to crime: Thinking globally, acting locally* (pp. 3–26). Boca Raton, FL: CRC Press.

Alpert, G. P., & Moore, M. H. (1993). Measuring police performance in the new paradigm of community policing. In G. P. Alpert & A. R. Piquero (Eds.), *Community policing: Contemporary readings* (pp. 215–232). Prospect Heights, IL: Waveland Press.

Alpert, G. P., & Piquero, A. (Eds.). (1998). *Community policing: Contemporary readings.* Prospect Heights, IL: Waveland Press.

Altschuler, D., Stangler, G., Berkley, K., & Burton, L. (2009, April). *Supporting youth in transition to adulthood: Lessons learned from child welfare and juvenile justice.* Washington, DC: Center for Juvenile Justice Reform. Retrieved from http://cjjr.georgetown.edu/pdfs/TransitionPaperFinal.pdf

American University. (2008). *Challenges and solutions to implementing problem-solving courts from the traditional court management perspective.* Washington, DC: U.S. Department of Justice, Bureau of Justice Assistance.

Atlas, R. I. (2008). *21st century security and CPTED: Designing for critical infrastructure protection and crime prevention.* Boca Raton, FL: Auerbach.

Avila, C., Lindsay, B., & Baker, K. (2011). *Reducing crime in Maravilla public housing.* Retrieved from http://www.popcenter.org/conference/conferencepapers/2011/avilaReducingCrimeinMaravillaPublicHousing.pdf

Barnes, G. (1995). Defining and optimizing displacement. In J. E. Eck & D. L. Weisburd (Eds.), *Crime and place.* Crime Prevention Studies (Vol. 4). Monsey, NY: Criminal Justice Press.

Barrows, H. S., & Tamblyn, R. M. (1980). *Problem-based learning.* New York, NY: Springer-Verlag.

Barthe, E. P. (2006). *Crime prevention publicity campaigns.* Response Guide No. 5. Washington, DC: Center for Problem-Oriented Policing. Retrieved from http://www.popcenter.org/responses/crime_prevention

Bayley, D. H. (1991). *Forces of order: Police behavior in Japan and the United States.* Berkeley: University of California Press.

Bayley, D. H., & Weisburd, D. L. (2009). Cops and spooks: The role of the police in counterterrorism. In D. L. Weisburd, T. Feucht, I. Hakimi, L. Mock, & S. Perry (Eds.), *To protect and to serve: Policing in an age of terrorism* (pp. 81–100). New York, NY: Springer-Verlag.

Benbenishty, R., & Astor, R. A. (2005). *School violence in context: Culture, neighborhood, family, school, and gender.* New York, NY: Oxford University Press.

Berlin, M. M. (2012). The evolution, decline, and nascent transformation of community policing in the United States: 1980–2010. In D. Palmer, M. M. Berlin, & D. K. Das (Eds.), *The global environment of policing* (pp. 27–48). Boca Raton, FL: CRC Press.

Berman, G., Rempel, M., & Wolf, R. V. (Eds.). (2007). *Documenting results: Research on problem-solving justice.* New York, NY: Center for Court Innovation.

Bittner, E. (1970). *The functions of the police in modern society.* Washington, DC: Government Printing Office.

Boba, R. (2001). *Introductory guide to crime analysis and mapping.* Washington DC: U.S. Department of Justice, Office of Community Oriented Policing Services.

Boba, R. (2003). *Problem analysis in policing.* Washington DC: Police Foundation.

Boba, R. (2009). *Crime analysis with crime mapping.* Thousand Oaks, CA: Sage.

Boland, B. (2007). *The response of Multnomah County to neighborhood crime: 1990–2005.* Alexandria, VA: National District Attorneys Association. Retrieved from http://www.ndaa.org/pdf/pub_multnomah_county_07.pdf

Bowers, K. J., & Johnson, S. D. (2003). *The role of publicity in crime prevention: Findings from the reducing burglary initiative*. Home Office Research Study, No. 272. London, England: Home Office.

Braga, A. A. (2002). *Problem-oriented policing and crime prevention*. Monsey, NY: Criminal Justice Press.

Braga, A. A. (2008). *Problem-oriented policing and crime prevention* (2nd ed.). Monsey, NY: Criminal Justice Press.

Braga, A. A., & Weisburd, D. L. (2010). *Policing problem places: Crime hot spots and effective prevention*. New York, NY: Oxford University Press.

Braga, A. A., & Winship, C. (2006). Partnership, accountability, and innovation: Clarifying Boston's experience with pulling levers. In D. L. Weisburd & A. A. Braga (Eds.), *Police innovation: Contrasting approaches and perspectives* (pp. 171–187). New York, NY: Cambridge University Press.

Braiden, C. (1992, November). Community policing: Nothing new under the sun. In *Community Oriented Policing and Problem Solving* (p. 21). Sacramento: California Department of Justice.

Braithwaite, J. (1999). Restorative justice. In M. Tonry (Ed.), *The handbook of crime and punishment* (pp. 323–344). New York, NY: Oxford University Press.

Braithwaite, J. (2002). *Restorative justice and responsive regulation*. New York, NY: Cambridge University Press.

Brown, L. P. (1985). Police-community power sharing. In W. A. Geller (Ed.), *Police leadership in America: Crisis and opportunity* (pp. 70–83). New York, NY: Praeger.

Bumbak, A. R. (2011). *Dynamic police training*. Boca Raton, FL: CRC Press.

Bureau of Justice Assistance. (1994). *Understanding community policing: A framework for action*. NCJ 148457. Washington, DC: U.S. Department of Justice. Retrieved from https://www.ncjrs.gov/pdffiles/commp.pdf

Bureau of Justice Assistance. (1995). *Drug abuse resistance education (D.A.R.E.)*. NCJ FS000039. Washington, DC: U.S. Department of Justice.

Bursik, R. J., Jr., & Grasmick, H. (1993). *Neighborhoods and crime: The dimensions of effective community control*. New York, NY: Lexington Books.

Butts, J. A., Bazemore, G., & Meroe, S. A. (2010). *Positive youth justice: Framing justice interventions using the concepts of positive youth development*. Washington, DC: Coalition for Juvenile Justice. Retrieved from http://juvjustice.org/media/resources/public/resource_390.pdf

Buzawa, E. S., & Buzawa, C. G. (2002). *Domestic violence: The criminal justice response* (3rd ed.). Thousand Oaks, CA: Sage.

Bynum, T. S. (2002). *Using analysis for problem-solving: A guidebook for law enforcement*. Washington, DC: U.S. Department of Justice, Office of Community Oriented Policing Services. Retrieved from http://www.cops.usdoj.gov/pdf/e08011230.pdf

California Highway Patrol. (2002). *SAFE: A safety and farm vehicle education program reducing farm labor vehicle collisions*. Retrieved from http://www.popcenter.org/library/awards/goldstein/2002/02–07%28W%29.pdf

Cambridge Systematics. (2011, November). *Crashes vs. congestion: What's the cost to society?* Bethesda, MD: Author. Retrieved from http://www.camsys.com/pubs/2011_AAA_CrashvCongUpd.pdf

Carter, D. L. (2004). *Law enforcement intelligence: A guide for state, local, and tribal law enforcement agencies*. Washington, DC: U.S. Department of Justice, Office of Community Oriented Policing Services.

Catalano, S., Smith, E., Snyder, H., & Rand, M. (2009). *Female victims of violence*. NCJ 228356. Washington, DC: U.S. Department of Justice, Bureau of Justice Statistics. Retrieved from http://bjs.ojp.usdoj.gov/content/pub/pdf/fvv.pdf

Center for Behavioral Health Statistics and Quality. (2011). *Results from the 2010 national survey on drug use and health: Summary of national findings*. Rockville, MD: U.S. Department of Health and Human Services, Substance Abuse and Mental Health Services Administration.

Center for Problem-Oriented Policing. (2000 et seq.). *Problem-Oriented Guides for Police*. Washington, DC: U.S. Department of Justice, Office of Community Oriented Policing Services. Retrieved from www.popcenter.org

Centers for Disease Control and Prevention. (2010). *Fact sheet: Understanding teen dating violence*. Retrieved from http://www.cdc.gov/violenceprevention/pdf/TeenDatingViolence_2010-a.pdf

Centers for Disease Control and Prevention. (2011). *Vehicle crash injury estimates*. Retrieved from http://www.cdc.gov/motorvehiclesafety/index.html

Chainey, S., & Ratcliffe, J. (2005). *GIS and crime mapping*. West Chester, England: Wiley.

Chamard, S. (2006). *Partnering with businesses to address public safety problems*. (Problem-Oriented Guides for Police, Problem-Solving Tools Series, No. 5). Washington, DC: U.S. Department of Justice, Office of Community Oriented Policing Services.

Charles, M. T. (2000). *Police training—Breaking all the rules*. Springfield, IL: Charles C Thomas.

Child Welfare Information Gateway. (2009, November). *Understanding the effects of maltreatment on brain development*. Washington, DC: U.S. Department of Health and Human Services, Administration for Children and Families. Retrieved from http://www.childwelfare.gov/pubs/issue_briefs/brain_development/brain_development.pdf

Cisneros, H. G. (1995). *Defensible space: Deterring crime and building communities.* Washington, DC: U.S. Department of Housing and Urban Development.

Clarke, R. V. (Ed.). (1993). *Crime prevention studies* (Vol. 1). Monsey, NY: Criminal Justice Press.

Clarke, R. V. (1997). *Situational crime prevention: Successful case studies* (2nd ed.). Albany, NY: Harrow and Heston.

Clarke, R. V. (1999). *Hot products: Understanding, anticipating and reducing demand for stolen goods.* (Police Research Series, Paper 112. Policing and Reducing Crime Unit). London, England: Home Office, Research Development and Statistics Directorate.

Clarke, R. V. (2000). Situational crime prevention: Successful studies. In R. W. Glensor, M. E. Correia, & K. J. Peak (Eds.), *Policing communities: Understanding crime and solving problems: An anthology* (pp.182–225). Los Angeles, CA: Roxbury.

Clarke, R. V. (2005). Seven misconceptions of situational crime prevention. In N. Tilley (Ed.), *Handbook of crime prevention and community safety* (pp.39–50). Cullompton, England: Willan.

Clarke, R. V., & Eck, J. E. (2003). *Become a problem-solving crime analyst: In 55 small steps.* London, England: Jill Dando Institute of Crime Science.

Clark, R. V., & Eck, J. E. (2005). *Crime analysis for problem solvers in 60 small steps.* Washington, DC: U.S. Department of Justice, Office of Community Oriented Policing Services.

Clarke, R. V., & Eck, J. E. (2007). *Understanding risky facilities.* (Problem-Oriented Guides for Police, Problem-solving Tools Series, No. 6). Washington, DC: U.S. Department of Justice, Office of Community Oriented Policing Services.

Clarke, R. V., & Weisburd, D. L. (1994). Diffusion of crime control benefits: Observations on the reverse of displacement. In R. V. Clarke (Ed.), *Crime Prevention Studies* (Vol. 3)(165–183). Monsey, NY: Criminal Justice Press.

Clear, T. R. (2007). *Imprisoning communities: How mass incarceration makes disadvantaged neighborhoods worse.* Oxford, England: Oxford University Press.

Clear, T. R., Hamilton, J. R., & Cadora, E. (2011). *Community justice* (2nd ed.). London, England: Routledge.

Cohen, D. (2001). *Problem-solving partnerships: Including the community for a change.* Washington, DC: U.S. Department of Justice, National Criminal Justice Reference Service.

Cohen, H. S., & Feldberg, M. (1991). *Power and restraint: The moral dimension of police work.* New York, NY: Praeger.

Collins, J. (2001). *Good to great: Why some companies make the leap . . . and others don't.* New York, NY: HarperCollins.

Community Policing Consortium. (1994). *Understanding community policing: A framework for action.* Washington, DC: U.S. Department of Justice, Bureau of Justice Assistance. Retrieved from http://www.ncjrs.gov/pdffiles/commp.pdf

Community Policing Consortium. (1998). *Understanding community policing: A framework for action.* NCJ 148457. Washington, DC: U.S. Department of Justice, Bureau of Justice Assistance.

Connors, E. F., Cunningham, W. C., & Ohlhausen, P. E. (1999). *Operation cooperation: A literature review of cooperation and partnerships between law enforcement and private security organizations.* Washington, DC: U.S. Department of Justice, Bureau of Justice Assistance.

Connors, T. D. (Ed.). (2011). *The volunteer management handbook: Leadership strategies for success.* Hoboken, NJ: Wiley.

Cordner, G. W. (1997). Community policing: Elements and effects. In R. G. Dunham & G. P. Alpert (Eds.), *Critical issues in policing: Contemporary readings* (3rd ed.) (pp. 451–468). Prospect Heights, IL: Waveland Press.

Cordner, G. W. (1999). Elements of community policing. In L. K. Gaines & G. W. Cordner (Eds.), *Policing perspectives: An anthology.* Los Angeles, CA: Roxbury.

Cordner, G. W. (2010). *Reducing fear of crime: Strategies for police.* Washington, DC: U.S. Department of Justice, Office of Community Oriented Policing Services.

Cordner, G. W., & Scarborough, K. S. (2003). Operationalizing community policing in rural America: Sense and nonsense. In Q. C. Thurman & E. F. McGarrell (Eds.), *Community policing in a rural setting: Innovations and organizational change* (2nd ed) (pp. 11–20). Cincinnati, OH: Anderson.

Cornish, D. B., & Clarke, R. V. (Eds.). (1986). *The reasoning criminal. Rational choice perspectives on offending.* New York, NY: Springer-Verlag.

Correia, M. E. (2000). Social capital and sense of community building: Building social cohesion. In R. W. Glensor, M. E. Correia, & K. J. Peak (Eds.), *Policing communities: Understanding crime and solving problems* (pp. 75–82). Los Angeles, CA: Roxbury.

Couper, D. C., & Lobitz, S. H. (1991). *Quality policing: The Madison experience.* Washington, DC: Police Executive Research Forum.

Crime and Violence Prevention Center. (1999). Lengthening the stride: Recognizing diversity as an asset. In *Community oriented policing and problem solving:*

Now and beyond (pp. 129–139). Sacramento: California Department of Justice.

Crowe, T. D. (1991). *Crime prevention through environmental design: Applications of architectural design and space management concepts.* (National Crime Prevention Institute). Boston, MA: Butterworth-Heinemann.

Davis, R. C., & Lurigio, A. J. (1996). *Fighting back: Neighborhood antidrug strategies.* Thousand Oaks, CA: Sage.

Decker, S. (2008, April). *Strategies to address gang crime: A guidebook for local law enforcement.* Washington, DC: U.S. Department of Justice, Office of Community Oriented Policing Services. Retrieved from http://www.cops.usdoj.gov/Publications/e060810142Gang-book-web.pdf

Delattre, E. J. (1994). *Character & cops: Ethics in policing.* Washington, DC: AEI Press.

Delisle, R. (1997). *How to use problem-based learning in the classroom.* Alexandria, VA: ASCD.

Diamond, D., & Weiss, D. M. (2004). *Advancing community policing through community governance: A framework document.* Washington, DC: U.S. Department of Justice, Office of Community Oriented Policing Services.

Dinkes, R., Kemp, J., Baum, K., & Snyder, T. (2009). *Indicators of school crime: 2008.* Washington, DC: U.S. Department of Justice, Bureau of Justice Programs. Retrieved from http://nces.ed.gov/pubsearch/pubsinfo.asp?pubid=2009022

Drucker, P. F. (1995). *Managing in a time of great change.* New York, NY: Truman Talley.

Drug Enforcement Administration. (2011). *Drugs of abuse: A DEA resource guide.* Washington, DC: Author.

Dunworth, T., & Mills, G. (1999, June). *National evaluation of weed and seed.* NCJ 175675. Washington, DC: U.S. Department of Justice, Office of Justice Programs.

Dunworth, T., & Saiger, A. (1993, July). *Drugs and crime in public housing: A three-city analysis, final report.* Washington, DC: U.S. Department of Justice, National Institute of Justice. Retrieved from http://www.icpsr.umich.edu/icpsrweb/ICPSR/studies/6235

Eck, J. E. (2002). *Assessing responses to problems: An introductory guide for police problem-solvers.* Washington, DC: U.S. Department of Justice, Office of Community Oriented Policing Services.

Eck, J. E. (2004). Why don't problems get solved? In W. G. Skogan (Ed.), *Community policing: Can it work?* (pp. 185–206). Belmont, CA: Wadsworth.

Eck, J. E., & Clarke, R. V. (2003). Classifying common police problems: A routine activity approach. In M. J.

Smith & D. B. Cornish (Eds.), *Theory for practice in situational crime prevention: Crime prevention studies, 16.* New York, NY: Criminal Justice Press. Retrieved from http://www.popcenter.org/library/crimeprevention/volume_16/TitlePages.pdf

Eck, J. E., & Spelman, W. (1987). *Problem solving: Problem-oriented policing in Newport News.* Washington, DC: U.S. Department of Justice, National Institute of Justice, Police Executive Research Forum.

Eck, J. E., & Spelman, W. (1989). A problem-oriented approach to police service delivery. In D. J. Kenney (Ed.), *Police and policing: Contemporary issues* (pp. 95–111). New York, NY: Praeger.

Eck, J. E., & Wartell, J. (1996). *Reducing crime and drug dealing by improving place management: A randomized experiment.* Washington, DC: U.S. Department of Justice, National Institute of Justice.

Eck, J. E., & Weisburd, D. L. (1995). *Crime and place.* Monsey, NY: Willow Tree Press.

Eck, J. E., & Weisburd. D. L. (1995). Crime places in crime theory. In J. E. Eck & D. L. Weisburd (Eds.), *Crime and Place* (pp. 1–33). Monsey, NY: Criminal Justice Press.

Eigenberg, H. M. (Ed.). (2001). *Women battering in the United States: Till death do us part.* Prospect Heights, IL: Waveland Press.

Eith, C., & Durose, M. R. (2011). *Contacts between police and the public, 2008.* NCJ 234599. Washington, DC: U.S. Department of Justice, Bureau of Justice Statistics. Retrieved from http://www.bjs.gov/content/pub/pdf/cpp08.pdf

Ellis, S. J. (2004). *The volunteer recruitment (and membership development) book.* Philadelphia, PA: Energize.

Feder, L. (Ed.). (1999). *Women and domestic violence: An interdisciplinary approach.* New York, NY: Haworth Press.

Felson, M. (2006). *Crime and nature.* Thousand Oaks, CA: Sage.

Felson, M., & Boba, R. (2010). *Crime and everyday life* (4th ed.). Thousand Oaks, CA: Sage.

Ferraro, K. F. (1995). *Fear of crime: Interpreting victimization risk.* Albany: State University of New York Press.

Finkelhor, D., Turner, H., Ormrod, R., Hamby, S., & Kracke, K. (2009, October). *Children's exposure to violence: A comprehensive national survey.* Washington, DC: Office of Juvenile Justice and Delinquency Prevention.

Fisher, B. S., & Sloan, J. J., III. (2007). *Campus crime: Legal, social, and policy perspectives* (2nd ed.). Springfield, IL: Charles C Thomas.

Flynn, D. W. (1998, July). *Defining the "community" in community policing.* Washington, DC: Police Executive Research Forum.

Folkemer, N. T. W. (2008, March). *Problem solving courts* (Road Map Series). Chicago IL: American Bar Association, Coalition for Justice.

Fox, J. A., & Burstein, H. (2010). *Violence and security on campus: From preschool through college.* Santa Barbara, CA: Praeger.

Frieze, I. H. (2005). *Hurting the one you love: Violence in relationships.* Belmont, CA: Wadsworth.

Gaines, L. K., & Kappeler, V. E. (2012). *Homeland security.* Upper Saddle River, NJ: Prentice Hall.

Gaines, L. K., & Swanson, C. R. (1999). Empowering police officers: A tarnished silver bullet? In L. K. Gaines & G. W. Cordner (Eds.), *Policing perspectives: An anthology* (pp. 363–371). Los Angeles, CA: Roxbury.

Gaines, L. K., & Kappeler, V. E. (2011). *Policing in America* (7th ed.). Waltham, MA: Anderson.

Gambetta, R., & Burgess, M. (2011). *Public safety programs for the immigrant community: 17 good practices in U.S. cities.* Washington, DC: National League of Cities and Municipal Action for Immigrant Integration. Retrieved from http://www.nlc.org/find-city-solutions/research-innovation/immigrant-integration

Geller, W. A., & Swanger, G. (1995). *Managing innovation in policing: The untapped potential of the middle manager.* Washington, DC: U.S. Department of Justice, National Institute of Justice, Police Executive Research Forum.

Gill, M., & K. Pease. (1998). Repeat robbers: How are they different? In M. Gill (Ed.), *Crime at work: Studies in security and crime prevention.* Leicester, England: Perpetuity Press.

Gladwell, M. (2000). *The tipping point: How little things can make a big difference.* Boston, MA: Little, Brown.

Glensor, R. W., & Peak, K. J. (2012). New police management practices and predictive software: A new era they do not make. In D. R. Cohen McCullough & D. L. Spence (Eds.), *American policing in 2022: Essays on the future of a profession* (pp. 11–17). Washington, DC: U.S. Department of Justice, Office of Community Oriented Policing Services.

Goldstein, H., & Susmilch, C. E. (1981). *The problem-oriented approach to improving police service: A description of the project and an elaboration of the concept.* Madison: University of Wisconsin Law School.

Goldstein, H. (1977). *Policing a free society.* Cambridge, MA: Ballinger.

Goldstein, H. (1990). *Problem-oriented policing.* New York, NY: McGraw-Hill.

Gordon, G. (1993). *Strategic planning for local government.* Washington, DC: International City/County Management Association.

Gosselin, D. K. (2009). *Heavy hands: An introduction to the crimes of domestic violence* (4th ed.). Upper Saddle River, NJ: Prentice Hall.

Government Accountability Office. (2005, October). *Community policing grants: COPS grants were a modest contributor to declines in crime in the 1990s.* GAO-06–104. Washington, DC: Author.

Graff, L. L. (2004). *Beyond police checks: The definitive volunteer and employee screening guidebook.* Dundas, ON, Canada: Linda Graff and Associates.

Grant, H. J., & Terry, K. J. (2005). *Law enforcement in the 21st century.* Boston, MA: Allyn & Bacon.

Greene, J. R. (2000). Community policing in America: Changing the nature, structure, and function of the police. In J. Horney, R. Peterson, D. L. MacKenzie, J. Martin, & D. P. Rosenbaum (Eds.), *Policies, processes, and decisions of the criminal justice system* (Vol. 3) (pp. 299–370). NCJ 182410. Washington, DC: U.S. Department of Justice, National Institute of Justice.

Greene, J. R., Bergman, W. T., & McLaughlin, E. J. (1994). Implementing community policing: Cultural and structural change in police organizations. In D. P. Rosenbaum (Ed.), *The challenge of community policing: Testing the promises* (pp. 92–109). Thousand Oaks, CA: Sage.

Grove, L. E., Farrell, G., Farrington, D. P., & Johnson, S. D. (2012, June 11). *Preventing repeat victimization: A systematic review.* Stockholm: Swedish National Council for Crime Prevention.

Guerette, R. T. (2006). *Disorder at day labor sites.* (Problem-Oriented Guides for Police, Problem Specific Guide Series No. 44). Washington, DC: U.S. Department of Justice, Office of Community Oriented Policing Services. Retrieved from www.popcenter.org/Problems/problem-disorder_daylabor.htm

Gwinn, S., Bruce, C., Cooper, J., & Hick, S. (Eds.) (2011). *Exploring crime analysis: Readings on essential skills* (2nd ed.). Overland Park, KS: International Association of Crime Analysts.

Harfield, C., & Harfield, K. (2008). *Intelligence: Investigation, community and partnership.* New York, NY: Oxford University Press.

Harocopos, A., & Hough, M. (2005). *Drug dealing in open-air markets.* Washington, DC: U.S. Department of Justice, Office of Community Oriented Policing Services.

Harries, K. (1999). *Mapping crime: Principles and practices.* Washington, DC: U.S. Department of Justice, National Institute of Justice.

Harvard University, John F. Kennedy School of Government, Program in Criminal Justice Policy and

Management. *Executive Sessions*. Retrieved from http://www.hks.harvard.edu/programs/criminaljustice/research-publications/executive-sessions

Heaton, P. (2010). *Hidden in plain sight: What cost of crime research can tell us about investing in police.* Santa Monica, CA: RAND.

Henry, V. E. (2002). *The CompStat paradigm: Management accountability in policing, business and the public sector.* Flushing, NY: Looseleaf Law.

Hesseling, R. B. P. (1995). Displacement: A review of the empirical literature. In R. V. Clarke (Ed.), *Crime Prevention Studies* (Vol. 3) (pp. 197–230). New York, NY: Criminal Justice Press.

Howell, J. C. (2006, August). *The impact of gangs on communities.* Washington, DC: U.S. Department of Justice, Office of Juvenile Justice and Delinquency Prevention. Retrieved from http://www.nationalgangcenter.gov/Content/Documents/Impact-of-Gangs-on-Communities.pdf

Howell, J. C., & Curry, G. D. (2009, January). *Mobilizing communities to address gang problems.* Washington, DC: U.S. Department of Justice, Office of Juvenile Justice and Delinquency Prevention. Retrieved from http://www.nationalgangcenter.gov/Content/Documents/NYGC-bulletin-4.pdf

Howell, J. C., & Egley, A., Jr. (2005, June). *Gangs in small towns and rural counties.* Washington, DC: U.S. Department of Justice, Office of Juvenile Justice and Delinquency Prevention. Retrieved from http://www.nationalgangcenter.gov/Content/Documents/Gangs-in-Small-Towns-and-Rural-Counties.pdf

Huddleston, C. W., III, & Marlowe, D. B. (2011). *Painting the current picture: A national report on drug courts and other problem solving court programs in the United States.* Alexandria, VA: National Drug Court Institute.

Jacksonville Community Council Inc. (2003). *Neighborhoods at the tipping point.* Jacksonville, FL: Author. Retrieved from http://www.jcci.org

Jeffery, C. R. (1977). *Crime prevention through environmental design* (2nd ed.). Beverly Hills, CA: Sage.

Jenkins, B. M. (2010). *Would-be warriors: Incidents of jihadist terrorist radicalization in the United States since September 11, 2001.* Santa Monica, CA: RAND.

Jenson, C. J., III, & Levin, B. H. (2005, January). *Neighborhood-driven policing: A series of working papers from the futures working group.* Proceedings of the Futures Working Group (Vol. I). Washington, DC: Federal Bureau of Investigation. Retrieved from http://www2.fbi.gov/hq/td/fwg/neighborhood/neighborhood-driven-policing.pdf

Jimerson, S., & Furlong, M. (Eds.). (2006). *The handbook of school violence and school safety: From research to practice.* Mahwah, NJ: Routledge.

Johnson, C. C., & Roth, J. A. (2003). *The COPS program and the spread of community policing practices, 1995–2000.* Washington, DC: The Urban Institute.

Johnson, D. R. (1981). *American law enforcement: A history.* St. Louis, MO: Forum Press.

Jones, A. A., & Wiseman, R. (2006). *Community policing in Europe: Structure and best practices—Sweden, France, Germany.* Los Angeles, CA: Los Angeles Community Policing. Retrieved from http://www.lacp.org/Articles%20-%20Expert%20-%20Our%20Opinion/060908-CommunityPolicingInEurope-AJ.htm

Jones, G., & Molina, M. (2011). *Crime analysis case studies.* Washington, DC: U.S. Department of Justice, Office of Community Oriented Policing Services.

Kalunta-Crumpton, A. (2009). Patterns of community policing in Britain. In D. Wisler & I. D. Onwudiwe (Eds.), *Community policing: International patterns and comparative perspectives* (pp. 149–164). Boca Raton, FL: CRC Press. Retrieved from http://www.crcnetbase.com/doi/abs/10.1201/9781420093599.ch7

Kappeler, V. E., & Gaines, L. K. (2011). *Community policing.* Cincinnati, OH: Anderson.

Karp, D. R., & Clear, T. R. (2000). Community justice: A conceptual framework. In *Criminal Justice 2000.* Washington, DC: National Criminal Justice Reference Service.

Katz, C. M., & Webb, V. J. (2004). *Police response to gangs: A multi-site study.* Washington, DC: U.S. Department of Justice, National Criminal Justice Reference Service. Retrieved from https://www.ncjrs.gov/pdffiles1/nij/grants/205003.pdf

Kelling, G. L., & Bratton, W. J. (1993). *Implementing community policing: The administrative problem.* Washington, DC: U.S. Department of Justice, National Institute of Justice. Retrieved from https://www.ncjrs.gov/pdffiles1/nij/141236.pdf

Kelling, G. L., & Coles, C. M. (1996). *Fixing broken windows: Restoring order and reducing crime in our communities.* New York, NY: Touchstone.

Kelling, G. L., Pate, T., Dieckman, D., & Brown, C. E. (1974). *The Kansas City preventive patrol experiment: A summary report.* Washington, DC: Police Foundation.

Kelling, G. L., & Sousa, W. H., Jr. (2001, December). *Do police matter? An analysis of the impact of New York City's police reforms.* (Civic Report 22). New York, NY: Center for Civic Innovation, Manhattan Institute.

Kennedy, D. M. (2006). Old wine in new bottles: Policing and the lessons of pulling levers. In D. L. Weisburd & A. A. Braga (Eds.), *Police innovation: Contrasting perspectives* (pp. 155–170). New York, NY: Cambridge University Press.

Kennedy, D. M. (2009). *Deterrence and crime prevention: Reconsidering the prospect of sanction.* New York, NY: Routledge.

Kennedy, R. F. (1964). *The pursuit of justice.* New York, NY: Harper & Row.

Kenney, D., & Watson, S. (1998). *Crime in schools: Reducing fear and disorder with student problem solving.* Washington, DC: Police Executive Research Forum.

Khashu, A. (2009). *The role of local police: Striking a balance between immigration enforcement and civil liberties.* Washington DC: Police Foundation. Retrieved from http://www.policefoundation.org/strikingabalance/strikingabalance.html

Khashu, A., Busch, R., Latif, Z., & Levy, F. (2005). *Building strong police-immigrant community relations: Lessons from a New York City project.* New York, NY: Vera Institute of Justice. Retrieved from http://www.vera.org/download?file=83/300_564.pdf

Kleinig, J. (1996). *The ethics of policing.* New York, NY: cambridge University Press.

Koper, C. S., Moore, G. E., & Roth, J. A. (2002). *Putting 100,000 officers on the street: A survey-based assessment of the federal COPS program.* Washington, DC: The Urban Institute. Retrieved from http://www.sas.upenn.edu/jerrylee/research/cops_levels.pdf

Kuhns, J. B., & Leach, N. R. (2012). *Model POP Curriculum.* Available from http://www.popcenter.org/learning/model_curriculum/

Lab, S. P. (1997). *Crime prevention: Approaches, practices and evaluations* (3d ed.). Cincinnati, OH. Anderson.

Labriola, M., Bradley, S., O'Sullivan, C. S., Rempel, M., & Moore, S. (2009). *A national portrait of domestic violence courts.* New York, NY: Center for Court Innovation.

LaFree, G., & Dugan, L. (2009). Research on terrorism and countering terrorism. In M. Tonry (Ed.), *Crime and justice: A review of research* (Vol. 38) (pp. 413–477). Chicago, IL: University of Chicago Press.

Langdon, L. (2010, October). *Gang units in large local law enforcement agencies, 2007.* NCJ 230071. Washington, DC: U.S. Department of Justice, Bureau of Justice Statistics. Retrieved from http://bjs.ojp.usdoj.gov/content/pub/pdf/gulllea07.pdf

Langworthy, R. H. (Ed.). (1999). *Measuring what matters: Proceedings from the Policing Research Institute meetings.* Washington, DC: U.S. Department of Justice, National Institute of Justice.

Law Enforcement–Private Security Consortium. (2009). *Operation partnership: Trends and practices in law enforcement and private security collaborations.* Washington, DC: U.S. Department of Justice, Office of Community Oriented Policing Services.

Leipnik, M., Bottelli, J., Von Essen, I., Schmidt, A., Anderson, L., & Copper, T. (2003). Apprehending murderers in Spokane, Washington using GIS and GPS. In M. Leipnik & D. Alpert (Eds.), *GIS in law enforcement: Implementation issues and case studies* (pp. 167–183). London, England: Taylor & Francis.

Lipsey, M. W., & Derzon, J. H. (1998). Predictors of violent and serious delinquency in adolescence and early adulthood: A synthesis of longitudinal research. In R. Loeber & D. P. Farrington (Eds.), *Serious and violent juvenile offenders: Risk factors and successful interventions* (pp. 86–105). Thousand Oaks, CA: Sage.

London, R. (2011). *Crime, punishment, and restorative justice: From the margins to the mainstream.* Boulder, CO: First Forum Press.

Lum, C. (2009, August). Translating police research into practice. *Ideas in American Policing, 11,* 1–16. Washington, DC: Police Foundation. Retrieved from http://www.policefoundation.org/content/translating-police-research-practice

Lum, C., & Koper, C. (2013). Evidence-based policing. In G. Bruinsma & D. L. Weisburd (Eds.), *The encyclopedia of criminology and criminal justice.* Springer-Verlag.

Lysakowski, M., Pearsall A. A., III, & Pope, J. (2009). *Policing in new immigrant communities.* Washington, DC: U.S. Department of Justice, Office of Community Oriented Policing Services. Retrieved from http://www.cops.usdoj.gov/RIC/ResourceDetail.aspx?RID=526

Manning, P. K. (1997). *Police work: The social organization of policing.* Prospect Heights, IL: Waveland Press.

Mason, G. (2004). *The official history of the metropolitan police.* London, England: Carlton.

Matthews, D. (Ed.). (2004). *Domestic violence sourcebook.* Detroit, MI: Omnigraphics.

Mazerolle, L., Soole, D. W., & Rombouts, S. (2007). *Crime prevention research reviews N0.1: Disrupting street-level drug markets.* Washington, DC: U.S. Department of Justice, Office of Community Oriented Policing Services. Retrieved from http://cops.usdoj.gov/files/RIC/Publications/e04072678.pdf

Mazerolle, L. G., Ready, J., Terrill, W., & Gajewski, W. (1998). *Problem-oriented policing in public housing: Final report of the Jersey City project.* Retrieved from http://www.ncjrs.gov/pdffiles1/nij/grants/179985.pdf

McCue, M. L. (2008). *Domestic violence: A reference handbook.* Santa Barbara, CA: ABC-CLIO.

McEwen, T., Ahn, J., Pendleton, S., Webster, B., & Williams, G. (2002). *Computer aided dispatch in support of community policing, final report.* NCJ 204025. Alexandria, VA: Institute for Law and Justice. Retrieved from https://www.ncjrs.gov/pdffiles1/nij/grants/204025.pdf

McGarrell, E. F., Chermak, S., & Weiss, A. (2002, November). *Reducing gun violence: Evaluation of the Indianapolis Police Department's directed patrol project.* NCJ 188740. Retrieved from https://www.ncjrs.gov/pdffiles1/nij/188740.pdf

McGloin, J. M. (2005, September). *Street gangs and interventions: Innovative problem solving with network analysis.* Washington, DC: U.S. Department of Justice, Office of Community Oriented Policing Services. Retrieved from http://www.cops.usdoj.gov/pdf/innovations/e09050001.pdf

Mears, D. P. (2010). *American criminal justice policy: An evaluation approach to increasing accountability and effectiveness.* New York, NY: Cambridge University Press.

Miller, L. S., Hess, K. M., & Orthmann, C. M. H. (2010). *Community policing: Partnerships for problem-solving* (6th ed.). Clifton Park, NY: Delmar.

Miller, R., & Aguilar, D. (2009, May). *Basic immigration enforcement training (BIET). Final report.* Lawton, OK: Cameron University and Advanced Systems Technology.

Moore, J., & Hagedorn, J. (2001, March). *Female gangs: A focus on research.* Washington, DC: U.S. Department of Justice, Office of Juvenile Justice and Delinquency Prevention. Retrieved from https://www.ncjrs.gov/pdffiles1/ojjdp/186159.pdf

Moore, M. H. (1995). *Creating public value: Strategic management in government.* Boston, MA: Harvard University Press.

Moore, M. H., & Trojanowicz, R. C. (1988). *Corporate strategies for policing.* Washington, DC: U.S. Department of Justice, National Institute of Justice. Retrieved from https://www.ncjrs.gov/pdffiles1/nij/114215.pdf

Morash, M., & Ford, J. K. (Eds.). (2002). *The move to community policing: Making change happen.* Thousand Oaks, CA: Sage.

Muhlhausen, D. B. (2001). *Do community oriented policing services grants affect violent crime rates?* (Report No. CDA01–05). Washington, DC: Heritage Foundation, Center for Data Analysis.

National Alliance for Model State Drug Laws. (2011). *Controlling methamphetamine precursors ephedrine and pseudoephedrine: A brief history of controls and current initiatives.* Santa Fe, NM: Author.

National Association of Drug Court Professionals. (2004). *Defining drug courts: The key components.* NCJ 205621. Washington, DC: U.S. Department of Justice, Bureau of Justice Assistance. Retrieved from https://www.ncjrs.gov/pdffiles1/bja/205621.pdf

National Crime Prevention Council. (2008). *Mobilizing the nation to prevent crime, violence, and drug abuse: Crime Prevention Coalition of America 2007 annual report.* Arlington, VA: National Crime Prevention Council.

Retrieved from http://www.ncpc.org/programs/crime-prevention-coalition-of-america/publications/mobilizing.pdf

National Crime Prevention Council. (2009). *Protecting what matters to you: National Crime Prevention Council 2008 annual report.* Arlington, VA: National Crime Prevention Council. Retrieved from http://www.ncpc.org/about/annual-report/NCPC-webFinal%20–2.pdf

National Crime Prevention Council. (2012). *Strategy: Gang prevention through community intervention with high-risk youth.* Retrieved from http://www.ncpc.org/topics/violent-crime-and-personal-safety/strategies/strategy-gang-prevention-through-community-intervention-with-high-risk-youth/

National District Attorneys Association. (2009). *Key principles of community prosecution.* Alexandria, VA: Author. Retrieved from http://www.ndaa.org/pdf/final_key_principles_updated_jan_2009.pdf

National Drug Intelligence Center. (2011). *National drug threat assessment.* Washington, DC: U.S. Department of Justice, National Drug Intelligence Center.

National Gang Center. (2012). *Has G.R.E.A.T. proven effective?* Retrieved from http://www.great-online.org/FAQ/HasGREATBeenProvenEffective.aspx

National Institute of Justice. (1973). *Neighborhood team policing.* Washington, DC: U.S. Government Printing Office.

National Institute of Justice. (2008, April). *Electronic crime scene investigation: A guide for first responders.* Washington, DC: U.S. Department of Justice, Office of Justice Programs. Retrieved from http://www.nij.gov/pubs-sum/219941.htm

National Institute of Justice. (2009). *What is an executive session.* Retrieved from http://www.nij.gov/topics/law-enforcement/administration/executive-sessions/what-is.htm

National Institute on Drug Abuse. (2010). *Drugs, brains, and behavior: The science of addiction.* NIH Pub Number: 10–5605. Bethesda, MD: Author.

National Institute on Drug Abuse. (2011). *Prescription drugs: Abuse and addiction.* NIH Pub Number: 11–4881. Bethesda, MD: Author.

Nerenberg, L. (2007). *Elder abuse prevention: Emerging trends and promising strategies.* New York, NY: Springer-Verlag.

New Jersey State Police. (2006). *Practical guide to intelligence-led policing.* New York, NY: Center for Policing Terrorism at the Manhattan Institute.

Newman, O. (1972). *Defensible space: Crime prevention through urban design.* New York, NY: MacMillan.

Newman, O. (1996). *Creating defensible space.* Washington, DC: U.S. Department of Housing and Urban Development.

Nicholl, C. G. (2000). *Community policing, community justice, and restorative justice: Exploring the links for the delivery of a balanced approach to public safety.* Washington, DC: U.S. Department of Justice, Office of Community Oriented Policing Services.

Nugent, M. E., Fanflik, P., & Bromirski, D. (2004). *The changing nature of prosecution: Community prosecution vs. traditional prosecution approaches.* Alexandria, VA: American Prosecutors Research Institute. Retrieved from http://www.ndaa.org/pdf/changing_nature_of_prosecution.pdf

O'Connell, J., Perkins, M., & Zepp, J. (2006). *Weed and seed performance measures: Analyzing and improving data resources final report.* Washington, DC: Justice Research and Statistics Association.

O'Keefe, G. J., & Reid, K. (1989). The McGruff crime prevention campaign. In R. E. Rice & C. K. Atkin (Eds.), *Public communication campaigns* (pp. 210–211). Newbury Park, CA: Sage.

O'Keefe, G. J., Rosenbaum, D. P., Lavrakas, P. J., Reid, K., & Botta, R. A. (1996). *Take a bite out of crime: The impact of the National Citizens' Crime Prevention Media Campaign.* Thousand Oaks, CA: Sage.

Oettmeier, T. N., & Wycoff, M. A. (1997). *Personnel performance evaluations in the community policing context.* Washington, DC: Community Policing Consortium. Retrieved from http://www.policeforum.org/library/human-resources-issues/Performance%20Eval%20in%20CP%20context.pdf

Office of Community Oriented Policing Services. (2009). *Community policing defined.* Retrieved from http://www.cops.usdoj.gov/Publications/e030917193-CP-Defined.pdf

Office of Community Oriented Policing Services. (2012). *What is community policing?* Retrieved from http://www.cops.usdoj.gov/default.asp?tiem=36

Office of National Drug Control Policy. (2011). *Epidemic: Responding to America's prescription drug abuse crisis.* Washington, DC: Author. Retrieved from http://www.whitehouse.gov/sites/default/files/ondcp/policy-and-research/rx_abuse_plan.pdf

Office of National Drug Control Policy. (2012). *National drug control strategy.* Washington, DC: Author. Retrieved from http://www.whitehouse.gov/ondcp/2012-national-drug-control-strategy

Ortmeier, P. J., & Davis, J. J. (2012). *Police administration: A leadership approach.* New York, NY: McGraw-Hill.

Osborne, D., & Gaebler, T. (1992). *Reinventing government: How the entrepreneurial spirit is transforming the public sector.* Reading, MA: Addison-Wesley.

Pate, A. M, Wycoff, M. A., Skogan, W. G., & Sherman, L. W. (1986). *Reducing fear of crime in Houston and Newark: A summary report.* Washington, DC: Police Foundation. Retrieved from http://www.policefoundation.co/sites/pftest1.drupalgardens.com/files/Pate%20et%20al.%20%281986%29%20-%20Reducing%20Fear%20of%20Crime%20in%20Houston%20and%20Newark%20%28Summary%20Report%29%20.pdf

Pattavina, A. (Ed.). (2005). *Information technology and the criminal justice system.* Thousand Oaks, CA: Sage.

Paulsen, D. J., & Robinson, M. B. (2009). *Crime mapping and spatial aspects of crime.* Upper Saddle River, NJ: Prentice Hall.

Peak, K. J. (2012). *Policing America: Challenges and best practices* (7th ed.). Upper Saddle River, NJ: Pearson.

Peak, K. J., Gaines, L. K., & Glensor, R. W. (2010). *Police supervision and management: In an era of community policing* (3rd ed.). Upper Saddle River, NJ: Prentice Hall.

Peak, K. J., & Glensor, R. W. (2011). *Community policing and problem-solving: Strategies and practices* (6th ed.). Columbus, OH: Pearson.

Pease, K. (1998). *Repeat victimisation: Taking stock.* Crime Detection and Prevention Paper 90. London, England: Home Office.

Peterson, M. (2005). *Intelligence-led policing: The new intelligence architecture.* NCJ 210681. Washington, DC: U.S. Department of Justice, Bureau of Justice Assistance. Retrieved from https://www.ncjrs.gov/pdffiles1/bja/210681.pdf

Pew Research Center. *Public's priorities for 2010: Economy, jobs, terrorism.* Retrieved from http://www.people-press.org/2010/01/25/publics-priorities-for-2010-economy-jobs-terrorism

Police Executive Research Forum. (1999, May). *Addressing community gang problems: A practical guide.* NCJ 164273. Retrieved from https://www.ncjrs.gov/pdffiles/164273.pdf

Police Executive Research Forum. (2010). *Police and immigration: How chiefs are leading their communities through the challenge.* Washington, DC: Author. Retrieved from http://policeforum.org/library/immigration/PERFImmigrationReportMarch2011.pdf

Police Executive Research Forum. (2012). *Voices from across the country: Local law enforcement officials discuss the challenge of immigration enforcement.* Washington, DC: Author. Retrieved from http://policeforum.org/library/immigration/VoicesfromAcrosstheCountryonImmigrationEnforcement.pdf

Police Foundation. (1981). *The Newark foot patrol experiment.* Washington, DC: Author.

Pollock-Byrne, J. M. (1989). *Ethics in crime and justice.* Pacific Grove, CA: Brooks/Cole.

Porter, P. G. (2009). *Volunteers: The volunteer experience with the retired senior volunteer program (RSVP)*. Seattle, WA: CreateSpace.

Porter, R. (2011). *Choosing performance indicators for your community prosecution initiative*. Washington, DC: Association of Prosecuting Attorneys. Retrieved from http://www.ndaa.org/pdf/final_key_principles_updated_jan_2009.pdf

Poyner, B. (1993). What works in crime prevention: An overview of evaluations. In R. V. Clarke (Ed.), *Crime Prevention Studies* (Vol. 1). Monsey, NY: Criminal Justice Press.

President's Commission on Law Enforcement and Administration of Justice. (1967). *The challenge of crime in a free society*. Washington, DC: Government Printing Office.

Punch, M., & van der Vijver, K. (2008). Community policing in the Netherlands: Four generations of redefinition. In T. Williamson (Ed.), *The handbook of knowledge-based policing* (pp. 59–75). Chichester, England: Wiley.

Putnam, R. D. (2000). *Bowling alone: The collapse and revival of American community*. New York, NY: Simon & Schuster.

Putt, J. (Ed.). (2010). *Community policing in Australia*. Canberra: Australian Institute of Criminology. Retrieved from http://www.aic.gov.au/publications/current%20series/rpp/100–120/rpp111.html

Quire, D. S. (1993). *Models for community policing evaluation: The St. Petersburg experience*. Tallahassee: Florida Criminal Justice Executive Institute. Retrieved from http://www.fdle.state.fl.us/Content/getdoc/3b38f54e-8fc3–467e-b90c-25264321d5db/Quire-Donald-abstract-Models-for-Community-Policin.aspx

Ratcliffe, J. H. (2008). *Intelligence-led policing*. Cullompton, England: Willan.

Ready, J., Mazerolle, L. G., & Revere, E. (1998). Getting evicted from public housing: An analysis of the factors influencing eviction decisions in six public housing sites. *Crime Prevention Studies, 9*, 307–327.

Reaves, B. A. (2010, December). *Local police departments, 2007*. NCJ 231174. Washington, DC: U.S. Department of Justice, Bureau of Justice Statistics. Retrieved from http://bjs.ojp.usdoj.gov/content/pub/pdf/lpd07.pdf

Reaves, B. A. (2011, July). *Census of state and local law enforcement agencies, 2008*. NCJ 233982. Washington, DC: U.S. Department of Justice, Bureau of Justice Statistics. Retrieved from http://bjs.ojp.usdoj.gov/content/pub/pdf/csllea08.pdf

Reaves, B. A. (2012). *Federal law enforcement officers, 2008*. NCJ 238250.Washington, DC: U.S. Department of Justice, Bureau of Justice Statistics. Retrieved from http://bjs.ojp.usdoj.gov/content/pub/pdf/fle008.pdf

Reno Police Department, & Police Executive Research Forum. (2012). *Police training officer program*. Washington, DC: U.S. Department of Justice, Office of Community Oriented Policing Services. Retrieved from http://www.cops.usdoj.gov/default.asp?Item=461

Repetto, T. A. (1974). *Residential crime*. Cambridge, MA: Ballinger.

Reuland, M., Morabito, M. S., Preston, C., & Cheney, J. (2006). *Police-community partnerships to address domestic violence*. Washington, DC: U.S. Department of Justice, Office of Community Oriented Policing Services. Retrieved from http://cops.usdoj.gov/files/RIC/Publications/domestic_violence_web3.pdf

Reuter, P. (Ed.), & National Research Council. (2010). *Understanding the demand for illegal drugs*. Washington, DC: The National Academies Press.

Reynolds, E. A. (1998). *Before the bobbies: The night watch and police reform in metropolitan London, 1720–1830*. Stanford, CA: Stanford University Press (original publisher, MacMillan Press Ltd., Hampshire, UK).

Rich, T. (1995). *The use of computerized mapping in crime control and prevention programs*. (Research in Action Series). NCJ 155182. Washington, DC: U.S. Department of Justice, National Institute of Justice.

Rich, T., Finn, P., & Ward, S. (2001). *Guide to using School COP to address student discipline and crime problems*. Washington, DC: U.S. Department of Justice, Office of Community Oriented Policing Services.

Robin, G. D. (2000). *Community policing: Origins, elements, implementation, assessment*. Lewiston, NY: Mellen Press.

Rosenbaum, D., Schuck, A, Graziano, L., & Stephens, C. (2008, January). *Measuring police and community performance using web-based surveys: Findings from the Chicago Internet project*. NCJ 221076. Chicago: University of Illinois, Center for Research in Law and Justice.

Roth, J., Ryan, J. A., & Koper, C. S. (2000, August). *National evaluation of the COPS program—Title 1 of the 1994 Crime Act*. NCJ 183643.Washington, DC: The Urban Institute.

Royal Canadian Mounted Police. (2012). *Community policing problem solving model*. Retrieved from http://www.rcmp-grc.gc.ca/ccaps-spcca/capra-eng.htm

Russo, T. (2009). *Predictive policing: A national discussion*. Retrieved from http://blogs.justice.gov/main/archives/385

Sadusky, J. (2004). *Bridging domestic violence intervention and community policing: Partnership and problem-*

solving tools. Washington, DC: U.S. Department of Justice, Office of Justice Programs, Office on Violence Against Women. Retrieved from http://www.vaw.umn.edu/documents/bridgingdv/bridgingdv.pdf

Sampson, R. (2002). *Bullying in schools.* Washington, DC: U.S. Department of Justice, Office of Community Oriented Policing Services.

Sampson, R., & Scott, M. S. (2000). *Tackling crime and other public-safety problems: Case studies in problem-solving.* Washington, DC: US Department of Justice, Office of Community Oriented Policing Services. Retrieved from http://www.cops.usdoj.gov/html/cd_rom/inaction1/Problem_Solving_Case_Study_toc_f.htm

Sampson, R. J. (1999). What "community" supplies. In R. F. Ferguson & W. T. Dickens (Eds.), *Urban problems and community redevelopment* (pp. 241–292). Washington, DC: Brookings Institution.

Santos, R. B. (2012). *Crime analysis with crime mapping* (3rd ed.). Thousand Oaks, CA: Sage.

Schafer, J. A. (Ed.). (2007). *Policing 2020: Exploring the future of crime, communities, and policing. Proceedings of the Futures Working Group,* Washington, DC: U.S. Department of Justice, Federal Bureau of Investigation. Retrieved from http://www.policefuturists.org/pdf/Policing2020.pdf

Schafer, J. A. (2001). *Community policing: The challenges of successful organizational change.* New York, NY: LFB Scholarly.

Schafer, J. A., Buerger, M. E., Myers, R. W., Jensen, C. J., III, Levin, B. H. (2012). *The future of policing: A practical guide for police managers and leaders.* Boca Raton, FL: CRC Press.

Schmerler, K., Perkins, M., Philips, S., Rinehart, T., & Townsend, M. (2011). *Problem-solving tips: A guide to reducing crime and disorder through problem-solving partnership* (2nd ed.). Washington, DC: U.S. Department of Justice, Office of Community Oriented Policing Services. Retrieved from http://cops.usdoj.gov/files/RIC/Publications/05060069_ProbSolvTips_0711_FIN.pdf

Schwartz, A. I., & Clarren, S. N. (1977). *The Cincinnati team policing experiment: A summary report.* Washington, DC: Police Foundation.

Scott, M. S. (2000). *Problem-oriented policing: Reflections on the first 20 years.* Washington, DC: U.S. Department of Justice, Office of Community Oriented Policing Services. Retrieved from http://www.cops.usdoj.gov/Publications/e03011022.txt

Scott, M. S. (2006). Implementing crime prevention: Lessons learned from problem-oriented policing projects. In J. Knutsson & R. V. Clarke (Eds.), *Putting theory to work: Implementing situational prevention and problem-oriented policing,* Crime Prevention

Studies (Vol. 20) (pp. 9–36). Monsey, NY: Criminal Justice Press.

Scott, M. S., & Dedel, K. (2006). *Clandestine methamphetamine labs* (2nd ed.). Washington, DC: U.S. Department of Justice, Office of Community Oriented Policing Services.

Scott, M. S., & Goldstein, H. (2005). *Shifting and sharing responsibility for public safety problems.* Washington, DC: U.S. Department of Justice, Office of Community Oriented Policing Services.

Scrivner, E. (2006). *Innovations in police recruitment and hiring: Hiring in the spirit of service.* Washington, DC: U.S. Department of Justice, Office of Community Oriented Policing Services.

Sedlak, A. J., & McPherson, K. (2010). *Nature of risk and victimization: Findings from the Survey of Youth in Residential Placement.* Washington, DC: U.S. Department of Justice, Office of Justice Programs, Office of Juvenile Justice and Delinquency Prevention.

Senge, P. (1990). *The fifth discipline: The art and practice of the learning organization.* New York, NY: Doubleday.

Senge, P., Kleiner, A., Roberts, C., Ross, R., Roth, G., & Smith, B. (1990). *The dance of change: The challenges to sustaining momentum in learning organizations.* New York, NY: Doubleday.

Shah, S., & Estrada, R. (2009). *Bridging the language divide: Promising practices for law enforcement.* New York, NY: Vera Institute of Justice. Retrieved from http://www.vera.org/content/bridging-language-divide-promising-practices-law-enforcement

Shaw, C. R., & McKay, H. D. (1942). *Juvenile delinquency in urban areas.* Chicago, IL: University of Chicago Press.

Shemella, P. (Ed.). (2011). *Fighting back: What governments can do about terrorism.* Stanford, CA: Stanford University Press.

Sherman, L. W. (1995). Hot spots of crime and criminal careers of place. In D. L. Weisburd & J. E. Eck (Eds.), *Crime and place, crime prevention studies* (Vol. 4) (pp. 35–52). Monsey, NY: Criminal Justice Press.

Sherman, L. W. (1998). *Evidence-based policing.* Washington, DC: Police Foundation.

Sherman, L. W., Farrington, D. P., Welsh, B. C., & MacKenzie, D. L. (Eds.). (2002). *Evidence-based crime prevention.* New York, NY: Routledge.

Sherman, L. W., Gottfredson, D., MacKenzie, D. L., Eck, J. E., Reuter, P., & Bushway, S. (1997). *Preventing crime: What works, what doesn't, what's promising: A report to the Attorney General of the United States.* Washington, DC: U.S. Department of Justice, Office of Justice Programs.

Sherman, L. W., Milton, C. H., & Kelly, T. V. (1973). *Team policing: Seven case studies*. Washington, DC: Police Foundation.

Simon, J. (2007). *Governing through crime: How the war on crime transformed American democracy and created a culture of fear*. New York, NY: Oxford University Press.

Skogan, W. G. (1990). *Disorder and decline: Crime and the spiral of decay in American neighborhoods*. New York, NY: Free Press.

Skogan, W. G. (2006). *Police and community in Chicago: A tale of three cities*. New York, NY: Oxford University Press.

Skogan, W. G., & Frydl, K. (Eds.). (2004). *Fairness and effectiveness in police: The evidence*. Washington DC: The National Academies Press.

Skogan, W. G., Hartnett, S. M., Dubois, J., Comey, J. T., Kaiser, M., & Lovig, J. H. (1999). *On the beat: Community and problem solving*. Boulder, CO: Westview Press.

Skolnick, J. H., & Bayley, D. H. (1986). *The new blue line: Police innovation in six American cities*. New York, NY: Free Press.

Skolnick, J. H., & Bayley, D. H. (1988). *Community policing: Issues and practices around the world*. Washington, DC: U.S. Department of Justice, National Institute of Justice.

Smith, E. L., & Farole, D. J. (2009). *Profile of intimate partner violence cases in large urban counties*. NCJ 228193. Washington, DC: U.S. Department of Justice, Bureau of Justice Statistics. Retrieved from http://bjs.ojp .usdoj.gov/content/pub/pdf/pipvcluc.pdf

Smith, P. T. (1985). *Policing Victorian London—Political policing public order, and the London metropolitan police*. Westport, CT: Praeger.

Sorensen, S. L. (1997). Smart mapping for law enforcement settings: Integrating GIS and GPS for dynamic, near-real time applications and analysis. In D. L. Weisburd & J. T. McEwen (Eds.), *Crime mapping and crime prevention* (pp. 349–378). Monsey, NY: Criminal Justice Press.

Sparrow, M. K. (1988). *Implementing community policing*. NCJ 114217. U.S. Department of Justice, National Institute of Justice. Retrieved from https://www.ncjrs .gov/pdffiles1/nij/114217.pdf

Sparrow, M. K., Moore, M. H., & Kennedy, D. B. (1990). *Beyond 911: A new era for policing*. New York, NY: Basic Books.

Starbuck, D., Howell, J. C., & Lindquist, D. J. (2001, December). *Hybrid and other modern gangs*. NCJ 189916. U.S. Department of Justice, Office of Juvenile Justice and Delinquency Prevention. Retrieved from http://www.nationalgangcenter.gov/Content/Documents/ Hybrid-and-Other-Modern-Gangs.pdf

Stevens, D. J. (2001). *Policing and community partnerships*. Upper Saddle River, NJ: Prentice Hall.

Stoloff, J. A. (2004). *A brief history of public housing*. Washington, DC: U.S. Department of Housing and Urban Development.

Substance Abuse and Mental Health Services Administration. (2005). *Successful strategies for recruiting, training and utilizing volunteers: A guide for faith- and community-based service providers*. Washington, DC: U.S. Department of Health and Human Services, Substance Abuse and Mental Health Services Administration. Retrieved from http://www .samhsa.gov/fbci/Volunteer_handbook.pdf

Sviridoff, M., Rottman, D., & Weidner, R. (2005). *Dispensing justice locally: The impacts, costs and benefits of the Midtown Community Court*. New York, NY: Center for Court Innovation.

Taft, P. (1986). *Fighting fear: The Baltimore County COPE project*. NCJ 103756. Washington, DC: Police Executive Research Forum.

Tampa Police Department. (2010). *Focus on four: Crime reduction plan*. Retrieved from http://www.tampagov .net/dept_police/Files/publications/FocusOnFour10print .pdf

Taylor, B., Heinen, B., Mulvaney, R., Weiss, D., Chapman, R., Scheider, M., Diamond, D., Cronin, C., & Conlon, A. (in press). *Community policing self-assessment tool: Documenting today and planning for tomorrow*. Washington, DC: U.S. Department of Justice, Office of Community Oriented Policing Services.

Taylor, R. B. (2001). *Breaking away from broken windows: Baltimore neighborhoods and the nationwide fight against crime, grime, fear, and decline*. Boulder, CO: Westview Press.

Terrill, R. J. (2009). *World criminal justice systems: A comparative survey* (7th ed.). Cincinnati, OH: Anderson.

Thibaut, J. W., & Walker, L. (1975). *Procedural justice: A psychological analysis*. Hillsdale, NJ: Erlbaum.

Thompson, A. C., & Wolf, R. V. (2004). *The prosecutor as problem-solver: An overview of community prosecution*. New York, NY: Center for Court Innovation. Retrieved from http://www.courtinnovation.org/sites/default/files/ prosecutor_as_ps.pdf

Thompson, M., Osher, F. C., & Tomasini-Joshi, D. (2008). *Improving responses to people with mental illness: The essential elements of a mental health treatment court*. New York, NY: Council of State Governments Justice Center.

Thurman, Q. C., & Zhao, J. (2003). *Contemporary policing: Controversies, challenges and solutions*. Los Angeles, CA: Roxbury.

Tilley, N. (Ed.). (2005). *Handbook of crime prevention and community safety*. Portland, OR: Willan.

Tonry, M. (1996). *Sentencing matters*. New York, NY: Oxford Press.

Travis, L. F., III, & Langworthy, R. H. (2008). *Policing in America: A balance of forces* (4th ed.). Upper Saddle River, NJ: Prentice Hall.

Trojanowicz, R. C. (1982). *An evaluation of the neighborhood foot patrol program in Flint, Michigan.* East Lansing: Michigan State University, The National Neighborhood Foot Patrol Center. Retrieved from http://www.cj.msu.edu/~people/cp/evaluate.html

Trojanowicz, R. C., & Banas, D. W. (1985). *Job satisfaction: A comparison of foot patrol versus motor patrol officers.* East Lansing: Michigan State University, National Neighborhood Foot Patrol Center. Retrieved from http://www.cj.msu.edu/~people/cp/jobsat.html

Trojanowicz, R. C., & Bucqueroux, B. (1990). *Community policing: A contemporary perspective*. Cincinnati, OH: Anderson.

Trojanowicz, R. C., & Bucqueroux, B. (1998). *Community policing: How to get started*. Cincinnati, OH: Anderson.

Trojanowicz, R. C., & Carter, D. (1988). *The philosophy and role of community policing.* East Lansing: Michigan State University, National Center for Community Policing. Retrieved from http://www.cj.msu.edu/~people/cp/cpphil.html

Trojanowicz, R., Kappeler, V. E., Gaines, L. K., & Bucqueroux, B. (1998). *Community policing: A contemporary perspective* (2nd ed.). Cincinnati, OH: Anderson.

Trojanowicz, R. C., & Moore, M. H. (1988). *The meaning of community in community policing.* East Lansing: Michigan State University, The National Center for Community Policing. Retrieved from http://www.cj.msu.edu/~people/cp/themea.html

Trojanowicz, R. C., & Smyth, P. R. (1984). *Manual for the establishment and operation of a foot patrol program.* East Lansing: Michigan State University, The National Center for Community Policing. Retrieved from http://www.cj.msu.edu/~people/cp/fpmanual.html

Trudeau, J., Barrick, K., Williams, J., & Roehl, J. (2010). *Independent evaluation of the national weed and seed strategy: Final report.* Washington, DC: U.S. Department of Justice, Office of Justice Programs. Retrieved from http://www.weedandseed.info/docs/reports/WnS_Final_Evaluation_Report.pdf

Tyler, T. R. (2006). *Why people obey the law*. Princeton, NJ: Princeton University Press.

Tyler, T. R. (2007). *Legitimacy and criminal justice: International perspectives*. New York, NY: Russell Sage Foundation.

Uchida, C. D. (2010). The development of the American police: An historical overview. In R. G. Dunham & G. P. Alpert (Eds.), *Critical issues in policing: Contemporary readings* (pp. 17–36). Long Grove, IL: Waveland Press.

Umbreit, M. S. (2001). *The handbook of victim-offender mediation: An essential guide for practice and research.* San Francisco, CA: Jossey-Bass.

United Nations Office on Drugs and Crime. (2011). *World drug report 2011.* New York, NY: Author.

United Negro College Fund. (2009, June). *Campus community policing at historically Black colleges and universities: Final evaluation report.* Fairfax, VA: Author. Retrieved from http://www.cops.usdoj.gov/Publications/e071026295-HBCU-Final-Report.pdf

U.S. Department of Education, & U.S. Secret Service (2002). *Threat assessment in schools: A guide to managing threatening situations and to creating safe school climates.* Washington, DC: Authors. Retrieved from http://www.secretservice.gov/ntac/ssi_guide.pdf

U.S. Department of Health and Human Services. (2001). *Youth violence: A Report of the Surgeon General.* Washington, DC: Author. Retrieved from http://www.surgeongeneral.gov/library/youthviolence/toc.html

U.S. Department of Homeland Security. (2011). *Implementing 9/11 Commission recommendations: Progress report 2011.* Washington, DC: Author.

U.S. Department of Justice. (2001). *Problem-solving partnerships: Including the community for a change.* Washington, DC: U.S. Department of Justice, Office of Community Oriented Policing Services. Retrieved from http://www.cops.usdoj.gov/pdf/e06011157.pdf

U.S. Department of Justice. (2001). *Toolkit to end violence against women website.* Washington, DC: U.S. Department of Justice, Office on Violence Against Women. Retrieved from www.ojp.usdoj.gov/vawo

U.S. Department of Justice. (2003). *Call management and community policing: A guidebook for law enforcement.* Washington, DC: U.S. Department of Justice, Office of Community Oriented Policing Services.

U.S. Department of Justice. (2004). *Forensic examination of digital evidence: A guide for law enforcement.* Washington, DC: U.S. Department of Justice, Office of Justice Programs. Retrieved from http://www.ojp.usdoj.gov/nij/pubs-sum/199408.htm

U.S. Department of Justice. (2005). *Intelligence-led Policing: The new intelligence-led architecture.* NCJ 210861.Washington, DC: U.S. Department of Justice, Office of Justice Programs. Retrieved from https://www.ncjrs.gov/pdffiles1/bja/210681.pdf

U.S. Department of Justice. (2005). *The weed and seed program.* Washington, DC: U.S. Department of Justice,

Community Capacity Development Office. Retrieved from http://www.ojp.usdoj.gov/ccdo/faqs.html

U.S. Department of Justice. (2007). *Digital evidence in the courtroom: A guide for law enforcement and prosecutors.* Washington, DC: Office of Justice Programs, National Institute of Justice. Retrieved from http://www.nij.gov/nij/pubs-sum/199408.htm

U.S. Department of Justice. (2007). *Investigation involving the Internet and computer networks.* NCJ 210798. Washington, DC: Office of Justice Programs, National Institute of Justice. Retrieved from https://www.ncjrs.gov/pdffiles1/nij/210798.pdf

U.S. Department of Justice. (2008, February). *Campus law enforcement, 2004–05.* NCJ 219374. Washington, DC: U.S. Department of Justice, Office of Justice Programs. Retrieved from http://bjs.ojp.usdoj.gov/content/pub/pdf/cle0405.pdf

U.S. Department of Justice. (2011, September). *Law enforcement guide to false identification and illegal ID use.* Washington, DC: U.S. Department of Justice, Office of Juvenile Justice and Delinquency Programs. Retrieved from http://www.udetc.org/documents/FalseIdentification.pdf

U.S. Department of Justice. (2012). *Community policing training and technical assistance.* Washington, DC: U.S. Department of Justice, Office of Community Oriented Policing Services. Retrieved from http://www.cops.usdoj.gov/default.asp?Item=1974

U.S. Department of Justice. (2012). *National gang threat assessment 2011: Emerging trends.* Washington, DC: Federal Bureau of Investigation, National Gang Intelligence Center. Retrieved from http://www.fbi.gov/stats-services/publications/2011-national-gang-threat-assessment/2011-national-gang-threat-assessment-emerging-trends

U.S. Department of Justice. (2012). *Predictive policing symposium: The future of prediction in criminal justice.* Washington, DC: Office of Justice Programs, National Institute of Justice. Retrieved from http://www.ojp.usdoj.gov/nij/topics/law-enforcement/predictive-policing/symposium/future.htm

U.S. Government Accountability Office. (2005, October). *COPS grants were a modest contributor to declines in crime in the 1990s.* GAO-06–104. Washington, DC: Author. Retrieved from http://www.gao.gov/products/GAO-06–104

U.S. Government Accountability Office. (2011, March). *Elder justice: Stronger federal leadership could enhance national response to elder abuse.* GAO-11–208. Washington, DC: Author. Retrieved from http://aging.senate.gov/events/hr230kb2.pdf

Verano, R., & Bezdikian, V. (2001). *Addressing school-related crime and disorder: Interim lessons from school-based problem-solving projects.* Washington, DC: U.S. Department of Justice, Office of Community Oriented Policing Services.

Volunteers in Police Service Program. (2008). *Citizen police academies: Introducing law enforcement to the community.* Retrieved from http://www.pdfio.com/k-2267486.html

Volunteers in Police Service Program. (2009). *Volunteer programs: Enhancing public safety by leveraging resources—A resource guide for law enforcement agencies.* Alexandria, VA: Author. Retrieved from http://www.policevolunteers.org/resources/publications/?fa=leveraging_resources

Volunteers in Police Service Program. (2010). *Missing persons: Volunteers supporting law enforcement.* Alexandria, VA: Author. Retrieved from http://www.policevolunteers.org/pdf/IACP_MissingFINAL_web.pdf

Volunteers in Police Service Program. (2011). *Volunteers in police service add value while budgets decrease.* Alexandria, VA: Author. Retrieved from http://www.policevolunteers.org/resources/pdf/volunteers_police_service_add_value_while_budgets_decrease.pdf

Wadman, R. C. (2009). *Police theory in America: Old traditions and new opportunities.* Springfield, IL: Charles C Thomas.

Walker, S. L. (1977). *A critical history of police reform: The emergence of professionalism.* Lanham, MD: Lexington Books.

Walker, S. L. (1980). *Popular justice: A history of American criminal justice.* New York, NY: Oxford University Press.

Walker, S. L. (1992). *The police in America: An introduction.* New York, NY: McGraw-Hill.

Walker, S. L., & Katz, C. M. (2008). *The police in America* (6th ed.). New York, NY: McGraw-Hill.

Washington State Patrol. (2012). *Community outreach: Problem oriented public safety.* Retrieved from http://www.wsp.wa.gov/community/pops.htm

Weinstein, S. P. (2011). *Community prosecution: A decade into the 21st century.* Retrieved from http://www.apainc.org/files/DDF/CP%20-%20Decade%20into%2021st%20Century%20FINAL.pdf

Weisburd, D. L. (2008, January). Place-based policing. *Ideas in Policing No. 9.* Washington, DC: Police Foundation. Retrieved from http://www.policefoundation.org/pdf/placebasedpolicing.pdf

Weisburd, D. L., Bernasco, W., & Bruinsma, G. J. N. (2009). *Putting crime in its place: Units of analysis in geographic criminology.* New York, NY: Springer-Verlag.

Weisburd, D. L., & Green, L. (1995). Measuring immediate spatial displacement: Methodological issues and problems. In J. E. Eck & D. L. Weisburd (Eds.), *Crime and place.* Crime prevention studies (Vol. 4) (pp. 349–361). Monsey, NY: Criminal Justice Press.

Weisburd, D. L., & McEwen, T. (1997). Crime mapping crime prevention. In *Crime Prevention Studies* (Vol. 8) (pp. 1–26). Monsey, NY: Criminal Justice Press.

Weisburd, D. L., Telep, C., Hinkle, J., &. Eck, J. E. (2008). *Effects of problem-oriented policing on crime and disorder.* Retrieved from http://www.ncjrs.gov/pdffiles1/nij/grants/224990.pdf

Weisel, D. L. (1990). *Tackling drug problems in public housing: A guide for police.* Washington, DC. Police Executive Research Forum.

Weisel, D. L. (2005). *Analyzing repeat victimization.* Washington, DC: U.S. Department of Justice, Office of Community Oriented Policing Services.

Weisel, D. L., & Painter, E. (1997). *The police response to gangs: Case studies of five cities.* Washington, DC: Police Executive Research Forum.

Weisheit, R. A., Falcone, D. N., & Wells, L. E. (1999). *Crime and policing in rural and small-town America* (2nd ed.) Prospect Heights, IL: Waveland Press.

White, M. B. (2008). *Enhancing the problem-solving capacity of crime analysis units.* Washington, DC: U.S. Department of Justice, Office of Community Oriented Policing Services. Retrieved from http://www.cops.usdoj.gov/Publications/e020827126.txt

Willis, J., Mastrofski, S., & Kochel, T. (2010). *Maximizing the benefits of reform: Integrating CompStat and community policing in America.* Washington, DC: U.S. Department of Justice, Office of Community Oriented Policing Services.

Wilson, J. M., & Grammich, C. A. (2008). *Police recruitment and retention in the contemporary urban environment: Conference proceedings.* Santa Monica, CA: RAND.

Wilson, J. Q. (1968). *Varieties of police behavior.* Cambridge, MA: Harvard University Press.

Wolf, R. V. (2007). *Principles of problem-solving justice.* New York, NY: Center for Court Innovation. Retrieved from http://www.courtinnovation.org/sites/default/files/Principles.pdf

Wolf, R. V. (2010). *Community prosecution and serious crime.* Alexandria, VA: National District Attorneys Association. Retrieved from http://www.courtinnovation.org/sites/default/files/documents/CP_SC.pdf

Wolf, R. V., & Campbell, N. (2004). *Beyond big cities: The problem-solving innovations of community prosecutors in smaller jurisdictions.* NCJ 213474. New York, NY: Center for Court Innovation. Retrieved from http://www.courtinnovation.org/sites/default/files/beyond_big_cities.pdf

Wolf, R. V., & Worrall, J. L. (2004). *Lessons from the field: Ten community prosecution leadership profiles.* Alexandria, VA: American Prosecutors Research Institute. Retrieved from http://www.courtinnovation.org/sites/default/files/cp_lessons_from_the_field.pdf

Woolfenden, S., & Stevenson, B. (2011). *Establishing appropriate staffing levels for campus public safety departments.* West Hartford, CT: International Association of Campus Law Enforcement Administrators. Retrieved from http://cops.usdoj.gov/files/RIC/Publications/e061122378_Est-Approp-Stfg-Levels_FIN.pdf

Wycoff, M. A., & Cosgrove, C. (2001, August 6). *Investigations in the community policing context, executive summary.* Retrieved from https://www.ncjrs.gov/pdffiles1/nij/grants/189569.pdf

Yin, R. (1979). *Changing in urban bureaucracies: How new practices become routinized.* Lanham, MD: Lexington Books.

Zahm, D. (2007). *Using crime prevention through environmental design in problem solving.* (Problem-Oriented Guides for Police, Problem-Solving Tools Series, No. 8). Retrieved from http://www.popcenter.org/tools/cpted

Zehr, H. (2002). *The little book of restorative justice.* Intercourse, PA: Good Books.

Websites

The following websites also provide portals to a vast array of publications relating to community policing and problem solving.

Administration on Aging, U.S. Department of Health & Human Services; http://www.aoa.gov

American Association of Retired Persons (AARP); http://www.aarp.org

American Bar Association Commission on Law and Aging; http://www.abanet.org/aging

Center for Problem-Oriented Policing; http://www.popcenter.org

Citizens Observer.com; http://www.citizenobserver.com

Clearinghouse on Abuse and Neglect of the Elderly, University of Delaware, Department of Consumer Studies; http://db.rdms.udel.edu:8080/CANE

Community Policing Consortium; http://www.communitypolicing.org

CrimeMapping, the Omega Group; http://www.crimemapping.com

D.A.R.E. America; http://www.dare.com

Evidence-Based Policing Matrix; http://gemini.gmu.edu/cebcp/Matrix.html

Futures Working Group; http://futuresworkinggroup.cos.
ucf.edu/index.php

Gang Resistance Education and Training (G.R.E.A.T);
http://www.great-online.org

International Network for the Prevention of Elder Abuse;
http://www.inpea.net

McGruff the Crime Dog; http://www.ncpc.org/about/about-
mcgruff/use-of-mcgruff

National Adult Protective Services Association; http://www
.apsnetwork.org

National Association of Citizens on Patrol; http://www
.nacop.org/index.htm

National Association of Triads; http://www.nationaltriad
.org

National Association of Youth Courts; http://www
.youthcourt.net

National Center for Community Policing. Publications;
http://www.cj.msu.edu/~people/cp/webpubs.html

National Center on Elder Abuse; http://www
.elderabusecenter.org

National Citizens Police Academy Association; http://www
.nationalcpaa.org

National Clearinghouse on Abuse in Later Life, a project of
the Wisconsin Coalition Against Domestic Violence;
http://www.ncall.us

National Committee for the Prevention of Elder Abuse;
http://www.preventelderabuse.org

National Crime Prevention Council; http://www.ncpc.org

National Gang Center; http://www.nationalgangcenter.gov

National Highway Traffic Safety Administration; http://
www.nhtsa.gov

National Institute of Justice; http://www.nij.gov

Nixle; http://www.nixle.com

Police Foundation; http://www.policefoundation.org

Police Futurists International; http://www.policefuturists.org

San Diego Family Justice Center model; http://www
.familyjusticecenter.org

U.S. Bureau of Alcohol, Tobacco, Firearms and Explosives;
http://www.atf.gov

U.S. Department of Homeland Security; http://www.dhs
.gov

U.S. Department of Justice, Community-Oriented Policing
Services; http://www.cops.usdoj.gov

U.S. Department of Justice, Office of Justice Programs;
http://www.amberalert.gov

USA on Watch, National Sheriffs Association; http://www
.usaonwatch.org

Volunteers in Police Service (VIPS), the International
Association of Chiefs of Police; http://www
.policevolunteers.org

Index

Entry titles and their page numbers are in **bold.**